# A COMPANION TO
# HENRY JAMES STUDIES

# *A COMPANION TO*
# HENRY JAMES STUDIES

*Edited by* DANIEL MARK FOGEL

**GREENWOOD PRESS**
Westport, Connecticut • London

**Library of Congress Cataloging-in-Publication Data**

A Companion to Henry James studies / edited by Daniel Mark Fogel.
    p.    cm.
    Includes bibliographical references and index.
    ISBN 0–313–25792–2 (alk. paper)
    1. James, Henry, 1843–1916—Criticism and interpretation.
    I. Fogel, Daniel Mark.
    PS2124.C55     1993
    813′.4—dc20     92–1129

British Library Cataloguing in Publication Data is available.

Library of Congress Catalog Card Number: 92–1129
ISBN: 0–313–25792–2

First published in 1993

Greenwood Press, 88 Post Road West, Westport, CT 06881
An imprint of Greenwood Publishing Group, Inc.

Printed in the United States of America

The paper used in this book complies with the
Permanent Paper Standard issued by the National
Information Standards Organization (Z39.48–1984).

10 9 8 7 6 5 4 3 2 1

For Leon Edel and Adeline Tintner

# Contents

# Acknowledgments

Thanks are due to many persons who aided in the preparation of this volume. For the suggestion that I commission and edit essays covering the whole spectrum of James studies, as a companion to his marvelous *Henry James Encyclopedia*, I am most grateful to Robert L. Gale. To my twenty contributors, for their wisdom and labor, and for their generosity, both intellectual and personal, I will feel a lasting debt. I am also grateful to the expert staff at Greenwood Press—notably Marilyn Brownstein, Maureen Melino, and Mark Kane—for guidance, patience, and unflagging professionalism. I want to thank Janet Whyde and Peter O'Neil for indexing *A Companion to Henry James Studies*. My wife, Rachel, and my children, Nicholas and Rosemary, have tolerated my sometimes consuming labor on this book with love and understanding; to them, too, I give thanks.

I have dedicated this book to Leon Edel and Adeline R. Tintner. Among all who have taught us about Henry James, they are the giants, standing out as unrivaled exemplars of sustained discovery and illumination, each in very different ways. I find that I am always still learning from them, as I am from my father, Ephim Fogel, whose death earlier this year has left me feeling very much like William James; he wrote, in a letter of farewell to his dying father, "All my intellectual life I derive from you." To many exceptional teachers, but especially to these three, I know I will be continually grateful for models of scholarship that will never cease to challenge and inspire.

# Introduction

*Daniel Mark Fogel*

This *Companion to Henry James Studies*, which is itself a companion to Robert L. Gale's *Henry James Encyclopedia*, presents twenty essays written specially for this volume and intended to provide both advanced students and scholars with a reference guide to Henry James studies in all—or nearly all—of the rich and multivariegated dimensions of the field. Two annotated lists in the appendices—one of Henry James's principal publications in book form, the other of landmarks of James criticism—are intended to reinforce and to supplement the reference value of the essays.

As we approach the 1993 sesquicentennial of Henry James's birthday (April 15, 1843), we can look back on a swelling tide of commentary on James's life and work with an ever increasing appreciation of his importance to American letters and to world literature. That importance rests not just on his nearly two dozen or so novels (22, counting the two posthumous, unfinished novels but not counting numerous novellas, some of which, like *In the Cage*, were originally published as single novels) and his 113 tales (including the recently discovered fragment "Hugh Merrow"). James's place in the history of modern literature also rests on his literary and cultural criticism and theory—on his great works of travel writing, notably *The American Scene*, perhaps the single most telling critique of American civilization between the present day and 1835, when Tocqueville's *Democracy in America* was published; on his prefaces to the New York Edition of his fiction, the most influential and penetrating body of work on the art of fiction in English; and on the extraordinary letters he wrote to hundreds of correspondents over the course of seven decades.

James's standing in world literature is by now well established. He has found his place in the company of the great novelists—Leo Tolstoy and Fyodor Dostoyevsky, Honoré de Balzac, Gustave Flaubert, and Marcel Proust, Charles Dickens and George Eliot, and Thomas Mann. Some such roll call must be sounded if we are to invoke his peers. Though other American novelists have written books at least as great as James's—Melville's *Moby Dick* comes immediately to mind—only one other American, William Faulkner, produced a body of work sufficient to place him as high as James in the pantheon of novelists. When one considers the complete person of letters, moreover, James and Faulkner part company, for if James is not one of our two or (if you wish to put forward another nominee) three finest novelists, he can still be claimed as our greatest literary critic, and if not our greatest critic, then one of our greatest writers of letters, and if not that, then one of our greatest theorists and critics of culture.

Henry James occupies a central position in the history of modern letters. He stands at a pivot point, looking at once backward to the distinctively nineteenth-century realistic novel and forward to the modern and postmodern novel of the twentieth century. In an unpublished manuscript of an essay on fiction, Virginia Woolf wrote, "The books of Henry James are in truth the bridge upon which we cross from the classic novel which is perfect of its kind to that other form of literature which if names have any importance should someday be christened anew—the modern novel, the novel of the twentieth century" (see my *Covert Relations* 112–15). The modern novelists to whom James has been of great importance are too many to list, but to name just a few, one might include some of the giants of modernism—Joseph Conrad and Virginia Woolf, for instance—as well as somewhat lesser lights such as Ford Madox Ford. And one would have to move forward in time to many contemporary and near contemporary writers who have acknowledged James's continuing presence and importance for them, among others Louis Auchincloss, Cynthia Ozick, and Philip Roth. The late Graham Greene devoted a long series of essays to James, declaring, "He is as solitary in the history of the novel as Shakespeare in the history of poetry" (30). James has also been important for such African-American novelists as Ralph Ellison and James Baldwin. Like Virginia Woolf, who kept a presentation photograph of John Singer Sargent's portrait of Henry James—signed by both Sargent and James—above her writing table at Asheham, Baldwin hung a signed copy of the same photograph (given to him by a grandson of William James) above his desk, for "James was his standard—the writer he thought of when he thought of the heights to which the novelist's art might aspire" (Leeming 47; and see Garnett 125).

Lest these introductory remarks seem to verge on the Jamesian equivalent of bardolatry, I should hasten to add that one need not turn James into a monument or build a cult of personality around him or even believe in that allegedly quaint institution The Author in order to find that something called Henry James is a center of extraordinarily vital activity—activity of thought and of feeling as well—in literary criticism and scholarship today. One may, in the manner of some poststructuralist critics, think of Henry James not as a person but as a set of discursive structures and strategies, finding that the field of discourse "Henry James" is among the richest and most rewarding for exploring concepts such as indeterminacy of meaning and undecidability—James's most famous ghostly tale, *The Turn of the Screw*, is a notorious case in point.

It is a truism that James's reputation has undergone ups and downs, during his lifetime and after. The bestsellerdom of *Daisy Miller* (1878) and the establishment of *The Portrait of a Lady* (1881) as an instant classic, for instance, preceded James's disappointment with the commercial failure of the big novels he wrote in the last half of the 1880s, *The Bostonians* and *The Princess Casamassima* (both 1886) and *The Tragic Muse* (1890). James's depression over the failure of the great collective edition of his fiction, the New York Edition (1907–9), has been amply documented. And yet from very early in his career, James's reputation has been almost continuously among the highest. Though the James "revival" of modern times is supposed to have begun in the 1940s, to have picked up momentum in the fifties, and to have been snowballing ever since, the dedication to James of famous special issues of the finest "little" literary magazines in earlier decades—the August 1918 Henry James number of *The Little Review* (which interrupted the serialization of James Joyce's *Ulysses*) and the 1934 issue of *Hound and Horn*, titled "Homage to Henry James"—belies the idea of revival.

It is nevertheless the case that the last three decades—the sixties, seventies, and eighties—have witnessed a spectacular (and, for the individual scholar or reader, a really unmanageable) avalanche of work on Henry James, much of it of extraordinarily high quality. In orientation, moreover, the best work on James runs the gamut from various modes of traditional scholarship and criticism to the full, often bewildering range of contemporary critical theories. From the stunning biographical scholarship and criticism of Leon Edel or the myriad, encyclopedic explorations of James's relation to the visual arts undertaken by Adeline Tintner to the theoretical examinations of James by commentators as diverse as John Carlos Rowe (Marxism and deconstruction), Paul Armstrong (phenomenology), Mark Seltzer (Foucauldian analysis), Elizabeth Allen (feminist theory), and Sharon Cameron (epistemology), from the stylistic studies of David Smit, Seymour Chatman, and Ralf Norrman to the intrepid archival research of Alfred Habegger (turned by Habegger to iconoclastic, feminist ends), from the neo-Aristotelian perspectives of Wayne C. Booth and Mary Doyle Springer to the philosophical pyrotechnics of Leo Bersani, Paul de Man, and J. Hillis Miller—these are long, long rows to hoe, and marvelously fertile ones at that.

So astonishingly diverse is the variety of critical and scholarly approaches with which Henry James has been treated in recent years that no single volume, even one as ambitious as this *Companion to Henry James Studies*, can hope to do justice to them all. What the *Companion* offers, I hope, is an eclectic range of critical perspectives on all areas of major interest to students of Henry James today. No attempt has been made to impose uniformity on the essayists, either in critical or methodological approach or in essayistic style. Each has been allowed to follow her or his own bent.

The first section of the *Companion*, devoted to criticism and theory, opens appropriately with Richard A. Hocks's concise history of criticism of Henry James. Three essays, by Sarah B. Daugherty, Daniel R. Schwartz, and Thomas M. Leitch, discuss various dimensions of Henry James's own practice as literary critic and as theorist of fiction: Daugherty concentrates on James's criticism of other writers, Schwarz on his theory of fiction, and Leitch on the complex and enduring legacy of James's prefaces to the New York Edition of his works. Finally, John Carlos Rowe discusses James's status as a critical theorist in the sense delineated by the Frankfort school of theory—not, that is, as a literary theorist but as a critic of society, one who uncovered in his fiction the ways in which bourgeois ideology victimizes and dispossesses human beings, notably, in Rowe's view, children such as Miles and Flora in *The Turn of the Screw* and Morgan Moreen in "The Pupil" and women such as Milly Theale in *The Wings of the Dove*.

The central (and by far the longest) section of the *Companion* is devoted to Henry James's fiction. The entire chronological development of James's fiction is treated in four essays: James W. Tuttleton on "The Early Years," James W. Gargano on "The Middle Years," Jean Frantz Blackall on "The Experimental Period," and Virginia C. Fowler on "The Later Fiction." The essay by Maqbool Aziz—"How Long Is Long; How Short Short!"—is the only piece in the *Companion* devoted to James's short stories (which James himself almost always called *tales*), but the shorter fiction figures in many other essays throughout the volume, including John Carlos Rowe's, Mary Doyle Springer's, Adeline Tintner's, and, among the four contributions that together trace James's entire career as a writer of fiction, most especially James Tuttleton's, which concentrates in its opening pages on James's apprenticeship to the art of fiction, an apprenticeship spent working chiefly within the comparatively compact scope of the short story and the novella.

The last four essays in the section on James's fiction treat special topics. Philip M. Weinstein places James in the context of the Continental novel by way of very telling comparisons and contrasts between, first, James on the one hand and Tolstoy and Flaubert on the other and then, second, between James again and Dostoyevsky and Proust. Weinstein aims at exploring a great deal of very rich territory, centering his discussion on a close examination of the construction of the gendered subject in James's fiction. Mary Doyle Springer works in her essay at the intersection of contemporary American and French feminist criticism and the formalist approach to James's fiction she has developed in her books *Forms of the Novella* and *A Rhetoric of Literary Character: Some Women of Henry James*. Adeline R. Tintner's "The Art in the Fiction of Henry James" is a concise, telling presentation of her wide-ranging scholarship on the use that James made of the visual arts, as set forth at far greater length in several of her books, most importantly in *The Museum World of Henry James*. And, finally, Anthony J. Mazzella considers a matter of recurrent interest to students of Henry James: the novelist's inveterate habit of revising his fiction, culminating in the extensive revision of his early novels and tales for the New York Edition; James made so many changes in the late versions of his early works that many readers feel he created virtually new works under the old titles.

The section on James's nonfiction opens with an essay by Lyall H. Powers on the uses of James's *Notebooks*; Powers coedited, with Leon Edel, *The Complete Notebooks of Henry James*. Darshan Singh Maini's eloquent exploration of Henry James's letter writing is virtually a capsule biography of James by way of his epistolarium. In an essay on one of the most important of James's many travel books, *English Hours*, Bonney MacDonald shows that James's preferences for the enclosed landscapes and interiors of England function as a vehicle for early discussion of style and aesthetics in his writing. Susan Carlson's essay on Henry James's plays provides a concise history of James's theatrical career and focuses on his treatment of women; Carlson shows how James at once revealed the social power of his strong female characters and exposed the societal constraints under which they labored while he himself worked within the dramatic tradition of the comedy of manners. Carol Holly discusses James's autobiographies, investigating the changing response of biographers and literary critics to Henry James's account of himself in *A Small Boy and Others*, *Notes of a Son and Brother*, and *The Middle Years*; her essay, the penultimate piece in the *Companion*, provides a kind of frame to the first essay, by Richard A. Hocks, in showing how responses to James's life-writing have been enriched and redirected over time with changing developments in literary criticism and theory. Finally, in "The Duality of *The American Scene*," Charles Caramello provides a challenging and trenchant analysis of the ambiguities, the strains, the flaws, and the greatness of James's sui generis account of his return to America after nearly a quarter of a century of expatriation.

Many of the essays in this volume were completed for the original deadline that I gave contributors in the fall of 1988, and most were completed within a year of that date. A few did not come into my hands until mid-year 1990. For a few of the essays, accordingly, the terminus for bibliographical coverage is 1987–88. Some of the essays that were completed later, however, and several for which the authors provided updates, refer to works published in 1989, 1990, and 1991. I am particularly grateful to Richard Hocks for supplementing the key first essay in the book, his history of James criticism, with an account of James studies through early 1991. As editor, I am solely to blame for what may perhaps be mistaken as failures by the contributors to acknowledge recent work. It is my conviction that readers will find the twenty essays in *A Companion to Henry James Studies* to be intellectually stimulating pieces that will wear well over time, aging very slowly indeed. At least a few of them, I believe, are bound to become classics of James criticism.

Approaching Henry James's sesquicentennial, we may ask ourselves what his meaning will be for readers in the twenty-first century as Henry James's world— very much the world of the nineteenth century, despite his having lived for much of the first two decades of the twentieth—becomes increasingly remote. Perhaps

James's fate will be like that of virtually all writers, a hostage to the fate of reading itself. As one who has found in Henry James's novels and tales a source of deep, renewable pleasure—pleasure above all in language and in the mysteries of human character—I would bet that James will have the power to delight and to teach us as long as language and character endure.

# A Note on Documentation

To ensure that readers would be referred to multiple versions of single titles by Henry James as little as possible (there are, for example, as many as ten versions of *Daisy Miller* currently in print in English), contributors were asked to refer to a single preferred text when citing important primary works; generally, following an old-fashioned rule of scholarship, contributors used first editions as the preferred texts unless there was some sound reason for establishing a later edition as standard. Most of the contributors were able to follow the editor's instructions in this matter. Thus, many key works by Henry James are cited, in the text and in the notes, with parenthetical page references to works identified by acronyms. Works so cited are listed in the Key to Frequently Cited Works by Henry James, which immediately follows.

The style of documentation throughout the *Companion* is the current style of the Modern Language Association. Endnotes are informative and substantive only. Bibliographical data for all the works cited parenthetically in the text and notes are provided in a single list of works cited, which covers the bibliography for all twenty essays in the volume. When more than one work by a single author appears in the list, parenthetic citations of work by that author include short titles. When different editions of a single secondary work are cited in different essays—for example, the 1918 and 1954 editions of Joseph Warren Beach's *The Method of Henry James*—the edition is identified in parenthetic citations by a date in square brackets following the page numbers.

Generally speaking, the list of works cited at the end of the volume does not include works by Henry James that are cited by acronym and listed in the Key to Frequently Cited Works by Henry James. Some James works, however, particularly those that are cited by acronym parenthetically with page references in some essays and that are also mentioned by title only in other essays, are included in both the list and the key.

# Key to Frequently Cited Works by Henry James

AA     *The Awkward Age*. New York: Harper and Brothers, 1899.

AB     *The Ambassadors*. New York: Harper and Brothers, 1903.

AM     *The American*. Boston: James R. Osgood, 1877.

AN     *The Art of the Novel: Critical Prefaces by Henry James*. Introduction by Richard P. Blackmur. New York: Scribner's, 1934.

AS     *The American Scene*. Ed. Leon Edel. Bloomington: Indiana U P, 1968.

AU     *Henry James, Autobiography*. Ed. F. W. Dupee. Princeton: Princeton U P, 1956.

BO     *The Bostonians*. London: Macmillan, 1886.

CP     *The Complete Plays of Henry James*. Ed. Leon Edel. Philadelphia: J. B. Lippincott, 1949.

CT     *The Complete Tales of Henry James*. Ed. Leon Edel. 12 vols. Philadelphia: J. B. Lippincott, 1962–64.

DM     *Daisy Miller: A Study*. New York: Harper and Brothers, 1878.

EH     *English Hours*. Boston: Houghton Mifflin, 1905.

EP     *The Europeans: A Sketch*. Boston: Houghton, Osgood, 1878.

FN     *The Future of the Novel: Essays on the Art of Fiction*. Ed. Leon Edel. New York: Vintage, 1956.

GB     *The Golden Bowl*. 2 vols. New York: C. Scribner's, 1904.

HA     *Hawthorne*. London: Macmillan, 1879.

HJL     *Henry James Letters*. Ed. Leon Edel. 4 vols. Cambridge: Harvard U P, 1974–84.

IC     *In the Cage*. Chicago: Herbert S. Stone, 1898.

LC-I      *Literary Criticism: Essays on Literature, American Writers, English Writers.* Ed. Leon Edel. New York: Library of America, 1984.

LC-II     *Literary Criticism: French Writers, Other European Writers, the Prefaces to the New York Edition.* Ed. Leon Edel. New York: Library of America, 1984.

LHJ       *The Letters of Henry James.* Ed. Percy Lubbock. 2 vols. New York: Scribner's, 1920.

NB        *The Notebooks of Henry James.* Ed. F. O. Matthiessen and Kenneth B. Murdock. New York: Oxford U P, 1947.

NN        *Notes on Novelists.* New York: Scribner's, 1914.

NO        *The Complete Notebooks of Henry James.* Ed. Leon Edel and Lyall H. Powers. New York: Oxford U P, 1987.

NS        *Notes of a Son and Brother.* New York: Scribner's, 1914.

NY        *The Novels and Tales of Henry James.* New York Edition. 24 vols. New York: Scribner's, 1907–1909.

OH        *The Other House.* New York: Macmillan, 1896.

PC        *The Princess Casamassima.* London: Macmillan, 1886.

PL        *The Portrait of a Lady.* Boston: Houghton Mifflin, 1886.

QS        *The Question of Our Speech, The Lesson of Balzac: Two Lectures.* Boston: Houghton Mifflin, 1905.

RH        *Roderick Hudson.* Boston: James R. Osgood, 1875.

SB        *A Small Boy and Others.* New York: Charles Scribner's Sons, 1913.

SF        *The Sacred Fount.* New York: C. Scribner's Sons, 1901.

SL        *The Selected Letters of Henry James.* Ed. Leon Edel. New York: Farrar, Straus and Cudahy, 1955.

SP        *The Spoils of Poynton.* New York: Houghton Mifflin, 1897.

TM        *The Tragic Muse.* London: Macmillan, 1891.

WM        *What Maisie Knew.* Chicago: Herbert R. Stone, 1897.

WW        *William Wetmore Story and His Friends.* 2 vols. Edinburgh and London: William Blackwood, 1903.

# I
# CRITICISM AND THEORY

# 1

# From Literary Analysis to Postmodern Theory: A Historical Narrative of James Criticism

## Richard A. Hocks

The criticism of Henry James has been among the most prolific in the academy, with its dizzying variety of approaches and counterapproaches as well as every hue of mixture in between, making the narrative of its history inevitably salta-tory.[1] The history of James criticism is also, in part, the history of modern criticism, with labyrinthine corridors of methodology, cultural analysis, and hermeneutical bias. Like the criticism of any major figure—Shakespeare, Dante, Goethe—James criticism has moved through at least three stages: that of explo-ration and assertion, both positive and negative; that of consolidation and full flowering; and that of revaluation or reinterpretation. Given the immensity of James criticism, alternative patterns may easily reveal themselves; one might be that of high reputation followed by an inevitable "kicking" period, followed in turn by renewal and panegyric reappropriation—in James's case this last period exhibiting a powerful "second wave." But whichever pattern one discerns, there is no disputing the Malthusian progression of James criticism, especially since the 1950s.

Although he never did recapture the momentary popularity accorded him by *Daisy Miller* in 1878 and though he was sorely disappointed by the sales of the New York Edition, on which he labored so hard from 1907 to 1909, James's critical reputation both during his lifetime and in the years immediately following his death in 1916 held up rather well. The person who probably did the most to discover and nurture the genius of James from his earliest years through his major phase was his fellow writer William Dean Howells, "one of James's 'first, warmest, truest' and most consistent admirers," who, because of his editorial positions, "rendered James great service by encouraging him, by publishing his fiction, by calling attention to it, and by interpreting and defending it" (Mordell 7). Howells wrote sixteen reviews and articles; indeed, James's early critics were often writers themselves: Joseph Conrad, Ford Madox Ford, H. G. Wells, Rebecca West, Vernon Lee, Virginia Woolf, and Mrs. Humphry Ward—who admired "the deep droughts from human life that [his work] represents . . . [for] there is scarcely anything in human feeling, normal or strange, that he cannot describe or suggest" (Ward 336). In 1905 Conrad denominated him "the historian of fine consciences" (Edel, *Twentieth Century Views* 15), but it was, most importantly, T. S. Eliot and Ezra Pound, in the 1918 memorial volume of *The Little Review*, who provided a platform for the most influential modernist writers to make their evaluation of James. Both lauded him in terms well beyond token respect for a predecessor. For Eliot, James was "the most intelligent man of his generation," a practitioner of "the deeper psychology," a writer whose greatness is seen "in his capacity for development as an artist" and in keeping his mind "alive to the changes in the world during twenty-five years"—this last concept similar to Pound's "make it new" proposal (Eliot, "In Memory" 45–46, 52). Six years later, Eliot went even farther, asserting that James's example was "not that of a style to imitate but of an integrity so great, a vision so exacting, that it was forced to the extreme of care and punctiliousness for exact expression." In a daring comparison, he affirmed that James gives away no profundity to Dostoyevsky and is "more useful, more applicable to our future" (Edel, *Twentieth Century Views* 56).

Pound's emphasis was on James's moral integrity, his "emotional greatness in [his] hatred of tyranny." But Pound paid special tribute to James's internationalism, the attempt to make "three nations intelligible one to another," the "struggle for communication," which is above all a "recognition of differences, of the right of differences to exist" (Pound, "Brief Note" 7–9). Such complementary praise by Eliot and Pound emblematizes certain important features about James. First, the praise comes from poets; James's late work in particular, as David Perkins and others have indicated, was to have a special impact on modern poetry. Second, Eliot and Pound epitomize modernism, and James's fiction in fact has come recently to be interpreted as more modern than nineteenth-century. Third, Pound's emphasis on James as an intellectual liberal fostering humane values is at once dated with wartime resonance yet sounds as timely and important as James Baldwin's recent veneration for James on much the same grounds.

The other major strand of early criticism comes from Elizabeth Cary, 1905, Joseph Warren Beach, 1918, and Percy Lubbock, 1921. These set the early tone for academic or "Jacobite" criticism by attending to theme and technique and exhibiting respect for James's New York Edition prefaces, thus establishing a pattern that would dominate scholarship and classroom alike for more than half a century of James studies. The titles alone by Beach and Lubbock bespeak serious preoccupation with Jamesian technique: *The Method of Henry James* and *The Craft of Fiction*. Beach's scrupulous analysis comes across in such pronouncements as these: "The *ideal* of James is clearly a combination, or rather a *fusion* of good taste with spiritual discernment, and perhaps the most complete, if not the most dramatic, instance of this fusion is . . . Lambert Strether. For him there seems to be no such distinction between esthetic and ethic as perplexes most of us mortals'' (Beach 158 [1918]). Lubbock went the next step and asserted that Strether's mind is ''fully dramatized'' and that James's ''art of dramatizing the picture of somebody's [inner] experience touches its limit. There is indeed no further for it to go'' (Lubbock 156, 171). *The Craft of Fiction* fully privileged and canonized James by applying principles gleaned from James's prefaces and evaluating major classic writers such as Tolstoy or Flaubert by ''Jamesian'' standards. More Jamesian than James, Lubbock's study codified ''point of view'' and the dramatic method in fiction, setting the stage for the great revival of James, and of formalist work on him, many years later. At the same time, Lubbock's prescriptiveness and conception of James as mandarin master-critic in the prefaces would prove the ultimate source against which many ''new wave'' Jamesians of the 1980s could rebel and deconstruct.

The ''kicking'' period for James came in the 1920s, when it became fashionable to be unfavorable to prewar work. Although Ernest Hemingway and especially Gertrude Stein themselves admired James, to others their sparer prose made James's late expressionism appear cumbersome and excessive; furthermore, D. H. Lawrence's sexual frankness made James seem unnecessarily delicate. On the other hand, James Joyce and Marcel Proust, who had more in common with him, seemed too obsessed on the one hand with minute detail and on the other with learned allusion and sexual audacity to really claim direct continuity with James. The stream-of-consciousness method, named and explained, ironically, by James's brother William in *The Principles of Psychology*, was, as interpreted and practiced by the moderns, more messy and wasteful than the writing of James, who sought not to *transcribe* the stream of thought but to *dramatize* it, largely through metaphor and adapted soliloquy. Yet in the twenties the newer approach seemed radical and spontaneous. In this milieu, Van Wyck Brooks's 1925 nationalistic critique of James as a type of failed American aesthete lacking in historical realism seemed plausible. For Brooks, James's deracinating pilgrimage abroad resulted in late novels for which only ''formal significance'' counts and which are otherwise mere ''exhalations of intellectual vapor . . . nebulae, shaped like planets, yet remain[ing] clouds of fiery mist'' (Brooks 140–41). This assessment not only recollected H. G. Wells's earlier 1914 attack in *Boon* but also set the tone for E. M. Forster's objection in 1927 that James's ''hour-glass'' symmetry in *The Ambassadors* was exquisite pattern at the ''enormous sacrifice'' of ''human life'' (Forster 219, 228). Edwin Muir then dismissed James (along with George Eliot and Joseph Conrad) in 1928, and Vernon Louis Parrington in 1930 deprecated his ''inner world of questioning and probing; even in his subtle psychological enquiries he remained shut up within his own skull pan'' (Parrington 241).

Although Parrington's dismissal of James as all ''nunace'' and subjectivism seemed to sound the nadir for Jacobitism, his objections, even if legitimate, could have no bearing on early fiction like *Daisy Miller*, *Washington Square*, *The American*, or *The Portrait of a Lady*. And in fact, the same year as Parrington's judgment, 1930, marked the beginning of James's revival, initiated by Cornelia P. Kelley's *The Early Development of Henry James*, a work that included the study of James as reviewer and critic—hardly Parrington's "skull pan." This re-recognition, if that is the right word, increased steadily from then on. In 1931, Constance Rourke in *Native American Humor* stressed James's humor and satire as the work of a "great experimental writer" who "greatly extended the areas of native comedy" with links to Nathaniel Hawthorne and Edgar Allan Poe as well as Mark Twain (Rourke 262). By 1934, four years after Parrington, James was being reaffirmed in two important publications: R. P. Blackmur in *The Art of the Novel* collected James's New York Edition prefaces between the covers of one book and wrote a brilliant introduction isolating and, in a fluid way, codifying James's aesthetic tenets, thus extending the approaches taken by Beach and Lubbock. *The Art of the Novel*, though now over fifty-seven years old, is still, remarkably, the standard source for James's Scribner prefaces (other than the New York Edition volumes themselves), with only James E. Miller, 1962, and William Veeder and Susan Griffin, 1986, as distant competitors. However, Leon Edel's Library of America volume of James's *Literary Criticism*, 1984, stands the best chance of becoming the new standard source. The other major 1934 publication was a special number of *Hound and Horn*, "Homage to Henry James," edited by Lincoln Kirstein, Yvor Winters, and Allen Tate, and containing thirteen essays, including noteworthy work by Stephen Spender, Marianne Moore, Edna Kenton, and Edmund Wilson, who contributed an important and provocative Freudian reading of *The Turn of the Screw*, "The Ambiguity of Henry James."

Clearly James was now taken seriously again, during a period when the specter of fascism was on everyone's consciousness, both because of his humanistic values and, explicitly, because of his treatment of evil. Newton Arvin in his *Hound and Horn* contribution stressed James's vision of a morally ugly world second to none in English fiction. In 1936, Graham Greene asserted that James was compelled to write by a "sense of evil religious in its intensity," with an imagination "clouded by the Pit," that he was a "social critic only when he was not a religious one," and that he stood alongside Shakespeare and Dante in his analysis of corruption (Edel, *Twentieth Century Views* 111, 117, 119). A similar note was struck that year by Stephen Spender in *The Destructive Element*, wherein he explored James's diagnostic anatomy of the political and moral corruption in society, his rendering of private sensibility as symptomatic of civilization's decadence, especially in late work such as the unfinished *Ivory Tower*. Interestingly, the onset of the Second World War was now an aid to the rise of James's status, a correlation many do not appreciate even now. By 1938, L. C. Knights ("Henry James") was arguing that James's narrative irony was an instrument for exhibiting the egoistic brutality and villainous self-righteousness perceived by his better "register" or "deputy" characters—as James called them in his prefaces. Knights's fusion between serious moral content and subtle technique would eventually dominate the sophisticated analysis of James's texts well into the 1980s, and even now has not entirely stopped.

The decade of the 1940s comprises the years when Jacobite criticism consolidated itself and indeed began to flower through the dominance of a few major critics, F. O. Matthiessen, Blackmur, and F. R. Leavis. Matthiessen's 1944 *Henry James: The Major Phase* instantaneously coined an expression for James's late work and also took a highly aesthetic-moral approach to the late novels, from *The Ambassadors* through *The Ivory Tower*, stressing character, theme, metaphor, and structure. Furthermore, Matthiessen's edition, with Kenneth Murdock, of James's *Notebooks*, 1947, was at least equally seminal work, for it opened up James as never before to scholars, teachers, and readers. The *Notebooks* volume was also, in certain ways, a companion work to *The Major Phase*, with its accute commentary linking notebook entries to developing ideas to completed works. In 1947, Matthiessen published a similarly helpful book with running commentary, *The James Family*, with selections from Henry Sr., William, Henry Jr., and Alice James.

R. P. Blackmur never published a full-length study of James, a project he constantly "deferred" for reasons probably as complex as his own James essays. But those very essays in the 1940s and 1950s, together with his earlier "Introduction" to the prefaces and his memorable chapter in the monumental *Literary History of the United States*, 1948, played an important role in the aesthetic-moral criticism of James. Essays like "The Loose and Baggy Monsters of Henry James," 1951, or "In the Country of the Blue," 1943, set new standards for rich "Coleridgean" commentary on James. If Matthiessen coined "the major phase," Blackmur came close with his depiction of the late trilogy of novels as "poetic dramas of the inner life of the soul at the height of its struggle" (Blackmur, *Golden Bowl* v).

F. R. Leavis's *The Great Tradition*, 1948, sounded a different note as he placed James with Jane Austen, George Eliot, and Joseph Conrad among the great English novelists, together with a fifth, D. H. Lawrence; James's "registration of sophisticated consciousness is one of the classical achievements," producing "an ideally civilized sensibility" (Leavis 1, 16 [1963]). And yet, this Blackmuresque assessment was reserved for James's work up through *The Awkward Age*, not the major phase, which, to Leavis, suffered from the "hypertrophy of technique." Leavis's bold claim aligned, astonishingly, Van Wyck Brooks's criticism of the late work with virtual Jacobite laudation! What this thesis really pointed up, however, besides new contextual appreciation for early and middle James, was the sheer quantity, the several "canons" within James's oeuvre. After all, how many authors could have their "major phase" dismissed and *still* be part of "the great tradition"? In certain respects, an American counterpart to Leavis during the same years was Yvor Winters, 1947, whose analysis of James's social and moral position was read respectfully yet never had the powerful impact here that Leavis did in England. Another major Jamesian event was the *Kenyon Review* Henry James number, 1943, a kind of companion volume to the *Hound and Horn* issue nine years earlier. This critical symposium, specially prepared and edited by Robert Penn Warren, featured essays by such luminaries as Katherine Anne Porter, Francis Fergusson, Jacques Barzun, Austin Warren, David Daiches, and Eliseo Vivas, as well as Blackmur and Matthiessen. Clearly James's position as one of the major writers in English and American fiction was fully secure some thirty years after his death. This was evident as well in the retrospective collection of secondary material edited by F. W. Dupee in *The Question of Henry James*, 1945, an even more diverse set of voices than those in either *Hound and Horn* or *Kenyon Review*.

The late 1940s and early 1950s also saw the emergence of Leon Edel as the uncontested dean of James studies—or, as Geoffrey T. Hellman put it in the title of his 1971 *New Yorker* profile of Edel, as "Chairman of the Board." Edel's Jamesian career began to take its distinctive shape with his two Sorbonne dissertations in the early 1930s, but his dominant—and dominating—position in the field may perhaps be dated from the publication of his monograph-length introduction to *The Complete Plays of Henry James*, 1949, and then from the publication of the first of the five volumes of his *Life of Henry James*, 1953–72 (later volumes were to win both the Pulitzer Prize and the National Book Award). Between 1949 and 1953, Edel published an important essay that exemplifies his method of "literary psychology" (as he calls it in *Stuff of Sleep and Dreams*, 1982). In that essay, "The Architecture of James's New York Edition," 1951, Edel uses biographical materials to illuminate the origins and structure of James's late, selective edition of his works. Generally speaking, Edel's approach to James's writing in *The Life* (and in his more than two hundred additional publications on James, whose prodigious output Edel himself appears to simulate) is psychobiographical. Edel is usually—and it must be said quite crudely—identified as a Freudian critic. One is more on the mark if one notes that Edel dra vs especially on Alfred Adler's emphasis on sibling rivalry in his analysis of the William James/Henry James relationship, on Carl Jung's ideas about the collective unconscious and about myth, and, most importantly, on the theories of the American therapist Harry Stack Sullivan, who departed from Freud's belief that the basic structure of one's personality is established during the first five years of life and who instead emphasized that significant personality change can occur at any time, depending to a great extent on one's relations with others. Thus, for example, Edel's reading of the redemptive power of love in the three great novels of James's major phase is supported by his interpretation of the new access to feeling that he believes James gained through his intense affection for the sculptor Hendrik Andersen. Interestingly, Edel's work has probably had greater impact on traditional James criticism than on the newer theoretical Jamesians, including the psychoanalytic ones who prefer "revisionist" Freudian thought like that of Jacques Lacan. Edel continues, nevertheless, to be a central point of reference—and of attack—for biographical critics of James, such as Alfred Habegger. Since, however, one might easily devote to

Edel's contributions to James studies an essay far longer than the present chapter, I hereby take recourse to recommending to the interested reader just such an essay, Daniel Mark Fogel's "Leon Edel and James Studies: A Survey and Evaluation," 1982 (adding the caveat that Edel has, since 1982, kept on publishing important James materials, including *The Complete Notebooks of Henry James* [coedited with Lyall Powers], *The Library of Henry James* [compiled with Adeline Tintner], the two volumes of James's own criticism in the Library of America [coedited with Mark Wilson], and a revised, one-volume edition of *The Life of Henry James*).

Apart from Edel, the criticism of Henry James in the 1950s continued in many respects along the same lines set in the 1940s, though branching out inevitably in various, largely unsurprising, directions. In 1951, F. W. Dupee's critical biography drew attention to James's cultural context; similarly, Henry Seidel Canby, also in 1951, compared and contrasted the lives, views, and work of James and Twain. This interest in the literary and historical context of James continued with Marius Bewley's *The Complex Fate*, 1952, a study that suggests various parallels in James's and Hawthorne's "Americanness," a train of thought extending back to T. S. Eliot's *Little Review* essay and, behind that, to James himself in his Hawthorne biography. Bewley later sought in 1959 to continue his discussion of James's cultural and international viewpoint in *The Eccentric Design*. "The complex fate," James's own locution, is that of the American who must fight "against a superstitious valuation of Europe" (*LHJ* I, 13). If any single statement could be said to condense James's "international theme," this is the one.

The fusion between art and cultural background was also the subject of Lionel Trilling's important 1951 essay on *The Princess Casamassima*; Trilling was the first to argue for both the social texture and genuinely political component of James's art, a position that was not to resurface until the 1980s, though it drew attention to a neglected novel that now shares the critical spotlight with James's most important fiction. More characteristic of 1950s criticism of James, however, in both academy and classroom were discriminating formalist approaches such as those found in *The English Novel*, 1953, by Dorothy Van Ghent, and in *The American Novel and Its Tradition*, 1957, by Richard Chase, who averred James's romance form to be "completely subdued and transmitted to suit his exacting novelistic purposes" (Chase 119). Formal analysis could also be found in Walter Allen's short critical history, 1955, the same year as R.W.B. Lewis's *The American Adam*, an obviously thematic study yet one that complemented Chase's. Still another formal-thematic analysis, by Edwin Bowden, 1956, had less impact than Lewis's, but it did begin to analyze James through the visual arts, an approach later developed with some success by Viola H. Winner, 1970, and ultimately dominated by Adeline Tintner in the 1980s.

Major books on James appeared at the end of the 1950s, much as they had at the beginning. Quentin Anderson's *The American Henry James*, 1957, was an audacious, thesis-ridden book (though often brilliant) seeking to connect

James's work with his father's eccentric philosophy despite Henry's own claims that he could never "enter into" his father's ideas. This study has never had a sympathetic audience in the academy, though it might have fared better had Anderson not insisted that James's "emblems" from his father's "system" were nothing short of prose allegories of Henry Sr.'s thought. Anderson's further reading of James as ahistorical, in contrast to the line of analysis epitomized, say, in Stephen Spender, was amplified later in his 1971 study, *The Imperial Self*. A more successful 1957 book than Anderson's was Frederick C. Crews's *The Tragedy of Manners*, an acute analysis of moral drama in the late novels. Crews's book was an engaged, searching analysis of the moral dimension in the late work arising inevitably from Jamesian method and technique. In 1959, Harold McCarthy's *Henry James: The Creative Process*, though citing no one else's work, furnished a satisfying overview of the major elements that compose the ground for James's aesthetic, including such fundamental formalist concepts as organic form, the drama of consciousness, felt experience, and dramatic substance.

In many ways, however, the most important study of the 1950s was Christof Wegelin's *The Image of Europe in Henry James*, 1958, a deceptively slim volume that explored the complexities of the international subject everyone had been talking, teaching, and writing about but had not yet put together. Wegelin's book took off from work like Marius Bewley's yet expounded a coherent and complex development of James's international fiction without falling into simplistic paradigms. His economy of expression and scrupulous distinction of Jamesian phases also allowed Wegelin to incorporate into his analysis many tales as well as novels. This book may still be perhaps the best single source for studying James's international theme.

By the 1960s James's reputation as "master" was so ensconced that criticism during the sixties and seventies was free to proliferate in myriad directions; so institutionalized or "academized" was James that ever widening numbers and kinds of studies emerged, one atop another. In 1960 Richard Poirier examined James's use of a comic discipline in the early fiction, but in 1961 J. A. Ward, in *The Imagination of Disaster*, followed the tradition of Graham Greene and Stephen Spender and addressed James's probing vision of evil and culture; among its many good features, this study attends to James's last tales, after the lead of Ezra Pound so many years before. Ward's second book on James, in 1967, sought to complement his *Imagination of Disaster* by its formal-aesthetic analysis of James's unity through germ and structure. Also in 1961, Wayne Booth's influential *Rhetoric of Fiction* pluralized the possibilities of "point of view" by showing with "intertextuality" (well before the term) that James's intentions in his notebooks were generally not realized but swerved in the finished work, thus creating "rhetorical" ambiguity, and likewise that authors seemingly omniscient were full of de facto point of view, "implied" authorship, and the like. Though evocative of the technical approaches of Beach and Lubbock forty years earlier, Booth's study probably anticipated *Rezeptionstheorie*. Despite Booth's polite suggestion of Jamesian "confusion" (based mainly on a couple of tales), both mastery and majesty of Jacobite criticism could be seen the same year, 1961, in Oscar Cargill's *The Novels of Henry James*, the first major synthesis, review, and evaluation of all previous scholarship on James's novels and still today a most insightful group of overview chapters on the major works. A somewhat comparable study, though with more of a "squatter" than "dandy" approach to James—a study that lacks Cargill's scholarship but that does include discussion of numerous tales—was S. Gorley Putt's *Henry James: A Reader's Guide*, 1966.

The lone voice against the kind of assessment found throughout the academy in Cargill, Ward, Poirier, Matthiessen, and Blackmur was Maxwell Geismar's 1962 frontal attack, *Henry James and the Jacobites* (the English title was *Henry James and his Cult*). Geismar's assault was essentially a reargument of H. G. Wells's *Boon*, 1914, and also of Van Wyck Brooks, to whom he dedicated the book. But to their old objections he added a diatribe against the academy for its veneration of James and, presumably, its regard for Jamesian method at the expense of other possibilities for the novel as a form. Ironically, Geismar's hostile thesis seemed only to clarify James's permanence at or near the top of the genre, for though Geismar was much discussed in classrooms and answered in print, his book retarded the proliferation of "Jacobite" scholarship and criticism not one iota. Indeed, the very same year, 1962, produced Dorothea Krook's *The Ordeal of Consciousness in Henry James*, a very powerful study of his moral and philosophical themes in fiction, from *The Portrait of a Lady* through the late novels and last tales. Krook was also among the many who placed James in the liberal humanistic tradition, as did C. B. Cox, 1963, and Naomi Lebowitz, 1965; Lebowitz went well beyond Cox to examine the full range of James's execution and to explore his fictive mode of personal relations.

The multidirectionality of James studies during this period can be seen easily in two entirely different 1964 Jacobite books. First, Robert Gale's *The Caught Image* rigorously analyzed James's dense figurative language by image-clusters with a thoroughness (including some statistical analysis) reminiscent of Caroline Spurgeon's study of Shakespeare. Gale's was the first detailed book-length study of the imagery in the corpus of a novelist: although critics like Matthiessen had attended to James's figurative language, *The Caught Image* fostered subsequent close attention to James's style. It was also, as things turned out, a mere presage for the most detailed informational volume ever published on the novelist, Gale's recent *Henry James Encyclopedia*, 1989.

The other 1964 study was Laurence Holland's *The Expense of Vision*, a heady, complex study of the relation of the New York Edition prefaces to several major novels. Holland's interest was in the way formal issues "reenact" not only literary but also historical ones, and in the way James *constructs* a vision often at the "expense" of *projecting* one in the traditional thematic or referential way. Though formalist in mode, Holland's book perplexed many a reader or reviewer at the time, but now it exhibits a "postmodern" tenor well in advance. Holland's sensibility, however, was as old as it was new, a paradox suggested by his dedication to Matthiessen's memory. The constant interest by now in James's "craft"—the long-ago Percy Lubbock term reiterated in Holland's subtitle—was pursued in studies by Sister M. Corona Sharp, Joseph Wiesenfarth (*Henry James and the Dramatic Analogy*), and Ora Segal, 1963 and 1969, who examined James's use of the confidant, the dramatic novel, and the registering observer—whether character, author, or narrative instrument. Joel Porte, 1969, submitted a more sophisticated presentation of Richard Chase's earlier romance thesis. Finally, Walter Isle's *Experiments in Form*, 1968, drew attention to the novels from 1896 to 1901, those after the drama period, showing their new direction toward twentieth-century experimentalism; his approach in effect refuted Geismar's notion that James had stultified the form of fiction.

Meanwhile, Leon Edel's superb 1963 collection of critical essays, *Henry James: Twentieth-Century Views*, enhanced the earlier "genre" of Dupee with an even better collection, both avoiding duplication and including several items hard to find elsewhere (some cited already in this chapter). Roger Gard, 1968, gathered and surveyed the responses to James's novels during his lifetime. The same year Sallie Sears's entirely different *Negative Imagination* probed with intensity James's "lifelong skepticism" and "polarization" of the "structures of his imaginative world" (Sears ix, ii), exploring unresolved tensions in the late novels. Finally, in 1970, Peter Buitenhuis re-refuted the Brooks-Geismar thesis by investigating solely James's novels and tales set in America and linking them extensively to James's nonfiction writings on America, creating—again before the term—another "intertextual" study. Buitenhuis's narrative of James the writer was, like the novelist's own depiction of *The Bostonians*, "a very *American* story."

Such immense diversification of James criticism continued with Viola Hopkins Winner's 1970 study of the importance of the visual arts in James's work, anticipating more extensive work by Adeline Tintner in the next decade. In *Henry James and the Naturalist Movement* (1971), Lyall Powers focused on the works of the 1880s to exhibit the Jamesian application of French "naturalists," and the next year James W. Tuttleton located James's earlier fiction within a broadly defined tradition of the American novel of manners. Also in 1972, Martha Banta's *Henry James and the Occult* examined with historical sophistication the use by a secular author of the technical resources of the supernatural. That same year, Seymour Chatman published the first rigorous, stylistic analysis of James's late prose style, a subject that reappeared in journal articles or as supporting evidence in book-length work but that was not reconsidered again systematically until Ruth Yeazell, 1976, and David Smit, 1988. Meanwhile, British criticism reemerged in 1972 with John Goode's edited collection, *The Air of Reality*, stressing, as its title indicates, James's powerful mimesis as well as cultural critique. Shortly after, William Veeder, 1975, showed James's awareness in the early fiction of the techniques of Victorian popular fiction: the issue of James and popularity would be taken up importantly in the 1980s.

Even as James studies expanded centrifugally from an older, tethered Jacobite foundation, the 1970s were also the beginnings of postmodernist analysis, even though the seminal studies were usually not recognized or built upon until the 1980s. Tzvetan Todorov, for example, wrote his two structuralist studies in 1971 and 1973, though the first, *The Poetics of Prose*, was not translated into English until 1977. Similarly, Fredric Jameson's *Marxism and Form*, 1972, though not a study of James, galvanized (as did later *The Political Unconscious*, 1981) James criticism into a revisionist view that James's supposed ahistorical-aesthetic stance was in fact firmly tied to actual historical processes. Other important studies for later postmodernist criticism of James were by Shlomith Rimmon-Kenan, whose highly technical metacommentary in 1977 on Jamesian ambiguity modernized the Edmund Wilson school of approach to works like *The Turn of the Screw* and *The Sacred Fount*, paving the way to new-wave approaches in the journals. Also, Wolfgang Iser's very brief 1977 study of "The Figure in the Carpet," claiming that the text comes to life in the reader, spawned—again mostly in journals—a spate of reader-response analyses of James's fiction generally and numerous applications to "The Figure in the Carpet" in particular. In hindsight it can now be seen that reader-response criticism was anticipated as early as Lubbock—and even James himself in the New York Edition prefaces. But if Lubbock, as said earlier, had out-Jamesed James, it can equally be said that many critics in the eighties have out-Isered Iser. Still another approach in the late 1970s that inaugurated important critical interests for the eighties were the aggressive feminist reading of *The Bostonians* by Judith Fetterley in 1978 and the more broadly based, quietly impressive fusion of rhetorical formal analysis with a feminist subject in the work of Mary Doyle Springer, also in 1978.

Just as the last years of the 1960s produced several significant studies in their own right on James, the same was true in the late 1970s. First, Ruth B. Yeazell's *Language and Knowledge in the Late Novels of Henry James*, 1976, showed attention to the mode of the late idiom that, though not as precise linguistically or technically as Chatman in 1972 (or again Smit in 1988), was otherwise a more satisfying critical commentary on the discriminating complexity of metaphor and syntax in James's late style. Second, *Henry James and the Experimental Novel*, by Sergio Perosa, 1978, was simply a brilliant analysis of James's experimentalism from the middle period through *The Sacred Fount* and the unfinished work, especially *The Ivory Tower*. Perosa's book was most original in introducing such productive conceptual ideas as James's fiction of "rival creation," his objectifying of subjective experience, and the somewhat iconoclastic view that the major-phase trilogy consolidates James's experimentalism rather than furthers it. Perosa went much further than Walter Isle ten years earlier in presenting James as the precursor to modern international fiction; indeed, James emerges, in Perosa's words, "as a great-uncle of postmodernism" (Perosa, *Henry James* 203), a claim greatly validated by the criticism of the 1980s. The third major book was Nicola Bradbury's 1979 *Henry James: The Later Novels*. Many critics, as earlier mentioned, have used reader-response in journal articles and, like Iser himself, have applied this approach to a given tale. But Bradbury presented a very close and complex analysis first of middle James, then of the great major-phase novels. She showed the intricate parallels among the characters' attempts at perception, the author's at expression, and the readers' at understanding, by pointing out the linguistic, formalist, and syntactic signals that allow these processes to occur. An added bonus was a final section touching on several of the difficult tales after *The Golden Bowl*. To date, Bradbury's is still the best application of *Rezeptionstheorie* to James's major fiction.

The reader of this chapter must understand two important features of James criticism in the 1980s. First, the quantity has become so massive as to number routinely over a hundred essays and book chapters per year, not counting the critical books, doctoral dissertations, edited textbooks, or biographical studies. Such acceleration and thickness have, of course, been gaining momentum steadily since the 1960s, a phenomenon perhaps less difficult to understand when one remembers that James's canon is at once extensive, experimentally "phased," and intricately wrought, combining Trollope-like quantity with Joyce-like tapestry.

The second important element of the 1980s is that, rather amazingly, James studies have experienced an ideological "second wave" (rather like the "second wind" of Lambert Strether in *The Ambassadors*). This has occurred because, more than any other American writer, poet, or novelist, James has become the receptacle for all the divergent, interlocking strands of postmodern critical theory—as distinct from "literary criticism"—a development that, as we have seen, got under way in the late 1970s. Admittedly, it would be false to suggest that all critical items published on James in the eighties are "theoretical"; there are still innumerable instances—to borrow from rhetoric-composition jargon— of "current traditional" approaches to James, some of which have been major contributions. But I think it is fair to say that the ideological center and critical hallmark of 1980s James studies resides with postmodern theory.

In 1981, Allon White introduced Jamesians to important ideas found in Roland Barthes and especially in L. Althusser's Marxist-Freudian concept of "symptomatic reading," yet the synergy of this theory was never matched by the actual examination of James's work, which remained simplistic. On the other hand, in 1980, Susanne Kappeler's "second hermeneutic" (after Propp, the formalist-structuralist) was perhaps slightly less impressive theoretically, yet her actual readings, especially of *The Sacred Fount*, were superior to White's. In retrospect, 1980–81 can be seen as emblematic of the geometrical expansiveness of perspectives on James first apparent in the 1960s. Alwyn Berland, 1981, in *Culture and Conduct in the Novels of Henry James*, vigorously argued for a James in the moral-humanist Victorian sage tradition of John Ruskin and Matthew Arnold—a "James" who would not (consciously) recognize himself in the proto-Lacanian mirror of Allon White. Also in 1981, James J. Kirschke tried, as had others before, to link James with the Impressionist Movement in art, mainly by pointing to many individuals in James's milieu who were associated with the movement, thus implicating James by association. Peter Stowell, 1980, came at James from exactly the opposite direction, by proposing a conceptual view of Impressionism and then comparing James with the only contemporary author with whom he had no connection, Anton Chekhov. The next year Anthony Hilfer showed, in his *Ethics of Intensity*, that one could still examine character in James without avoiding recent theory and sacrificing intellectual complexity (the "interaction" of ethos and pathos) or the resources of comparatist analysis.

The great versatility of James criticism can be appreciated still another way: the same prolific year, 1981, also produced three "traditional" books of considerable merit, each totally unlike the others yet each a kind of final, consolidating copestone to an aspect of James's stupendous "first wave" criticism. One of these was Sarah B. Daugherty's *The Literary Criticism of Henry James*, an unpretentious model of old-fashioned literary history, thoroughly informed on James's broad critical milieu. By intentionally skipping the prefaces and by her historical approach, Daugherty provided the ideal complement to work such as Lubbock's, Blackmur's, and McCarthy's. The second book was R W.J. Wilson's *Henry James's Ultimate Narrative*, the first book-length study of the tactics of technique in one work, *The Golden Bowl*. Wilson drew out the possibilities found in such fine analysis as that of Yeazell and Bradbury, creating a study with two interesting implications. First, he presented *The Golden Bowl* as *the* book in James's canon, much as Lubbock had *The Ambassadors* sixty years earlier. Second, his study insinuated that James's last published novel alone deserved the stature of, say, *Ulysses*, a proposal that seems excessive yet at certain moments almost plausible when one encounters chapter after chapter, essay after essay, written on it during the 1980s. The third book was Daniel Mark Fogel's *Henry James and the Structure of the Romantic Imagination*, an engaging and exquisitely written study. Fogel's romantic structure permeating James is "the design of spiral return" (Fogel, *Henry James* 5), as enunciated in M. H. Abrams's monumental *Natural Supernaturalism*; more generally, however, Fogel's analysis capped the long-esteemed tradition of reading James's later fiction "Coleridgeanly," though Fogel expanded his base to include and incorporate the great nineteenth-century Romantic poetic tradition more generally. Interestingly, however, it was less the Romantic structure per se that most distinguished the richness of this study, since Fogel's conceptual position stood at the apex of a great, well-articulated approach enunciated by others; it was rather his fresh application of the conceptual viewpoint to several late novels, always making the design look different with each reading—such as the transformation of pervasive marine imagery in *The Wings of the Dove*, linking it to *The Tempest* (a work that drew some of James's finest critical formulations), as well as the convincing "ascending spiral" of Milly Theale's ultimate rationale of forgiveness.

A good example, after Wilson, of a *Golden Bowl*–focused study was Ralf Norrman's strenuous *Insecure World of Henry James's Fiction*, 1982, a sometimes jargon-laden yet ambitious look at the variety of performative language in

James, such as "unuttered utterances" or "emphatic affirmations." The same verbal hypertrophy Leavis had condemned in the fifties was now, in the eighties, perceived as the rhetorical clue to James's radical ambiguity. Residual formalism, however, still governed Norrman's study, with his underlying concept of chiastic inversion. Also by 1982, the impact, through reprints, of Shoshana Felman's astonishing 1977 "Turning the Screw of Interpretation" began to be felt. Felman's very long essay was a brilliant analysis of James's tale through the conceptual prism of French theory—Lacan, Derrida, Foucault. If we take into account the original date of 1977, Felman's was among the first radical, poststructuralist readings of James, even though Foucault, like Todorov, is a structuralist; that is, Felman showed that one could address the subject matter of a structuralist like Foucault—in this case, madness—and interpret it through a poststructuralist lens.

The years 1983–84 blossomed into the *anni mirabiles* for "second wave" James studies, bringing to fruition the new mode of analysis first introduced in the late 1970s. Feminist criticism of James reappeared in 1982 in Alfred Habegger's *Gender, Fantasy, and Realism*, an iconoclastic analysis of James and Howells as "sissies," and more extensively in 1984 with studies by Elizabeth Allen and Virginia Fowler. Allen's view of a woman's place in James was that she experiences a tension from both performing and questioning her signifying activity until, with the late novels, she learns to manipulate the "mystification" imposed on her. In *Henry James's American Girl: The Embroidery on the Canvas*, Fowler depicted the woman in James's work as a person whose function as a repository of culture becomes emotionally crippling when abandoned by men to live within her subjective self—until that very self, as with Maggie Verver, can be newly born, acquire the necessary ingredients of deception, and become no longer the graceful "embroidery" on another's canvas but, like James himself, an "embroiderer." Feminist criticism since Fetterley and Springer through Allen and Fowler continues apace, of course, in journals and at conferences. The most recent controversial addition to this body of criticism is once again Alfred Habegger's. His *Henry James and the "Woman Business,"* 1989, presents the thesis that James was essentially paternalistic, primarily because he could not overcome his allegiance and quasi-affinity to the benighted, indeed bizarre views about women held by his father.

Still another new-wave view of James acknowledges his lifelong concern for sales and professional popularity, a view opposed to James as pure aesthete and monastic artist. Marcia Jacobson proposed this view in 1983, picking up on some threads from Veeder. The same idea was resubmitted in 1985 by Anne T. Margolis and in 1986 by Michael Anesko, who proposed that James's "friction with the market" (James's own phrase) was even productive of his artistic independence. Interestingly, Leon Edel and Lyall H. Powers's recent edition of the *Notebooks*, 1986, gives credence to the Jacobson-Margolis-Anesko position even while it somewhat weakens Edel's own earlier thesis that the New York Edition was a kind of temple of art. Moreover, James's own mining and transmutation of popular fiction has been the subject of one of Adeline Tintner's studies, as we shall see. Of course, everyone agrees that James was hurt in the very magazine of his being, so to speak, by the pathetically poor sales of the New York Edition. It all seems bitterly ironic from the perspective of James criticism, for those Scribner's prefaces on which he worked so carefully have been explicated and reexplicated, mythologized and demythologized, reified and deconstructed; the effort now seems at times like a growth industry, yet it hardly earned James any money beyond base bachelor subsistence at the turn of the century.

Again in 1983, Edward Wagenknecht published a handbook, *The Novels of Henry James*, designed to update the work done by Oscar Cargill and S. Gorley Putt, though, almost inevitably, Wagenknecht sacrificed both the richness of Cargill's overview and the resources of Putt's critical commentary just to cover major sources, give plot summaries, and survey criticism. These same years were not without their new collections of James essays in the tradition of *Hound and Horn* or *Kenyon Review*; in 1983, *Modern Fiction Studies* published twelve original essays covering different aspects from the earliest stories in the 1860s to the *Autobiography*; and in 1984 Ian F. A. Bell edited and contributed to *Henry James: Fiction as History*, a group of eight original essays exhibiting historicist, Marxist, deconstructionist, and Lacanian methodology while interpreting James.

The Ian Bell collection may imply to the reader of this chapter that the "second wave" of James criticism was now valorized; in fact, however, there were three major books in the same 1983–84 span that, more than any others, have defined theoretical criticism of Henry James for the 1980s as a whole. The first of these, Paul Armstrong's *The Phenomenology of Henry James*, 1983, is a beautifully written, highly perceptive, and philosophically illuminating analysis of the relation between James's fiction and the twentieth-century philosophical school that parallels his work more than any other. By using selected but important novels from *Roderick Hudson* to *The Golden Bowl*, Armstrong also managed to provide an admirable introduction to some of the thought of Husserl, Merleau-Ponty, Binswanger, Heidegger, and Sartre. This work of critical acumen was followed in 1987 by Armstrong's epistemological study of modernism, which included extended commentary on a novel, *The Ambassadors*, not discussed in the earlier book. The second major study was Mark Seltzer's *Henry James and the Art of Power*, 1984, a book that demonstrates, with a fresh and highly visible conceptual framework, that James's text is anything but nonpolitical, as earlier formalist critics would have it; rather, James exhibits a politics of the novel by probing the interconnection between art and power. Seltzer treated only three works, *The Princess Casamassima*, *The Golden Bowl*, and *The American Scene*, but these are major texts; more important, he exhibited a creative use of structuralist Foucauldian and Bakhtinian theory in a book that also makes as much use of "intertextual" material (like H. G. Wells's *The Future in America*) as any other study that I know of on James.

The last of these "big three" 1983–84 new-wave studies was John Carlos

Rowe's *The Theoretical Dimensions of Henry James*, 1984, a study of extraordinary virtuosity and almost unlimited importance for any postmodern study of Henry James. This book has rightfully been called "a kind of *summa* in which each chapter tests a major contemporary theory in application to James's work" (Bradbury, *Bibliography* 3); yet its real hallmark is its being, in Rowe's own language, "a productive work of deconstruction." Without question, Rowe's is *the* deconstructionist magnum opus on James; it is characterized by a dazzling "mobility," not merely from one theoretical approach to another but throughout the critical narrative. Yet the result is an astonishingly integrated argument—one might say "unified" if the term were not inimical to Rowe's anti-formalism. Not only is James used successfully as the prism by which to explore literary mastery, anxiety of influence, feminism, psychoanalysis, Marxism, and reader-response criticism, but (were this not enough) Rowe's mobility enables him to deconstruct each critical school along with James! His regnant antiformalism, moreover, is never critical "pluralism" but is an authentic application of a Nietzschean "genealogy" of both James's fiction and the academy. Rowe likewise illustrates, as did Felman, the strategic use of a structuralist like Foucault ("What is an Author?") by a post-structuralist and even brings to the fore and refocuses provocative works by other theorists such as Peter Brooks, David Carroll, Seltzer, and Felman. *The Theoretical Dimensions of Henry James* is a unique book, even while it epitomizes the resources and acumen of American deconstruction. It is unique because no deconstructive theoretician in the 1980s is still as much a "Jamesian" as Rowe; and no Jamesian is quite so nimble a theoretician.

It perhaps sounds as if nothing of much importance has occurred critically since John Rowe, but such is not the case: James is simply too much the lifeblood of the academy itself. A number of works from 1985 to 1989 have already been cited incidentally in this chapter, but one should add other contributions. Vivien Jones's 1985 study of James's "protean" criticism, for example, complements the earlier work of Daugherty and McCarthy. In 1986, John Auchard showed that if the subject is "silence" and the approach conceptually sophisticated, it is still possible to make a plausible thematic argument. Also in 1986, however, Donna Przybylowicz's *Desire and Repression* exhibited the potent combination of Lacanian psychoanalysis with Marxist critique in the examination of a disparate group of James's late writings. Like Seltzer (and unlike Armstrong or Rowe), Przybylowicz tends to hammer the reader with jargon, yet her book remains, with Felman's "Turning the Screw," the best Lacanian work extant on Henry James, though one anticipates considerably more in the future.

The veteran critic James W. Gargano, author of numerous fine journal pieces on James for many years, published and introduced in 1987 a two-volume collection of major criticism on the early and late novels. Similar in conception to the earlier models by Dupee and Edel, Gargano nevertheless also commissioned original work by Daniel Mark Fogel and Barton Levi St. Armand. The year 1986 also marked the publication of Adeline Tintner's major work, *The*

*Museum World of Henry James*. Ever Since the 1940s, Tintner has in a sense buffeted the winds of increasingly theoretical criticism and persisted in an "old-fashioned" (but also quite creative) source-and-analogue approach to James. Although Tintner's articles appeared without let or hindrance for decades, it is interesting that her hefty book versions have come out during the heyday of critical theory. Like Frost's west-running brook, *The Museum World* was followed in 1987 by *The Book World of Henry James*, and in turn by *The Pop World of Henry James*, 1989, mentioned earlier. Tintner's mining of transmuted sources for James is prodigious, and though it sometimes seems as if James (or anyone) could not possibly have so many different explicit sources or analogues as Tintner attributes to him, even a portion of them makes Tintner's Jamesian well capacious. She also collaborated in 1987 with Leon Edel in *The Library of Henry James*, not a critical argument but a most valuable resource and research tool for future critical-biographical work and supportive of the sort of genetic criticism she herself practices well.

Other theoretical criticism continues. In 1987, Martha Banta edited and contributed to several fine reassessments of *The American*, the book James once declared flawed by romance. The caliber of Banta's collection is very high, indicated just by the contributors: Peter Brooks, John Carlos Rowe, Carolyn Porter, Mark Seltzer, and Banta herself. Newer work includes David Smit, mentioned earlier, who in 1988 wrote the first thorough and acute stylistic analysis since Chatman or Yeazell. Susan Mizruchi, also in 1988, exhibited the resources of a new complex historicism for James studies; and Dale M. Bauer, also in 1988, provided a most original collaboration of feminist and Bakhtinian theory to readdress the "ultimate" novel—at least for the eighties—*The Golden Bowl*.

James's tales, an impressive body of work in their own right, have never elicited anything like the book-length work done on the novels; even James's criticism has more books written on it. This truth, however, is misleading inasmuch as a vast critical literature on the tales can be found in the journals and, of course, in portions of many studies on the novels. Meanwhile the criticism of one particular tale, *The Turn of the Screw*, is so extensive that it probably competes with the printed work on *Hamlet*. This critical phenomenon has been aided and abetted by the interpretive literature having assumed the status of "primary literature," generating its *own* theoretical analysis: Felman and Rimmon are examples of this development, although one notes a recent book-long resubmission of the traditional—that is, anti-hallucinatory, anti-Freudian, anti-ambiguity—approach to the tale by Peter Beidler in 1989.

The most satisfying book on the tales as a whole is still Krishna Baldev Vaid's meticulously well defined study in 1964 of James's technique, a work that is "dated" only if, say, Joseph Warren Beach is dated. In 1966 Putt discussed a number of the tales in his *Reader's Guide*, and James Kraft examined the very early tales—those before 1880—in 1969. Edward Wagenknecht in 1984 published a handbook–companion volume on the tales, with the same format as his

1983 guide to the novels. And in 1988, Richard Gage wrote a thematic study of James's metaphorically titled short story sequences.

When one tries to assess all the criticism written on Henry James over, say, the last two decades, both books and articles, the area that seems to stand out the strongest is comparatist or parallel analysis. As unique as scholars deem James's work, they are compelled to examine his work in relation to some other figure, whether literary, philosophical, or even visual artist; indeed, the parallel is usually employed to isolate or clarify his uniqueness. Parallels with visual art have tended to cluster around the Impressionists or, as with Ralph Bogardus, James's collaboration with Coburn. Tintner's work is, strictly speaking, usually genetic rather than comparative, yet the number of visual and literary parallels she finds in James is astonishing.

Comparative analysis really goes back to T. S. Eliot's "Hawthorne Aspect" in *The Little Review*, and truly Hawthorne remains a rich and luminous vein of study with James. Analyses by Marius Bewley and many others were summarized and resubmitted by Robert Emmet Long's *The Great Succession* in 1979. But whereas Long traced the relation up to the mid–1880s, Richard Ruland the same year extended it throughout James's career. This modulating, career-long relation to Hawthorne has been the keynote for important recent historicist work by Richard Brodhead, 1986, and Gordon Hutner, 1988, in two Hawthorne studies with a great deal to say about James. Mizruchi's work is of a somewhat similar stamp, and Rowe's "anxiety of influence" segment within his *Theoretical Dimensions* is also provocative James-Hawthorne criticism.

James's kinship with the work of George Eliot goes back to Leavis, but Richard Freadman's *Eliot, James, and the Fictional Self*, 1986, explored with great sophistication and theoretical insight the two authors' modes of narration and conception of character. A sensitive and exploratory study of James and Robert Browning was penned by Ross Posnock in 1985; a more conventional literary approach was *James and Conrad*, by Elsa Nettels, 1977, a subject frequently found in journal articles. Berland's study, already cited, is among the best on James and Matthew Arnold; Stowell's is probably the only parallel with Anton Chekhov. Numerous scholarly discussions of James and Honoré de Balzac were capped by William W. Stowe's 1983 theoretically oriented study of the territory of consonance between the two, though Peter Brooks was still productively exploring James's Balzacian "openness" as recently as 1987.

Articles on James and Ivan Turgenev constantly appear, but Dale Peterson's *The Clement Vision*, 1975, was a good, if momentary, overview. James's relation with Robert Louis Stevenson and Edith Wharton were more personal than literary, though the relation with Wharton was both, as Millicent Bell showed in 1965. Another complex personal-aesthetic relationship was with Gustave Flaubert: David Gervais, 1978, explored their contrasting views of tragedy, though with a decided Flaubertian bias. The Émile Zola connection was an inevitable element in Lyall Powers's 1971 study, already cited, and Michael Egan, 1972, elaborated the aesthetic connection with Henrik Ibsen. Critical literature seems to pair James with, or play him off against, virtually everyone: Sand, Dickens, Goethe, Maupassant, Pater, Ruskin, Wilde, Garland, Crane, the Goncourts, Howells, Daudet, Irving, Poe, Milton, Dante, Joyce, Pound, T. S. Eliot, Fitzgerald, Cather, Bellow, O'Connor, Waugh, Percy, Fowles, Drabble, Bowen, Roth. Critics also parallel him with Stein, Woolf, Greene, Marianne Moore, Stevens, Nabokov, Williams, Frost, Proust, Musil, and—more than one might expect—Shakespeare. It sometimes appears there are no literary authors who are *not* compared with James.

In the philosophical sphere, Stephen Donadio in 1978 showed a creative parallel between James and Nietzsche, uniting them under the aegis of the transcendental artist who fuses the authorial self with the mastery and power of art. Donadio, following Nietzsche, redefined Jamesian perception as an act of will. No one has ever written a book on James and Emerson, despite innumerable Emersonian issues throughout James's fiction, but Quentin Anderson, as we saw, tried to assert the oneness between James and his father's neo-Swedenborgian thought.

My own 1974 study, *Henry James and Pragmatistic Thought*, was the first comprehensive examination of the important connection between the novelist's work and his brother-philosopher's thought, challenging the prevailing views of opposition held by Matthiessen and Ralph Barton Perry. My study examined William's thought "through Henry's own eyes"—literature and philosophy through the epistemology of knowing that William named "ambulation," and meeting in aesthetics. William was the pragmatist, Henry the pragmatism, though Henry's "deep structure" remained neo-Coleridgean in its network of polarity and polar-predominance. My book was "theoretical" in its extensive use of Barfieldian history of consciousness and in its conceptual dialogue between ambulation and polarity. But it was not theoretical in the postmodern mode of the 1980s. At bottom it was a phenomenological work: first, because James's inner mind was conveyed—not only what he thought but how he thought; second, because that very mentality or consciousness is, in William's language, "transitional," a function rather than an entity in its fluid relations with experience; third, because the line of congruence between Henry's quasi-supernaturalism and William's radical empiricism anticipates phenomenology itself. *James and Pragmatistic Thought* anticipated work like Fogel's (the polarity side) and Armstrong (the ambulation side). This stance between the brothers' work has been periodically reiterated—Jacques Barzun in 1983, Courtney Johnson in 1987— and is routinely found in journal essays.

In certain respects, a comparable study to mine was John Carlos Rowe's 1976 *Henry Adams and Henry James*, which explored, through these two seminal minds, a crisis of thought between the Civil War and the beginnings of modernism, sociohistorical factors evolving into epistemological ones. Rowe's interest recollected an abiding subject probed earlier by Blackmur but never fully developed. In another direction, Rowe anticipated his brilliant *Theoretical Dimensions* by showing both the historical and the philosophical process by which James became a radically modern novelist. Rowe's 1976 study was similar to mine in exploring interconnections between historical, philosophical, and stylistic issues.

Time and again I have stressed throughout this chapter the immense, geometrical diversification of journal articles. The *Henry James Review*, founded in 1979, is most notable for its fine balance between contemporary analysis and traditional scholarship, with features such as its distinguished series of Centennial Essays on specific James texts. The *Review*'s existence parallels and simulates the development of James scholarship from the "first wave" on through the second; somehow it has avoided the kind of provinciality or one-dimensionalism too often present in journals devoted to the work of a single figure. Any student or fledgling scholar who wishes to obtain a flavor of James criticism would do well to begin with the *Henry James Review*. The sheer quantity of work now amassed on James can be so intimidating that it might be helpful to note here some of the bibliographical tools that could help chart one's way. Robert Gale's *Eight American Authors* and bibliographies by Linda J. Taylor, Dorothy M. Scura, John Budd, and Nicola Bradbury are all helpful in different ways for different periods of scholarship. And of course Gale's *A Henry James Encyclopedia*, 1989, mentioned before and ideal for beginning and seasoned Jacobite alike, manages to "foreshorten" (as James himself would say) more helpful information on James than any other single volume ever published. Also, the James chapter of *American Literary Scholarship*, published yearly by the Duke University Press, provides a continuing overview of James scholarship. More substantial analysis will be found in the "Analytic Bibliographical Essays" published intermittently in the *Henry James Review*, though these are not as regular and predictable as are the *Scholarship* chapters, which appear about eighteen months after the end of the year covered—that is, June 1990 for 1988 scholarship. Some combination of these research tools can help the would-be Jamesian negotiate the mountain of work done and being done on James. For instance, the history of essays alone on James is a rich one. Besides those mentioned throughout this chapter, one thinks of outstanding "'single essay" contributions like Robert Reilly's on James's morality of fiction, 1967, like Ian Watt's first-paragraph explication of *The Ambassadors*, 1960, or like René Wellek's 1958 essay on James's organic aesthetics. Superb essays in the last two decades are so plentiful that it would be simply a slight to those not mentioned if I were to list any—though occasionally certain ones, like Wolfgang Iser's, have had considerable influence.

Any history is necessarily a partial narrative in content and emphasis and in its inevitable fragmentation as time continues and closure is deferred. With respect to continuing historical assessment, it might be appropriate to close with a glance at the "Henry James" in the 1948 *Literary History of the United States* and then his counterpart in the *Columbia Literary History of the United States* in 1988. R. P. Blackmur's venerable chapter conveyed James's intellectual and cultural crosscurrents in a way that actually anticipates the cross-disciplinary approaches that have vastly increased since Blackmur's era. Ruth B. Yeazell, on the other hand, focuses more directly and sequentially on the fiction itself, exhibiting fine critical discrimination reminiscent at times of earlier formal analysis of the Blackmur period, or shortly after it. And yet Yeazell brackets her commentary with James's autobiographical texts in a way that reflects recent biographical theory very different from the "intellectual history" of the Blackmur period. Moreover, Yeazell's personal and text-focused approach conveys the "portal" effect enunciated by the editors of the Columbia volume, reflecting their "modest postmodernism"; that is, whereas Blackmur's grand essay gave us a Ptolemaic illusion of the totality of James's life, work, and intellectual milieu, Yeazell's narrative perspective is inevitably Copernican. The massive proliferation of James studies, especially in the last three decades, makes it now seem impossible to view him with anything but Copernican humility; and yet, the very boldness of some contemporary methodology sometimes gives the counter-illusion that the critic has momentarily glimpsed the central cosmology of James's mind and art. Thus, I find it difficult to say whether the next James chapter in *Literary History* forty years hence will be closer to Blackmur or Yeazell, though it will certainly be different from either.

Since completing this chapter approximately two years ago, I can report, to no one's surprise, that James criticism shows nary a sign of abatement, though it is somewhat difficult to discern any particular dominant ideological or critical path. From the massive scholarship written more recently, one might cull the following books for brief mention: Sharon Cameron's *Thinking in Henry James*, 1989, a philosophically sophisticated look at James's meta-consciousness in the fiction; David McWhirter's *Desire and Love in Henry James*, 1989, an updated thematic study with generous readings of the last three novels; Adeline Tintner's patented and ongoing sources-cum-transmutation explanation of James's creativity in *The Pop World of Henry James: From Fairy Tales to Science Fiction*, 1989; and Lynda S. Boren's fluidly eclectic theoretical approach, *Eurydice Reclaimed: Language, Gender, and Voice in Henry James*, 1989. All the same, I suspect the two most important "impact" volumes of 1989 are likely to remain Gale's magnificent *Encyclopedia* and Alfred Habegger's much-researched though pugnaciously argued *Henry James and the "Woman Business,"* both mentioned earlier in this chapter.

James studies in 1990 have been extremely fruitful and represent at their best, once again, almost an ease with critical approaches of entirely different methodology and presupposition. Daniel Mark Fogel's *Covert Relations*, 1990, is a compelling and fascinating anxiety-of-influence analysis of James on *both* James Joyce and Virginia Woolf, two giants of modernism so often talked about in the same conversation with James but hitherto never comprehensively explored. Susan M. Griffin's *The Historical Eye: The Texture of the Visual in Late James*, 1991, illustrates the resources of interdisciplinary criticism as she connects late James with both art history and William's *Principles of Psychology*. My own *Henry James: A Study of the Short Fiction*, 1990, is the first critical overview of the tales since Krishna B. Vaid in 1964. Jonathan Freedman's *Professions of Taste*, 1990, explores more comprehensively than anyone else James's relations with Walter Pater, Oscar Wilde, and British aestheticism. Equally thorough in its "solidity of specification" is Philip Horne's *Henry James and Revision*, 1990, a careful exposition that in many ways bucks the recent trend of interpreting the New York Edition as a contingent, problematic, market-oriented project and instead reemphasizes its nuanced artistry. I might also note such projects as *New Essays on* The Portrait of a Lady, edited by Joel Porte, 1990, which, like the 1987 *New Essays on* The American, edited by Martha Banta, shows how surprisingly susceptible James's early fiction is to contemporary theory, especially, in this instance, psychoanalysis. Analogously, there is by this time a sort of quietly amassed library of critical volumes treating individual James works, illustrated most recently and best by Peter Beidler's and Terry Heller's studies on *The Turn of the Screw*, 1989, and Daniel Mark Fogel's study of *Daisy Miller*, 1990. Finally, perhaps I can designate if not a new critical trend, at least a fresh and rich subject for recent James studies. Bonney MacDonald's *Henry James's Italian Hours*, 1990, examines with elegant perspicacity James's evolving perception and attendant style between his early and late writings on Italy; similarly, coeditors James W. Tuttleton and Agostino Lombardo collected thirteen original essays in *"The Sweetest Impression of Life": The James Family and Italy*, 1990. So perhaps the next "trend" in James studies could actually be the oldest of Jamesian ideas—internationalism—only now increasingly carried out in criticism itself that comes from India and Japan as well as Europe. Thus, for example, *The Magic Circle of Henry James: Essays in Honour of Darshan Singh Maini*, edited by Amritjit Singh and K. Ayyappa Paniker, 1989, might be said to join hands spiritually, if not geographically, with Tuttleton and Lombardo's *"The Sweetest Impression of Life."*

## NOTE

1. I wish to express my indebtedness to Alan W. Bellringer, whose *Henry James* (New York: St. Martin's, 1988) included a slim but helpful model for my addressing the early years of James criticism, and to Nicola Bradbury, whose *Annotated Critical Bibliography of Henry James* (New York: St. Martin's, 1987) allowed me a handy reference guide when working outside the library, and a few of whose annotations I have occasionally paraphrased in part.

# 2
# James as Critic and Self-Critic

## Sarah B. Daugherty

Like many creative writers, James wrote criticism in order to defend his art and "secure [himself] a niche in the pantheon of letters" (Maini, "Writer as Critic" 190). But he was more than an apologist for his own practice; he was the most important critic of fiction in the nineteenth century. During his lifetime he published five critical volumes—*French Poets and Novelists* (1878), *Hawthorne* (1879), *Partial Portraits* (1888), *Essays in London and Elsewhere* (1893), and *Notes on Novelists* (1914)—and over three hundred reviews, commentaries, and prefaces, a definitive edition of which has recently been compiled by Leon Edel (*LC*-I and *LC*-II). All these pieces, from minor notes to major essays, testify to James's interest in the novel, the novella, and the short story as literary forms. As he noted in 1864, English and American literature had suffered from "the absence of any critical treatise upon fiction," whose "vague and desultory canons" had not yet been codified (*LC*-I, 1196). In the fifty years that followed, James himself developed a poetics of fiction that was to influence future generations of critics. Yet he was not primarily a theorist, nor was he as dogmatic a formalist as were his most ardent disciples. Though sometimes condescending to writers whose objectives differed from his—Mark Twain and D. H. Lawrence, for example—he made a conscious effort to avoid a priori pronouncements. And most of his judgments have withstood the test of time; as his chief exemplars he chose writers whom we still regard as canonical while he dismissed scores of lesser, and now forgotten, talents.

James's lifelong commitment to "precious discriminations" (*LC*-II, 1316) originated in his sense of cultural mission. The periodicals that published most of his early reviews—the *Atlantic*, the *North American Review*, and the *Nation*— were founded by Eastern critics who hoped to raise American intellectual standards. As James later wrote of his first mentor, Charles Eliot Norton, the would-be "representative of culture" had a crucial role to play in "a young roaring and money-getting democracy, inevitably but almost exclusively occupied with 'business success' " (*NN* 415). Hence, like his Brahmin elders, James followed the example set by Matthew Arnold, who combated the Philistinism of "the fat-headed respectable public" (*LC*-I, 716). In his early years James aspired to educate the Americans as Arnold had the British; and when he moved to England in 1876, he continued to champion "the ideal" on both sides of the Atlantic.

His theories of fiction were likewise influenced by these aspirations. To an extent he was a realist, seeking to give the novelist "a legitimate role as a social historian" and "dismissing as irresponsible any apology for him as a mere dabbler in make-believe" (Anesko, *Friction* 88). James's most famous defense of realism occurs in "The Art of Fiction" (1884). Replying to Sir Walter Besant, a popular writer who stressed the need for entertaining stories, he argued that "the only reason for the existence of a novel is that it does attempt to represent life" and that "the air of reality" is "the supreme virtue of a novel—the merit on which all its other merits . . . helplessly and submissively depend" (*LC*-I, 46, 53). He was suspicious, therefore, of his own taste for romantic fiction or, as he called it, "the novel irresponsible" (*LC*-I, 1202). Granted, a writer who could "improvise" might lull the reader into accepting falsehood or fantasy: he wrote of George Sand, for example, that one "floats along the limpid current of her prose" as one might glide "in a gondola past a painted landscape" (*LC*-I, 41). But as James questioned "the Romantic self's potential for unconditional subjectivity and freedom" (Posnock 10), so he distrusted the Romantic artist's "free play of . . . unchallenged instinct" (*LC*-II, 1057). The "sense of fluidity," he remarked, "is fundamentally fatal to the sense of particular truth" (*LC*-II, 759).

James's comments on narrative technique—a subject that always fascinated him—reflect his belief in the novelist's proper role as "historian." As William Goetz has observed, his objections to first-person narration ("in the long piece . . . a form foredoomed to looseness" [*LC*-II, 1315] ) were related to his fear of the "abyss of romance"; only through third-person narration could an author maintain a degree of objectivity, showing his characters' "relations" to each other and to his own controlling consciousness (Goetz 24–27). James also argued against the sentimental style popularized by Charles Dickens and his imitators— the "injudicious straining" after effects that left "nature and reality at an infinite distance behind and beside them" (*LC*-I, 221). Above all, he disapproved of the Victorian novelists' betraying their "sacred office" (*LC*-I, 46) by using narrators who drew attention to the fictive nature of their works: "It is impossible to imagine what a novelist takes himself to be unless he regard himself as an historian and his narrative as a history. It is only as an historian that he has the smallest *locus standi*. As a narrator of fictitious events he is nowhere; to insert into his attempt a backbone of logic, he must relate events that are assumed to be real" (*LC*-I, 1343). James would have been bemused, no doubt, by the playfulness of today's antirealists.

But his commitment to realism was qualified by his belief in "the importance of the ideal" (*LC*-I, 714); and, paradoxically, his conservatism linked him with the modernists of the next generation, who emphasized the artist's personal vision rather than commonly held views of "reality" (Jones, *James the Critic* ix). James's theories of human nature caused him to reject fiction he thought "silly, or stale, or unclean": for example, in reviewing a novel that dramatized a woman's sexual aversion to her husband, he protested, "Beasts and idiots act from their instincts; educated men and women, even when they most violate principle, act from their reason, however perverted, and their affections, however misplaced" (*LC*-I, 57, 592). This comment anticipates James's strictures against the French naturalists as well as his own concern with his characters' more complex motives. But if he was shocked by novels with too much passion, he was bored by those with too little. The fiction of Anthony Trollope, who dealt with "average" experience and whose characters had few "adventures," was a case in point: "He is an excellent, an admirable observer. . . . But why does he not observe great things as well as little ones?" James asked (*LC*-I, 1313, 1314). As for his friend William Dean Howells, James publicly approved of his "love of . . . the familiar and vulgar elements of life" but privately deplored his "realism war," calling him "as little as possible of a critic" (*LC*-I, 502; *HJL* III, 204). And in writing of domestic novels such as those of Harriet Beecher Stowe and Helen Hunt Jackson, James always lamented the vulgarity and dreariness of bourgeois life. Stephen Donadio hardly exaggerates, then, in stating that James believed the practice of realism—or at least of the low mimetic mode—to be "essentially servile" (207).

James was therefore isolated from the generation of realists to which he ostensibly belonged. Moreover, as Marcia Jacobson has noted, the development of a mass market for fiction in the 1880s and 1890s undermined the writer's authority "as a spokesman for his whole culture." In *The Bostonians* (1886) and *The Princess Casamassima* (1886), James did attempt to be a "historian" of American and British political movements—only to face rejection by a public eager for more reassuring explanations of social change (Jacobson 5, 141).

Quite naturally, then, James's criticism reflects his growing faith in the validity of the writer's personal point of view. In "The Art of Fiction," he rejected Besant's dictum that an author must write from observation alone: with sufficient imagination he or she could "[convert] the very pulses of the air into revelations" (*LC*-I, 52). Further, he argued that "the deepest quality of a work of art will always be the quality of the mind of the producer" (*LC*-I, 64). Interestingly, this statement reflects the theories of his brother William, who had argued in "Great Men" that the individual mind functions independently of the environment.

Thus the appreciation of individual writers became the most important of James's critical principles: an author's "particular organism," he wrote in 1888, "constitutes a *case*, and the critic is intelligent in proportion as he apprehends and enters into that case" (*LC*-II, 524). This approach limited James's development as a theorist, but it made him a more flexible critic than others (notably Howells and Émile Zola) who were burdened by "the oppressive *à priori*" (*LC*-I, 651). Of all the cases James dealt with, the most important were those of Nathaniel Hawthorne, George Eliot, Ivan Turgenev, and Honoré de Balzac, the novelists who most directly influenced his own fiction (Veeder and Griffin 5). In retrospect, we can see that James was not quite the disinterested critic he sometimes claimed to be, for like all major writers, he experienced the conflicts that Harold Bloom has memorably termed "the anxiety of influence." But his essays on these writers afford us the greatest insights into James's own "case" and the scope and limits of his perspective.

Hawthorne was a literary ancestor whom James was at first reluctant to acknowledge. To an extent Hawthorne embodied the provincialism that the self-styled cosmopolitan sought to escape; and, on a deeper level, he provided a model that James imitated even while attempting to preserve "the illusion of originality" (Rowe, *Theoretical Dimensions* 32). In 1879 James was asked to write a biography of his predecessor for Macmillan's English Men of Letters series—an invitation that paid tribute to his fame in his adopted land, for he was the only American contributor, just as Hawthorne was the only American subject. Looking backward, James stressed Hawthorne's predicament as a writer in a country lacking most of "the items of high civilization": "no palaces, no castles, nor manors, nor old country-houses, nor parsonages, nor thatched cottages, nor ivied ruins" (*LC*-I, 351, 352). To Howells, these were the "dreary and worn-out paraphernalia" of sentimental fiction; but to James, they symbolized the "manners, customs, usages, habits, forms" that the novelist, as would-be historian, had a vocation to represent (*HJL* II, 267). The ivied ruins were also emblems of the picturesque—a word that appears repeatedly in James's early writings. In 1871 he had still believed that America was "to a certain point a very sufficient literary field," though one that would "yield its secrets only to a really *grasping* imagination. . . . To write well and worthily of American things one needs even more than elsewhere to be a *master*. But unfortunately," he added, "one is less!" (*HJL* I, 252). By 1881, however, he had given up this challenge, though not his aspiration to mastery: "My choice is the old world— my choice, my need, my life" (*HJL* II, 328). Thus the "moral" he drew in *Hawthorne*—"that the flower of art blooms only where the soil is deep, . . . that it needs a complex social machinery to set a writer in motion" (*LC*-I, 320)— was derived as much from his experience as from his reading.

James's portrait of Hawthorne was likewise colored by his own creative ambitions. His emphasis on the small number of Hawthorne's works reflects his desire to be a more "abundant producer" and to achieve greater success in the literary marketplace (*LC*-I, 345; Anesko, *Friction* 66). And his exaggeration of Hawthorne's simplicity—his claim that the romancer had "no general views that were in the least uncomfortable" (*LC*-I, 340)—resulted from James's self-consciousness as a writer of the post–Civil War generation. The "good American," he said, "will be a more critical person than his complacent and confident grandfather. He has eaten of the tree of knowledge" (*LC*-I, 428). In particular, James chided Hawthorne for retreating into allegory, "one of the lighter exercises of the imagination" (*LC*-I, 366). For Hawthorne and the other Romantics, of course, allegory had been no mere exercise but a serious attempt to dramatize transcendent values. James, however, was enough of a realist to demand that the balloon of romance be tethered to the earth: we need, he claimed, "to feel beneath our feet the firm ground of an appeal to our own vision of the world, our observation" (*LC*-I, 422).

But if James criticized Hawthorne for his flights into metaphysics, he praised him for delving into the motives of his characters and exploring the abysses beneath commonplace experience. The "charm" of Hawthorne's works, James conceded, "is that they are glimpses of a great field, of the whole mystery of man's soul and conscience. They are moral, and their interest is moral; they deal with something more than the mere accidents and conventionalities, the surface occurrences of life" (*LC*-I, 368). For James, as for Hawthorne, moral truth resulted from "the deeper psychology," the mental drama that occurred as characters became aware of their complex relations with each other. As an example, James cited the characterization of Hilda (*The Marble Faun*), the "somewhat rigid New England girl" who loses her innocence as she learns of her friends' crime: "She has done no wrong, and yet wrong-doing has become a part of her experience, and she carries the weight of her detested knowledge upon her heart" (*LC*-I, 446). The same could be said of James's own American innocents, from Isabel Archer to Milly Theale. Increasingly, then, he valued the example of a writer more profound than the realists of his own generation—a writer who perceived "a life of the spirit more complex than anything that met the mere eye of sense" (*LC*-I, 459).

Among British authors, George Eliot stands alone as the novelist James most admired. Because her fiction had the "rich density of detail" lacking in Hawthorne's works, he devoted many pages of his reviews to her "paintings" of bourgeois and rustic life. Initially, however, he dismissed her as a "feminine"—though "a delightfully feminine"—writer. He noted, "She has the microscopic observation, not a myriad of whose keen notations are worth a single one of those great synthetic guesses with which a real master attacks the truth" (*LC*-I, 911). If James was sexist in classifying Eliot with the lesser "painters," one may share his impatience with such heroes as Felix Holt and Adam Bede, monotonously virtuous characters in whom "passion proves itself feebler than conscience" (*LC*-I, 915). But James was moved by her depiction of flawed, passionate women victimized by a patriarchal culture: Maggie Tulliver, "worth a hundred of her positive brother, . . . yet on the very threshold of life . . . compelled to accept him as her master"; Dorothea Brooke, "yearning for a motive for sustained spiritual effort and only wasting her ardor and soiling her wings against the meanness of opportunity"; and Gwendolen Harleth, personifying "youthfulness—its eagerness, its presumption, its preoccupation with itself" but developing a conscience as a result of her tragic marriage (*LC*-I, 929, 959, 989).

As numerous critics have recognized, Dorothea and Gwendolen became significant models for James's Isabel Archer.

Partly in self-defense, however, he continued to emphasize the distinction between his own aesthetics and those of his predecessor. He contended that Eliot's "drawing" was superior to her "composition," calling *Middlemarch* "a treasure-house of details, but . . . an indifferent whole" (*LC*-I, 907, 958). Although James was correct in noting the structural flaws in Eliot's weaker fiction, this comment illustrates his prejudice against the social, as versus the psychological, novel. In *Middlemarch*, as the title implies, Eliot attempted to deal with an entire community, whereas in *The Portrait of a Lady*, James was primarily concerned with the depiction of his superior protagonist. The contrast suggests the difference between British and American novels, as well as that between male and female writers: James tended to idealize his heroines, whereas Eliot—perhaps more realistically—showed the full extent to which her characters were bound by their ties to others, whose stories might deserve equal attention and sympathy.

Not surprisingly, James also complained that Eliot's novels lacked "the great dramatic *chiaroscuro*" (*LC*-I, 960). Hence he heightened the melodrama in his fiction (making Osmond, for example, a far worse villain than Casaubon) and carefully selected details to prevent the effect of anticlimax (allowing us to witness Isabel's decision to return to Osmond but not the outcome of that decision, as we might in an Eliot novel). It appears, then, that James developed a certain resistance against Eliot, as evidenced both by his fiction and by his somewhat condescending reviews. But Eliot deserves to be called James's literary mother, for she taught him to see the dramatic potential in women's stories rather than in more traditional male "adventures." To quote a famous line from "The Art of Fiction," "It is an incident for a woman to stand up with her hand resting on a table and look out at you in a certain way" (*LC*-I, 55).

Ivan Turgenev exercised an influence that James acknowledged more gratefully. Unlike Eliot, the Russian novelist was a master of literary form, and he was also a "delightful, mild, masculine" mentor (*LC*-I, 1015) at a time when James felt isolated from his male peers. ("Turgénieff is my man," announces James's persona in a dialogue on Eliot's *Daniel Deronda* [*LC*-I, 982]). James met Turgenev during the winter of 1875–76, when both writers became members of the literary circle of Gustave Flaubert. But despite his admiration for their craftsmanship, James pronounced Flaubert and his followers—including Alphonse Daudet, Edmond de Goncourt, and Émile Zola—"a queer lot, and intellectually very remote from my own sympathies" (*HJL* II, 20). The key problem was that the French, who often depicted sexual promiscuity, undermined the ideals of human character that James had espoused during his decade as a critic and writer of fiction. (He made allowances for Flaubert's Madame Bovary, who was "powerfully conceived" though "naturally depraved," but strenuously objected to Zola's Nana: "The figure of the brutal *fille*, with nothing but devouring appetites and impudences, has become the stalest of the stock properties of French fiction" [*LC*-II, 173, 870].) Turgenev, however, resembled James in being an outsider who appeared to know "strange and far-off things" beyond the ken of his French confreres (*LC*-II, 1015). And again like James, the Russian novelist affirmed the value of morally sensitive characters: "he holds that there are trivial subjects and serious ones, that the latter are much the best, and that their superiority resides in their giving us absolutely a greater amount of information about the human mind" (*LC*-II, 973).

If James admired Turgenev's psychological penetration, one reason was that the authors had similar conceptions of male and female roles. In Turgenev's fiction, as James noted, "It is the women and young girls . . . who mainly represent strength of will—the power to resist, to wait, to attain" (*LC*-II, 982). This statement applies equally to James's writings, from "Madame de Mauves" to *The Golden Bowl*. And Turgenev's men, like James's "poor sensitive gentlemen," are typically "natures strong in impulse, in talk, in responsive emotion, but weak in will, in action, in the power to feel and do singly" (*LC*-II, 1250, 977). (Indeed, Neshdanoff of *Virgin Soil* was the direct inspiration for Hyacinth Robinson of *The Princess Casamassima*: "the 'aesthetic' young man, venturing to play with revolution, finds it a coarse, ugly, vulgar, and moreover very cruel thing; the reality makes him deadly sick" [*LC*-II, 1005].) The resemblance here is more than coincidental: as exiles from their native countries, and as male authors working in a genre dominated by women, James and Turgenev developed a typology of characters reflecting some of their own anxieties.

Not only did Turgenev furnish a gallery of useful portraits, but he also gave James lessons in the art of composition. Unlike Eliot, who philosophized too much and had a weakness for rounded plots, Turgenev began with a "vision of some person or persons, . . . interesting him and appealing to him just as they were and by what they were" (*LC*-II, 972, 1072). He had affinities with the French insofar as he was "a story-teller who [had] taken notes" and paid careful attention to detail; "an idea, with him, is such and such an individual, with such and such a nose and chin, such and such a hat and waistcoat, bearing the same relation to it as the look of a printed word does to its meaning" (*LC*-II, 968–69, 977). But he surpassed the French in his feeling for "the poetry" and "the strangeness" inherent in his figures, preferring evocative diction to words and phrases that were "too striking, or too complete" to convey this sense of mystery (*HJL* II, 26). Moreover, as Dale Peterson has observed, Turgenev's was a poetic rather than a scientific realism, one that depended on "the play of perspective and the 'point of view' " and that emphasized "the power of human perception to extract felt value even from the most constricting . . . of circumstantial realities" (2–3). James especially admired Turgenev's avoidance of generalizing commentary: "the poet never plays chorus; situations speak for themselves" (*LC*-II, 983). And because he used his protagonists as structural "centers," Turgenev's works were "remarkable for concision"—a virtue lacking in the English novel, which, James lamented, "has come in general to mean a ponderous, shapeless, diffuse piece of machinery" (*LC*-II, 974; *LC*-I, 497). In his prefaces, written some thirty years later, James expounded the lessons he had learned from the Russian master. To be sure, he sometimes complained that Turgenev took life "terribly hard" (*LC*-II, 992); but as Peterson has aptly noted, both writers superimposed a "comedy of mind" upon their overt "tragedy of manners" (116).

The relationship between James and Honoré de Balzac was more complex and problematical. Hawthorne, Eliot, and Turgenev impressed the critic as "great consciences and great minds." James noted, "They care for moral questions; they are haunted by a moral ideal." Balzac, however, was primarily "a great temperament—a prodigious nature" (*LC*-II, 47). James credited him with establishing "the realistic, descriptive novel" as the most characteristic of French literary genres; hence Flaubert and his followers, "the new votaries of realism," were "the grandsons of Balzac" (*LC*-II, 168, 1012). But James regretted that this "historian," though greater than his descendants, had failed to represent "superior virtue, intellectual virtue" (*LC*-II, 44). Especially in Balzac's female characters, James found "the sexual quality . . . inordinately emphasized and the conscience . . . inordinately sacrificed to it"; even the novelist's supposed saints were capable of taking lovers or exchanging their honor for money (*LC*-II, 62).

Nonetheless, thanks to "the incomparable vividness of his imagination" (*LC*-II, 36), Balzac transcended James's usual moral categories. The case for Balzac's greatness had been made by Hippolyte Taine, whose study James acknowledged as the only one "worthy of its subject" (*LC*-II, 31). Balzac, Taine had argued, was not merely a realist but a "realistic romancer" who attempted to derive universal truths from the data he observed. Beneath the social history of nineteenth-century France, Balzac sought "the eternal history of the soul" (*LC*-II, 49; Taine, *Balzac* 121). Following Taine's lead, James noted that Balzac transformed his characters into types and his settings into symbols. Thus the author's Père Goriot became another King Lear, the personification of "distracted paternal love," while the "shabby Maison Vauquer" became "the stage of vast dramas, . . . a sort of concentrated focus of human life, with sensitive nerves radiating out into the infinite" (*LC*-II, 59, 60). And because Balzac's characters were larger than life, James accepted—though with some trepidation—Taine's argument that such powerful figures were to be admired, even if they were magnificently corrupt or vicious. " 'Balzac loves his Valérie,' " wrote James, quoting Taine's defense of the depraved Madame Marneffe (*LC*-II, 63). Peter Brooks has perceptively written of the philosophy underlying Balzac's—and James's—taste for hyperbolic rhetoric. Unlike their more skeptical contemporaries, who embraced materialism and the new science, both authors were driven to "push *through* manners to deeper sources of being," putting readers in touch with "the conflict of good and evil played out under the surface of things." Perhaps inevitably, melodrama provided a means of representing the sacred in an era when Christianity had lost its unifying force and mythmaking had become the act of the individual artist (Brooks 4, 15–16).

In the 1870s, James was bemused by Balzac's "extraordinary union of vigour and shallowness,'' praising the novelist's ''power'' but deploring his grossness and vulgarity (*LC*-II, 66, 68). As he wrote his own fiction, however, James used Balzac's works as sources more often than those of any other writer (Tintner, *Book World* 246). And during his major phase at the turn of the century, he followed Balzac's example by giving full value to such characters as Kate Croy and Charlotte Stant, reprehensible though their actions were. (As he explained in the preface to *The Golden Bowl*, he discarded ''the muffled majesty of authorship'' in order to ''get down into the arena'' and ''live and breathe and rub shoulders'' with his antagonists [*LC*-II, 1323].) Naturally, then, he paid tribute to the master from whom he had ''learned . . . more of the lessons of the engaging mystery of fiction than from any one else'' (*LC*-II, 121). In 1902 he likened himself to a prodigal son returning to ''the parental threshold and hearthstone''; and in 1905, lecturing to an American audience on ''The Lesson of Balzac,'' James called him ''the father of us all'' (*LC*-II, 91, 120). Balzac, he said, surpassed the timid Anglo-Saxons because he entered into his characters' consciousness, their ''very skin and bones,'' and also because he was aware of his method and purpose: ''the fusion of all the elements of the picture, under his hand, is complete—of what people are with what they do, . . . of all the parts of the drama with each other'' (*LC*-II, 132, 135). Once more, James followed Taine, who had praised fiction in which the greatest force received the greatest development (*Philosophie* 345)—that is, in which the most passionate characters were most fully dramatized, along with the conditions that made them what they were.

Hawthorne, Eliot, Turgenev, and Balzac were thus the authors who most influenced James, and theirs were the cases he used as touchstones in dealing with lesser writers. Reading his essays on these four novelists, one sees the validity of Daniel Schwarz's claim that James helped establish a humanist tradition of Anglo-American criticism—a tradition whose later exponents include F. R. Leavis and Wayne Booth. All these critics sought order in response to historical chaos, and all subordinated their aesthetic to their moral values, even while discussing form as a revelation of the meaning inherent in the subject (Schwarz 1–3). In James's view, Hawthorne, Eliot, and Turgenev were chiefly notable for their moral imagination: not only did they create ethically conscious characters, but they also made the consciousness—and often the conscience— into the thematic and formal center of their fiction. James's remark on Eliot's Dorothea suggests the value he attached to such characterizations: ''we believe in her as in a woman we might providentially meet some fine day when we should find ourselves doubting of the immortality of the soul'' (*LC*-I, 959–60). The same could not be said of Balzac's figures, yet James came to admire the novelist's visionary power, his ability to dramatize hidden spiritual values. As Peter Brooks has argued, Balzac too may be regarded as a humanist whose belief in the sacred contrasted sharply with the ''attitude of deconstructive and stoic materialism'' adopted by Flaubert and the novelists who followed him (198).

During his later years, James gained sufficient self-confidence to praise the authors whom he had regarded as antagonists. He conceded that Flaubert, despite his cynicism, was a master of literary style. "His life was that of a pearl-diver, breathless in the thick element while he groped for the priceless word, and condemned to plunge again and again" (*LC*-II, 309). Likewise he applauded Zola as a writer of epic, albeit malodorous, fiction. "His personality is the thing that finally pervades and prevails, just as so often on a vessel the presence of the cargo makes itself felt for the assaulted senses" (*LC*-II, 873). William Veeder has observed that the use of metaphor in James's later essays was a mark of the critic's increased flexibility. Whereas his early pronouncements were often dogmatic, his later style discourages simple moralism while avoiding the opposite extreme of simple relativism (Veeder, "Image as Argument" 174).

But if James became a more sophisticated critic, it is also true that the scope of his interests narrowed as he assumed the role of master in his own right. In the 1890s he virtually abandoned the practice of reviewing popular novels, preferring to write lengthy essays on authors he admired. As a writer who had tried but failed to reach a mass audience, he developed a certain scorn for the periodicals, which he likened to trains that could not run unless all their seats were occupied, if only by stuffed mannequins (*LC*-I, 95). Then, too, he discovered that instructive "cases" were increasingly difficult to find. In France, the imitators of Balzac and Flaubert were decidedly inferior to the originals; hence James wrote retrospective essays on the authors of "his own house . . . his own youth and the irrecoverable freshness of its first curiosities and its first responses" (*LC*-I, 112). In the United States, a generation of local-color writers, including Hamlin Garland, Bret Harte, and Mary Wilkins Freeman, had shown that America might indeed yield its secrets to a grasping imagination. James praised these authors in a series of "American Letters" (1898) yet acknowledged the difference between his perspective and theirs. "I have lost touch with my own people," he later confessed to Garland (Garland 93). In Britain at the turn of the century, the most fashionable writers were the novelists of "saturation," including Arnold Bennett, Compton Mackenzie, and H. G. Wells. James likened their art to the squeezing of an orange—a metaphor suggesting both the richness of life and the crudity with which they treated it (*LC*-I, 132). As for the younger, less famous authors who submitted their works to him, his response was to imagine how their novels might be rewritten in Jamesian fashion, with a central character as the controlling consciousness.

Thus, among his later critical writings, the most important by far are his prefaces to the New York Edition of his own *Novels and Tales* (1907–9). To an extent, as Thomas Leitch has noted, James's purpose was to advertise "the authority of his imaginative vision" (24). Just as James had praised the characters of Hawthorne, Eliot, and Turgenev, so he now called attention to the superior qualities of his own creations: "I confess I never see the *leading* interest of any human hazard but in a consciousness . . . subject to fine intensification and wide enlargement" (*LC*-II, 1092). (Indeed, he excluded some works from the edition—*Washington Square* and *The Bostonians*, for example—to which this principle would not easily apply, and he revised others to increase the scope of the central consciousness [Leitch 26, 29].) His characters' sense of their experience, he maintained, transformed mundane events "into the stuff of drama or, even more delightful word still, of 'story' " (*LC*-II, 1083). He also stressed his attention to "architecture," because "composition alone is positive beauty" (*LC*-II, 1315). True, he conceded, there might be "life" in the sprawling novels of William Makepeace Thackeray, Alexandre Dumas, or Leo Tolstoy, "but what do such large loose baggy monsters, with their queer elements of the accidental and the arbitrary, artistically *mean*?" (*LC*-II, 1107).

Yet the prefaces undermine the legend of James as formalist master—a myth perpetuated, at times, by the novelist himself and accepted as truth by his more dogmatic disciples. In these essays, however, James acknowledged the limits of his own vision, as when he referred to the "abysmal" mysteries presented to him by modern tourists and American businessmen (*LC*-II, 1218, 1203). And in a famous passage, he argued that the "house of fiction" has innumerable windows, each one created "by the pressure of the individual will" of the artist (*LC*-II, 1075). Many commentators have noted that James's concern with point of view, both in his fiction and in his criticism, shook the philosophical foundations of the realistic novel; to adopt perspectivism as a ruling principle is to deny the existence of "a 'true point of view' " (Jones, *James as Critic* 122; Posnock 180).

Even when writing of his achievements, James was often less than authoritative. Though delighting in "the story of [his] story," he confessed to lapses of memory concerning the origins of some of his works, the "buried germ" of which he could not "disinter" (*LC*-II, 1309, 1241). (*The Tragic Muse*, for example, he called "a poor fatherless and motherless, a sort of unregistered and unacknowledged birth" [*LC*-II, 1103].) More crucially, he recognized the gap between intention and execution: "one's plan, alas, is one thing and one's result another" (*LC*-II, 1294). A passage in the preface to *The Awkward Age* sums up numerous references to the times when his material had mastered him:

The little ideas one wouldn't have treated save for the design of keeping them small, the developed situations that one would never with malice prepense have undertaken, the long stories that thoroughly meant to be short, the short subjects that had underhandedly plotted to be long, the hypocrisy of modest beginnings, the audacity of misplaced middles, the triumph of intentions never entertained—with these patches, as I look about, I see my experience paved: an experience to which nothing is wanting save, I confess, some grasp of its final lesson. (*LC*-II, 1122)

Readers of James's fiction, with its multiple ambiguities, do learn a lesson here: like all creative writers, the novelist could not fully control the structure of his texts or the play of his language, thus creating interpretive problems that can never be resolved. (Is Maggie Verver a saint or a witch? What are we to make of Strether's final act of renunciation?) In revising his earlier works, James did try to unearth their "buried secrets." But some "intentions," he conceded, were "buried too deep to rise again," whereas others were "not much worth the burying" (*LC*-II, 1046). And as he revised, he wrote new texts posing new interpretive conundrums.

Moreover, despite his fame as a formalist, James wavered on the issue of how much formal control he should try to achieve. In "The Art of Fiction," he suggested that "life *without* rearrangement," which touches "the truth," might be preferable to life "*with* rearrangement," which could be a mere "compromise and convention." He added, "Catching the very note and trick, the strange irregular rhythm of life, that is the attempt whose strenuous force keeps Fiction upon her feet" (*LC*-I, 58). And in the preface to *The Portrait of a Lady*, he made a crucial concession even as he admired the "square and spacious" house he had built for his heroine. "I would rather, I think, have too little architecture than too much—when there's danger of its interfering with my measure of the truth" (*LC*-II, 1072). There appear to have been two Jameses: a formalist who wanted to control the "appetites and treacheries" of his material, and an anti-formalist who celebrated its "expansive, . . . explosive principle" (*LC*-II, 1278). John Carlos Rowe, who has written of the deconstructive potentialities of James's fiction, cites James's remark that the novel appears "more true to its character in proportion as it strains, or tends to burst, with a latent extravagance, its mould" (*LC*-II, 46). If James was ambivalent about "the impulse toward completed meaning," he surely cleared the way for those who would seek its undoing (Rowe, *Theoretical Dimensions* 7).[1]

A word should also be said concerning the role James never assumed—the role of explicator of his own fiction. Indeed, the clues provided by his prefaces have served to provoke debate rather than resolve it. *The Turn of the Screw* furnishes an example: those who believe in the ghosts can cite James's defense of the "fairy-tale pure and simple" against "the mere modern 'psychical' case"; those who doubt the governess can cite his hint that her "explanation" of the "anomalies and obscurities," unlike her "record" of them, may be far from "crystalline" (*LC*-II, 1183, 1182, 1185). In any event, James placed the burden of interpretation on the reader. "Make him *think* the evil, make him think it for himself, and you are released from weak specifications" (*LC*-II, 1188). To be sure, James might be taken aback by theorists who argue that "the birth of the reader" entails "the death of the author"; he was still too much the master for such self-effacement. But as he reread his own novels and stories, he realized that there were "more of the shining silver fish afloat in the deep sea of [his] endeavour than the net of widest casting could pretend to gather in." Consequently, he asked his readers to collaborate with him, inviting them "to dream again in [his] company" (*LC*-II, 1338).

Looking back at James's criticism, one notes a paradox. In relation to his contemporaries, he was something of a conservative; yet from our perspective, his writings seem prophetic, whereas theirs seem dated, if not outmoded. (Contrast, for example, "The Art of Fiction" with Howells's *Criticism and Fiction* or Zola's *Le roman expérimental*.) His earliest reviews are marked by the seriousness—and sometimes the stridency—of a young conservative trying to bring order out of chaos. In an increasingly democratic society, he championed "the ideal" against the vulgar; and in an increasingly secular age, he affirmed his "faith in human will and in character" (Cargill 375). Because of this faith, he stands apart from nineteenth- and twentieth-century critics who view the novel as an endless play of signifiers. "To use current terms," writes Daniel Schwarz, "James believed in the metaphysics of presence" (23).

Yet circumstances conspired to make James a more liberal, forward-looking critic than he set out to be. The resistance he encountered from his readers led him to see that his perspective, however intelligent, was only one among many. And his admiration for other writers led him to define the role of the critic as "the real helper of the artist, a torch-bearing outrider, the interpreter, the brother" (*LC*-I, 98). Given the breadth of his reading, he invites today's critics to place his fiction in multiple contexts: if his concern for the "deeper psychology" links him with the "Anglo-Saxons," his concern for literary style allies him with the French.

Finally, James perceived that his works were subject to many interpretations and that his role as master was far from absolute. He might well be surprised at some of the readings his fiction has been given, but he would applaud criticism that is "creative and mature." Such criticism, he believed, would foster not only the appreciation of old masters but also the development of new ones. As he wrote in "The Future of the Novel," "A community addicted to reflection and fond of ideas will try experiments with the 'story' that will be left untried in a community mainly devoted to travelling and shooting, to pushing trade and playing football" (*LC*-I, 106). Those of us who claim membership in the first community, even as we live in the second, may well acknowledge James as the father of us all.

## NOTE

1. See also Sharon Cameron's recent book *Thinking in Henry James*, especially chapter 2, "The Prefaces, Revision, and Ideas of Consciousness" (32–82). According to Cameron, the prefaces sometimes imply that consciousness is centered and unitary; but contradictions exist both within the prefaces and between them and the novels, which dramatize the radical dissemination of consciousness.

# 3
## James's Theory of Fiction and Its Legacy

*Daniel R. Schwarz*

In this essay I shall place Henry James's "The Art of Fiction" within the context of the period in which he wrote, his critical corpus, and the current theoretical debate. James is the first figure whom we can isolate as a major source of the way we have read and taught fiction in England and America for the past fifty years. We can trace back to Henry James the dilemma of Anglo-American novel criticism: how to focus on technique without sacrificing subject matter. Much of the novel criticism of this century has been trying to resolve these two factors into an aesthetic. Given that novels seem to create imagined worlds with a distinct time, space, and causality that mimes that of the real world, it seems as if subject matter ought not to be ignored. But given that novels are, like other literary forms, works of art composed of words, we cannot ignore technique. Though most "formal" critics of the novel do not neglect content in determining meaning, focus on one nevertheless always seems to be at the expense of the other. James provides a paradigm for those who believe that novels have a particular artistic and thematic vision and that the author shapes that vision into a formal pattern for a particular audience. First and foremost, James is a pluralist in his criticism. "The only obligation to which in advance we may hold a novel . . . is that it be interesting" (*LC*-I, 49).

For those of us who believe that it is time to recenter the subject, the author, and the anterior world, James provides crucial arguments. Yet he never forgets the role of the reader. For James, anterior reality is a source of fiction. "The only reason for the existence of a novel is that it does attempt to represent life" (*LC*-I, 46). The novelist is as occupied with looking for truth as is the historian: "to represent and illustrate the past, the actions of men, is the task of either writer, and the only difference that I can see is, in proportion as he succeeds, to the honor of the novelist, consisting as it does in his having more difficulty in collecting his evidence, which is so far from being purely literary. It seems to me to give him a great character, the fact that he has at once so much in common with the philosopher and the painter; this double analogy is a magnificent heritage'' (*LC*-I, 47). James's morality is a morality of art that values form, but form in the service of content. In James, we hear echoes of Shelley claiming that ''the poet is the unacknowledged legislator of the world'' and of Arnold's high seriousness.

The stature of James's criticism of the novel surely depends on James's stature as a novelist. As Sarah B. Daugherty notes, ''James's Prefaces, though they have been rigidly interpreted by Percy Lubbock and others, constitute his presentation of his own case, not a set of formulae to be applied to the works of other novelists'' (139). We should remember that his discussion of method and theory is shaped by his own experience of writing novels and, in the case of the prefaces, in response to his memory of his own novels. Still, his writing about the aesthetic of the novel provided an example for discussing the art of the novel, particularly point of view, and for the humanist perspective that has dominated Anglo-American formal criticism of the novel. While James looks forward to concern with form and technique, he provides continuity with the high seriousness of Arnold, who argued for the central place of criticism and defined it as a disinterested act of mind. As Daugherty has shown, James accepts Arnold's definition of criticism—''to know the best that is known and thought in the world.'' ''For him, the literary critic was not the narrow formalist, but rather the cultural, social, and moral critic.'' James wished, like Arnold, ''to remain aloof from the vulgar herd, to observe the world from an intellectual height, to see life steadily and see it whole'' (Daugherty 3–4).

According to William K. Wimsatt, Jr., and Cleanth Brooks, James and Flaubert ''display, in reaction against romantic inspirationalism, a concern for craftsmanship, and a stress upon form as opposed to the exploitation of privileged 'poetic' materials'' (686). But James's focus on art was in part a reaction to naturalism, which focused on heredity and environment in shaping human character and on the drab life of the lower-middle and lower classes. That art controls life and that form discovers the moral significance of theme are part of the New Critical credo for which James has been regarded as a source. Wimsatt and Brooks iterate an orthodoxy of New Criticism when they remark, ''The general principle governing the relation of individual word to the total work is not changed simply because these are poems and not novels'' (686). For them, James is a spokesman in defense of this position when he writes, ''A novel is a living thing, all one and continuous, like any other organism, and in proportion as it lives it will be found, I think, that in each of the parts there is something of each of the other parts'' (*LC*-I, 54). By stressing the relationship between form and content in his criticism and by creating works that required the most attentive and intense kind of reading, James provides a precedent for the view later articulated by Mark Schorer: that technique discovers the values of subject matter. By example and critical tenet, James's insistence on the fusion of style and substance and of form and content has been adopted as a premise of the onto-logical approach of New Criticism and the rhetorical approach of Chicago Ar-istolelian criticism. James's attention to aesthetic matters—craft, unity, technique—made him a favorite of New Criticism, and his interest in narration has made him an important figure in traditional and recent rhetorical criticism.

James's interest in technique and form is influenced by the concept of art for art's sake, which Gautier, Baudelaire, and Mallarmé made prominent in France and which Pater, Wilde, and Yeats imported and developed in England. James can sound like a devotee of art for art's sake, one who is indifferent to the moral implications of reality and content. When, in the preface to *The Spoils of Poynton*, he speaks of "technical subterfuges and subleties" as "the noblest part of *our* amusement," James is something of an aesthete and connoisseur. "My prime loyalty was to the interest of the game, and the honour to be won the more desirable by that fact. Any muddle-headed designer can beg the question of perspective, but science is required for making it rule the scene" (*AN* 137). Whatever sense of fun informs this passage, it still seems to value artistry for its own sake and to patronize moral values and content.

For James, it is the imagination that mediates between life and art. The artist was not, as the naturalists seemed to regard him, a passive, objective observer:

Experience is never limited, and it is never complete; it is an immense sensibility. . . . It is the very atmosphere of the mind; and when the mind is imaginative—much more when it happens to be that of a man of genius—it takes to itself the faintest hints of life, it converts the very pulses of the air into revelations. . . . [Experience is] the power to guess the unseen from the seen, to trace the implication of things, to judge the whole piece by the pattern, the condition of feeling life in general so completely that you are well on your way to knowing any particular corner of it. (*LC*-I, 52–53)

The notion of art as a separate reality is in the Romantic tradition and reminds us that James has continuities with those, from Coleridge through Wilde and Stevens, who sought to build in art an alternative space and who believed that literature can create ghostlier demarcations and keener sounds than the real world.

James borrows a good deal of his critical terminology and something of his sense of the artist as a special figure from the visual arts. In "The Art of Fiction," he wrote, "A psychological reason is, to my imagination, an object adorably pictorial; to catch the tint of its complexion—I feel as if that idea might inspire one to Titianesque efforts" (*LC*-I, 61). Perhaps the interest in Europe, and particularly in Paris, in Impressionism and, later, in the more self-conscious experiments in rendering reality more accurately and more closely—such as Cubism, Fauvism, and post-Impressionism—was a factor in his use of termi-nology from painting and sculpture. After all, the prefaces were written in 1907–9 when Cézanne, Matisse, and Picasso were challenging traditional concepts of reality with their foreshortening, their abandonment of traditional perspective, and their inquiries into the relationship between three-dimensional reality and two-dimensional painting. James felt that "a picture without composition slights its most precious chance for beauty" (*AN* 84). He saw himself as a painter of consciousness, as someone who caught the evanescent processes of the mind and who imposed, by means of deft brush strokes, order and meaning. He often used the term *painter* interchangeably with *writer*. Comparing himself to a painter, he wrote, "Sketchily clustered even, these elements gave out that vague pictorial glow which forms the first appeal of a living 'subject' to the painter's consciousness; but the glimmer became intense as I proceeded to a further analysis" (*AN* 141).

James borrowed the term *foreshortening* from painting in order to, as James E. Miller puts it, "indicate that infinitely complex task of evoking a sense of reality. . . . [B]oth space and time are for the writer a challenge of perspective; and picture, scene, and dialogue will all be determined by the total strategy for foreshortening" (12). In other words, for the purpose of arousing interest, the artist will reorganize material according to the artistic demands of intensity, economy, and composition. Because James conceived of his novels in spatial terms and wanted to "build" a shape or design that would hold, he also used architectural images with their three-dimensional implications (*AN* 109). Thus he describes *The Portrait of a Lady* as "a structure reared with an 'architectural' competence" (*AN* 52). He recalls his plan for *The Awkward Age* in spatial terms: "The neat figure of a circle consisting of a number of small rounds disposed at equal distance about a central object. The central object was my situation, my subject in itself, to which the thing would owe its title, and the small rounds represented so many distinct lamps, as I liked to call them, the function of each of which would be to light with all due intensity one of its aspects" (*AN* 110).

James's "The Art of Fiction" (1884), perhaps his most important single piece of criticism of the novel, was a response to Walter Besant's "The Art of Fiction" (1884). Because Besant's published lecture expressed some of the critical shibboleths of the day, James chose the same title as Besant. Though James became more interested in technique as his career progressed, he never abandoned the credo expressed in "The Art of Fiction" that "a novel is in its broadest definition a personal, a direct impression of life: that, to begin with, constitutes its value, which is greater or less according to the intensity of the impression" (*LC*-I, 50). As Daugherty wrote, "Despite his abiding interest in the art of fiction his discussion of technique was always related to his concern for 'life' " (193–94).

At the center of James's criticism is an interest in life in every aspect, even if in his work we feel that the focus is on the manners and morals of the upper-middle class. In a passage that can be read only autobiographically, he says of himself that "he incurs the stigma of labouring uncannily for a certain fullness of truth" (*AN* 154). In the preface to *The Princess Casamassima*, he asserts that the novelist "report[s] with truth on the human scene; to do so, the novelist requires the sense of life and the penetrating imagination" (*AN* 76, 78). The quest for realism is related to the quest for life and truth. Life was the raw material of art. As Miller puts it, "Life was the source of art, direct and first-hand impressions made up the materials, and the personal and individual consciousness shaped them into a unique image and a form that constituted their value" (3).

Content, then, is far more important to James than to some of his followers. Usually, James did not give priority in his criticism to technique. In "The Art of Fiction," James asserts: " 'The story,' if it represents anything, represents the subject, the idea, the *donnée* of the novel; and there is surely no 'school' ... which urges that a novel should be all treatment and no subject. There must assuredly be something to treat" (*LC*-I, 59). Of subject matter, the key question asks, "Is it valid, in a word, is it genuine, is it sincere, the result of some direct impression or perception of life?" (*AN* 45). The artist must not be content with creating isolated palaces of art remote from either the reader's or his own life. For James, then, the human aspect is central, and he is nowhere more compelling than when discussing *What Maisie Knew*. "No themes are so human as those that reflect for us, out of the confusion of life, the close connection of bliss and bale, of the things that help with the things that hurt, so dangling before us for ever that bright hard medal, of so strange an alloy, one face of which is somebody's right and ease and the other somebody's pain and wrong" (*AN* 143). As Daugherty wrote, "His conception of character as center, for example, derived not merely from an aesthetic ideal but from a humanistic philosophy" (194).

James directed the novel away from its traditional emphasis on plot, an emphasis derived from neoclassicism and the novel's epic and romance antecedents. James regarded character, not plot, as central to the novel. This relates to what Oscar Cargill calls "his faith in human will and in character" (325). In England and America, James contributed to the making of an aesthetic that values character over plot and values the English novel of manners and morals over novels that emphasize either a romance component or a historical perspective or polemical vision. James's interest is in "a man's specific behavior" rather than plot. "What a man thinks and what he feels are the history and the character of what he does" (*AN* 66). Thus he preferred fiction in which character was the center, and he felt a lack of structure when the attention was more diffuse. In James, according to James E. Miller: "The matrix of character and action is consciousness. The consciousness becomes the key to fictional interest and feelings, meditations, inner responses, flow of thought surge to the fore as major material for representation" (16). He wrote in the preface to *The Princess Casamassima*, "I confess I never see the *leading* interest of any human hazard but in a consciousness (on the part of the moved and moving creature) subject to fine intensification and wide enlargement" (*AN* 67). Not only is James's interest in the motives and psyche of characters, but he is also certain that the only conceivable interest for reading is our interest in other human beings. In an essay on Trollope (1883), he wrote: "Character, in any sense in which we can get at it, is action and action is plot, and any plot which hangs together, even if it pretends to interest us only in the fashion of a Chinese puzzle, plays upon our emotion, our suspense, by means of personal references. We care what happens to people only in proportion as we know what people are'' (*LC*-I, 336).

James was at his best not as a theorist but when dealing with specific examples in his work and that of others. After "The Art of Fiction," James rarely posited universal standards and usually insisted on evaluating authors on their own terms. As Daugherty wrote, "Despite his increasing interest in technique, James became less preoccupied with theoretical formulations and more tolerant of aesthetic diversity" (139). This nominalism, this insistence on responding to texts on their own terms as "cases," as James would call them, was an important influence on the critical practice of allowing a text to generate its own aesthetic rather than either applying an a priori standard or looking for specific thematic patterns. Perhaps as an expression of nineteenth-century American optimism, James was relatively tolerant of all kinds of forms and styles. Style is judged according to its efficiency, and form according to its unity. Content is not judged in terms of whether it satisfactorily illustrates a position or demonstrates an ideology but rather on whether it reflects human life as that life is actually lived.

That James's criticism eschews dogmatism, and speaks in general for flexibility and open-mindedness, is illustrated by his critical style. He rarely wrote as if he believed he could promulgate a credo or set of rules. The qualifications, circumlocutions, hesitations, and intricacies of his own style reinforce his pluralism even while implicitly acknowledging the impossibility of precision in aesthetic matters. In all his criticism, but most notably in the prefaces, the modest tone, qualifications, sensitivity, tolerance, and judiciousness speak for his humanism. As he puts it, "The house of fiction has in short not one window, but a million" (*AN* 46). As he notes in "The Art of Fiction," we cannot tell the writer what to write or how. "We must grant the artist his subject, his idea, his *donnée*: our criticism is applied only to what he makes of it" (*LC*-I, 56).

James's discussion of the art of fiction revolved around the artist's relation to his art, the presence of the artist in his work, and the importance of the artist's discovering values. As Miller wrote: "James's presence in the form of the first-person singular is felt throughout his work, and he contended that as a matter of fact an author could not escape his work because he left his stamp everywhere. . . . Although the author's 'spiritual presence' was always distinctive though largely unconscious, his 'rendering' of his subject was a matter of acute consciousness" (11–12). To use current terms, James believed in the metaphysics of presence and believed that language evokes an anterior reality. Thus, whereas James has been adopted by rhetorical critics and New Criticism, his aesthetic principles are often surprisingly expressionistic and derive from the creative process that precedes the work. James sees a relationship between "felt life"— the author's perception of experience—and "the 'moral' sense of a work of art"; the artist's sensibility provides the "projected morality" (*AN* 45).

R. P. Blackmur summarizes James's central tenets in his introduction to *The*

*Art of the Novel*, his 1934 collection of James's prefaces to the New York Edition of his work.

Life itself—the subject of art—was formless and likely to be a waste, with its situations leading to endless bewilderment; while art, the imaginative representation of life, selected, formed, made lucid and intelligent, gave value and meaning to, the contrasts and oppositions and processions of the society that confronted the artist. . . . Then everything must be sacrificed to the exigence of that form, it must never be loose or overflowing but always tight and contained. There was the "coercive charm" of Form, so conceived, which would achieve, dramatise or enact, the moral intent of the theme by making it finely intelligible, better than anything else. (*AN* xxxviii)

James called attention to the importance of form at a time when talk about real life dominated discussion of fiction. Before we agree with Miller that for James, "form is everything—whether it is called execution, treatment, technique—which is done to the unrefined lump of life, the patch of actual experience, to turn it into the finished work of art, product of the imagination" (17), we must stress that James sought organic or "found" form as a way of focusing "interest." As René Wellek notes, "The harmony of form and substance is James's constant requirement" (316). But perhaps by focusing on form, Blackmur underestimates James's commitment to life and essential humanistic values. James believed in the inseparability of style and meaning. Though for the later James a complex style was essential to present the complexities of life, he felt that style must always be a means of understanding experience.

We should look more closely at James's standards, even while acknowledging that he is rarely concerned with proposing specific tenets. James believes that the intensity of the creative process is the source of economy, organic unity, and, hence, artistic excellence. Intensity of creative effort produces within the imagined world intensity that is usually lacking in day-to-day life: "Without intensity, where is vividness, and without vividness where is presentability?" (*AN* 66). In the preface to *The Tragic Muse*, James wrote, "I delight in deep-breathing economy and organic form, and economy and organic unity derive from the intensity of the creative process" (*AN* 84). The artist tries "to preserve for his subject that unity, and for his use of it (in other words for the interest he desires to excite) that effect of a *centre*, which most economise its value" (*AN* 37–38). Economy means, as Miller wrote: "Making everything 'count' to the utmost. . . . [It has] no reference to size or length but full relevance to architecture and shape" (19). James frequently refers to what he calls "the rule of an exquisite economy" (*AN* 129). Of such long novels as *War and Peace*, he asks, "What do such large loose baggy monsters, with their queer elements of the accidental and the arbitrary, artistically *mean?*" (*AN* 84).

For James, "interest" is crucial. To arouse interest, the artist must discover *representative* experience: "The art of interesting us in things . . . can *only* be the art of representing them'' (*AN* 9). James never loses sight of arousing and maintaining the interest of the reader. Verisimilitude is a value based on the assumption that the reader will respond to what he or she believes is real. Yet interest is not simply interest in the subject matter; but, rather, it includes a sense on the part of the artist of the reader's interests. In a sense, the artist represents the reader and prepares a text that, when its technique and subject matter fuse into a whole, will appeal to the reader. James admires the "preserved and achieved unity and quality of tone. . . . What I mean by this is that the interest created, and the expression of that interest, are things kept, as to kind, genuine and true to themselves'' (*AN* 97). Thus aesthetic concepts are inextricably related to content and the reader's response to it. James is extremely conscious of *earning* the reader's attention, and he realizes that he needs to create characters in whom we are "participators by a fond attention'': "The figures in any picture, the agents in any drama, are interesting only in proportion as they feel their respective situations; since the consciousness, on their part, of the complication exhibited forms for us their link of connection with it'' (*AN* 62). Frequently, James thinks of himself as a surrogate for the reader. When he speaks of "we" and "us," he is making common cause with the community of readers that he as an artist seeks.

The emphasis on point of view is central in James's criticism of the novel as well as in his fiction, where he modified the traditional omniscient narrator of Victorian fiction. His interest in point of view is related to his concern about intensity, interest, and realism. In part James's standard is realism—the sense that art can imitate the essence of life, what J. Hillis Miller calls a Platonic sense of reality. According to Wayne Booth: "The process most like the process of life is that of observing events through a convincing, human mind, not a godlike mind unattached to the human condition. . . . [I]f the experience is to be more intense than our own observations, the mind used as an observer must be 'the most polished of possible mirrors' '' (*Rhetoric* 45 [1983] ). James depends in his major works on what he calls "intense *perceivers* . . . of their respective predicaments'' as "mirrors of the subject'' (*AN* 70–71). For him, "A subject residing in somebody's excited and concentrated feeling about something—both the something and the somebody of course being as important as possible—has more beauty to give out than under any other style of pressure'' (*AN* 128). In fiction he believes "the person capable of feeling in the given case more than another of what is to be felt for it, and so serving in the highest degree to *record* it dramatically and objectively, is the only sort of person on whom we can count not to betray, to cheapen or, as we say, give away, the value and beauty of the thing'' (*AN* 67).

Reading James's criticism shows us how broad his interests were, how seldom he let himself become enmeshed in narrow discussion of narrative perspective, and how point of view is only part of James's aesthetic heritage. Anticipating later phenomenological criticism, he understands that the teller is like a reader of experience in the sense that the teller disentangles what he or she perceives in life as the reader does in the text. Proposing an important analogy, James equates his dramatized consciousness with a reader of "the pages of life."

The teller of a story is primarily, none the less, the listener to it, the reader of it, too; and, having needed thus to make it out, distinctly, on the crabbed page of life, to disengage it from the rude human character and the more or less Gothic text in which it has been packed away, the very essence of his affair has been the *imputing* of intelligence. The basis of his attention has been that such and such an imbroglio has got started—on the pages of life—because of something that some one has felt and more or less understood. (*AN* 63)

By shifting focus from external action to the drama of consciousness, James foreshadowed interior monologue and stream of consciousness. James was interested not simply in point of view as a technique but in dramatized consciousness as action. As James E. Miller wrote: "For life itself, the important terms are *immediacy* and *application*: for art, these become *reflection* and *appreciation*. We are involved in the action of life, and must act and apply; we are interested in the action of fiction (if we are), and appreciate it most intensely in its reflection on the feelings and thoughts of characters" (16).

When James argued that novels were incremental to the reader's experience and enlarged the scope of the reader's life, he introduced a staple of humanist criticism of the novel that is somewhat different from Horace's "to teach and to delight." In "Alphonse Daudet," he wrote, "The success of a work of art, to my mind, may be measured by the degree to which it produces a certain illusion; that illusion makes it appear to us for a time that we have lived another life—that we have had a miraculous enlargement of experience" (*LC*-II, 242). But James sometimes stressed that the imaginative worlds of novels provided alternative places to which readers could escape. The novel frees the reader from everyday self by providing us with the world of another consciousness.

The concepts of romance and realism are crucial to James's criticism. He certainly saw himself in the tradition of nineteenth-century realism. As Daugherty wrote, "James accepted the premise underlying all realistic fiction—that it is the task of the novelist to deal with life around him, not with fantasy, mythology, or philosophy" (186). Wimsatt and Brooks note that James was enough of an Aristotelian to give "a picture of a real and objective and external world" (692). In "The Art of Fiction," James wrote, "The air of reality (solidity of specification) seems to me to be the supreme virtue of a novel" (*LC*-I, 53). In the preface to *The American*, he wrote that realism "represents to my perception the things we cannot possibly *not* know, sooner or later, in one way or another. . . . The romantic stands, on the other hand, for the things that, with all the facilties [*sic*] in the world, all the wealth and all the courage and all the wit and all the adventure, we never *can* directly know" (*AN* 31–32). By contrast, the romance lets us loose from the real and operates "in a medium which relieves it, in a particular interest, of the inconvenience of a *related*, a measurable state, a state subject to all our vulgar communities" (*AN* 33).

In his concept of romance, James includes the fairy tale, the ghost story, or any fictional experience in which the author's imagination—particularly his fancy—takes precedence over our empirical sense of psychological and social reality. Romance represented to James a vacation from seriousness and from intense study of character. James anticipated the crucial distinction between English novels and American romance, a distinction that D. H. Lawrence made in *Studies in Classic American Literature* (1923) and that Richard Chase later developed in *The American Novel and Its Tradition* (1951). "The people [in Hawthorne's *The Scarlet Letter*] strike me not as characters, but as representatives, very picturesquely arranged, of a single state of mind; and the interest of the story lies, not in them, but in the situation, which is insistently kept before us, with little progression" (*LC*-I, 404). James believed that the romance frees the artist from reality, from fact, and from observation. Because romance implies something of a play world, it also frees the artist from the rigorous concept of mimesis that insists that art should imitate life. Thus James becomes more an aesthete and a romantic when speaking of fairy tales or the wonderful. He rejects pure genres—"romance" and "novel" or "novel of character" and "novel of incident." "The only classification of the novel that I can understand is into that which has life and that which has it not" (*LC*-I, 55). He admired Balzac, Scott, and even Zola for fusing realistic and romantic impulses, and in his fiction, James always tempered his own romance elements with a strong realistic component.

James believed in literary criticism of fiction as an intellectual activity and felt that it could educate novelists and readers. In James's criticism, as Wellek wrote: "The contrast between the English novel and the French novel is drawn so sharply that the English appear as the blundering formless prudish psychologists and moralists and the French as the shallow, immoral masters of the surface and of sensations. . . . James himself aims at righting the balance; he himself is creating the psychological, moral novel which is also a work of art and form" (306–7). James believed that the comparative positions of French and English novels had much to do with the differing state of criticism in these two nations. "The authors of the English studies appear to labor, in general, under a terror of critical responsibility; the authors of the French, on the contrary, to hunger and thirst for it" (Daugherty 150). Because of his appreciation of the French novelists, culminating in his acknowledgment of Balzac as his artistic patriarch and master, James also influenced the tendency to value the European novel—particularly the French novel—despite its bent for the sociological at the expense of the psychological, and to patronize the English novel as less artistic and less inclusive.

To understand James's heritage we need to examine Percy Lubbock's codification of James's practice and theory. In his foreword to *The Craft of Fiction*, Mark Schorer aptly summarizes Lubbock's achievement: "He gave the criticism of the novel not only terms by means of which it could begin to discuss the question of how novels are made ('the only question I shall ask'), but also a model of the way that the question might plausibly be put.'' James's criticism, especially the prefaces, is the Bible, and Lubbock's *The Craft of Fiction* (1921) is the Talmud or *Midrash*. Lubbock's book, along with Joseph Warren Beach's *The Method of Henry James* (1918) and *The Twentieth-Century Novel: Studies in Technique* (1932), did much to turn James's musings on his method as a novelist into an aesthetic with rigid rules. Yet it is ironic that Lubbock and Beach sought to codify James's suggestions, for James himself cautions about theorizing on art. ''Mysteries here elude us, . . . general considerations fail or mislead, and . . . even the fondest of artists need ask no wider range than the logic of that particular case. The particular case, or in other words, his relation to a given subject, once the relation is established, forms in itself a little world of exercise and agitation'' (*AN* 121). James often thought that a characteristic of novels was their freedom from rules and categories; James E. Miller notes that this freedom gives the novelist room for experimentation and innovation: ''Such freedom *from* rules and regulations and freedom *for* experimentation and creation should prove exhilarating for both writers and their audience'' (26). As we have seen, James objected to the imposition of extrinsic standards on a work based on critics' preconceptions about what a novel should be. Subscribing to the latitudinarianism of the later James, Lubbock maintains, ''The best form . . . makes the most of its subject'' (*Craft of Fiction* 40 [1957]). But in practice, as we shall see, Lubbock has a hierarchy of methods, and his paradigm is James's later method of having an omniscient narrator render the consciousness of characters even to the point of effacing himself.

Lubbock's codification of James stresses several concepts crucial to twentieth-century criticism of the novel. Lubbock used James to argue that a book is ''a process, a passage of experience,'' revealing its form—or rather, partially revealing its form, because that form is ''an ideal shape with no existence in space'' and lacks ''size and shape'' and therefore can be approached only imperfectly (*Craft of Fiction* 15, 22 [1957]). Lubbock realized that the reading of fiction is a linear process and that patterns take shape and then dissolve or recede, only to be replaced by new patterns that do the same. Lubbock's opening sentences make a telling point about the folly of conceiving of fiction in spatial terms: ''To grasp the . . . form of a book, to . . . survey it at leisure—that . . . effort . . . is perpetually defeated. . . . As quickly as we read, it melts and shifts in the memory; . . . when the last page is turned, a great part of the book . . . is already vague and doubtful'' (*Craft of Fiction* 1 [1957]). Using the qualification and suspension of predicate that are characteristic of the mature Jamesian style, Lubbock describes the ineffability of form to the perceiver in a medium that is temporally defined. Because of the length of the novel, the reader cannot retain everything; impressions of character, theme, and language inevitably displace one another rather than build toward an architectonic whole.

By using much of the Jamesian vocabulary, Lubbock forges a link to his master. Unlike James, Lubbock at times seems to feel that point of view *is* the craft of fiction, that method in fiction is ''governed by the question of the point

of view" (*Craft of Fiction* 251 [1957]). Lubbock prefers the dramatized consciousness of the narrator to other methods. "In the drama of his mind . . . there
is no narrator; the point of view becomes the reader's once more. The shapes
of thought in the man's mind tell their own story. And that is the art of picture-
making when it uses the dramatic method" (*Craft of Fiction* 256 [1957]). And
this dramatic method works best if a third-person narrator is retained, because
he can range over time freely. "The seeing eye is with somebody in the book,
but . . . the picture contains more . . . because it is the author's as well. . . . [The
author] keeps . . . hold upon the narrator *as an object*; the sentient character in
the story . . . is not utterly subjective" (*Craft of Fiction* 258–59 [1957]).

Lubbock focused on James primarily as a formal and technical master and
neglected his interest in truth and life. That Lubbock faults *War and Peace* for
its lack of unity shows us his commitment to organic unity at the expense of the
quality and breadth of content. "The chapters [of *War and Peace*] refuse to
adapt themselves . . . to a broad and single effect . . . they will not draw together
and announce a reason for their collocation" (*Craft of Fiction* 52–53 [1957]);
for "the uncertainty of Tolstoy's intention is always getting between the reader
and the detail of his method" (*Craft of Fiction* 59 [1957]). (Nor did James
himself fully respond to Tolstoy's concept of form.) Basically, Lubbock zeroes
in on James's concept of organic form. In "the well-made book . . . the subject
and . . . form coincide" (*Craft of Fiction* 40 [1957]). He indicts Tolstoy for failing
to integrate "into one design" the historical material with "the drama of the
rise of a generation": "a comeliness of form . . . [would have made *War and
Peace*] a finer, truer . . . picture of life" (*Craft of Fiction* 31, 40–41 [1957]).

For Lubbock, more than for James, form and unity are values in themselves,
distinct and separate from how they convey meaning. The shift in emphasis is
one of degree, not kind, but it is obvious that content plays a much smaller role
in Lubbock than James. Lubbock wrote to redress the balance between form and
content at a time when he justifiably felt that matters of form and artistry had
been neglected. Yet if we read Lubbock carefully, we discover that, despite his
stress on form, he understands the importance of content. Notwithstanding his
emphasis on artistry, Lubbock has not abandoned the content of the work and
is interested in the feelings of the author, the consciousness of the teller, the
issues that the novel presents, and the richness and variety of the imagined world.
Technique is perceived as a way not only to artistic unity but also to seeing and
feeling the external world; unity usually revolves around and is in service to
meaning. Indeed, though Lubbock's focus is on isolating the originality of
James's technique, we should recall how he recapitulates the *content* of the
James novels he discusses—most notably *The Ambassadors* and *The Wings of
the Dove*—as if Lubbock cannot quite eschew plot even if he wants to.

As for James, characterization is crucial to Lubbock's concept of form. Indeed,
Lubbock seems to diminish the role of plot even further. Following James,
Lubbock insists that characters must be chosen not because they are exceptional,
but because of their universality. At one point, it is on the basis of characterization

that Lubbock differentiates between the scenic, by which he means a dramatized scene in which the major characters take part, and the panoramic, an overview of the characters' experiences. An artist's attention alternates between "the incidents of his tale" and the shape and hue they take "in somebody's thought" (*Craft of Fiction* 71 [1957]); if he is a polished artist he alternates according to "*some* plan" (*Craft of Fiction* 72 [1957]), and for Lubbock, the best plan is one that always keeps the reader's interest in mind.

*The Craft of Fiction* has its hagiographic aspect. Lubbock is unstinting in his praise for James. Yet Lubbock acknowledges that because of James's idiosyncrasy, the methods of "the only real *scholar* in the art" may well be seen just as "a part of his own original quiddity" (*Craft of Fiction* 186–87 [1957]). Simply put, James showed how to treat "dramatically" an "undramatic subject." In Lubbock's argument, *The Ambassadors* and *The Wings of the Dove* become the quintessence of fiction, the position to which the history of the novel moves. Lubbock dialectically resolves thesis and antithesis—on the one hand, scenic or dramatic, and on the other, pictorial or panoramic. "Everything in [*The Ambassadors*] is now dramatically rendered . . . because even in the . . . description . . . nobody is reporting his impression to the reader. . . . And yet *as a whole* the book is . . . pictorial, an indirect impression received through Strether's . . . consciousness" (*Craft of Fiction* 170 [1957]). Basically, James is credited for discovering a technique that uses the best features of scene and panorama. For Lubbock, this is fiction's version of splitting the atom. He wrote that only in James's later novels is "a pictorial subject . . . thus handed over . . . to the method of drama, so that the intervention of a seeing eye and a recording hand . . . is practically avoided altogether" (*Craft of Fiction* 185 [1957]). This statement reveals a concept of action that values the drama of consciousness over events and episodes.

E. M. Forster's *Aspects of the Novel* (1927) was a response to James's critical legacy and Lubbock's codification and simplification of that legacy in *The Craft of Fiction*. Forster believes that critics have overstressed point of view. By speaking in compelling terms of the elements that he thinks are crucial, Forster rescued the novel from the dogmatism of James and Lubbock. Point of view is not the most important "aspect" but merely one of many secondary ones that do not deserve a separate chapter. The absence of a chapter on "point of view" probably affected the direction of subsequent criticism. With Lubbock (whom he has mentioned a few lines previously) in mind, Forster remarks that critics feel the novel "ought to have its own technical troubles before it can be accepted as an independent art" (79 [1954]). For Forster, a novelist's "method" resolves" into the power of the writer to bounce the reader into accepting what he says" (Forster 78–79 [1954]). By discussing point of view in a few pages in the second chapter, entitled "People," he is emphasizing that point of view, whether in the form of a persona or omniscient narrator, is significant only insofar as it expresses a human voice. Parting company with James and Lubbock, Forster wrote, "The creator and narrator are one" (56 [1954]).

E. M. Forster's warning about self-conscious art is a deliberate attempt to separate himself from the James aesthetic. "The novelist who betrays too much interest in his own method can never be more than interesting; he has given up the creation of character and summoned us to help analyse his own mind, and a heavy drop in the emotional thermometer results" (80 [1954]). Though Forster accepted the classical notion of an efficient plot, we should note that the terms *economical* and *organic* derive from the James influence. "[In the plot] every action or word ought to count; it ought to be economical and spare; even when complicated it should be organic and free from dead matter" (Forster 88 [1954]). But the meaning of plot depends on the active participation of a responsive reader. "Over [the plot] . . . will hover the memory of the reader (that dull glow of the mind of which intelligence is the bright advancing edge) and will constantly rearrange and reconsider, seeing new clues, new chains of cause and effect, and the final sense (if the plot has been a fine one) will not be of clues or chains, but of something aesthetically compact, something which might have been shown by the novelist straight away, only if he had shown it straight away it would never have become beautiful" (Forster 88 [1954]). This is the very kind of active reader that R. S. Crane had in mind in his famous 1952 essay "The Concept of Plot and the Plot of *Tom Jones*" and is the active reader on whom recent reader-response theorists depend. Forster conceived of the structure of the novel as a continuous process by which values are presented, tested, preserved, or discarded rather than as the conclusion of a series that clarifies and reorders everything that precedes. He understood that the importance of a linear pattern within the imagined world relates to the temporal experience of reading the novel. He knew that even if the greatest novels expand infinitely as if they were atemporal, "it is never possible for a novelist to deny time inside the fabric of his novel" (Forster 29 [1954]). For when one "emancipate[s] fiction from the tyranny of time . . . it cannot express anything at all" because "the sequence between the sentences" is abolished and then "the order of the words," until there is no sense (Forster 41–42 [1954]). Thus he pointed criticism of the novel away from James's spatial conception of form, a concept derived more from James's understanding of painting, sculpture, and architecture than from Coleridge's organic form. Forster helped keep alive temporality as a critical concept in the years when discussion of novel form in spatial terms predominated due to the influence of James and later Joseph Frank (Rosenbaum, "*Aspects*" 63).

In *The Rhetoric of Fiction* (1961), Wayne C. Booth is responding both to James and the codification of James by Percy Lubbock in *The Craft of Fiction*. Booth wrote at a time when New Critics had adopted the Jamesian aesthetic for their own purposes and insisted on the superiority of telling to showing. Booth is ambivalent about the example of James. On the one hand, Booth shows that James himself is not the formalist critic that some of his followers have made him out to be, because he is not interested in the dramatic for its own sake but as part of the intensity that all good fiction requires. Booth appropriates James to his cause by arguing that James never thought that the author should be banished; rather, he was concerned with how "to achieve an intense illusion of reality, including the complexities of mental and moral reality" (*Rhetoric* 50 [1983]). But, on the other hand, Booth has misgivings about James's pursuit of a rhetoric in the service of realism rather than for the purpose of eliciting specific effects. "From the beginning James's passion for the reader's sense of traveling in a real, though intensified, world dictates a general rhetoric in the service of realism, rather than a particular rhetoric for the most intense experience of distinctive effects" (*Rhetoric* 50 [1983]).

Booth insists that James's method of "push[ing] all summary back into the minds of the characters" has its price (*Rhetoric* 173 [1983]). The author surrenders the ability to be an "unequivocal spokesman" (*Rhetoric* 175 [1983]). And this, finally, is the difficulty of modern literature and the focus of Booth's last chapter, "The Morality of Impersonal Narration." "As unreliability increases, there obviously can come a point at which such transformed information ceases to be useful even in characterization of minds, unless the author retains some method of showing what the facts are from which the speaker's interpretations characteristically diverge" (*Rhetoric* 175 [1983]). Booth rejected the then fashionable argument that fiction had evolved from simpler to higher forms and that Flaubert or James represented a turning point. Comparing James to Austen in the *Emma* chapter, he wrote, "By combining the role of commentator with the role of hero, Jane Austen has worked more economically than James, and though economy is as dangerous as any other criterion when applied universally, even James might have profited from a closer study of the economies that a character like Knightley can be made to achieve" (*Rhetoric* 253–54 [1983]).

In this period of shrill, polemic, critical debate between opposing factions who seem to be, to paraphrase Arnold, armies of the night contending "on a darkling plain," does James not remind us that the ethics of reading require that we suspend our beliefs and enter into the author's imaginative world rather than single-mindedly apply an external critical grid to each text? He understands the need for a pluralistic aesthetic that attends to demands of mimesis and of form. Perhaps we should conclude by recalling the tonality of James's theories. That the tone of "The Art of Fiction" is dialogic in nature reminds us that the master novelist did not always speak in a master voice. "Art lives upon discussion, upon experiment, upon curiosity, upon variety of attempt, upon the exchange of views and the comparison of standpoints" (*LC*-I, 44–45). James's emphasis on the relationship of art and life provides a paradigm for those who are skeptical about the claims of recent theory that there is nothing outside the text and that the concepts of author, anterior reality, and historical contexts are fictions. His work is central to a tradition that believes that reading is a transaction between a human reader and a human author. James understands that novels are human observations of other humans presented in an artistic form for the consumption of human readers.

# 4
# The Prefaces

*Thomas M. Leitch*

At the age of sixty-two, Henry James wrote to Charles Scribner's Sons "to arrange for a handsome 'definitive edition' of the greater number of [his] novels and tales," a collection to include revised texts of a wide selection of James's long and short fiction, each volume to include "a freely colloquial and even, perhaps as I may say, confidential preface or introduction," the whole production to be called "the New York Edition if that may pass for a general title of sufficient dignity and distinctness" (*HJL* IV, 366, 367, 368).[1] James's magisterial tone here conceals his frankly economic interest in the project, his wish that the sales of the New York Edition would provide what he described to Edith Wharton as "the bread of my vieux jours" (Bell, *Edith Wharton and Henry James* 167)— a pension for James's declining years.

Judged in practical terms, the New York Edition was a stunning failure almost from the day in December 1907 when the first volumes appeared. The novelist's agent, J. B. Pinker, forced him to engage in humbling and sometimes expensive negotiations with several publishers for rights to reprint his earlier work. James's desire for a "handsome" edition with large type and generous margins severely restricted the number of novels and tales he could include, and even though Scribner's allowed him to expand the edition from the sixteen volumes they had originally proposed to twenty-three, the revised texts of the New York Edition overflowed these boundaries into a twenty-fourth volume.[2] James thereupon suffered the further indignity of reshuffling his introductory remarks into new contexts, with the result that his analysis of "Fordham Castle" and some of his remarks on "Julia Bride" ended up in the wrong preface.[3] Though the completed edition, with its elegant plum-colored bindings and its photographic frontispieces by Alvin Langdon Coburn, was opulent enough to give its author a thrill of pride, that thrill was virtually his only reward, since the New York Edition not only failed to make money but also absorbed most of James's energy for two years, during which he undertook no new work.[4]

Only as a literary monument was the New York Edition successful, but here James's success, though posthumous, outstripped even his expansive desires. James's painstaking selection and revision of his work decisively altered the way a generation of critics defined his career, even when they preferred to work with the earlier, unrevised texts. More important, his "freely colloquial and . . . confidential" (*HJL* IV, 367) prefaces have become widely recognized as the first substantial contribution in English to the poetics of fiction.

James's 1905 letter to Scribner's already hints at this intention when it indicates that each preface will be "representing, in a manner, the history of the work or the group, representing, more particularly, perhaps, a frank critical talk about its subject, its origin, its place in the whole artistic chain, and embodying, in short, whatever of interest there may be to be said about it" (*HJL* IV, 367). James's reference to his whole artistic chain and his hint that the prefaces will give a comprehensive account of each work point in a new direction echoed in Scribner's prospectus for the edition, which describes it as "an elaborate edifice whose design and execution are absolutely unique in their kind owing to their complete unity of effect" (quoted in Edel, "Architecture" 169). James told Howells, "It will be long before I shall want to collect them together . . . and furnish *them* with a final Preface" (*LHJ* II, 99); even so, the eighteen prefaces are clearly planned as a unified series, the closest James would ever come to a systematic theory of fiction.

The approach to the prefaces as an exposition of a coherent theory of fiction, first systematically explored by Leon Edel in 1931, gained more direct influence from R. P. Blackmur's 1934 essay on the prefaces, reprinted as the introduction to the volume *The Art of the Novel*, in which all eighteen prefaces were collected for the first time. Both Edel and Blackmur see James's theoretical aims as essentially rhetorical. In preface after preface, James recalls and defines the subject of the novel or tale at hand, discusses the potential that made it a promising subject, and proceeds to analyze the way he has treated the subject in order to realize this potential as fully and economically as possible. The distinction between the given subject and its development—what James variously called the essence and the form or the matter and the manner (*AN* 53, 324)[5]—implies a rhetorical theory of fiction most straightforwardly developed in the preface to *The Ambassadors*, which Blackmur took as a model for the series. James begins by recounting the remark ("Live all you can; it's a mistake not to. . . . I'm too old—too old at any rate for what I see") and the speaker and situation (a man past middle age addressing a much younger friend in a garden in Paris) that provided his germ; then he proceeds to explain the way in which this single episode suggested the growth of the novel; finally he analyzes the way in which he has chosen to treat his subject. The rhetorical basis of James's argument is clearest when, considering what was to become Lambert Strether's exhortation to-Little Bilham in the Paris garden, he describes his search for a motivating character and circumstances.

Where has he come from and why has he come . . . ? To answer these questions plausibly . . . was to possess myself of the entire fabric. At the same time the clue to its whereabouts would lie in a certain *principle* of probability: he wouldn't have indulged in this peculiar tone without a reason; it would take a felt predicament or a false position to give him so ironic an accent. One hadn't been noting ''tones'' all one's life without recognising when one heard it the voice of the false position. The dear man in the Paris garden was then admirably and unmistakably *in* one—which was no small point gained; what next accordingly concerned us was the determination of *this* identity. . . . He would have issued, our rueful worthy, from the very heart of New England—at the heels of which matter of course a perfect train of secrets tumbled for me into the light. . . . I accounted for everything—and ''everything'' had by this time become the most promising quantity—by the view that he had come to Paris in some state of mind which was literally undergoing, as a result of new and unexpected assaults and infusions, a change almost from hour to hour. (*AN* 313–14)

In its relentless inductiveness, this sounds like nothing so much as Poe's account of the genesis of ''The Raven'' in ''The Philosophy of Composition.'' The difference, of course, is in the tone: Poe is a magician trying to impress an audience, whereas James, as so often in the prefaces, speaks with a hushed exaltation that suggests an extraordinary intimacy between his audience and himself. But even when James goes on to discuss the technical problems arising from his decision to remain within Strether's consciousness throughout the novel by using a third-person narrative that would have no access to anyone's thoughts but the hero's, his analysis recalls Poe. In fact, though the preface to *The Ambassadors*, which James considered his most successful novel, is the most closely reasoned and, in some ways, the most attractive of them all, it is quintessential rather than representative because it is so single-mindedly empirical.

Most of the prefaces carry on their theoretical arguments largely through generalizing excurses on technique, on the kinds of fiction, and on the novel as a literary and artistic form. Readers who are not Jamesians frequently find these general excurses the most compelling passages in the prefaces; they are certainly the most quotable.

Really, universally, relations stop nowhere, and the exquisite problem of the artist is eternally but to draw, by a geometry of his own, the circle within which they shall happily *appear* to do so. (*AN* 5)

The balloon of experience is in fact of course tied to the earth, and under that necessity we swing, thanks to a rope of remarkable length, in the more or less commodious car of the imagination; but it is by the rope we know where we are, and from the moment that cable is cut we are at large and unrelated: we only swing apart from the globe— though remaining as exhilarated, naturally, as we like, especially when all goes well.

The art of the romancer is, "for the fun of it," insidiously to cut the cable, to cut it without our detecting him. (*AN* 33–34)

The house of fiction has . . . not one window, but a million—a number of possible windows not to be reckoned, rather; every one of which has been pierced, or is still pierceable, in its vast front, by the need of the individual vision and by the pressure of the individual will. (*AN* 46)

Only make the reader's general vision of evil intense enough, I said to myself . . . and his own experience, his own imagination, his own sympathy (with the children) and horror (of their false friends) will supply him quite sufficiently with all the particulars. Make him *think* the evil, make him think it for himself, and you are released from weak specifications. (*AN* 176)

These passages arise in particular contexts (discussions of given novels or tales) that they seem to transcend because of the power of their rhetoric and imagery; and it is largely on the basis of such detachable observations, rather than the architectural design of the prefaces as a group, that James first received attention as a theorist of fiction.

The typical preface, then, treats the same topics as the preface to *The Ambassadors*, but more freely, discursively, even rhapsodically. The prefaces to the middle volumes of the edition, those containing James's shorter stories, are more fragmentary and unbalanced than the others—just as in those novels with a "makeshift middle" (*AN* 302), James has a habit of going on at such length about the first story in each volume that he has much less time for the others— and any one of the prefaces to the other novels, to *Roderick Hudson* or *The American* or *The Portrait of a Lady* or *The Tragic Muse* or *The Awkward Age*, is more representative of the series than the preface to *The Ambassadors*. Hence the preface to *Roderick Hudson*, and the entire series, begins with an announcement having the air of a program: " 'Roderick Hudson' was begun in Florence in the spring of 1874, designed from the first for serial publication in 'The Atlantic Monthly,' where it opened in January 1875 and persisted throughout the year. I yield to the pleasure of placing these circumstances on record, as I shall place others, and as I have yielded to the need of renewing acquaintance with the book after a quarter of a century" (*AN* 3). Such passages often blossom into surprisingly fervent invocations of "the great Paris harmony" (*AN* 27) outside James's window as he wrote *The American* or "the good fog-filtered Kensington mornings" (*AN* 85) which greeted the author of *The Tragic Muse*, invocations that show James's devotion to recreating his own past. He is not only giving his readers background material but also allowing them to overhear some nostalgic reminiscences, essaying brief autobiographical flights in preparation for *A Small Boy and Others* (1913) and *Notes of a Son and Brother* (1914).

It is true that James clearly feels a responsibility to provide certain kinds of background information to his audience, as he shows when he remarks his inability to "say what, in the summer of 1873, may have put 'Madame de

Mauves' '' into his head. He acknowledges, '' 'Louisa Pallant,' with still subtler art, I find, completely covers her tracks.'' And he notes, ''Blankness overtakes me, I confess, in connexion with the brief but concentrated 'Greville Fane' '' (*AN* 196, 197, 234). But since he goes on in each case to recall something about the circumstances under which each story was written, he is evidently apologizing for a different kind of omission: his inability to account for the way the story was first suggested to him, the seed from which it grew, the germ he treats so fully and proudly in the preface to *The Ambassadors*. These germinal ideas characteristically mark the center of the prefaces as well as the works they introduce, though sometimes, as in the preface to *The Golden Bowl*, they are brought up only briefly and abstractly. James's germs take a wide variety of forms. Sometimes, as in *Roderick Hudson*, *The Tragic Muse*, and James's international stories, the subject seems to be given as ''one of the half-dozen great primary motives'' (*AN* 79). *The Tragic Muse*, for example, marks James's first attempt to ''do something about art''—specifically, about ''the conflict between art and 'the world' '' (*AN* 79), a conflict to which he repeatedly returned in his shorter tales of the 1890s.

More often, James's novels and stories are presented as attempts to display or work out the complexities of leading figures like Isabel Archer and Hyacinth Robinson. The case of Hyacinth, who ''sprang up for me out of the London pavement'' (*AN* 60) and whose plot is defined in terms of the potential conflict implied by his situation as a sensitive outsider—''I got my action . . . under the prompt sense that the state of feeling I was concerned with might develop and beget another state, might return at a given moment, and with the greatest vivacity, on itself'' (*AN* 71–72)—is relatively simple, but that of Isabel is revealingly complex. James both indicates and reenacts this complexity in the preface to *The Portrait of a Lady*, a novel developed from ''my grasp of a single character—an acquisition I had made, moreover, in a fashion not here to be retraced.'' The paradox in Isabel's conception lies for James in its combination of vividness and indeterminacy. ''I saw it as bent upon its fate, some fate or other; *which*, among the possibilities, being precisely the question. Thus I had my vivid individual—vivid, so strangely, in spite of being still at large, not confined by the conditions, not engaged in the tangle, to which we look for much of the impress that constitutes an identity.'' James asks, ''If the apparition was still all to be placed how came it to be vivid?'' He answers with a series of figures. Isabel is described as a given value that has been ''take[n] over straight from life'' and ''to that extent . . . *been* placed'' by ''the imagination that detains it, preserves, protects, enjoys it, conscious of its presence in the dusky, crowded, heterogeneous back-shop of the mind very much as a wary dealer in precious odds and ends,'' ready ''to disclose its merit afresh as soon as a key shall have clicked in a cupboard-door.'' Having established himself as an antiquarian or broker whose shop constitutes his aspiring heroine's placement, James changes his figure, describing his ''outfit for the large building of 'The Portrait of a Lady' '' as beginning with ''this single small corner-stone, the conception of a certain young woman affronting her destiny.'' He continues a little inconsistently, ''It came to be a square and spacious house . . . but . . . it had to be put up round my young woman while she stood there in perfect isolation'' (*AN* 47–48).[6] This discussion, which begins as an attempt to describe Isabel's conception in autobiographical terms by revisiting the scene of composition and tracing ''the history of the growth of one's imagination'' (*AN* 47), proceeds to interpret the novel by rehearsing its major conflict, which opposes Isabel's conception of herself as a figure of pure potential to whom every point of contact with circumstance would mark a limitation of freedom to Gilbert Osmond's and Madame Merle's belief in the expressiveness and intrinsic value of appearances, surfaces, material objects, and social rituals. Even James's figures, which define Isabel first as a precious object in the hands of a collector and then as an isolated figure in a building erected around her, recapitulate the action of the novel, echoing her imprisonment just as James's earlier reference to the many-windowed house of fiction echoes her aspirations to freedom and vision.

Isabel's peculiar combination of vividness and undefined potential, which James refers first to his own undefined relation to his figure and then, by implication, to her engagement with the world of her novel, indicates James's preference for taking his subjects as given, indefinable or unplaceable except in terms of the tale that treats the novelist's idea by exhibiting ''the related state, to each other, of certain figures and things'' (*AN* 5). The most promising subjects are precisely those that necessarily imply a narrative development and so cannot be defined apart from that development.

James's simultaneous insistence on isolating his subjects in order to define them for analysis and on refusing to define them apart from their development in the completed novel or tale is even more pronounced in the stories whose subjects are based on particular situations or anecdotes he has overheard. He begins the preface to *The Awkward Age* by remarking: ''I recall with perfect ease the idea in which 'The Awkward Age' had its origin, but re-perusal gives me pause in respect to naming it. The composition, as it stands, makes . . . so considerable a mass beside the germ sunk in it and still possibly distinguishable, that I am half-moved to leave my small secret undivulged'' (*AN* 98). At length, however, he overcomes his reticence enough to identify as the germ of the novel ''the difference made in certain friendly houses and for certain flourishing mothers by the sometimes dreaded, often delayed, but never fully arrested coming to the forefront of some vague slip of a daughter,'' and the consequent ''account to be taken, in a circle of free talk, of a new and innocent, a wholly unacclimatised presence, as to which such accommodations have never had to come up'' (*AN* 99–100, 101). Such a subject seemed especially promising because of its myriad possibilities, but these very possibilities now made it difficult to define as a subject: ''Though the relations of a human figure or a social occurrence are what make such objects interesting, they also make them, to the same tune, difficult to isolate'' (*AN* 101). The same problem appears in James's discussion of *What Maisie Knew*, whose nominal subject, the fate of a child whose divorced parents have remarried and wish to have her off their hands, James cannot bring himself to call a subject until he has proceeded to sketch a treatment, a line of development, a network of relations that give out "that vague pictorial glow which forms the first appeal of a living 'subject' to the painter's consciousness" (*AN* 141). When is a subject not a subject? Before it has received "the sacrament of execution" that "indissolubly marries" subject and form (*AN* 115–16). Hence James, writing on the anecdote that gave him the idea for *The Spoils of Poynton*, notes the "fineness . . . that communicates the virus of suggestion, anything more than the minimum of which spoils the operation" and recalls how, having heard at a Christmas Eve dinner about the struggle of a widow and her son over her late husband's house and furnishings, he noted the promise of the situation, only to observe, in the reported action of the adversaries, "clumsy Life again at her stupid work" (*AN* 119, 121). The point here is not simply that art is more shapely and satisfying than life but rather that though James defines subjects as a priori possibilities for treatment, he conceives of that treatment as committed to exhibiting relations and developments without which the subject is not a subject after all.

James's treatment of his subjects accordingly takes as its explicit rule the injunction "Dramatise, dramatise!" (*AN* 265), which James applies especially to his shorter tales. Richly promising heroes and heroines are dramatized by being put in situations that bring them into conflict with their world or that manifest their divided natures; such subjects depend on a conflict between a sensitive consciousness, "the troubled life mostly at the centre of our subject" (*AN* 67), and the social circumstances it confronts. But the external situations and conflicts suggested by the anecdotes behind *The Spoils of Poynton* and *What Maisie Knew* also need to be dramatized by being lodged in a sensitive awareness of their potential value. Whether James begins with a subject like Isabel Archer or Hyacinth Robinson or a situation like that of *The Awkward Age* or the international tales, his fiction, long or short, tends to take the form of a dialectical interplay between a perceiving consciousness and its world.

James is often critical of his procedures in developing this interplay. In the second half of *Roderick Hudson* "everything occurs . . . too punctually and moves too fast"; the relationship between the hero and heroine of *The American* is so briefly and weakly depicted that when "it takes a great stride . . . the author but appears to view that but as a signal for letting it severely alone"; Nick Dormer, in *The Tragic Muse*, is "not quite so interesting as he was fondly intended to be"; *The Wings of the Dove* "offers perhaps the most striking example I may cite . . . of my regular failure to keep the appointed halves of my whole equal" (*AN* 12, 38, 96, 302). But these criticisms are always technical and rhetorical; they always apply to his treatment of a particular subject, never to his choice of subjects, the evanescence of his principals' consciousness, the relative thinness of physical action in his stories—in short, never to the strictures that critics had been applying to his work for nearly thirty years. James often gives the impression of rising above debate because he characteristically answers his critics by redefining the terms of the argument. The preface to *The Portrait of a Lady* indicates some of the differences between his definition of a "subject" and the ideas of theme or character or situation with which it is usually identified. Although James presents his subjects as raw material to be exhibited through a given fictional treatment, identifying them as subjects already amounts to treating them in a certain specific way, as he suggests when he explains that if Newman had taken revenge on the Bellegardes, "there would be no subject at all, obviously,—or simply the commonest of the common," for Newman's final position as "a strong man indifferent to his strength and too wrapped . . . in *other* and intenser, reflexions for the assertion of his 'rights' '' was "of the essence and constituted in fact the subject" (*AN* 22). Only Newman's renunciation of vengeance makes his situation an appropriate subject. Similarly, Maisie's position as "a tennis-ball or a shuttlecock" in her parents' ruined marriage did not become a subject until James postulated "the chance of happiness and of an improved state . . . for the child, round about whom the complexity of life would thus turn to fineness, to richness. . . . Sketchily clustered even, these elements gave out that vague pictorial glow which forms the first appeal of a living 'subject' to the painter's consciousness" (*AN* 140, 141). These hints about how subjects are constituted are made most general and explicit in James's discussion of *The Spoils of Poynton*, in which he describes the way the battle over the spoils "wanted, for treatment, a centre," which took the form of the ever more interested observer Fleda Vetch, who, by registering "the felt beauty and value of the prize of battle, the Things," thereby "marked her place in my foreground at one ingratiating stroke. She planted herself centrally, and the stroke, as I call it, the demonstration after which she couldn't be gainsaid, was the simple act of letting it be seen she had character." Having imagined Fleda as someone who "would understand" the importance of the spoils to Mrs. Gereth, James defines "the progress and march of my tale" as "that of her understanding," and concludes: "A subject residing in somebody's excited and concentrated feeling about something—both the something and the somebody being of course as important as possible—has more beauty to give out than under any other style of pressure" (*AN* 126, 127, 128).

This line of argument involves James in redefining not only "subject," but "story" as well. Isabel's famous vigil by the fire in chapter 42 of *The Portrait of a Lady*, which "is a representation simply of her motionlessly *seeing*, and an attempt withal to make the mere still lucidity of her act as 'interesting' as the surprise of a caravan or the identification of a pirate," becomes a scene that "throws the action further forward than twenty 'incidents' might have done" (*AN* 57).[7] Although Isabel's "adventures are . . . mild," and "without her sense of them, her sense *for* them . . . they are next to nothing at all," the novel shows "their mystic conversion by that sense . . . into the stuff of drama or . . . of 'story' '' (AN 56). In his concluding remarks to the final volume of his shorter tales, James is still more direct:

A human, a personal "adventure" is no *a priori*, no positive and absolute and inelastic thing, but just a matter of relation and appreciation—a name we conveniently give, after the fact, to any passage, to any situation, that has added the sharp taste of uncertainty to a quickened sense of life. Therefore the thing is, all beautifully, a matter of interpretation and of the particular conditions; without a view of which latter some of the most prodigious adventures, as one has often had occasion to say, may vulgarly show for nothing. (AN 286)

James's consistency in defining his subjects and stories in terms of his principals' finely perceptive awareness of their situations amounts to an explication of his own career and its development, an identification of the figure in his carpet. On no point is James more insistent than his conception of his fiction "not as my own impersonal account of the affair in hand, but as my account of somebody's impression of it—the terms of this person's access to it and estimate of it contributing thus by some fine little law to intensification of interest'' (AN 327). In his opening preface, James announces, probably to the surprise of many of his most devoted readers, that "the centre of interest throughout 'Roderick' is in Rowland Mallet's consciousness, and the drama is the very drama of that consciousness.'' In the preface to *The Princess Casamassima*, he lists other such "intense *perceivers*" as Christopher Newman, Isabel Archer, Fleda Vetch, Maisie Farange, Vanderbank, Merton Densher, Lambert Strether, Maggie Verver, and Prince Amerigo (AN 16, 70–71). At times, as in the prefaces to *The Portrait of a Lady*, *The Awkward Age*, and *The Ambassadors*, the pattern of Jamesian fiction seems to resolve simply into the history of a sensitive consciousness. More often, however, as in the prefaces to *The Princess Casamassima*, *The Tragic Muse*, and *The Wings of the Dove*, James emphasizes the dialectical interplay between moral consciousness and its objects. It is the nature of suffering or bewildered agents, figures placed in a false or anguished position, to attempt to transform the worlds that oppose their desires through an act of imaginative consciousness. This act can lead to acts of heroic unselfishness (as in the case of Fleda and Maisie) or to insuperable contradictions that destroy the principal (as in the case of Hyacinth Robinson) or to an attempt to rescue other characters from the temptations they are indulging (as in the case of Lambert Strether and Maggie Verver), or, more often, to a final renunciation (as in the case of Rowland Mallet, Christopher Newman, Isabel Archer, and Merton Densher), but in each case the focus of the novel is on the moral development of the principals.

Because this paradigm is central both to James's account of his own work and to his theory of fiction, the prefaces compose not only an exposition of that theory a propos of James's fiction but also a critical praxis, a retrospective attempt to define James's career in terms of a consistent line of development that becomes a model for all prose fiction. At times the exemplary status James is claiming for his work becomes explicit, as when he dismisses *The Newcomes*, *The Three Musketeers*, and Tolstoy's well-known novel *Peace and War* as "loose baggy monsters" whose absence of a governing central consciousness produces "queer elements of the accidental and the arbitrary" so wasteful of potential meanings that such novels "artistically *mean*" less than his own novels, which are governed by "a deep-breathing economy and an organic form" (*AN* 84). More often, however, James's claims for his own novelistic practice as consistent and exemplary are left implicit, his visionary program for fiction and the theory of fiction passed off as disinterested exposition.

Over the past twenty-five years, critics of James, provoked largely by Laurence B. Holland's analysis of the prefaces, have tended to read them less as an exposition of the theory of fiction and more as a praxis or program for reading. Holland's James, and the James of more recent critics, is not the disinterested theorist of Blackmur and Edel because in writing the prefaces, James is creating a new way of thinking about his work, not explaining a coherent pattern that was there all along. Accordingly, the fundamental importance these recent critics ascribe to the prefaces is less architectonic or expository than dramatic, and the dominant rhythm they find is turbulent. Taking exception to the " 'calm' and order" Blackmur finds characteristic of the prefaces, Holland contends, "The strength as well as the tenor of the essays derives rather from the euphoria and anxieties of James's intimate involvement with his fiction" (155 [1964]).

Holland thus makes the prefaces sound different not only from the prefaces analyzed by Blackmur and Edel but also from the prefaces of any earlier novelists. Scott's prefaces to the Waverley novels use the convention of direct address to the audience to discuss the historical background of the work at hand. This practice is abbreviated and more sharply focused by Dickens, who added prefaces to each of his serialized novels on their first book publication and subsequent editions, briefly explaining the factual background of the book and his aims in writing and sometimes defending himself on particular points of controversy (the unromanticized portrayal of thieves in *Oliver Twist*) or scientific possibility (the spontaneous combustion of Krook in *Bleak House*). These three impulses— giving factual background, clarifying one's aims and intentions, and defending oneself—continued as the goals of prefaces as late as the collected editions of Hardy (1912) and Conrad (1920). Such prefaces are occasional essays, which usually subsume questions about composition and artistic procedure under the claim of truth to life and which so often and so closely press the author's pose as historian that the straight-faced whimsy of Conrad's tone, for example, sometimes approaches that of L. Frank Baum in his prefaces to the later stories about the land of Oz.

James's impulse in his prefaces was different, largely because he had not enjoyed an unusual popular success—a success that would confirm his status as the leading American novelist of his day—since *Daisy Miller*. In revisiting the scenes of his earlier fiction, he could not assume a readership who shared his sentimental attachment to Nancy and Rose Maylie or who remembered the furor caused by the publication of *Jude the Obscure*. Though James's prefaces are clearly intended for an audience that has already read the books they introduce, James's relation to that audience is far more complex than Dickens's or Conrad's. Because the prefaces are everywhere, as James told Howells, "a sort of plea for Criticism, for Discrimination, for Appreciation on other than infantile lines" (*LHJ* II, 99) of James's fiction and fiction generally, James seems in a state of constant despair over the lazy practices of readers. The "finer idiosyncrasies of literary form seem to be regarded as outside the scope of criticism," he observes with exasperation, and he concludes that the advantage of scenic composition is that "we feel, with the definite alternation, how the theme *is* being treated. That is we feel it when, in such tangled connexions, we happen to care. I shouldn't really go on as if this were the case with many readers" (*AN* 157, 158). It is unclear whether James thinks the readers of the prefaces belong to the few who already care about the formal characteristics of fiction or whether he is trying to persuade them to care. What is clear is that James believes most readers, even most of his readers, are indifferent to questions about fictional form, since they assume, as he had observed in "The Art of Fiction," that "a novel is a novel, as a pudding is a pudding, and that our only business with it could be to swallow it" (*LC*-I, 44).

But the frankly adversarial stance of such passages is complicated by the unusual intimacy James adopts in many others. Since he believes that his novels have never been read with the kind of critical attention and appreciation they deserve, he poses throughout the prefaces as his own ideal reader, who will correct the inattention of earlier readers by showing how the novels should be read, which questions should arise and what sort of criticism the fiction invites and supports. This procedure departs not only from that of any other, earlier introducer of his or her own work but also from James's own procedure in analyzing the work of other writers, whom he had always approached as a member, however penetrating, of a critical community.[8] By assuming the role, instead, of his own best audience, James can show the ways in which his fiction is exemplary.

Hence James's analyses of his own novels and tales and his consequent arguments about novels and stories generally can be recast as the latest phase in James's continuing attempt to redefine himself for his audience and, correspondingly, to redefine an audience for himself. Like James's notebooks, the prefaces adopt an argumentative yet meditative tone that seems to predicate an audience not congruent with their author but closer than anyone outside him; especially in their inveterate reminiscences of the scenes of composition and their passionate excurses on general matters, they seem intended to be overheard rather than addressed to a clearly defined audience. Throughout the notebooks, James had habitually dramatized his relation to himself by splitting himself into parts, addressing himself in the second person and externalizing technical problems through dialogue and rumination. In the prefaces he dramatizes the problem of his relation to his audience in the same way, anticipating his audience's reaction by splitting himself into author and ideal audience and adopting a confidential tone often reminiscent of the notebooks, as when he asks himself where his ideas for several of his short stories have come from:

One's notes, as all writers remember, sometimes explicitly mention, sometimes indirectly reveal, and sometimes wholly dissimulate, such clues and such obligations. The search for these last indeed, through faded or pencilled pages, is perhaps one of the sweetest of our more pensive pleasures. Then we chance on some idea we *have* afterwards treated; then, greeting it with tenderness, we wonder at the first form of a motive that was to lead us so far and to show, no doubt, to eyes not our own, for so other; then we heave the deep sigh of relief over all that is never, thank goodness, to be done again. Would we have embarked on *that* stream had we known?—and what mightn't we have made of this one *hadn't* we known! How, in a proportion of cases, could we have dreamed "there might be something"?—and why, in another proportion, didn't we *try* what there might be, since there are sorts of trials (ah indeed more than one sort!) for which the day will soon have passed? (*AN* 258–59)

Passages like this, whose syntax and rhetorical mode align the speaker much more intimately with other readers than with the author whose tracks the speaker is following, emphasize not the authoritative exposition of James's fictional theory but the dramatic status of the New York Edition as the climactic Jamesian fiction.

The project James ascribes to his fiction—a series of encounters between an imaginative consciousness and the intransigent circumstances that beset it—has this revisionary drama as its logical outgrowth. Since "the teller of a tale is primarily . . . the listener to it, the reader of it, too" (*AN* 63), the relation between James and the surrogate principals whose impressions of their experience James has been at such pains to render becomes reversible. If Strether is "a man of imagination" (*AN* 310), like James, James is equally like Strether, a superbly sensitive consciousness struggling to appreciate and so redeem a sequence of bewildering but exhilarating experiences.[9] Hence James presents himself not only as the author who has arranged his novels in a way to be set forth in the prefaces but also as a reader, following the example of his heroes, who will provide in turn an example for his readers.

Embarking on the first of the prefaces, James interrupts his assurances about "the continuity of an artist's endeavour" throughout his work and his intention "to take this mark [of relevance] everywhere for granted" to define his own position not as commentator but as fascinated reader. "Addicted to 'stories' and inclined to retrospect, he fondly takes, under this backward view, his whole unfolding, his process of production, for a thrilling tale, almost for a wondrous adventure" (*AN* 4). The melodramatic imagery that has earlier marked the imagination of his apparently inactive principals now settles on the figure of James himself and remains attached to him throughout the prefaces, converting "his protagonist's adventure in the novel into a technical adventure for the author executing it, the adventures being intimately if mysteriously connected'' (Holland 156 [1964]).[10]

The conflict between these two stances—James the magisterial commentator on his collected fiction and James the excited explorer of ''the buried, the latent life'' (*AN* 342) represented by his earlier work—is never fully resolved; the drama of the prefaces stems from James's attempt to resolve it, tempered by his intermittent acknowledgment that this attempt must ultimately remain incomplete. James adopts several strategies to insure that the New York Edition will be the most successful of all his fictional accomplishments. He recovers earlier failures of authority by recasting them in more congenial terms, most notably in the case of the ''supersubtle fry'' (*AN* 221) who composed the ranks of his fictional artists and writers. Instead of defending them as ''represented eminent cases'' of actual artists, James redefines them as ''in *essence* an observed reality'' whose power is a function of ''operative irony'' (*AN* 221, 223, 222). ''If the life about us . . . refuses warrant for these examples, then so much the worse for that life,'' rules James, and he defends his ''high and helpful public and, as it were, civic use of the imagination'' in aiding such ''true meanings to be born'' (*AN* 222, 223, 224). More generally, reediting his earlier works allows James to redefine his career retrospectively, discovering in each of his earlier works intimations of the 1907 James. Though some of these intimations are incomplete, ''redolent of good intentions baffled by a treacherous vehicle'' like the melodramatic story of *The American*, James more often finds that ''the march of my present attention coincides sufficiently with the march of my original expression'' to justify the sense of ''the exemplary closeness of 'The Awkward Age,' '' for example, as ''treasure quite instinctively and foreseeingly laid up against my present opportunity for these remarks'' (*AN* 344, 335, 116). Instead of imposing his later aesthetic, with its thematic emphasis on the relation between consciousness and its objects, on his earlier works, James sees himself as gratifyingly rediscovering this aesthetic as nascent from the beginning in all the works he has chosen to include in the New York Edition.

James's labors in preparing the edition transpose the problem of defining a subject as unformed yet already formed into a new key. James sees his earlier work as so much '' 'old' matter,'' a series of subjects to be ''re-accepted, re-tasted, exquisitely re-assimilated and re-enjoyed—believed in, to be brief, with the same 'old' grateful faith (since wherever the faith, in a particular case, has become aware of a twinge of doubt I have simply concluded against the matter itself and left it out)'' (*AN* 339–40). The older novels and tales thus become subjects marked by their exquisite potential, an ''uncanny brood'' of possibly ''awkward infants'' whose condition might well require that ''a stitch should be taken or a hair-brush applied'' (*AN* 337–38) to bring out the value James sees himself as once having brought out in Isabel Archer.

At the same time, James is aware that not every story justifies his confidence in his work as a whole, for ''criticism after the fact was to find in [his fiction] arrests and surprises, emotions alike of disappointment and of elation: all of which means, obviously, that the whole thing was a *living* affair'' (*AN* 342). But this uneven success of his earlier work, his sporadic failure to rediscover his 1907 principles in every one of his earlier novels and tales, does not strike James as a shortcoming; instead he sees it as the greatest charm and adventure of the New York Edition, which thereby becomes ''a *living* affair,'' an opportunity for him to infuse his work with new imaginative vitality by reviewing, reconsidering, and revising it. ''The thing done and dismissed has ever, at the best, for the ambitious workman, a trick of looking dead, if not buried, so that he almost throbs with ecstasy when, on an anxious review, the flush of life appears,'' James announces of *The Awkward Age* (*AN* 99). If reperusal does not always awaken that flush of life, it is equally true that the revising reader's discernment of the flush of life may simply ally him nostalgically with the fondly self-deluded author of the original work. James acknowledges this problem by transforming the standards by which his work is to be judged, in one of the most exultant passages of the prefaces:

> Again and yet again, as, from book to book, I proceed with my survey, I find no source of interest equal to this verification after the fact, as I may call it, and the more in detail the better, of the scheme of consistency ''gone in'' for. As always—since the charm never fails—the retracing of the process from point to point brings back the old illusion. The old intentions bloom again and flower—in spite of all the blossoms they were to have dropped by the way. This is the charm, as I say, of adventure *transposed*—the thrilling ups and downs, the intricate ins and outs of the compositional problem, made after such a fashion admirably objective, becoming the question at issue and keeping the author's heart in his mouth. (*AN* 318–19)

This passage links three adventures: the adventure of Strether and James's other imaginative heroes, the adventure of the author bent on solving his technical problems by discovering a method of treatment that will do the greatest justice to his promising subject, and the adventure of the revising editor and ideal reader in coaxing the story back to life by ''following critically, from page to page, even as the red Indian tracks in the forest the pale-face, the footsteps of the systematic loyalty I was able to achieve'' (*AN* 115), and so completing a chain of identifications with the working novelist and each surrogate consciousness. Linking these adventures throughout the prefaces through the act of rereading has the effect of creating a new fiction, parallel but superior to the original novels and tales. ''There is the story of one's hero, and then, thanks to the intimate connexion of things, the story of one's story itself. I blush to confess it, but if one's a dramatist one's a dramatist, and the latter imbroglio is liable on occasion to strike me as really the more objective of the two'' (*AN* 313).

By defining the process of rereading as an adventure, James is able to redeem his earlier failures and incomplete successes. In discussing the commercial failure of *The Awkward Age*, whose publisher told him, ''I've never in all my experience seen [a book] treated with more general and complete disrespect,'' James consoles himself by recalling "the rich reward of the singular interest attaching to the very intimacies of the effort" (*AN* 108, 109). Elsewhere, his tone is more admonitory than consolatory. Comparing the schematism of *The Awkward Age* to that of Ibsen's problematic plays, James argues that a reader who strives to appreciate such imperfect works but finds them simplified "almost to excruciation" or "enfeebled by remarkable vagueness" is never simply to be caught "in the act of a mistake. He is to be caught at the worst in the act of attention, of the very greatest attention, and that is all, as a precious preliminary at least, that the playwright asks of him, besides being all the very divinest poet can get" (*AN* 113). When James rules that "the essential property" of an imaginative or broadly poetic form is "to give out its finest and most numerous secrets, and to give them out most gratefully, under the closest pressure" (*AN* 346), he is not only generalizing his own example of rereading in order to exhort his readers to a greater appreciation of fictional technique and a closer attention to the problems of rendering reality, but he is also attempting to elevate the artistic status of the novel, intensify the audience's pleasure, and rescue himself as novelist from his incidental failures, since "an imputed defect is never, at the worst, disengageable, or other than matter for appreciation" (*AN* 118). It is no wonder that James, reviewing the body of his short fiction, concludes that "what longest lives to [the storyteller's] backward vision, in the whole business, is not the variable question of the 'success,' but the inveterate romance of the labour" (*AN* 287)—a romance the prefaces now make directly available to the responsive reader.

For this reason James never sees himself as rewriting his earlier work for the New York Edition; he is rather revising it, that is, reseeing it, rereading it. On the one hand, he contends that the act of rereading "caused whatever I looked at on any page to flower before me as into the only terms that honourably expressed it"; but he concludes this sentence by acknowledging, "so many close notes, as who should say, on the particular vision of the matter itself that experience had at last made the only possible one" (*AN* 339). Whenever he speaks of revising his earlier work, James strikes both these notes, tempering his positivism with a suggestion that he is not improving his fiction, or even necessarily doing justice to the figure that forms the leading subject of his career, but rather reawakening the potential of his work by affording it the appreciative attention it deserves and inviting his reader to do the same. In the final preface, over half of which is devoted to "this infinitely interesting and amusing *act* of re-appropriation," James gradually makes this invitation more explicit. "What has the affair been at the worst, I am most moved to ask, but an earnest invitation to the reader to dream again in my company and in the interest of his own larger absorption of my sense?" (*AN* 336, 345). The reader's acceptance of this invitation completes the equation, which James has been urging throughout the prefaces, between seeing and doing, writing and moral action. Just as he had presented his sensitive heroes and heroines as engaged by dint of their inquiring imaginations in an essentially active relationship with their fictional worlds, he

now concludes that "to 'put' things is very exactly and responsibly and interminably to do them" (*AN* 347) because the acts of vision and revision engage
other people in an actively interpretive community.

The prefaces have left a complex legacy. Despite the indifferent sales of the
New York Edition, James succeeded more completely through his prefaces than
through his revisions in creating an Authorized Version of his work, a way of
seeing his career as a consistent whole and so of vindicating his status as the
exemplary American novelist of his time. James's relatively systematic exposition of his critical principles encouraged a generation of critics, headed by
Percy Lubbock and Joseph Warren Beach, to distill more systematic theories of
fiction, a tendency that continues in the theoretical work of Mark Schorer and
Wayne C. Booth, who, though resisting the particular dogmas of Lubbock and
Beach, still operate within a Jamesian framework, and in the influential textbook
of Cleanth Brooks and Robert Penn Warren. The attempt to derive a systematic
poetics of fiction from James reaches an apotheosis in James E. Miller's analytical
anthology of passages from a wide range of James's criticism. In the meantime,
R. P. Blackmur and others had secured James's more general position as the
preeminent theorist of the novel. The most pervasive legacy of the prefaces,
however, has been still broader, in the response to James's plea for aesthetic
appreciation of the novel. James's frequent collapsing of the distinction between
subject and form, his defense of the novel as a responsible literary mode, his
assertion that the greatest works of art are those that require and reward the
closest attention, his account of revision as reseeing—all of these tendentious
arguments have become the platitudes not of the theory of fiction, but of the
common reader's experience. They represent a kind of influence that James the
novelist never had or hoped to have, a legacy that is likely to endure even beyond
that of the novels and tales the prefaces were designed to introduce.[11]

## NOTES

1. Michael Anesko has traced the negotiations between James and his publishers
back considerably further. "As early as the summer of 1904 he had been approached,
or so his agent [J. B. Pinker] claimed, with various proposals regarding a collected
edition." In fact, "Pinker and [Scribner's Senior Editor E. L.] Burlingame had discussed
the possibility of a collected edition of James's work in April 1900, but the matter was
dropped later in the year" (Anesko, *"Friction with the Market"* 144, 238).

2. See Anesko (*"Friction with the Market"*) 144–62 for a detailed account of James's
negotiations with Scribner's and a chart showing the migration of many of the short
stories in volumes 13–17 to other volumes in the edition, culminating in the appearance
of volume 18. For an earlier view arguing that James had planned the edition from the
beginning to occupy twenty-three volumes, the number chosen to echo that of Balzac's
*Comédie humaine*, see Edel, "Architecture" 169.

3. See *AN* 275–77, a passage from the preface to volume 18, though "Julia Bride"
appears in Volume 17 and "Fordham Castle," as James notes, in Volume 16. *AN*

continues this confusion by omitting "Fordham Castle," "Julia Bride," and "The Jolly Corner" from the headnotes listing the works collected in each volume.

4. James wrote William Dean Howells on December 31, 1908: "I've just had the pleasure of hearing from the Scribners that though the Edition began to appear some 13 or 14 months ago, there is, on the volumes already out, no penny of profit owing me— of that profit to which I had partly been looking to pay my New Year's bills! It will have landed me in Bankruptcy—unless it picks up; for it has prevented my doing any other work whatever" (*LHJ* II, 119). Anesko notes, "James's literary income in 1908 was smaller than it had been in 25 years" (*"Friction with the Market"* 241; see also 177). Seven years later, James estimated to Edmund Gosse that his total earnings from the edition amounted to some fifty pounds (*LHJ* II, 497). Hershel Parker's research shows that James's energy was not utterly exhausted by the New York Edition, since he was completing what proved to be a greatly abbreviated version of his projected two-volume *The American Scene* as he prepared the revisions and wrote the prefaces for the first four volumes of the New York Edition (Parker, "Henry James 'In the Wood' " 496–500).

5. See Hardy 30–50 for an extended discussion of the rhetorical implications of this distinction.

6. See Veeder ("Image as Argument") on James's use of figures, and especially on their logical inconsistencies, throughout his criticism.

7. Cf. the much earlier passage in "The Art of Fiction" (*LC*-I, 60–62) in which James defends "An International Episode," and by implication the *Portrait* as well, on these grounds.

8. The closest analogue may be Fielding's chapters introducing each of the eighteen books of *Tom Jones* by giving his readers some idea of how to read them. Fielding, however, is anticipating his readers, not correcting them.

9. See Feidelson and Leitch for more detailed discussions.

10. Richard Chase observes, for example, that Isabel's "tragic recognition" is figured "in images that belong as much to melodrama as to tragedy" (126).

11. The foregoing essay was written during the summer of 1988. Since then, academic discussions of the prefaces, not surprisingly, have been shaped even more decisively by the second of the two paradigms I develop here; recent critics have been less and less inclined to take the prefaces as a systematic exposition of James's theory of fiction (or a series of analyses of individual novels and tales) and have been more intent on emphasizing their historical and biographical contexts and their own revisionary fictive status. This stance, which informs Philip Horne's *Henry James and Revision*, is most clearly apparent in two recent reconsiderations of the prefaces: Inka Mülder-Bach's "Genealogy und Stil: Henry James's *Prefaces*," and Margaret Ellen Brown's unpublished dissertation, "The 'Unabashed Memoranda' of the Prefaces: Henry James's Letter to the World." I wish also to acknowledge here the force of two earlier essays that had escaped my attention when I first wrote: Stuart Culver's "Representing the Author: Henry James, Intellectual Property, and the Work of Writing," in *Henry James: Fiction as History*, edited by Ian F. A. Bell, and Wendell P. Jackson's "The Theory of the Creative Process in the 'Prefaces' of Henry James."

# 5
# Henry James and Critical Theory

## John Carlos Rowe

Theory never aims simply at an increase of knowledge as such. Its goal is
man's emancipation from slavery.
— Max Horkheimer, "Postscript" to "Traditional
and Critical Theory" (1937)

Of the many literary moderns who have been cited as forerunners of "critical
theory," Henry James and T. S. Eliot have been the most influential in Anglo-
American schools of criticism. Such a claim may merely remind us of how
profoundly the New Criticism has shaped even its most vigorous adversaries; I
need not detail just how influential James and Eliot have been for the New
Critics. Yet the specific use of "critical theory" to designate a social theory
complemented by a specific political practice comes not from Anglo-American
schools of literary criticism but from the social and cultural work of the Frankfurt
School. For Adorno, Horkheimer, Marcuse, and Benjamin, Bertolt Brecht would
be a far better example than James or Eliot of the literary author as critical
theorist. For these same theorists and the heirs of their Marxist traditions of
cultural criticism, any claim for the importance of James and Eliot in the development of twentieth-century critical theories would be simply another indication of how often that term is confused with "literary theory" or "aesthetics."

Yet, this confusion of critical and literary theory is part of the academic history
of "critical theory," and it will thus be my focus in this essay. Those who agree
with my judgment of James's and Eliot's influence generally point to the great
volume of "criticism" written by both authors. Each played an important role
in defining the terms of subsequent schools of academic criticism, most of them
admittedly "literary" schools and movements. Eliot, more clearly than James,

established the framework for Anglo-American New Criticism. James's essays on Impressionism (literary and visual), naturalism, the theory of the novel, and a wide range of authors were less specifically adapted to a particular school of criticism, though they have been used with great authority by the New Critics.

James and Eliot did not write *only* literary criticism, though their other non-fiction works are often classified with the former, if only in obedience to the publisher's convention of treating a literary author's "nonfiction" in this category. Eliot's *Notes toward the Definition of Culture* (1948) and James's *The American Scene* (1907) are clearly works of cultural criticism that critically interpret European and American societies, respectively, in terms of a utopian conception of how society *ought* to be organized. These are arguably works of "critical theory." In the case of James, we might add other examples, including his twenty dispatches for the *New York Tribune* from 1875 to 1876, collected as *Parisian Sketches* (1957) by Leon Edel and Ilse Dusoir Lind, and perhaps *William Wetmore Story and His Friends* (1903), if we read that curious volume as James's anthropology of American expatriates in Europe. Bits and pieces of the other travel writings might be included, as well as selected essays and reviews, but the list would still be modest, given the great volume of James's other writings. In a similar sense, Eliot's own claims to status as "critical theorist" would be slim indeed, if based only on specific expository prose concerned with social and cultural theory. The vast majority of Eliot's prose deals with literary and philosophical topics.

On this spare evidence, then, it would seem best to revise my initial claim and argue instead that James had a profound influence on twentieth-century *literary* theory. That would be the safe course to follow, but only because it is already so well trodden. Virtually every new academic book on James either explicitly or implicitly makes such a claim, and the sheer number of scholarly works on James would thus give evidence of his influence. Given the enormous diversity of the arguments for James's influence, it would be foolish to attempt any survey in such a brief essay. Instead, I propose sticking to my quixotic introductory evaluation of James and exploring what it might mean to talk of Henry James as critical theorist.

At stake in such an argument is James's role in the development of Marxist and various post-Marxist theories, including in the latter category feminism, New Historicism, and deconstruction. Each of these kinds of "critical theory" is in one way or another a "social theory" before it is a "literary," "aesthetic," or "philosophical" theory. I shall not attempt to "survey" these theories and their relative judgments of James's role in modern art and culture; instead, I shall make reference along the way to such theories as I try to work out James's fit to the narrow bounds of "critical theory" as it has been defined by the Frankfurt School and as it has influenced the political aims of post-Marxist and poststructuralist theories. In using James in this fashion, I am also interested in the possible relation among these diverse, often heterogeneous, versions of "critical theory." My contention is that insofar as James can be understood as a "critical theorist," the James so constructed will help us understand what such theories might have in common. Even before beginning this work, however, I want to write clearly that James's very unfitness for a Marxist definition of "critical theory" must also be part of our interest. Despite his great sensitivity to the subtleties of ideological manipulation and control, James was no Marxist. However we may justify the attention he pays to a newly empowered bourgeoisie and a fading aristocracy, generally on the grounds that these are the classes through which we understand the powers of ideology, I cannot absolve James from his neglect of that "grey immensity" of the European and American "underclass." Yet to label James simply a "bourgeois writer," implying thereby that he merely legitimated capitalist cultural values, is to miss entirely James's critical dimension— one that has a prophecy for our own age that is still unrecognized.

For traditional Marxists, James typifies bourgeois mystification. James's valorization of "aesthetic experience," his relentless abstraction, his studious refusal of concrete details, and his fictional concentration on middle-class manners seem to identify him unmistakably as just another author intent on justifying the bourgeoisie's right to rule. It is this general Marxist interpretation of James that is behind Fredric Jameson's more sophisticated criticism: "Jamesian point of view, which comes into being as a protest and defense against reification, ends up furnishing a powerful ideological instrument in the perpetuation of an increasingly subjectivized and psychologized world, a world whose social vision is one of a thoroughgoing relativity of monads in coexistence.... This is the context in which the remarkable transformation of Henry James from a minor nineteenth-century man of letters into the greatest American novelist of the 1950s may best be appreciated" (*The Political Unconscious* 221–22).[1] Aside from the sheer rhetorical pleasure of labeling Henry James "a minor nineteenth-century man of letters," Jameson means that James is merely one among many who contributed to the legitimation of bourgeois values, simply another figure caught up in what David Lloyd has termed the "aesthetic ideology" framed by romantic idealism and developed in nineteenth-century "intellectual history" from Hegel to Matthew Arnold and carried on by such modern disciples as T. S. Eliot and Henry James.[2]

At the other end of the spectrum, there is the deconstructive James, enormously popular in the past decade and quite clearly a central modern literary figure in the so-called American version of deconstruction. The label "American" may be unjust, since it refers more specifically to the work of the "Yale School," best represented in the work of Geoffrey Hartman, J. Hillis Miller, Paul de Man, and Harold Bloom.[3] Only Miller has interpreted James in any sustained manner, but Henry James as modernist heir of Romanticism is certainly implicit in the formulation of deconstruction as developed by de Man, Hartman, and Miller, as well as in the poetics of influence developed by Bloom.[4] More important, of course, has been the adaptation of the theories of Hartman, Miller, de Man, and Bloom on the interpretation of the strategic, even systematic, verbal ambiguity of Henry James to the more general deconstructive thesis of linguistic undecidability. That Henry James understood his mind-numbing prose, especially in the writings of the Major Phase, to be working out such an insight into the essential nature of language is one of the distinguishing characteristics of American deconstruction's reading of him.[5] This, of course, is what distinguishes so-called American deconstruction from Continental poststructuralism: the former "literarizes" deconstruction by celebrating writers who are themselves "proto-deconstructive" theorists; the latter has little interest in literary authors, except as useful examples, and sticks to the fundamental insight of deconstruction that *every* "author" must be read as a critical fiction in need of deconstruction (including the deconstructive critic's own bid for authority). Even in that case, however, the deconstruction of "Henry James" is an interesting issue even for deconstructive critics who do not follow the literary lead of the Yale School, since "Henry James" has been subject to such a wide variety of influential literary critical constructions. And since those constructions have been in many cases fundamental to our thinking about "modern art" and even "modern culture," the deconstruction of Henry James becomes a topic of far more than merely local literary interest.

Feminist interpretations of Henry James cannot be as easily generalized as those of Marxists and deconstructive theorists. On the one hand, James has often appeared to be one of the few masculine moderns to be eminently concerned with the problems facing modern women. Insofar as the majority of his novels and tales are organized around the difficulties confronting intelligent young women in predominantly patriarchal societies on both sides of the Atlantic, he seems a likely ally for feminist politics and an apt subject for feminist literary criticism. It is worth noting that several of the most important contemporary feminist theorists paid careful and often sympathetic attention to James's fiction early in their careers. Jane Tompkins's "Introduction" to *Twentieth-Century Interpretations of "Turn of the Screw"* appeared in 1970, and it is a far cry from her compelling critique of nineteenth-century canonical American literature in *Sensational Designs: The Cultural Work of American Fiction, 1790–1860* (1985). James is appropriately treated in *Sensational Designs* as the heir of the elitist and decidedly patriarchal literary traditions of Hawthorne and the Transcendentalists, but he is also given credit for taking seriously "domestic space," in the manner of more popular writers like Susan Warner or more recognizable feminist precursors like Jane Austen (Tompkins, *Sensational Designs* 185). Susanne Kappeler's intricate post-Freudian psychoanalytical reading of James in *Writing and Reading in Henry James* (1980) can be read as a sort of preface to her recent *Pornography of Representation* (1989). And the elements of Juliet Mitchell's important contributions to feminist psychoanalysis are sketched in her 1972 essay "*What Maisie Knew*: Portrait of the Artist as a Young Girl," in which the occlusion of psychic insight that describes Maisie's education is made equivalent to James's own artistic process.[6]

On the other hand, James's narratives lead these intelligent young women relentlessly toward sacrifice, exile, or death (often all three at the same time, as in the case of Daisy Miller and Milly Theale). Those who "succeed" do so only in the most problematic ways, often by accepting the patriarchal terms of their societies and learning to "play the game." And politically committed women, like Oliver Chancellor in *The Bostonians*, or women with their own careers, like Henrietta Stackpole in *Portrait of a Lady*, are relentlessly mocked by James for having "missed" something deeper and more profound about the real bases for social interaction. It is not just *The Bostonians* that troubles those feminists who judge James to be the ultimate version of patriarchal "aestheticism," but the subtler ways in which James sets his feminine characters up for the finest triumphs only to steal their fire in the last analysis.

The "failure" of James's feminine protagonists is almost always the occasion for James's own bid for power, his insistence that as author he has succeeded where these fragments of his imagination have failed. Thus Isabel Archer is only "true" to herself in those moments of intense reflection when she comes "closest" to James himself. And serious women writers, like Margaret Fuller or George Sand, are judged by James to have failed because they did not write enough or well enough. Despite the convincing arguments of William Veeder regarding the uses James made of nineteenth-century popular fiction, especially the great wealth of popular fiction written by women, James confirms his critical reputation for literary elitism by repeatedly trivializing the work of popular women writers.[7] Alfred Habegger (*Henry James and the "Woman Business"*) has demonstrated quite convincingly how ambivalent James was on the "woman question," in both its specific political and its more general cultural and social dimensions. Just what is at stake for those feminists most critical of Henry James is the degree to which he used his feminine characters and apparent feminist sympathies for the sake of his own bid for literary power and mastery. In this regard, of course, James is all the more insidious insofar as his conservative values are disguised in liberal rhetoric.[8]

For New Historicists too, James is an equivocal figure, on the one hand simply victimized like all others by his "times" but on the other hand capable of comprehending at least partially the boundaries of the ideological prison in which he lived and worked. In some cases, such knowledge makes James *more* responsible for ideological complicity than he is in traditional Marxist judgments. This is the sort of case made by Mark Seltzer in *Henry James and the Art of Power* (1984). In this same regard, James is a crucial figure for New Historicists, since he wrote in such a critically transitional historical period. Rather than simply effecting the literary transition from the prevailing literary realism of the later Victorian period to the literary impressionism of the early modern novel, James worked with other artists and scholars to textualize social reality. Like Oscar Wilde's Vivian in "The Decay of Lying" (1889), James argues that "life imitates art far more than art imitates life," or in his own words, "It is art that *makes* life, makes importance, for our consideration and application" (*HJL* IV, 770).

This apparently charming iconoclasm, this bid for mere *literary* authority, especially in an age in which the arts appeared to be increasingly irrelevant, has a more insidious dimension insofar as it helps pave the way for postindustrial societies, in which the laws of economic production are determined more by immaterial than material commodities. In our own economy, information, services, entertainment, and fashion are no longer secondary effects, by-products, of industrial production but are the central activities of more than two-thirds of the work force. Thus James's and Wilde's "fictions" may be said to anticipate the "paradigms" of the marketeer, the "models" of the computer programmer and artificial intelligence experts, and even the "development plans" of the contractor or Pentagon officer. Behind the New Historicist's concern with the powers of representation in whatever historical period is just this contemporary question of how *we* are controlled and constrained by elaborate, surprisingly "artistic," modes of social signification. In that regard, of course, James must be considered a crucial figure, either for his anticipation of a coming age dedicated to semiotic controls or for his modest contributions to our adaptation to such a reality principle.

The argument that the unconscious of a literary author's work finds its visible manifestation in institutional practices and procedures, like the Elizabethan stage and court for Stephen Greenblatt or the institutions of criticism in our own modernity, seems to me to be essential to the politics of New Historicism.[9] By the same token, such a position argues against any effort to theorize an author like Henry James as a "critical theorist." After all, "critical theory" involves active ideological analysis that is predicated on a theory of utopia, of social transformation in light of the failings of contemporary reality, which are most often the consequences of institutional constraints. Such a definition is in keeping with the Frankfurt School's prevailing Marxist understanding of the uses of intellectual activity for the purposes of social emancipation. For New Historicists, it leaves most literary authors trapped within the discursive limits of their own historical—that is, ideological—moments, and it assigns the work of cultural criticism to that ultimate avant-garde: the political scholar.

We are thus dealing with a spectrum of judgments of Henry James that range from the sympathetic to the thoroughly critical, leaving "Henry James" in his old, familiar position of "radical ambiguity," variously "available" for interpretation and contemporary use. Such a view might well be considered the encompassing perspective, which might well relegitimate the name of "Henry James" as that modern most suitable for the title "theorist," literary or critical. However we evaluate James's literary contributions, he remains an important figure in our most powerful methods of interpretation and aesthetic evaluation, virtually inescapable as the "master" of the modern novel. In a sense, that was the issue, if not the conclusion, of my own *Theoretical Dimensions of Henry James*, and in that regard I was simply following the lead of post-Freudian psychoanalytical critics like Shoshana Felman, who finds in James the sort of rhetoric best suited to elicit interpretation while escaping the reader's authoritative control. This, I think, also reflects a prevailing deconstructive interest in James, elements of which can be found in Frank Kermode's definition of the "modern classic," which seems so appropriate to James's literary oeuvre and its twentieth-century influence (Kermode 114).

I have claimed that some of these differences might be negotiated by reconsidering James as "critical theorist" in his own right rather than as constructed by various critical theories. In this regard, I turn to a work that is at once the most appropriate for understanding what we mean by "critical theory" and the least likely to make the case for Henry James: Max Horkheimer's 1937 essay "Traditional and Critical Theory" (translated by Matthew J. O'Connell et al., in *Critical Theory: Selected Essays*, 1982). It is the locus classicus of "critical theory" as a specific discipline, especially in its formulation by the Frankfurt School. There is simply no chance that the reader will take Horkheimer's "critical theory" for "literary" or "aesthetic" theory; indeed, the essay is written against such idealist adaptations of what must be understood as a unique blend of social theory and political action, of ideological analysis and a utopian project. In fact, Horkheimer published his "Postscript" to the essay in another 1937 issue of the journal he edited (from 1932 to 1941), *Zeitschrift für Sozialforschung*, an issue that included Herbert Marcuse's "Philosophie und Kritische Theorie," as if to challenge his colleague's greater sympathy for the philosophical foundations for "critical theory." For Horkheimer, "critical thinking" must replace "philosophy."

For Horkheimer, "traditional theory" encompasses bourgeois individualism, rationalism, and nationalism: "Bourgeois thought is so constituted that . . . a logical necessity forces it to recognize an ego which imagines itself . . . autonomous. Bourgeois thought is essentially abstract, . . . its principle . . . an individuality which inflatedly believes itself . . . the ground of the world . . . , an individuality separated off from events" (210). In many regards, this definition suits James's authorial practice quite precisely. If the "autonomous subject" of Romantic idealism was no longer socially available in James's own era, then writers like James sought to reconstruct it in and through the "autonomous" world of art. This is the formalist James, so dear to the New Critics, committed "eternally but to draw, by a geometry of his own, the circle within which [relations] shall happily *appear*" to cohere (*AN* 5). The fractured, alienated self may well be James's topic in most of his novels and tales, but it may be redeemed by an authorial act that gives the appearance of coherence and "integrity." When Strether "advises" Little Bilham in Gloriani's garden in *The Ambassadors*, he is responding to the modern individual's fear of social determinism. "Live all you can; it's a mistake not to" is glossed by Strether: " 'The affair of life . . . [is] at the best a tin mould, either fluted and embossed, with ornamental excrescences, or else smooth and dreadfully plain, into which a helpless jelly, one's consciousness is poured. . . . Still, one has the illusion of freedom" (*AB* 149–50).

Horkheimer goes on to include under "traditional theory" the "direct contrary" of such radical and finally "bourgeois" individualism. The traditional, then, includes any view of the individual as an "unproblematic expression of an already constituted society; an example would be a nationalist ideology. . . . In the internally rent society of our day, such thinking, except in social questions, sees nonexistent unanimities and is illusory" (210). For James, the cosmopolitan writer, the forerunner of the high-modern American "expatriates" in Europe, such a view appears inimical, unless we begin to take seriously the "Americanness" of Henry James in relation to his international pretensions. Indeed, the "American" identity that James condemns from *The American* to *The Golden Bowl* focuses on the provincial, isolationist American identity that we associate with Christopher Newman's and Adam Verver's naïveté, sometimes charmingly mystified as their "innocence." We know, of course, that such innocence is no longer a virtue in adult life, and James makes it abundantly clear that in adults it must be taken for ignorance, if not downright evil.

But against such naifs, James pits the "knowledgeable" Americans, who learn how to adapt European values to American interests. They include Christina Light, victimized in *Roderick Hudson* only to learn how to exploit more finely as the Princess Casamassima, Basil Ransom in *The Bostonians*, and Maggie Verver in *The Golden Bowl*, among a long list of others, in which James includes his own name. For it is his own cosmopolitanism that is as profoundly involved with America's emerging social and political power as the melodramas these characters arrange. Given America's imperial ambitions in the early modern period—including John Hay's "Open Door" policy in the Far East, our annexation of the Philippines, our negotiated "control" of Central America and the Caribbean in conjunction with the various treaties covering the Panama Canal, and our role in the First World War—James's "cosmopolitanism" must be read in terms of America's geopolitical ambitions in the same period. There is a special suitability, I think, to what otherwise must appear as a rather tenuous analogy, since America developed a "new" brand of imperial domination, distinctly different from the costlier and even less efficient colonial policies of the nineteenth-century European imperial powers. Unlike England, France, and Germany, America did not seek to control materially its "territories," except in such cases as the Canal Zone and the Philippines. Instead, America sought "spheres of influence," in which our foreign policy was based on "winning hearts and minds" to the American way and, of course, the American "self."

James's "cultivated" Europeans are generally impoverished, increasingly desperate scions of the old aristocratic orders; his "new" Europeans include bourgeois characters as vulgar as their American equivalents. Only his new Americans have a chance at adapting to a new age in which national identity, hereditary titles, and material wealth will be replaced by cosmopolitanism, intelligence, imagination, and the sort of "spiritual" wealth that his predecessor Walt Whitman associated with the power of the self to emulate and even incorporate others. This is the traditional site of Jamesian compassion and humanity, as well as its insidious subtext, psychological control and domination—the subjective equivalent of American imperialism. Thus far, James suits only the "traditional theory" of Horkheimer's essay, and the prospect for Henry James as "critical theorist" appears gloomy indeed.

Horkheimer's definition of "critical thinking" and its "theory" is predictably Marxist, focused as it is on the responsibilities of the individual to his/her identification with some collectivity and to his/her commitment to the production of social reality. For Horkheimer, critical thought does not pertain to the individual alone or to aggregations of individuals. "Its subject is . . . a definite individual in . . . real relation to other individuals and groups, in . . . conflict with a particular class, and, finally, in the resultant web of relationships with the social totality and . . . nature. The subject is no mathematical point like the ego of bourgeois philosophy; his activity is the construction of the social present" (210–11). Horkheimer's last point seems pointedly directed at writers like Henry James, whose literary production has been so adaptable to philosophical reflection. Dorothea Krook's *The Ordeal of Consciousness in Henry James* (1962), Richard Hocks's *Henry James and Pragmatistic Thought* (1974), Paul Armstrong's *The Phenomenology of Henry James* (1983), and Sharon Cameron's recent *Thinking in Henry James* (1989) are only a few examples of the many scholarly books that explore the fundamentally philosophical nature of James's writing. Even Horkheimer's reference to "the subject" as "no mathematical point like the ego of bourgeois philosophy" seems directed at the Henry James who could insist on the "abstractness" of the philosophical subject, its status as the mere "ado of consciousness" in that hopelessly abstract (and deliberately awkward) word he used to describe Isabel Archer's subjectivity in his Preface to *The Portrait of a Lady* in the New York Edition.

As Horkheimer points out in his "Postscript" to "Traditional and Critical Theory," the two philosophical models for the essay are Descartes and Marx. "Theory in the traditional sense established by Descartes . . . organizes experience in the light of questions which arise out of life in present-day society" (244). Horkheimer refers, of course, to the rationalist tradition represented by Cartesian thought, its "logic"—systematic doubt—and the intellectual history it initiated—an intellectual history intent on proving the unprovable: the essential rationality of mind and its a priori status with respect to experience and even the empirical data given to us by the natural world. Horkheimer's Marxian conception of critical theory is thus quite understandably critical of rationality, technology, and the authority of the sciences. "The critical theory of society . . . has for its object men as the producers of their own historical way of life in its totality. The real situations which are the starting-point of science are not regarded simply as data . . . to be predicted according to the laws of probability. . . . Objects, the kind of perception, the questions asked, and the meaning of the answers all bear witness to human activity and the degree of man's power" (244). To be sure, this view hardly dismisses technology, insofar as "human activity" and the "degree of man's power" may well find science and technology to be primary tools. Even so, it is as human tools that science and technology are to be understood, rather than as the paradigms for "consciousness-in-itself,"

that "absolute ego" in whose evolving "spirit" man might achieve victory
"over the dumb, unconscious, irrational side" of his nature (Horkheimer 245).

Quite the contrary, Horkheimer understands these tools to be properly put to
use in "work in society, and the class-related form of this work puts its mark
on all human patterns of reaction, including theory. The intervention of reason
in the processes whereby knowledge and its object are constituted . . . does not
take place therefore in a purely intellectual world, but coincides with the struggle
for certain real ways of life" (245). Now, the least likely category in which to
explore James's status as as critical theorist would seem to be his contribution
to any class consciousness beyond bourgeois class consciousness—his "consciousness" of consciousnesses, as it were—with which his work is traditionally
associated by Marxists. If there is any "class conflict" in James, it appears to
involve the struggle of the bourgeoisie to define itself against the lingering claims
of the landed gentry, and in this work the myth of "classless" America seems
to serve James quite well. Often enough the bourgeoisie merely imitates what
it understands to be the signs of aristocratic privilege and distinction. Christopher
Newman buying up bad copies of European paintings, Adam Verver "stocking"
his American museum with the fragments of European art history, Gilbert Osmond laboring at his own copies of antiquities, the narrator of *The Aspern Papers*
snooping about for unpublished manuscripts—all are examples of James's own
critique of the "culture industry." Such dilettantism, if not commodity fetishism,
is the antithesis of what Horkheimer means by "the struggle for certain real
ways of life"; nothing could be more illusory or more the property of a "purely
intellectual world."

But such "collectors" and fetishists are easy enough for James to caricature;
even Newman in *The American*, early as that novel is, serves primarily as an
occasion for exploring the subtler ways in which the bourgeoisie legitimates its
authority. "Manners" hardly covers the repertoire of discursive tricks through
which the crude powers of this ruling class are disguised. James understood
better than any of his contemporaries how profoundly bourgeois "capital" resides
in its command of representation, rather than in money or lands. And it is in
this regard that James's ideological criticism still seems contemporary and justifies in part the elaborate abstractions of his prose style, even as such an insight
calls for a critique of its own medium, of the novelist's techniques and values
as parts of the problem so analyzed.

For Horkheimer, such a defense would make sense only when supported with
evidence of James's identification with proletarian interests and his contributions
to the formation of such a class consciousness. To be sure, the traditionally
defined proletariat lingers only on the margins of James's fictional worlds, as
long as we understand the "working class" in these traditional terms. Yet I
would agree with recent cultural critics that such a narrow definition ignores the
labor of those whose work is the most likely to be exploited, in part because
such work has no properly established "exchange value." In this group I would
include James's women and children, the two groups in James most likely to

be victimized by bourgeois authority. In this context, James also recognized how fundamentally women experience their dispossession through the everyday use of language and how their access to language is always conditioned by patriarchal rhetoric, even when used by other women. But it is also the unacknowledged labor of women in birth, child rearing, and education to which James's fiction calls attention.

Contemporary feminists have pointed out that one of the fundamental omissions from traditional Marxist theory is the work of women, in both the work force and the domestic world. So much of James's fiction is given over to the bourgeois work of courtship and marriage that we tend to forget the central roles that children play in his fiction. In its obsession with its own forms, rituals, and powers, bourgeois society ignores its children. The "Principino" in *The Golden Bowl* is just what the name suggests: a mere bibelot, another "collectible" for the Ververs. Maisie Farange, of course, dramatizes the confusions and alienation experienced by children attempting to adjust to family relations and parental roles that seem to change overnight. In *The Turn of the Screw*, such alienation turns fantastic for Miles and Flora, whether we accept the "truth" of what the governess reports or simply her madness. In either case, these children, orphaned by their parents and emotionally abandoned by their uncle, are left to grow up in a world that seems hostile to their interests. We forget that Verena Tarrant in *The Bostonians* is, after all, little more than a child when her father first pushes her before a revivalist audience; to the very end, she grows little, except in her capacity to mime, like Maisie, the rhetoric of what she can only guess controls adult behavior and values. There are many other examples of children given center stage by James yet marginalized by their parents and other adults of the bourgeois world. I select these familiar fictional children in part because they so self-evidently work, and work hard, either for their parents' and guardians' material profit or simply for the sake of a little attention and affection. The trivialization of the work of children goes hand in hand with the patriarchal disregard for the labor of women, both in reproduction and in the work of child rearing, in addition to the more demonstrable forms of work performed by women in Victorian society. Indeed, in addition to the labor of the factory, of the sweatshop, and of "cottage industry," we must list the work of governesses, servants, and "cultivated companions," despite the subtleties of class divisions that traditionally separate such drudging and unrewarded labors.

Like bourgeois women, James's children of the middle class are more than just alienated; they are imprisoned, psychologically abused, and in some cases, quite literally killed by the pressures or neglect of their parents. In this regard, Pansy Osmond is one of the most familiar examples, shut away in an Italian convent for her "edification" when in fact she is hidden as the visible sign of her father's adultery with Madame Merle. Isabel "goes back" to Osmond as much for Pansy's sake as for any commitment to middle-class marriage, but "saving" Pansy is much harder work than James knows how to articulate; it can be left only as a "prospect" for Isabel at the very end of the novel. Pansy's prison extends well beyond that convent, and in this regard she anticipates the pathetic fate of Tina Bordereau, locked up with her "great-aunt" (or mother) in their ruined Venetian palazzo, only to be offered to a "publishing scoundrel" as a guarantee that Juliana might reach beyond the grave to keep this niece/ daughter in bondage to Juliana's fantastic secret. Like Tina, Pansy has value as an exchangeable commodity, whether such value is determined by Gilbert Osmond, Lord Warburton, or even Ned Rosier.

Whether Tina "develops" finally, in open rebellion against the lies of Juliana and the treachery of the narrator, hardly matters when we consider her wasted life. The fires that consume Aspern's "papers"—"There were so many," she taunts the narrator in one of those rare moments that satisfy James's reader with justice achieved—have already consumed Tina, no matter how "beautiful" she appears at the very last to the zealous editor. In a similar fashion, the horror of the governess in *The Turn of the Screw* is the hint that Douglas offers that she too has never grown up, that his "love" for her might well have been returned by her if only on the evidence of her "gift" of that manuscript, her most terrible secret. The equivalence of women and children in this bourgeois economy is not an effect of James's paternalism but of the virtual hostility its social world expresses to the "development" and "growth" either of women or children.

Children in James generally represent cases of arrested development, of the failure of maturation and acculturation, to the point that we are inclined to forget them, unwilling as we are to engage the ugly truth they reveal. The extremity of this parental abuse of children is murder, and it is of murder that we must judge the Ambients' finally fatal struggle over the "morality" of little Dolcino in "The Author of Beltraffio," just as it is murder with which both the governess and the uncle must be charged in the death of Miles in *The Turn of the Screw*. In another of those tragic and perverse stories, "The Pupil," Morgan Moreen dies of a "broken" or "weakened" heart (it matters little which) when his parents agree to give him to his tutor, Mr. Pemberton. He understands as well as the others that he is Mr. Pemberton's delayed "payment," in one of those marvellously perverse ironies in James—that the "reward" for Pemberton's care and education of this extraordinary boy is the boy himself. It is, of course, just what Morgan has seemed to want all along. As Mrs. Pemberton wails, "But I thought he *wanted* to go to you!" (*NY* XI, 577). Even the most casual reader, Pemberton included, knows that what the child most wants is the care and attention of his parents.

Such children understand their young years to involve work, often very hard work, which they are willing to perform, if only it will bring them a proper return. Yet like the tutor, Mr. Pemberton, these children are never paid for their labors. Aware of the boy's pain and confusion from living with parents whose lives are dedicated to a life of leisure and luxury that they cannot afford, Mr. Pemberton proposes, if somewhat in jest, "We ought to go off and live somewhere together" (*NY* XI, 545). The bond that unites the tutor and his charge is their sense that their labors are not respected, that they are mere victims of a confidence game they both understand with perfect clarity but somehow are powerless to escape. When Pemberton elaborates, "I'd get some work that would keep us both afloat," Morgan replies promptly: "So would I. Why shouldn't *I* work? I ain't such a beastly little muff as *that* comes to" (*NY* XI, 545). And yet it is a "beastly little muff," or "bungler," that best represents Morgan's image of himself, or at least what his parents have led him to believe of himself. Yet in his choice of words, in the decisively American idiom Morgan chooses— *muff*, like *bungler*, comes from a baseball term still current today—Morgan rebels ever so slightly in the "cultivated" Italy where the vulgar term is uttered.

What "child labor laws" might be enacted to protect such children, dispossessed and possessed by the fantastic adult world around them? James's representation of these bourgeois children is perhaps his most profound indictment of the bourgeoisie's lack of a proper historical consciousness, its failure to develop those means through which it might transform and renew itself. And yet we hardly notice how the children in Henry James's fiction are as orphaned, abandoned, and abused as the fictional children in Mark Twain's work. Isabel Archer in *Portrait*, Milly Theale in *The Wings of the Dove*, and even Chad Newsome in *The Ambassadors* are young adults who have experienced in their own ways just such dispossession and who have been scarred for life. It is a "neglect" or repression that we cannot attribute to James, but it may well be a consequence of our own reading habits as bourgeois readers, intent as we are on the "serious" business of adult relations and mindless of the work our children must every day perform.

I have suggested that these children are workers as alienated from their labor of acculturation as the children of sweatshops and factories. They remind us again of how profoundly James's bourgeois women are dispossessed, cast in roles either as confining as that Bronzino painting Milly views at Matcham— "dead, dead, dead"—or as perversely conventional as Maggie's "triumphant" role as the prince's wife and her father's daughter at the end of *The Golden Bowl*. When Milly Theale leaves the offices of Sir Luke Strett in *The Wings of the Dove*, she plunges into the "grey immensity" of London, a "grey immensity" that "had somehow become her element" (*NY* XIX, 247). Her long walk through working-class London has often been analyzed as one of the rare moments in James in which high society must confront the underclass world on which it builds its palaces. To be sure, it *is* a little sentimental, even an indulgent insight for the doomed Milly to recognize in the exhausted lives of those around her a metaphor for her own fate.

There is nonetheless a serious dimension to her recognition that her own mortality links her not just with "common humanity" but with precisely those for whom the daily question is one of survival, of the "practical question of life" (*NY* XIX, 250). Her mental gestures are significant, even as they connect her with her fictional predecessor Hester Prynne. "It was as if she had to pluck off her breast, to throw away, some friendly ornament, a familiar flower, a little old jewel, that was part of her daily dress; and to take up and shoulder as a substitute some queer defensive weapon, a musket, a spear, a battle-axe—conducive possibly in a higher degree to a striking appearance, but demanding all the effort of the military posture'' (*NY* XIX, 248).

James repeats the military metaphor again in his account of Milly's "march" through the London slums. At first, it is merely a sign of her fortitude, her strength of will in the face of her own doom, but soon enough it becomes her identification with the working classes. "She found herself moving at times in regions visibly not haunted by odd-looking girls from New York, duskily draped, sable-plumed, all but incongruously shod and gazing about them with extravagance; she might, from the curiosity she clearly excited in the by-ways, in sidestreets peopled with grimy children and costermongers' carts, which she hoped were slums, literally have had her musket on her shoulder, have announced herself as freshly on the war-path'' (*NY* XIX, 249). Seeing herself imaginatively (a "sable-plumed" New York girl) in the whores of London, she is driven to military solidarity with these outcasts. Even in her extremity, her rebellion is finally trivial. Coming out on the familiar lawns of Regents' Park, "she looked for a bench that was empty, eschewing a still emptier chair that she saw hard by and for which she would have paid, with superiority, a fee'' (*NY* XIX, 250).

Perhaps Olive Chancellor's or Tina Aspern's rebellion is more significant, but they are all doomed in the end to just such glimmers of solidarity with the oppressed. It is the "nameless fear" that the governess senses in Miles and Flora and that binds her to them, too tightly to be sure but nonetheless in a sympathy that initially indicates how much their exploitation partakes of that belonging to the more demonstrable "working class." The governess fears those ghosts of Peter Quint and Miss Jessel in the same sense that she struggles with Mrs. Grose for authority: all are servants, however much authority they are respectively granted by their master. Their "work" does not belong to them, and even Miss Jessel's "pregnancy" carries with it a "horror" of illegitimacy and immorality that steal even that work from her. It is fitting that her pregnancy should remain merely a "rumor," never confirmed by James's text.

These sympathies for the "exploited" labor of bourgeois women and children may seem indulgent in their own right if we take into account the sorts of exploitation experienced daily by industrial workers in nineteenth-century Europe and America. But James's point is that the most insidious exploitation works through the psychological and verbal practices that make a "musket, a spear, or a battleaxe" appear just what they are for Milly's imagination: anachronistic weapons with which to combat a subtler enemy. It is Maud Lowder at her account books who reminds James of Britannia, armed not so much with martial weapons as with quills for the ledgers. And the uncle in *Turn of the Screw* decorates his apartment with "trophies of the hunt," but one conducted clearly by way of the verbal blandishments and billets-doux that in part seal his contract with the governess. The bourgeois pen is mightier than the sword, and it is James's rather accurate prophecy that the power of late capitalism will find itself best in the rhetorical legerdemain that we too often treat reductively as the "manners" of high society.

It is little coincidence, I think, that the few proletarians to assume central roles in James's fiction are occupied in daily tasks intimately connected with this emergent rhetorical power, with the "discourse" of the bourgeoisie. Hyacinth Robinson in *The Princess Casamassima* is a bookbinder, and the telegraph operator in *In the Cage* is merely another circuit in the communications system of the ruling class. The sources of capital may be repressed, if only to disguise the sheer vulgarity of that nameless "commodity" on which the Newsomes' fortune is based in *The Ambassadors*. Yet as Newman's own entrepreneurial history makes clear in *The American*, the power of the bourgeoisie has little to do with actual production, with "commodities" per se. Leather, washtubs, or railroads, oil or the stock market, Newman knows the "trick" of making money. More often than not, such a "trick" is rhetorical, a sleight of hand by which the labor of another may become your own.

In the case of James's imaginative, intelligent young women, such trickery aims at their very vitality and "bloom." It is the fertility of such women, both intellectually and physically, that the ruling class seeks to possess. *The Sacred Fount* is not just metaphorically a narrative of vampirism; it quite graphically describes the possession of others that is the work of the ruling class. Understood exclusively in terms of the limited opportunities available to Isabel Archer, Milly Theale, and even the mystified Maggie Verver, such exploitation and alienation hardly compare with that of the vast and largely unrecognized underclass in James's fiction. Yet when we add to this company James's fictional children, and the extent to which his most promising young adults still bear the scars of such childhoods, there is a rather numerous fictional company capable of the sort of "class consciousness" that Horkheimer demands for "critical theory."

Such a class consciousness must appear contrived insofar as it is shaped primarily from within the bourgeoisie. It is clear enough that James feared the "masses," especially the immigrants to America for whom he could at once express sympathy for their socioeconomic oppression and contempt for their lack of "development" and "cultivation." *The American Scene* gives ample evidence of James's fears of immigrant cultures. It would be wrong to force this adaptation of Horkheimer's Marxist definition of "critical theory" to suit James's ambivalence regarding the rapid demographic and cultural changes in modern America. Yet for all his conservative commitments to such dangerous clichés as national integrity, the special "tone" of a "culture" or "civilization," there is a social utopianism in James that meets the requirements of Horkheimer's "critical theory," precisely because such utopia is predicated on the common interests discovered through shared labor. That utopian dimension rests squarely in our capacities to control our means of communication and thus to produce our own representations. In this regard, James anticipates the central questions facing us in our postmodern condition, in which the powers of social speech seem every day to move further from the control of the ordinary citizen.

James's utopianism is nowhere better expressed than in his commencement address to the graduating class at Bryn Mawr College on June 8, 1905: "The

Question of Our Speech.'' From Marxist, feminist, and New Historicist perspectives, it is a troubling, if not nasty, little talk, filled with James's fears of
what immigration will do to the "American idiom" and his appeals to his women
auditors for whom "voice" and "tone" are matters of special importance. Add
to all of this James's unspoken assumption that the *vox Americana* must be
monolingual, cannot be thought of as other than "American English," and you
have the elements of a very strong case against James as "critical theorist,"
certainly in the twentieth-century context in which I have been developing that
term. From a New Historicist perspective, James is simply too utterly imbued
with the inherited values of "Western civilization" to entertain any alternative
to it. Along with this civilization come those "torch-bearers," those "articulate
individuals," among whom he counts himself in the example of his speech (*QS*
49). Against such a standard of "articulation," James pits "the common schools
and the 'daily paper,' " traditional enemies of the high-culture ideals that he
and many of his modernist followers would develop so elaborately, especially
in the face of dramatic changes in the class structures of Europe and America
at the turn of the century (*QS* 44).

I cannot leave aside these problems in James's appeal to his bourgeois auditors
to "purify" the language and emulate the "tone" that distinguishes French or
Italian and their correlative cultures and arts. Yet even amid these fears and
prejudices, James recognizes that the common aim of those dispossessed must
be to achieve some control over the means of their communication. Insofar as
James celebrates the social and political powers of language, he treats verbal
communication as the chief basis for the formation of what a proper critical
theorist would term "class consciousness." To be sure, for James it remains
"national" consciousness, the *vox Americana*, full of all the mystifications of
a nationalism repugnant to Horkheimer and the Frankfurt School, as well as to
many so-called Americanists in our contemporary period. Even so, James's
"nationalism" begins with the recognition of a shared alienation from the means
of social articulation and thus discursive power:

All the while we sleep the vast contingents of aliens whom we make welcome, and whose
main contention, as I say, is that from the moment of their arrival, they have just as
much property in our speech as we have, and just as good a right to do what they choose
with it—the grand right of the American being to do just what he chooses 'over here'
with anything and everything: all the while we sleep the innumerable aliens are sitting
up (*they* don't sleep!) to work their will on their new inheritance and prove to us that
they are without any finer feeling or more conservative instinct of consideration for it,
more hovering, caressing curiosity about it, than they may have on the subject of so
many yards of freely figured oilcloth, from the shop, that they are preparing to lay down,
for convenience, on the kitchen floor or kitchen staircase. (*QS* 44–45)

Certainly James recoils from his own excessively material metaphor for language, with its insistence on the sheer instrumentality of language, which for
these "innumerable aliens" remains simply "convenient" and "wonderfully

resisting 'wear' . . . an excellent bargain: durable, tough, cheap" (*QS* 45–46). The metaphor is overdetermined with an anti-Semitism that surfaces more explicitly elsewhere in "The Question of Our Speech" and cannot be ignored. Bought as it is "cheaply" in a "shop" for practical use in the kitchen, James's extended metaphor suggests how the immigrants' use of the *vox Americana* may only reinforce their essential privacy, their confinement to the provincialism of the tenement and the exploitation of those more "articulate." Even such a generous interpretation suggests that James endorses a "melting-pot" thesis, through which the immigrants' "access" to American society depends on a certain acculturation to "proper" American English.

Yet the "influences of example and authority" are not so easily identified by James as they might be by more "traditional theorists" appealing to the conservators of European culture: "I grant you here that I am at a loss to name you particular and unmistakable, edifying and illuminating groups or classes, from which this support is to be derived; since nothing, unfortunately, more stares us in the face than the frequent failure of such comfort in those quarters where we might, if many things were different, most look for it" (*QS* 48). James prefers instead to insist on simply "a consciousness, an acute consciousness" of "formed and finished utterance, wherever, among all the discords and deficiencies, that music steals upon your ear" (*QS* 50). James's reluctance to specify that "class" or "group" from which we might expect the models for cultivated speech stems from his own democratic sentiments, tainted with the prejudices of his age and his own cultivated experience. Troublesome as this ideal must be in his articulation, it still carries with it a certain conviction that the ultimate social capital is communication and the capacity for and access to those means of representation from which his victimized characters are so often banned.

It is prosperity, of a sort, that a hundred million people, a few years hence, will be unanimously, loudly—above all loudly, I think!—speaking it, and that, moreover, many of these millions will have been artfully wooed and weaned from the Dutch, from the Spanish, from the German, from the Italian, from the Norse, from the Finnish, from the Yiddish even, strange to say, and (stranger still today) even from the English, for the sweet sake, or the sublime consciousness, as we may perhaps put it, of speaking, of talking, for the first time in their lives, *really* at their ease. (*QS* 42)

The "consciousness" of "proper speech" that he advises his auditors to "cultivate" is thus not necessarily English but rather a social discourse that makes this diverse population capable of communicating. Of course, James has in mind the development of "American English" that will eventually take the place of "English" and thus incorporate those elements of immigrants' speech that may be made to serve the purposes of verbal "discrimination and selection," of judgment and precise evaluation. Just who are to be the arbiters of what should be "retained" and what "suppressed" in this development of the *vox Americana* is left deliberately vague by James, but we can read clearly enough his implication. That he himself might be counted one of the judges of such linguistic propriety, even as he liberally embraces the ideal of a language capable of responding "from its core, to the constant appeal of time, perpetually demanding new tricks, new experiments, new amusements," goes without saying (*QS* 46).

But what remains compelling about James's formulation of a social utopia predicated on popular access to the most sophisticated modes of communication is the possibility of reconceiving class consciousness in these general terms: that is, the shared interests of those members of a society effectively dispossessed of these very means of social communication. This is precisely the situation of James's bourgeois women and children, who are victimized insofar as they are required to speak a language that expresses only their powerlessness or dispossession. Milly Theale's recognition of her mortality is less a consequence of her visit to Sir Luke Strett than it is the result of her experiences in the social world of London. "She" has no voice, and it is entirely fitting that the "voice" she finally chooses can be articulated only by others, in her absence. If such is the case, then her identification with the underclass of London is more political than sentimental, and James's politely biased address to these Bryn Mawr graduates may suggest a subtler bond they share with the immigrants arriving in America.

There is nonetheless a great distance separating such symbolic "identification" of bourgeois women with the working class from the ideal of diverse peoples "speaking . . . *really* at their ease," in which both "ease" and "reality" are assumed to have some equivalence insofar as they are produced by such peoples. The hint in James that the true "economic production" of a society is its capacity to communicate among its many cultural and ethnic differences seems confirmed in his repeated references to the "economy" and "property" of language in "The Question of Our Speech." Even so, James remains a victim of his own contemporary and class-specific situation insofar as he insists on what he terms a "conscious" speech that is "imitative." "Conscious, imitative speech—isn't that more dreadful than anything else?" James poses rhetorically his auditors' objections to what must be understood idiomatically as the stilted and elaborate speech of his European aristocratic models. "It's not 'dreadful,' I reply, any more than it's ideal: the matter depends on the stage of development it represents. It's an awkwardness, in your situation, that your own stage is an early one, and that you have found, round about you—outside of these favoring shades—too little help. Therefore your consciousness will now represent the phase of awakening, and that will last what it must" (*QS* 51). Unable to make the leap to the formation of either a class or, even more narrowly, a national consciousness based on its own means of representation, James reverts at the last to those cultural traditions that so often serve to prop up the artist's bid for authority. "The Question of Our Speech" is James's version of Eliot's "Tradition and the Individual Talent," which more than any other essay by the moderns shaped our twentieth-century justifications of the modernist avant-garde.

This much of James's endorsement of human language remains perfectly defensive, specific to the patriarchal and bourgeois ideology of his age. Yet insofar as his fiction focuses on those who find such traditional ''access'' to language, social or personal, to exclude them in their own social particularity and in the real conditions of their labor, James contradicts his own conservative impulses. Recognizing that the work of socialization, the work of child rearing, and the child's own ''work'' of acculturation have something in common with the more material work of the proletariat, he discovers the elementary terms for such an expansive ''class consciousness'' in our access to and competency in that elusive ideal of ''conscious speech.''

In this regard, James anticipates those post-Marxians who understand the powers of the ruling class to reside less in its control of the material world of wealth and capital than in the property of language and the powers of representation. Insofar as his fiction attempts to work out the ethical terms by which we might judge and interpret the ''speech'' of others in the interests of a more democratic language, he was a critical theorist in the best sense. There is a hint of just this political dimension to James's theory of language in J. Hillis Miller's conclusions on the ways that James's style calls attention to the necessity by which any speech-act invokes the common laws of language—''laws'' of interpretation and judgment that must be said always to exceed any particular text. For Miller, the ''unreadability'' of the text, literary or otherwise, must be understood in precisely its relation to the invocation of such a ''law.''

The text in this specific sense is unreadable. It does not transmit its own law legible in it. Its law cannot be read within it but remains in reserve. . . . The critic or reader is tempted to make this one text the ground of a universal legislation for all mankind as readers, though the text neither offers nor claims any authority for that move. The text is not the law nor even the utterance of the law but an example of the productive force of the law. We respect or ought to respect not the example but the law of which it is an example, the ethical law as such. (121)

The ''law'' to which Miller refers is the productive necessity of language, which works only insofar as it encompasses a more ''goodly company,'' circulates without exhaustion or consumption, and thus remains ever historical. It is one of the ways in which Marx and Engels's promise of men and women experiencing their own ''real, sensuous activity'' as producers of their social worlds might be approached. And in the lie it gives to Cartesian rationalism, to ''idealists'' of all sorts, the ethics of speech as real, material communication offers a finer justice than Reason.

Some such ''law'' is what governs the utopian social order of a ''classless society'' dreamt in the Marxist imaginary, and it has affinities with James's own flawed respect for the social prospects of a language genuinely produced and cultivated by ''the people.'' That we have formalized James's writings as literary experiments in language or dismissed those writings as unproblematic contributions to bourgeois ideology is only a measure of how dismally we have failed to understand what James meant by the redeemed society that an easier speech might bring: "the perfect possession of this highest of civilities, the sight, through the narrow portal, of the blue horizon across the valley, the wide fair country in which your effort will have settled to the most exquisite of instincts, in which you will taste all the savor of gathered fruit" (*QS* 51–52). It is a grand vision, touched a bit with his father's Swedenborgian sentiments and social idealism. James was the master when he delivered these lines, but I would like to think that something of Morgan Moreen's rebelliously childish slang—"I ain't such a beastly little muff as that"—still echoed in James's ear.

## NOTES

1. I quote this passage because it strikes me as a central argument against those who continue to write about James as the master of the modern novel. To write today at all about James, in whatever temper, is to contend with this judgment and then not only for the sake of overturning its criticism. In "Modern Art and the Invention of Postmodern Capital," I fundamentally agree with Jameson in his judgment of James, and yet this essay defends James by way of certain qualifications of his social and political inclinations. I do not mean to be contradictory but simply to write with a "good conscience" about James. That means understanding the extent to which his mastery, irony, and formalism have realized the conservative political implications of his thought and even his habits (he was *cultivated*, to be sure), even as his critique of ideology anticipates our more sophisticated understanding of the discursive modes of hegemonic control. It is not I, but James, who fosters such contradictions.

2. See Lloyd, "Arnold, Ferguson, Schiller," 2.

3. Wallace Martin cogently describes the American reception of both deconstruction and the Yale School in the 1970s:

> Although many American critics thought that the theoretical revisionism of Miller, de Man, and Bloom in the early 1970s resulted from their acceptance of ideas current in Continental criticism, others interpreted it as an essentially defensive maneuver, intended to ward off the threat of a more radical critique of literature (Riddel, "A Miller's Tale"). From one point of view, de Man's and Miller's argument that literature demystifies or deconstructs all attempts to accord it a special status can be seen as an attack on the Anglo-American critical tradition and on literature itself. From another point of view, this argument may be intended to save literature from irremediable deconstruction: it acknowledges the validity of anti-idealistic theories and claims that literature has already anticipated them. (xviii–xix)

It is in this latter regard that the deconstructive James has generally had the widest appeal, and it is a version of deconstruction now in need of critique, especially as far as the modernism that James represents is concerned.

4. J. Hillis Miller's *The Ethics of Reading*, based on his René Wellek Library Lectures at Irvine in 1985, is only one place where he treats James at length. I have attempted to demonstrate the adaptability, as well as some of the limitations, of Bloom's map of misreading for James's subsumption of his predecessors in *The Theoretical Dimensions of Henry James*.

5. A full bibliography of such deconstructive readings of James would be a scholarly project in its own right. Good examples include my own *Henry Adams and Henry James* (1976), which I have repeatedly criticized, Henry Sussman's *The Hegelian Aftermath* (1982), Shoshana Felman's "Turning the Screw of Interpretation" (1977), and Susanne Kappeler's *Writing and Reading in Henry James* (1980).

6. "In his theoretical writing James juxtaposes the pictorial and the dramatic technique: the picture and the scene. In *What Maisie Knew* they merge because both are only aspects of the dominant theme of playing with reflections. The novel is not a drama nor a painting but it is, in an important sense, a shadow-puppet show or, despite its precinema imagery, a film. So is Maisie's view of her world" (Mitchell 170).

7. See Veeder, *Henry James*, esp. ch. 1.

8. In *The War of the Words*, the first volume of *No Man's Land*, Sandra Gilbert and Susan Gubar use Vernon Lee's caricature of Henry James, in the character of Marion in Lee's novella "Lady Tal," to explain quite precisely the ambivalence women writers— both his contemporaries and many of his subsequent critics—feel toward James's authority. I can only refer my readers to Gilbert and Gubar's interpretation, which is too long even to paraphrase in this note (*The War of the Words* 214–216).

9. "There are, of course, further institutional strategies that lie beyond a love for the theater. In a move that Ben Jonson rather than Shakespeare seems to have anticipated, the theater itself comes to be emptied out in the interests of reading. In the argument made famous by Charles Lamb and Coleridge, and reiterated by Bradley, theatricality must be discarded to achieve absorption, and Shakespeare's imagination yields forth its sublime power not to a spectator but to one who, like Keats, sits down to reread *King Lear*. Where institutions like the King's Men had been thought to generate their texts, now texts like *King Lear* appear to generate their institutions. The commercial contingency of the theater gives way to the philosophical necessity of literature" (Greenblatt 444–45). As Shakespeare goes, so goes James. It is in this dialectic between textuality and institutional practices that I find New Historicism's politics (which its critics insist are nowhere to be found) to have the greatest cogency and relevance for our contemporary situation.

# II
# HENRY JAMES'S
# FICTION

# 6
# The Early Years

*James W. Tuttleton*

In his autobiographical reminiscence *A Small Boy and Others* (1913), Henry James said that the hit-or-miss education he had received as a boy was best calculated to produce the spectatorial vocation of the novelist. But short stories, rather than the novel, constituted his immediate apprenticeship, for—as he confessed years later—he had had, "from far back," a fascination with the "whole 'question of the short story' " (*AN* 178), and it was this genre, with its special demands, that first roused his imagination and indeed continued to feed it throughout his lifetime.

However, between 1864—the date of his first short story ("A Tragedy of Error")—and 1880, the period of James's apprenticeship covered by these introductory remarks, James experimented with other literary forms as well. His first experiments with the short story—as collected in *A Passionate Pilgrim and Other Tales* (1875)—are perhaps most fully understandable if they are seen in the context of James's personal life and other contemporaneous literary productions. This is especially the case because as he composed the stories that were to make up this volume, James was also wandering about Europe and writing essays and articles, for the *Atlantic Monthly* and the *Nation*, on the customs and conventions, the architecture and art, the landscape and peoples of England, France, and Italy—nonfiction periodical journalism eventually gathered into *Transatlantic Sketches* (1875).

Likewise, his later tales during this apprenticeship period—eventually collected in *The Madonna of the Future and Other Tales* (1879), *A Bundle of Letters* (1880), and *The Diary of a Man of Fifty* (1880)—are also chronologically intermingled with early efforts at literary criticism like *French Poets and Novelists* (1878), biographical writing like *Hawthorne* (1879), and his first tentative explorations of both the novel form—in *Watch and Ward* (1871), *Roderick Hudson*

(1875), *The American* (1877), *Confidence* (1879), and *Washington Square* (1880)—and "the beautiful and blest *nouvelle*" (*AN* 220)—in *The Europeans* (1878) and *Daisy Miller* (1878). What I am trying to suggest is that the transformation of Henry James from an inexperienced apprentice to a major writer of international distinction was an organic development that simultaneously reflects a growing mastery of several genres.

During this apprentice period, through the year 1880, James wrote nearly 40 short stories (out of a career total of 112). Most of them may be set aside here as youthful efforts at finding a fictional voice, locating his real themes, and creating the audience for his art. Indeed, when he prepared his first volume of tales for publication—*A Passionate Pilgrim and Other Tales* (1875)—he retained only the best: "The Last of the Valerii," "Eugene Pickering," "The Madonna of the Future," "The Romance of Certain Old Clothes," "Madame de Mauves," and the title story, "A Passionate Pilgrim." Even some of these, as he later confessed, were reprinted in the New York Edition only as a testament to his personal circumstances in the 1870s. Nevertheless, these early tales reflect the nascent formulation and rapid evolution of his thought about the four great subjects of both his long and short fiction in the early period: (1) the social and moral conditions of American life; (2) the rich discovery, by the traveling American, of the complex cultural life of Europe and its effect on the aesthetic and moral sense; (3) the nature and demands of the artistic life; and (4) the plight of the American free spirit, usually a young woman, ground (as he would put it) in the very mill of the conventional.

Many of the early stories and novels reflect the social perspective of "A Bundle of Letters" (1879), where the character Louis Leverett speaks his author's mind in saying, "I am much interested in the study of national types; in comparing, contrasting, seizing the strong points, the weak points, the point of view of each" (*CT* IV, 442). Out of his comparisons of the social and moral differences between America on the one hand and England, Italy and France on the other arose James's greatest early theme as a portraitist of manners, what he called "The Americano-European legend." This legend, namely the international theme, is sometimes explored neutrally, sometimes with sympathy for the American abroad, sometimes with sympathy for the European confronting American vulgarity. At times James satirically deflates American cultural naïveté and moral rigidity; yet sometimes, in defending American innocence, he brings into question an impenetrable European sensibility so complex as to seem (or be) morally duplicitous.

His creative method, in other words, was that of an "operative irony" in which his theme in one tale might be just the reverse of his theme in another tale, what he called "the possible other case, the case rich and edifying where the actuality is pretentious and vain" (*AN* 222). Sometimes, in fact, the operative irony is evident in a single tale or novel: a presumptive theme or thesis is subtly qualified by a suggestive counterstatement. But however impartial his ironical method, there is no doubt that in the comparison and contrast of the New and the Old World, Europe ultimately appealed to him as a place to live and work because it offered greater complexity of social relations as material for fiction and because, as Herbert Croly once remarked, Europe meant for him "life itself raised to a higher power, because more richly charged, more significantly composed, and more completely informed" (Dupee, *Question of Henry James* 29). That this decision was immensely important to James is suggested in the urgency of his notebook entry, where, after some crisscrossing of the Atlantic, he announced: "I have made my choice, and God knows that I have now no time to waste. My choice is the old world—my choice, my need, my life" (*NB* 23).

"A Passionate Pilgrim" (1871) is exemplary of James's original response to Europe. In this tale of the American's enchanted discovery of the Old World, the picturesque English town and countryside are described at length with a "natural affection" induced as much by James's reading of English literature as by direct observation. Here the traveling American, the dying Clement Searle, luxuriates in an England prepared for him, as for the narrator, "in visions, in dreams, in Dickens, in Smollett, and Boswell" (*CT* II, 227–28). Reflecting a nostalgia for England reminiscent of Irving's *The Sketch Book*, Searle undertakes to emotionally appropriate what Hawthorne had called "our old home." James offers a sharp contrast between the picturesque antiquity of England, in all its ancient loveliness, and "the naked background of our own education, the dead white wall before which we [Americans] played our parts." Searle remarks: "We [Amercans] are nursed at the opposite pole. Naked come we into a naked world." In contrast is an English landscape of picturesque villages, quaint old churches, ancient colleges, and lovely sheep meadows. "We greeted these things," the narrator remarks, "as children greet the loved pictures in a story-book, lost and mourned and found again" (*CT* II, 251). As the title may indicate, the ardor of the culture-starved American, on his first journey to Europe, has a quasi-religious implication of worship.

Yet at the same time, America is not without possibilities. Searle commends "a certain heroic strain in those young [American] imaginations of the West, which find nothing made to their hands, which have to concoct their own mysteries, and raise high into our morning air, with a ringing hammer and nails, the castles in which they dwell" (*CT* II, 293–94). (James indeed had just such an American imagination.) Searle dies before his claim to an English estate can be settled. But in willing some of his belongings to the penniless Englishman Rawson, who has wheeled him about Oxford, the dying Searle makes possible Rawson's departure for America in a kind of reverse passionate pilgrimage where an enchanted American culture may, just may, be created de novo. Personally, however, James was not willing to wait for this desirable consummation. Despite its criticism of the cultural nudity of America, the tale was immensely popular in America. William Dean Howells, at the *Atlantic*, remarked that James's tales "had characteristics which forbad any editor to refuse them," and he ranked "A Passionate Pilgrimage" above James's other short stories because of its dramatic power and "rich poetical qualities" (347, 349).

In "The Last of the Valerii" (1874), James's response to Europe is also double-edged with ironic implication. In this tale, the image of "Europe" was that held by his elder brother, the American pragmatist William, who found the Continent to be resonant with echoes of the historical evils of the pagan era. Indeed, the blood-soaked history of Europe, about which William complained, is palpably manifest in the ancient ruins through which Henry strolled. "The Last of the Valerii" concerns an American wife and an Italian count, her husband. Conte Valerio is to all appearances an excellent husband, although, to the narrator of the tale, he seems "nothing but senses, appetites, serenely luxurious tastes." Since the Count has an aversion to Catholicism and reveals in fact a pagan disposition, the question posed by the narrator is whether or not he "had anything that could properly be termed a soul" (*CT* III, 95.) The question is answered when Martha proposes an archaeological excavation at the Villa Valerio, in hopes of turning up some salable artifacts. The count protests. " 'Let them lie, the poor disinherited gods, the Minerva, the Apollo, the Ceres you are so sure of finding,' he said, 'and don't break their rest. What do you want of them? We can't worship them. Would you put them on pedestals to stare and mock at them? If you can't believe in them, don't disturb them. Peace be with them!' " (*CT* III, 98).

Still, she persists, and the workmen eventually turn up an ancient marble statue of Juno. Thereupon the count appropriates the statue, will not sell it, and erects it in a moonlit casino. There, in secret and by night, he prostrates himself before it. As the ancient pagan passion for the goddess overcomes the count, he worships her, even to the point of making blood sacrifices at her altar. As the narrator remarks on "the strange ineffaceability of race-characteristics," the Count Valerio reverts to "the faith of his fathers" and surrenders to "the old ancestral ghosts" (*CT* III, 116). In this reversion to the old gods (or mental derangement, depending on one's point of view), Count Valerio utterly neglects his anguished wife. In due course, however, Martha takes charge and privately orders the Juno reburied in the layered soil of the ancient villa. This act seemingly brings the count back to his senses, and they are reconciled—the story turning out happily. But as the narrator remarks, the count "never became, if you will, a thoroughly modern man" (*CT* III, 122). He secretly retained the broken-off marble hand of the Juno for occasional private devotions. In this tale James creates, like Hawthorne before him in *The Marble Faun*, a neutral territory in which romance may flourish, in order to demonstrate how the past may bizarrely erupt into the present, how superstition remains deep-rooted in the race, and how, in modern Europe, ancient ways of thinking and feeling may resurface in the modern sensibility.

In "Madame de Mauves" (1874), however, the forceful American wife, married again to an Old World aristocrat, produces a tragic rather than a happy outcome. In this story, an American woman, Euphemia Cleve, has married a distinguished Frenchman, the Baron de Mauves, whose subsequent infidelity absolutely estranges her. An American visitor, Longmore—who falls in love with the aloof but beautiful Madam de Mauves—is invited by the baron's sister to attach himself to Euphemia. He, however, declines the adulterous suggestion and returns to America. Later he learns that the baron, moved by Euphemia's fidelity to him, has repented his unfaithfulness and has thrown himself upon her forgiveness. But, in her inflexible moral resentment, she refuses to accept her repentant husband, whereupon the baron blows out his brains. Although the way is now clear to commence his suit, Longmore does not return to France to act on his love for her. The tale makes much of the ethical purity of the beautiful Madame de Mauves, but the puritanical absoluteness of her moral sense is too much even for the American Longmore. As the narrator remarks, "The truth is, that in the midst of all the ardent tenderness of his memory of Madame de Mauves, he has become conscious of a singular feeling,—a feeling for which awe would be hardly too strong a name" (*CT* III, 209). Thus, in tracing the strong and weak points of this Franco-American conflict of temperament and values, James shows that the morally angular American woman's uncritical marriage to a European husband, elegant but ethically promiscuous, produces fatal consequences for both. All of the characters are denied forgiveness and love, including Longmore himself.

If James's earliest aim was to become a novelist, he had before him the example of Hawthorne in America, as well as Balzac, Flaubert, Turgenev, Daudet, George Eliot, and the Goncourt brothers in Europe—some of whom he met in Paris in 1875–76 and all of whom he studied assiduously and whose effect on his apprenticeship is partly celebrated in *French Poets and Novelists* (1878). They set a high standard because of their keen intelligence of art, and James wanted nothing more than to embody in himself their commitment to aesthetic perfection. The standard they set, however, was not matched in James's first novel, *Watch and Ward*, written in America in 1870 after his return from a year in Europe. He had high hopes for it, telling his editor at the *Atlantic*, where it was serialized in 1871, that it was "one of the greatest works of 'this or any age' " (Edel, Introduction to *Watch and Ward* 14). But in fact it had manifest defects that delayed him in republishing it until 1878, when he extensively revised it for its first book edition. Despite these improvements and a few decent reviews—the *New York Times* grouped James with "the very few leading romance writers of England and America" (Gargano, *Early Novels* 32)—James never again reprinted it in his lifetime and spoke as if *Roderick Hudson* were his first novel.

Despite its limitations, *Watch and Ward* is nevertheless a spirited performance for a first novel. Based on the Pygmalion theme, the tale recounts the adoption of the orphaned Nora Lambert, age twelve, by the bachelor Roger Lambert, age twenty-nine. Convinced that by supervising her education he can eventually produce for himself the perfect wife, Roger oversees the girl's training only to discover, later on, that other men have also become interested in this charming young woman. After many trials and tribulations for them both, Nora does eventually marry Roger, whose steadfast love finally wins the day. Reflecting

aspects of domestic sentimental fiction of the time, especially in the figure of
the first pious but then rebellious young ward, James's novel dramatizes what
was to become the major theme of more mature fiction like *The Portrait of a
Lady*, *The Bostonians*, and *The Awkward Age*—namely, the problem of marriage
for the naïve young heroine.

*Roderick Hudson* (1875), James's second novel, revives the international
theme by reconstructing, in part, James's passionate pilgrimage to Italy in 1869.
Here the wealthy Rowland Mallet, visiting Northampton, Massachusetts, makes
the acquaintance of Roderick Hudson, a young sculptor of such promise that
Rowland offers to take him to Italy to study art. They depart for Europe, leaving
behind Mary Garland, Roderick's fiancée (with whom Rowland has secretly
fallen in love). In Italy, Roderick's talent begins to flourish, and he has produced
a number of promising sculptures when he meets and falls in love with the
beautiful Christina Light. Christina's mother wants to marry her off to wealth
and a title, certainly not to a penniless artist. Roderick's thwarted passion for
Christina and the grandeur of European sculpture begin to destroy him as man
and artist. Rowland tries to revive his inspiration and to retrieve him from the
moral debauchery into which Roderick is sinking. But when Roderick asks for
money in order to effect an assignation with Christina, Rowland—confessing
that he loves Mary Garland—denounces Roderick for heartless egotism. Roderick
then disappears into a storm and is later found dead at the base of a cliff.

That James clearly intended Roderick to be a type of pure artistic egotism, a
latter-day New England Shelley, is evident in the sculptor's being half-mad over
Ideal Beauty and willing to sacrifice everyone, including himself, and every
social and moral convention in order to achieve its realization. The moral norm
of the novel mediates a conception of the destructive egotism of the Romantic
temperament and the acute consciousness that social living requires a degree of
selflessness and deference to the sensibilities of others. The novel thus tests the
viability of the notion of Romantic genius, as exemplified in Roderick, against
other values dramatized in the novel. James seems principally concerned with
how the American small town and the foreign colony in Rome may assimilate,
if at all, the egotism of this genius. In this respect, James may have had in mind
Emerson's observation in the essay "Manners": "Society will pardon much to
genius and special gifts, but, being in its nature a convention, it loves what is
conventional, or what belongs to coming together. That makes the good and bad
of manners, namely what helps or hinders fellowship" (*Essays* 360).

In James's comments on Northampton we are meant to understand the American small town as restrictive and inhibiting to budding aesthetic genius. But in
the "heterogeneous society" in Rome, few such inhibitions exist, and there is
no sufficient cause for Roderick to behave, in his social relations, as if society
were in a conspiracy against his manhood and an enemy to his creativity. James
describes Roderick as wholly without manners: loud, rude, interruptive, contradictory, with the effect that most of those in Rome, as in Northampton, think
him insufferably conceited. What saves him from the consequences of his boorish

behavior is his occasional charm, a quality that James reports rather than demonstrates. His indifference to convention, which Christina associates with the "sacred fire" of the artist, enchants this American *cappriciosa*, who just as imperiously violates the custom of the country in Rome, even while invoking its protection.

If Roderick's violations of the accepted norm of civilized conduct bring him under criticism from his patron, Rowland Mallet, Roderick's defense of himself is the romantic principle that artists have so often invoked to sacrifice moral conventions in their pursuit of the sensual life. If society wants beautiful works of art, he argues, artists must be granted freedom from constraints on their conduct, exemptions from the moral norm that governs others. He absolves himself of his transgressions, but even so, a paralyzing sense of guilt prevents him from producing his sculptures. His disintegration—gambling, drinking, and unspecified attention to women memorable only for certain graceful lines—is, in fact, the effect of self-indulgence masquerading as artistic freedom. For Rowland Mallet—and for James, if the example of his biography is any clue—the artist owes to his passions only as much deference as any other man should accord them, and no more; in fact, as Rowland remarks, the artist is no doubt much better off for leading a quiet life.

The crisis between the two men, narrated by James with great dramatic intensity, is brought to a head by Rowland's refusal to give Roderick enough money to follow Christina. As Roderick wanders away from Rowland into the mountains, accusing himself of only stupidity in not seeing Rowland's love for Mary, Rowland reflects, "It was egotism still: aesthetic disgust at the graceless contour of his conduct, but never a hint of simple sorrow for the pain he had given" (*RH* 469). We are left to wonder, therefore, whether Roderick's death expresses the selfless motives Oscar Cargill has supplied for him: "an effort to square himself with his patron, or to free him in relation to Mary Garland" (37n). For Roderick has been presented to us as "never thinking of others save as they figured in his own drama," of possessing an "extraordinary insensibility to the injurious effects of his own eloquence," of being "perfectly indifferent" to "sympathy or compassion." In a sharply phrased comment on Emerson's apotheosis of the self-reliant individual, James wrote: "The great and characteristic point with him was the perfect absoluteness of his own emotions and experience. He never saw himself as part of a whole; only as the clear-cut, sharp-edged, isolated individual, rejoicing or raging, as the case might be, but needing in any case absolutely to affirm himself" (*RH* 391–92). When Roderick finds that his desire is blocked, he dies, probably a suicide—though the motives as well as the actual circumstances of his death are, as Cargill concedes, wonderfully ambiguous.

Though Rowland Mallet has sometimes been faulted as a Jamesian "meddler" whose benevolent interference in Roderick's life, like Ralph's manipulation of Isabel Archer, virtually ruins the protagonist, it is more accurate to say that he embodies personal and social standards superior to those of Northampton society and to the Roman colony, standards superior, certainly, to the destructive egotism of the Emersonian individualist. Rowland perfectly balances a civilized appreciation of aesthetic values with a fine moral sensibility. If he calls himself "the most rational of men," he also has a generous heart, instanced by his offering to take Roderick with him to Europe. A man of leisure, he yet believes in the application of genius. Although he has been called a passive spectator of life and Roderick the active participant, it is Rowland who initiates the journey to Italy and who feels the responsibility for his young protégé that such an offer implies.

Above all, Rowland embodies a commitment to civilized manners that stands in admirable contrast to Roderick's coarse and impulsive individualism; it is a code of manners, moreover, squarely based on a sensitivity to moral claims. "Discord was not to his taste; he shrank from imperious passions, and the idea of finding himself jealous of an unsuspecting friend was absolutely repulsive. More than ever, then, the path of duty was to forget Mary Garland" (*RH* 102). If Roderick calls himself "a Hellenist," Rowland is no "Hebraist." Conscience he does indeed have, but above all he strives for disinterestedness. In Arnold's terms, he is one of the Children of Light, with the saving sense of beauty. A cultivated social sense is also his, but he is by no means, like the later Gilbert Osmond, suffocating in his deference to the merely conventional. Rowland "enjoyed a quiet corner of a drawing-room beside an agreeable woman," James wrote, "and, although the machinery of what calls itself society seemed to him to have many superfluous wheels, he accepted invitations and made visits punctiliously, from the conviction that the only way not to be overcome by the ridiculous side of most of such observances is to take them with exaggerated gravity" (*RH* 91–92).

Perhaps this statement best expresses James's perception about the nature of our social experience: that groups of people constitute themselves as polite society; that an ordered social observance can be extremely agreeable; that insistence on such rites is, *sub specie aeternitatis*, absurd; but that their agreeableness makes them worth observing with (as he refined the phrase in the New York Edition) an "ordered gravity." The quality of Rowland's social and moral perceptions makes him by far the most interesting character in the book, certainly of far more interest to Christina Light than Roderick Hudson cares to admit. Rowland is, in fact, as James later remarked in the preface, the real center of the novel: "My subject, all blissfully, in the face of difficulties, had defined itself—and this in spite of the title of the book—as not directly, in the least, my young sculptor's adventure. This it had been but indirectly, being all the while in essence and in final effect another man's, his friend's and patron's, view and experience of him" (*AN* 15).

Early in *Roderick Hudson*, Rowland Mallet remarks, "It's a wretched business, ... this practical quarrel of ours with our own country, this everlasting impatience to get out of it" (*RH* 29–30). His characterization of Northampton's aesthetic thinness suggests a partial reason; counterbalanced against the American small town is James's first response to Rome, as indicated in this famous 1869 letter to his brother William: "At last—for the first time—I live! It beats everything: it leaves the Rome of your fancy—your education—nowhere. It makes Venice—Florence—Oxford—London—seem like little cities of pasteboard. I went reeling and moaning thro' the streets, in a fever of enjoyment. . . . The effect is something indescribable. For the first time I know what the picturesque is" (*HJL* I, 160). James likewise has Rome impress the young American sculptor by "the element of accumulation in the human picture," by its "infinite superpositions of history" (*RH* 85), by the density of a high old tradition in arts and society. The "dusky swarming purlieus of the Ghetto" strike Roderick as "weighted with a ponderous past" and "blighted with the melancholy of things that had had their day" (*RH* 249). The Vatican especially fascinates Roderick, as it did James, as "what he had been looking for from the first, the sufficient negation of his native scene." James presents Rome, much after the manner of Hawthorne, as "the immemorial city of convention." He calls the pope, in fact, "the most impressive convention in all history . . . visible to men's eyes in the reverberating streets, erect in a gilded coach drawn by four black horses" (*RH* 85). In fact, the American's response to Italy in this novel is the test of the authenticity of his cultural and aesthetic values.

To James in the mid–1870s, the spectacle of the American's "assimilation" of Europe was rich ground for reflection, for he had seen hundreds of American travelers giving Europe the once-over but managing to miss any real experience of its complex culture—treating it "as a vast painted and gilded holiday toy, serving its purpose on the spot and for the time, but to be relinquished, sacrificed, broken and cast away, at the dawn of any other convenience" (*AN* 189). He wrote to his mother in 1869: "What I have pointed at as our [American] vices are the elements of the modern man with *culture* quite left out. It's the absolute and incredible lack of *culture* that strikes you in common travelling Americans. The pleasantness of the English comes in a great measure from the fact of their each having been dipped into the crucible, which gives them a sort of coating of comely varnish and colour. They have been smoothed and polished by mutual social attrition. They have manners and a language. We lack both" (*HJL* I, 152). James wanted nothing less than to appropriate for himself and to embody in Rowland an international culture that is symbolized by Europe. But it might as well be remarked that in James's fiction, "Europe" comes to be an invented landscape, an imagined standard of civilized existence, which he defined for his friend Grace Norton as a standard of "wit, of grace, of good manners, of vivacity, of urbanity, of intelligence, of what makes an easy and natural style of intercourse!" (*HJL* II, 239–40). He thought he could assimilate this standard by living in Italy, but the experiment failed. As he told Grace Norton in 1874:

I have been nearly a year in Italy and have hardly spoken to an Italian creature save washerwomen and waiters. This, you'll say, is my own stupidity; but granting this gladly, it proves that even a creature addicted as much to sentimentalizing as I am over the whole *mise en scène* of Italian life, doesn't find an easy initiation into what lies behind it. Sometimes I am overwhelmed with the pitifulness of this absurd want of reciprocity between Italy itself and all my rhapsodies about it. (*LHJ* I, 36–37)

France, he thought, might be a more suitable ground for his aesthetic project, so he settled in Paris in 1875.

*The American* (1877), James's next novel, was a product of James's mistaken belief that only a few months' residence in Paris had turned him into "an old, and very contented, Parisian" who had "struck roots into the Parisian soil," and was "likely to let them grow tangled and tenacious there" (*LHJ* I, 48). In fact, however, during his year of residence in Paris in 1875, he never had a proper entrée into the exclusive society of the Faubourg St. Germain, where the aristocrats lived. And he languished, discontented, in the society (largely) of the American colony in Paris. But his knowledge of the Théâtre Français, as well as of the fiction of Balzac, Flaubert, Turgenev, and the Goncourts, and a lively imagination of what must be going on within those forbidden aristocratic *hôtels*, induced James to assume a familiarity with the Faubourg and to claim it as a fictional setting. *The American* illustrated a distinctive Jamesian donnée of this early period: "the situation, in another country and an aristocratic society, of some robust but insidiously beguiled and betrayed, some cruelly wronged, compatriot, the point being in especial that he should suffer at the hands of persons pretending to represent the highest possible civilisation and to be of an order in every way superior to his own" (*AN* 22).

In this novel, the compatriot is a young American millionaire, Christopher Newman—whose name suggests that he is meant to be the new man of egalitarian America, a Christopher Columbus in reverse, discovering the alien strangeness of the Old World. His wealth secured, he goes to Paris to appropriate culture and to cap his fortune with the best aristocratic wife money can buy. But his ignorance of hierarchical class arrangements and of the social forms observed in polite French society makes his attempts to marry the aristocratic Claire de Cintré, the daughter of an impoverished family with an eight-hundred-year-old name, a spectacle rich in social comedy. To secure permission to marry her, he must of course pass the test with the old Marquise de Bellegarde, who rules the family with absolute authority, and her son the Marquis Urbain de Bellegarde, who transcendently patronizes an American utterly oblivious to his social marginality in France. Paradoxically, the family accept Newman, out of an initial avidity for his fortune, but then reject him, out of a returning disgust at his commercial vulgarity. As such, the novel dramatizes the victimization of the innocent but overreaching American at the hands of an aristocratic family whose treachery is the stuff of rankest melodrama.

James clearly intended Newman to be a comic example of the American "national mould." Innocent of art and culture, Newman has only recently discovered in Europe "a very rich and beautiful world" that had "not all been made by sharp railroad men and stock-brokers" (*AM* 95). Since he is "baffled on the aesthetic question," Raphael, Titian, and Rubens constitute "a new kind of arithmetic" and inspire Newman, "for the first time in his life, with a vague self-mistrust" (*AM* 6). James describes Newman as having that typically American "vagueness which is not vacuity, that blankness which is not simplicity, that look of being committed to nothing in particular, of standing in an attitude of general hospitality to the chances of life, of being very much at one's own disposal, so characteristic of many American faces. It was our friend's eye that chiefly told his story; an eye in which innocence and experience were singularly blended" (*AM* 7).

A feature of this definition of the American is his innocent belief that "Europe was made for him, and not he for Europe" and that the world "was a great bazar, where one might stroll about and purchase handsome things" (*AM* 82). If Madame de Cintré is the handsomest thing in Paris, Newman believes that she is his for the asking because, though he does not have a title, he is—as Americans were fond of describing themselves—"nature's nobleman." But as Valentin de Bellegarde remarks, a man who has manufactured washtubs "cannot marry a woman like Madame de Cintré for the asking" (*AM* 144). In this respect, Newman is an illustration of James's criticism—in the *Nation* essay "Americans Abroad" (1878)—that there is "a profound, imperturbable, unsuspectingness on the part of many Americans of the impression they produce in foreign lands" and that "it may sometimes provoke a smile, when the impression produced is a good deal at variance with European circumstances" (Tuttleton, *The American* 360).

If Newman is meant to synthesize the unsuspecting characteristics of the American national character—especially the typically American attitude toward will and work, money and power—these were qualities that James deplored in all Americans, whether at home or abroad. Yet in a letter to Thomas Sergeant Perry, James recorded a more favorable view of the fluid potentiality of the American identity as it came to consciousness of the fixed condition of national types in the Old World.

To be an American is an excellent preparation for culture. We have exquisite qualities as a race, and it seems to me that we are ahead of European races in the fact that more than either of them we can deal freely with forms of civilization not our own, can pick and choose and assimilate and in short (aesthetically &c) claim our property wherever we find it. To have no national stamp has hitherto been a regret and a drawback, but I think it not unlikely that American writers may yet indicate a vast intellectual fusion and synthesis of the various National tendencies of the world. (*HJL* I, 77)

Even so, as "Americans Abroad" makes plain, "Americans in Europe are *outsiders*; that is the great point, and the point thrown into relief by all zealous efforts to controvert it. As a people we are out of European society." The effect of the Americans' exclusion from the magic circle was that "to be known in Europe as an American is to enjoy an imperfect reciprocity" (Tuttleton, *The*

*American* 359). Excluded from the inner sanctum of the Faubourg, James complained in his notebook: "I couldn't get out of the detestable *American* Paris. . . . I saw, moreover, that I should be an eternal outsider. I went to London in November, 1876" (*NB* 26). James's settlement in London produced considerably better social results. Indeed, as a consequence of his brilliant "conquest of London," as Edel has called it, he was received into the highest circles of English society and became a central figure in London letters. But, as he later warned Edith Wharton, the real material of an American expatriate should be the Anglo-American, not the Franco-American, subject. Furthermore, because he did not know European aristocracies intimately, he later tended to stage his conflicts between Americans traveling abroad and expatriate Americans who had congregated in colonies.

Frederick Sheldon characterized these groups in "The American Colony in France," which appeared in the *Nation* in April 1878. According to Sheldon, the great cities of Europe were filled with

single ladies who have come to study for prima donnas or for "general culture," with no visible means of support; married ladies without their husbands (many American families, like their mercantile houses, having branches on this side); widows of the class called *vedova pericolante* in Italy, sometimes alone, sometimes with a daughter, pretty, dressy, not bashful, *qui s'habille et babille*; and young girls travelling together without chaperonage or duennage, *sans puer* and all, of course, *sans reproche*; but no amount of conscious rectitude will get them the respect of other people who are accustomed to draw certain inferences from certain appearances. (258)

These remarks had the effect of suggesting to James the fictional possibilities of American colonies abroad. Sheldon's account of the unattended girl abroad and the American colony, with its "idle, aimless existence," its tea and gossip, its "little gradations of rank and its *grandes dames*" who unite in sneering at those they call "low Americans," is so suggestive a model for Mrs. Costello's American colony in Rome that it clearly must have provoked James to imagine the heroine of *Daisy Miller* (1878).

What most interested James at this period was what he called, in "Americans Abroad," the "great innocence of the usual American tourist" who was totally ignorant of the impression he produced in violating the customs of the country. The American, he remarked, "takes all sorts of forms, some of them agreeable and some the reverse, and it is probably not unfair to say that by sophisticated Europeans it is harshly interpreted. They waste no time in hair-splitting; they set it down once for all as very vulgar. It may be added that there are a great many cases in which this conclusion hardly seems forced" (Tuttleton, *The American* 361). In *Daisy Miller*, James presents us with just such a case: a conclusion as to the vulgarity of this socially unformed young woman seems hardly forced. But what James's subtle art asks us to do is to split hairs on precisely this point: to weigh the unsuspecting innocence of Americans traveling abroad against the view of Europeans (and Europeanized Americans like Mrs. Costello and her circle) that innocence counts for less than punctilious adherence to the custom of the country.

In this wonderfully foreshortened tale, the charming, free-spirited, and vivacious Daisy Miller of Schenectady intrigues Frederick Winterbourne, a Europeanized American in Geneva, and she is likewise taken with him. Yet she seems to be a flirt, a coquette, and he cannot quite tell if she is virtuous. "He felt that he had lived at Geneva so long that . . . he had become dishabituated to the American tone" (*DM* 24). His aunt and the other American women abroad find Daisy's conduct, in accepting the company of men without a chaperon, to be reprehensible. They do not split hairs, and they advise Winterbourne to do likewise. Since she must be immoral, they ostracize her from their social life. Too late, Winterbourne learns that the independent and capricious young girl is virtuous and that she loved him. But by then she has died of Roman fever contracted on an imprudent nighttime visit, with her male companion Giovanelli, to the Colosseum.

Some American readers were outraged with Daisy's behavior and saw James's tale as an affront to American girlhood, but others championed her as a free spirit destroyed by bankrupt European social conventions. Howells, for one, defended the tale in that "so far as the average American girl was studied at all in Daisy Miller, her indestructible innocence, her invulnerable new-worldliness, had never been so delicately appreciated" (347). But more than nationalistic considerations came into play in the controversial reception of this tale. James, Howells, Twain, and other developing writers of the time had come to constitute a new school of "realists" whose aim was to displace the idealistic romanticism and sentimentalism of midcentury writing. Insisting on author-effaced presentation of characters who are more or less like those we know and who are engaged in actions of an ordinary kind and seen from a clinical or at least impartial and not wholly sympathetic perspective, these realists demanded a rigorous verisimilitude in fictional representation. Howells, as the editor of the *Atlantic*, had given over its pages to these new writers, and the absence in James's work of ideal characters engaged in noble actions had offended many genteel readers. James's portraits of Christopher Newman and Daisy Miller sparked endless discussions of the cultural differences between America and Europe and of the new realism that ironically probed these matters. *Daisy Miller* gave James an international celebrity that made the *nouvelle*, as he called it, "the most prosperous child of my invention" (*AN* 268). Though he was never again to equal the popularity he enjoyed at this point in his career (except perhaps in *The Portrait of a Lady* [1881], which developed *Daisy*'s themes at greater length), in this heroine "James had discovered," as Edel has remarked, "nothing less than 'the American girl'—as a social phenomenon, a fact, a type" (Edel, *Henry James: The Conquest* 309). "All unaware he had written a small masterpiece" (Edel, *Henry James: A Life* 216).

As James was later to observe in the preface to the New York Edition of

"Lady Barbarina," "On the interest of *contrasted* things any painter of life and
manners inevitably much depends, and contrast, fortunately for him, is easy to
seek and to recognise; the only difficulty is in presenting it again with effect, in
extracting from it its sense and lesson." For James, there was "no possibility
of contrast in the human lot so great as that encountered as we turn back and
forth between the distinctively American and the distinctively European outlook"
(*AN* 198). Hence, in his next tale, "An International Episode" (1878), he devised
an engaging little comedy of manners balancing the drama of the unsuspecting
European aristocrat in America against the knowing American pilgrim in Europe.
In part 1 of the tale, Lord Lambeth and Percy Beaumont travel to New York
and Newport, sites that offer James a rich opportunity to satirize the vulgarity
of American life at hotels and wealthy resorts. Lord Lambeth falls in love with
Bessie Alden but is summoned home when his mother learns of his interest in
the American girl. In part 2, Bessie travels to England, meets the Lambeths,
and is proposed to—but she rejects Lord Lambeth on the ground that he is too
shallow for serious marital consideration. Champions of Daisy Miller found
much comfort in the spectacle of a savvy American girl rejecting an English
lord.

This tale makes it plain that James was reacting against the Englishman Laurence Oliphant, who had written a satire on American manners in New York City
called *The Tender Recollections of Irene Macgillicuddy* (1878). It dealt with
what James, in his review of it, described as Oliphant's chief criticism of New
York high life: "the eagerness and energy displayed by marriageable maidens
in what is vulgarly called 'hooking' a member of the English aristocracy."
Though exasperating to James, Oliphant's novel nevertheless suggested to him
that it was "possible, after all, to write tales of 'American society.' " Oliphant
had shown that there were types, vivid local color, and "a considerable field
for satire." But why, he asked, "should it be left to the cold and unsympathetic
stranger to deal with these things? Why does not native talent take them up—
anticipate the sneers of foreign irony, take the wind from its sails and show us,
with the force of real familiarity, both the good and the evil that are to be found
in Fifth Avenue and on Murray Hill? Are we then so dependent upon foreign
labor that it must be left to the English to write even our 'society stories?' "
(*LC*-I, 1192–93).

James rewrote Oliphant's story from a more cosmopolitan viewpoint, em-
bodying in it his consciousness of the warping limitations of any provincial bias.
The tale, as I have remarked, comes down to an American girl's rejecting an
English lord, one of Arnold's "barbarians" who makes more for anarchy than
for culture. British readers who had taken pleasure in James's satire on the
American girl in *Daisy Miller* did a doubletake at "An International Episode,"
and James was publicly criticized by Mrs. F. H. Hill, whose husband edited the
London *Daily News*, on the ground that his portrait of the two Englishmen was
untrue to English character. Further, she condemned James's portrait of
snobbish English ladies. "Perhaps he does not consider that English manners

are pretty, and we have no doubt he has had ample means of judging" (Daniels 26).

Mrs. Hill's remark points to how successfully, by 1878, James had ensconced himself in English high society. Indeed, in that season, James had dined out more than a hundred times. He could not let pass the insinuation that he had cultivated English society for the purpose of satirizing it, and he remonstrated with Mrs. Hill, denying that he had meant to "make a resumé of my view of English manners." He complained of "the bother of being an American" when English novelists of manners, like Trollope, Thackeray, and Dickens, "were free to draw all sorts of unflattering English pictures, by the thousand. But if I make a single one . . . sinister rumours reach me as to what I think of English society" (*HJL* II, 221–22). He expressed annoyance too that English readers saw no harm in his pictures of disagreeable Americans—saw, in fact, a "natural fitness" in them. And he told his mother that although he had been "very delicate," he would "keep off dangerous ground in the future. It is an entirely new sensation for them (the people here [in London]) to be (at all delicately) *ironised* or satirised, from the American point of view, and they don't at all relish it. Their conception of the normal in such a relation is that the satire should be all on their side against the Americans; and I suspect that if one were to push this a little further one would find that they are extremely sensitive" (*LHJ* I, 67–68).

James's desire to defend the American and his manners against unsuspecting European superciliousness influenced, as we have seen, "An International Episode." But though tragedies, as James said, "arrest my attention more" and "say more to my imagination," he realized that he could not publish yet another story of an "evaporated marriage," if only because Howells, his editor at the *Atlantic*, did not wish to give his readers a succession of New-World defeats at the hands of the Old. Hence, James next promised Howells "a very joyous little romance" (*HJL* II, 105).

In *The Europeans* (1878), the Baroness Münster, whose morganatic marriage to a European prince is about to be dissolved, and her brother Felix Young, a bohemian young artist, come to America to seek their fortunes among their American cousins, the New England Wentworths. Eugenia, the baroness, is playing for time, before her divorce, hoping to land an American husband. The wealthy American businessman Robert Acton nearly proposes but finally does not; and at the end Eugenia returns to Europe, apparently intent on holding the prince to his vows. Felix, however, wins the hand of Gertrude Wentworth, and the novel concludes with their wedding and that of three other couples as well: the marriage of her sister Charlotte to the Unitarian minister Mr. Brand; the marriage of her brother Clifford to Lizzie Acton, Robert's sister; and Acton's reported marriage to "a particularly nice young girl" (*EP* 281).

Several sources of conflict generate the social comedy of this short novel: Europe vs. America; Felix vs. Eugenia; and Gertrude vs. the Wentworths. Mr. Wentworth and his family are convinced that "this country is superior in many respects'' (*EP* 56) to England and Holland; if Eugenia is the wife of a prince, Mr. Wentworth believes that '' 'we are all princes here' '' (*EP* 71). If New England life is colorless and lacking in romance (Gertrude has sought escape in the *Arabian Nights* when Felix suddenly materializes before her), Europe is by implication rich in the aristocratic and picturesque. And if these antebellum New Englanders are interested in morals, ''the great questions in life,'' the Europeans are more interested in manners, those highly stylized conventions that nevertheless express every nuance of feeling.

Oscar Cargill has remarked that *The Europeans* is a tale in which ''a pair of 'corrupt' Europeans, brother and sister, are immersed in an American experience, purifying in inverse ratio to their 'cosmopolitanism' '' (62). This remark unfairly characterizes Felix, the moral norm of the novel. To understand the complexity of James's treatment of the international theme in this novel, we must grasp the nature of the ''Europeanism'' of Eugenia and Felix. We must study their remarkably different ways of looking at life.

First, Eugenia and Felix are not identified with any specific country; Felix, in fact, admits to having lived in every city in Europe. They are both almost totally deracinated from any *patria* and from the moral and social orientation such a native land provides. They are children of Americans: their father was born in Sicily, but of American parents; their mother was a Bostonian. Felix was born in France, Eugenia in Vienna. They are the nephew and the niece of Mr. Wentworth; their American connection constitutes the basis for their visit to Boston. It is not merely that James needs a motive to get them to Boston that he makes them the children of Americans. That they are Europeanized children of Europeanized Americans constitutes a significant element in James's characterization of them. T. S. Eliot once observed, ''It is the final perfection, the consummation of an American, to become, not an Englishman, but a European— something which no born European, no person of any European nationality, can become'' (Dupee, *Question of Henry James* 109). This Europeanizing process, in other words, requires the deliberate effacement of the attitudes, customs, and manners that are distinctive to the country where they originate. One must erase from one's character and conduct whatever might conceivably be called provincial. ''If you have lived about,'' James remarked in the same year that *The Europeans* was published, ''you have lost that sense of the absoluteness and the sanctity of the habits of your fellow-patriots which once made you so happy in the midst of them. You have seen that there are a great many *patriae* in the world and that each of these is filled with excellent people for whom the local idiosyncrasies are the only thing that is not rather barbarous. There comes a time when one set of customs, wherever it may be found, grows to seem to you about as provincial as another'' (*PP* 75–76).

James in *The Europeans* is preoccupied with what happens when unsuspecting Europeanized Americans come to a provincial New England incapable of grasping their complex cosmopolitanism. ''You are a foreigner of some sort,'' says Gertrude, trying to fix Felix's national identity. But James is not interested in our understanding Felix and Eugenia in terms of a national provincialism; he wishes us to understand them as simply foreign, foreign to New England, as intruders with a disturbing and different view of the world. In this respect, "Europe" constitutes a metaphor for the romance of the strange and faraway, the rich and ambiguous, the mysterious and indefinite. "Of some sort—yes; I suppose so," says Felix. "But who can say of what sort? I don't think we have ever had occasion to settle the question. You know there are people like that. About their country, their religion, their profession, they can't tell" (*EP* 38). That this kind of cosmopolitanism was James's goal for himself is suggested in an observation that he once made to Edmund Gosse: "Nothing at this hour would give me more pleasure than if an intelligent stranger, deigning to cast a glance on my productions, should say that he was mystified—couldn't tell whether they are the work of an American writing about England or of an Englishman writing about America. I think that even *now* such a stranger might be a little mystified & I believe he will be still more so in the future" (James, *Selected Letters of Henry James to Edmund Gosse* 59). The "Europeanness" of these two strangers prevents us from establishing a provincial identity for them; James's technique is thus a way of reinforcing the mystery of personality, one of the Hawthornian ideas underlying his characterization of Eugenia, Felix, and Gertrude.

Both European visitors are fortune hunters—one literally, the other figuratively. Eugenia is ambitious, exploitative, even cynical in the candor with which she weighs the Wentworths in the matrimonial future she plans for herself. But fortune, for Felix, is a metaphor for the wealth that experience brings. Eugenia insists that the Wentworths be rich. Felix agrees that it will be pleasanter if they are rich, but he counts on their being "powerful, and clever, and friendly, and elegant, and interesting, and generally delightful!" (*EP* 14). Eugenia has an eye on the main chance; Felix has his eye open to possibilities of almost every kind. He accompanies Eugenia to America in search of enlarged opportunities for consciousness, freely receptive to the impressions and experiences opening up before him.

Felix's attitudes are a continuous exasperation to the baroness. Full of high spirits and comic wit, he is often called frivolous and consents to be so described; but the vocabulary of those who regard him in this way is inadequate to Felix's high sense of joy, whereas the spectacle of Eugenia's attempt to adapt herself to the Wentworth society is rich in ironies that cut both ways. James "ironizes" both the calculated artifices she employs and the studied plainness and angularity of New England social life that render her arts ineffectual. Her behavior is an utter enigma to everyone, but her power is evident in her sense of art. She decorates the cottage Mr. Wentworth gives her with portieres suspended in the doorways, wax candles distributed about in unexpected places, and "anomalous draperies" disposed over the sofas and backs of chairs. Charlotte and Gertrude are bewildered by Eugenia's "copious provision of the element of costume." "India shawls suspended, curtain-wise, in the parlor door, and curious fabrics, corresponding to Gertrude's metaphysical vision of an opera-cloak, tumbled about in the sitting places" (*EP* 80). On Gertrude the effect of Eugenia's intention is to awaken her to the charm of conscious art as a means of enriching an otherwise colorless life. " 'What is life, indeed, without curtains?' she secretly asked herself," and James comically remarks that she had been "leading hitherto an existence singularly garish and totally devoid of festoons" (*EP* 81). What is significant here is not the actual properties of Eugenia's theatrical arrangement—indeed, the India shawl, the curious fabrics, and the "remarkable band of velvet, covered with coarse, dirty-looking lace" (*EP* 80) are actually rather pathetic improvisations from Eugenia's trunk of stage props. What is significant is Gertrude's awakening "metaphysical vision" after the long sleep of Thoreauvian simplifications: her perception of the meaning of Eugenia's conscious refinement of nature, her conscious rearrangement of the world in terms of art and design—an aesthetic response to life that James nearly always associates with Europe as opposed to New England.

This tension between nature and art, provoked in the Wentworths by Eugenia's grand style, troubles the Wentworths in another way. Their anxiety stems from Eugenia's boredom with them, her irritation at a manner of life so plain and unadorned that it provides her art little material to work with. But Gertrude's awakening instinct for the difference between Eugenia's social style and their moral reality allows her to interpret Eugenia to her baffled relations. Gertrude's first insight occurs on the occasion of their introduction, when Eugenia remarks on the girls' handsomeness. This compliment pleases Gertrude, though she cannot yet say why, for she knows it to be untrue. Later she realizes that flattery may be employed to create good feeling, which perhaps cannot be realized in the airless atmosphere of absolute truth.

Eugenia acts unconsciously, unsuspectingly, on the assumed value of flattery, and it comes as an irritating surprise to her that these Americans do not recognize the value, even the necessity, as one of the graces of civilized living, of an occasional fib spoken with a fine intention. When Acton introduces her to his mother, an invalid steeped in the moral absolutism of Emerson, Eugenia declares that Robert has told her a great deal about his mother. "Oh, he talks of you as you would like, . . . as such a son *must* talk of such a mother!" It is a graceful remark; it is meant to please, but it simply isn't true. Acton has never even mentioned his mother.

Mrs. Acton sat gazing; this was part of Madame Münster's "manner." But Robert Acton was gazing too, in vivid consciousness that he had barely mentioned his mother to their brilliant guest. He never talked of this still maternal presence—a presence refined to such delicacy that it had almost resolved itself, with him, simply into the subjective emotion of gratitude. And Acton rarely talked of his emotions. The Baroness turned her smile toward him, and she instantly felt that she had been observed to be fibbing. She had struck a false note. But who were these people to whom such fibbing was not pleasing? If they were annoyed, the Baroness was equally so; and after the exchange of a few civil inquiries and low-voiced responses she took leave of Mrs. Acton. (*EP* 135)

In this passage one may observe James's double point of view, an operative irony that lays bare the weaknesses of both positions. To Mrs. Acton, who knows that her son is not the kind to speak gracefully about his mother, Eugenia's flattery is sheer prevarication. But the passage also implies a judgment on a society so meticulous in its observance of truth that graceful but meaningless civilities are unacceptable.

Richard Poirier has remarked, "At the end of the novel James's compassion and admiration are given more to Eugenia than to her American friends" (*Comic Sense* 144). And insofar as Eugenia may rectify what James believed to be active deficiencies in the culture of New England, she is a positive energy in the novel. She brings color, civility, charm, and conscious art to a community that is plain, dull, and devoid of sophistication. But Eugenia is no ideal heroine. She fails to make her fortune in the New World because she is not above using devious means to realize her financial and matrimonial ambitions. Acton declines to propose because he senses that she is not honest, that her polite fibs may conceal something more profoundly deceitful. This is indeed the case. For she tells him that she has renounced her marriage (and by implication is therefore free to accept his proposal), but she tells Felix that she has not done so. We cannot know which is in fact the case, and it probably does not matter. But it is inescapably true that Eugenia is lying to one of these men, and whichever one it is, the lie is too serious to warrant her enjoying the reader's full esteem.

In fact, James's point of view, so self-effacing in the later novels, is nowhere more intrusive than in his directing us to a negative judgment on Eugenia's cynical opportunism. "It is my misfortune that in attempting to describe in a short compass the deportment of this remarkable woman I am obliged to express things rather brutally. I feel this to be the case, for instance, when I say that she had primarily detected such an aid to advancement in the person of Robert Acton, but that she had afterwards remembered that a prudent archer always has a second bowstring" (*EP* 173). Clifford Wentworth, the callow son of the household who has been rusticated from Harvard for drinking, is Eugenia's second bowstring.

In her final breach of manners, she undertakes to make this heir to the Wentworth fortune fall in love with her—under the guise of civilizing him, of giving him a set of decent manners. In presenting her motivation, James is subtle: he has the difficult task of making her motives clear without causing us to detest her.

Eugenia was a woman of finely-mingled motive, and her intentions were never sensibly gross. She had a sort of esthetic ideal for Clifford which seemed to her a disinterested reason for taking him in hand. It was very well for a fresh-colored young gentleman to be ingenuous; but Clifford, really, was crude. With such a pretty face he ought to have prettier manners. She would teach him that, with a beautiful name, the expectation of a large property, and, as they said in Europe, a social position, an only son should know how to carry himself. (*EP* 173–74)

It is part of the beauty of James's characterization that while Eugenia is an adventuress, we cannot call her simply that. Though she does eye Clifford as a possible husband (she is thirty-three), she does have a disinterested social ideal for him that, in any case, is worth his realizing. Even so, she fails because she is, like Americans abroad, too unsuspecting of the impression—here of dishonesty—that she makes. Her only recourse is therefore to return to the Old World.

For Felix, however, the angular conservatism of the New England milieu is no impediment to success. In the novel's concern with values, Felix suggests that a vivid moral sense, a passionately joyful affirmation of life, and a sophisticated style of behavior may create a paradigm of the ideal relation between manners and morals. On several counts he is innocent of precisely those moral lapses and social "oversights" that alienate the community from Eugenia. If he suggests, for instance, that Eugenia civilize Clifford Wentworth, Felix is manifestly preoccupied with what James calls "the work of redemption." He is not prepared for the puritan conclusion to which Mr. Wentworth unerringly leaps. Nor is he ready for the construction that Eugenia places on his educational proposal, and the idea of her trying to ensnare Clifford in matrimony suddenly looms before him. "The idea in prospect had seemed of the happiest, but in operation it made him a trifle uneasy. 'What if Eugenia—what if Eugenia'—he asked himself softly; the question dying away in his sense of Eugenia's undetermined capacity" (*EP* 150).

Yet it is Felix who first begins to wake Gertrude from the trance she has been in, to open her up to the delight of self-knowledge, to the naturalness of being herself. It is he who guides Mr. Brand into an awareness that he really ought to marry Charlotte. And it is Felix who reveals to Mr. Wentworth the secret that joy and a sense of moral and social responsibility may coexist harmoniously. *The Europeans* thus dramatizes the triumph of Felix Young's view of life as an opportunity to be faced with delight, realized through the artifice of elaborate form, and enjoyed for the formal arrangements that constitute its beauty. Though Felix is doubtless idealized (he is meant to turn Hawthorne's New England gloom on its head), he serves as a foil to Eugenia (in his union of social grace *and* moral sensitivity) and to the Wentworths (in his commitment to enriching romance, color, mystery, and charm). The novel thus finely balances the strengths and limitations of European culture and exposes to purifying laughter the still vestigial, provincial, and narrow moralism implicit in New England plain living and high thinking.

James set *The Europeans* in the New England of the 1830s–1840s, partly because he did not wish to rouse the ire of contemporary American critics and partly because composing his biography *Hawthorne* (1879)—written for the English Men of Letters series—had immersed him in the era in which Hawthorne had been formed. As he reflected on the Salem romancer, James came to see that the absence of social detail in Hawthorne's notebooks "documented," as it were, the cultural thinness of the environment in which Hawthorne had lived. As James remarked to his English readers, such a thinness of cultural forms would not have faced a young Englishman or Frenchman aspiring to become a writer. And to press home to his English audience "the negative side of the spectacle on which Hawthorne looked out," James launched into his famous enumeration of "the items of high civilization, as it exists in other countries, which are absent from the texture of American life": no state, sovereign, court, aristocracy, etc. Salem seemed so isolated to James, and New England culture so impoverished, that the most distinctive adjective he could ascribe to Hawthorne was "provincial." But in fact, as he observed in the biography, "it takes so many things, as Hawthorne must have felt later in life, when he made the acquaintance of the denser, richer, warmer European spectacle—it takes such an accumulation of history and custom, such a complexity of manners and types, to form a fund of suggestion for the novelist" (*HA* 42). The absence of those "items of high civilization" in America that nourish the novelist of manners, like Eliot and Thackeray, accounts for why Hawthorne cared for "the deeper psychology" of the individual and also accounts for the romance form in which he wrote. These absent elements of high culture also help to explain why James expatriated to Europe and devoted himself, by contrast, to the novel.

Howells said that he could foresee, "without any very powerful prophetic lens, that Mr. James will be in some quarters attainted of high treason" (Kirk and Kirk 166), and indeed, the attack on James's *Hawthorne* by American critics was prompt, shrill, and chauvinistic. James found their reactions "a melancholy revelation of angry vanity, vulgarity and ignorance. I thought they would protest a good deal at my calling New England life unfurnished, but I didn't expect they would lose their heads and their manners at such a rate" (*NB* 29n). Howells himself gave *Hawthorne* the most thoughtful response:

After leaving out all those novelistic "properties" as sovereigns, courts, aristocracy, gentry, castles, cottages, cathedrals, abbeys, universities . . . , by the absence of which Mr. James suggests our poverty to the English conception, we have the whole of human life remaining, and a social structure presenting the only fresh and novel opportunities left to fiction, opportunities manifold and inexhaustible. No man would have known less what to do with that dreary and worn-out paraphernalia than Hawthorne. (Kirk and Kirk 169)

But having cut himself adrift from the provincialism of every nation in favor of an international cosmopolitanism, James was not of a mind to agree with Howells. He could not sympathize with his editor's "protest against the idea that it takes an old civilization to set a novelist in motion—a proposition that seems to me so true as to be a truism." He told Howells, "It is on manners, customs, usages, habits, forms, upon all these things matured and established, that a novelist lives—they are the very stuff his work is made of" (*LHJ* I, 71–74).

*Confidence*, which James published in 1879, is like *Roderick Hudson* and several other early tales in the pairing of two young bachelors, here Bernard Longueville and Gordon Wright. In this case, the wealthy Gordon has become

attracted to Angela Vivian, but he lacks confidence and is unwilling to act on
his feelings for this complex woman until Bernard has advised him as to whether
she is after his money. Bernard travels to Germany to meet them and commences
a "scientific study" of the woman, so as to determine whether Gordon should
marry her, meanwhile enjoying the game of seeing whether Angela can keep up
her act of sincerity. Eventually he advises Gordon that she is not right for him,
and so appears to produce a breakup of the couple, after which Gordon departs
for foreign climes. Later Gordon marries Blanche, a silly girlfriend of Angela's.
Some time later, Bernard again meets Angela, falls in love with her, and announces their impending marriage to Gordon and Blanche. At this, Gordon, who
has become disenchanted with his wife, denounces Bernard for misleading him
about Angela, whom he swears to love. Needless to say, the comedy of errors
is worked out in the end, in the most improbable way, with Angela's effecting
the reconciliation of Gordon and Blanche. As F. O. Matthiessen and Kenneth
B. Murdock note, this leaves Bernard "free to marry Angela as placidly as the
hero of any sentimental tale in the magazines of James's day" (*NB* 7). The
whole bit of plot business is achieved with mirrors, leading the *Spectator* reviewer
to wonder, "What could Mr. James be thinking of?" (Gargano, *Early Novels*
45). *Confidence* is generally regarded as one of James's weakest novels; it was
not reprinted in the New York Edition.

In his next book, *Washington Square* (1880), James undertook "a tale purely
American." Writing it, however, made him "feel acutely the want of the 'paraphernalia' " (*LHJ* I, 73). James had in mind to do this tale as a *nouvelle*, "the
main merit and sign [of which]," for him, was "the effort to do the complicated
thing with a strong brevity and lucidity," indeed with "a frugal splendor" (*AN*
231). But an example of the difficulty confronting James in *Washington Square*
was the setting. If, as he once remarked, "to name a place, in fiction, is to
pretend in some degree to represent it" (*AN* 8), how could he handle the exposition, how could he represent what this square meant to New York social
history? He felt he could not assume the reader's familiarity with it. Thus the
work is marked by something rare in James—a lengthy prosaic exposition,
running to several pages, accounting for the historical importance of the setting
and those who populate it. That James felt obliged to lard his story with several
pages of expository narration about the place indicates his felt problem with the
paraphernalia of the American setting. America might "to a certain point [be]
a very sufficient literary field." But as James told Charles Eliot Norton: "It will
yield its secrets only to a really *grasping* imagination. . . . To write well and
worthily of American things one need even more than elsewhere to be a *master*.
But unfortunately one is less!" (*LHJ* I, 30–31).

Despite James's view that the book did not match up to his best (it was not
included in the New York Edition), *Washington Square* has nevertheless remained a relatively popular novel. This tale concerns Catherine Sloper, the very
shy, stolid, and motherless daughter of the wealthy, urbane, bitterly ironic Dr.
Austin Sloper. Into her life comes the young Morris Townsend, who courts her

for her money, but when he finds out that her father intends to disinherit her if she marries him, he abandons her. After Dr. Sloper's death, Townsend renews his suit, tempted even by the small bequest her mother had left her, but she rejects him, preferring to live on in Washington Square as an old maid. As such, the tale is rich in pathos for the plain but willing young woman who is caught between her love for the scoundrel Townsend and her wish to please a sardonic father who has in fact never liked her.

Although hers is a poignant story, it is plain that Catherine will resemble Isabel Archer in the extent to which James subjects her to an analytical scrutiny that cannot blur for us her negative qualities—her unimaginativeness, docility, simplicity, lack of taste in dress, even her gluttony, since she is overweight. Nevertheless, these are not as fully emphasized as her virtues of trust, obedience, and love. James always preferred to the simple heart those characters who have a more acute sensibility and greater analytical depth, members of the "supersubtle fry." Of the characters here, only Dr. Sloper is sufficiently brilliant, at least in his withering irony, to be classed as such. Most readers have seen him as a sadistic fiend who denies to his daughter an experience that might have been less empty than her eventual lifetime of repetitive and meaningless fancywork. Others have argued that Catherine "created" the emptiness of her life, in which case the doctor cannot be seen as the fiend in human form that he is sometimes made out to be. F. R. Leavis, one of the latter, has remarked, "I should have said that the whole point of the story depends upon the not obscurely presented datum that the father's ironic dryness covered something very different from 'cruel egotism' " (cf. Putt 47). Even so, Catherine is not obtuse. She has an ill-understood intuition about Mrs. Penniman's ridiculous romanticism, and her grasp of her father's cruelty eventually becomes as sure as her instinct for the punishingly right way to refuse him. Few of James's tales deal so poignantly with a trusting innocence cruelly abused. But in Catherine he gives us a woman the essence of whose pathos is that "she seems never more than numbly conscious of what she feels. The whole story is a miracle in monotone; of the monotonous in life treated unmonotonously" (Gargano, *Early Novels* 48). As a reformulation of some aspects of *Eugenie Grandet*, yet set in New York, the novel seems a sufficient negation of James's feeling that art blooms only where the soil is deep.

Toward the end of this apprentice period, James wrote to William in 1878 from London:

If I keep along here patiently for a certain time I rather think I shall become a (sufficiently) great man. I have got back to work with great zest after my autumnal loafings, and mean to do some this year which will make a mark. I am, as you suppose, weary of writing articles about places, and mere potboilers of all kinds; but shall probably, after the next six months, be able to forswear it altogether, and give myself up seriously to "creative" writing. Then, and not till then, my real career will begin. After that, *gard a vous*. (Edel, *Henry James: A Life* 215)

But, in retrospect, it is clear that well before 1878, James's real career had already begun. He had mastered the formal demands of the short story, the *nouvelle*, and the novel. He had also written controversially in the biographical mode, and his literary criticism was (and still is) illuminating. His travel sketches, though frankly written for pelf, turned out to be brilliant examples of the impressionistic mode, and his cultural criticism provoked animated debate then and now. Moreover, his portraits of Christopher Newman, Rowland Mallet, and Roderick Hudson, not to speak of Catherine Sloper, Daisy Miller, and other American heroines, showed him to be an acute psychological observer and the social historian, par excellence, of his time. In an essay of 1882 entitled "Henry James, Jr.," Howells issued what was intended to be an interim report on James's achievement. It may usefully be taken here as a summary of James's apprenticeship up through *Washington Square*.

Arguing that James had inaugurated a new school of analytical realism, deriving from Hawthorne and George Eliot, Howells tried to lay to rest the slipshod old-fashioned fiction of Thackeray, Dickens, Fielding, Trollope, and Reade. James, Howells argued, was now "universally recognized" because he was "a very great literary genius" (347, 354). The vigor of his prose, his brilliant characterization, his "finished workmanship," "the luminous and uncommon use of words, the originality of phrase, the whole clear and beautiful style" (346–47) marked how far the art of fiction had come from the fumbling efforts of his predecessors. "No other novelist, except George Eliot," Howells remarked, "has dealt so largely in analysis of motive, has so fully explained and commented upon the springs of action in the persons of the drama, both before and after the facts." Reflecting the realism of Daudet rather than of Zola, James's fiction gave rich evidence of "a metaphysical genius working to aesthetic results" (349). Howells's dismissive comment about James's clumsy predecessors raised a storm of protest in which James was smeared by the same tarbrush laid on Howells. But there can be no doubt that James had indeed achieved, by this time, major status as a writer of fiction. Subsequent generations of readers have affirmed Howells's high praise. Though most of his best work lay ahead of him, by 1880 James had indeed served a brilliant apprenticeship and was ready for the mature art of *The Portrait of a Lady*, *The Bostonians*, *The Princess Casamassima*, and the later triumphs of the major phase.

# 7
# The Middle Years

*James W. Gargano*

Henry James's middle years begin with the success of *The Portrait of a Lady* (1881), reach midcareer with the depressing popular failures of *The Bostonians* and *The Princess Casamassima* (both published in 1886), and end with *The Tragic Muse* (1890), a novel James described in 1905 as terminating "my earlier period" (*HJL* IV, 367). Writing to William Dean Howells in 1888, James bewails that, having fallen "on evil days," he is "still staggering a good deal under the mysterious and [to me] inexplicable injury wrought—apparently—upon my situation by my last two novels, the *Bostonians* and the *Princess*, from which I expected so much and derived so little." He goes on with some exaggeration, "They have reduced the desire and demand, for my productions to zero" (*HJL* III, 209). At the end of the decade, James, now permanently settled in England and nearing fifty, felt discouraged enough to pursue a second career as a dramatist, from motives that, he confessed to his brother William, were "exclusively mercenary" (*HJL* III, 209).

From a twentieth-century perspective, the years following the appearance of *The Portrait* stand out as a highly productive time that saw the publication not only of the three formidable novels but also of numerous critical essays and eighteen tales, among them such minor masterpieces as "The Author of Beltraffio," "The Aspern Papers," "The Liar," and "A London Life." Remarkable for their clarity and engagement with social issues, the three novels have been characterized by Edmund Wilson as works in which James "gives his clearest and most elaborate criticism of life" and in which "his heroes and heroines have professions, missions, practical aims" (402). In the 1880s, James certainly demonstrated a creative vigor and willingness to experiment that became distinctive watermarks of his career. *The Portrait* added a profoundly psychological dimension to the international theme and, as Laurence Holland puts it, achieved a fusion of plot, character, imagery, and moral intention through "a carefully measured visual strategy that is one of James's most impressive contributions" to English fiction (43 [1982]). *The Bostonians*, James's only major novel devoted to the American scene, wittily examines the feminist movement through a strange if not abnormal sexual triangle and introduces into his work, under the influence of French naturalism, literal and circumstantial descriptions of places and details of his characters' appearance and dress. If *The Bostonians* keeps a polite distance from what its author thought to be the "uncleanness" of naturalistic fiction, it nevertheless deals in a suggestive way with the peremptory nature of sexual passion. *The Princess Casamassima*, a panoramic novel with a vivid English setting, documents a sensitive bookbinder's attempt to come to terms with his illegitimate birth and social disadvantages through involvement in subversive political action. Even more naturalistic than its predecessor, *The Princess* reads today like an elegy for the beauty and traditions painfully evolved by civilized society and now endangered by what Yeats called "mere anarchy" or the "blood-dimmed tide" that is "loosed upon the world." *The Tragic Muse*, another English novel, explores in its broad canvas the not always compatible claims of art and public service, freedom and conventional securities. As if in reaction to the pessimism of *The Princess*, James dramatizes the issues with a less stern realism and a tolerant comedic spirit that result in what Leon Edel characterizes as a "large mural of English life and art" (*Middle Years* 255).

The last three novels and many critical essays of the middle years reveal, as Lyall Powers has definitively shown (in *Henry James and the Naturalist Movement*), that James was energized and permanently influenced by French naturalism without adopting what he regarded as its sometimes reportorial tedium, its sexual crudities, and, especially in the case of Zola, its hostility to the refinements of art.[1] He admired Daudet's distinctive style of naturalism as resolving its "discoveries in pictorial form" (*LC*-II, 229), but his admiration must have been only a natural reflex to someone who had already revealed a painterly eye and hand in *Roderick Hudson*, *The American*, and, preeminently, *The Portrait*. Irrepressibly witty in *The Bostonians* and *The Tragic Muse*, he could temper his respect for Zola by noting the "extraordinary absence of humor" from his works and "the melancholy dryness of his execution" (*LC*-II, 869, 870). In an 1883 essay, he objects to the limited vision of the naturalists by offhandedly remarking that Trollope, whose artistry and prosiness he disparages, "tells us, on the whole, more about life than the naturalists in our sister republic" (*LC*-II, 134). Always ambivalent about his French confreres, vacillating between panegyric and stricture, he missed in all of them, except Daudet, that "poetical touch" that "modifies . . . the hardness of consistent realism" (*LC*-II, 230). On the other hand, he never ceased to pay tribute to the uncompromising honesty that the naturalists, in contrast to English writers, brought to the observation of life.

The psychological and environmental determinism that enters into James's concept of character from the beginning of his career hints at an early temperamental bias toward naturalism, perhaps reinforced by his reading of Balzac and his followers. *Roderick Hudson*, *The American*, and *Washington Square* contain naturalistic elements, and *The Portrait*, though it lacks the solidity of specification of *The Bostonians* and *The Princess*, presents a heroine strongly conditioned by her milieu, her inner compulsions, and her heritage. James's movement toward naturalism was gradual, and his acceptance of it was never wholehearted. Even the two saliently naturalistic novels are also novels of manners, richly revealing the Jamesian sensibility and dealing with his major themes: the quest for identity by a "self" racked by dualities and contrary proclivities; the central role of consciousness in the intellectual and sensuous growth of character; the social milieu as an arena where action is the expression of incomplete men and women consciously or unconsciously using one another to gratify their mostly illusory desires or private ideals; and the inevitability, for sensitive men and women, that experience will impose a compromise with or escape from a world that does not foster or cherish impractical idealism.

Though my discussion will concentrate on James's themes, the novels published during the middle years reveal that he approached the writing of each of his works with the zeal of an artist intent on ordering the diversity of his fictional world into an aesthetically satisfying form. *The Portrait* is noteworthy in the history of English and American fiction for the meticulous symmetry of its episodes, its highly functional visual strategies, and the skill with which its characters, settings, and image patterns are woven into a seamless design. Its technical virtuosity has led F. R. Leavis to extol it, along with *The Bostonians*, as one of "the two most brilliant novels in the language" (153 [1960]), and Arnold Kettle declares that its fully conscious art makes the novels "which precede it, except for those of Jane Austen, seem a trifle crude" (53). In addition to its formal elegance, *The Portrait* is distinctly innovative in utilizing point of view not only to record its heroine's feelings and impressions about life but also to render, most effectively in her night-long vigil in chapter 42, what William Veeder calls "the illusion of mental process" (*Lessons* 206).

Alike experimental in their naturalism and pointed social criticism, *The Bostonians* and *The Princess* differ conspicuously in their narrative development. Unusually straightforward and reportorial, *The Bostonians* dramatizes each of its major incidents with an amplitude of detail and authorial commentary that leaves little room for ambiguity. In sharp contrast, *The Princess* opens with realistically rendered scenes but finally shifts to indirection in dealing with the significant events of its hero's life: his introduction to the leader of the anarchist movement is clouded in mystery; his epiphanic visits to Paris and Venice are dramatized through letters and reverie; and his suicide is presented as a fait accompli. In addition, James treats the activities of his socially subversive organization with mere hints and suggestiveness that ultimately amount to evasion. Nevertheless, his steady but not complete adherence to Hyacinth Robinson's point of view gives a depth and complexity to the hero's inner life that relates him more closely to Isabel Archer than to the protagonists of *The Bostonians*. In *The Tragic Muse*, James copes with the difficulty of dramatizing three lives crowded with vicissitudes by distilling many incidents into his characters' impressions of them. He thus affords insight into his characters' sensibilities, multiplies modes of perception, and achieves economy by freeing himself from the literal representation of events. In *The Princess* and *The Tragic Muse*, he sometimes describes persons and places with a copious realism, but he tends increasingly to convert the occurrences of the external world into the stuff of his protagonists' consciousness. He anticipates, though without his later control and psychological tension, the exploration of the subconscious that distinguishes many of his works of the 1890s and of the major phase.

Because of its concern with an American girl abroad, *The Portrait of a Lady* is often and justifiably seen as the culmination of James's first creative period. He himself called Isabel Archer, his heroine, "a female counterpart of Newman" (*HJL* II, 179), the hero of *The American*; like her, Newman comes to know the limitations and spiritual reserves of his nature in a complex European world. Yet James's study of Isabel eschews the old-fashioned melodrama of *The American*, with its duel, deathbed confession and heartless aristocratic villains, and dwells on the consequences resulting from a lovable girl's hope of finding the realization of vague dreams in the real world. To S. Gorley Putt's pinpointing of the "new element" in *The Portrait* as an "interest . . . now focused entirely on the minds and feelings of his characters" (159), it may be supererogatory to add that the intensest, tenderest, and most honest focus is on Isabel, whose portrait, according to Leon Edel, belongs "in the great gallery of the world's fiction" (*Conquest of London* 433).

The portrait of Isabel derives much of its strength and appeal from James's intention "that the young woman be herself complex" (*NY* III, xvii). In attempting to achieve this complexity, James made her so diverse that her contradictory qualities can be more easily experienced than reconciled. To begin with, she has an American past, a spiritual-psychological history adumbrated by James as he pictures her, in a revealing flashback, in her Albany house. The young woman whom James mildly satirizes as trying to read German philosophy in a room full of rejected furniture has not outgrown the child who once imagined a fantasy land on the other side of a bolted door that she knows to open on commonplace reality. She is an Americana, with more established traditions and more intellectual values than the ingenuous Daisy Miller: she is independent and imaginative, high-minded to the point of moral austerity, ignorant of evil, and avid for self-improvement. In all the tergiversations of her life, her choices and decisions will be complicated by a shaping, provincial heritage that will itself be reshaped by the actualities of an older, less innocent world.

It is the brightest and most captivating side of his American heroine that James shows in her first appearance at Gardencourt, her uncle's English estate. Her spontaneity and excited responsiveness to her surroundings immediately impress her cousin Ralph Touchett and Lord Warburton as altogether original qualities. But there is more to her than artless, virginal charm, and much of it exposes her confusions and dualities. When she defines "her idea of happiness" as a "swift carriage, of a dark night rattling with four horses over a road that one can't see" (*PL* 144), she strikes her friend Henrietta Stackpole as romantically reckless; on the other hand, she sounds a note of timidity in shrinking from the "cup of experience" as a "poisoned drink" (*PL* 130). She is capable of feeling, at different times and with equal convictions, that she suffers from frigidity and that "if a certain light should dawn she could give herself completely" (*PL* 44). Compared with the brassy Henrietta, she has superfine delicacies, but she cannot suppress an "American" impertinence and sense of importance. With a redundant fund of life and little experience, she sets out on her European initiation with, in Tony Tanner's words, no knowledge of "what her self is, or what it may do" (Tanner, "Fearful Self" 150).

James increases the complexity of his portrait by presenting Isabel with a mixture of unsparing objectivity and indulgence that arouses in the reader ambivalent feelings of pity and affection. Conscious that his dissection includes all that can be said against her, he disarmingly admits, as early as chapter six, that she is "an easy victim of scientific criticism" (*PL* 43) who nevertheless deserves affection. His analysis of the delight she takes in her "sublime soul" and the "tangle of vague outlines" (*PL* 42) she mistakes for thoughts has a satiric bite that effectively removes her from the pedestal occupied by many nineteenth-century heroines. In fact, James is so thoroughgoing in making her a collaborator in her own tragedy that Putt suspects him of harboring a subconscious animosity against her as well as the other characters in the novel (159). On the other hand, James's love for his heroine is so evident that Charles Thomas Samuels blames him for losing his objectivity and siding with her against her husband (110). Philip M. Weinstein goes even further by deploring James's supposed identification with Isabel's moral fastidiousness in her final adherence to exalted, inelastic, and unrealistic concepts of duty (70).

The ambiguous effect of James's "direct appeal to charity" (*PL* 88) for Isabel serves, I believe, an artistic and tonal purpose in putting her engaging New-World presumptions in an ominous perspective of future misery. James's apologies for her in the sixth and twelfth chapters suggest that a threatening cloud hangs over her even as she strikes her admirers as a golden possibility set aside for mysterious purposes. Readers who are privy to James's foreshadowing as well as to Isabel's recurrent dread about herself see more than the worshipful Goodwood and Warburton and the idealizing Ralph, who exalts his cousin as "finer than the finest work of art—than a Greek bas-relief, than a great Titian, than a Gothic cathedral" (*PL* 52). The appeal for charity is James's amelioration of the "hardness . . . of consistent realism," a plea for Isabel against her own audacities and benightedness, and a promise that she will ultimately prove worthy of the tolerance extended her. Without the appeal, the first part of the novel might seem, despite its dazzling style and humorous interludes, a long preparation for catastrophe instead of a prelude to pain and spiritual awakening. The first part of *The Portrait*, then, contrasts Isabel's presumptuous self-sufficiency with the stronger forces, both temperamental and exterior, working against her.

James's logic is to create the first of his two portraits, that of a promising girl who possesses the psychic resources to recover from the doom she seems to court. The young American dressed in black who makes her "appearance in the doorway" at Gardencourt in the second chapter of the novel harmonizes into the informal outdoor setting and creates a paradise around her. She certainly differs from the lofty lady of the second part who, "dressed in black velvet" and looking "brilliant and noble" in her formal world, is "framed in the doorway" of the ominously named Palazzo Roccanera (*PL* 321). Ironically, however, the vivacious girl is taking her first inevitable steps toward disenchantment, whereas the splendid lady will wrest from her anguish a sense of selfhood and freedom. The two portraits are equally lifelike, but in the latter the doomed innocence of the former is replaced by a haunted inwardness that becomes the source of strength.

To maintain his ambivalence, James organized the first part of *The Portrait* in terms of three intrusions into Isabel's life: Mrs. Touchett's decision to transplant her niece from Albany to Europe; her son's plan to give Isabel the fortune she needs to live expansively; and Madame Merle's intrigue to manipulate her into marrying Gilbert Osmond, Merle's onetime lover. The unworldly Isabel fully believes her aunt's fiction that she is traveling in Europe at her own expense, and she has no inkling that Ralph is responsible for her uncle's generosity. Moreover, she is arrogantly convinced that she is a free agent as she walks into the trap expertly set by Madame Merle. The three actions are so linked that Isabel seems to be moved about without a will of her own. Her rejection of Caspar Goodwood's and Warburton's proposals of marriage may suggest that she is, after all, an independent spirit who makes her own choices, but it merely proves that her imagination and high-mindedness are working against her: she resists the tangible temptations of wealth, status, and sexual appeal because she entertains a nebulously Emersonian vision of existing, in Tanner's phrase, "at the height of sheer communion with ideal beauty" ("Fearful Self" 208). With her sights set on transcendent gratifications, she shares with Newman and James's later hero Strether a peculiarly American imagination capable of transforming reality into ethereal, finespun ideality. Given Isabel's headlong imagination, it is difficult to entertain Arnold Kettle's suspicion that her attraction to a bloodless aesthete like Osmond is not only improbable but also an authorial fraud practiced on the reader (Kettle 30). In fact, she is so ready to idealize his isolation, poverty, and exquisite relationship with his doll-like daughter as insignia of superiority that, as Richard Poirier maintains, her "marriage to Osmond is the most predictable thing that could happen to her" (*Comic Sense* 218).[2]

Of the many scenes foreshadowing the confluence of circumstance and character that determines Isabel's tragedy, four may be briefly noted because their counterparts recur in the second part of the novel. The first, in chapter 22, shows Madame Merle and Osmond arranging Isabel's future with the cynicism of practiced predators. Significantly, it is Isabel's glimpse of a reenactment of this scene that, in the second part of the novel, arouses her doubts about her husband's past relation to Madame Merle. Another scene binding the first and second parts of the novel together occurs in chapter 24 and dramatizes Isabel's visit to Osmond's Florentine villa, where her imagination "supplied the human element" to his "dry account" of his "simple" and "negative" existence (*PL* 232, 231). James's premonitory comment as she enters the court ("the place . . . looked somehow as if, once you were in, it would not be easy to get out") is an almost obtrusive prefiguring of her future imprisonment in the Palazzo Roccanera and the impossibility of her permanent escape from it (*PL* 221). The third scene, in which, in chapter 25, the Count Gemini threatens to expose Madame Merle's plot, foreshadows the countess's climactic revelation at the end of the novel and intimates that Isabel will be walking into what the countess calls in the New York Edition "a steel trap" (*NY* IV, 87). The fourth critical scene, in which Ralph bitterly tells Isabel that in marrying Osmond she will be "put into a cage" (*PL* 299), takes place in chapter 34 and contrasts with the poignant deathbed scene between the cousins in the next to last chapter of the book. Speaking through Ralph, James makes one of his severest indictments of Isabel, but even it contains a grudging tribute to her idealizing imagination: "It was wonderfully characteristic of her that she had invented a fine theory about Gilbert Osmond, and loved him, not for what he really possessed but for his very poverties dressed out as honours" (*PL* 305). Each of the above-mentioned scenes from the first part of *The Portrait* predicts trouble for Isabel, whereas those from the second part indicate that she awakens from innocence into knowledge.

A summary look at the first thirty-five chapters of the novel reveals that Isabel is immersed in a society in which incomplete selves seek fulfillment through other incomplete selves. Mrs. Touchett brings her niece to Europe partly because Isabel will do her credit as an attractive companion, and the invalid Ralph tries to be whole by empowering his cousin to soar toward ideals he can only vicariously enjoy. Madame Merle manipulates Mrs. Touchett and Isabel to make up for thwarted ambition, and Osmond's initial interest in Isabel springs from her newly acquired fortune. Isabel herself subconsciously desires a high priest who will give authority to her artistic and spiritual longings and dedicate her burdensome wealth to noble uses. Yet, though James makes all his characters "pardonable" even while they are accomplices in one another's destinies, he insists on the moral distinction between the Touchetts' and Isabel's benign motives and Madame Merle and Osmond's coverup of the truth about their relation to each other. In expressing the amoral principle that guides her conduct, Madame Merle acts as if Isabel's happiness does not count in her scheme of things: "I don't pretend to know what people are meant for. . . . I only know what I can do with them" (*PL* 210). Osmond, likewise, has no scruples about remolding Isabel and sacrificing her "very bad" opinions to accord with his egotistical plans for her (*PL* 250).

The nervous and taut Isabel portrayed in the second part of the novel has lost her earlier piquancy and has become a drawing-room ornament whose manner, dress, and surroundings reflect her husband's aestheticism while her inner life is an active inquiry into the causes of a chronic spiritual malaise. James now focuses on his heroine's expanding consciousness as her only sure route to personal salvation. Isabel's early drama of expectation has been converted into one of intuitions, suspicions, and sad insights into human motives and character: the "future" of the fatalistic first part has happened, only to be understood in a sort of bitter postmortem. To show the new direction he is now taking, James plays variations, stressing Isabel's increased understanding of her dilemma, on important episodes and scenes from the first part of the novel. The first action of the second part reveals her tentative steps toward independence when she frustrates her husband's scheme to marry the unwilling Pansy to Lord Warburton. For all the differences in their situations, Pansy clearly resembles the earlier Isabel in being treated by Madame Merle and Osmond as a pawn in their game of social exploitation. The divided Isabel acts, at times, as if she has been cowed into sharing her husband's and Madame Merle's assumption that Pansy's preferences should not interfere with her marriage to a man of wealth and title. Nevertheless, for all her loyalty to Osmond, she sounds Warburton's motives and helps him to infer that his love of Pansy is a sham, a device to be near Isabel. The rescue of Pansy, though it does not guarantee the girl's happiness, is an act of initiative and intelligence that introduces a positive note into the novel.

James carefully leads up to what Viola Hopkins Winner calls the "tragically affirmative" ending (143) by examining Isabel's slow progress toward understanding Madame Merle, Osmond, and her own character and predicament. In a brief scene in chapter 40 that looks back to Madame Merle's visit to Osmond in chapter 22, Isabel picks up an impression, "like a flicker of light" (*PL* 357), as she comes on the couple communing together in mute companionship. In an instant, she alertly seizes an "image" that she stores in her consciousness as a portent of evil. Isabel's education advances by such evanescent glimpses, but she is also capable of sustained and honest inquiry. In chapter 42, which James admired as one of the high points of *The Portrait*, Isabel's unsparing analysis of herself and Osmond is a movement toward enlightenment, a ruthlessly honest survey of her married life, and a proof that she knows more about her husband's past connection with Madame Merle than she can admit to herself. Her progress toward comprehension of her situation is all but complete when, in detecting the passionate excess in Madame Merle's interest in Pansy, she exclaims: "Who are you—what are you? . . . What have you to do with my husband?" (*PL* 453).

James masterfully dramatizes how Isabel's half-conscious knowledge surfaces when the Countess Gemini, whose hints in the first part of the novel remained cautiously veiled, tells Isabel that Pansy is Madame Merle's child. Even before the countess becomes explicit, Isabel is so prepared for an ugly truth that she feels "a foreboding which made her heart beat" (*PL* 475). When the countess is disposed a little to "play with her subject" (*PL* 475), Isabel assumes that something "horrible" is about to be divulged. Her "lips" express "vague wonder," and in trying to follow the countess's elucidation, she forces the countess, as if hearing her owns doubts verbalized, to speak slowly and factually. When she is asked if she had never suspected that Madame Merle had been Osmond's mistress, she equivocally confesses: "I don't know. Something has occurred to me. Perhaps it was that" (*PL* 476). In a sense, Isabel has known and not known but has been afraid to clear up the ambiguities that have tortured her consciousness. With the disclosure of Pansy's illegitimacy, however, she translates knowledge into her boldest action by defying Osmond and going back to Gardencourt, in a scene that recalls her debut in Europe, to be with her dying cousin.

Consistent with the muted optimism of the last chapters, James intends Isabel's full consciousness of evil and betrayal to energize her into purifying the atmosphere in which she has breathed doubts and imagined terrors. In wordlessly communicating her new knowledge to Madame Merle, she wins a major victory and drives a secret and disruptive member out of the family. The lie at the heart of the household, a metonomy for the larger society, has been dispelled, and Isabel's subliminal fears can be assigned to a specific cause that she can now begin to deal with. The question in *The Portrait* is not so much whether or not Isabel achieves freedom but what kind of freedom. There is little doubt that Osmond is sensitive enough, on reflection, to deduce from Madame Merle's self-banishment and his wife's defiance that his duplicity has been exposed, that his invocations of such high-sounding words as *honor* will no longer have their old resonance. It is to an altered Osmond that Isabel, no longer a mere object in his palace of art, will return.

Still, critics continue to ask why, with what she knows, does she goes back at all?[3] The reasons, which are many, grow out of Isabel's feelings, traditions, and the "moral" climate of her society. To begin with, James gives dramatic prominence to her promise that she will not desert Pansy, who, she tells the Countess Gemini, "has become mine" (*PL* 479) and whom she calls at their last parting, "my child" (*PL* 488). Moreover, as Dorothea Krook points out, "Isabel Archer takes a 'sacramental' view of marriage, as a 'sanctified' union which is to be regarded as . . . indissoluble" (358). In addition, in her reconciliation with her cousin on his deathbed, a scene that contrasts with the scene of alienation in chapter 24, she experiences the kind of love that James perhaps felt for his cousin Minny Temple and that Merton Densher will feel for Milly Theale, a love like that of Stransom for the beatified Mary Antrim. In what Joseph Wiesenfarth calls "the great love scene" in *The Portrait* ("A Woman" 24), the cousins together face Ralph's error in making her a rich woman, and they join in a "religious" recognition that their love has a value abiding beyond pain. James means Ralph's prophecy that Isabel "will grow young again" (*PL* 507) to endow her with a bequest of love and life, youth and regeneration, that is more substantial than the fortune Ralph importuned her father to leave her.

The near juxtaposition of the deathbed scene and the scene in which Isabel succumbs to Goodwood's passionate kiss implies that James intended to contrast examples of spiritual and physical love. James shows acute psychological insight in having Isabel, who has normal sexual susceptibilities, submit to an ardent physical appeal when she is exhausted from the strain of exaltation and an overcharged consciousness. He does not, however, intend Goodwood's kiss to be an epiphany illuminating an approved romantic way out of her troubles with her husband. Instead, the kiss represents for James a subjection, a loss of the independence that Isabel has gained throughout the second part of the novel. As she frees herself from Goodwood and impulsive sexual "temptation," she does not turn her back, as some critics contend, on a creative future; rather, she rejects a man whose sexual intensity does not make him less narrow, socially maladroit, or unaesthetic, a man who urges the last claim of her past on her. As she settles that claim and understands the fear he has formerly aroused in her, she is ready to live within the constraints of a loveless marriage with her commitment to Pansy before her and with a complete vision of the forces that have molded but not destroyed her. For James, the vision is worth the travail.

In *The Bostonians*, James abandoned the international theme that had made him famous and adapted the literary methods of French naturalism to the writing of a "very American tale, a tale very characteristic of our social conditions" (*NO* 20). Presciently identifying "the most salient and peculiar point" of American life as "the situation of women, the decline of the sentiment of sex, the agitation on their behalf" (*NO* 20), James gave his narrative added social resonance and dramatic tension by making his "hero," Basil Ransom, a virile Confederate veteran from Mississippi and his main female characters, Olive Chancellor and Verena Tarrant, representatives of New England's reformist tradition. James felt proud enough of his experiment in naturalism to urge Grace Norton, "Do like *The Bostonians* . . . ; it is something like Balzac!!!" (*HJL* III, 75). It is, in fact, almost Balzacian in the passage minutely detailing the view of Boston seen from Olive Chancellor's window, in James's description of the unprepossessing street on which Ransom lived in New York, and in the *tour-de-force* depiction of Marmion's hotel and environs. Still, James departs from naturalistic objectivity and betrays his bias against feminism by showing it as arising from the American male's abdication of a vital social role. Having no legitimacy in itself, feminism has sprung up to fill the vacuum created by the American businessman's unbalanced preoccupation with moneymaking. It has been widely observed that except for Ransom, the men who appear in *The Bostonians* hardly represent the social spectrum of American males and that they merit their insignificance. With a sometimes good-natured but often acerbic satire that does not mask his authorial prejudice, James's description of the acclaimed oratrix, Mrs. Farrinder, reduces her husband to an afterthought; Verena's suitor, Henry Burrage, indulges the aptitudes of a dilettante while his mother manages his courtship of Verena; Verena's father shows enterprise enough to pass for a mesmerist and to collect handsome checks for allowing Olive to "adopt" his daughter; and Matthias Pardon, a buffoonish reporter, would like to marry Verena in order to turn her into a celebrity rather than a wife.

James also jeopardizes his realistic method by parodying the female champions of feminism with sometimes cruel animus. The venerable Miss Birdseye, whom some sensitive Bostonians took as a malicious caricature of Elizabeth Peabody, Hawthorne's sister-in-law, is introduced as a comic figure whose "sad, soft, pale face . . . looked as if it had been soaked, blurred, and made vague by exposure to some slow dissolvent" (BO 26). She is chronically inept in speech, convinced that humbugs like Selah Tarrant have great gifts, and as out of touch with reality in her old age as she was in her crusading youth. In denying that he meant to satirize Miss Peabody, James affirmed that his fictional character was "treated with respect throughout" (HJL III, 70); yet, if she finally achieves dignity in death near the end of the novel, she gives the impression of having lost her way in a labyrinth of misplaced confidences and good intentions. Though presented with more depth, Olive Chancellor fights for the liberation of women with an obsessiveness that derives from a motiveless hatred of men. Her ardor to "possess" a female friend, the nervous demands she makes on herself and others, and her yearning for martyrdom link her crusading to pathology rather than to enlightened thought. Of course, Verena does little to establish feminism as an intellectual and cogent body of ideas: from her first outpourings, James makes clear that she excites her audience because of her theatricality, her youthful prettiness, and the compelling "bird notes" of voice. Her effusions, which Ransom dismisses as rodomontade, are made up of shopworn and emotive notions alien to her warm and unreflective nature. As she entrances both Ransom and Olive, Verena exercises the gifts of a radiant actress triumphing over a bad script.

Instead of researching the woman question with the patience of a Zola, James probably relied on imagination prodded by keen but limited observation and, according to Marcia Jacobson, on a host of secondary fictional sources (Jacobson 20–40). His very American novel surveys a restricted segment of the American scene with brilliance, but feminism is soon belittled into a doctrinaire faith presided over by a sick priestess.[4] As soon as Olive embodies the movement, the novel becomes a typical Jamesian drama of conflicting personalities. It does not take Basil Ransom long to perceive that Olive is a "spinster as Shelley is a lyric poet" (BO 18) and that Verena is made for love and marriage. Verena's frank and amiable relations with men contrast markedly with Olive's belief that women can be sufficient unto themselves.

Because James locates the fundamental weakness of the feminist movement in the diversity of human nature, Olive is safe in her psychological investment in Verena only as long as the latter is unaware of her real, complex self. James insists that, even as Verena progresses from her father's tutelage to Olive's, she has little or no sense of selfhood and certainly no ideas of her own. She is amenable to living in Olive's elegant home, embarking with her on an unrelenting course of study, and having her career as a public speaker laid out for her. Feminism may have been James's original subject when he conceived The Bostonians, but as he wrote it became secondary to his greater interest in the process by which Verena gradually gains selfhood and freedom from Olive's psychic oppression. Certainly Verena is no Isabel Archer; yet she resembles her and other Jamesian protagonists in having to achieve her "identity" after being victimized by a false estimate of herself. Like Isabel, too, she must shake off a tyranny that, though exerted without the predatory purpose of Osmond and Madame Merle, turns her from an independent being into a satellite. Verena, however, effects a more complete escape than Isabel and—a rare instance in James—finds salvation in a man whose sexual magnetism is one of his virtues.

As in *Washington Square* and the later *What Maisie Knew*, James associates the first manifestation of individuality in his heroine with the practice of dissimulation. From the moment Verena chooses not to tell Olive of her meeting with Basil Ransom at Cambridge, dreading to surrender "the only thing that was all her own" (*BO* 288), she preserves an element of personal liberty and keeps a part of her self inviolate. She even compounds her deception when she sends Ransom an invitation to her New York lecture. James documents another stage in Verena's emancipation when, during her New York visit, she acknowledges the expansive urges of her own nature and the cramping limitations of Olive's. Her mild hedonism as she looks forward to dining at Delmonico's and attending an opera leads her to silent protests against her companion's unaccommodating somberness: "Olive's earnestness began to appear as inharmonious with the scheme of the universe as if it had been a broken saw" (*BO* 296). James even alerts his readers, as if it were a crucial occasion, to Verena's serious impatience with Olive's worry that a long stay in New York will weaken her feminist resolve: the "tremulous, tentative tone" of Olive's speech "produced the first manifestation of impatience—the first, literally, and the first note of reproach—that had occurred in the course of their remarkable intimacy" (*BO* 300). As she awakens to New York's seductions, Verena responds with more ardor to Ransom's masculine appeal. In commenting on her new emotional susceptibility, James calls attention both to her feelings and to her consciousness of these feelings: "she was beginning to perceive that he produced a peculiar effect upon her" (*BO* 316). Elizabeth McMahan correctly interprets James in arguing that the "opponents of Olive's brand of feminism" triumph because "they have human sexuality on their side," but she misreads him in explaining Verena's attraction to Ransom by numbering Verena among the host of women who "have never had their capacity for thought developed" (242). The fact is that Verena falls in love *because* her long-stifled consciousness has begun to take in more of the world's variety.

The climax of the New York scenes takes place when Ransom convinces Verena that the champion for feminism that she fancies herself "isn't you." "That description of herself as something different from what she was trying to be, the charge of want of reality, made her heart beat with pain" (*BO* 337). Obviously, Verena's panic rises from a realization that Ransom's perception is a true one. Ironically, as she entertains the notion that her opinions are borrowed and theoretical, she has no doubt that her real self confronts the aggressive Ransom who, under the guise of refuting her arguments, is in fact making love to her. The generalization behind James's drama seems to be that women, or for that matter men, who live with a full sense of the world's attractions cannot confine themselves in the straitjacket of any all-consuming ideology. Or as William McMurray sums up James's moral meaning, "In pretending to absolutist forms in our activity, we risk spiritual death" (344).

James intended Verena to be seen as someone who, with considerable help from Ransom and the negative example of Olive, arrives at a repudiation of what is for her "the hollow and factitious ideal with which her family and her association with Olive Chancellor had saddled her" (*BO* 384). Nevertheless, the concluding scenes of the novel at Cape Cod and in Boston are full of conflict and tension rather than facile resolution, for though Verena has begun to understand herself, she naturally finds it painful to break her old union with Olive. She does not, as some critics contend, move without struggle from Olive's dominance to Ransom's; instead, she passes through a period of divided loyalty during which she tries to satisfy the opposing claims on her. She flees from New York after the realization that she loves Ransom; at Cape Cod, she submits to her lover's pressure only to escape when Miss Birdseye's death recalls her to a sense of mission; and even before she turns her back on the audience ready to make her famous, she begs Ransom, on Olive's behalf, that she be allowed to address the public one last time. Though Verena confesses that she is glad when she gives up her career, James points out that she is "in tears" and projects that marriage will not be the serene state promised by Ransom (*BO* 449).

James's ending not only puts Ransom's hyperbolic promises in ironic perspective but also raises the question as to whether he, like Olive, will inhibit Verena's growth. James's narrative voice often patronizes Ransom for his provincial taste and his reiteration of reactionary ideas, and Ransom shows anything but the mettle of a hero when he considers marrying Mrs. Luna, Olive's inane sister, who would be able to support him while he writes polemics against the spirit of the age. Moreover, his failure as a lawyer and his quixotic decision to marry on the strength of one article accepted by an obscure journal may not augur brilliant social opportunities for his wife. Irving Howe certainly exaggerates in assuming that he will make Verena "unhappy ever after" (*Bostonians* xxviii), but Howe is right in dispelling the belief that Ransom has the stature of a chivalric hero. On the other hand, Ransom's recurrent laugh at the fatuity he observes has a tonic ring in a world of impostors like Tarrant and unpardonable journalists like Matthias Pardon. James may distance himself from Ransom's more outrageous rhetoric and sometimes bullying manner, but James clearly sympathizes with Ransom's attacks on the feminization of society, and James means his readers to admire the Southerner's hatred of the crass commercialization of Verena's talent. Moreover, Ransom's promises to Verena dwell on the ampler life she will have with him rather than on any desire to keep her as a cloistered household goddess.

Due allowance made for its social pertinence as an exposé of America's appetite for quackery and the distractions served up by its publicists and promoters, *The Bostonians* dramatizes with seriocomic deftness the role of love in

Verena's salvation. Love develops despite ideological differences and other powerful counterforces, and it triumphs not because it is rational or prudent for the
lovers to submit to it but because it is elemental and overbearing. In fact, Verena
seems in most of her few meetings with Ransom to act in accordance with inner,
passional compulsions that she does not understand. She betrays her best friend
and protectress, from whom she has promised to keep no secrets, and she is
powerless to avoid emotional entanglements even when she thinks she wants to.
Fleeing from New York to Cape Cod, she not only writes to Ransom but is
careful to include her address in her letter to him; constantly preparing for a
public career that he would loathe, she listens to antifeminist diatribes and talks
to him about their life after marriage. After leaving Cape Cod, she hides from
him so that he cannot prevent her public lecture, but when he snatches her from
the footlights, she clings to him and declares herself "glad."

Ransom, for all his vaunted reasonableness, is as much the victim of his love
as is Verena. His love at first sight conflicts with his amusement at her feminist
simplicities. His calculated decision to marry Mrs. Luna is, ironically, overturned
when he hears that Verena has returned from Europe. In New York he takes
Verena to Central Park and does not suspect that underneath the current of his
didactic conversation he is absurdly making love to her. Even though he has
assured himself that he is too poor to marry, he follows her to Cape Cod on the
strength of a rosy prevision of literary success. Above all, James leaves no doubt
that Ransom, with his rationalist appeal to the editor of the *Rationalist Review*,
does not see Verena with the scientific eye of Dr. Prance, who once diagnosed
her as "anaemic" and later thinks of her as a "slim" affair. If Ronald Wallace
is too severe in labeling Ransom as James's "self-deceived protagonist as hero,"
Wallace is one of the few critics who sees in the erratic behavior of the lovers
the stuff of comedy promising a relatively happy ending (35).

James's conclusion may even hint that Olive, in her desperate surrender to
her longed-for martyrdom, may find the voice she has hitherto lacked in her
reliance on Verena. When abandoned by her protégée, she rises from prostration,
and "like the heroine that she was," braves the crowd she imagines will greet
her with hisses (*BO* 447). Surprisingly, however, instead of making her the
martyr she has yearned to be, the audience accepts her with "respectful" silence
and a disposition to listen. James's reticence about the success or failure of
Olive's address may not justify optimistic assumptions about her future, but his
obvious sympathy with her heroic effort humanizes her, and his insistence on
the audience's attentiveness permits the inference that she may no longer need
a mouthpiece.

James did not design the climactic scenes of *The Bostonians* to pass pessimistic
judgment on his three main characters. They have instead launched out into new
lives and face new trials in their careers. The ending of the novel, like that of
*The Portrait*, may appear unsatisfactory to readers who expect from their author
a definitive statement about the future course of the characters' lives. James,
however, avoids conclusiveness and is content to organize an action whose

resolution opens into continuing possibilities that do not foreclose vistas or cancel futurity with sentimental bromides.

James found ample warrant for the dark vision of *The Princess Casamassima* in the violence that plagued both England and the Continent before and while he wrote his novel. W. H. Tilley and others have detailed the assassinations that occurred from the early to the mid 1880s; among others, the murder of Czar Alexander II in 1881; the killing of Lord Frederick Cavendish and Thomas Burke in Dublin in 1882; the dynamiting of two underground railways in London in 1883 and of part of Victoria Station in 1884; and the explosion of bombs in 1885 in the House of Commons, Westminster Hall, and the Tower of London.[5] Well aware of England's difficulties at home and abroad, James grieves in a letter to Grace Norton in 1885: "the country is gloomy, anxious, and London reflects its gloom. Westminster Hall and the Tower were half blown up two days ago by Irish dynamiters." He leaves no doubt as to how much he was affected by the continuing threats to his adopted country. "The possible *malheurs*, reverses, dangers, embarrassments, the decline in a word of old England, go to my heart" (*HJL* IV, 66, 67).

As Tilley demonstrates, *The Princess* owes much of its inspiration to the widely publicized appearance during the last quarter of the nineteenth century of mysterious international organizations devoted to abolishing existing institutions and class structures. Nevertheless, the creative impulses behind this or any other novel, as James's preface to the New York Edition implies, are too numerous, private, or vague to trace. Despite his reticence about his literary and autobiographical sources, critics have speculated that his plot and characters are indebted to Ivan Turgenev's *Virgin Soil*, the English working-class novels of George Gissing and Walter Besant, and the realistic works of Balzac and Zola.[6] Leon Edel persuasively relates Hyacinth Robinson's sense of social alienation to James's personal crises when he wrote *The Princess* (*Middle Years* 192). Still, James's own version of the experience that animates his novel affords a rich initiation into its dense, creative world. In declaring that *The Princess* "proceeded directly, during the first year of a long residence in London, from the habit and the interest of walking the streets" (*NY* V, v), James accounts for the vivid, unlabored specificity of his descriptions of the city's streets and neighborhoods. This command of place contributes to the authenticity of the novel and enables James to delineate social gradations with a sure hand: the dinginess of Lomax Place fixes the unenviable status of plucky Amanda Pynsent, Hyacinth Robinson's foster mother, even as it establishes the indelible cockneyism of Millicent Henning as she relies on her beauty to rise in the world; Audley Court, entered through a "narrow alley" between "high, black walls" (*PC* 88), defines the constricted milieu of Paul Muniment, Hyacinth's conspiratorial friend; the princess's residences in the "genteel vacancy" of South Street, Mayfair, and Madeira Crescent, a "mean and meagre and fourth-rate" street (*PC* 403), measure her descent as she seeks contact with the "people"; and Hyacinth's course through London includes a fateful union (presented with naturalistic detail) with his dying mother at Millbank prison, visits to Lady Aurora in Belgravia, and an introduction to radicalism at the shabby Sun and Moon tavern in Bloomsbury.

If, as James maintains, his hero "sprang . . . out of the London pavement" (*NY* V, v), he also sprang into being as a sympathetic alter ego possessing James's passion for a larger life without James's opportunities. Hyacinth's torment at his deprivation amid the omnipresent seductions of London sharpens his sensibilities and makes him, like James, a person on whom nothing is lost. Perhaps recalling his own eagerness for social acceptance, James notes that his hero "wanted to drive in every carriage, to mount on every horse, to feel on his arm the hand of every pretty woman" (*PC* 125). He further endows Hyacinth with a fondness for literature and the theater, a flair for dress, and a love of nature that, at moments, brings tears to his eyes. Thus, despite his upbringing in Lomax Place in the home of a poor seamstress, he shares with his creator the aesthetic and intellectual attributes to insure "that he should fall in love with the beauty of the world" (*NY* V, xii). James records the expansion of Hyacinth's consciousness in terms that may shed light on his own experiences in England, but he never compromises his objective portrait of a fatally divided protagonist adrift in a society chronically riven by inner discords. Because Hyacinth's quest for selfhood ends in a vision rather than a realization of his potential, *The Princess* is the grimmest novel of James's middle years. Isabel Archer, at least, outlives her anguish and has the consolation of Ralph's memory, the support of Pansy's love, and a realistic view of Osmond that may be a source of power in her relations with him. Verena Tarrant unshackles herself from psychological bondage, marries for love, and, despite the certain problems she will face, is "glad" to have found her true self. Only Hyacinth is trapped in a dilemma for which there is no solution except suicide.

James planned his novel in terms of a social and biological determinism so enforced by polarities that a tragic denouement was inevitable. First of all, though Hyacinth's London tolerates social fluidity, the distance between the "happy few" and the lower classes is "so vast and preponderant, and so much the law of life" that any hope of bridging the gap appears chimerical (*PC* 470). Second, with a plebeian French mother of questionable morals and an aristocratic father who never acknowledged him, Hyacinth reflects in his parentage the irreconcilable extremes of society. Insisting on his antinomies with a vengeance, James endows Hyacinth's two surrogate parents with opposed political views, his foster-mother encouraging him to think himself an aristocrat and her confidant, Mr. Vetch, passing himself off as a socialist. It follows almost too logically that James's protagonist, like his society, is made up of inimical elements. Hyacinth is troubled about his identity, wishing in alternating moods to be accepted by society's fortunate minority and to overturn the status quo. His internal strife becomes so acute that he doubts whether he will ever achieve wholeness. "There were times when he said to himself that it might very well be his fate to be divided to the point of torture, to be split open by sympathies that pulled him in different ways" (*PC* 126).

James further intensifies the dualisms in *The Princess* by making two of Hyacinth's revolutionary friends pull him in contrary directions. Eustache Poupin initiates Hyacinth into the subtle art of bookbinding but also overwhelms him with a stream of revolutionary rhetoric. Hyacinth cannot help observing that Poupin has his own contradictions, for, though he often contemns the establishment and despises the bourgeois institution of marriage, he is an exemplary worker and lives conventionally with his congenial helpmate. That James makes each step in his hero's career a progress in two opposed directions is further evident in Hyacinth's equivocal relation with the glamorous but jaded princess, who seeks new sensations in her experiment in political terrorism. Whereas she uses him to escort her into the haunts of poverty, her natural gentility and sophistication give him an insight into a sumptuous way of life known to him only in fiction and dreams. Because of her, Captain Sholto invites him to his chambers, where Hyacinth sits "drinking in enchantments" (*PC* 199) as he listens to talk about Paris, Albania, and Madagascar. Paradoxically, his visit to Medley, an English country house, to enlighten the princess blunts his revolutionary zeal and converts him into a lover of the opulence and beauty he is pledged to destroy.

James gives more dramatic poignancy to his hero's divided nature by contrasting him to Paul Muniment, under whose influence Hyacinth agrees to perform an act of violence required by the anarchist movement. Hyacinth's respect for Muniment's equanimity and dedication to revolutionary principles is proof of the "fallible consciousness" that Sister Jane Marie Luecke attributes to him (274–80), but it also represents a deep psychological discontent with his own ambivalence, a longing to simplify himself through total commitment to a cause. Despite Muniment's "sanity," he has a fundamental kinship to such single-minded exploiters of innocence as Madame Merle and Olive Chancellor. Having subscribed to an abstract idea, Muniment has no compunction about proposing his friend for a mission leading to certain death. As he sees the world grow dearer to Hyacinth, he makes no attempt to save him from the folly of his oath to Diedrich Hoffendahl, the mysterious czar of the revolutionary underworld. It is Muniment's implacability in discounting sentimental ties as not worth a "feather beside our service" that leads the princess to compliment him as a "most extraordinary man" (*PC* 498). What the fallible Hyacinth does not know and what James underlines with sharp emphasis is that Muniment has won stability and unity by divesting himself of part of his humanity: when Hyacinth, for example, exults in the "immense deal of affection between them," James notes, "he did not even observe . . . that [the affection] was preponderently on his own side" (*PC* 436). The princess herself discovers that, though Muniment has used her as a lover and accepted her money for the cause, he remorselessly discards her when her funds dry up. In the next to last chapter, after twice praising Muniment as a first-rate man and once as a "most remarkable man," she blurts out her final appraisal of him, "Ah, you *must* be a first-rate man— you are such a brute!" (*PC* 583).

Muniment symbolizes the power of a compelling abstraction for men and women trapped in painful dualisms, but equally important, by introducing Hyacinth to Hoffendahl, he helps Hyacinth to see that in addition to the visible divided society that people experience every day of their lives there is another society operating "subversively beneath the vast smug surface" (*NY* V, xxii). Hoffendahl, an even more monolithic figure than Muniment, so affects Hyacinth that he is haunted by an apocalyptic vision of the unreality of ordinary life.

People go and come, and buy and sell, and drink and dance, and make money and make love, and seem to know nothing and suspect nothing . . . ; and iniquities flourish, and the misery of half the world is prated about as a "necessary evil," and generations rot away and starve in the midst of it, and day follows day, and everything is for the best in the best of possible worlds. All that is one-half of it; the other half is that everything is doomed. In silence, in darkness, but under the feet of each one of us, the revolution lives and works. It is a wonderful, immeasurable trap, on the lid of which society performs its antics. (*PC* 308)

The pervasive and fundamental division in Hyacinth and his society is also apparent in Paris, where his love of beauty is most fully satisfied: "it came over him that the most brilliant city in the world was also the most blood-stained" (*PC* 362–63). Paris unites, as he does, a spirit of hedonism and a legacy of violence. He may sit in the "most dandified cafe in Paris" (*PC* 361) and surrender like a voluptuary to the city's art, but everywhere he goes he is accompanied by still another hereditary ghost, that of his revolutionary grandfather, who had died knowing "the ecstasy of the barricades" (*PC* 363). In an adolescent way, Hyacinth may have fatalistically reenacted his grandfather's deed when he mounted a chair in the Sun and Moon and proclaimed his willingness to die for his ideals.

There is a solid grain of truth in John P. O'Neill's contention that the rigid design of the novel, rather than Hyacinth's character, places him in a situation from which there is no life-saving exit (58). It is not so much, as William Stowe contends, that Hyacinth has taken in more data than he can "process" (97), but that, beginning with his heredity, too many snares have been set for him. Yet James attempts to rescue his novel from its determinism by introducing into the final chapters a concept of freedom intended to be affirmative. He does this by making Hyacinth see that the world does not essentially change but continually repeats itself in new cycles of aggression and revenge, of cruelty that begets violence. His grandfather's heroism at the barricades, his mother's vengeance against her lover, and Hoffendahl's projected acts of terrorism are part of an unending pattern from which Hyacinth must deliver himself. Having fallen in love with the monuments of thought and beauty that the best aspirations of humanity have created, he redefines himself by rejecting the dichotomies of father and mother, the former's libertine acceptance of social inequities and the latter's resort to crime to rectify injustice. In championing values that have humanized mankind, he tries to find wholeness outside the arena of social strife and disassociates himself from the princess and Muniment's imperious egotism and reduction of life to abstraction.

James brilliantly implies that the pattern that Hyacinth repudiates is once again repeating itself in the relationship between Sholto, an aristocratic rake on the prowl for pretty women, and Millicent Henning, Hyacinth's last hope before he kills himself. One of James's most vivid female characters, Millicent makes up for her cockneyism and untutored taste by her statuesque beauty and a robust health that make her Hyacinth's almost fraternal companion during his London walks. Although he at times suspects her of an intimacy with Sholto, he returns to her, again and again, with naïve trust. In his last conversation with her, he tells her about his ancestry and feels her sympathy diffuse ''a sense of rest, almost of protection'' (*PC* 529). If at times she has the impressiveness of a beautiful Amazon, at other times she can be a reassuring mother figure and, in the New York Edition, a sexual partner who surrenders as he draws her ''closer and closer—so close . . . he felt her yield with a fine firmness . . . and with the full mass of her interest'' (*NY* VI, 346).

With a subtlety that has largely escaped critical notice, James suggests that Millicent and Sholto, coming as they do from different social strata, may be repeating the drama that led to Hyacinth's mother's crime and all its consequences. Peering into Millicent's future, James emphasizes his vision of life as a series of repetitive acts when she exclaims, on hearing of the murder of Hyacinth's father, ''Well, that's the way I'd have served him too!'' (*PC* 528). Millicent's declaration links her with Hyacinth's mother and with all the other exponents and perpetrators of violence in the novel. If Hyacinth obeys Hoffendahl's mandate, he will be helping to perpetuate a continuing history of bloodshed and will bear ''the personal stain'' of provoking the ''public reappearance . . . of the imbrued hands of his mother'' (*PC* 587). Hyacinth feels an intense ''loathing of an idea of *repetition*'' when his ''summons came'' (*PC* 589), and honorably sacrifices himself rather than be involved in a cycle of continuing atrocities.

James, then, concludes his novel with a mitigation, if not a cancellation, of the determinism with which it began. He gives Hyacinth a measure of freedom in his last act, but the fact must be faced that it is a freedom exercised in a harrowingly coercive situation. The last chapter does deal with Hyacinth's resolution to emancipate himself from an oath that would violate his highest values, but his mood just before his suicide, after he has seen Millicent exhibiting the ''long, grand lines'' of her figure to Sholto (*PC* 589), is one of disillusionment. James undoubtedly admires his hero's final, defiant courage, but the ugly fact remains that the world has failed one of its gifted spirits.

James's primary concern with Hyacinth's social-aesthetic initiation and his own limited knowledge explains his indirect treatment of the organization and machinations of the anarchist movement. His concern also explains why this novel, so full of life and brilliance that Lionel Trilling could judge it an ''incomparable representation of the spiritual circumstances of our civilization'' (92

[1948]) cannot be included among James's greatest fictional successes. Remarkable as the scenes are at the Sun and Moon, the anarchist movement remains a vague donnée rather than a reality. Hoffendahl is talked about but never seen, and James forgoes the inviting opportunity to dramatize Hyacinth's sole meeting with him. In fact, Hyacinth describes it only once, and despite the powerful impression it made on him, he rarely thinks about it with the fear and trembling it should inspire. Of the three other characters who are admitted to Hoffendahl's presence, Poupin is too amiably ludicrous to be taken seriously as a revolutionary, and Schinkel and Muniment have little to say about the machinery and agenda of the cause they serve. In short, the forces that presumably threaten to overturn society are compounded of shadow and mist, lacking substance.

*The Tragic Muse* differs most conspicuously from its immediate predecessors in containing three distinct narrative movements. In the preface to the New York Edition, James prides himself on the artistry with which he fused the stories of Nick Dormer's rejection of politics for art and Peter Sherringham's refusal to resign his diplomatic post for the stage by making Miriam Rooth, his tragic muse, "a link between the other two cases" (*NY* VII, xiv). Of course, the usual Jamesian symmetries are at work to cement interconnections: Nick and Peter are cousins and contemporaries and face similar dilemmas; with neat parallelism, the former is in love with the latter's sister, Julia Dallow, and Peter is expected by the Dormers to marry Nick's sister Biddy; finally, Peter falls in love with the unaccommodating Miriam, who falls in love with the unresponsive Nick. James knits his characters and incidents together even more firmly by permitting his master of the revels, Gabriel Nash, to all but manage Dormer's destiny, introduce Miriam to the cousins, and vex Sherringham with unwelcome truths that interfere with and ultimately destroy his romantic dreams about Miriam.

To achieve compactness and unity for a novel that tells three complex stories, James often departed from the realistic directness of *The Bostonians*, resorting to techniques that he hoped would insure economy without sacrificing density. Dorothea Krook, who prefers *The Tragic Muse* to *The Bostonians* and *The Princess*, praises James for focusing on essentials and excluding irrelevant scenes that might, in the case of Dormer, merely "document" his political career (70). James skips over Nick's campaign for a parliamentary seat, dwelling retrospectively on his hero's remembrance of it as a time of high sport, windy oratory, and exhilarating cooperation with his backer, Julia Dallow. James gives no graphic description of political rallies, with their assemblage of solid citizenry; he never shows Nick consorting with fellow parliamentarians and overlooks a whole session of parliament in which Nick presumably participated; and he avoids representing any meeting between Nick and his constituents when Nick resigns his seat in the House of Commons. Instead of rendering the political scene circumstantially, James embodies the spirit of politics in the intense but narrow-minded Julia, in Nick's quintessentially British mother, Lady Agnes, and in Mr. Carteret, a wealthy bachelor who reduces politics to crotchet. Finally, Nick is motivated from the grave by his father, Sir Nicholas, whose abortive career he promised to redeem—a promise made in a deathbed scene James does not choose to reconstruct. Thus, though Dormer feels himself "two quite distinct human beings, who have scarcely a point in common," his political interests and affiliations are so subordinated to his determinant passion for art that his psychic split has little dramatic credibility (*TM* 166). Ultimately his contest is less with himself than with outside forces.

Miriam's early progress from a histrionic ranter to an accomplished actress is traced in a series of vivid scenes, and her personality is conveyed through her pungent speech, but in James's overall portrait of her she is seen, except in one scene, through the eyes of other characters. The means by which she becomes a professional actress and gains acclaim are left obscure until, ten months after the event, she tells Dormer how she made her debut. Miriam's relations with her theater managers and fellow actors, relations that indicate she has precociously adopted the ways of a prima donna, are given only passing attention, and James forgoes the opportunity to "do" a big scene when he hurries past her first dramatic hit, preferring to examine it, after the performance, from Sherringham's point of view. Her offstage assumption of piquant roles, a trait that links her to the many-faceted Princess Casamassima and to Madame de Vionnet in *The Ambassadors*, is frequently filtered through Sherringham's sensibility. Above all, James's decision to deal suggestively and delicately with Miriam's love for Dormer "robs the exuberant girl," as Pelham Edgar notes, "of the full expression of her nature" (284).

Considered by W. R. Macnaughton as "one of the most interesting characters ever created by James" ("In Defense" 7), Sherringham achieves more vividness than Dormer because his life is more thoroughly explored and because he indulges more ardent emotions than James attributes to his artist hero. In Miriam's presence, he becomes "subject" to her spell, and while tenaciously clinging to the proprieties, he appreciates every nuance of her artistry and responds with a lover's abandon to her beauty and social genius. He cannot tame his emotions as easily as Nick does, and almost to the end of the novel he deceives himself into believing that he may give up all for love. Aware of its splendor as well as its vulgarity, Peter has a love-hate relationship with the theater, whereas Nick from the beginning treats Parliament as a bitter pill he may have to swallow. Before Peter marries Biddy Dormer and capitulates to a certain bedrock philistinism in him, he has the appeal of someone whose bifurcated nature is real and who discovers unruly and even perverse elements in himself. Perhaps what keeps Peter from being a fully rounded character is that one half of his life—the prosaic, bureaucratic part of him—seems an authorial convenience rather than a solid reality.

James's economies and indirection may account for the slackening of the narrative pace of the novel after the opening scenes in Paris, in which all the main characters are assembled and sketched with unobtrusive art and sparkling wit. Of course, *The Tragic Muse* contains other perfectly wrought scenes, in which each detail of setting, dialogue, and authorial innuendo contributes to the enhancement of theme and action. The scene of Dormer's proposal to Julia craftily plays the lovers' barely suppressed sexual feelings against their controversy over a dull magazine article in a slightly absurd "temple" on an island titillatingly secluded and close enough to Julia's house to afford her an escape. With equal art, James humorously exaggerates the disparity between Dormer and Mr. Carteret, his political sponsor, whose butler Nick finds magisterially intimidating and whose house impresses him as containing furniture and other objects so oversized that they disconcert his sense of scale. Still, the finish and exquisite "tone" of James's best scenes cannot keep the novel from becoming a cerebral artifice whose polarities, evasions, and ordered scenic arrangement prove devitalizing. It is not surprising that Daniel Schneider judges the novel "as icily conceived and executed" (*The Crystal Cage* 49), that Viola Hopkins Winner derogates it as "thin and bloodless" (24), and that Daniel Mark Fogel describes it as so "oppositional" that it "threatens to fly apart" (*Henry James and the Structure* 173).[7]

Yet *The Tragic Muse* is an engaging and amusing work if considered as a human comedy dealing with the compromises men and women must make in contending with the often conflicting claims upon them. Nick Dormer's love of art prevents him from being a serious parliamentarian and thus from pleasing Lady Agnes, Julia, and Mr. Carteret. Peter's life is so entwined with Biddy Dormer and Miriam and so ruled by his love for the theater, his ambitions, his sense of social decorum, and his sexual passion that he is fated to lapse into compromise. Even Miriam, who will not be deflected from her goal, makes concessions to mercenary managers and an unintelligent public, and she marries a combination booking agent and minor actor whom she treats like a lackey. The multiplication of cases illustrating the inevitable limitations on human freedom and possibility suggests that James entertains, albeit only playfully, an ideal of complete liberation from complexity and conventional restraints.

That ideal is embodied in Gabriel Nash, whom most critics have taken with a seriousness that belies his role in the novel.[8] Assuming that Nash is meant to be a realistic character, D. W. Jefferson, for example, objects to him as "unplaceable" (125), when it is clearly James's intention to make him too unattached to be a credible citizen of the real world. Robert S. Baker, too, condemns Gabriel's sterile egocentricity by classifying him as a Paterian aesthete even though Nash turns aside, with a weary reproof, Biddy Dormer's question as to whether he is an aesthete. In fact, he touches the world like a spirit taking on temporary existence to perform an assigned mission. If James keeps him from being too ethereal by giving him a past, Nash quickly disowns and wishes to obliterate it. He comes into the novel like a mysterious stranger or apparition— "he appeared" when Nick, under the spell of art in Paris, is in need of a guardian angel. Since Nash is never explained through serious self-analysis or authorial commentary, he baffles more than elucidates when he compares himself to a "merman wandering free" (*TM* 104) or when he allies himself to the immortals by affirming that he is unaging and does not live in the nineteenth century. James plays a witty game of mystification by giving Nash the powers of a seer and by having him materialize at opportune times to influence Dormer and Sherringham. James never shows him at home and never hints that he has family connections or obligations that might impede him from roaming to Spain or Samarcand when the fit comes on. Nash's only affiliation is with the Anonymous Club, of which he is the sole member and which has its headquarters in some unlikely street. Even more enigmatically, since he never needs doctors and is "innoculated" against disease, he seems to gain health from his avoidance of sordidness and his exposure to natural beauty. Despite Dormer's occasional suspicion that his friend may be a poseur, Nash finally arouses in him "the sense of the transient and occasional, the likeness to vapour or murmuring wind or shifting light" (*TM* 465). With an almost surreal attempt to enhance the mystery surrounding Nash, James emulates Hawthorne in having Dormer imagine that, when Nash quits society, he dissipates into thin air and his likeness fades from the canvas on which his portrait was roughly sketched. Undoubtedly, James implies that Nash places too great a value on "being" to be permanently implicated in the earnest strivings and cross-purposes through which human beings fashion their destinies.

Divine agent, Mephistophelean busybody, or comic spirit, Nash treats Dormer's life as if it were one of his experiments, and he relishes each twist of his plot. Promising to "bother" Dormer to the end, he plies him with subversive notions and prods him to defy convention. He manifests a Jamesian sense of fun as he first disparages Dormer's entrance into politics and then encourages him to seek election so that he can edify the world by resigning his seat in the House of Commons. His prognostications often have authorial resonance and authority, as when he makes good on his promise that after Julia has put Nick in Parliament, "I'll pull you out" (*TM* 113). In one of the most critical scenes in the novel, he interposes with a fateful knock on Dormer's studio door, confesses that he was guided by "miraculous" instincts, and accuses Nick of a "great wrong" in subordinating his art to politics. In this brief scene, which James introduces as dramatizing "a turn of the tide in Nick Dormer's personal situation" (*TM* 240), Nash effectively keeps his promise to end Dormer's political career. At another time, he mischievously arranges to have Miriam sit for Dormer, thus causing Julia, who sees his hand in the arrangement, to break off her engagement.

Although Nash is fallible and, in a few instances, human enough to resent personal criticism, he clearly serves as James's *magister ludi*. He not only directs Dormer through the maze of his early career but also, in the brilliant conversation in chapter 36, forces the love-sick Sherringham to face disquieting realities about Miriam's future life as a celebrity lionized and then destroyed by a public hungry for sensations. Nash's intuition that Miriam has fallen in love with Dormer proves to be sound, and his prediction that she will marry someone who will contribute to her success is borne out when she becomes Dashwood's wife. Another of Nash's predictions, that Dormer will lapse into a polished painter of country-house habitués, seems to become a reality when Dormer is reconciled to Julia and paints her portrait. Moreover, at the end of the novel, Julia has begun a campaign to recapture the man she has pursued, rejected, and, at last, decided to have. In telling Dormer's fortune, Nash has foreseen that Dormer's sister Biddy will join Julia against him in the eternal scheme, not of the individual woman but of the whole "sex," to snare man into marriage. Nash softens his prediction into a warning of what will happen "if you don't take great care" (*TM* 469), and James, too, refuses to be definite about his artist's future, though Dormer finds himself sketching "the whole company" at one of Julia's parties (*TM* 473).

As Ronald Wallace observes, the novel cannot go on after Nash has escaped from a world where possibility has hardened into decision, where careers have become the business of life (10). Vagrant, elusive, and finally unclassifiable, Nash is the enemy of the settled condition and routine. Complaining that existence is flawed into banality by "repetition" and "recurrence," he envisions a world in which men and women make a single appearance in a given time and place and then move on in a series of experiences with novel scenes and persons. He regards his past not as determining his present but as part of a sequence of phases in an unending quest for self-renewal through fresh adventures. Nash perhaps embodies for James an idealized, etherealized freedom that exposes the limitations of what Gabriel calls the clumsiness of the human condition. Though he is content to "be," all the other characters must adjust to a society that exacts harsh terms even from the relatively free artist. For example, as much as Miriam may wish to experiment with ever changing roles, she can gain acclaim only by long runs that require repetition and recurrence. Dormer, whose liberty she envies, appears at the close of the novel to be unable to extricate himself from the claims of the past.[9] As for the minor characters, young and old, they are creatures of circumstance who accept their confining views as valid social standards. Lady Agnes is a well-bred philistine and xenophobe who deplores art and can discover nothing to amuse her during a holiday in Paris. Her daughter Grace is an unattractive image and a hollow echo of her mother, and Mr. Carteret lives and dies embalmed in political preoccupations. Having invented a genteel past for herself, Miriam's mother courts respectability with a tenacity that turns her into a fatuous eccentric controlled by a single idea.

James, then, uses Nash to measure the freedom of the other characters in *The Tragic Muse*. Gabriel's candor in championing the arts and above all the art of living at the expense of utilitarian and conventional behavior affronts Lady Agnes, fills Julia with disgust, and causes Sherringham to view him with a mixture of fascination and repulsion. In her headlong rush to celebrity, Miriam dismisses him as inconsequent, but Dormer more intelligently heeds the wisdom in his paradoxes and impertinences. Biddy Dormer, for all her ingenue charm, shows her habit of thinking in categories when she tries to dismiss Nash as an aesthete. Of course, James is aware that his flesh-and-blood characters are being contrasted to a fictional convenience meant to expose the limitations of his worldlings. Whereas others are rooted in place and occupation, Nash is free and fugitive; whereas others strive to earn money or win lovers, he has no need to make a living and is, it appears, immune to sexual desire; and whereas others are accosted by ugliness and mindful of fate, he looks on the earth as a pleasure ground where he will never grow old or die. Emanation of the ideal though he may be, however, he allows James to tell a tale of men and women enmeshed in their individual and collective egos and destinies. His ultimate unreality gives a poignant reality to James's vision of human incompleteness and the tragicomedy of human endeavor.

Nash's ability to escape from deterministic contingencies reveals how thoroughly the protagonists of *The Portrait*, *The Bostonians*, and *The Princess*, as well as those of *The Tragic Muse*, are caught in the web of circumstance and psychological compulsion. Isabel Archer's spiritual freedom is qualified by fundamental renunciations, and Hyacinth Robinson achieves liberty only as he turns a gun against himself. The end of *The Bostonians*, especially in its emphasis on Verena's emancipation from Olive, suggests that she and Ransom will be happier in their marriage than Isabel and Osmond or Sherringham and Biddy Dormer, but James cannot resist the temptation to foreshadow some dark passages in their future. Nash, then, is paradoxically the bright vision that haunts the inevitable chiaroscuro of reality. He resembles Felix Young, the irrepressibly happy youth of *The Europeans*, who takes his bride from the gloom and repression of her native New England to some never-never land beyond the seas. An even purer abstraction than Felix, Nash covets neither wife nor fortune and revels in selfhood in a world where the Isabels, Verenas, Hyacinths, Dormers, and Sherringhams grasp at ideal selves that evaporate in the very quest for them.

## NOTES

1. Powers's analysis (in *Henry James and the Naturalist Movement*) shows James modifying his naturalistic techniques as he moves from the detailed, almost Balzacian documentation of *The Bostonians* to the more selective descriptiveness of *The Princess* and *The Tragic Muse*. Powers also discusses the role of heredity as a factor in determining the careers of James's major characters.

2. Donald Mull describes Osmond as "the actualization of [Isabel's] flights and aspirations" (105). For Tony Tanner, Osmond functions as "Isabel's anti-self" ("Fearful Self" 210).

3. A few representative interpretations of the famous, controversial ending indicate that there is no critical consensus about its thematic meaning. Seeing Isabel as a sort of decadent, John Auchard asserts, "The vector of Isabel Archer is not only away from vitality but towards something contrary to vitality, inevitably as ghastly as the young man's attraction to the vacancy of the absent Maud-Evelyn" (62). Philip Weinstein emphasizes her refusal to give herself and the world a second chance in her retreat to "inner superiority" (68). F. W. Dupee finds her return to Osmond "an austere decision but inescapable in the light of her character and quest"; he also considers the ending as proof that James "is more Puritan . . . than Hawthorne in *The Scarlet Letter*" (*Henry*

*James* 124, 125 [1973]). Christof Wegelin more affirmatively regards Isabel's flight from Goodwood as a movement "not so much into Osmond's prison as into the freedom of her duty" (71).

4. Leavis dismisses "the political interest" as "incidental" (135 [1960]), and Michael Swan argues that the politics of *The Bostonians* is subordinate to the "psychological relationship between [Olive and Verena]" (75).

5. With sharply different emphases, Lionel Trilling, Oscar Cargill, and Mark Seltzer, as well as Tilley, deal significantly with the political realities that inform *The Princess* (Trilling, *Liberal Imagination* 58–92 [1948], Cargill 146–73, Seltzer 25–58, and Tilley throughout).

6. Oscar Cargill (146–73) and Marcia Jacobson (41–61) have thoroughly studied James's indebtedness to other writers.

7. Leon Edel explains James's "omissions" as part of his dramatic technique: "he boldly put together his story by scenic alternation, not by telling the reader everything, but by letting the scenes explain themselves, as in a play" (*The Middle Years* 263).

8. Pelham Edgar conjectures that Nash might be taken as "a projection of Nick Dormer's own mind" (288).

9. D. J. Gordon and John Stokes maintain, "Miriam and Nick are . . . in a trap, for what they represent depends absolutely upon the condition of their experience" (162).

# 8
# The Experimental Period

## Jean Frantz Blackall

The "experimental period" is a fascinating one for the student of James.[1] Here we see him, with kaleidoscopic brilliance and rapidity, breaking away from his anchorage in the Victorian novel and developing the technical and stylistic resources that he will bequeath to the twentieth-century novel. Ambivalence is a characteristic attitude in both James and his characters. And ambiguity is a characteristic of James's fictions both because he cultivated indeterminate effects for demonstrable reasons—for example, to mystify, entice, or implicate the reader; to represent the mind groping toward an *éclaircissement*—and because the rapid evolution of donnée materials into new forms during the process of composition caused transformations in point of view and emphasis within the works. "It is not unusual in James for the overtones of one novel to become the themes of the next" (Dupee, *Henry James* 192 [1951]). The nineties fictions were written very rapidly—under the duress, at times, of publishers' deadlines and also of an exuberant outburst of imaginative energy—and perhaps for these reasons, evolution within these texts is especially acute. In four instances, *The Spoils of Poynton*, *What Maisie Knew*, *The Sacred Fount*, and *The Awkward Age*, James meant to write a short story, only to have the material "[grow] by a rank force of its own" into a short novel (*HJL* IV, 251). In two instances, *Poynton* and *The Turn of the Screw*, a functional character moved from the periphery to a central position in the narrative, becoming the protagonist. Readers' resultant perplexity may account in some degree for the burgeoning criticism of particular texts out of all proportion to their intrinsic merits in the canon. *Poynton* is a problematic book because of the rarefied attitudes of its heroine and its mixed tone: *The Turn of the Screw* is a *tour de force* rather than a major work; and *The Sacred Fount* is, as S. Gorley Putt remarks, "the very last novel one would wish to see placed in the hands of a newcomer to James's fiction," though it has its attractions (258). The most fully realized of these fictions are *The Turn of the Screw* and *In the Cage*, two distinguished *nouvelles*; *The Awkward Age*, a brilliant exemplar of what is yet an excessively artificial structural and narrative method; and *What Maisie Knew*, which is the happiest fusion of experimental rigor with human value. The experimental period also rewards scrutiny when we consider not only the technical virtuosity but also the substance of these fictions. What new material did James exploit during the nineties, and how do these often painful, often perplexing works reveal the preoccupations of the author? Alternative designations for this phase of James's career are the "English period" and the "treacherous years."

The year 1895 is a line of demarcation in James's professional career. During his five-year attempt to establish himself as a playwright in the early nineties, he wrote only short works of fiction, twenty tales altogether. But with the failure of his play *Guy Domville* in 1895, James dedicated himself anew and with religious fervor to the writing of novels. He wrote in his notebooks on January 23, 1895: "I take up my *own* old pen again—the pen of all my old unforgettable efforts and sacred struggles. To myself—today—I need say no more. Large and full and high the future still opens. It is now indeed that I may do the work of my life. And I will" (*NB* 179). Yet, with his characteristic economy, the wish never to squander effort or time, James pondered how the theatrical experience might be relevant to the writing of fiction. "Has a *part* of all this wasted passion and squandered time (of the last 5 years) been simply the precious lesson, taught me in that roundabout and devious, that cruelly expensive, way, *of the singular value for a narrative plan too* of the . . . divine principle of the Scenario?" (February 14, 1895) (*NB* 188).

Thus James formulated the analogy that would dominate his conception of novelistic form ever after. The well-made novel, like the well-made play, should be scenic in design, fashioned in structural blocks and built up according to a carefully plotted dramatic scenario, with preparation, crisis, and denouement. Writing fictions during this period shorter than the expansive canvases of the late eighties and the turn of the century, he concentrated on form, dramatic encounter, point of view, modes of exposition. The author, like the dramatist withdrawing into the wings, would increasingly exploit the resources of the dramatist. What the reader can be made to see and hear on stage is the experience offered. Stage properties, costumes, and settings assume ever increasing, often symbolic, importance. Character groupings, entrances and exits, and body language may accentuate or define relationships. Houses project the characters and attitudes of their owners in a perceptible form. Dialogue becomes "organic," bearing the burden of exposition. To facilitate the latter end, James introduced *ficelles*, characters belonging to the exposition rather than to the substance of the fiction. The *ficelle* is employed as "the reader's friend" (*AN* 322–24) to assist, through conversation, in drawing out the attitudes and in forming the views of principal characters by providing an audience and a respondent. Examples of such functionaries are Mrs. Wix in *Maisie*, Mrs. Jordan in *Cage*,

Mrs. Grose in *Screw*, and the Duchess in *The Awkward Age*. (For a fuller definition, see Sharp xxiii, xxvii–xxviii.)

Concurrently, overt authorial presence increasingly yields to a focus in the subjective experience of a pivotal character (a ''central consciousness'') from whose angle of vision a third-person narrative is told or who himself performs as a first-person narrator. For by interposing ''a definite created sensibility . . . between the reader and the felt experience which is the subject of the fiction,'' James objectified that subject; ''his subject really was not what happened but what someone felt about what happened'' (*AN* xvii–xviii). The dramatic scene filtered through the sensibility of a central character becomes the means of objectifying that sensibility. ''James is passing over from the dramatisation of events to the dramatisation of states of mind and soul, the conditions of what is happening below the surface of the dialogue and the action'' (Egan 32 [London]). James's intense preoccupation with point of view in the experimental fictions and thereafter in turn leads to the selection of unusual perspectives—that of a child (*Maisie*), that of a young woman deprived by class (*Cage*) or by lack of worldly experience (*Screw*) of the knowledge to interpret her experiences cogently, that of an obsessed narrator consumed by the desire to justify his own intellectual artifact (*Fount*), and so on. James came to delight in the sheer difficulty of solving a technical problem, in finding means to express a mind at work: ''I so despair of tracing her [Maisie's] steps that I must crudely give you my word for its being, from this time on, a picture literally present to her'' (*WM* 360).

Thus the spectacle of a mind at work on a scene objectively rendered is the entertainment that James offers his reader. Yet the reader is never permitted for a moment to remain passive. We are drawn into the fiction in an effort to assimilate meaningful details, physical and abstract. Through the agency of the narrator or central consciousness, we are impelled to enter into the mental processes being enacted—stepwise, reflective, and fragmented though these may be and however interrupted by the give-and-take, the subterfuge, of dialogue. Evoking an analogy with Brechtian drama, Sergio Perosa suggests: ''We watch, as it were, through the actor *into* the action. In a rather similar way, though the point must not be overstressed, James's narrator is actually involved in the action but detached from it; he performs his role in the story, but, more crucially, he acts as intermediary for the reader, providing him not with a full intepretation of the scene but with hints and clues that the reader himself must interpret. In both cases much more is required of the spectator or reader than mere acquiescence in the facts presented'' (*Experimental Novel* 50).

Certain characteristics of James's fiction are accentuated or at times initiated by the technical experimentation of the postdramatic years. There is an aggravated tendency toward mixed tone, a strange fusion of the comical and the tragic. There are stylistic changes, associated, it would seem, with James's efforts to maximize expressiveness by indirect means. And there is an increasing ambiguity, which is the product both of the evolution of James's initial idea (his donnée, or given) during the process of composition and of his stylistic evolution. In *Strange Alloy* (a work appropriately deriving its title from James's preface to *Maisie*), Ellen Douglass Leyburn makes a general argument for James's characteristic "amalgam of laughter and pain in [his] portrayal of the complexities of reality" (xvii), including *Poynton* and *The Awkward Age* among her exemplary texts. This sort of fusion is particularly characteristic of the fiction of the nineties. Again and again James takes up a comical, ironical, or circumscribed subject—in the interest, it would seem, of focusing on a technical problem—only to have the work move toward a more serious perception of character and circumstance thereafter as objective realities are registered inwardly by sentient protagonists.

Stylistic changes are most notable in augmented verbiage, in the stylization of dialogue, and in the treatment of figurative language—also in the variation of sentence rhythms, as F. W. Dupee remarks in his beautiful, succinct account of the evolution of James's style in the nineties (*Henry James* 193–96 [1951]). The ratio between matter and verbiage begins to modify. In seeking to externalize mental process through dialogue or first-person narration, James proliferates the number of words he needs to tell even the simplest tale, and the focus of a narrative within the consciousness of a central character results in what James called (in speaking, specifically, of first-person narrative) "terrible *fluidity*" (*AN* 320–21). "James's overtreatment is not only a cherished habit and an indulgence of his later, mannered style: it is implied in and a consequence of his experimental method itself. He wanted to confront, search, and combine too many things and too many possibilities, to pursue all possible threads, to squeeze every drop of meaning out of every technical and expressive potentiality" (Perosa, *Experimental Novel* 65). Yet Ronald Wallace's insistence on the comical aspect of verbal elaborations, for example, "repetition, exaggeration, and deflation" (112), is also to be regarded. Seymour Chatman's analysis of James's stylistic characteristics during the major phase is immensely suggestive for the reader of the nineties fictions as well. He isolates for discussion such elements as deixis, ellipsis, hyperbole, James's peculiar use of expletives, and so on. Chatman identifies earlier critics concerned with style, D. W. Jefferson and R. W. Short, as being among those who have noticed "the curious mixture of colloquial and formal diction in James" (106 [1986]). He observes James's "attempt to catch the mind at work, in all its uncertainty, indeed, assuming uncertainty to be its ordinary lot, experience to be essentially fluid, and so the narrative task necessarily approximative" (41 [1986]). In effect, James is working toward "stream of consciousness" technique, though he maintains a degree of logical and dialectical continuity within his representation of thought sequences that one does not associate with the later technique.

The dialogue of James's plays has sometimes been associated with that of Restoration comedy in its cadence, "style and bite," and these qualities come over into the fictional dialogue (Granville-Barker, quoted in *CP 69, 765;* cf. *CP* 295, Wallace 112). Sentence rhythms are variable, language is colloquial, and characters indulge in stichomythic exchanges and tease each other with ambiguous pronouns. Conversation becomes a drawing-room sport, with its apotheosis in Mrs. Brookenham's salon in *The Awkward Age* (see Krook 150–51). In the winter of 1896–97, it is usually claimed, when James was in the middle of writing *Maisie* (Edel, *Treacherous Years* 176), he adopted the practice of dictating aloud to a typist. Beyond this point, all of his fictions would be dictated, so that the speech is literally colloquial, addressed to the ear. The reader is often well advised to read complex passages aloud, both for their intrinsic beauty and as a mode of clarification. (See *CT* 10:13 for another fine account of the style in evolution.)

But James is writing fiction, nonetheless, not drama, and available to him as a writer of fiction is a richer and more elaborated figurative language than one commonly hears on stage. The three titles James considered for the second of these novels, "The House Beautiful" (*NB* 208), "The Old Things" (*NB* 247), and "The Spoils of Poynton," cause one to see the house proliferating in his perception from an aesthetic object to a material object to a figurative object, the booty in a battle waged for possession. The latter idea will permeate and color the language of the finished work, as the whole contest for possession between Mrs. Gereth and her son is translated into metaphoric expression. "She was still prepared to fight. What indeed was her spoliation of Poynton but the first engagement of a campaign?" (*SP* 92). James's imagery is on the whole more organic than allusive. It grows out of and together with the "subject" in hand, which may be consciously apprehended, as in the instance of *Poynton*, or intuitively felt, as appears to be the case in *The Other House*, a Victorian fiction incongruously peppered with classical tropes and epithets: "like the priestess of a threatened altar" (*OH* 175), "wine-dark doors" (*OH* 318). When James's subject is a child (Maisie), that child interprets the world in terms of games and playthings. A telegraphist who works in a wire cage invokes images relating to a cage to characterize her own position in relation to the world outside. Thus "in the cage," "the figure in the carpet," and "the sacred fount" are governing metaphors in the tales of which they are a part. Such titles anticipate major phase titles such as *The Wings of the Dove* and *The Golden Bowl* in their figurative domination of the works or in their transformation of physical aspects of the fictions into figurative ones, symbolic objects. This proliferation of figurative language will lead, eventually, to the vegetable metaphors of the late period. (For a rich descriptive survey of James's metaphoric language dissociated from any interpretive thesis, see Gale, *The Caught Image*. Cf. Holder-Barrell and Laitinen on figurative language in *Poynton*.)

As regards structure, we may observe that James's earlier confrontation of America and Europe is metamorphosed during these years into the confrontation of innocence versus experience, naïveté versus worldliness, good versus evil, in different specific terms. Children and young women are the counterparts to naïve and vulnerable Americans abroad; and parents, surrogate parents, ghosts, and a gilded but corrupt sophisticated adult society generate the mysterious ambiance, like the Europe of the early fictions, into which these creatures must venture and where they must attempt to survive. According to Tony Tanner: "The enforced response, the 'process of vision' of the candid outsider, attracted him as a theme not because it was American, nor even because it was moral and innocent, but because it allowed him to study what he elsewhere calls 'the strain of observation and the assault of experience.' It permitted him to scrutinize unanticipated collisions of sensibility and data when those collisions were at their freshest, their most revealing, their most meaningful" (*Reign* 267). In any event, this strategy of confrontation may be understood as a means for dramatizing the material outwardly, in the structure of the work. For these works, like those of James's whole career, illustrate his characteristic polarizing imagination and his exploitation of confronted opposites in the interest of generating dramatic intensity through antagonistic wills. The opposition of the old versus the new is yet another such paradigm, one scrutinized by Daniel Schneider in *The Crystal Cage* (41–43). (See also Peter Brooks 157, 167, and *passim* on the "melodrama of consciousness" in James's later fiction.)

Hence we see that a characteristic form for these fictions is that of a contest between two opponents over an object at an ever increasing price. The object may be human, material, or abstract. Maisie's parents and surrogate parents literally grapple over her physical presence. Mrs. Gereth does battle with her son and his fiancée to see who will possess Poynton, the house and its contents. The narrator of *Fount* argues with an opponent till the small hours of the morning over whose version of reality is true. James then attains a variety of tones and effects depending on the point of view he selects: that of the object, for example, Maisie; that of one of the antagonists, the *Fount* narrator, say, or the governess in *Screw*; or that of an observer character who becomes implicated in the contest in progress, for example, "divided Vanderbank" (*AN* 71) of *The Awkward Age*, and the equally divided Fleda Vetch of *Poynton*, who are respectively pressed to cast their allegiance with the mother or the daughter, the mother or the son. James was ever mindful of the energy generated by dramatic confrontation, and an awareness of such a pattern is extremely helpful in perceiving the inward dynamics of these works.[2]

Alternative designations for this phase of James's career direct our attention to subject matter and to the author within the works. The English period draws attention to the fact that, without exception, all the novels and *nouvelles* of these years, and most of the stories, are localized to England, and that not one of the longer works treats the celebrated international theme that James exploits in the early novels and again in the major phase. This preoccupation with English themes may indicate, in keeping with the experimentation of the later eighties, James's attempt to find new subject matter after his early exploitation of the international theme. Whereas the long novels of the eighties look for new material in broad social themes—the feminist movement, anarchy, politics, the theater— those of the nineties continue to examine social themes but in more intimate, domestic contexts. These originate in such topics as the expropriation of the English widow in *Poynton*, "the situation of the mother *deposed*, by the ugly

English custom, turned out of the big house on the son's marriage and relegated''
(*NB* 137); the consequences for the child of the death of the mother or the divorce
of the parents (in *The Other House* and *Maisie*); the problems of being a governess
(in *Screw*) or a telegraphist engaged to a grocer (*Cage*); how one amuses oneself
at country-house parties on weekends (*Fount*); or in *The Awkward Age*, the
dilemma for a sophisticated English mother of having to integrate a supposedly
naïve teenage daughter into her own social life. Undoubtedly, James is, at one
level, continuing his exploration of new materials for fiction and utilizing the
cumulative knowledge of English manners that twenty years' residence in England had afforded. Certain passages in his notebooks indicate his persistent
interest in the evolution of contemporary British society, for example, his notation
on February 27, 1895, of "the 2 most striking social notes" discerned by a
French social critic, "Brada," in her *Notes sur Londres*: "the masculinization
of the women" and "the demoralization of the aristocracy—the cessation, on
their part, to take themselves seriously; their traffic in vulgar things, vulgar
gains, vulgar pleasures—their general vulgarization" (*NB* 192). This could virtually be a statement of James's own thematic interests in *Maisie* or *Cage* or
*The Awkward Age*. S. Gorley Putt, who regards the novels of the nineties as
being "in effect a sustained commentary on the society of the nation in which
[James] had chosen to live," characterizes their "social content" as a "[dis-
section of] the rotting head of the smelly fish of late Victorian and Edwardian
England" (243; cf. Ward, *Imagination* 78), and Richards, in his introduction to
*Poynton*, enumerates particular elements of contemporary decadence perceived
by James (xii–xv).

The "treacherous years" is Leon Edel's designation for this phase of James's
career. Approaching these fictions from the perspective of the biographer, Edel
argues that James's recurrent choice of vulnerable protagonists, neglected and
abused children, young or vulnerable women, manifests a regression into childhood feelings as he struggled to recover from the burden of defeat and personal
humiliation involved in his theatrical fiasco and to achieve detachment from the
London social world from which he felt excluded after his withdrawal to Rye
in 1897 (*Treacherous Years* 248–50). "James performed imaginative self-
therapy" by assuming the disguise of a female child (*Treacherous Years* 264).
The increasing age and maturity of the vulnerable protagonists mark his gradual
return to an adult and analytic stance in the spectator figures of Mr. Longdon
in *The Awkward Age* and the narrator of *Fount* (*Treacherous Years* 250–53).
James's concurrent obsession with technical mastery during these years is his
reassertion of rational form, his authority as a writer, on confused emotions
(*Treacherous Years* 109–10). Edel's Freudian readings have had great influence
in causing other interpreters to approach the fictions of the nineties as illuminating
excursions into—or emanations from—James's psyche. One of the most illuminating of these is Thelma Shinn's tracing of the theme that she discerns as
uniting all the principal fictions of the nineties, "the struggle between passive
and passionate love and its effect on art and the artist" (136). Philip Sicker, in

his chapter entitled "The Disturbed Midnight," argues, "James' preoccupation during the late 1890s with matters of point of view and form . . . is not so much a novelist's interest in literary style as a man's response to the horror of self-entrapment" (75). Like their creator, the characters of the late nineties fictions are isolated within their subjective consciousnesses. Artists in life, they seek to impose the illusion of order on their evanescent impressions and to define a personal identity by acts of imagining directed toward beloved objects outside: "a sense of identity was possible only if the changing beloved could be transformed into an unchanging image" (Sicker 78). Daniel Schneider's identification of the figure in James's carpet as being freedom versus enslavement is also formulated on a biographical premise, James's own sense of being "a divided self." Schneider observes that James's earlier pitying attitude toward the escapist tendencies of victimized and threatened protagonists (slaves) is qualified in the postdramatic years as James became more critical of such impulses in himself. "In the nineties a sharp irony deeply qualifies the pity we might feel for such a protagonist. Both the caged telegrapher of 'In the Cage' and Fleda Vetch of *The Spoils of Poynton* are presented as sentimentalists and idealists who again and again take flight into a world of dreams. . . . If the soul is threatened by 'the other' and unable to compete on practical terms, it can choose to live in a world in which there is no question of competition—a world of fantasy, a house of fiction. We arrive, thus, at the preoccupations that were to produce *The Sacred Fount*" (*Crystal Cage* 65–66).

Now that the experimental character of the nineties fictions as regards scenic structure and point of view is an established sentiment, readers are discovering new perspectives from which to regard them. Recent approaches that have yielded new readings of these works include interest in James's relationship to the contemporary marketplace and his efforts to communicate with a popular audience; inquiry into James's attitudes toward feminist issues; a fascination with the centrality of absence, silence, and verbal blanks as a constitutive element; and a host of contemporary theoretical approaches. Responding both to the psychological critics (Edel and, before him, Geismar and Wilson) and to those preoccupied with James's formal experimentation (especially Wiesenfarth and Isle), Marcia Jacobson argues in *Henry James and the Mass Market* that when James "returned to the novel in the late nineties, he did not withdraw 'into a dreamy interior world' [quoting Wilson] or devote himself to abstract 'experiments in form' " (99). The fiction of the nineties is neither psychologically regressive nor obsessively experimental. Rather, she proposes, the fiction of the eighties and the nineties is unified by James's consistent effort to address a popular audience in his version of its own terms. The fashionable marriage question and the child-centered novel concern him in *Maisie* and the English dialogue novel and the new woman novel in *The Awkward Age*. Anne Margolis concurs in arguing for James's reactive awareness of the literary environment and in questioning Edel's "regressive" reading of the nineties fictions, though she is no less ingenious than he in formulating a personal relationship between

James and his characters. Because his own relationship to the Anglo-American reading public was problematic, James's experimentation involved his displacing onto his characters the burdens of supersubtlety, fineness, and indiscretion that caused him trouble in his own attempts, as novelist, to win a popular audience. Thus the reader confronts the heroic perversities of a Fleda Vetch, or Maisie's "improper" curiosities, or Mrs. Brookenham's ruthless exposure of her daughter Nanda, or Nanda's own outspokenness, rather than such attitudes in the author. "James appears to be calling upon his characters [Maisie and Nanda Brookenham in this instance] to act in his behalf, to challenge the timidity of the English-speaking novelist and liberate the Anglo-American novel by undermining the 'great difference . . . between what they [the English-speaking public] talk of in conversation and what they talk of in print' [quoting James]" (Margolis 129). So disguised and distanced behind his characters, James meanwhile persevered in his impulse toward educating his audience by refusing to offer such sops as the indecent liaison or the conventional happy ending and by treating forbidden themes. Adultery is the new thematic material that Margolis discerns as being broached in the nineties, a topic that will become central to the major phase fictions. Patricia Meyer Spacks makes a rather similar point from the reader's perspective, using *Maisie* to illustrate how the "gossipy" character of the realistic novel, distanced through narrative voice, permits the reader to satisfy voyeuristic and salacious curiosities without, as it were, being contaminated. Thus gossip draws the reader, and narrative distance protects the reader. "Initially the reader [in company with the narrator] can feel superior (as the gossip feels superior), not only to Maisie but to the other actors in the drama—superior in knowledge but also in sophistication, specifically worldly knowledge, and in interpretive power" (Spacks 217). However, by the end of the fiction, James's "gossip" changes character, and the reader is more seriously engaged. "By the final chapters, one feels the same avid interest in the movements of Maisie's psychic life that another novelist might engender in a couple's erotic arrangements" (Spacks 221). Such an argument would be equally suggestive of James's technique in *Cage*, *Awkward Age*, and *Fount*.

Though James has long been celebrated for his sympathetic and perceptive representations of female character (see, e.g., Springer 2–3 and Wagenknecht, *Eve* ix), the nature of his attitudes toward feminism has become a subject of inquiry only recently. Is he ambivalent in his attitude toward women? Is he subtly sexist in perpetuating stereotypes and in romanticizing female suffering rather than challenging patriarchal structures? Or does he in fact expose power structures that both subordinate women and entrap them within representational roles? Such matters are addressed apropos of nineties fictions in studies by Elizabeth Allen, Carren Kaston, and John Carlos Rowe, whose collective sentiment is that feminist issues are intrinsic to James's novels. "James claims for himself a certain authority regarding the representation of women, insofar as their social situation is a central problem in his fiction from *Daisy Miller* to *The Ivory Tower*" (Rowe, *Theoretical Dimensions* 87). Moreover, since these writers examine nineties heroines in a continuum that includes earlier and later fictions, one effect of their studies is the suggestion that the vulnerable and naïve heroines of the nineties are not necessarily isolated in a midnight phase of James's imaginative life but are variations in an ongoing interpretation of female character and experience. According to Shine: "The passivity that characterized the victimized children of the 1880's is not in evidence in those of the following decade. In the 90's James's fictional children are conspicuous for their energetic response to experience. A distinctive group of eager, curious, and remarkably active little girls loom large in the stories of the last half of the decade. . . . Between 1895 and 1900 James seems to be following the evolution of the female child from cradle to adulthood" (75). That is not to deny, as Rowe also remarks, that "James's uncanny ability to represent the complex psychologies of women . . . is in part attributable to his identification with their marginal and powerless situations" (*Theoretical Dimensions* 90). Rowe's illumination of feminist issues in *Poynton* would be relevant as well to *Maisie* or *Cage* as regards the marginalized existence of female characters, their emotional dependency on men, and their dependency on male power either literally or (for Fleda) in a fetishized form (102–4). Allen suggests a feminist reason for James's interest in vulnerable young girls during the nineties in her account of the particular dilemma of both Maisie and Nanda Brookenham of *The Awkward Age*. As young girls, both are arbitrarily impressed with an acceptable social role or identity. "Both function as signs of innocence and ignorance in corrupt societies" (Allen 118). But the imposed symbolic identity is inadequate to contain and express their developing intelligence and complexity. "The assertion of self, of unconventional values and of a rejection of social patterns was to be more incongruous and difficult in the very young girl than in any other figure" (Allen 122). Thus both are disappointed in their attempt to achieve a relationship with a beloved man based on a "union of perception," a bond of intelligent sympathy—a fate they share, Allen intimates, with both Fleda Vetch of *Poynton* and the telegraphist of *Cage* (123). Kaston discerns a more positive evolution by juxtaposing *Poynton*, *Cage*, and *Maisie* (in context with other novels). Fleda Vetch's "ambassadorial consciousness" precludes her imagining a personal self or accommodating her own desires. She simply lives through and in her sympathetic identification with the needs of other characters, her own identity "constituted largely by what it mirrors. . . . This image of the self as a reflector, of consciousness as a mirror, receiving its identity from outside of itself, closely resembles and helps us to understand the stereotypical feminine self scrutinized by feminists" (Kaston 68). The telegraphist escapes a similar fate in her relationship to her wealthy customers, leaving the "cage" of melodramatic and erotic fantasizing about them to embark, tentatively, on "shared fictionalizing" with her humble fiancé, Mr. Mudge (Kaston 120), that is, on a shared process of imaginative exchange. According to Kaston, "Such collaboration—shared fictionalizing, or the mutual creation of experience—is the essence of feminism" (15). Maisie begins where Fleda ends, by repudiating an ambassadorial function, when she refuses to be a messenger of insult between her warring parents. Eventually she extricates herself from the parental figures' imaginative power over her and frames a personal demand, that she and her stepfather "go away together, just the two of them" (Kaston 128). Thus, Kaston argues, "Instead of constituting a 'leak' or victimizing dissipation of power, instead of disabling her or rendering her 'sterile,' as James says they do Fleda (*Prefaces*, p. 131), consciousness and vision coupled with the desires of the personal self confer power on Maisie and ready her for fictions of her own" (136).

Studies by Tzvetan Todorov, John Auchard, and Nicola Bradbury provide an illustrative sampling of perspectives on a phenomenon that, according to Bradbury, is adumbrated in the early fictions, developmental in the nineties, and fully evolved in the late period. That is the centrality of silence, absence, void—a topic that writers examine with regard both to style, in the form of verbal blanks or the literal absence of speech, and to structure, in the form of an "absent cause" (Todorov, "Structural Analysis" 74) or a "fertile gap" (Auchard 38), a negative presence that instigates imaginative activity in both characters and readers. In two seminal essays, one devoted to James's tales of 1892–1903 and the other to language in *The Awkward Age*, Todorov applies a structuralist poetics to James's fiction, making a similar point about his treatment of language and his treatment of structure. In either instance, both characters and readers are implicated in a quest, persistently prolonged, for an elusive truth or essence. "The secret of James's tales is . . . precisely this existence of an essential secret, of something which is not named, of an absent, overwhelming force which puts the whole present machinery of the narrative into motion. . . . On the one hand he deploys all his strength to reach the hidden essence, to unveil the secret object; on the other, he constantly moves it further and further away. . . . The cause is that which, by its absence, gives rise to the text" ("Structural Analysis" 75). This absent cause may variously be perceived as a secret to be penetrated, a ghost (does it exist or not?), death (which "makes a character become the absolute and absent cause of life" ["Structural Analysis" 89]), or a work of art, as the truth to be sought after. Or again, the inexplicit language of *The Awkward Age* is like that of the Delphic oracle, "which neither speaks nor is silent, but suggests. . . . Everything happens as if the characters were activated by two opposing forces, and participated simultaneously in two processes with contrasting values: . . . they try to penetrate words, to get behind them, to seize the truth; but . . . the possible failure of this quest is as if neutralized by the pleasure they take in *not* saying the truth—in condemning it forever to uncertainty" ("Verbal Age" 363–64). In a study historically, socially, and thematically oriented, Auchard places silence in James within the context of late nineteenth-century symbolist and decadent expression and sensibility; it is both an antimaterialistic manifestation and "a delicately balanced emblem of modern man's existential ambiguities" (3). Auchard argues: "Silence, as structure, relates to other 'negated' forces in the fiction, those which move against obvious statement, against presences, against things, against the assertions of positivism. Even ghosts, as visitations that live as absences, become part of the progress of Henry James away from phenomena and the word'' (3). Within this context, Auchard considers tales of the nineties, including *Cage*, *Screw*, and *Poynton*. He suggests that Todorov's structural model of the quest pertains only to stories like *Cage* and *Screw*, which are ''variations of detective fiction genres,'' and that James's developing intentions move beyond this model (39). Comparing these two works, he throws out the fascinating suggestion that their heroines (who are superficially rather dissimilar) resemble each other in both living within the cages of their imaginations. ''Is life that is lived for silent, ghostly forces, for solidifying or abstracted symbolist silences, life at all, or is it foolish, fictive, comic, morbid?'' (Auchard 47). In *Poynton*, Auchard discerns a reeducation of the heroine away from things as the goal of a life toward the discovery ''that suggestive absences can matter as positive values'' (76–77; cf. 83). Bradbury prefaces her study of the late fictions with a chapter on the ''development of silence as a means of expression'' in four earlier novels, including *Maisie*, *Awkward Age*, and *Fount*. ''During the 'dramatic' period . . . James extended the scope of silence as a means of specifically 'not saying' things'' (Bradbury, *Later Novels* 34), that is, silence became the expression both of the unsayable and the unspeakable (''what cannot be put into words and what is deliberately concealed'' [Bradbury, *Later Novels* 11]). Concurrently, Bradbury argues, James developed ''inner silence'' as representing ''an image of the inviolate integrity of the individual'' (*Later Novels* 18, 34); for example, Maisie develops her sense of selfhood by learning to conceal her thoughts (20). *Fount* is ''a demonstration by default of the values of silence'' because here the reader is denied a ''space of silent understanding'' with the author (Bradbury, *Later Novels* 34, 33). (See too Norrman's anatomy of various kinds of ''blanks'' [in *Techniques of Ambiguity*] as being among James's ambiguity-creating devices, with particular reference to *Cage* and *Screw*; Millicent Bell's persuasive demonstration that ''the relation of silence to speech is the central issue'' in *Maisie* [''Les Mots'' 329]; and Rimmon's fascinating study, theoretical and applied, of the relationship between gaps and the creation of narrative ambiguity in James's experimental fiction.)

Richard Hocks suggests that methodological pluralism in approaches to James has to do in part with ''his 'transitional' moment in literary history, whereby his genius for experimentation still allied itself successfully with his mimetic presuppositions'' (''James Studies 1981'' 29). The aggravated merger of experimentation with mimesis during the nineties may explain why theoretical studies have converged with particular intensity on these evolutionary texts, above all on *Screw*, *Fount*, and ''The Figure in the Carpet,'' for these works have proven most resistant to traditional interpretive strategies. Shlomith Rimmon (now Rimmon-Kenan), Christine Brooke-Rose, Shoshana Felman, and Susanne Kappeler, to cite a few influential voices, all use one or more of these works as exemplary texts. Taken together, their studies may be read as illustrating recent mainstream theoretical movements, structuralist (Rimmon, Brooke-Rose), psychoanalytic (Felman), and *Rezeptionstheorie* (Kappeler). These writers converge in such sentiments as the nonmimetic character of James's texts, their indeterminacy, their self-reflexive character, and James's strategic implication of the reader as a collaborator in the making of the fiction. "By leaving a central gap open and encouraging the reader to search for clues, group evidences, and weigh them against each other, the ambiguity makes the reading process dynamic or, in modern Structuralist-Marxist parlance, prevents the reader from being merely a passive consumer and turns him into an active producer of the text" (Rimmon 228). Rowe's *Theoretical Dimensions*, though not devoted exclusively to the experimental fictions, enacts a dynamic confrontation with six disparate theoretical approaches to James and provides the most spacious and authoritative theoretical overview to date. (See also Rowe's illuminating review of Kappeler.) Existing apart from the *Screw* and *Fount* obsession, but a catalytic theoretical text as well, is Paul Armstrong's application of phenomenological and existential concepts to James's fiction. Armstrong uses *Maisie* to illustrate the convergence of "all of the major aspects of experience that preoccupy James's imagination" (*Phenomenology* x), namely, "the 'impression,' the imagination, freedom, personal relations, and the politics of daily life" (*Phenomenology* ix). In a narrower focus, Charles Anderson scrutinizes "the politics of experience" in *Poynton*. Integrating Marxist theory into his argument, Anderson observes how the things, as the embodiment of "human investments of meaning and value," "serve conflicts over power for the sake of individual ascendancy" (192).

## THE THIRD-PERSON CENTRAL CONSCIOUSNESS: *THE SPOILS OF POYNTON, WHAT MAISIE KNEW,* AND *IN THE CAGE*

These three works are all dramas of renunciation or of loss, a characteristic Jamesian theme relentlessly developed in the fictions of the nineties. "Psychologically, the order [in James's fictions] is from innocence through involvement and responsibility to renunciation, for that is the pattern of Henry James's psychology of experience" (Granville Jones xi). Hence in all three works, a vision of what might have been frames the protagonist's acceptance of what is. Fleda Vetch, Maisie, and the telegraphist, each in different specific terms, must relinquish the possibility of a preferred relationship with the central male figure. Each has, as it were, a vision of escape from all the contingencies of her personal circumstances and yet must at last seek refuge in an alternative relationship based on a community of suffering or, for the telegraphist, on the hard economic fact of her need for support. The principal male characters—Owen Gereth, Sir Claude, Captain Everard—also resemble each other in being young men who are genial and accommodating but also weak. Their weakness is associated with their susceptibility to women, who draw them by sexuality and govern them by stronger wills than their own. (Vanderbank of *The Awkward Age* is another of this company, though he has a more complex inner life than the other three.) Hence the reiterative pattern in these fictions is that the "dark lady," seductive and willful, draws the male character away from the protagonist, who does not, herself, desire power or sex so much as a bond of intelligent sympathy, of shared understanding, with the male character (cf. Elizabeth Allen 123).

In technique these fictions are similar in there being a more overt authorial presence within the works than is felt elsewhere. In *Maisie*, for example, there is a lessening of distance caused by the persona's intermittent exclamations over the rigors of telling the tale from a child's point of view. There are intrusions into Maisie's thoughts. "There was literally an instant in which Maisie fully saw—saw madness and desolation, saw ruin and darkness and death" (*WM* 289–90). And the foreknowledge implicit in this passage is that of the authorial persona, not Maisie. In both *Maisie* and *Cage*, ironic humor depends in part on the discrepancy between the recorded responses of the naïve heroine and a more sophisticated, worldly or sexually aware, voice recording these perceptions. "They were in danger, they were in danger, Captain Everard and Lady Bradeen: it beat every novel in the shop" (*IC* 85). In his chapter on *Poynton*, Kenneth Graham asserts that the authorial presence, a "unity of personal tone," is never entirely dissociated from James's dramatic rendering of his material. "The Jamesian narrative mode is never really one of a totally 'sunk' point of view—within Fleda's 'theatre of consciousness,' say. It is an extraordinary mixture of meditative authorial monologue and dramatized action and dialogue, both of the latter being nevertheless essentially within the former, and never entirely detached from that one presiding, intelligent voice" (Graham 129–30; cf. Philip Greene, 362–63). Outside the fictions, James's "meditative authorial monologue," in his own person in the notebooks, is especially rich and informative in his treatment of *Poynton* and *Maisie*, together with *The Other House*. These early entries, written as James was devising a new technique, provide the fullest, most detailed practical demonstration of his development of a scenario.

Significant moments in James's inception of *Poynton* (*NB* 136–37) indicate that he origir ally conceived of his subject objectively, as a drama centered in "things." A widow, Mrs. Gereth, is dispossessed by law of her home and its furnishings in favor of her son Owen when he inherits his father's estate. Mrs. Gereth's situation is complicated by the fact that Owen's fiancée is a romp and a boor in Mrs. Gereth's esteem—and no doubt in James's as well (*AN* 131)—whereas Poynton has become an aesthetic treasure and an expression of the character of its owners through the elder Gereths' careful amassing and deployment of fine antique furnishings over years. Hence the objective situation that James conceived was a contest for the art treasures of Poynton between Mrs. Gereth, an unwilling victim, and Mona Brigstock, Owen's fiancée, who feels that what belongs to Owen comes with him. The solution that Mrs. Gereth proposes to herself is to find a suitable alternate for Mona. Her candidate is Fleda Vetch, a girl modest in means and accomplishments but whose aesthetic sensibility is, nonetheless, equal to Mrs. Gereth's own. Fleda is a willing worshipper in Mrs. Gereth's aesthetic shrine and is sympathetic to Mrs. Gereth's personal dilemma. But gradually Fleda's sense of fair play and her awakening love for Owen, who is a stupid but decent fellow, qualify her allegiance to Mrs. Gereth. Goaded by Mrs. Gereth and deferred to by Owen, she becomes an unwilling ambassador between the two disputants after Mrs. Gereth "steals" the gems of the Poynton collection and installs them in the dower cottage, Ricks. Thus Fleda emerges as the subjective center through whose consciousness the reader perceives the contest, and the story in turn becomes that of Fleda's divided allegiance between the mother and the son (*NB* 215–18). By the time that James wrote his retrospective preface, therefore, he was most concerned to celebrate Fleda as his heroine, the "free spirit" in whose supersubtle consciousness the drama is played out (*AN* 129–30). To Fleda, Mrs. Gereth in her fanaticism is as discordant a note as Mona in her boorishness. To steer a middle course, therefore, Fleda renounces both Poynton and Owen, who has made his love for her known. She resists the bribe that Mrs. Gereth's confident restoration of the treasures to Poynton entails, and she insists that Owen shall first disengage himself from Mona without Fleda's own intervention, a task beyond his powers. Fleda's posture of detachment is underscored by a disastrous fire at Poynton, which occurs just as she arrives there to select a farewell present from Owen, who is meanwhile honeymooning with Mona.

Hence we see that what began as a comical drama (see Graham 130–31, Wallace 80–88, Nathan), a sort of tug-of-war between Mona's big feet and Mrs. Gereth's sharp tongue, has become something approaching tragedy or, at least, a drama of loss. To preserve her own integrity, Fleda has refused to take an active part in detaching Owen from Mona, and together with Mrs. Gereth she retreats to the dower cottage at last. Moreover, that drama ultimately focuses in Fleda's loss of Owen and of Poynton, not in the trials of the superseded widow. Fleda has herself superseded Mrs. Gereth as protagonist, and the drama has moved inward, to become that of Fleda's divided allegiance and thwarted passion. "Fleda finds herself the mediator of a struggle for possession that functions on several levels, each to some extent corrupt, and all of which work against her own determination to find relationships that are not possessive at all" (See 128). Such evolutions in the making of James's novel obviously multiply the perspectives from which the reader must respond, complicate the tone of the story, and give rise to the questions that have preoccupied critics—above all, the question of how to read the heroine: Is Fleda the admirable "free spirit" that James perceived her to be or an overscrupulous neurotic? Is the fire at the end a melodramatic flourish or an implied comment?

The case for Fleda is represented by Paula Marantz Cohen, who challenges the frequently invoked analogy with Jane Austen's heroines. Fleda has to pay her way: she has no fortune, no real home, no maternal figure to applaud and approve. Thus Fleda must really suffer the consequences of her choice, and this is the "new brand of heroism" that Cohen celebrates. "Fleda's scruples do not pretend to win her the kind of practical benefits that the Jane Austen heroine thought to be her due. They lose Fleda both the husband and the things, a destiny the reverse of Elizabeth Bennet's. But . . . the loss represents neither the failure of a pragmatic philosophy nor the triumph of a philosophy of self-denying social altruism. Instead, the material and conventional loss corresponds to the survival of the self as integral, undiminished, uncompromised—in a word, free'' (Cohen 114). And this, of course, is what James claimed for his heroine, that however unproductive of effects, "only intelligent, not distinctively able" (*AN* 131), she was yet a "free spirit" (*AN* 129–30). Other studies that affirm Fleda's character and attitude include those by Auchard, Alan Bellringer (*Spoils*), Dupee, Greene, Graham, Jule Kaufman, and Wagenknecht (*Novels*). Alwyn Berland speaks for the unconverted in arguing that Fleda is a problematic character because "her renunciation, far from asserting the primacy of human values over 'things,' ends by bringing misery to every single major character in the novel. Her renunciation seems never to have to surmount the imperatives of passion or of strong emotional commitment, and so seems boringly exquisite" (56). Other negative judgments leveled against Fleda are that she is an ethical relativist and a self-deluding visionary, therefore an unreliable interpreter of her experiences (McLean); that she is a sexual phobic imposing a medieval code of honor on herself and others (Stein, "The Method"); that she is legalistic and sophistical in her posture of self-denial and nonintervention (Baym "Fleda Vetch"); and that she is inconsistent, incessantly oscillating between idealism and acquisitiveness (Schneider, *Crystal Cage* 54–55). David Lodge provides an incisive résumé and commentary on the opposed critical camps, weighted toward the negative view of Fleda (5–10). His sentiment is that the positive readings are likely to be intentionalist, endorsing James's own interpretation of his heroine. Out of this context emerges Lodge's own fashionable view that *Poynton* anticipates James's later fiction in "aspir[ing] to the condition of ambiguity" (6). A neatly poised middle view is Charles Palliser's demonstration that "James's attitude toward his heroine is a complex mixture of sympathy and irony" (37). Interpreters generally agree that the catastrophic fire at the end is good theater, but they interpret it variously, in accordance with their sentiments about the novel and characters: Did Mrs. Gereth burn Poynton to prevent Mona's "thumbing 'her' treasures" (Putt 245)? Or did James himself burn Poynton, as a judgment on Fleda, who as "author" of her own fate "promotes a design that entails her own absence" (Kaston 4, 81)? Is it an implicit judgment on Mona's curatorial neglect (Wagenknecht, *Novels* 146–47)? Is it a purification (Auchard 82), the precondition of a new imaginative community, purged of things, between Fleda and Mrs. Gereth (Cohen 115–16)? Or is it James's own "retribution wreaked on a world in which a Fleda Vetch strives to be scrupulously moral but appears foolish or mad, confounds everyone, and cuts a ridiculous figure" (Granville Jones 131)? Or is it simply "enigmatic" (Richards, Introduction to *Spoils* x)?

The overall proportioning of *Maisie* intimates the character of James's amplification of his donnée. The first third of the novel covers about nine years, and the last third, five days. The three final chapters treat the events of a single day. This modification in James's handling of time signals his characteristic turning from an objective situation inward, into the mental activity of the central character, a little girl, as she grows older. Initially, James perceived Maisie, like the inanimate "things" from which *Poynton* developed, as a "bone of contention" (*NB* 127; cf. *AN* 127). Maisie Farange is a "shuttlecock" or a "tennis-ball" (*AN* 140), batted back and forth between her divorced parents in a game for possession, which subsequently becomes a game to divest one's self of a burdensome object. Out of this game Maisie emerges with a new set of surrogate parents, her father's second wife, "Mrs. Beale," and her mother's second husband, Sir Claude, assuming the parental roles of their delinquent spouses, Beale Farange and Ida Farange. But thus, ironically, Maisie brings her stepparents together in a new liaison as the Faranges regroup too, with the other partners left in the background. It was the neat symmetry of these couplings that fascinated James, as well as the opportunity for the play of ironic wit dependent on the discrepancy between the child's perceptions and the adult truths being enacted before her (*AN* 127, 134). This ironic potential is sustained in the finished novel by James's establishing a sort of premise in the opening chapter, that the experiences through which Maisie should pass would leave her unspoiled (*WM* 5; cf. 81, 167).

As his thinking about the novel developed, however, James discovered "the second of the golden threads of [his] *form*" in "the tenderness [Maisie] inspires" (*NB* 238). Her guileless wish to bring together her stepparents is not merely ironic in effect because it is motivated by love, and she inspires tenderness in them, in Sir Claude especially, who will become her admirer and her advocate at the end, so guiding the reader's responses (*WM* 458–70). Gradually, as Maisie grows older and learns more—if not about adult sexual behavior, then about fair play and not being used and keeping one's word and not breaking promises—she is pressed into the need to make choices. On the brink of adolescence and the last day of her novel, Maisie is faced with the same sort of crisis of choice that preoccupies Fleda Vetch through many days. The outer game of shuttlecock has gradually been superseded by an inner buffeting and divisiveness within Maisie's own consciousness, and the pace of the fiction has adjusted downward to the slower tempo of the decision-making process. Reluctantly, Maisie takes leave of Sir Claude, who is enthralled by Mrs. Beale, and disappears in the company of her governess, Mrs. Wix, whom James described to himself in his working notes as an "honest frump," characterized by "old dingy decencies" and an "old-fashioned conscience" (*NB* 237, 257–58), a vignette that resurfaces in the finished novel (e.g., *WM* 454–55). This is not to say that Maisie espouses the moralistic rigidity of Mrs. Wix any more than she does the amiable weakness of Sir Claude. Mrs. Wix is a deus ex machina figure, as Mr. Longdon will be in *The Awkward Age*, to provide an uncontaminated refuge for the heroine after she has defined her own position.

Technically, *Maisie* is a tour de force. The "most delightful difficulty" (*AN* 144) James undertook in this fiction was centering his narrative in a child. "Small children have many more perceptions than they have terms to translate them; their vision is at any moment much richer, their apprehension even constantly stronger, than their prompt, their at all producible, vocabulary" (*AN* 145). Hence

James explains in his preface that he restricted himself to Maisie's range of experience, to "the occasions and connexions of her proximity and her attention," and that he also utilized "Maisie's terms . . . since her simpler conclusions quite depend on them," but that he retained an adult presence: "our own commentary constantly attends and amplifies" (*AN* 145–46). Armstrong describes the effect that James thus achieves: "The narrator's irony calls upon the reader to join Maisie in the hypotheses she projects but at the same time to criticize them and to learn the necessity of suspicion even while appreciating the reasons for her faith. This dialectic inducts the reader into the double motion of belief and doubt" (*Phenomenology* 15). (Armstrong's important phenomenological reading is supplemented and amended by Williams 39–40, 42.) An added complexity is that James undertook to represent a child in the process of maturing over time. Merla Wolk traces how the narrator's modifying distance toward Maisie corroborates "her growing mastery of her situation" (203), and Blackall (in "Moral Geography") illustrates how James uses physical settings and encounters associated with these settings to objectify Maisie's mental evolution in "picture[s] literally present to her" (*WM* 360).

There has been a notable evolution in responses to this work. Earlier commentators debated whether or not Maisie is spoiled or contaminated by her exposure to a corrupt adult world, the majority view being no, and they pondered the related question of what, exactly, Maisie did know. (See bibliographical notes in the Hynes, Blackall, and Smith articles for résumés of critical positions.) Later studies are more concerned with how Maisie knows, with the process or means by which she acquires knowledge. For example, Geoffrey Smith notes, "If precisely what Maisie knows is unclear, *how* she knows is not: she learns by observing behavioral patterns and testing words against actions" (235). Moreover, critics associate this process enacted within the fiction with both the reader's experiences in engaging with the text and the author's practices and attitudes in creating it. Thus Maisie becomes a metaphorical artist or, for the reader, an instigator and guide. The "artist" figure is persistently invoked by Tanner, who sees Maisie, the telegraphist of *Cage*, the *Fount* narrator, and others as figures whose wonder and detachment from the world are preconditions for insight. "For James, the artist figure *had* to remove himself from the world in order to attain to a true vision of the Whole" (Tanner, *Reign* 308). William Nance perceives Maisie as James's own "collaborator in the creation of the novel" (88) and frames his account of the important Boulogne scenes as a "myth of the artist." Nance states: "The mythic French world is Maisie's self-created *fiction* in which she lives for a time, following the blue river of truth to the fullness of knowledge. What she must renounce is *romance*, the insidious world created by pure desire" (101). Wolk associates the question of how the artistic imagination functions with the epistemological questions raised by the novel: "Questioning the sources of knowledge is central to the exercise of the artistic imagination for James, and it is for this subject that the relationship between Maisie and the narrator [the topic of

Wolk's article] has special significance'' (196). Working from the premise that ''for the Jamesian reader, as for the Jamesian heroine [i.e., Maisie], participation in a James novel is a process of initiation into vision'' (168), Juliet Mitchell provides a deft impressionistic reading of the ''glass-mirror-spectacle'' (183) and games imagery of the novel. Another form that such an initiation might take is suggested in Kenny Marotta's argument that Maisie's demands within the novel are consistent with James's own hopes as expressed in his ''Question of Our Speech'' lecture in 1905. ''Maisie asks for fidelity to language—fidelity in the senses both of verbal self-consistency and of consistency between the word and the act; and by calling for it, she makes it possible for anyone who will respond'' (Marotta 502–3). Randall Craig likewise suggests a parallel between the effect Maisie exerts on characters within the fiction and on readers outside it: ''Maisie's development has a concomitant effect on those around her. . . . If readers are to reach an understanding of the novel, they must replicate Maisie's interpretive and linguistic proficiency'' (''Read[ing] the unspoken'' 208–9). (See also Craig's ''Reader-Response Criticism,'' where he further develops his hermeneutic theoretical context, again with reference to *Maisie*.)

*Cage* is one of the few works that James did not mention in his writer's notebooks, possibly because it is in effect a retreatment of the donnée for an earlier story, ''Brooksmith'' (1891). The idea common to both is the exclusion of a humble character from the tenuous relationship to the beau monde that affords each one entertainment and a sense of self-worth. '' 'You continue to see good society, to live with clever, cultivated people: but I fall again into my own class, I shall never see such company—hear such talk—again' '' (*NB* 64). This is the lament, in James's notation of the ''Brooksmith'' *donnée*, of a lady's maid on the death of her kind mistress, but he subsequently developed it around the ''fatal experience'' of a male character, an '' 'intelligent' butler [Brooksmith] present at rare table-talk, rather than that of the more effaced tirewoman'' (*AN* 283). Thereafter the insistent image of the telegraphist's cage in the corner of the local grocery store was to provide a superb vantage point from which to represent a young woman's entrapment, her exclusion from, yet visual access to, the world of privilege. In his preface to *Cage*, James records that his waiting at the small local postal-telegraph office had seemed to him ''to take place in a strong social draught, the stiffest possible breeze of the human comedy. . . . So had grown up for speculation . . . the question of what it might 'mean,' . . . for confined and cramped and yet considerably tutored young officials of either sex to be so free, intellectually, of a range of experience otherwise quite closed to them'' (*AN* 154). In any event, *Cage*, like ''Brooksmith,'' is one of the exceptional fictions in which James scrutinizes class divisions and indicates his awareness of the other nation of the poor and faceless and anonymous. His heroine is nameless because she has in effect no identity (cf. Ward, *Search for Form* 64; see Sicker 78) apart from her role, her function, to receive and transmit the telegrams thrust through the bars by heedless dandies such as Captain Everard.

She has no social identity outside her own class, which she chooses for the present to ignore in the person of her dreary fiancé, Mr. Mudge, a stalwart grocer. Mr. Mudge and a little gray home in Chalk Farm are her fate, postponed. Meanwhile, in Mayfair she still sees things (*IC* 64), and what she sees is the stuff that dreams are made of—Captain Everard, resplendent, genial, Olympian in her esteem, and a gentleman requiring her assistance. Perhaps James's experience of having delved into the intense inner life of Fleda Vetch played some part in the evolution of the later tale, for James perceived Fleda as seeing the "protected error" of the possibility of a relationship between herself and Owen and taking it into the cage within her own breast and cherishing it there (*SP* 130).

Older readings of *Cage* emphasize its social commentary, underscoring James's wide-eyed perception of social inequities and exclusions in contrast to his more characteristic option for the terrain of the novelist of manners. This view places the telegraphist in the company of Hyacinth Robinson and his impoverished benefactors in *The Princess Casamassima*, of Mrs. Wix in her abject economic dependency, and, of course, of Brooksmith. It underscores the pathos of the tale. The social reading calls attention to such passages as the opening paragraphs of chapter five, or this one about the telegraphist and her friend Mrs. Jordan: "Reality, for the poor things they both were, could only be ugliness and obscurity, could never be the escape, the rise" (*IC* 216). L. C. Knights, Morton Dauwen Zabel, and Albert Friend are among those who have developed the darker view of the *nouvelle*. Heath Moon updates and redefines the social theme in arguing that the telegraphist is a would-be saviour of the old order, in the person of Captain Everard. "Both [she and the governess in *Screw*] harbour fantasies of being the object of special recognition, noticed for exemplary dedication, since for both, loyalty to the gentlemanly class is inseparable from romantic school-girlish yearnings" (Moon 33). Nonetheless, as "school-girlish yearnings" intimates, *Cage* is another of James's strange alloys. Perceiving the company the telegraphist keeps in the New York Edition, her tale sandwiched in with those of precocious children such as Morgan Moreen of *The Pupil* and Maisie, we are alerted once more to the ironies evoked by the discrepancies between a naïve vision and a more objective one. Childlike but not a child, "Mrs. Wix compensates for ugliness and poverty by romance" (Mitchell 186), and so does the telegraphist. Thus she is fair game for an ironic narrator. In emphasizing satirical aspects, E. Duncan Aswell and Charles Thomas Samuels (150–54) are most emphatic; see also J. A. Ward (*Search for Form*) and Blackall ("*In The Cage*"). Ralf Norrman (in *Techniques of Ambiguity*) provides a good general account of the *nouvelle*, including a survey of criticism to 1977. As the telegraphist's own stock has depreciated, new attention has been paid to Mr. Mudge, neglected until Joel Salzberg identified him as the telegraphist's "redemptive fate." Salzberg dignifies Mudge as "the vehicle by which his fiancée is redeemed from her own solipsistic imagination, as well as from demeaning poverty'' (63), a sympathetic reading that has since been reaffirmed by both Stuart Hutchinson and Wagenknecht (*Tales*).

The telegraphist has also been perceived as being an artist figure, who imaginatively integrates and transforms snippets of life outside the cage as these reach her in the telegrams she processes and in Everard's desultory conversations. Lacking real knowledge of Everard and his world, she invents a self-gratifying vision in which she can live imaginatively. Tanner takes her most seriously as the "Jamesian artist, though seen in comic and pathetic perspective" (*Reign* 313). For Sicker she is a hubristic "artist of life," "James' vision of the artistic imagination gone wild" (80–81). And Aswell invokes the metaphor of the artist to argue that the telegraphist is self-deluded, naïve, and inferior, her "attempts to impose 'artistic' control" on the lives of other characters thus doomed to failure (376). In short, she becomes, in his reading, the *artiste manqué*. Naomi Schor's perception of the telegraphist as an "interpretant" creating her own fiction is the "artist" thesis in a new guise: the girl's interpretation "is a 'creative' rather than critical activity; the young woman is not content merely to encode and decode, rather she delights in filling in the gaps, piecing together the fragments, in short, adding something of her own to the faulty, often trivial texts at hand. . . . In no other fiction of interpretation . . . [that Schor considers] is interpretation more closely linked to the production of the tale" (171). Schor's treatment of *Cage* as an allegory of reading represents a new direction in the treatment of this work.

## FIRST-PERSON NARRATORS: *THE TURN OF THE SCREW* AND *THE SACRED FOUNT*

Critical controversies focus and converge on these two tales, together with "The Figure in the Carpet" (1896), most obviously because they are first-person narratives. Thus any reader dissatisfied with the narrator's account can postulate the narrator as being unreliable or limited and can proceed, from the text, to invent an alternative set of hypotheses to account for the data provided. To the believers, the narrator is authoritative, an observer and agent of transmission of an objective reality, literal or figurative, which overtly exists within the tale, though the data available may be incomplete or only partially understood by the narrator or in any case unverifiable according to any external norm provided the reader. This stance produces readings of *Screw* as a supernatural tale and takes the narrating governess at her own assessment, as a would-be protector or "saviour" of the children in her charge at Bly, an isolated country house, children who are threatened by evil specters. *The Fount* becomes the story of an acute and compassionate observer who is moved, by the unexplained depletions and flourishings of persons he contemplates at a weekend house party at Newmarch, to form an imaginative structure to account for these changes. According to his hypothesis of "the sacred fount," the youthful (Mrs. Brissenden) or clever

(Gilbert Long) people are in effect vampires, consuming the essence of those counterparts who appear to be aging (Guy Brissenden) or mentally depleted (May Server). Thus like an artist, perhaps a surrogate for James as author, the narrator interprets and imposes form on the social data available to him and, in so doing, emulates his creator. Counterarguments and readings arise from those unbelievers who ponder the personal qualities and attributes of the narrator characters. Under scrutiny, both are anonymous. Both are peripheral within the societies they inhabit, she separated by class and role, he by his observer's stance. Both are self-dramatizing in their assumed roles of protector and interpreter, and both are solicitous of those whom they appear to victimize. Obsessive in their need to be right, both are manipulative in their interpretation of data. They "see" things they do not look at. They overinterpret, dismiss, or arbitrarily complete the remarks of other characters, and they are committed to the production of a text that attests to and justifies their own behavior. From this vantage point, the governess appears to be a hysteric, insecure in her first job and perhaps in love with her employer; she hallucinates the ghosts out of her own insecurities and her desire to perform heroically. It is she and not the ghosts whom the children have to fear. Her male counterpart emerges as a madman or *artiste manqué* or comic butt of the author's ironic joke, at best an object of authorial self-parody, the fabricating voyeuristic consciousness gone wild. Feminist critics might well ponder the respective fates of these two characters, the governess having emerged in a critical consensus as a candidate for psychoanalysis and her male counterpart commonly celebrated as an authorial surrogate, engaging in James's own art of imaginative fabrication. Do matters of gender, the characters' sexual identities, their relative status in the social hierarchy, and their power relative to that status affect the authority with which these characters address the reader? In any case, visited with such antithetical options, or simply under the influence of deconstructionist theory, the critical frontier nowadays asserts that these works are irreconcilably ambiguous, that they dramatize an aporia, or that "[James's] values are positively all blanks" (*AN* 177); they are structured around an absence or an emptiness.[3]

Bruce Robbins, in a helpful résumé of such views relative to the *Screw*, remarks: "The new consensus is succinctly put by Allon White in *The Uses of Obscurity*: 'the important thing is surely the difficulty of ever knowing whether the governess is deluded, not that she is or is not deluded—it is the "undecidability" of the text which operates so powerfully to make it so unsettling' (131). Undecidability, obscurity, uncertainty, indeterminacy—these terms seem to restore the authority of James's blankness by announcing a definitive break with the naive passion for single interpretation" (193). Moreover, in the eyes of many contemporary critics, the narrative is understood to comment self-reflexively on its own strategies. For example, "By constantly undermining and restoring his narrator's credibility, James transforms a narrative which is potentially either a ghost story or a mystery tale about a demented governess into a very subtle fiction about the process of fiction itself" (Cook and Corrigan 65). See Kevin

Murphy's "Unfixable Text" for a similar argument on authorial strategy, or Dieter Freundlieb for the contrasting view that indeterminacy originates in the disparate "knowledge frames" of readers rather than in authorial strategies. Brooke-Rose exhaustively demonstrates the "non-methodology" and multilayered "misreadings" (Part 1, 292) of those traditional readings of *Screw* collected by Gerald Willen and Robert Kimbrough, as a preliminary to her own analysis of the tale "as an unusually perfect example of what Todorov (1970) calls the Pure Fantastic, that is, a narrative in which the ambiguity of natural and supernatural explanation is preserved throughout and beyond the text, the two hypotheses running parallel, equivalent and undecidable" (Part 3, 517 n.). The idea that the tale thematizes hesitation and thus induces hesitancy in the reader's responses to it is subtly argued within two frames of reference, intellectual history and evolving critical theory, by Tobin Siebers.

Countermovements within the vast critical literature restore the *Screw* to its Victorian context and examine its imaginative links with *Jane Eyre*. For example, Elliot Schrero, in responding to "deconstructive or ironic readings," as illustrated in Rimmon and Felman, postulates that "James meant to show the hapless case of two abandoned orphans, not the fate of reading," an objective rendered clear when the modern reader is aware of certain "cultural allegiances [that] controlled the play of textual meaning" for James's contemporaries (261). Schrero elucidates Victorian assumptions as to the corruption of servants, the moral duties of governesses (as parental surrogates), and the horror of sexual misconduct. In a more hypothetical but provocative reading, Jane Nardin suggests that the evil atmosphere omnipresent in the tale may be traced not only to demons and neuroses but also to "cruel and destructive pressures of Victorian society, with its restrictive code of sexual morality and its strong sense of class consciousness, upon a group of basically sane and decent individuals" (132). For other social perspectives on the tale, see studies by Heath Moon, Rowe (*Theoretical Dimensions*, e.g., 123–24), and Robbins (195–97). The inherence of *Jane Eyre* in *Screw*, persuasively argued by E. A. Sheppard and Adeline Tintner ("Henry James's Use of 'Jane Eyre' "), is deftly updated by Linda Kauffman in her perception of Miss Jessel (one of the ghosts) as the governess's "dark double," the Bertha in her attic (181–82).

The *Fount* is an intellectual playground for addicted Jamesians and, more recently, an exemplary text for theorists. An enumeration of disparate approaches may suggest the speculative energy that has been lavished on this work. Regarding its origins in a vampirish donnée, Edel places it within the canon as one of James's recurrent treatments of "sex as a depleting force" ("Introductory Essay" xxv–xxix; cf. "Introduction to *SF*" 9–11). Regarding its vampire theme within a literary continuum, E. A. Sklepowich sees it as "socializ[ing] the Gothic," and its "gossipy" narrator as an "urbane version" of the Gothic villain, stalking reputations. "The serene Newmarch is a kind of haunted house in which the pursuit is not by mad monks and monsters but by Dame Rumor, here found in the person of the ambiguous narrator" (Sklepowich, "Gossip" 112–13). Perceived within an American literary context, the *Fount* illustrates an evolutionary sophistication, since Hawthorne, in "the writer's approach to matters of psychic vampirism" (Banta, *Henry James and the Occult* 103). Indeed, the novel looks back to Hawthorne and may be read as a thematic analogue to *The Blithedale Romance* (Beebe, Babiiha), the governing idea in both works being "the immanence (and imminence) of death in life" as represented in a pervasive imagery of masks and veils (Keyser 110, 106). But the *Fount* also looks forward to the twentieth-century novel in its themes of malaise, alienation, and salvation through art (Isle 232) and to the "game-like fictions of Sarraute, Beckett, and Robbe-Grillet. . . . In *The Sacred Fount* there are some of the elements found in the modern experimental novel: an anonymous narrator whose reliability gradually erodes; an intricate, intellectual construct created to order the social microcosm; glimpses of an almost entropic world; elliptical conversations; and a jigsaw-puzzle plot" (Sklepowich, "Gossip" 113). Most specifically, James's novel has been associated with Nathalie Sarraute's *nouveau roman*, *Portrait d'un inconnu* (Bouraoui). In both works, "the novel form is used to question and 'contest' the novel itself, to write 'the novel of a novel that is not written, that cannot be written'—'to destroy it under our eyes while seeming to build it.' The aims and the method adopted in the two novels seem to be the same, if the unknown and unnamed protagonist of *Portrait d'un inconnu* too spies on the lives of others and tries to find their possible 'law,' if he too is puzzled and baffled by their actions and relations, by the role he can play in them, if he resorts as well to half sentences and *sous-conversation*, endlessly connecting and achieving nothing" (Perosa, quoting Sartre's preface to Sarraute's *Portrait*, *Experimental Novel* 103).

James's work differs, however, in having been persistently identified with an aesthetic experience. The *Fount* narrator is perceived not merely as a social spy and a drawing-room detective but also, in the views of many readers, as a figure of the artist, whether he be understood as a type of the Jamesian artist (Krook; Tanner, "Henry James's Subjective Adventure"; Lebowitz; Weinstein), as the object of authorial self-parody (Follett was first to express this view, but see especially Holland's version of ironic self-scrutiny), or as the *artiste manqué* (e.g., Ranald; Blackall, *Jamesian Ambiguity*, ch. 4; Richards, "*The Ambassadors*"). Yet Kappeler invites a rethinking of the figure "from artist to critic." Of the narrator as creator of the theory of the sacred fount, she wrote: "The 'death' of the creative artist—the completion of his work—leaves him in the unprivileged position of a reader, which thus is, strictly speaking, the end of his *être artiste*; but we have also shown him to be, *qua* artist, some kind of a model critic. . . . It is indeed curious that the narrator should not be acknowledged for his interpretative faculties by his *confrères*" (158–59). Yet perhaps he has: "I agree with Bellringer [in "*The Sacred Fount*"] that James's observer arrives at 'truth' rather than delusion and that decency and the special nature of his knowledge keep him from making embarrassing disclosures" (Gargano, "James's *The Sacred Fount*" 49). Central to the work, as it is to criticism of the work, is the strange portrait of "The Man with the Mask," which the narrator and his fellow guests contemplate and discuss in chapter 4. Does it represent the theme of appearance and reality (Edel, "Introductory Essay" xvi–xx) or that of life and death, as the characters themselves speculate? "May [it] suggest *all* of the characters as their lives interwine in the writer's [i.e., the narrator's] imagination" (Bouraoui 98)? Or, as Susan Winnett suggests (221–22), does it thematize whatever reading commentators devise to resolve the exegetical problems that the book poses? Doesn't it, rather, as she goes on to argue, self-reflexively reiterate and mirror the irresolvable quest enacted within the fiction? "There is no issue in the novel represented in the painting except that of undecidability determined by the structure of the novel and capable of undermining the closure of any thematic argument" (Winnett 222; cf. Rimmon 223–26).

## THE DRAMATIC NOVELS: *THE OTHER HOUSE* AND *THE AWKWARD AGE*

Juxtaposed, *The Other House* (1896) and *The Awkward Age* (1899) frame the experimental period in the sense that they reveal the immense distance James traversed technically within these few years. *The Other House* marks the transition from playwriting to the writing of dramatic fiction in the most rudimentary, explicit way. Adapted from a play scenario (*OH* xi), this novel is obviously structured in three acts. Its action occurs on a highly visualized stage set, Tony Bream's modern mansion and Mrs. Beever's Victorian counterpart being opposed as "other houses" to each other, the two separated by a stream in which the climactic murder of Tony's daughter, Effie, will occur. The characters, with the sole exception of Rose Armiger, the murderess, lack the roundness that one associates with even James's supporting characters, Mrs. Wix, say, or the sturdy Mr. Mudge. The exposition is so largely conveyed through dialogue that James subsequently converted the novel into a stage play with relatively little change. (The drama has been published by Edel in *CP*; the original scenario is lost [*OH* xi].) And finally, its actual matter is the most melodramatic James ever rendered, a circumstance appropriate to its being written for a popular weekly, the *Illustrated London News*. James omitted it from the New York Edition. Perhaps the exceptional praise that Tanner accords this work in his introduction to James for the general reader implicitly underscores the popular and accessible aspects of the novel: "It is an unusual—and powerful—work in the James canon. For in it he presents us with an almost unmitigatedly evil female figure . . . Rose Armiger, who goes far beyond the other women whose complex motivations result in destruction (Christina Light, Madame Merle, Kate Croy). She not only plots and cheats and lies and deceives; she murders a child and then tries to fix the blame on the Good Heroine" (*Henry James: The Writer and His Work* 82).

Originally entitled "The Promise," this novel recounts the consequences, as it were, of a mother's curse. Tony's wife, Julia, was so unhappy in her relationship to her own stepmother that on her deathbed she elicits a vow from her husband not to remarry during the lifetime of their child. Thereafter, Tony Bream is loved by two women, Rose Armiger and Jean Martle, despite their both having other suitors, Dennis Vidal and Paul Beever, respectively. Rose, the "Bad Heroine," perceives the "Good Heroine" (*NB* 140), Jean Martle, as a rival, and Tony's daughter, Effie, as an obstacle. Distrait, Rose at last murders the child and attempts to fix the blame on Jean, in order to bring about her own union with Tony. The novel ends with Rose, her guilt discovered, being led away by Dennis Vidal, who now views her with horror. Jean and Tony are left to live happily ever after, if such is imaginable.

Despite its obvious melodrama, *The Other House* is an interesting work for the student of James because its bold strokes expose the substratum of the fully realized fictions. Here character types, motivations, and situations are less subtly veiled, and certain undigested elements in the language and crafting of the novel tell us something about James's fusive imagination. The rather arbitrary posing of the "other" houses against one another, for instance, crudely approximates the subtler opposition of Buckingham Crescent and Beccles in *The Awkward Age* as projections of the owners' respective life-styles and value systems. (Compare, for example, *OH* ch. 13 with *AA* ch. 24.) Julia Bream is a rudimentary form of those characters who inhabit the works from which they are absent— such as Jeffrey Aspern, Maud-Evelyn, and Acton Hague of "The Altar of the Dead." Their hovering presence illustrates one of the ways in which James's sense of the past operates. Julia Bream's deathbed wish in a sense predetermines the actions of the characters present on stage. The deceased Lady Julia of *The Awkward Age* is a much subtler manifestation of such a presence, the symbol in Mr. Longdon's mind, and Vanderbank's, of all that is missing in the modern salon world of Mrs. Brookenham. It is toward the idea of Lady Julia, unknown to herself, that Nanda Brookenham gropes in her attempt to define an authentic self. Isle generalizes other such instances in observing that "most of the characters [in *OH*] are . . . Jamesian types; they reflect his central preoccupations and reappear in various mutations in later novels. It is enlightening to study the early forms of figures like Sir Claude . . . , Vanderbank . . . , or even Merton Densher and Kate Croy'' (45, 48–51; cf. Putt 309–12).

Rose Armiger is, however, a special case. J. A. Ward, whose theme is James's pervasive consciousness of evil, notes a change in James's attitude in his treatment of her: ''James continues to convey the horror of evil, and yet divests the evildoer of the simple blackness that often takes the place of realistic characterization in the early works. . . . Rose's tremendous passion and vitality, her grace and style are inseparable from her cruelty. James treats Rose's evil as a psychologist rather than a moralist, and in doing so makes her heinous crime believable'' (*Imagination* 4). This intermixture of spiritual force and destructive potential implies a source, which Leon Edel was first to observe, in Rose's association for James with the actress Elizabeth Robins and, through Robins, with the Ibsen heroines, especially Hedda Gabler, whom Robins popularized in England in the eighties and nineties (*OH*, intro., part v; cf. Egan 59–64 [London]). Thus, through the overt linkage of Rose Armiger with the Ibsen heroines, we discern one imaginative source for the dark ladies of James's late fiction, another being the Greek tragic heroines—Medusa perhaps, who is mentioned in the text, but surely also Medea, the murderess of children. Daniel Lerner and Oscar Cargill have developed the Grecian connection with reference to plot devices and to character prototypes, among them the choral characters of Dr. Ramage and Mrs. Beever ("Grecian Urn"; cf. Cargill 209–12). The Ramage/ Beever functionary reemerges in a subtilized form in such hypothetical witnesses as the "ingenious observer" or the "attentive spectator" invoked in *The Awkward Age*, and Mrs. Beever in the more integral character of Mr. Longdon.

Criticism of this work is rather heterogeneous and sparse. For an exhaustive résumé touching on many of the salient issues, see Edel's introduction, later incorporated into *The Treacherous Years*. Muriel Shine's treatment of the child Effie as a scapegoat figure used metaphorically to externalize the tensions between the Good and Bad Heroines illuminates the subtler aspects of the language of the novel (78–81), and Thelma Shinn, in her compelling exploration of the "mythic" substructure of the novel, goes still further in symbolizing Effie as innocence, art, and the artist. Gerard Sweeney explains the "failure" of the novel as a consequence of James's modifications of his donnée materials in the course of writing. "These changes involve the coupling of a revised center with the original ending" (Sweeney 216) and consequent diminution of the character of Mrs. Beever (cf. Isle, 46–47, 64–66). Sweeney's association of Mrs. Beever with Mrs. Gereth of *Poynton* affords another interesting instance of the imaginative overlapping characteristic, especially, of these fictions of the nineties.

*The Awkward Age* is a library in one volume. Lacking a designated central consciousness, it so completely develops the point of view of several pivotal figures, their individual "cases" (*AN* 105), that it changes character read from their respective angles of vision. James began with Mrs. Brookenham and with the dilemma of the modern fast-set mother confronted with the need to integrate her adolescent daughter (of an awkward age or born into one) into life "downstairs." So frequently right about his own achievement, James celebrated "Mrs. Brook" as "the best thing I've ever done" (*LHJ* I, 333). She is one of his greatest characters, the consummate actress, a social chameleon, though less accessible to the reader than an Isabel Archer or a Maggie Verver because of James's astringently dramatic technique of presentation. Mrs. Brook is accessible, except for brief descriptions of dress and manner, mainly through her words and deeds, which are veils in themselves. The opposite side of the mother's problem of assimilation is, of course, the daughter's feelings and fate at being assimilated into a decadent and artificial salon world. The novel ends, characteristically, with Nanda Brookenham's taking leave of her mother's sphere in an attempt to realize her own identity in the anachronistic refuge of lost values and spiritual refinements that Mr. Longdon offers her in a formal adoption. Longdon once loved Nanda's grandmother Lady Julia and discerns her reflection (not her essence) in Nanda. Hence he is the natural antagonist of Mrs. Brookenham, opposing her risqué wit and social opportunism with moral reflectiveness and the ideal of a harmonious and peaceful life-style, symbolic of a lost Edenic past. Between them in type and moral sensibility stands Vanderbank, who, though undesignated, is de facto the central consciousness of the novel because he is the character made to choose. On Van's choice depends not only his own but also Nanda's fate, for loving Van, she will follow him where he leads, though herself a "Gainsborough" type (AA 120–21) with a compromising infusion of modern manners. (For a particularly sensitive reading of Nanda's plight, see Krook.) While Nanda, in Longdon's presence, belatedly awakens to her un-realized self, Van labors to realize his better self. He is lured to this test by Longdon's offer to dower Nanda, should Van choose her and relinquish his place at her mother's right hand. Meanwhile, in the salon, Vanderbank performs as Apollo (AA 105) to Mrs. Brookenham's moon (AA 427), for she draws young men about her as the moon draws the tides (AA 103). A social magnet, Mrs. Brook exercises a submerged lure of sexuality transformed into words, and her being identified with Diana is a half truth, like Madame de Vionnet's pink parasol. All of the characters in The Awkward Age can be grouped according to these paradigms of the new and the old, the superficial and the genuine, the brilliant and the moral, all of them in some degree divided selves, except for the Brook-enhams' son Harold and a décolletée hostess, Tishy Grendon, who represent the naked extremes of modernism. (For a fine, multifaceted perspective on the novel, see J. A. Ward, Imagination.)

James assists the reader to perceive these interacting perspectives at play by naming the separate books of the novel for ten characters, each of whose presence or point of view or life-style predominates at that moment as it is focused in a given social occasion, scenically presented. He describes this technique in a famous passage in his preface: "I drew on a sheet of paper . . . the neat figure of a circle consisting of a number of small rounds disposed at equal distance about a central object. The central object was my situation, my subject in itself, to which the thing would owe its title, and the small rounds represented so many distinct lamps, as I liked to call them, the function of each of which would be to light with all due intensity one of its aspects" (AN 110; cf. 116). James's comment has caused interpreters to scrutinize the architectonic form of the novel as the expression of its content. How may the many interpretive "lamps" of discriminated social occasions and characters be understood to illuminate the central subject of "the awkward age"? Eben Bass pioneered this topic in his analysis of the schematic structure of the novel, and Walter Isle offers an elab-orated treatment of structure in Experiments in Form (see esp. 176–78, 184–93). Many interpretive possibilities depend on how the reader interrelates these narrative blocks; for example, Daniel Mark Fogel's delineation of the structural pattern of the novel as a Hegelian spiral with a descending movement is enhanced by his reading of the architecture. "Nanda," the final book, "returns upon the first ["Lady Julia"] at a different level, so that the novel is framed by Lady Julia's evocations [as the standard of feminine grace and propriety according to which the masculinized modern woman will be found wanting] and by a vision of Nanda as preeminently Lady Julia's granddaughter" (Fogel, *Henry James and the Structure* 18–19). Arnold Davidson demonstrates other "calculated contrasts" around which James structures subsections of his narrative and identifies certain "reading clues" whereby James indirectly assists the reader to interpret what is seemingly objectively rendered. Francis Gillen goes furthest in this direction, showing how even in this novel, James's most dramatic, the author enters into his fiction and controls the reader's responses, thus belying his own theoretical postulate of strictly scenic presentation.

In his preface, James also calls attention to the other experimental objective that he fixed on in *The Awkward Age*, his attempt to write a novel in which dialogue would largely bear the burden of exposition. His ideal was "really constructive dialogue, dialogue organic and dramatic, speaking for itself, representing and embodying substance and form" (*AN* 106). James began with a popular model in the *roman dialogué* as written by French contemporaries "Gyp" and Henri Laveden (*AN* 106–8), but characteristically he diverged from Gyp's frivolity, producing a dialogue that is stylized, abstract, allusive, and often opaque, in keeping with the evolving late style. Thus the language of *The Awkward Age* is a fascination for modern theorists preoccupied with James's style, with his modes of expressing but also withholding meaning. An earlier instance is H. K. Girling's fine essay on the meanings of "wonder" and "beauty" as created by their contexts. "James seeks to exploit the ambiguity of such words, particularly their ambiguity in fluent conversations, where in certain situations, polite and 'empty' phrases, or familiar and hard-worked colloquialisms may be filled with subtleties of meaning and depths of pathos for those who can decode them" (Girling, " 'Wonder' and 'Beauty' " 372). For Tzvetan Todorov, *The Awkward Age* marks a moment in the history of the novel for its "study of language through the use of language." "I would compare it," he remarks, "to the great novels which follow it and which our modern mind holds in much more reverence, for the fact that it explores thoroughly a path opened by language but unknown to literature—that it pursues this exploration further than had ever been done before, or than has been done since. *The Awkward Age* is an exemplary book in that it represents—rather than tells about—the obliquity of language and the uncertainty of the world" ("Verbal Age" 371). Stuart Culver designates the topic of the novel as a question of "conversational ethics." The Late Victorians' "Continental interest in talk for its own sake," as illustrated here in Mrs. Brookenham's salon, "would appear to compromise British moral philosophy as James has described it, which locates the individual's intrinsic value in what lies behind his verbal self-representation, not in that representation alone." Thus "the moral demand for reserve and restraint and the aesthetic interest in free exchange (i.e., the play of forms for their own sake)" are set at odds when the figure of the "pure young virgin" enters the adult drawing room (Culver, "Censorship" 370–73). Culver uses this formulation of the "awkwardness" of *The Awkward Age* as the occasion for a response to Todorov's treatment of the language of the novel: "This reading ultimately

rests on . . . the [Continental] belief that appearances and formal surfaces are
what is finally essential'' (''Censorship'' 376). ''Speeches [quoting Todorov]
'do not *evoke* events external to themselves; they *are* events' '' (''Censorship''
377). Culver observes further that for Bersani (''Jamesian Lie''), as for Todorov,
''Jamesian talk . . . is no longer tied to external criteria of truth such as reference
or intention, but is, rather, constitutive of that truth'' (''Censorship'' 386).

   *The Awkward Age* is a more human and humane novel than the scrutiny of
its innovative technique alone would suggest. In its articulated display of diverse
modes of human expression and response it is in effect James's *Vanity Fair* and
may remind us of his apprenticeship in the Victorian era. From the sublime in
Nanda and the brilliant in Mrs. Brook, it arrives at the ridiculous in such minor
characters as Little Aggie and Tishy Grendon, who are the comical caricatures
of the other two. It is Thackerayean in its merger of laughter and pain, frivolity
and judgment. Sklepowich is particularly sensitive to this balance in his account
of the games its characters play: ''The novel's ambiguous statement about the
morality of manners arises primarily from the confrontation between Longdon's
and Mrs. Brook's opposing attitudes to social gamesplaying. Longdon, the gra-
cious ghost of a former London, . . . functions as a moral norm in a world where
marriage has become both business and game and friendship a meaningless
formality'' (''Gilded Bondage'' 188–89). *The Awkward Age* is also Thackerayean
in its rendering of society as a spectacle and an entertainment. ''The social entity
is more literally the hero than in any of the novels,'' Dupee remarks (*Henry
James* 197 [1951]), and he celebrates this novel as ''the most elaborate expression
of James's preoccupations in the '90's,'' as ''one of his masterpieces, and clearly
the chief work of its period'' (196).[4]

## NOTES

   1. This chapter deals with the principal fictions of the experimental period, which are
listed in the order in which they were written, with dates of first book publication in
parentheses: *The Spoils of Poynton* (1897), *The Other House* (1896), *What Maisie Knew*
(1897), *The Turn of the Screw* (published with another *nouvelle, Covering End*, in *The
Two Magics*, 1898), *In the Cage* (1898), *The Awkward Age* (1899), and *The Sacred
Fount* (1901). All these works, except *The Other House* and *The Sacred Fount*, were
reprinted (with revisions) in the selective New York Edition of James's works (1907–9),
together with his prefatory comments. Short stories written during these years were first
published in book form in these collections: *Embarrassments* (1896), *The Soft Side* (1900),
and *The Better Sort* (1903). The texts of the stories as they first appeared in book form
have been reprinted, together with introductory remarks and data on original magazine
publication, in *The Complete Tales of Henry James*, ed. Leon Edel, volumes 9–11. James
revised fifteen of the short stories written from 1896 to 1901 for the New York Edition,
among the best known or most highly regarded of these being ''The Figure in the Carpet,''
'' 'Europe,' '' ''Paste,'' ''The Real Right Thing,'' ''Miss Gunton of Poughkeepsie,''
and ''The Beldonald Holbein.''
   2. Books devoted exclusively to James's fictions of the nineties are Joseph Wiesen-

farth's *Henry James and the Dramatic Analogy* (1963) and Walter Isle's *Experiments in Form* (1968). Michael Egan, in *Henry James: The Ibsen Years* (1972), mentions all the principal works except *In the Cage* and treats *Other House*, *Spoils*, and *The Turn of the Screw* at some length. Wiesenfarth and Egan develop the theatrical analogy. Egan argues for Ibsen's influence on the scenic design, atmosphere, themes, and characters of James's fictions after 1895, and especially for James's "gradual assimilation of Ibsen's symbolic manner" (29; cf. 67–70 [London]). Wiesenfarth develops the theatrical analogy with specific reference to the qualities of intensity, economy, and objectivity, qualities that James associated with the drama and attempted to incorporate into the fictions. He identifies those critics most concerned with "the dramatic nature of James's novels" before his own study (xii) and includes a selective bibliography of materials of the 1920s–1960s pertinent to the four works he treats (*Spoils*, *Maisie*, *Awkward Age*, and *Sacred Fount*). To those he mentions should be added Ronald Peacock's fine perspective essay in *The Poet in the Theatre*. In a broader-based study, Isle prefaces his exegetical chapters on the five novels of the nineties with two important general chapters, the one defining their experimental character as being illustrative of a move from the Victorian toward the modern novel and the other placing them within the context of James's theatrical writing during the early nineties. Isle examines experimental aspects with reference to character, structure, and themes. Joseph Warren Beach, in his seminal, pioneering study of *The Method of Henry James* (1918; 2d ed. 1954), provides a descriptive (in part 1) and evolutionary (in part 2) account of all the nineties fictions. S. Gorley Putt's *Henry James: A Reader's Guide* (1966) includes all the novels and stories, grouped in discursive essays according to salient themes. Oscar Cargill, in *The Novels of Henry James* (1961), and Edward Wagenknecht, in *The Novels of Henry James* (1983), both include wide surveys of pertinent secondary materials, together with personal responses and commentary. Wagenknecht's companion books on the *Novels* and the *Tales* (1984) are the best single source for an overview on multiple aspects of the fictions, including origins, sources, publication data, plot, structure, and a generous discussion of individual characters. Leon Edel, in the *Treacherous Years* (1969, 1977, 1985) section of his authoritative biography of James, provides the personal, social, and cultural context within which these works were produced, together with substantial interpretive commentary on individual works. General collections of essays that include nineties fictions are Tony Tanner's *Henry James: Modern Judgements* (1970); John Goode's *The Air of Reality* (1972); Lyall H. Powers' *Henry James's Major Novels* (1973); and James W. Gargano's *Critical Essays on Henry James: The Late Novels* (1987), which includes contemporary reviews and comments.

3. There are two notable book-length studies of *The Turn of the Screw*, one by Thomas Mabry Cranfill and Robert Lanier Clark, Jr., arguing for a "nonapparitionist" reading of the tale (i.e., the governess hallucinates the ghosts), and one by E. A. Sheppard, calling for an "apparitionist" reading (there are real ghosts in the tale). The Cranfill/Clark volume has an excellent bibliography of materials up to 1965. Elizabeth Sheppard's volume is especially interesting for its account of contextual materials, including James's knowledge of contemporary developments in psychical research, his place in the "tradition" of the ghostly tale, and the association of *The Turn of the Screw* with *Jane Eyre*. Though the apparitionist reading, which of course works to validate the governess, is now commonly discounted, it has been updated trenchantly and energetically, at times hilariously, by Wagenknecht (*Tales* 1984). Collections of essays are Gerald Willen's *Casebook* (1960), which includes the last revised version of Edmund Wilson's influential

Freudian essay "The Ambiguity of Henry James"; and a Norton Critical Edition, edited by Robert Kimbrough (1966), which includes an enumeration and comment on the principal textual variants among editions and an annotated bibliography of still other studies of the tale. Taken together, these volumes offer a generous selection of disparate views and important critics, Edel, Heilman, et al. to 1965. James's own most important comments on the tale are to be found in *NB* 178–79, 299; *HJL* IV, 84, 86, 88, 251; and the author's preface, *NY* XII.

Exclusion of *The Sacred Fount* from the New York Edition results in its having no author's preface. James's own most sustained comment on the novel is to be found in a letter in response to Mrs. Humphry Ward's perplexities as to his intention (*HJL* IV, 185–86). For consideration of James's letter, see Leon Edel, "An Introductory Essay," xxx–xxxi, and "Introduction" to *The Sacred Fount*, 9, 14; Jean Frantz Blackall, *Jamesian Ambiguity*, 68, 144–52; and James Gargano, "James's *The Sacred Fount*," 50–53, 57–58. There are also two brief passages in James's notebooks that clearly establish the vampirish donnée (*NB* 150–51, 275). For a generous citation and commentary on secondary materials from a traditional versus a modernist point of view, compare Wagenknecht (*Novels*, to 1983) and Blackall (*Jamesian Ambiguity*, to 1965) with Kappeler, who argues from the premise that "the general secondary literature . . . [to 1980] lacks method and discipline" (198). Martha Banta *(Henry James and the Occult)* also provides copious citation and discussion of secondary materials pertaining to both *The Turn of the Screw* and *The Sacred Fount* (to 1972).

4. For a counterview, and a formulation of some of the problematic issues that the novel poses for many readers, see Schneider's article, which is prefaced by an enumeration of critical responses up to 1978.

Two notable books on *The Turn of the Screw* have appeared since the above essay was completed. Peter G. Beidler's *Ghosts* reaffirms the apparitionist reading on the ground of contextual research into nineteenth-century attitudes. Beidler argues that in the later part of the century, ghosts were taken seriously even by sophisticated readers and, moreover, that James, in his portrayal of the ghosts and the children, was aware of documented accounts of demonic possession. Terry Heller reiterates the "true ambiguity" of James's work, drawing on Lacanian psychoanalytic theory and the reader-response theory of Wolfgang Iser. His exemplary introductory text provides a succinct, lucid overview of critical responses to *Screw* from 1898 into the 1980s.

Alfred Habegger offers another overview of the fictions of the nineties (*Henry James and the "Woman Business"* 233–35), oriented to the thesis that James, throughout his career, appropriated and rewrote American women's popular fiction of the midcentury. Previously unrecorded contemporary periodical reviews of five experimental fictions (*What Maisie Knew, In the Cage, The Turn of the Screw, The Awkward Age,* and *The Sacred Fount*) are identified and quoted at length by Arthur Sherbo in "Still More on James" (101–8). Sharon Cameron discusses passages from *Maisie* in an important book on James's representation of consciousness and includes a briefer treatment of *Fount: "The Sacred Fount* fulfills the ultimate Jamesian fantasy of the omnipotence and omnipresence of thinking or consciousness" (161).

The author thanks Lee A. Talley most warmly for her painstaking labor in the preparation of this chapter.

# 9
# The Later Fiction

*Virginia C. Fowler*

In October of what he referred to as the "monstrously numbered" new century (*HJL* IV, 128), Henry James responded to a letter from his friend W. Morton Fullerton with the following description of his own life: "The port from which I set out was, I think, that of the *essential loneliness of my life*—and it seems to me to be the port also, in sooth to which my course again finally directs itself! This loneliness (since I mention it!)—what is it still but the deepest thing about one? Deeper about *me*, at any rate, than anything else: deeper than my 'genius,' deeper than my 'discipline,' deeper than my pride, deeper, above all, than the deep countermining of art" (*HJL* IV, 170). Though James was at the time of this letter engaged in the writing of *The Ambassadors*, with whose lonely hero he himself identified, his insistence that loneliness remains "the deepest thing about one" reflects a conviction that both suggests a modernist view of the self and permeates much of James's fiction, especially the fiction of the late phase. This fundamental loneliness of the self results from its essential isolation in a world it can know only through its own perceptions, which it must, in James's fiction, accept as legitimate and act on as though there were indeed a validating authority outside itself. What was to become a prominent feature of modernist epistemologies had for James so compelling an experiential basis in his own life as to influence his fiction—and especially his later fiction—stylistically, formally, and thematically.

In his youth, as he remarks in *A Small Boy and Others*, the recognition of a gap between the self and others was a source of joy and delight. "They were so *other*—that was what I felt; and to *be* other, other almost anyhow, seemed as good as the probable taste of the bright compound wistfully watched in the confectioner's window" (*SB* 101). Similarly, James's own personal loneliness no doubt resulted in part from his predilection to be an observer of life more than a participant in it; contrasting himself as a child with his brother Wilkie, he concludes, "One way of taking life was to go in for everything and everyone, which kept you abundantly occupied, and the other way was to be as occupied, quite as occupied, with the sense and the image of it all, and on only a fifth of the actual immersion" (*SB* 164). Although this temperamental tendency served him well as an artist, it also gave shape to the vision of human life and the human condition informing his fiction. And increasingly, in the later fiction, that condition includes the painful isolation of the individual from others, the difficulty of accurately interpreting and understanding the behavior of others, and yet the yearning for a connection—for love—that is rare and, when it does occur, transitory. No doubt those who, like Wilkie, "go in for everything and everyone" may experience loneliness and alienation, but in James's fiction they are rarely given representation and certainly not as the protagonist or central consciousness. Particularly in the late fiction, James's characters resemble their creator in experiencing "only a fifth of the actual immersion" in life.

The completed novels of James's "late phase"—*The Sacred Fount* (1901), *The Ambassadors* (1903), *The Wings of the Dove* (1902), and *The Golden Bowl* (1904)—become less and less populated until, in *The Golden Bowl*, we find a world inhabited essentially by only four characters, though it is also true, as James wrote in the preface, that we "really see about as much of them as a coherent literary form permits" (*AN* 330). Yet the epistemological uncertainties experienced by the characters and the reader alike are complicated and multiplied in these late novels, making us increasingly aware of the disjunction between self and other, self and world. This thematic concern is both reflected in and created by James's experimentation with point of view and his development of an ornate and sometimes ponderous style that has frequently come under critical attack.

James's preoccupation with point of view is, of course, evident in his earliest fiction. But in the later novels, his methods of presentation are crafted so as to make us as keenly aware of the "*process* of vision," as he says of *The Ambassadors* (*AN* 308), as we are of the vision itself. And, more even than in the earlier fiction, his reflectors are individuals "on whom nothing is lost" (*LC*-II, 53). William R. Goetz has in fact argued: "The chronological development of James's art is in part such a refinement of the reflector method as to allow the characters' minds increasingly to approximate the magisterial intelligence and sensitivity of that of their creator. Or more accurately, since the novels themselves are the place where James's growth in intelligence and self-consciousness occurs, the technique of the reflector contributes to, as much as it mirrors, James's understanding of his own grasp of the world" (7). Since one mark of the human condition in the late fiction is the fundamental isolation of the self and the absence of any authority, reality seems to be defined and constituted by the self's perceptions. The gradual unfolding of these perceptions becomes the subject of the fiction,and though James continues to be concerned with the moral dimensions of human action, he is, as Paul B. Armstrong observes, "less interested in where the line between [right and wrong] lies than in how one draws it, and with what legitimation'' (*Phenomenology* 6).

For the centers of consciousness whose perceptions effectively constitute the "adventure" and excitement of the last three novels, and for the reader as well, the process of drawing that line becomes far more complex and difficult than it is in works from James's early and middle periods. Because these centers of consciousness do acquire the "intelligence and sensitivity" of James himself, they tend in the late fiction to find the world more complex and ambiguous than do those in the earlier fiction; the confusion experienced by Winterbourne over Daisy Miller is a simple matter by comparison with the confusion created by Milly Theale in those around her. We may reasonably infer that this growing complexity of the reality represented in the late fiction is a correlative of James's own vision of life in his later years. As he wrote in a letter to the sculptor Hendrik Andersen, dated September 4, 1913, the world "is so far vaster in its appalling complexity than you or me, or than anything we can pretend without the imputation of absurdity and insanity to do to it, that I content myself . . . with living in the realities of things, with 'cultivating my garden' (morally and intellectually speaking), and with referring my questions to a Conscience (my own poor little personal), less inconceivable than that of the globe" (*HJL* IV, 682). As, apparently, in James's own life, it is entirely within the individual consciousness (and conscience) that the moral implications of the late fiction are to be found.

Similarly, the style that characterizes the late fiction attempts to render the "appalling complexity" of the world and yet to render it as clearly as is possible. James's "late style," to which his brother William was one of the first, but hardly the last, to object, is highly abstract, relying on metaphors more common to poetry than to prose; like other readers, Ruth Bernard Yeazell noted that "the disparity between vehicle and tenor which makes so many of James's late images metaphysically surprising suggests a world in which connections are not easily made" (*Language and Knowledge* 46). Highly figurative, James's late style demands of its reader an active participation; we must ourselves become those "on whom nothing is lost" if we are to grasp the late fiction. We are obliged to allow the repetition of images and metaphors in different contexts to create within our own minds the associative meanings that both clarify and complicate the text for us. The characters of the late fiction thus accrue more meanings for us than can easily be delineated, taking on the three-dimensionality and complexity of actual people. The images and metaphors used by and about Milly Theale, for example, or Maggie Verver, are so plentiful and worked through so many variations that we can never reduce these characters to a single set of qualities or traits. This figurative style is partly what creates the ambiguities inherent in the late fiction, so that our readings of the texts become, as William W. Stowe has argued, analogous to "our experience of the world, as a model for the interpretation of life itself" (169).

Another stylistic and formal feature of the late fiction that has in recent years begun to receive critical attention is the punctuation of the text with silences. These may be wordless moments charged with an almost mystical significance that words are inadequate to express, as when Milly Theale comes face to face with the Bronzino portrait. Or they may function to prevent the total collapse and disintegration of both social and personal relationships, as in Maggie Verver's refusal verbally to confront Charlotte or Adam. In this latter instance, silence preserves Maggie's world, and the words that the characters do use reveal nothing of the reality of their situation. Nicola Bradbury argues that James uses silence as a means of expression in his earliest fiction but that the instances of silence are more numerous and of more kinds in the late fiction (see *Later Novels* 32–35). Correlative to this use of silence is the omission of crucial conversations from the text and the inclusion of endless reflection about the meaning of these conversations. What Sir Luke Strett actually says to Milly Theale, for example, is not provided for us; instead, after Milly's visit, we follow her thoughts about all that Sir Luke's words—and the silences between them—might have meant.

William James complained that in *The Wings of the Dove*, Henry had "reversed every traditional canon of storytelling (especially the fundamental one of *telling* the story, which you carefully avoid)" (Matthiessen, *James Family* 338). But James's method and style in the late fiction reveal that his interest is less in "telling the story" than in showing what the story means for its principal actors. As he was to write in "The Lesson of Balzac," "There is no such thing in the world as an adventure pure and simple; there is only mine and yours, and his and hers—it being the greatest adventure of all, I verily think, just to *be* you or I, just to be he or she" (*LC*-II, 135). In the late fiction, James is almost exclusively concerned with showing us his characters' "point of pressing consciousness," their "process of vision," as a means of allowing us to know who these characters are. The interior workings of his characters' minds become the locus of both interest and meaning. Thus James eventually, and with a tone of considerable exasperation, wrote to his brother:

I mean to try to produce some uncanny form of thing, in fiction, that will gratify you, as Brother—but let me say, dear William, that I shall be greatly humiliated if you *do* like it, and thereby lump it, in your affection, with things of the current age, that I have heard you express admiration for and that I would sooner descend to a dishonoured grave than have written. Still, I *will* write you your book, on that two-and-two-make-four system on which all the awful truck that surrounds us is produced, and *then* descend to my dishonoured grave. . . . But it is, seriously, too late at night, and I am too tired, for me to express myself on this question—beyond saying that I'm always sorry when I hear of your reading anything of mine, and always hope you won't—you seem to me so constitutionally unable to "enjoy" it, and so condemned to look at it from a point of view remotely alien to mine in writing it, and to the conditions out of which, *as* mine, it has inevitably sprung—so that all the intentions that have been its main reason for being (with *me*) appear never to have reached you at all. (*HJL* IV, 382–83)

Because James's "intentions" in the late fiction are to show us the process by which his characters confront, sort out, and formulate equations far more complex and far less stable than "two-and-two-make-four," even themes and characters familiar from his earlier fiction now assume different meanings and functions. For example, in *The Ambassadors, The Wings of the Dove*, and *The Golden Bowl*, he turns again to the international material that proved such a rich resource at the beginning of his career, and in the latter two, he takes up again the figure of the American Girl, whose earliest incarnations had been Daisy Miller and Isabel Archer. But the international material is no longer simply a tool of social analysis and criticism; instead, the gap between Americans and Europeans becomes, as Armstrong has said, "both a manifestation of and a metaphor for the gap between the Self and the Other" (*Phenomenology* 144). In the working out of this metaphor, Europe remains "the Other" because James could not ultimately deny his American identity. But the American "Self" in these late novels is no longer simply innocent and vulnerable, though it has learned how to use the guise of innocence to attain power. Further, in *The Wings of the Dove*, the Self becomes an Other to the Other; we watch Kate Croy, Merton Densher, Susan Shepherd Stringham, and the other characters all attempt to reduce for interpretation the character of Milly Theale. At the same time, we watch Milly Theale discover the value of self-consciously using these interpretive objectifications (American Girl, princess, dove) to her own advantage. The international material thus dramatizes the complex, dynamic interactions of the Self and the Other and reveals a gap that can rarely be traversed, let alone bridged.

The innocence of the American Girl is also presented as a more complex matter in the late fiction than it had been in the early. Milly Theale and Maggie Verver are aware of their innocence, self-conscious of it, in a way that Daisy Miller or Isabel Archer never were. In the case of Maggie Verver, innocence, she discovers, can be used to assert her right to power. And though the reader has minimal access to Milly Theale's motivations, this "dove" clearly makes her power felt by Kate and Densher, without leaving them any grounds on which to object. Thus the line between James's "good heroines" and his "bad hero-ines"—between Milly Theale and Maggie Verver on the one hand and Kate Croy and Charlotte Stant on the other—is less clearly delineated than it is, for example, between Isabel Archer and Madame Merle.

The interior world represented in the late fiction is, then, as treacherous and uncertain a place as the exterior world in which the characters move—the openly and crassly commercial world of Lancaster Gate, for example, where "nobody . . . does anything for nothing" (*NY* XIX, 160). The ambiguity for which James has so often been noted is pervasive in the late fiction. We are able, certainly, to make moral distinctions between the characters, but we are not allowed to feel consistently comfortable about those distinctions, nor do we feel as though making those distinctions definitively settles the issues raised. Characters as conveniently repugnant as Gilbert Osmond simply do not occupy much of the stage in the late fiction. Instead, the fiction makes moral judgments less com-forting because it obliges us to know and understand the pressures acting on all of the characters. As James asks in "The Lesson of Balzac," "How do we know given persons, for any purpose of demonstration, unless we know their situation for ourselves?" (*LC*-II, 132). Despite the fabulous wealth of some of the late characters, and despite the exotic language used to render them, James's late fiction works hard and successfully to "represent life," and the life it represents is as complex and uncertain as the human mind.

James has often been attacked for his failure to represent human sexuality as an integral part of human beings. The fairness of this attack is questionable even in regard to his early fiction, but in regard to the late fiction it ceases to be in any way legitimate. Yeazell argues in fact that from the late nineties onward in James's novels, "sexual passion becomes the central mystery, the hidden knowledge, which the Jamesian innocent must at last confront" (*Language and Knowledge* 20). Although I would quarrel with Yeazell about James's use of sexual passion to represent "the central mystery" or the "hidden knowledge," there is certainly no question that sexual passion is a key element in the minds and lives of James's late characters. As the most intimate human bond possible, it assumes transformative powers in both *The Sacred Fount* and *The Ambassadors*, capable of creating both positive effects (as in Chad Newsome) and detrimental ones (as in Guy Brissenden). The human desire for intimacy, for ways out of the loneliness of the self, that sexuality represents seems in the late James both necessary and yet terribly vulnerable to misuse. The rejection of such intimacy on the part of a character like John Marcher, of "The Beast in the Jungle," is tantamount to a rejection of life itself. Yet it also can easily become one more instrument of power, which is the case in *The Wings of the Dove*, where Merton Densher uses sexual intimacy as payment for his cooperation in Kate Croy's plot. The gap between the Self and the Other that sexual intimacy promises to bridge or at least narrow must, it seems, be respected for the safety of the Self that it ultimately preserves. Never a casual matter in James's fiction, sexual passion ultimately operates as a symbol of the quality of relationship between his characters. In none of the late novels is a solution discovered to the dangers of rejecting intimacy, on the one hand, and the dangers of engaging in it, on the other; at best, as in *The Golden Bowl*, these opposing dangers exist in tension to each other. One must turn to a story like "The Jolly Corner" for the possibility of such a solution. In many ways, sexual passion is given the ambiguous symbolic status attaching to marriage in *The Portrait of a Lady*; clearly, intimacy in human relationships is something about which James experienced a lifelong ambivalence. In the late fiction at least, however, sexual passion becomes the perhaps more appropriate symbol of that intimacy.

Begun in 1900, *The Sacred Fount* originated in a story suggested to James by Stopford Brooke, and was first sketched out in his notebooks in February 1884: "The notion of the young man who marries an older woman and who has the effect on her of making her younger and still younger, while he himself becomes her age. When he reaches the age that *she* was (on their marriage), she has gone back to the age that *he* was.—Mightn't this be altered (perhaps) to the idea of cleverness and stupidity? A clever woman marries a deadly dull man, and loses and loses her wit as he shows more and more. Or the idea of a *liaison*, suspected, but of which there is no proof but this transfusion of some idiosyncrasy of one party to the being of the other—this exchange or conversion?'' (*NO* 88). The completed novel accordingly gives us one couple, the Brissendens, for whom the sacred fount has worked its transformation: Mrs. Brissenden, considerably older than her husband, has since their marriage become increasingly youthful and attractive in appearance while her young husband has correspondingly aged dramatically. There is, further, a man once dull and aloof who has now become intelligent, witty, and friendly. The quest that the first-person narrator undertakes is to identify the woman who may have effected this transformation in Gilbert Long.

Often considered James's most difficult work, *The Sacred Fount* does not approach this vampire theme straightforwardly or directly, and in fact nowhere is the radical alteration of the original "germ" of a novel more evident. For what interested James was not so much the subject of the novel but the possible approach to or presentation of it.

*The Sacred Fount* is one of the few works for which James employed a first-person point of view, including, on the verge of the late period, "The Turn of the Screw." As in that ambiguous tale, the real subject of interest in *The Sacred Fount* is the narrator, whose perceptions of the transformations in his fellow houseguests at a weekend country-house party are all the reader is given. One very quickly becomes aware that the narrator's purpose—to identify the woman who has transformed Gilbert Long—is designed and presented by James to engage the reader in a mystifying, maddening, and ultimately futile course of detection. Our search for the mysterious woman is guided by the narrator's perceptions about his fellow guests; these perceptions constitute our only "clues" in the case, and they are broken off at the end of the novel by the narrator's encounter with Mrs. Briss, who, after rejecting his theories, says to him, "My poor dear, you *are* crazy, and I bid you good-night!" (*SF* 318).

Critical opinion about this anomalous novel has been divided on the issue of its intended seriousness. Dorothea Krook, for example, argues that it "is James's most serious and most exhaustive study of the creative imagination, and of the moral and philosophical difficulties inherent in its characteristic opera-tions"(183). Laurence B. Holland, in what is perhaps still the most fruitful discussion of the novel, argues that the novel takes "the form of parody" in order "to control the unintended parody that James's art threatens to become and to measure the pressures that motivate it" (183 [1964]). Thus, it is not just "the authority of the Narrator . . . but also the authority of James's imagination . . . and the authority of the enigmatic novel itself which is challenged by the parody, the presentational form which renders an account in this case only to call into question its own validity" (Holland 183–184 [1964]).

Certainly *The Sacred Fount* is, by any measure, a transitional work between the novels of the late nineties and those of the new century. Its development of the epistemological theme of appearance and reality, particularly since determining the relationship between them is the principal demand placed on the reader as well as the narrator, groups it with novels like *What Maisie Knew* and *The Awkward Age*. And its focus on the transformative powers of intimacy for the two couples involved would become an important aspect of *The Ambassadors*, written just after James completed *The Sacred Fount*. Significantly, James explains in the preface to *The Ambassadors* why he did not use the first-person point of view in that novel. Allowing Strether to be "at once hero and historian" might well have made possible a greater "variety"; but he concludes, "Suffice it, to be brief, that the first person, in the long piece, is a form foredoomed to looseness, and that looseness, never much my affair, had never been so little so as on this particular occasion" (*AN* 320). Technically, *The Sacred Fount* did indeed provide James the opportunity to gauge the dangers inherent in his increasing interest in the mental workings, the "process of vision," of the individual self. The three big novels of the late phase indeed document his growing belief that reality cannot be divorced from (may not even have an existence apart from) the mind perceiving it.

At the same time, it is difficult to regard *The Sacred Fount* with the same interest and seriousness that one brings to either the novels that precede it or those that follow. James himself dismissed it, in a letter to Mrs. Humphry Ward, as not "worth discussing," as "a remarkably accidental" book, "the merest of jeux d'esprit," written for the money it would bring in as a "single magazine installment" (*HJL* IV, 185–86). When it grew longer than he had originally intended, he nevertheless wanted to complete it so as not to have wasted the writing he had already invested; and as he said in a letter to William Dean Howells, he had what amounted to a superstitious need to complete projects he began (*HJL* IV, 251). "So, only," he continues in his letter to Mrs. Ward, "it was that I hatingly finished it; trying only to make it—the one thing it *could* be, a *consistent* joke. Also, for a joke it appears to have been, round about me here, taken rather seriously. It's doubtless very disgraceful, but it's the last I shall ever make!" (*HJL* IV, 186). In a similar vein, he rather shamefacedly acknowledged to W. Morton Fullerton that Fullerton was "perfectly right about such stuffs as the *Sacred Fount*—I can't, the least little bit, afford to write them; they lead to bankruptcy straight—and serve me right thereby. *That jeu d'esprit* was an accident, pure and simple, and not even an intellectual one. . . . It was a mere *trade*-accident, *tout au plus*—an incident of technics, pure and simple" (*HJL* IV, 197–98). James's subsequent decision to exclude it from the New York Edition (the only novel after *The Bostonians* so treated) was, one cannot help thinking, sound. Though not without merit, *The Sacred Fount* does not approximate the achievement either of the experimental novels of the nineties or of those that followed it.

Written before *The Wings of the Dove*, though published after it, *The Ambassadors* was regarded by James himself as "quite the best 'all round,' of all my productions" (*AN* 309). Though it bears some resemblance to *The Sacred*

*Fount*, it is far superior to the earlier novel and quite justifies James's pride in it. A reflective outsider observing the passions of others and trying to piece together what his observations might mean, the transformative powers of love, the highly charged and evocative setting—all these elements are present in both novels. But whereas they combine to suggest a morally and rationally suspect *artiste manqué* in *The Sacred Fount*, one whose interest in others reflects neither a responsiveness to them nor a desire for the self-knowledge they may promote, in *The Ambassadors* these elements together create an ordinary, though sensitive and educated, man who discovers relatively late in life the narrowness and emptiness at the core of his being. As James says in the preface, his hero has "missed too much, though perhaps after all constitutionally qualified for a better part" (*AN* 308). Like the narrator in *The Sacred Fount*, Lambert Strether must try to discern the reality behind the appearances he confronts in Paris; but unlike that narrator's motivations, which serve intellectual amusement and speculation, Strether's need to understand eventually engenders a recognition of the implications for himself of what he sees. "*Would* there yet perhaps be time for reparation?—reparation, that is, for the injury done his character; for the affront, he is quite ready to say, so stupidly put upon it and in which he has even himself had so clumsy a hand? The answer to which is that he now at all events *sees*" (*AN* 308).

Strether's superiority to the narrator of *The Sacred Fount* is to no small extent the result of James's decision not to employ the first-person point of view but instead to make his hero the controlling center of consciousness in a story communicated by an omniscient narrator. We see everything through Strether's consciousness, but he is not allowed himself to narrate the story. As a result, the text invites our sympathetic responses to Strether and allows us to believe in his perceptions and to care about the way they affect him. Rather than questioning the reliability of our hero (as we do in *The Sacred Fount*, where hero and narrator are one and the same), we are instead able to enter into his experience; his "process of vision" becomes our own.

Equally important in the distinction between *The Ambassadors* and *The Sacred Fount* is that the sacred fount theme is subordinated to the more important theme of regret for opportunities lost, which is so poignantly suggested in Strether's advice to little Bilham to "live all you can." These words constituted, in fact, the seed of the novel; some such statement was attributed to William Dean Howells and was reported to James by his friend Jonathan Sturges late in 1895. As James's initial notebook entry reveals, the image of Howells giving some such advice to Sturges, during a brief stay Howells made in Paris, worked immediately and profoundly on James's imagination: the initial entry sketches out virtually the entire novel (*NO* 140–42.) It clearly struck a responsive chord in James, one that he had in fact sounded several years earlier in "The Middle Years" and that is also to be heard in his portrayal of Mr. Longdon in *The Awkward Age*. These years during the 1890s, when James's fondest ambitions for success in the theater were so totally destroyed, made him keenly aware of the life he had sacrificed for his art and of the fact that age itself was closing off the opportunities of youth. These realizations receive most eloquent articulation in "The Middle Years," in which his hero, Dencombe, concludes: "A second chance—that's the delusion. There never was to be but one. We work in the dark—we do what we can—we give what we have. Our doubt is our passion and our passion is our task. The rest is the madness of art" (*NY* XIII, 209).

Such an elegiac tone is one of the most striking qualities in *The Ambassadors*, a tone that for James necessitated Paris as the setting of the novel. As he admonishes himself in the initial notebook entry, his hero's "live all you can" advice would be successful only if rendered in a setting reverberating with meaning. "But think of the place itself again first—the charming June afternoon in Paris, the tea under the trees, the 'intimate' nook, consecrated to 'artistic and literary' talk, types, freedoms of (for the *desoriente* elderly American) an unprecedented sort; think above all of the so-possible presence of a charming woman or two, of peculiarly 'European' tradition, such as it had never yet been given him to encounter. Well, this is what the whole thing, as with a slow rush the sense of it came over him, made him say" (*NO* 142).

The figure of Strether, then—who, James wrote to Jocelyn Persse, bore "a vague resemblance" to himself (*HJL* IV, 286)—"*is* the subject, the subject itself" of *The Ambassadors* (*HJL* IV, 221). Strether serves both as the reflector, or central consciousness, of the novel and as its hero. The novel is structured in such a way, and other characters share the stage with Strether in such a way, as to assist his movement toward the central recognition of the life he has missed. As in *The Wings of the Dove* and *The Golden Bowl*, James's composition in *The Ambassadors* is marked by repeated scenes and incidents and by paired characters. We are thus given two delegations to Paris, both on behalf of the powerfully absent Mrs. Newsome, to rescue her son from the pernicious influence that has made him linger in Paris and refuse to return to the responsibilities awaiting him in Woollett. Strether's failure to complete his mission, because the certain knowledge he brought with him to Paris becomes in his mind a false conception of Chad's situation, results in the arrival on the scene of Sarah Pocock's more effective delegation.

Just as Strether's ambassadorial journey to Paris is repeated and commented on by Pocock's journey, his growth in awareness and his change in loyalties are marked through the four balcony scenes in the novel: his first visit to Chad's apartment is preceded by his long, meditative vision, from the street below, of the balcony on which Chad's friend little Bilham is smoking; his discovery of young Mamie Pocock on the balcony of the Pocock hotel, which leads him to see her as an ally; his visit to Chad's apartment late in the novel, during which, as he awaits Chad's return, he himself hangs over the balcony and, later, shares an intimate conversation with Chad; and his final visit to that same apartment, which is preceded by his vision from the street below of Chad smoking on the balcony, making Strether himself feel as though "his last day were oddly copying his first'' (*NY* XXII, 305). As William M. Gibson has shown, ''Each of these balcony episodes embodies a major discovery or decision for Strether and together they chart the rise and fall of his sense of freedom and of the value of youth'' (309).

In a similar fashion, the novel sets up its characters in a variety of contrasting pairs—Strether/Chad, Mrs. Newsome/Mme de Vionnet, Mamie Pocock/Jeanne de Vionnet, Waymarsh/Strether, etc. The logically patterned composition of the novel is what makes for its strict unity and its almost perfect symmetry, the most striking aspect of which is the way that Strether and Chad have changed places at the end of the novel.

What initially shatters Strether's certainty about the rightness of his mission is, first, the fact that Chad has undergone what Strether sees as a positive transformation into a more ''civilized'' human being and, second, his inability to assess the ''virtuous attachment'' that little Bilham tells him unites Chad and Mme de Vionnet (*NY* XXI, 180). Aware from the moment of his arrival in Liverpool of a ''personal freedom . . . he hadn't known for years'' (*NY* XXI, 4), Strether finds in ''the vast bright Babylon'' of Paris (*NY* XXI, 89) ''civilized'' life such as Woollett had never dreamed of. Yet he recognizes that ''almost any acceptance of Paris might give one's authority away'' (*NY* XXI, 89) because it would create a bond between himself and Chad that would jeopardize them both. Woollett and its representative, Mrs. Newsome, so far across the ocean, become a palpable presence in the novel long before Sarah Pocock arrives to embody them. Increasingly, Strether comes both to identify Chad with the son he lost through his own selfish neglect (*NY* XXI, 84) and to regard him as an older brother and even a rival.

What Strether's prolonged stay in Paris presses on him is an awareness of having grown old without ever having experienced youth. As he says to little Bilham: ''it's as if the train had fairly waited at the station for me without my having had the gumption to know it was there. Now I hear its faint receding whistle miles and miles down the line. What one loses one loses; make no mistake about that'' (*NY* XXI, 217–18). Later, after Pocock's arrival in Paris, Strether realizes that his having ''missed'' what life might have offered him in his youth was not an anomalous accident of his youth but indeed a proclivity of his very character. ''It came to him in fact that just here was his usual case: he was for ever missing things through his general genius for missing them, while others were for ever picking them up through a contrary bent. And it was others who looked abstemious and he who looked greedy; it was he somehow who finally paid, and it was others who mainly partook'' (*NY* XXII, 185–86). What he ''pays'' for in Paris is his loyalty to his own vision of Chad and Mme de Vionnet, his refusal to recant that vision in deference to the vision of Woollett. The price is his own marriage to Mrs. Newsome and the security for his old age that such a marriage would have insured. Yet, as he realizes, his faith in his own vision has prompted him to no decisive action, such as himself taking up a life in Paris like Chad's; in fact, he recognizes ''that he would have been held less monstrous had he only been a little wilder. What exposed him was just his poor old trick of quiet inwardness, what exposed him was his *thinking* such offence'' (*NY* XXII, 201).

Strether's attempt at least to enjoy, through his vicarious identification with Chad, the inward experience of what he has missed is of course doomed from the outset both because Chad himself is far more limited than Strether wants to believe him and because Chad's ''virtuous attachment'' to Mme de Vionnet cannot mean what Strether has wanted it to mean. Though Strether remains to the end incapable of judging Chad and Mme de Vionnet as Woollett would do, he also remains incapable of embracing the knowledge that he is eventually forced to confront. His adolescent reluctance to see the sexual component of Chad's relationship with Mme de Vionnet ties him to the American Girls of James's last two novels; as little Bilham says, Strether is ''not a person to whom it's easy to tell things you don't want to know'' (*NY* XXI, 202). Strether should have realized, as he himself reflects after his fateful encounter with Chad and Mme de Vionnet in the country, that ''intimacy, at such a point, was *like* that— and what in the world else would one have wished it to be like? It was all very well for him to feel the pity of its being so much like lying; he almost blushed, in the dark, for the way he had dressed the possibility in vagueness, as a little girl might have dressed her doll. . . . He foresaw that Miss Gostry would come again into requisition on the morrow; though it wasn't to be denied that he was already a little afraid of her 'What on earth—that's what I want to know now— had you then supposed?' He recognised at last that he had really been trying all along to suppose nothing'' (*NY* XXII, 266).

''Intimacy, at such a point,'' is something that Strether ultimately rejects for himself, just as he has done throughout his life. He has wanted, as this passage reveals, to believe against all reasonable supposition that Chad and Mme de Vionnet have shared a ''virtuous attachment,'' and through their efforts to encourage that belief, they have made their intimacy, once it is revealed, appear to be like ''lying.'' Their efforts in the country to perpetuate the illusion have represented a ''quantity of make-believe'' that ''disagreed with his spiritual stomach'' (*NY* XXII, 265). Yet as the passage above makes evident, for everyone except Strether, the reality of the relationship has been so clear as to suggest Strether's need to believe in the appearances out of some fear of or revulsion to the reality behind them.

Strether's final encounter with Mme de Vionnet reveals, moreover, that passion itself, and in particular passion from a woman, is what so frightens him. ''It might have made Strether hot or shy, as such secrets of others brought home sometimes do make us; but he was held there by something so hard that it was fairly grim. This was not the discomposure of last night; that had quite passed— such discomposures were a detail; the real coercion was to see a man ineffably adored. There it was again—it took women, it took women; if to deal with them was to walk on water what wonder that the water rose?'' (*NY* XXII, 285). What Strether has ''missed'' in life is thus something he ultimately has not wanted and that he can only, this late in his life, refuse again. The Other, represented for Strether by the beautiful Mme de Vionnet, is fascinating and desirable but must be kept at a distance; the loneliness and isolation of the self are thus preferable to the danger of connection and intimacy with the Other.

Like John Marcher of "The Beast in the Jungle," who loses the possibility of life as it is embodied by May Bartram because he waits for the significant event (the beast) that will suddenly charge his life with meaning, Lambert Strether rationalizes his refusal of the love offered him by Maria Gostry by arguing that "to be right," he must "not, out of the whole affair, . . . have got anything for" himself (*NY* XXII, 326). In the tale, however, Marcher's horrified recognition of what he has missed climaxes the story, leaving the reader with a sense that, could the past repeat itself, Marcher's insight would prompt him to different action. *The Ambassadors*, by contrast, forces us to consider that at some profound level of his being, Strether has preferred to miss "the train at the station." Though he comes in the course of the novel to see what he has missed, the reader realizes (whether Strether does or not) that his "missing" might as well have been a refusal. What he is obliged to carry back to Woollett with him is his recognition that there had after all *been* a train at the station.

Though James's first notebook entry for *The Wings of the Dove* was written November 3, 1894, in his preface to the New York Edition he stated, "I can scarce remember the time when the situation on which this long-drawn fiction mainly rests was not vividly present to me" (*AN* 288). If we turn to his autobiographical writings, we find not only abundant evidence of the picturesque appeal of the subject matter of the novel to James's imagination even when he was a child but also, in his reminiscences about his cousin Mary (Minny) Temple, the specific roots of the central character of the novel. Minny Temple, who died at the age of twenty-four from tuberculosis, clearly became, as the autobiography reveals, for James the symbol of all the conflicting values and traits that were to inform his fictional American Girls, of whom Minny was also the prototype. "Death, at the last," he wrote, "was dreadful to her; she would have given anything to live—and the image of this, which was long to remain with me, appeared so of the essence of tragedy that I was in the far-off aftertime to seek to lay the ghost by wrapping it, a particular occasion aiding, in the beauty and dignity of art" (*NS* 515).

The autobiographical source of Milly Theale's character, and the intensity and ambivalence of James's feelings about Minny Temple, may account at least in part for the unusual, complex structure of *The Wings of the Dove*. Just as Minny had represented so many things to Henry James (her death, he said, marked "the end of our youth"), so James envisioned her fictional counterpart from the first in terms of the meanings and values she would represent for others. "If one had seen," he remarks in the preface, "that her stricken state was but half her case, the correlative half being the state of others as affected by her" (*AN* 294), then the "law of composition" for the novel would need to be that of "successive centres" as the reflectors of the narrative. *The Wings of the Dove* thus has a unique place among James's late novels in the point of view it employs. Instead of a single consciousness, as in *The Ambassadors*, or the two consciousnesses of the prince and the princess in the parallel halves of *The Golden Bowl*, *The Wings of the Dove* moves from one consciousness to the next, making it, in Edward Wagenknecht's words, "even more difficult than it usually is with James to distinguish clearly between these persons and an unnamed narrator or hypothetical observer" (*Novels* 203). Moreover, the central figure of Milly Theale does not enter the novel until the third book and disappears before the last one.

The effects of this unusual structure are varied, but chief among them are uncertainty about the subject of the novel and, consequently, an apparently unavoidable distortion in any analysis of the novel. The novel is "about" Milly Theale, but it is also "about" Kate Croy, Merton Densher, and the interrelationships among the three of them. John Goode has argued that the triangularity inherent in the relationships of the characters "emphasizes the social concern of the novel: it is not the other person which most matters, it is the other person's relationship to someone who is related to you, and the ultimate concern of the novel is the way in which one person's geometry squares with everybody else's" ("Pervasive Mystery" 247). This triangularity makes *The Wings of the Dove* James's most exhaustive study of the fragility and potential destructiveness of personal relationships. The self's needs are here imaged as impossible of fulfillment without the violation of the Other. As a consequence, nowhere in James's fiction are moral and psychological imperatives more inextricably enmeshed. The individual's survival can be insured only through retreat into the self or through a closing down of the empathetic impulses that can bond individuals together.

As in *The Ambassadors*, the international theme in *The Wings of the Dove* becomes a metaphor for the distances separating the Self from the Other. Yet both here and in *The Golden Bowl*, that distance has been increased by the American characters' fabulous wealth, which gives them a power and also a responsibility that the Americans in the early international fiction lacked. Their "innocence" is presented in ironic juxtaposition to the power their wealth provides them, and they become complicitous in the plots devised to exploit or abuse them. In *The Wings of the Dove*, the deception that Kate and all the other characters practice on Milly Theale can work only because of Milly's enormous desire to be deceived. Like Lambert Strether, Milly so willingly accepts the story given her that we are obliged to find some merit in Kate's argument to Densher, late in the novel, that Milly "never wanted the truth. . . . She wanted *you*. She would have taken from you what you could give her and been glad of it, even if she had known it false. You might have lied to her from pity, and she have seen you and felt you lie, and yet—since it was all for tenderness— she would have thanked you and blessed you and clung to you but the more. For that was your strength, my dear man—that she loves you with passion" (*NY* XX, 326). Where Kate errs, perhaps, is in thinking that Milly's illness is irreversible and fatal. As the ambiguous treatment of Milly's illness suggests, her death is in part an act of will. Sir Luke Strett insists that she could live if she "would take the trouble to do" so (*NY* XIX, 246), but Milly herself concludes, "It was perhaps superficially more striking that one could live if one would; but it was more appealing, insinuating, irresistible in short, that one would live if one could" (*NY* XIX, 254). Milly's tragedy lies not in her dying or in her suffering at the hands of the "hard English gang" she encounters, but in the discrepancy between her wealth and her spiritual and psychological deficiency. It is this deficiency that can make her feel like "a poor girl—with her rent to pay" (*NY* XIX, 253). Yet unlike Isabel Archer, whose inheritance is a burden and who does not know what to do with money, Milly Theale understands the power of her fortune, and she succeeds, through her bequest to Merton Densher, in defeating her rival.

At the same time, Kate Croy's willingness to deceive a dying girl in order to gain her fortune makes Kate—and Densher—corrupt as well. As Sallie Sears observes, in the late fiction "there is no one and nothing to blame and yet no one is blameless" (164). The social world itself is so totally corrupt in *The Wings of the Dove* that personal relationships cannot escape that corruption. The world of Lancaster Gate that both Kate and Milly choose to inhabit is a world in which nobody "does anything for nothing" (*NY* XIX, 160), a world ruled over by Maud Lowder, "Britannia of the Market Place," who, with "her florid philistinism" and "a reticule for her prejudices as deep as that other pocket, the pocket full of coins stamped in her image," was to Kate "unscrupulous and immoral" (*NY* XIX, 31). That both Kate and Milly somehow mistake Lancaster Gate as a place where life could flourish indicates not simply the deceptive appearances of the social world but, more important, the extent to which Kate and Milly have unwittingly absorbed the values inherent in that world.

Readings that see this complex text as a story of redemption, figuring Milly Theale, the Christ-like dove, as the redeemer, and Merton Densher as the recipient of that redemption, are obliged to overlook the many ways in which the text resists such interpretation (representative, redemptive readings include those by Quentin Anderson [*The American Henry James*], Dorothea Krook [*The Ordeal of Consciousness in Henry James*], R.W.B. Lewis ["The Vision of Grace"], and F. O. Matthiessen [*Henry James: The Major Phase*]). William R. Macnaughton has recently pointed out the difficulty of explaining the Christian allusions in the novel and of determining "James's attitude toward them. What is peculiar about some of them is that they seem almost frivolous or parodic, as if James were daring us (and perhaps himself) to take them seriously" (*Later Novels* 96). The difficulty in viewing Milly Theale as, for example, a dove who spreads her wings in protection and redemption of the world that she, through her death, leaves behind is that she self-consciously adopts the role of dove, just as she does the roles of princess and American Girl. When Kate Croy pronounces Milly a dove, Milly "found herself accepting as the right one, while she caught her breath with relief, the name so given her. She met it on the instant as she would have met the revealed truth; it lighted up the strange dusk in which she lately had walked. *That* was what was the matter with her. She was a dove. Oh *wasn't* she?'' (*NY* XIX, 283). Milly immediately begins to act like a dove and to discover ''the measure of the success she could have as a dove'' (*NY* XIX, 284).

In a similar fashion, she self-consciously assumes the role of princess (for Susan Stringham) and of American Girl (for Merton Densher), and what becomes clearer as the novel progresses is not that these roles are designed by Milly to conceal or protect a different identity but that, on the contrary, they mask an inner core of emptiness. If she is a symbol of Otherness to the characters surrounding her, each of whom attempts a reductive, simplistic interpretation of that symbol, she nevertheless has no subjectivity or self for herself. She becomes, in fact, a greater presence in the novel the more she is absent from it, just as she is more real, in her death, for Merton Densher than she was in her life. Thus, as John Auchard has observed, ''Although Milly Theale's condition, as the heiress of the ages, suggests plenitude, it is her disinherited and negated state which distinguishes her'' (100).

Milly Theale, ''heiress of all the ages'' yet doomed to an early death by a mysterious illness, experiences herself in juxtaposition to Kate Croy, whose ''talent for life'' makes her a striking contrast to Milly. As I have argued elsewhere (Fowler 83–105), Milly's illness is presented by James as symbolic of some sort of inner deficiency that makes her unable to withstand ''the whole assault of life'' (*NY* XIX, 125). James claims in the preface that, like Lambert Strether, she yearns for life; she wants ''to 'put in' before extinction as many of the finer vibrations as possible, and so achieve, however briefly and brokenly, the sense of having lived'' (*AN* 288). The text of the novel itself, however, shows us less of Milly's desire for life than James's preface and his notebook entries claim. What we see instead are her passivity, her withdrawal, her increasing isolation, and her fear. From the outset, she experiences her difference from Kate in terms of a deficiency within herself, a deficiency that is tied to her identity as a woman. Kate, Milly explains early in the novel to Lord Mark, is ''better than any of you. She's beautiful'' (*NY* XIX, 164). Kate is ''difficult,'' whereas Milly seems to herself ''easy'' to understand (*NY* XIX, 166). Kate would be certain to be the object ''of some probably eminent male interest'' (*NY* XIX, 173). The ''handsome girl'' with her ''talent for life,'' Kate ''would never in her life be ill; the greatest doctor would keep her, at the worst, the fewest minutes'' (*NY* XIX, 258). Kate, Milly claims, is ''the handsomest and cleverest and most charming creature I ever saw, and . . . if I were a man I should simply adore her. In fact I do as it is'' (*NY* XX, 163).

Kate, on her side, similarly regards Milly as all that she herself is not and even asks her at one point, ''What help, with your luck all round, do you need?'' (*NY* XIX, 260). Just as Kate's beauty is what distinguishes her for Milly, Milly's wealth is her most significant attribute for Kate. ''She couldn't dress it away, nor walk it away, nor read it away, nor think it away; she could neither smile it away in any dreamy absence nor blow it away in any softened smile. She couldn't have lost it if she tried—that was what it was to be really rich. It had to be *the* thing you were" (*NY* XIX, 121). For Kate, Milly's fortune liberates her from the constraints imposed by being female. "It might have proved a test of one's philosophy not to be irritated by a mistress of millions, or whatever they were, who, as a girl, so easily might have been, like herself, only vague and cruelly female" (*NY* XIX, 176). As the narrator observes at one point, Milly and Kate "each thought the other more remarkable than herself" (*NY* XIX, 173).

Both Kate and Milly suffer the constraints of being female, though those constraints are different for each. As Elizabeth Allen has argued, "Kate and Milly both undergo the same processes as women, their difference lying in their response" (153). As a woman, Kate's only available means of defining herself is in relation to men, and since she is poor, her only value for men is in her beauty. Despite her desire for the freedom and power that money alone could give her, she is a sister and daughter of fierce loyalties, as her offer to her father in the opening chapter reveals. But both her father and her sister, the pathetic Miriam Condrip, want her to work for their advantage by allowing her Aunt Maud's patronage to shape a successful marriage for her. "It was through Kate that Aunt Maud should be worked, and nothing mattered less than what might become of Kate in the process" (*NY* XIX, 34). On her side, Kate enjoys the experience of life that Aunt Maud's patronage affords her, but she balks at the bartering of her beauty for a wealthy husband. In love with the penniless Merton Densher, Kate values her right to marry for love more than she values the potential wealth she might acquire by allowing Aunt Maud to get the highest bid for her hand in marriage. She wants to be faithful to Densher and yet somehow acquire a fortune as well. Unlike Densher, Kate has a "talent for life" and an under-standing of the forces shaping and controlling her world, just as she has a capacity for perception and an appreciation for nuance, both of which he lacks. As she says to him before he leaves for America: "There are refinements. . . . I mean of consciousness, of sensation, of appreciation. . . . No, . . . men *don't* know. They know in such matters almost nothing but what women show them" (*NY* XIX, 99).

If Kate's value and identity in the world is her beauty, then Milly is similarly deprived of subjectivity by her wealth. Like Kate, Milly is conscious of the roles others thrust on her and of the identities they shape for her. She learns how to act out the roles of princess, of American Girl, of dove, aware that the power of her fortune is the basis for her success with the crowd of Lancaster Gate. Ironically, what she wants more than anything, including Densher or his love, is to be, like Kate, a "handsome girl" with a "talent for life." It is in fact debatable whether she is more injured by the knowledge that Kate and Densher are lovers or by the fact that Kate has withheld this information from her.

Perhaps because Kate is presented to us with such sympathy in the first book of the novel, we can never see her as the "bad heroine" in quite the same way that we do characters like Serena Merle or Charlotte Stant. And both Kate and

Milly are betrayed by their feeling for the third member of this triangle, Merton Densher, who is really so undeserving of the love both of them feel for him.

Merton Densher's "transformation" by the ghostly love of Milly Theale is key to those readings that view the novel as a story of redemption. Though most readers recognize Densher's moral and intellectual ineptitude in the early parts of the novel, few have wanted to deny his spiritual and moral growth by its end. In a sense, James's text is at odds with itself in regard to Densher, since it is through his consciousness that the final part of the novel is presented. The autobiographical connections between Milly Theale and Minny Temple and, perhaps, those between Merton Densher's reaction to Milly's death and James's reaction to Minny's death have also complicated readings of the novel. Yet the emotional ambivalence of the text toward the figure of Milly Theale notwithstanding, Merton Densher nonetheless emerges as the least sympathetic character of the triangle.

From the outset, Densher is the passive male observer so common in James's fiction, similar in this regard to Lambert Strether. He is the man of thought, whereas Kate is the woman of action. In love with Kate, he consents to conceal their love from Aunt Maud, yet he hopes that he will not be obliged himself to lie to her, in which instance "it will be left all to" Kate (*NY* XIX, 98). Similarly, he agrees to play his passive role in Kate's plan to deceive Milly, but he scruples to participate actively. Though he apparently accedes to Kate's wishes as long as he can maintain his sense of himself as untainted, in reality he perceives the two of them in a struggle for power. "Something [was] made doubly vivid in him by the whole present play of her charming strong will. What it amounted to was that he couldn't have her—hanged if he could!—evasive. He couldn't and he wouldn't—wouldn't have her inconvenient and elusive. He didn't want her deeper than himself, fine as it might be as wit or as character" (*NY* XX, 19).

Densher's need to assert his will with Kate becomes most pressing when Kate announces her plan to leave Venice and to have Merton stay behind—on the basis of the possibility that Milly might offer to marry him.

"Well," he said, "I'll stay, on my honour, if you'll come to me. On *your* honour."

Again, as before, this made her momentarily rigid, with a rigour out of which, at a loss, she vaguely cast about her. Her rigour was more to him, nevertheless, than all her readiness; for her readiness was the woman herself, and the other thing a mask, a stop-gap and a "dodge." She cast about, however, as happened, and not for the instant in vain. Her eyes, turned over the room, caught at a pretext. "Lady Wells is tired of waiting: she's coming—see—to *us*."

Densher saw in fact, but there was a distance for their visitor to cross, and he still had time. "If you decline to understand me I wholly decline to understand you. I'll do nothing."

"Nothing?" It was as if she tried for the minute to plead.

"I'll do nothing. I'll go off before you. I'll go tomorrow."

He was to have afterwards the sense of her having then, as the phrase was—and for vulgar triumphs too—seen he meant it. She looked again at Lady Wells, who was nearer, but she quickly came back. "And if I do understand?"

"I'll do everything."

She found anew a pretext in her approaching friend: he was fairly playing with her pride. He had never, he then knew, tasted, in all his relation with her, of anything so sharp—too sharp for mere sweetness—as the vividness with which he saw himself master in the conflict. "Well, I understand."

"On your honour?"

"On my honour."

"You'll come?"

"I'll come." (*NY* XX, 230–31)

Densher's need for this physical proof of his bond with Kate is not created by any anxiety growing out of their deception of Milly. On the contrary, his desire for such proof begins when he returns from America, and it takes the form of an impatience with the restrictions on passion that the delay of their marriage necessitates. He resents the "respect" for Kate that prohibits him from asking her back to his rooms, and he questions the legitimacy of Kate's expecting such respect. "Compressed and concentrated, confined to a single sharp pang or two, but none the less in wait for him there on the Euston platform and lifting its head as that of a snake in the garden, was the disconcerting sense that 'respect,' in their game, seemed somehow—he scarce knew what to call it—a fifth wheel to the coach" (*NY* XX, 5). Densher is aware, moreover, of having subtly forced Kate to be aware of his needs and to pay for delaying their marriage: "he had already suffered Kate to begin finely to apply antidotes and remedies and subtle sedatives. It had a vulgar sound—as throughout, in love, the names of things, the verbal terms of intercourse, were, compared with love itself, horribly vulgar" (*NY* XX, 6).

Throughout the stay in Venice, Densher feels his masculinity is somehow challenged or threatened by the fact that he is surrounded by women; he "was glad there were no male witnesses: it was a circle of petticoats; he shouldn't have liked a man to see him" (*NY* XX, 209). Unlike Kate or Milly, however, both of whom are cast in roles, Densher, by his maleness, is allowed the luxury of consistent subjectivity. As Elizabeth Allen has argued, "Not only does his subject status free him from the need to understand the process of representation and its manipulative potential, it prevents him from possessing a full understanding of what it is to be 'other' and therefore of projection into the suffering of another consciousness" (157).

Far from understanding Kate's situation, Densher in fact consistently reduces her to the level of object. The metaphor he most repeatedly uses for Kate is that of a book. " 'The women one meets—what are they but books one has already read? You're a whole library of the unknown, the uncut.' He almost moaned, he ached, from the depth of his content. 'Upon my word I've a subscription!' " (*NY* XX, 62). His and Kate's dealings with Milly interest him more than they disturb his conscience. "Mere curiosity, even, about his companion, had now for him its quick, its slightly quaking, intensities. He had compared her once, we know, to a 'new book,' an uncut volume of the highest, the rarest quality; and his emotion (to justify that) was again and again like the thrill of turning the page" (*NY* XX, 222).

Densher's actions at the end of the novel seem the result not of any transformation or redemption he has experienced as a result of Milly's bequest. Having acted his part in the plot against Milly, he now wishes not simply to exonerate himself by refusing the bequest but also to assert once more his mastery over Kate. He will marry Kate without the money, but not with it. Moreover, he will not deny that he is in love with Milly's memory, yet he apparently believes that this mourning after the lost opportunities represented by Milly would not interfere with marriage to Kate. It is Kate who has the strength and the insight to recognize the impossibility of their marriage because, as she says, "We shall never be again as we were!" (*NY* XX, 405).

At the end of *The Wings of the Dove*, James manages to create an overwhelming sense of loss—in his readers as well as his characters. The novel suggests, in fact, that loss is the most definitive human experience. Sears has argued that in the late novels, James's "imagination so orders reality that the possibilities for happiness that face each character inevitably have an either-or quality about them, and yet the characters are all the kind of people for whom the alternative to the fulfillment of their desires is an empty, pointless existence" (72). Certainly *The Wings of the Dove* suggests that human happiness is not possible, in part because it always seems to necessitate a violation of the Other. In this regard, the book is the darkest of the late novels, and its darkness seems in large part the result of the unrealized potential for greatness in both Milly Theale and Kate Croy.

Written during 1903 and published late in 1904, *The Golden Bowl* was James's last completed novel (except for *The Outcry* [1911], a novel James based on his 1909 play of the same name) and in many regards his most brilliant. Perhaps, as Bradbury suggests, "it completed his *oeuvre*" because "he had taken the novel form as far as he could, or even as far as it could then go" (*Later Novels* 4); it certainly may be said to bring together many of the most important themes, figures, and techniques of his long career. In it, he takes up the international theme by which his career had first been launched and makes it much more central than it had been in either *The Ambassadors* or *The Wings of the Dove*. For the first time in his major fiction, he imagines an actual uniting of American and European that not only does not result in the destruction of either but actually generates an offspring. In *The Golden Bowl*, James's fascination with the enigmatic relationships of appearance and reality, of power and innocence, of the individual and society, is given its greatest range. In its reliance on figurative language, *The Golden Bowl* continues the late style of *The Ambassadors* and *The Wings of the Dove*, yet carries that style further than ever before. In it, the possibilities and limitations of language are tested to their breaking point. It is small wonder that James wrote his agent that *The Golden Bowl* was "the best book, I seem to conceive, that I have ever done," even though its eventual unpopularity (and his disappointment with the sales of the New York Edition) led him later to conclude that it had been "the most arduous and thankless task I ever set myself" (*HJL* IV, 591).

A part of the arduousness of writing *The Golden Bowl* undoubtedly lay in the subject itself: for what more horrifying deception is conceivable than a husband's adultery with his own mother-in-law? The betrayal and violation of another human being had been an abiding theme in James's fiction, and in the fiction of the nineties he had dramatized the betrayal and violation suffered by children at the hands of adults. In *The Golden Bowl*, he presents comparably intimate relationships, but in this instance the characters are all adults—and they are not destroyed by the betrayal and violation. Clearly, however, at the center of the whole problematic of Self and Other is just this recognition and fear of the human capacity to deceive, betray, and violate the Other. James is finally, in this crowning novel, able to imagine the possibility of life after betrayal.

As we have seen, both *The Ambassadors* and *The Wings of the Dove* use the international structure as a way of developing their concerns, but in both those novels, the international aspect of the subject is of far less significance than it had been in such earlier work as *The Portrait of a Lady* and as it is in *The Golden Bowl*. *The Golden Bowl* introduces James's most fantastically wealthy Americans and his most aristocratic European ever. Furthermore, the Americans in this novel are not represented by one of James's "long and lean," passive and intellectual American men, like Lambert Strether, nor solely by his spontaneous and innocent American Girl. The Girl in this instance has attached to her a father, and not one of the absent fathers of business so typical of James's other fiction. Thus, the relationship between the American Girl, the symbol and repository of America's "best" cultural values, and her father, the producer of the money she so carelessly spends in Europe, is made central in this novel. James had from the outset of his career shown concern for his homeland's devotion to "business," to the making of money, and the American man who symbolized that devotion came in for a good deal of his satiric criticism. *The Golden Bowl* is, however, his first presentation of that American businessman's relation to and responsibility for the American Girl.

The self-indulgent, emotionally incestuous relationship between Adam and Maggie Verver is presented in *The Golden Bowl* as the source of Maggie Verver's innocence and, ultimately, of her failure to establish a sense of identity. The Maggie Verver of the first half of the novel is very similar to Milly Theale in having a core of emptiness and nothingness. But in *The Golden Bowl*, James suggests that this is not a permanent or fatal deficiency; Maggie has no mysterious illness to which she can retreat. Although her relationship with Adam has the potential to be similarly disabling, she confronts the exploitation others would make of this and, unlike Milly Theale, decides not to die but to live. James's most positive treatment of the American Girl, Maggie rejects the bond to her father and claims an adult marital relationship for herself. She is the only one of the American Girls who possesses and accepts sexual passion, and in fact this passion propels her into selfhood.

Adam Verver represents James's most disquieting presentation of the acquisitive nature of Americans, who believe that there is nothing—culture, tradition, even people—that money cannot buy. Possessing "the spirit of the connoisseur," Adam Verver sets out "to rifle the Golden Isles" (*NY* XXIII, 140–41) of the art treasures he has the money to purchase. As Viola Hopkins Winner has shown, Adam's attempt to purchase art—and the history of the culture that produced it—is "wrong" because it is based on a purely aesthetic and acquisitive attitude toward art rather than on a recognition that art is "an expression of human life" (166). Adam Verver is confident that he can buy any piece of art he wants, house it all in his museum in American City, and thereby provide his native country with the "culture" and "tradition" it lacks. He similarly appropriates people. He purchases Prince Amerigo as a husband for Maggie, just as he would an expensive painting: "the instinct, the particularly sharpened appetite of the collector, had fairly served as a basis for his acceptance of the Prince's suit" (*NY* XXIII, 140). Later, he buys the penniless Charlotte Stant to be his wife, not out of any desire for marital intimacy but to make Maggie feel better about having herself married the prince. Adam's acquisitive, dehumanizing attitude is initially shared by Maggie, who explains to her husband-to-be that he is "one of the things that can only be got over here. You're a rarity, an object of beauty, an object of price" (*NY* XXIII, 12).

Although both Maggie and Adam Verver display a far more exaggerated form of American acquisitiveness than any of James's other Americans, the difference is one of degree, not kind. It represents an approach to the Other that denies the Other's subjectivity and therefore that precludes the possibility of any genuinely intimate relation to the Other. We see a similar spirit in Milly Theale's desire to find in Europe a sense of having lived and in her approaching Kate Croy and Merton Densher as two more elements of the European scene. We also see this spirit in Lambert Strether's relegation of Mme de Vionnet to the status of symbol—albeit a symbol of all that is associated in his mind with tradition, the past, and "culture." The Americans in all three novels have a tendency to view the English and Europeans they encounter as exotics—which is beautifully captured in Strether's response to hearing Mme de Vionnet speak French: the "result was odd, fairly veiling her identity, shifting her back into a mere voluble class or race to the intense audibility of which he was by this time inured. When she spoke the charming, slightly strange English he best knew her by he seemed to feel her as a creature, among all the millions, with a language quite to herself, the real monopoly of a special shade of speech, beautifully easy for her, yet of a colour and a cadence that were both inimitable and matters of accident" (*NY* XXII, 261).

The problem resulting from the encounter of Americans and Europeans is the form in which James casts the larger problem of Self and Other, and of individual and society. Because national differences seem, in their appearance, so clear, both the Americans and the Europeans of the late fiction accept those appearances as congruent with the reality of the individual. In *The Golden Bowl*, as nowhere else, James exhaustively dramatizes the incongruities between appearances and reality, incongruities that both Maggie Verver and Prince Amerigo (and the other characters as well) are forced to discover. As Armstrong writes, in one of the best discussions to date of *The Golden Bowl*: "James believes . . . that to know someone or something means to pay equal attention to both the individual and the type. To know the Prince's type is not to know his individuality because his past history may influence but cannot encompass the private self he is still always becoming. His type is nothing more than the ground on which his individual freedom is thrown" (*Phenomonology* 143). Maggie's discovery in the course of the novel is not simply, then, the discovery, as Fanny Assingham claims, of " 'what's called Evil—with a very big E: for the first time in her life' " (*NY* XXIII, 385). Nor is it simply the discovery that appearances may be manipulated to conceal realities. Most important, what she learns is that the personal relationship of marriage requires her to deal with her husband as a subject, not an object, to be willing to extend to him the same status of subject that she wants for herself.

What enables her to discover this, and to act on it, is her own decision to live not as a solipsistic extension of her father but as an independent self. The ultimate source of her decision is, of course, Henry James himself, who in this novel determined to create an American Girl able and willing to withstand "the whole assault of life," not as a detached observer but as a fully engaged participant. In this regard, *The Golden Bowl* registers a triumph of the possibility for human connection, both in the private realm and—because of the representative status of Maggie and the prince—in the social realm.

Because Maggie Verver is endowed with a positive force, a nascent "talent for life," her foil, Charlotte Stant, emerges as a much more typical "bad heroine" than does Kate Croy. Just as Milly Theale learned to see herself in contrast to Kate Croy, so Maggie Verver inclines to define herself in contrast to Charlotte Stant. But Maggie inherits some of Kate's "talent for life" and also some of her intelligence, so that, unlike Milly Theale, Maggie becomes the actor, the doer, the controller of the others. Given Maggie and Adam's unwitting complicity in the adultery, Charlotte is made to pay an extraordinarily high price for wanting to appropriate the prince for herself. Banished to America and a life with Adam Verver, whose "silken noose" entwines her beautiful neck, Charlotte is deprived not only of the prince but also of any knowledge or understanding of the situation she finds herself in. She is sacrificed, as Maggie explains to the prince, for their survival: "It's as if her unhappiness had been necessary to us—as if we had needed her, at her own cost, to build us up and start us" (*NY* XXIV, 346). This kind of statement is what makes Maggie Verver so unsettling and unappealing a character to some readers; she uses Charlotte in much the same way Kate Croy proposed to use Milly Theale. And yet this kind of quality, in the Jamesian universe, seems necessary to any decision to engage in life rather than withdraw from it. In the emotional economy of James's fiction, especially the late fiction, the individual's flourishing seems always dependent on the suffering of another— which is perhaps why James was so reluctant to create a hero or heroine who would in fact choose to flourish.

The figure of Maggie Verver, who determines to live, whatever the cost to herself, her father, the prince, or Charlotte, bears a resemblance of sorts to the figure of James himself in his famous Galerie d'Apollon dream that he describes in his autobiography. The text of the dream, to which James refers as "the most appalling yet most admirable nightmare of my life," reads as follows:

The climax of this extraordinary experience—which stands alone for me as a dream-adventure founded in the deepest, quickest, clearest act of cogitation and comparison, act indeed of life-saving energy, as well as in unutterable fear—was the sudden pursuit, through an open door, along a huge high saloon, of a just dimly-descried figure that retreated in terror before my rush and dash (a glare of inspired reaction from irresistible but shameful dread), out of the room I had a moment before been desperately, and all the more abjectly, defending by the push of my shoulder against hard pressure on lock and bar from the other side. The lucidity, not to say the sublimity, of the crisis had consisted of the great thought that I, in my appalled state, was probably still more appalling than the awful agent, creature or presence, whatever he was, whom I had guessed, in the suddenest wild start from sleep,the sleep within my sleep, to be making for my place of rest. The triumph of my impulse, perceived in a flash as I acted on it by myself at a bound, forcing the door outward, was the grand thing, but the great point of the whole was the wonder of my final recognition. Routed, dismayed, the tables turned on him by my so surpassing him for straight aggression and dire intention, my visitant was already but a diminished spot in the long perspective, the tremendous, glorious hall, as I say, over the far-gleaming floor of which, cleared for the occasion of its great line of priceless vitrines down the middle, he sped for *his* life, while a great storm of thunder and lightning played through the deep embrasures of high windows at the right. (*SB* 196)

Like James in his dream, Maggie Verver, awakened from her state of sublime innocence and indifference, succeeds in "surpassing" Charlotte and the prince "for straight aggression and dire intention." In the language of the novel, she is "innocence outraged," the lamb who suddenly becomes the aggressor—in order to save her own life. Maggie's own most triumphant moment of "turning the tables on" Charlotte occurs during the evening of bridge at Fawns. Maggie, walking on the terrace, watching the others play cards, and meditating on "the horror of the thing hideously *behind*" their harmless appearance, suddenly senses that Charlotte has left the card game to seek her out. "The splendid shining supple creature was out of the cage, was at large" (*NY* XXIV, 239). Charlotte has come to inquire whether she has inadvertently offended Maggie in some way, since Maggie's appearance seems to have changed. Trapping Maggie through deliberately false language, Charlotte forces her to admit, "I accuse you—I accuse you of nothing" (*NY* XXIV, 250). But Maggie has only pretended that she is still the naïve and innocent young girl she once was, and she manages to inspire terror and retreat in Charlotte by reassuring Charlotte that she has never held any grievance against her and, finally, by asking Charlotte to seal their talk by giving Maggie a kiss—in the full view, the "high publicity" of the others. Just as James in his dream discovered the success he could enjoy by taking an offensive, rather than a defensive, stance, because such aggression is just what his "visitant" least expects, so he presents Maggie Verver's success as the result of her surprising Charlotte by being herself something other than her appearance had suggested. Charlotte and the prince have been able to deceive Maggie through their manipulation of appearances and observances of the "forms"; and Maggie in turn defeats Charlotte through comparable manipulations and observances. In so doing, she not only defeats her rival but also achieves a sense of self that will allow her to establish herself in a more intimate relation to another than any other character in the late James.

If we consider the endings of the last three novels, the difference of *The Golden Bowl* becomes quite clear:

"Then there we are!" said Strether.

But she turned to the door, and her headshake was now the end. "We shall never be again as we were!"

" 'See'? I see nothing but *you*." And the truth of it had with this force after a moment so strangely lighted his eyes that as for pity and dread of them she buried her own in his breast.

Whereas both *The Ambassadors* and *The Wings of the Dove* end with a severance of a tie, a parting of ways with no hope of reunion, the final embrace in *The Golden Bowl* projects an intimacy that will last beyond the end of the novel. Yet the threat to the Self that the embrace also reflects remains an inherent part of Maggie's relationship to Amerigo. The desire to transcend the confines of herself that has enabled Maggie to wage battle for her marriage and her life must, to be fulfilled, risk the exposure of herself that will inevitably ensue. Or, as Armstrong puts it, "The contradiction between conflict and care remains unresolved. . . . In fact, contesting each other's claims up to the very end, both terms of this contradiction express themselves in the final embrace on which the curtain falls" (*Phenomenology* 184).

This fragility of personal relationships is presented in the novel as a result and function of the epistemological and linguistic limitations of the human condition. Once she begins to realize that appearances do not necessarily mean what she had thought, knowledge becomes for Maggie "a fascination as well as a fear" (*NY* XXIV, 140). Like Strether, whose "process of vision" eventually forces him to confront not only the "truth" of Chad's relation to Mme de Vionnet but the "truth" of his own life as well, Maggie's journey to knowledge forces her to confront both the truth of the relation between Amerigo and Charlotte and the truth about her own participation in allowing that relation to develop. The key difference, of course, is that Chad's relation to Mme de Vionnet has not constituted a betrayal of Strether in the same way that Amerigo's relation to Charlotte does of Maggie. And unlike Milly Theale, who "turns her face to the wall" and dies when the truth of Kate's relation to Densher is revealed to her, Maggie determines to live with that knowledge, regain her husband's loyalty, and yet do so without destroying the fabric of their lives. Knowledge, in fact, is what empowers her because Amerigo's knowing that she knows will render her a different person in his eyes. " 'Yes, look, look,' she seemed to see him hear her say even while her sounded words were other—'look, look, both at the truth that still survives in that smashed evidence and at the even more remarkable appearance that I'm not such a fool as you supposed me. Look at the possibility that since I *am* different there may still be something in it for you—if you're capable of working with me to get that out' " (*NY* XXIV, 187–88).

Among the truths Maggie discovers, then, is the "truth" of her own appearance to the others. She thus becomes self-conscious in a way she had never been before; she watches herself playing her part in the drama of their lives and learns that she can in fact alter the script and control the plot: she is not condemned to a particular role. Gabriel Pearson has said that just this "sharp gap that seems to open between the self as perceived by others and as experienced by itself" constitutes "one of the disconcerting depths in this novel" (320). This self-consciousness differs from that displayed by Milly Theale. Milly assumes the roles that others have tried to assign to her and to this extent transcends them, but she uses such self-conscious role playing as a purely defensive maneuver; others are thus always in control of the script. Maggie, in contrast, comes to recognize in others a greater complexity than Milly ever does, and yet Maggie nevertheless so successfully manipulates appearances as to gain control over the script itself. To do this, she is forced to become aware of the continually shifting relations among the members of the two marriages. From moment to moment, she must calculate what her father knows, what the prince knows, and what Charlotte knows.

The efficacy of James's late style is nowhere more apparent than in his re-creating for the reader these same uncertainties. Especially in the second half of *The Golden Bowl*, where we are trapped almost entirely in Maggie's consciousness, the prose renders us helpless as readers to know any more definitively the "truth" of what each of the characters knows than does Maggie herself—not to mention that the text sometimes forces us to question Maggie's conclusions as well. Moreover, because the "truth" of the adultery is so horrifying, it is a truth that cannot be spoken. To bring it out into the open would be to destroy their lives and their world. Thus, language becomes a way of concealing knowledge rather than revealing it, and silence comes to be more communicative of truth than speech is. For, ultimately, Maggie is determined to preserve her world by maintaining—and forcing the others to maintain—the appearance that everything is perfectly as it should be. Thus, the real reasons for Adam and Charlotte's removal to America are never spoken—by any of the characters. All of them live in terror of what Adam may, in fact, know, but his silence is even more profound than Maggie's. This sacrifice of the bond with her father is, of course, the highest price Maggie must pay for her marriage and her life.

In *The Golden Bowl*, then, James finally confronts the violation and destructiveness that may ensue from intimacy, and he asserts the power of the Self to withstand those threats and live beyond their pain. To do so requires of the Self an energetic counteraggression, a willingness, that is, to relinquish innocence and claim the rights—and responsibilities—of power. In so doing, the Self enters the fallen world of time and accepts the conditions of being human.

# 10

# How Long Is Long; How Short Short! Henry James and the Small Circular Frame

*Maqbool Aziz*

The exclamatory edge in the title of this essay is not just for the lark: it is intended to draw attention to a considerable critical scandal—the shockingly poor status often accorded, in formal study of literature, to the ancient and important literary genre variously called *short story, tale, novella, nouvelle*, etc.[1] As these terms in themselves quite graphically indicate, the theoretical urge behind the appellations has only one purpose—to institute an order of demarcation between the supposedly superior claims of the novel and all the rest, which are *less* than the novel. Indeed, all too often academic discussion of the shorter and the lesser form tends to degenerate into inevitable considerations of its length in relation, in particular, to its more elevated and honored sister, the novel.[2] There is nothing wrong with this: novels are longer than short stories, and any consideration of their relative length is a perfectly legitimate starting point for more substantive evaluations. Lately, however, the matter has been complicated by yet newer scales of classification. Thus, for instance, the following, though near enough in length, often turn up under beguiling, generic guises: Hemingway's *The Old Man and the Sea*, Lawrence's *St. Mawr*, Anita Brookner's *Hotel du Lac*, James's *The Siege of London* and *In the Cage*, and, say, Graham Greene's *Dr. Fischer of Geneva*. The first is deemed a "short novel," the second is considered a "novella," the third a "novel proper," the fourth and fifth "tales" (*In the Cage* was originally treated as a novel), and the last a "prose parable." Clearly, something more metaphysical and mystical than considerations of length is needed to give a semblance of order to the proliferating identities and appellations. As matters stand, one could, in fact, in any consideration of James's own short fictions, add yet another turn to this general, acritical screw. One might say that if Kipling's "Mary Postgate" or "The Gardener," or Hemingway's "A Clean Well-Lighted Place," or Maupassant's "Two Friends," or Kafka's

"A Hunger Artist," or Joyce's "Araby" are all classic short stories, then, surely, Henry James never attempted any. By the same token, if *Hotel du Lac* is a novel, then, surely, James wrote many more novels than we give him credit for. Many of his "tales" are longer than many a slim novel of today, whereas none are quite as skimpy as the classical short stories listed above. There is, in short, no real escape from the following questions: In the realm of fiction, how long after all is long; how short, short? Which is better, the long or the short? Does length really matter as a category of criticism?

Any cursory survey of academic study and teaching of literature should indicate that considerations of length have played a major role in shaping literary curricula, which, in turn, have influenced the field of academic publishing. The shorter works of modern masters such as James, Conrad, Lawrence, and Faulkner, to name only a few, rarely receive anything more than a very short shrift in the classroom; similarly, few elicit interpretive studies entirely devoted to themselves. The manner in which this state of affairs can distort aesthetic and critical standards may be gleaned from the established, high reputation of a profoundly tedious work such as *The Sacred Fount* and the almost total neglect of such sparkling works by James as *The Siege of London* and *In the Cage*.

It would be quite wrong to attribute this state of affairs to this or that merely managerial whim of the School of English. As with most matters of this kind in literary-critical discourse, the making of this peculiar prejudice too can be traced back to the Greeks—or, better still, to our misconceptions and distortions of the ancient Greek context. Were it not for the age-old literary terrorism of the epic—as we taught ourselves to *mis*take the epic to be—life today would have been much simpler and the fortunes of the shorter narrative altogether different. Fielding's supremely awkward early attempt to define the novel— "comic epic poem in prose"—nicely underscores the point. His decision to seek refuge with the epic for the new species of "romance" he had attempted is, of course, perfectly understandable. In the century of its evolution, with its ludicrous and largely make-believe preoccupation with things "classical" and "Augustan," the newly evolving "novel" simply could not have escaped the tyranny of the epic, especially in an age in which the genesis of the epic was virtually unknown.

Ever since that first stranglehold, the epic has held menacing sway over all areas of literature; it has determined, even dictated, most terms and categories of literary criticism, quite as it has given rise also to numerous misconceptions. With the similarly "classical" weaponry of "history" there to assist it, the majesty of the epic has been the mainstay of the novel's extraordinary critical prestige, needless to say, against the lowly stature thus accorded all the shorter forms.[3] As a consequence, therefore, not only have we forgotten that the short narrative (short story, ballad, fable, parable, etc.) is of an older vintage than all longer narrative forms (the epic, the romance, the novel, compilations such as histories, etc.), but we have also come to believe that the fake antiquity of the longer narrative is a guarantee also of its aesthetic superiority and excellence. Our critical disdain of the mere "tale" has become a reflex response.

Few would dispute that a *short* tale is infinitely more *natural*—and, therefore, aesthetically more appealing because it is immediately completer—than the epic, the romance, or the novel. Indeed, when these longer species wish to engage the attention of the reader-listener under conditions of verisimilitude, they always resort to the strategies of the shorter modes: the epic and the romance with their episodes; the novel with its episodes, chapters, segments, installments. The "naturalness" and intrinsic orderliness of the shorter mode may well be the secret of its breathtaking longevity—nearly four thousand years of unbroken existence in a dozen or more linguistic and cultural contexts. From the Vedic tales to the Sanskrit tales of the *Panchatantra*, to the tales of the Old Testament, to the *Jatakes* (tales) of the Buddhist world, and on to the treasure troves of the Persian *Hazaar Dastaan* and its sister, the celebrated Arabic compendium *Alf Laila Wa Laila* (the so-called Arabian Nights), and then on to its reincarnation in Boccaccio's *Ten Nights* (*Decameron*), there's plenty. And, of course, we need no reminding that the Greek *muthos* ("myth") is after all a short "plot"— a short fiction!

It is wrong to speak of the short story as a "junior" among literary forms. Quite the opposite seems more accurate. Whereas the history of most literary forms shows periods of turbulence and transformation, the progress of the shorter mode has been a model of integrity and constancy. The problematic status of the short tale, Jamesian or otherwise, in the contemporary academic world is due not to the genesis or the peculiarly circumscribed character of the genre. Rather, it has its roots in the shoddy development of the scales of literary criticism—scales according to which "substance" has often been seen, and still is seen, as an exclusive by-product of the notions of "length" and "scope." Substance, length, and scope together constitute that menacing buzz word of modern criticism, the dreaded "complexity"—the foster-mother, we might add, of the no-less-frightful "profundity." How can a mere "short" claim to be either complex or profound![4] As a colleague of mine, asked to give a lecture on a set of tales by various authors, nervously complained, "But tell me what is there to say about a 'short story' "!

"A lot—a stupendous lot," Henry James would have said, responding quite angrily to such slight done to his "small circular frame," his "beautiful and blest nouvelle," his "shorter form." He contributed no less than 112 of these, in varying mode and length, and he well believed a gathering of "good little tales" was an achievement substantive enough for any writer to claim he had presented, in miniature form, a record of his time. James's devotion to the form was complete and unceasing: he could never dream of "renouncing the nouvelle." In later years, when his novel writing began to show signs of wear and tear on the imagination, he was able to turn out several exquisite *nouvelles*.

James's delightful critical evaluation—one of his early critical masterpieces—

210 Henry James's Fiction

of the tales of Maupassant (an author who was a principal source of his own immediate inspiration) provides a useful way into James's own handling of the "condensed form." James is well aware of the initial difficulty the British reader might find with the shorter form. "The little story is but scantily relished in England, where readers take their fiction rather by the volume than by the page, and the novelist's idea is apt to resemble one of those old fashioned carriages which require a wide court to turn round. In America, where it is associated pre-eminently with Hawthorne's name, with Edgar Poe's, and with that of Mr. Bret Harte, the short tale has had a better fortune. France, however, has been the land of its great prosperity, and M. de Maupassant had from the first the advantage of addressing a public accustomed to catch on, as the modern phrase is, quickly" (*LC*-II, 534–35). James then proceeds to tell his British reader, who may have difficulty "catching on," something about the general artistic procedure of M. de Maupassant:

[Maupassant] fixes a hard eye on some small spot of human life, usually some ugly, dreary, shabby, sordid one, takes up the particle, and squeezes it either till it grimaces or till it bleeds. Sometimes the grimace is very droll, sometimes the wound is very horrible; but in either case the whole thing is real, observed, noted, and represented, not an invention or a castle in the air. M. de Maupassant sees human life as a terribly ugly business relieved by the comical, but even the comedy is for the most part the comedy of misery, of aridity, of ignorance, helplessness and grossness. When the laugh is not for these things, it is for the little *saletés* (to use one of his own favorite words) of luxurious life, which are intended to be prettier, but which can scarcely be said to brighten the picture. (*LC*-II, 536).

If M. de Maupassant "fixes a hard eye on some small spot of human life," then a distinguished Russian contemporary of his has, to the young critic in James, his interest elsewhere. In 1897, a year before the publication of *In the Cage*, James provides an equally penetrating evaluation of Turgenev; the passage quoted below occurs in a discussion of Turgenev's "condensed" compositions. The image of a "patch" (or "spot") of experience that might be squeezed to draw blood (presumably of significance and meaning) is common to both evaluations, even though there is a gap between the two of almost a decade:

[Turgenev's] vision is of the world of character and feeling, the world of the relations life throws up at every hour and on every spot; he deals little, on the whole, in the miracles of chance,—the hours and spots over the edge of time and space; his air is that of the great central region of passion and motive, of the usual, the inevitable, the intimate— the intimate for weal and woe. No theme that he ever chooses but strikes us as full; yet with all we have the sense that their animation comes from within, and is not pinned to their backs like pricking objects used of old in the horse races of the Roman carnival, to make the animals run. Without a patch of "plot" to draw blood, the story he mainly tells us, the situation he mainly gives, runs as if for dear life. (*LC*-II, 1031)

In the Maupassant passage, "spot" is clearly a measure in a scale of time and space; in the Turgenev passage, "patch" is a measure, rather, of perception, meditation, and reflection. Maupassant's "small spot of human life," relying as it does on the "miracle of chance," makes for a story of incident, whereas Turgenev, more interested in "the great central region of passion and motive," gives us a story of character—but not character in any conventional sense of the word. There is an inevitability in all human behavior, as there is an inevitability in all human situations. Almost all aspects of character in the tales and novels of James are aspects of this inevitability; and its "animation," in particular works of fiction, "comes from within."

James's own practice, to which these and similar other distinctions in his criticism repeatedly allude, appears to be a synthesis of three traditions of the shorter form: the *conte* of Maupassant; the *nouvelle* of Turgenev, Maupassant, and George Eliot; and the moral tale of Hawthorne. His ultimate decision to call his shorter works "tales," rather than "stories" or "'novellas," may well be his way of pointing to an intended and achieved synthesis, in his work, of the modes he himself was most influenced by.

The designation—"tale"—is sanctified and given a touch of finality in the New York Edition of the *Novels and Tales of Henry James*. The term, of course, had made its appearance with the very first book, a collection of stories, published by James: *A Passionate Pilgrim and Other Tales* (1875). The first collective edition of the shorter works, however, is not called "tales" but "stories": *Stories Revived* (1885).[5] One of the stories revived, *A Passionate Pilgrim*, had made an earlier appearance in the garb of a "tale," just as another, *Daisy Miller*, had once been called "a study." The classificatory difficulty here is all too obvious: the critic is advised to stay away from the shifting sands of "stories," "tales," "novellas," "studies," etc. (How long is long; how short, short!)

Yet if we consider the question in the light of James's quiet reflections on Maupassant, Turgenev, and other practitioners of the art, and bear in mind that the term *tale* is imbued with a definite "tonal" peculiarity—consider the difference between "a tale told by an idiot" and "a story told by an idiot"—we can begin to detect a theoretical justification in James's choice. The term *tale* seems to fit James's reworking of a familiar mode more accurately than any of the other appellations. The tonal peculiarity that clearly stands out in James's shorter works has to do with pace and contour, which create the typical Jamesian resonance, rather than with any mere "patch of plot." In the typical Jamesian tale, the contour is often circular—a "small circular frame." Sometimes, as in *The Siege of London*, it is quite literally circular; that is, at the end of the imaginative journey, the mind returns to the opening frame and its mood. Whereas the contour is circular, the pace of a typical Jamesian tale is controlled so as to create a cumulative effect that is neither too languorous nor too brisk. Thus one might say that James's tales carry and convey a sense, an aura, of "treatment" that one normally associates with novels and novel writing, and a terseness and sharpness of focus that is often the special preserve of the anecdote.

As the buoyancy of the *conte* merges with the principle of development, a small and circular frame is born.

Needless to add, in the large body of James's work, individual instances of all measures of "pace," "stretch," and "contour" are available. Such early masterpieces as "The Madonna of the Future" and "Four Meetings," for instance, point straight to the practice of Maupassant rather than to that of Turgenev. The vast majority, however, of James's own condensed compositions follow a course of their own, in which two of James's favorite binary oppositions—incident and character; idea and form—coalesce to order a form that is free of the temptations and terrors of "overdoing." Linearity having been dispensed with, it is in the blest circularity of the "tale" that James is most at home and in his very own. To some readers, however, this same circularity comes as a bit of a shock. It causes them to wonder and exclaim: "But where is the story? Did anything happen at all?!''

Virtually nothing happens when the much married Mrs. Nancy Headway of the backwaters decides to lay siege to the glitterati of London of another day; nothing of much consequence happens when the simple girl behind the telegraph counter, caught in a cage as it were, begins to look a little too closely at the same glitterati as they send secret telegraphic messages to one another; nothing happens when the original of Eliot's J. Alfred Prufrock, having found Mrs. Worthingham worth precious little, decides to go back to his old, somewhat crapy Cornelia to raise "the overwhelming question." Yet a great deal happens to the alert reader. James pursues his fictional characters and incidents only insofar as these enable him to go after a hundred complacencies of the reader. It is the reader who must make the happening happen, must do his or her own share of the work—or the circle of inevitability will not weave the intended illusion. "In every novel," James observed, "the work is divided between the writer and the reader; but the writer makes the reader very much as he makes his characters. When he makes him ill, that is makes him indifferent, he does no work; the writer does all. When he makes him well, that is, makes him interested, then the reader does quite half the labor. In making such a deduction as I have just indicated, the reader would be doing but his share of the task; the grand point is to get him to make it. I hold that there is a way."[6] It comes as a small shock to remember that James had formulated his "grand point" about the collaborative art of fiction when he himself had yet to compose his first major work of fiction. Even more startling is the fact that he had a perfectly sound and plausible reason for proposing the ideal working liaison between the reader and the novelist.

It would appear James had early made an important choice for himself—the choice of a particular brand of realism with which he intended to counteract the long specter of *the odd* on English narrative and dramatic prose. There is something of Matthew Arnold's strictures on Chaucer in James's precocious assault on Dickens, roughly of the same date as the theoretical formulation quoted above. The mainspring of the two criticisms—Arnold on Chaucer and James on

Dickens—seems almost identical; and so does the intended moral. Chaucer will not do because "high seriousness" is lacking in him; quite in the same spirit, Dickens must be rejected because he is not much of a philosopher. The crucial passage in James's criticism of Dickens is worth quoting in some detail:

If we might hazard a definition of [Dickens's] literary character, we should . . . call him the greatest of superficial novelists. We are aware that this definition confines him to an inferior rank in the department of letters which he adorns; but we accept this consequence of our proposition. It were, in our opinion, an offense against humanity to place Mr. Dickens among the greatest novelists. . . . He has added nothing to our understanding of human character. . . . He is master of but two alternatives: he reconciles us to what is commonplace, and he reconciles us to what is odd. The value of the former service is questionable; and the manner in which Mr. Dickens performs it sometimes conveys a certain impression of charlatanism. The value of the latter service is incontestable, and here Mr. Dickens is an honest, an admirable artist. But what is the condition of the truly great novelist? For him there are no alternatives, for him there are no oddities, for him there is nothing outside of humanity. He cannot shirk it; it imposes itself upon him. For him, alone, therefore, there is a true and a false; for him alone it is possible to be right, because it is possible to be wrong. Mr. Dickens is a great observer, and a great humorist, but he is nothing of a philosopher. Some people may hereupon say, so much the better; we say, so much the worse. For a novelist very soon has need of a little philosophy. . . . the author must *understand* [emphasis added] what he is talking about. (*LC*-I, 856–57)[7]

Coming from a young man of twenty-three, about a master who had already been writing novels and tales for longer than all the years of the green youth, these strictures no doubt contain something quite "brattish." (Strangely enough, young James's view of Dickens had quite an impact on some later criticism of fiction: F. R. Leavis's celebrated first dismissal of Dickens, in *The Great Tradition*, owes a great deal to James. It, in fact, reproduces the sentiments just quoted.) Yet when we look back over the half century of James's own practice of the art of fiction, the essential point of his criticism stands out in sharp relief. From medieval drama through Chaucer, Shakespeare, and Ben Jonson, through Restoration comedy, Fielding, and Jane Austen, down indeed to the bustling world of Dickens's own character types, literary realism in English literature, in the novel in particular, seems to have relied rather too heavily on the beguiling attractions and charms of the odd in human character and situations.

James's example amply demonstrates he has no interest in the "oddities" of life and experience—a work as thoroughly Dickensian as *In the Cage* has no odd type in it—for the obvious reason that oddities of character and situation, even when perfectly real and engaging, do not contribute to "our understanding of human character." The *understanding* of it—the author's as well as the reader's understanding of it—and not the representational figure per se, is what really matters, what should matter to the novelist and the reader. The ritual of the art of fiction for James is to get together with the reader and make the artist's observations and presentments bristle with the life of understanding. To say this is not to repeat the cliché that Henry James is a psychological novelist. Rather, to say this is to reassert (with James himself) that, unlike the Dickens of his early criticism, he himself certainly is a philosophical novelist—but in the "right real" sense of that much abused adjective. James's thought (his philosophizing, that is) *dwells* in his fiction, as his fiction *dwells* in his thought. It is this indwelling of thought with representation that we take back with us and that enables us to challenge our complacencies, as we take leave of Mrs. Nancy Headway, or White-Mason, or the caged girl, in order to return to the glare of our day.

The insistence on the ideal of understanding is absolutely crucial: its manifestation in the tales and novels is James's unique contribution to the art of fiction. All issues of technique, form, point of view, structure, and length are means toward this single and singular end. An insatiable curiosity about human affairs—the emphasis must fall on the word *human*, since James is singularly devoid of any interest in, say, nature—impels all the operations of thought, therefore giving all the particularities of the imagined experience the greatest attention and focus. This pursuit of the minute particular, of course, has its drawbacks: it demands from the reader a devoted attention; and it can leave a grossly misleading impression of the artistic intention. In a piece curiously entitled "A Prediction in Regard to Three English Authors," T. S. Eliot, who owed so much to James's tales and novels, goes to the heart of the matter. Eliot sees in James's *thought* the qualities he admires in the poetry of the English metaphysical poets: the active collaboration between thought and emotion, in the interest, of course, of *understanding*.

James has suffered the usual fate of those who, in England, have outspokenly insisted on the importance of technique. His technique has received the kind of praise usually accorded to some useless, ugly, and ingenious piece of carving which has taken a very long time to make; and he is widely reproached for not succeeding in doing the things that he did not attempt to do. With "character," in the sense in which the portrayal of character is usually expected in the English novel, he had no concern; but his critics do not understand that "character" is only one of the ways in which to grasp reality: had James been a better hand at character, he would have been a coarser hand altogether, and would have missed the sensibility to the peculiar class of data which were his province.

Eliot goes on to make a startling comparison—though the surprise soon disappears as we look at the suggestion in the light of Eliot's view of the metaphysicals:

The example which Henry James offered us was not that of a style to imitate, but of an integrity so great, a vision so exacting, that it was forced to the extreme of care and punctiliousness of exact expression. . . . James did not provide us with ideas, but with another world of thought and feeling. For such a world some have gone to Dostoievsky [the one of loose and baggy monsters, according to James], some to James; and I am inclined to think that the spirit of James, so much less violent, with so much more reasonableness and so much more resignation than that of the Russian, is no less profound, and is more useful, more applicable for our time.[8]

"An integrity so great, a vision so exacting," in an imaginative world that is a "world of thought and feeling": it is a pity that so much James criticism, instead of giving its attention to the "care and punctiliousness of exact expression"— with which the novelist orders his "peculiar class of data" toward a final synthesis of thought and feeling in the presented case—for so long has been preoccupied with abstracting and extracting formulations out of, and away from, the coherent and composite world of the fictions. The critic in James himself would have proceeded to assess the actual working of *thought* in the particularities of a tale or a novel. The process of "indwelling" of thought in James's work, then, compels the critic to disregard all shortcuts, all the mundane categories and questions of criticism—questions of length, or development (a highly dubious proposition at the best of times), or technique and character and philosophy, in the awkward senses of the three terms. The critic must do, with the author, his own share of the work. Needless to say, the ideal of criticism here being endorsed stands the risk of exposing the limits of criticism itself. How can one unveil the working of thought in, say, *The Siege of London* or *In the Cage* or *Crapy Cornelia* without wanting to rewrite the tales? This is not the place to explore the complex implications, for criticism and epistemology, of this question. Something more modest, however, a brief rereading perhaps of a few aspects of the tales, seems quite in order. *The Siege of London* has a wider focus that is gradually narrowed down (the top of a cone spiraling down to its point) as the subject is contained within the circular form of the tale. *In the Cage* takes the opposite course: the point of the cone spirals outward yet is contained within the circular frame. The narrative movement in *Crapy Cornelia* is largely horizontal.

Since the publication in 1934 of Edmund Wilson's influential essay on *The Turn of the Screw*, entitled "The Ambiguity of Henry James," the word *ambiguity* (together with the critical notion that has been thrust on it) has become the watchword of James studies. The treacherous word has been used to point to a variety of virtues and vices in James. Indeed, James's ambiguity is sometimes invoked and served up with such ambiguity that one knows not how to deal with ambiguity. When it is seen as a characteristic mark of his strength, the point of reference often tends to be the so-called open-endedness of his tales and novels. When, however, it is invoked to slight his achievement, the ambiguity becomes a natural and logical consequence of his bad prose and tedious thinking. The English word derives from the seventeenth-century Latin *ambiguous*, which carries the sense of "going here and there." Its primary sense is much closer to "uncertainty" than "multiplicity of meaning." The peculiar critical connotation forced on the word by modern criticism, itself a by-product of modernistic relativism, is a recent phenomenon.

If it is true that "care and punctiliousness of exact expression" is dear to James the writer, and if *understanding* is the ideal his art strives for, then surely ambiguity cannot possibly have any real place in the Jamesian scheme. The function of his art is precisely to conquer and counter ambiguity. Why, then, does a writer as deliberate, as meticulous, as thoughtful, as careful about minute particulars, as certain of his moral vision as is James continue to invite the charge, or approbation, of ambiguity? Could it be that what is mistaken for ambiguity is a different kettle of fish?

What creates the impression of ambiguity is, in fact, the preponderance of *tacit* signifiers in James's tales and novels—the preponderance, that is, of things that are not said but that still mean as much as those that are actually said. Whereas the stated signifiers work in the open, on stage, the tacit signifiers work with and around the reader, contributing to the factor of tolerance—so to speak— in the composition. *Tolerance* derives from another eighteenth-century Latin word, *tolerare*—"to sustain." In its epistemological sense, the term refers to that factor surrounding an object, or a composition, or an idea, which not only provides the necessary perspective to the truth contained in the subject but also prepares the way for it to reveal itself on its own. It is this factor that, in the final analysis, coaxes the inevitabilities in the "great central region of passion and motive" to "animate" themselves "from within"—the mere "patch of plot" being just the starting point. Thus what we have in James is not ambiguity, either accidental or intentional, but a crucial dimension of depth—a multilayered and multidimensional "wroughting" of the imagined world to give it the maximum of authenticity. James's "cases" may not always be "real," or interesting—they are rarely not authentic as imaginative experience. As James's prefatory remarks to *The Turn of the Screw* show, he is chiefly interested in the question of the authenticity of the sense of evil and fear that he wishes to conjure up through the governess: James has little interest in her pathology per se.

There are a hundred ways in which the tacit signifiers are made to work on the active, collaborative mind of the reader. From punctilious attention to detail to careful balancing of one kind of detail against another to careful orchestrating of tonal variations, both in the speaking voice and in the actual, rhythmic pacing of the prose, to the many metaphoric underpinnings of theme, idea, and image: one could make a long list of the ways in which James's literary thought tries to come to grips with the fullness of a particular case. The risk of "overdoing," of which James was ever so conscious, pertains to this area of artistic deliberation rather than to the mechanics of the plot.

Here is how the opening section of *In the Cage* arrests our attention and begins to work on our minds:

It had occurred to her early that in her position—that of a young person spending, in framed and wired confinement, the life of a guineapig or a magpie—she should know a great many persons without their recognising the acquaintance. That made it an emotion the more lively—though singularly rare and always, even then, with opportunity still very much smothered—to see any one come in whom she knew, as she called it, outside, and who could add something to the poor identity of her function. Her function was to sit there with two young men—the other telegraphist and the counter-clerk; to mind the "sounder," which was always going, to dole out stamps and postal-orders, weigh letters, answer stupid questions, give difficult change and, more than anything else, count words as numberless as the sands of the sea, the words of the telegrams thrust, from morning to night, through the gap left in the high lattice, across the encumbered shelf that her forearm ached with rubbing. This transparent screen fenced out or fenced in, according to the side of the narrow counter on which the human lot was cast, the duskiest corner of a shop pervaded not a little, in winter, by the poison of perpetual gas and at all times by the presence of hams, cheese, dried fish, soap, varnish, paraffin, and other solids and fluids that she came to know perfectly by their smells without consenting to know them by their names.

The barrier that divided the little post-and-telegraph-office from the grocery was a frail structure of wood and wire; but the social, the professional separation was a gulf that fortune, by a stroke quite remarkable, had spared her the necessity of contributing at all publicly to bridge. When Mr. Cocker's young men stepped over from behind the other counter to change a five-pound note—and Mr. Cocker's situation, with the cream of the ''Court Guide'' and the dearest furnished apartments, Simpkin's, Ladle's, Thrupp's, just round the corner, was so select that his place was quite pervaded by the crisp rustle of these emblems—she pushed out the sovereigns as if the applicant were no more to her than one of the momentary appearances in the great procession; and this perhaps all the more from the very fact of the connection—only recognised outside indeed—to which she had lent herself with ridiculous inconsequence. She recognised the others the less because she had at last so unreservedly, so irredeemably, recognised Mr. Mudge. But she was a little ashamed, none the less, of having to admit to herself that Mr. Mudge's removal to a higher sphere—to a more commanding position, that is, though to a much lower neighborhood—would have been described still better as a luxury than as the simplification that she contented herself with calling it. He had, at any rate, ceased to be all day long in her eyes, and this left something a little fresh for them to rest on of a Sunday. During the three months that he had remained at Cocker's after her consent to their engagement, she had often asked herself what it was that marriage would be able to add to a familiarity so final. Opposite there, behind the counter of which his superior stature, his whiter apron, his more clustering curls and more present, too present, h's had been for a couple of years the principal ornament, he had moved to and fro before her as on the small sanded floor of their contracted future. She was conscious now of the improvement of not having to take her present and her future at once. They were about as much as she could manage when taken separate.

She had, none the less, to give her mind steadily to what Mr. Mudge had again written her about, the idea of her applying for a transfer to an office quite similar—she couldn't yet hope for a place in a bigger—under the very roof where he was foreman, so that, dangled before her every minute of the day, he should see her, as he called it, ''hourly,'' and in a part, the far N.W. district, where, with her mother, she would save, on their two rooms alone, nearly three shillings. It would be far from dazzling to exchange Mayfair for Chalk Farm, and it was something of a predicament that he so kept at her; still, it was nothing to the old predicaments, those of the early times of their great misery, her own, her mother's and her elder sister's—the last of whom had succumbed to all but absolute want when, as conscious, incredulous ladies, suddenly bereaved, betrayed, overwhelmed, they had slipped faster and faster down the steep slope at the bottom of which she alone had rebounded. Her mother had never rebounded any more at the bottom than on the way; had only rumbled and grumbled down and down, making, in respect of caps and conversation, no effort whatever, and too often, alas! smelling of whisky.
(*IC* 1–6)

Few opening movements in modern English fiction could rival this chapter for its quiet daring and audacity. James wants this first frame of his tale to speak volumes to the reader—*silently*, even as an oil canvas would to an attentive spectator. The "silence" matters, for the controlling image enunciated by the very title recommends it and anticipates it. Very much as a sense of evil is to mark and determine the interest in *The Turn of the Screw*, claustrophobia permeates *In the Cage*, at least in one sense. The prose itself works toward this effect. Its crowded, congested texture and halting, interrogative rhythms speak for the theme and the interest of the theme. Contrary to the impression taken by Leon Edel (*Treacherous Years* 235), there is nothing Sherlock Holmesian about the writing, simply because the narrative does not pose a problem to be solved. Indeed, it could be argued that the tale is devoid even of any theme in the conventional sense of the term. Its peculiar, charged texture is emblematic of a condition of experience that the writer wishes to convey to the reader. He is not trying "to get to the truth" of any problem. Thus we get the "feel," the "aura" of the subject, together with its potentialities, long before the subject is fully in focus. Before we are able to grasp the minute particulars, ordered as these are with searing economy, and before we are given any signal of recognizability to help us place the personage at the center of the scene, a sense of her powerful presence already begins to overwhelm us. The function that the thought—I do not mean the act of thinking—is called on to perform has little to do with the flaunting of an appropriate social observation. Its potency is expended in an effort to organize the resources of the language—interpolatory clauses, metaphorical asides, alliterative jingles, rhythmic pauses, sheer whimsies of sentiment, etc.—in a manner that will coax the reader to attend to the intriguing predicament of the unnamed heroine.

In an important sense, our introduction to the girl in the cage is our initiation into the final phase of what has come to be known as Victorian civilization, a civilization that—a rudimentary technology at its beck and call, its inherent injustices now fortified with a machinery—would begin the assault on the individual that is still with us. The Dickensian/Victorian ambience is nicely reflected by the personages that crowd about the girl as well as the places they come from and go to. The Dickensian flavor of Mr. Cocker, Mr. Buckton, Mr. Mudge, Mrs. Bubb, Mrs. Jordan, Lady Bradeen, Lord Rye, Lady Agnes, Captain Everard, Gussy, Cissy, Fritz, Simpkin's, Ladle's, Thrupp's, Suchbury, Monkhouse, Whiteroy, etc., is unmistakable. But James's immediate interest in the local-color possibilities of this world is not of the order of any easy, comic, or satirical gain: he needs the sociohistorical ambience in order to *understand* the main case. The extraordinary confidence with which the opening data are assembled and presented clearly shows James has already pondered the case.

In the first of the three paragraphs, the prose is largely austere. It stays close to the objects and ideas it wishes to capture. Though a sinister note is introduced in the very first sentence, with the highly evocative and emblematic images of the "guinea pig" and the "magpie," and though there are some highly suggestive leaps of the imagination here and there—"words as numberless as the sands of the sea," "the narrow counter on which the human lot was cast," etc.—these instances here create certain necessary reverberations that will expand and augment what is to follow in the next two paragraphs and will, in fact, resonate there.

The static first frame suddenly begins to bloom as James surely and deliberately begins to widen the context against which the plight of the heroine must be perceived, understood, evaluated. This context has a definite social and historical dimension. James—preeminently a social novelist—does not *portray* social issues, mores, or problems: he makes a literary and creative *use* of his unusually keen sense of society. He deploys the sense imaginatively in order to come to grips with forces that impel his fictional characters into action. Suggested early in the opening paragraph, the metaphor of "the barrier" between the grocery and the post office is picked up to construct the hierarchical ladder in Mr. Cocker's establishment: what it means, has always meant, might still mean to the bird in the cage. The brief sketch of Mr. Cocker is charged with the social dimension. So is the magnificently launched fortune of Mr. Mudge. The passage is worth going back to in order to assert how intimately James knows his characters and the peculiarities and stresses that inform their passage through life. Only a steady act of meditation could have made the following possible. The apple of our young lady's eye has been removed to a higher sphere:

He had, at any rate, ceased to be all day long in her eyes, and this left something a little fresh for them to rest on of a Sunday. During the three months that he had remained at Cocker's after her consent to their engagement, she had often asked herself what it was that marriage would be able to add to a familiarity so final. Opposite there, behind the counter of which his superior stature, his whiter apron, his more clustering curls and more present, too present, h's had been for a couple of years the principal ornament, he had moved to and fro before her as on the small sanded floor of their contracted future. She was conscious now of the improvement of not having to take her present and her future at once. They were about as much as she could manage when taken separate.

The nuances of tone and therefore meaning, the sudden shifts in the angle of vision as well as articulation, the blending of the light and the dark in the speaking voice—a proper appreciation of these features would require a sentence-by-sentence parsing of the passage. Yet the general drift is obvious enough. It is the psychological vulnerability of Mr. Mudge and his betrothed that the passage dwells on. What enables James to capture the tenuousness of the emerging link between the once "principal ornament" of Mr. Cocker's establishment and the new recruit is the real measure of thought that has gone into the composition. Although a veritable world of human affairs has already been conjured up, other than the "hams, cheese, dried fish, soap, varnish, paraffin," and the frail barriers, nothing of any props, or mere ideas, is within view. We are truly in a world of thought and feeling.

Though we may feel we are already in full possession of the case in *In the*

*Cage*, are already privy to the minds of the girl, Mr. Mudge, and Mr. Cocker, the picture needs several shades to deepen its perspective. The present predicament of the girl—should she or should she not seek a transfer to Mr. Mudge's new appointment at Chalk Farm—leads the thought inevitably to the girl's other, earlier predicaments. The brief, though deeply moving, glance backward at the girl's other predicaments, of another day, brings the overture to a powerful climax. The effect resembles a neat little overture in which the notes capture not so much a series of facts but a myriad of unstated emotions and anxieties. And so, as James begins to reflect on the girl's past, the reader senses layers of crucial significance, meanings, and perspective being added to the case—with an extraordinary economy and controlled compression. The manner in which James goes about the business, here as well as in the refrain in chapter 5 of the tale, gives us a good idea of the alliance of thought and feeling with which, throughout, the presentment is charged. James's grasp of the past terrors of the girl's life is that authentic center of the composition—such centers are present in almost all his works—around which all the other fiddles and flutes, the violins and the wind instruments of this orchestra of scenes must make their music. The musical metaphor is borrowed from James's preface to *In the Cage*, and it has a special point. Though less in evidence in his own critical vocabulary, where the language of painting and architecture predominates, musical structures shape many of the small circular frames, are in a sense their chief technical hallmark. Here then are the two sentences that, at this stage, telescope the girl's past of want, bereavement, dissipation, decay—in short, her other predicaments:

It would be far from dazzling to exchange Mayfair for Chalk Farm, and it was something of a predicament that he so kept at her; still, it was nothing to the old predicaments, those of the early times of their great misery, her own, her mother's, and her elder sister's—the last of whom had succumbed to all but absolute want when, as conscious, incredulous ladies, suddenly bereaved, betrayed, overwhelmed, they had slipped faster and faster down the steep slope at the bottom of which she alone had rebounded. Her mother had never rebounded any more at the bottom than on the way; had only rumbled and grumbled down and down, making, in respect of caps and conversation, no effort whatever, and too often, alas!, smelling of whisky.

Henry James was a radical thinker, quite in the same way as, for his own age, Shakespeare was a radical thinker (consider *Othello* and *Lear*). Yet there continues to persist the appalling myth that James wasted a lifetime pretending to be a European aristocrat; that his central preoccupation was little more than a fantasy of wealth, prestige, nobility, and lots of servants: that, in short, he was an earlier-day author of "Dallas," and also a player in it. This estimate of James is largely the contribution of the lazy reader who fails to pay adequate attention to the dialectic of James's literary thought—who fails, that is, to see that James's lifelong passion for his art is fiercely moral, fiercely human. Whatever of "the patch of plot" there is in *In the Cage*—or in any other fine work by James—is there to highlight, to bring into proper relief, the caged girl's moral and human dilemma. In most of James's tales, this preoccupation of the writer receives the clearest articulation, often, as here, in the very opening section or chapter.

In section 5 of *In the Cage*, the narrative returns to the "other predicaments" of the girl in order now to give the theme a present focus: the "other" predicament is now a present predicament. The metaphorical force of the phrase "in the cage" has already turned a mere literalism into so many different cages in a whirl. Her present predicament is of course a consequence of her past predicaments; the two together are now pulling her into yet another cage—her fantasies surrounding Captain Everard. The quite dazzling section 5 of the tale sets in motion an extraordinary social vision with definite metaphysical implications; and it is ordered in a prose that is rarely far from the density of great poetry. Here then is writing of Shakespearean grandeur and an analytical precision that is quite simply unique. It would be foolish to say that section 5 of *In the Cage* comes to us from the point of view of the caged girl: the section is an unusually eloquent instance of the "indwelling" of thought in fiction. The girl now is well familiar with the mind-forged manacles of her glittering clients; she sees the glitter, is even tempted by the claims it can make on one's powers of fantasy, yet she is blessed with the vision of the terrors of social and actual reality. The section is worth quoting in full:

This was neither more nor less than the queer extension of her experience, the double life that, in the cage, she grew at last to lead. As the weeks went on there she lived more and more into the world of whiffs and glimpses, and found her divinations work faster and stretch further. It was a prodigious view as the pressure heightened, a panorama fed with facts and figures, flushed with a torrent of color and accompanied with wondrous world-music. What it mainly came to at this period was a picture of how London could amuse itself; and that, with the running commentary of a witness so exclusively a witness, turned for the most part to a hardening of the heart. The nose of this observer was brushed by the bouquet, yet she could never really pluck even a daisy. What could still remain fresh in her daily grind was the immense disparity, the difference and contrast, from class to class, of every instant and every motion. There were times when all the wires in the country seemed to start from the little hole-and-corner where she plied for a livelihood, and where, in the shuffle of feet, the flutter of "forms," the straying of stamps and the ring of change over the counter, the people she had fallen into the habit of remembering and fitting together with others, and of having her theories and interpretations of, kept up before her their long procession and rotation. What twisted the knife in her vitals was the way the profligate rich scattered about them, in extravagant chatter over their extravagant pleasures and sins, an amount of money that would have held the stricken household of her frightened childhood, her poor pinched mother and tormented father and lost brother and starved sister, together for a lifetime. During her first weeks she had often gasped at the sums people were willing to pay for the stuff they transmitted—the "much loves," the "awful" regrets, the compliments and wonderments and vain, vague gestures that cost the price of a new pair of boots. She had a way then of glancing at the people's faces, but she had early learned that if you became a telegraphist you soon ceased to be astonished. Her eye for types amounted nevertheless to genius, and there were those she liked and those she hated, her feeling for the latter of which grew to a positive possession, an instinct of observation and detection.

There were the brazen women, as she called them, of the higher and the lower fashion, whose squanderings and graspings, whose struggles and secrets and love-affairs and lies she tracked and stored up against them, till she had at moments, in private, a triumphant, vicious feeling of mastery and power, a sense of having their silly, guilty secrets in her pocket, her small retentive brain, and thereby knowing so much more about them than they suspected or would care to think. There were those she would have liked to betray, to trip up, to bring down with words altered and fatal; and all through a personal hostility provoked by the lightest signs, by their accidents of tone and manner, by the particular kind of relation she always happened instantly to feel.

There were impulses of various kinds, alternately soft and severe, to which she was constitutionally accessible and which were determined by the smallest accidents. She was rigid, in general, on the article of making the public itself affix its stamps, and found a special enjoyment in dealing, to that end, with some of the ladies who were too grand to touch them. She had thus a play of refinement and subtlety greater, she flattered herself, than any of which she could be made the subject; and though most people were too stupid to be conscious of this, it brought her endless little consolations and revenges. She recognised quite as much those of her sex whom she would have liked to help, to warn, to rescue, to see more of; and that alternative as well operated exactly through the hazard of personal sympathy, her vision of silver threads and moonbeams and her gift for keeping the clues and finding her way in the tangle. The moonbeams and silver threads presented at moments all the vision of what poor *she* might have made of happiness. Blurred and blank as the whole thing often inevitably, or mercifully, became, she could still, through crevices and crannies, be stupified, especially by what, in spite of all seasoning, touched the sorest place in her consciousness, the revelation of the golden shower flying about without a gleam of gold for herself. It remained prodigious to the end, the money her fine friends were able to spend to get still more, or even to complain to fine friends of their own that they were in want. The pleasures they proposed were equalled only by those they declined, and they made their appointments often so expensively that she was left wondering at the nature of the delights to which the mere approaches were paved with shillings. She quivered on occasion into the perception of this and that one whom she would, at all events, have just simply liked to *be*. Her conceit, her baffled vanity were possibly monstrous; she certainly often threw herself into a defiant conviction that she would have done the whole thing much better. But her greatest comfort, on the whole, was her comparative vision of the men; by whom I mean the unmistakable gentlemen, for she had no interest in the spurious or the shabby, and no mercy at all for the poor. She could have found a sixpence, outside, for an appearance of want; but her fancy, in some directions so alert, had never a throb of response for any side of the sordid. The men she did follow, moreover, she followed mainly in one relation, the relation as to which the cage convinced her, she believed, more than anything else could have done, that it was quite the most diffused.

She found her ladies, in short, almost always in communication with her gentlemen, and her gentlemen with her ladies, and she read into the immensity of their intercourse stories and meanings without end. Incontestably she grew to think that the men cut the best figure; and in this particular, as in many others, she arrived at a philosophy of her own, all made up of her private notations and cynicisms. It was a striking part of the business, for example, that it was much more the women, on the whole, who were after the men than the men who were after the women; it was literally visible that the general attitude of the one sex was that of the object pursued and defensive, apologetic and attenuating, while the light of her own nature helped her more or less to conclude as to the attitude of the other. Perhaps she herself a little even fell into the custom of pursuit in occasionally deviating only for gentlemen from her high rigour about the stamps. She had early in the day made up her mind, in fine, that they had the best manners; and if there were none of them she noticed when Captain Everard was there, there were plenty she could place and trace and name at other times, plenty who, with their way of being "nice" to her, and of handling, as if their pockets were private tills, loose, mixed masses of silver and gold, were such pleasant appearances that she could envy them without dislike. *They* never had to give change—they only had to get it. They ranged through every suggestion, every shade of fortune, which evidently included indeed lots of bad luck as well as of good, declining even toward Mr. Mudge and his bland, firm thrift, and ascending, in wild signals and rocket-flights, almost to within hail of her highest standard. So, from month to month, she went on with them all, through a thousand ups and downs and a thousand pangs and indifferences. What virtually happened was that in the shuffling herd that passed before her by far the greater part only passed—a proportion but just appreciable stayed. Most of the elements swam straight away, lost themselves in the bottomless common, and by so doing really kept the page clear. On the clearness, therefore, what she did retain stood sharply out; she nipped and caught it, turned it over and interwove it. (*IC* 31–38)

There is one curiously violent image in the chapter. The experience of watching how London amused itself was like the twist of a "knife" in the girl's "vitals." The image is the climactic point not only of the passage but of the whole "queer extension of her experience, the double life that, in the cage, she grew at last to lead." This, then, is the essence of the story of the girl in the cage: the "double life" that leads to an anguish of awareness that is like the twist of a knife in her vitals.

In every respect, chapter 5 of *In the Cage* is an extension, albeit a richer, a more elaborate and complex, extension of chapter 1. In neither is there any significant play of primary action: both rely almost entirely on the secondary narrational data—the recollection. The Wordsworthian notion of "recollection in tranquility" is not altogether out of place here, for, as in Wordsworth, the recollection in the tale also moves toward a reshaping of observed reality. I am deliberately using the term "recollection" for what some might call character analysis or analysis of scene or situation. Analysis involves objectivity and codification: nothing of the kind is being attempted here. What we have here is James in his Keatsian garb, changing himself to *become* all and every entity of the composition. This is the standard mode of all of James's forays into the "action" of his tales as well as his novels. It is the first-person narrator (James— to spot the single occurrence of the "I" of the narrator, one has to read the passage very slowly) who is speaking here for the many layers of the experience of the girl. The one reality she has so violently experienced is, of course, easy to abstract and state: the caged girl is both attracted to and repelled by the "golden shower" that will not rain on her. This is what the novelist has *understood* of the case of the girl. He shall dramatize a part of it, but he has also set himself the much more difficult task of telescoping, for the reader's understanding, the myriads of tensions in her soul. Thus the primary action is suspended, and we are given, instead, a feast of tacit signals, some articulated directly, others not, that bring to surface and into focus a host of feelings, emotions, fears, vanities, sensations, anxieties, resolves, loves, hates—and much more. Using the frailest of dramatic vehicles, in these two segments in particular but also in the tale as a whole, James manages to bring within the conscious grasp of the girl (and the reader) a vision of moral squalor every bit as squalid as the one that was to be the share of little Maisie. This is the ''peculiar class of data'' to which Eliot wanted to draw our attention.

Since there is to be an orchestration between the fiddles and the flutes of the various scenes and chapters in the tale, naturally the blocks of recollection cannot be said to be self-contained: they must issue from, and interact with, all the other elements, such as the scenic and dramatic blocks. Yet the recollections, in the many forms in which they come and with their own dynamic of pace, tempo, and tone, do remain the signal feature of a James tale. In itself, what exactly is there of significance in the dramatized cavortings of a Captain Everard, or a Lady Bradeen, or a Mrs. Jordan—or the silent specter of a nameless girl in a cage? They can only represent the world of ''men'' from which the reader, if the author is at all anything of a ''philosopher,'' must move toward ''man''— toward general moral and social truths. Without a palpable presence of these latter in the thoughts of James, James's tales would fail to make the kind of impact they make on the collaborative reader.

Needless to say, the commentary offered above is wholly inadequate: chapter 5 of *In the Cage* in particular would require an analytical essay to itself. I have confined myself to drawing attention to that procedure, that facet of the art of James by which the narrated experience in his tales acquires the air of authenticity and significance and by which the artist's vision gets its necessary moral and social geogr. phy. In a large body of work such as the tales of James, it is only to be expected that such a procedure would vary.

The 112 tales of James may be said to fall into two broad categories, in one large grouping of which the tale-teller, like Coleridge, appears as a ''subtle-souled psychologist'' who unmasks characters and situations to reveal the emotional truth of his chosen subjects. Tales like *In the Cage*, indeed most of the shorter fictions from the mid–1880s on, are the work of James as the ''subtle-souled psychologist.'' There is then the other James—James as the cultural anthropologist, the very first of the breed in fiction. In conventional critical parlance, the tales and novels that are the work of this second side of James are often remembered as ''international tales'' or ''tales of cultural contrast.'' Though adequate in a limited way, both designations carry an aura of superficiality and lightness that is wholly inappropriate when the point of reference is such masterpieces as, among others, ''Madame de Mauves,'' *Daisy Miller*, ''Four Meetings,'' ''Lady Barbarina,'' ''An International Episode,'' and *The Siege of London*. James's international tales are not tales so much as they are what he himself came very close to calling them: "studies"—studies in cultural anthropology, conducted in the mode of fiction. In *The Siege of London* we have this other aspect of the art and thought of James.

The two tales, *In the Cage* and *The Siege of London*, and therefore the two lines of interest, are entirely different in character—and the difference is not to be explained by the gap of years between the two works. (It is for this reason that I have deliberately reversed the chronology.) Whereas the thought and writing in *In the Cage* are syncretic, striving for effects of crystalline sharpness and density and for taut and strung rhythms, even in the scenic blocks, *The Siege of London* aims for a halting, rather languorous pace, since this allows for the right kinds of exactitudes in the tale's relentless pursuit of a variety of verisimilitudes—visual, moral, social, historical, even sartorial. If the art of the "subtle-souled psychologist" is necessarily inward-looking, the cultural anthropologist in James cannot but look steadily at what is "out there." Thus, for instance, a few paragraphs may suffice to "place" the future Mrs. Mudge in her psychological cage; such economy would be fatal to the central interest in *The Siege of London*. And so we get nearly twenty pages of meticulously ordered circumstance, both past and present, of several characters, to prepare us for the sieges to begin.

Here, again, a quick backward glance at Dickens, whose lesson was ingrained on James's mind, is useful. Dickens's many examples of social anthropology, as it were, though enormously interesting and engaging in a dozen ways, are often not wholly believable. Though the schoolmaster's utilitarian rhetoric in *Hard Times* is authentic, the character who delivers it is not a character but, to borrow James's own term, a mere "figure." The charge of stereotyping is at the heart of James's youthful strictures on Dickens; and his criticism has a direct bearing on his own handling of the theme of cultural differences between nations. He was well aware that the slightest slip of the imagination could turn one of his national types into stereotypes. It is a mark of his greatness that, though he spent half a century making up stories about Americans and Europeans, there are no stereotypes in James.

In essence, the creative strategy that avoids these pitfalls in *The Siege of London* is quite similar to the one that gives us the rarified experience in *In the Cage*: a careful, prior assessment of the intellectual and emotional possibilities of the subject in hand. Our brief consideration of two passages from *In the Cage* has shown how James's imagination is in full command of the many implications of the spirit (of the girl) in turmoil. There is, however, an important, not entirely technical, difference between the way the fictional imagination grapples with the subject in *In the Cage* and how it courts the interest in *The Siege of London*. The art of *In the Cage* is largely the art of the close-up, to which the packed language gives the necessary "length." Consider, for instance, the enormous range of the following, a single sentence, from *In the Cage*: "She quivered on occasion into the perception of this and that one whom she would, at all events, have just simply liked to *be*." Behind the extraordinary notion of "quivering" into perception, there lies a fullness of empathy and comprehension and an unusual ability to yoke together heterogeneous ideas. In *The Siege of London*, however, the imagination operates differently: it *lingers* over objects, situations, and characters, so that the perspective thus achieved removes all possibilities of reductiveness. Indeed, the whole issue of conflicting cultural conditionings is so thoroughly pondered in advance that some readers, expecting to meet bold and crude contrasts, tend to be confused and take back a wrong impression of, in particular, Mrs. Nancy Headway. The angry and awkward controversies that sprang up in the wake of the publication of *Daisy Miller* and ''An International Episode'' were caused by the presence of a similar ''tolerance factor'' in those works.

The way in which the imagination lingers over its objects is best seen in the very opening of *The Siege of London*. Set in a theater, the scene introduces the theatricality of Mrs. Nancy Headway through the spectacular image and metaphor of ''watching''—the reader-as-spectator watches over spectators watching still other spectators, while all are watching a play that, in turn, resembles the life of Mrs. Headway. As if this were not enough of a cluster, after the lengthy preamble, Mrs. Headway's figure is slowly brought into focus through the lens of a binocular. Thus established, the watch becomes the controlling metaphor of the tale and closely corresponds to the image of the ''siege'' introduced in the title: those under siege are being watched, just as those being watched are, of course, under siege.

The elaborate structural strategem with which the tale opens should alert the reader to an important aspect of James's tales of cultural contrasts: because of the very nature of the enterprise, in these tales his vision is particularly exacting and comprehensive. The counterpointing of perspective suggested in the opening of the tale is even more of a necessity in the delineation of the international characters. James ponders these from so many different angles of vision that the resultant images acquire an integrity of their own that, in turn, demands autonomous judgments from the reader. The complex presentment of the much-named Mrs. Nancy Headway—and of the agents whose perceptions furnish the data— is a good case in point.

Although it is only proper that the emotional weight of the tale should fall on the shoulders of Mrs. Headway, *The Siege of London*, in fact, is not ''about'' Mrs. Headway; though Mrs. Headway stands at the midpoint, she stands there in direct relation to the ado being made about and around her. Therefore, the tale is as much about her as it is about Littlemore, Sir Arthur Demense, Lady Demense, even Waterville and Mrs. Dolphin. The arrangement allows James to bring all and everything under his imaginative scrutiny. We are first properly introduced to Mrs. Headway through Littlemore's reminiscences of his past association with her, which contain the following close-up: ''She was a genuine product of the wild West—a flower of the Pacific slope; ignorant, absurd, crude, but full of pluck and spirit, of natural intelligence and of a certain intermittent haphazard felicity of impulse'' (141).[9] The short segment outlines the moral terms by which not only Mrs. Headway but all the personages of the tale are to be judged: that is, the polarity between culture and nature, the old order and the new. But since James sees Mrs. Headway first and foremost as a human being, and not an embodiment of any theorem, the issue is not to be taken at its face value in any simplistic manner. In the very starkness of Littlemore's formulation, there lies the important element of ''unease''—but not uncertainty—that colors his impression and similar other impressions. Could it not be that Littlemore's ''knowingness,'' his mask of maturity and sophistication, in itself is just a little absurd, rather crude, and based on ignorance? Signals of this kind continue to plague, or bless, our changing and shifting perceptions of Mrs. Headway through-out the tale—and sometimes they come from very awkward quarters, in a very awkward fashion.

A lengthy, leisurely account of the history of Sir Arthur Demense at first looks purely narrational in character, and it proceeds in that fashion for almost two pages, until we come to the following and realize, with not a little jolt, that the narrating voice in fact has changed in tune quite radically:

It pleased Sir Arthur to believe he was romantic; that had been the case with several of his ancestors, who supplied a precedent which he would scarce perhaps have ventured to trust himself. He was a victim of perplexities from which a single spark of direct perception would have saved him. He took everything in the literal sense; a grain of humor or of imagination would have saved him, but such things were never so far from him as when he had begun to stray helplessly in the realm of wonder. He sat there vaguely waiting for something to happen and not committing himself to rash declarations. If he was in love it was in his own way, reflectively, inexpressibly, obstinately. He was waiting for the formula which would justify his conduct and Mrs. Headway's peculiarities. He hardly knew where it would come from; you might have thought from his manner that he would discover it in one of the elaborate *entrées* that were served to the pair when she consented to dine with him at Bignon's or the Café Anglais; or in one of the luxurious band-boxes that arrived from the Rue de la Paix and from which she often lifted the lid in the presence of her admirer. (168–69)[10]

The dazzling richness of the effects achieved here reminds us of the prose of *In the Cage*; yet the perceptions here have an elasticity and flexibility about them that is all their own. In the quiet yet razor-sharp critique of Sir Arthur there is something of the ferocity of a Swift: by comparison, Littlemore's starkness appears quite tame. Mrs. Headway is not present in the passage in any direct way; yet by implication, the passage is a very crucial gloss on her conduct and character, as it is a cartoon (in the literal meaning of the word) of Sir Arthur. In the light of such a devastating indictment of culture and tradition, for a while at any rate, Mrs. Headway stands out as a ''flower of the Pacific slope.''

The counterpointing continues when, a few lines below the passage just quoted, the narrating voice turns its attention toward Mrs. Headway herself. What follows is a passage of extraordinary brilliance. The brilliance can easily be misconstrued as being a feature of the style—it so happens that the ''desert'' image in the passage is indeed a later addition. In point of fact, however, the real beauty of the passage resides in James's grasp of the tussle between two orders of life and in his astonishing ability to imagine, so accurately, where and how the "flower of the Pacific slope" would make her personal adjustment in what is a sociohistorical crisis (that is how, in their completely separate ways, both Mrs. Dolphin and Lady Demense see the case). Here is the passage:

She talked about her past because she thought it the best thing to do; she had a shrewd conviction that it was somehow better made use of and confessed to, even in a manner presented and paraded, that caused to stretch behind her as a mere nameless desert. She could at least a little irrigate and plant the waste. She had to have *some* geography, though the beautiful blank rose-coloured map-spaces of unexplored countries were what she would have preferred. She had no objection to telling fibs, but now that she was taking a new departure wished to indulge only in such as were imperative. She would have been delighted might she have squeezed through with none at all. A few, verily, were indispensable, and we needn't attempt to scan too critically the more or less adventurous excursions into poetry and fable with which she entertained and mystified Sir Arthur. She knew of course that as a product of fashionable circles she was nowhere, but she might have great success as a child of nature. (169–70)[11]

The two passages occur in a lengthy single block and challenge each other: the decadent romanticism of Sir Arthur stands nicely exposed to a Whitmanesque sensibility. In both, we again see James slipping under the skin of his characters. What he finds there are strictly human attributes: the uncertainties and reticences of Sir Arthur and the calculated daring of Mrs. Headway. The two passages neither confirm nor deny the veracity of Littlemore, our first witness; they simply add to the ever changing scale of *our* perceptions of Mrs. Headway.

The watch, of course, is still on. Here, to mention one more gaze of many, is Waterville, quite literally watching Mrs. Headway as he himself is being scrutinized by the author and the reader. The occasion is a social gathering at the Demense house, where Waterville is one of the guests. He is looking from a distance at Mrs. Headway, who is talking to an army officer. The staging of the scene takes us back to the staging of an actual staging with which the sieges begin:

Mrs. Headway got on in perfection with her warrior; Waterville noticed her more than he showed; he saw how that officer, evidently a cool hand, was drawing her out. Waterville hoped she would be careful. He was capable, in his way, of frolic thought, and as he compared her with the rest of the company said to himself that she was a very plucky little woman and that her present undertaking had a touch of the heroic. She was alone against many, and her opponents were a serried phalanx; those who were there represented a thousand others. Her type so violated every presumption blooming there that to the eye of the imagination she stood very much on her merits. (196–97)

The plucky little woman, the bloom of the "Pacific slope," confronted with the blooming presumptions of those who have come to watch her! Again and again, the imagination returns to the person of Mrs. Headway, lingers on this or that or the other perception of her until we begin to realize that it is *she* who is under siege, and not the nobility of Warwickshire—or are they both? Speaking of George Eliot (the passage is quoted in full elsewhere in this essay), James draws our attention to the "union of the keenest observation with the ripest reflection" in her novels and stories. James's excursions into fictionalized cultural anthropology precisely reflect this quality—an acute awareness at once of the human, the cultural, and the historical dimensions of character and incident.

Whereas *In the Cage* and *The Siege of London* may be said to represent two broad lines of James's fictional thought in the shorter form, the lesser known *Crapy Cornelia* represents a third, quite unusual variation. The variation is most in evidence in some of the tales of the closing decades of James's career—in works such as "The Bench of Desolation," "The Altar of the Dead," "The Tone of Time," and "Owen Wingrave." These are not tales so much as they are meditations strung on the frailest of narrative structures.

What is character but action; what is action but character? The thought occurred to James early in his life and remained the ideal to be attained throughout his career. His work is a record of the ways in which he himself tried to bridge the gap between the two categories. In *Crapy Cornelia*, the attempt is made to "internalize" action to a degree that action seems almost to have become merely a feature of character. The narrational data is reduced to two short visits and a dialogue; the latter is presented in such a mode that the "talking" seems to be taking place in the head of someone, rather than on the stage. Yet the impression of the one life recounted in the tale could not be completer. Perhaps it was this internalization of action that T. S. Eliot had in mind when, celebrating the art of James, he remarked that the conventional conception of character was not the only route to representational reality. Perhaps, having spotted the seed of a new artistic and narrative departure in the late works of James, in *Crapy Cornelia* in particular, Eliot decided to fashion the most celebrated internalized tale in verse on the model of his master!

There is little evidence that Eliot ever met James. Ample evidence, however, exists of James's profound influence on Eliot. In his essay alluded to earlier in this paper, Eliot acknowledges James's influence on his literary career. From the long-established culture of American expatriates in Europe, Eliot had singled out James as the nearest to him in literary as well as personal temperament and, therefore, as the most suitable model. A dormant Calvinistic-cum-Catholic streak in James, which may be the source of the peculiar sense of evil and doom in him—"Everything's terrible, *cara*—in the heart of man," Prince Amerigo tells Maggie in *The Golden Bowl*—had a powerful romantic fascination for Eliot. So had that other aspect of late James—the long procession of failed lives. In *Crapy Cornelia*, White-Mason is one such (nearly) failed life.

The correspondence between Henry James's White-Mason and Eliot's J. Alfred Prufrock is so startling that it is difficult to attribute it to a mere coincidence. The correspondence is not confined to the "mid-life crisis," so to speak, of the two personages: it extends to a good deal of the actual phrasing of the works and to all their psychological ambience. *Crapy Cornelia* was published in 1909, when James was sixty-six years of age. He had good reason to ponder the phenomenon of failed lives: at that age people are prone to do just that. Eliot's "Love Song of J. Alfred Prufrock" was published in 1915; it is very likely the poem was written at some time during 1912 and 1913. At the time, Eliot was in his early twenties. Clearly *his* middle-aged hero has no basis in lived experience. It is entirely fictional, imagined—borrowed! To be sure, there is one very fundamental difference between the two characters: whereas White-Mason lives and suffers within history, the prudent frock of Eliot sings of the death of history. If, in the end, James's White-Mason realizes that he could "have hummed no wedding-march" (337) with his worthless Mrs. Worthingham, even the mermaids would not sing for Eliot's admirer of the lady in whose rooms "women come and go/talking of Michaelangelo."

It is "half-past five" (325), early evening or late "afternoon" (323), when we come upon White-Mason. He is a middle-aged New Yorker who would like to be reminded "he wasn't so old" (326). He is wearing "his hat, his necktie, his shirt-cuffs" (325). For some time he has been sitting on his "chair of contemplation" (323), hoping to break "the charm of procrastination" (324). The procrastination has to do with his proposal of marriage, which he would like to take to Mrs. Worthingham in order to "put . . . the question that had lapsed the other time, the last time" (324), when he had tried to propose to her.

Mrs. Worthingham is a society lady whose apartments reflect the "lustre of her own polished and prosperous person" (329). Friends flit in and out of her place: "what friends she had—the people who so stupidly, so wantonly stuck!" (324). It was because of the presence of these others that White-Mason got nowhere on that last occasion. Though he feels just a little "immobilized" (324), "he wouldn't put it off again . . . the idea of proposing to Mrs. Worthingham" (325). However, had he been able to formulate the question, he wonders, would it "have done"? Perhaps "It *wouldn't* have done" (326), after all!

After much procrastination and talking with himself, White-Mason gets up, tidies up his necktie and his shirt cuffs, leaves the park, and "entering, with very little space to traverse, one of the short new streets that abutted on its east side" (326), begins to stroll in the direction of Mrs. Worthingham. At the temple of Mrs. Worthingham, with her own "rings and brooches and bangles and other gewgaws" (329), on the one hand, and the modern, vulgar opulence of her apartment, on the other, "expensive objects" seem to come "shrieking" (327) at him: he feels almost " 'snap-shotted' on the spot" (327). He is surprised to find his old friend, the simple, loyal, unassuming, rather crapy Cornelia Rasch also visiting Mrs. Worthingham. The modern, "knowing" airs of Mrs. Worthingham contrast sharply with the endearing, old-fashioned simplicity and honesty of White-Mason's crapy Cornelia. He feels paralyzed once again; once again he fails to ask Mrs. Worthingham "the important question." His "gallantry" is "paralyzed" (342), and he returns to the park for a "second brooding session"

(341). On the chair of contemplation, he reconstructs the scene in which he came very near to proposing: "It was as if he had sat and watched himself—that came back to him: Shall I now or shan't I? Will I now or won't I?" (341). He is becoming increasingly aware he has always "known" the likes of Mrs. Worthingham, for whom "every blest thing coming up . . . in any connection, [is] somehow matter for . . . general recreation" (338).

White-Mason's meditation, a near soliloquy in the first half of the tale, continues for some time. Finally, however, he decides to pay a visit to Cornelia Rasch instead. It is his encounter with his own past, through the agency of Cornelia Rasch, that saves him from drowning. The two talk about their past together, their shared experiences; having thus recovered the sense of the past through Cornelia, White-Mason is saved from the vulgar, fickle, and flashy glitter of Mrs. Worthingham.

No such redemption awaits White-Mason's younger brother, J. Alfred Prufrock: no mermaid-Cornelia will sing for him. He is fated to see his Cornelias "riding seaward on the waves," singing not to him but "each to each." This is the only departure—and it is very significant indeed—from what is otherwise, in the poem by Eliot, a near copy of James's *Crapy Cornelia*. One is tempted to say that even the celebrated opening image of the poem—the evening "etherised upon a table"—might have been inspired by White-Mason's memory of "his sentient state on his once taking ether at the dentist's" (351).

Eliot freezes Prufrock's procrastination and veils the identity of his places and personages in the experimental, modernistic fashion. From Eliot's redoing of the James tale, it would appear that he intended a reinterpretation rather than a parody or an imitation of James's work. The interpretation has a historical point, but in the heavily cultivated cynicism of the poet of twenty-five, there is something clearly inauthentic and contrived.

J. Alfred Prufrock, a New Englander of sorts, is procrastinating when we come upon him. It is late afternoon-evening, indeed "the evening is spread out against the sky" (l. 2), and both "the afternoon, the evening" (l. 75) are soon to go to sleep peacefully. Our hero is middle-aged, beset with the fear that he is "growing old" (l. 120); "a bald spot" has appeared "in the middle of his hair" (l. 40). His collar is "mounting firmly to the chin" (l. 43); his "necktie rich and modest" is "asserted by a simple pin" (l. 44). He has been procrastinating long; he has been a victim of "a hundred indecisions," "a hundred visions and revisions" (ll. 32–33). He must break this charm now and, traversing the "half-deserted streets" (l. 4) of the vicinity, must now "go and make" his "visit" (l. 12).

The visit has to do with a woman whose name is not revealed but whose composite picture is drawn through two or three telescoped details, which leave us in no doubt that she is a copy of the type represented by Mrs. Worthingham. And the object of Prufrock's visit, of course, is identical to the trial White-Mason had to face. Prufrock, too, wishes to put to his lady friend what is for him an "overwhelming question" (l. 10). Quite like the hubbub in the temple of Mrs. Worthingham, the establishment of the unnamed lady of poor Prufrock is frequented by many friends; "among the porcelain" (l. 89), "women come and go talking of Michaelangelo" (ll. 13–14). There is much matter for "general recreation": there are "the cups, the marmalade, the tea" (l. 88). Quite like the feeling White-Mason experiences, the feeling of being "snap-shotted," as it were, Prufrock imagines himself "formulated, sprawling on a pin, pinned and wriggling on the wall" (ll. 57–58).

Prufrock is unable to roll his determination "toward" the "overwhelming question" (l. 93). As a consequence, his "ridiculously agitating experience" deepens. He too begins to find excuses for his paralysis—perhaps "it wouldn't have done" after all; "would it have been worth it after all, Would it have been worth while" (ll. 99–100). Slowly, as paralysis of his gallantry takes over, Prufrock's will begins to spiral downward, quite as the awareness that he has "known them all already, known them all" (l. 49) seems almost to be the only ray of light. In the end, however, since there is no Cornelia to pull him out of his despondency, Prufrock drowns in the welter of his own consciousness.

*Crapy Cornelia* is James's most passionate plea for order in a world beginning to look extremely disorderly at the turn of the century. Several of the meditational tales of the period are veiled pleas for the same thing. James's White-Mason locates a route to order, with his revived belief in the livingness of the past against the encroaching terrors of "modernism." In a deeply moving short meditation, White-Mason contrasts the "furnished" and "fed" and "advised" and "sanitated" and "manicured" and "advertised" face that Mrs. Worthingham and the glitterati of the future might represent—as they indeed do today, in the 1990s—with the culture of innocent tradition as it is represented by his rather plain and crapy Cornelia Rasch. "In *his* time, when he was young or even when he was only but a little less middle-aged, the best manners had been the best kindness, and the best kindness had mostly been some art of not insisting on one's luxurious differences, of concealing rather, for common decency, a part at least of the intensity or the ferocity with which one might be 'in the know' " (338–39). This coherent moral vision, based as it is on the ideal of common humanity and common decency and baffling as it might be for "the women who come and go, talking of Michaelangelo," contrasts violently with Prufrock's desire to have been "a pair of ragged claws, scuttling across the floors of silent seas" (ll. 73–74). What *Crapy Cornelia* says so eloquently is that, without a definite point of reference in memory and history and tradition, consciousness can be an unbearable burden. Eliot's strange critique of the tale in "The Love Song of J. Alfred Prufrock" graphically presents the other, the pathological alternative. In this way, Eliot pays his compatriot a glorious tribute and at the same time enunciates the disturbing dawning of the new age.

Henry James was the last great connoisseur of the past as the living present in the history of modern Anglo-American literature. His belief in continuity had as its basis not any ideological framework but the living, concrete thought of an imaginative writer, almost half a century of the work of a true philosopher-novelist. *Crapy Cornelia* and several other tales of this kind are James's several sermons on the waning of the trust in the principle of continuity. Young Eliot's decision to construct his first major poem on the philosophical argument of *Crapy Cornelia* is, perhaps, a curious acknowledgment that, after many waste lands, one day, half a century later, with an ideological paraphernalia to buttress him, Eliot too would be returning to the crapy Cornelia of a Christian society. For James's tales, it should suffice to say that one of them marks some very crucial transitions and transformations in modern English literary history.

## NOTES

1. *The Siege of London* first appeared in *Cornhill Magazine* 47 (1883): 1–34, 225–56. The tale was extensively revised for the New York Edition. *In the Cage* first appeared in a book edition in 1898 (London: Duckworth and Company; Chicago: Herbert S. Stone). It was lightly revised for the New York Edition. *Crapy Cornelia* first appeared in *Harper's Magazine* 119 (1909): 690–704. In a uniform final version, all three works are available only in *The Novels and Tales of Henry James*, ed. Percy Lubbock (London: Macmillan and Company, 1921–23); all textual references to *The Siege of London* and *Crapy Cornelia* are to this edition. *The Siege of London* appears there in volume XI, *Lady Barbarina, Etc*; *Crapy Cornelia* appears in volume XVIII, *Maud Evelyn, Etc.*

2. A very curious recent study of the relationship between various literary forms, with special reference to the shorter mode of fiction, is John Bayley's *The Short Story*.

3. In the sense in which it is used by Herodotos, the word *history* (*historia*) means *research*—that which has been researched and is not a figment of the imagination. This elevated concept of history was what lay behind the use of the word in the titles of many early novels: it was supposed to confer on the form a special respectability. Since few had actually read Herodotos, the fact that a good deal of Herodotos was in fact pure fiction was completely ignored. The evolution of literary forms is riddled with ironies. Few of those who speak of *War and Peace*—or, for that matter, of *The Portrait of a Lady* or *Bleak House* or *Middlemarch*—as an epic novel ever realize that Tolstoy's book is almost twice the length of all three Western epics put together.

4. The abbreviated form "short" for "short story" has something quite disparaging about it. See my "Mr. Amis's Merchandise" and "Shorts, Knickers, or Novels."

5. *Stories Revived* is the first multivolume edition of James's tales. Issued in three volumes, it contains fourteen of his early tales in their first extensively revised form.

6. This passage appears in a brilliant—still one of the best—early critical evaluation of George Eliot: Henry James's "The Novels of George Eliot" (1866). See *LC-I*, 912–32.

7. This passage (from James's 1865 review of Dickens's *Our Mutual Friend*) needs to be read in the light of the following by James on the novels of George Eliot:

> She has over them [Dickens and Thackeray] the great advantage that she is also a good deal of a philosopher; and it is to this union of the keenest observation with the ripest reflection, that her style owes its essential force. She is a thinker,—not, perhaps, a passionate thinker but at least a serious one; and the term can be applied with either adjective neither to Dickens nor to Thackeray. The constant play of lively and vigorous thought about the objects furnished by her observation

animates these latter with a surprising richness of colour and a truly human interest. It gives the author's style, moreover, that lingering, affectionate, comprehensive quality which is its chief distinction. (*LC*-I, 926)

8. "A Prediction in Regard to Three English Authors, Writers Who though Masters of Thought, Are likewise Masters of Art" was originally published in English in *Vanity Fair* (February 1924), 29, 98. The English version is a translation of a version that first appeared in French as "Lettre d'Angleterre" in *Nouvelle Revue Française* (November 1923), 619–25. A section of the English version is reprinted in *Henry James: A Collection of Critical Essays*, ed. Leon Edel (Englewood Cliffs, N.J.: Prentice Hall, 1963), 55–56.

9. The first book version reads "far West" for "wild West"; "audacious" for "absurd"; and "good taste" for "felicity of impulse."

10. In the first book version, "literal sense" is followed by a short sentence that simply reads, "He had not a grain of humour." The reconsidered assault of the imagination on Sir Arthur is fiercer.

11. The thrust of the first book version is identical to what we have here. The "desert/irrigation" image is a later addition. Also, in the book version, we read: " . . . better to make a good use of it than to attempt to efface it. To efface it was impossible, though that was what she would have preferred." Similarly, Mrs. Headway's "more or less adventurous excursions into poetry and fable" reads simply "the ingenious re-arrangements of fact."

# 11
# A Round of Visits: James among Some European Peers

## Philip M. Weinstein

My title may suggest a social call rather than an academic scrutiny. Like Mark Montieth in James's story from which I take my title, I have time for only a few visits, and these must be brief if they are too transpire within the confines of a single trip. Rather than consider questions of influence or of literary schools, I intend to place James within a European context that his work does not usually solicit. I will not visit Balzac and Turgenev, George Eliot and Hawthorne—the writers he arguably learned the most from; likewise I will not visit Realism and Naturalism, Impressionism and Modernism—the literary movements he has been best situated within: his relation to these houses of fiction and their larger grounds is already well documented.[1] Instead, James will visit in these pages two Russian novelists whose accomplishment he could never assimilate—Tolstoy and Dostoevsky—and two French ones whose devotion to form came before and after his own—Flaubert and Proust.[2]

These roughly contemporary European figures join James as compelling novelists of consciousness and its projects. My aim is to explore their construction of the subject by attending to the ideological matrices within which subjectivity itself comes into being. This is an essay, then, on the problematic of the represented subject.[3] The canonical nature of my choices can hardly be blinked, though I do compare "the master" with other "masters" with whom he is usually not compared. Other writers might of course be suggested, but an analysis of the practice of these four serves to silhouette the lineaments of James's own practice. Among the many ways an essay such as this can fail is to treat each writer at the level not of practice but of summary, to pretend that their work is unified, its effects totalizable, its place in "tradition" open to definitive assignment. At the risk of lengthening these visits without making them profound, I shall attend to some of the intricacies—and even contradictions—of discrete novelistic behavior, and I shall immerse the reader in the specific tone and texture of five different verbally woven worlds.

How do these texts represent the subject? In what ways do gender norms and ideological subtexts affect such representation? These questions govern the analyses that follow. I group my first three novels—Flaubert's *Madame Bovary,* Tolstoy's *Anna Karenina,* and James's *The Golden Bowl*—around the rendering of women within the thematic frame of adultery. The second three novels—Dostoevsky's *The Brothers Karamazov,* James's *The Golden Bowl* again, and Proust's *Recherche*—I approach by way of certain "staged" encounters that tend to typify the subject's experience of the social world.

What is at stake in the representation of adultery may be suggested by brief citations on marriage by Tony Tanner. "Marriage . . . is a means by which society attempts to bring into harmonious alignment patterns of passion and patterns of property" (*Adultery* 15). Arguing that these patterns include the realms of nature, family, society, and metaphysics (the church), Tanner sees the hypnotic appeal of the adulterous wife for fictional treatment as grounded in her inscription in these concurrent yet conflicting roles. "The figure of the wife ideally contains the biological *female,* the obedient *daughter* (and perhaps sister), the faithful *mate,* the responsible *mother,* and the believing *Christian,* and harmonizes all the patterns that bestow upon her these different identities" (*Adultery* 17). When she budges, the whole social fabric wobbles—its precarious contractual basis emerges into view—and focus on her enables a larger picture of society's symbolic orders sustaining crisis.

These commentaries begin by analyzing the first scene of illicit embrace or consummation and conclude by assessing the latent or overt judgment being brought to bear. I attend throughout to the woman's subjectivity as formed by the kinds of language made available to her to think through her experience, and I note as well the text's ways of positioning her transgressive act. We begin our round of visits by turning to the scene in *Madame Bovary* of Emma's yielding to Rodolphe.

The shades of night were falling; the horizontal sun passing between the branches dazzled the eyes. Here and there around her, in the leaves or on the ground, trembled luminous patches, as if humming-birds flying about had scattered their feathers. Silence was everywhere; something sweet seemed to come forth from the trees. She felt her heartbeat return, and the blood coursing through her flesh like a river of milk. Then far away, beyond the wood, on the other hills, she heard a vague prolonged cry, a voice which lingered, and in silence she heard it mingling like music with the last pulsations of her throbbing nerves. . . .

She repeated [once she has returned home]: "I have a lover! a lover!" delighting at the idea as if a second puberty had come to her. So at last she was to know those joys of love, that fever of happiness of which she had despaired! She was entering upon a marvelous world where all would be passion, ecstasy, delirium. (116–17)[4]

The difference between two kinds of experience—and two kinds of prose for rendering them—is stark here. Emma's intercourse registers with metaphoric intensity: the interplay of dazzling light and darkness, ambient silence pressed against the cry of a bird and the pulsing of her nerves, sweetness oozing from the trees and the coursing of her own milk-like blood. Her incarnate processes momentarily mesh with natural process; Flaubert's lyrical prose suggests speechless release, encounter, satisfaction. But the language Emma then employs to possess mentally what she has just experienced bodily has the opposite effect. It empties out the experience, dislodges it from its concrete setting in space and time, immerses it within literary scenarios whose only locus is not here–not now. "So at last she was to know" ("'elle allait donc posséder''); the real has become a metonymic sign of what has not yet arrived: passion, ecstasy, delirium.

Literature holds out the real-life promise of these heady states. Reading, like love itself, proposes a narrative form for our unmapped bodily impulses. As Leo Bersani claims, "The various sorts of intelligibility which literature brings to the life of the body are Flaubert's subject in *Madame Bovary*" (*Astyanax* 90). Emma disastrously conflates the body so glamorously mapped by literary codes with the body so plotlessly molded by life in space and time—conflates them in such a way, as we have just seen, that the embodied experience slips away into its fantasy displacement. But Flaubert keeps us aware of these differences insofar as his prose affords us—through the site that is Emma—an extraordinary penetration into her bodily sensations and desires.[5] Emma's subjective mental life, by contrast, is romantically packaged from our first entry into her consciousness until our last. Her mind's teeming projects never escape from the glazed essentialist scripts of her culture: the language of intense tableaux, of supreme emotional states. Adultery itself is but the predictable romantic antidote to predictable realistic drudgery: in Charles Baudelaire's words, "the tritest theme of all, worn out by repetition, by being played over and over again like a tired barrel-organ" ("Madame Bovary" 339) ("la donnée la plus usée, la plus prostituée, l'orgue de Barbarie le plus éreinté" [*Oeuvres* 1:651]).

Triteness reaches heights in Flaubert that were not to be attempted again until Joyce, and this is so because both writers were so keenly attuned to the code behind the speech, the language game behind the language utterance. *Madame Bovary* opens on a scene of instruction in Latin—a scene in which Charles's "*ridiculous sum*" inaugurates a lifetime of submission to linguistic authority, what Tanner calls "an education in loss" (*Adultery* 251). Charles's childhood failure with Latin resurfaces in his midcareer medical crisis—how to determine whether Hippolyte's clubfoot is an equinus, varus, or valgus—and this gap between uncertain material practices and the authoritative linguistic terms that signify them recurs often in the text.

Men such as Bournisien, Homais, Lheureux, and to a lesser extent Léon and Rodolphe ignore the gap or profit from it. Sheltered and confined within the authority of their factitious institutional idiom, they appear, like Homais, "as calmly established in life as the gold-finch suspended over his head in its wicker cage" (52).[6] Emma, by contrast, suffers a kind of exposure from the space between her wordless experience and the linguistic resources she has available for articulating it. By the end she has disintegrated under the relentless pressure of abusive discourses. She watched at the inventory as "they examined her dresses, the linen, the dressing-room; and her whole existence, to its most intimate details, was stretched out like a cadaver in an autopsy before the eyes of these three men" (215).[7] In this prophetic image, she emerges as the inventoried victim of three discursive practices: the bad debt of credit-debit economics, the decomposing body of scientific laboratory analysis, and the wrecked heroine of romantic mythology.

Adultery fails, but marriage in this novel fares little better. Emma's darkest discovery is that adultery and marriage are equally boring, routine-saturated arrangements. The few sympathetic portraits—Justin, Emma's widowed father, Dr. Larivière—are solitary males: the first hopelessly in love, the second a survivor of lost love, the third professionally beyond the reach of love. Wives and servants, for their part, seem to be nearly interchangeable. Exchanged for dowry, devoted to their husbands' enterprises, taken up by their duties, all the wives—except Emma—have been emptied of their own erotic energies, become almost speechless, transferring on their children their "scattered, broken little vanities" (5).

No other woman in *Madame Bovary* enjoys/suffers the complexities of an inner life: Flaubert's choice to make Emma the only female subject transforms her at once into an object. Yet the composite female rejection of Emma on the verge of her crisis—Madame Tuvache and Madame Caron joining in their scornful "Women like that ought to be whipped" (223)—reveals, beyond its brutality, these women's common plight. Unlike Homais and Lheureux and Bournisien, unlike Léon and Larivière—men grounded in the viability of a profession, socialized by its confraternity, provided life narratives by its goals—they have only "Madame" to cling to. Their fragile identity lodges within their married state, and they turn as one on Emma for betraying it.

Flaubert's narrative stance of generous unbelief rarely leads him to castigate Emma. Rather, he tends to find his way into his heroine with an understanding that has passed through and emerged on the other side of cliché. Emma, for example, sees through the clichéd arias of *Lucia di Lammermoor*—"she knew now how small the passions were that art magnified" (162)—yet moments later, despite her awareness, she swoons before the "poetic power of the acting" (163) ("la poésie du rôle qui l'envahissait" [*Oeuvres* 1:498]). This contradiction is telling, for it reveals the power of cliché as somehow immune to one's knowledge that it is cliché: a revelation that only an author alert to cliché's intrinsic role in language-as-system could afford to grant his heroine.[8]

Tolstoy and James, for different reasons, shun the equation of speech with cliché as energetically as Flaubert pursues it. Tolstoy's belief in a fresh, cliché-free space of thinking and talking, of the subject in control of his or her own discourse, imposes, indeed, a different treatment of his heroine. We turn now to the crucial scene in *Anna Karenina*, in which Anna and Vronsky's love is first consummated:

That which for nearly a year had been Vronsky's sole and exclusive desire . . . had come to pass. Pale, with trembling lower jaw, he stood over her, entreating her to be calm, himself not knowing why or how.

"Anna, Anna," he said in a trembling voice, "Anna, for God's sake! . . . "

But the louder he spoke the lower she dropped her once proud, bright, but now shame-stricken head, and she writhed, slipping down from the sofa on which she sat to the floor at his feet. . . .

"My God! Forgive me!" she said, sobbing and pressing Vronsky's hand to her breast. . . . He felt what a murderer must feel when looking at the body he has deprived of life. The body he had deprived of life was their love, the first period of their love. . . . But in spite of the murderer's horror of the body of his victim, that body must be cut in pieces and hidden away, and he must make use of what he has obtained by the murder.

Then, as the murderer desperately throws himself on the body, as though with passion, and drags it and hacks it, so Vronsky covered her face and shoulders with kisses. . . . At last, as though mastering herself, she sat up and pushed him away. Her face was as beautiful as ever, but all the more piteous.

"It's all over," she said. "I have nothing but you left. Remember that."

"I cannot help remembering what is life itself to me! For one moment of that bliss . . . "

"What bliss?" she said with disgust and horror, and the horror was involuntarily communicated to him. "For heaven's sake, not another word!"

She rose quickly and moved away from him.

"Not another word!" she repeated, and with a look of cold despair, strange to him, she left him. She felt that at that moment she could not express in words her feeling of shame, joy, and horror at this entrance on a new life, and she did not wish to vulgarize that feeling by inadequate words. Later on, the next day and the next, she still could not find words to describe all the complexity of those feelings, and could not even find thoughts with which to reflect on all that was in her soul. . . . But in her dreams, when she had no control over her thoughts, her position appeared to her in all its shocking nakedness. . . . She dreamt that both at once were her husbands, and lavished their caresses on her. . . . And she was surprised that formerly this had seemed impossible to her, and laughingly explained to them how much simpler it really was. . . . But this dream weighed on her like a nightmare, and she woke from it filled with horror. (136–37)[9]

I have quoted this scene at length because it inaugurates their passion as a scene of guilt. Suddenly their intercourse takes place, and Tolstoy visits it just at the moment of completion. This timing has less to do with fear of censorship than with the strategic omission of any love scenes that might precede this one, scenes of growing intimacy, of entry into an intoxicating (if terrifying) bond. Unlike Flaubert, who takes his reader into the transforming power of Emma's intercourse, Tolstoy permits no lyricism here. He is not about to allow his lovers (and with them his reader) to enjoy this first lovemaking.

Instead we witness disaster, Anna's guilt before God. Tolstoy ensures that we see, beyond the two lovers, the offended absent parties as well: God above, her husband outside. At this moment of physical union, Anna and Vronsky suffer an agonizing disunion. (Not that Flaubert's text proposes union either: Rodolphe's petty plot of exploitation is revealed to us before he takes his first step.

But Flaubert's text constructs the experience of intercourse in such a way that its force nonetheless registers, despite the meanness of the male who makes it possible.) Tolstoy uses murder as a figure for what the man has done to the woman. He momentarily evades the brutal logic of his metaphor by saying that it was not Anna but "their love" that Vronsky had deprived of life, but he then resumes the metaphor: Vronsky's kisses and embraces are so much hacking at a corpse.

To image their initial intercourse as murder is to see the beginning as already the end.[10] "It's all over. . . . I have nothing but you left." Yet, it is just beginning: six hundred pages follow this scene, with Anna clinging to Vronsky, a corpse hanging on to her murderer. It is over in other ways as well. When Vronsky shifts to the language of desire, Anna cuts him dead: "What bliss? . . . For heaven's sake, not another word!" The two have no common language for what they have just experienced together. Emma and Rodolphe, by contrast, share precisely the same language, though he knows it is but a language of empowerment whose referent is unreal, and she takes it for an open sesame to the realm of passion. Anna, however, is caught, as it were, speechless—exposed between two inadequate linguistic options. It is either "bliss" or "my God!"—either the high-society discourse of carnal delight or the religious discourse of spiritual guilt. Vronsky is at home in the former discourse, but Anna's finer mesh of desire and judgment can be satisfied with neither of these languages. Yet Tolstoy imagines for her no other, and this absence of a language that would articulate to herself and to Vronsky her blend of guilt and renewal is crucial. Without it, she must rely on the words of others (their codes of assessment) for knowing what she is up to, and this means, increasingly, that she opts for the de-realizing language of pure guilt.

Anna and Vronsky's burgeoning misunderstanding of each other eventually becomes suicidal for Anna. Long before the suicide, though, Anna has revealed her incapacity to find a language with which to say herself. Here she is responding to Vronsky's suggestion that she tell her husband she is leaving him:

"Very well; suppose I do so!" she said. "Do you know what the result will be? I will tell it you all in advance," and an evil light came into her eyes which a minute before had been so tender. " 'Ah, you love another and have entered into a guilty union with him?' " (mimicking her husband, she laid just such a stress on the word *guilty* as Karenin himself would have done). " 'I warned you of the consequences from the religious, civil, and family points of view. You have not listened to me. Now I cannot allow my name to be dishonoured . . . ' " my name and my son she was going to say but could not jest about her son . . . " 'my name to be dishonoured' and something else of that kind," she added. "In short, he will tell me clearly and precisely in his official manner that he cannot let me go, but will take what measures he can to prevent a scandal. And he will do what he says, quietly and accurately. . . . He is not a man, but a machine, and a cruel machine when angry," she added, picturing Karenin to herself with every detail of his figure and way of speaking, setting against him everything bad she could find in him and forgiving him nothing, on account of the terrible fault toward him of which she was guilty. (172–73)

In this resonant passage, she enters fully into Karenin's point of view; she speaks Karenin, she is Karenin. If Tolstoy denies her any language of her own, he amply provides her with her husband's, and she knows every judgment it will pass upon her. She thus appears as a *me*, not an *I*, an object and not a subject, a receiver of others' annihilating discourses and not a discoverer of an appropriate one of her own. She is *spoken*; she does not speak herself. She can come at her own springs of feeling and intelligence only through the heavily judgmental prism of her patriarchal culture's discourse on adultery. She conspires, therefore, in her own alienation: she cuts herself in half, figuratively in her dreams and in her voicing her husband's attack on her, literally at the end of the novel when she hurls herself in the path of an oncoming train. In a word, since her consciousness has access only to the language of indictment, she can speak and think only her own suicide.

If we shift from the language of subjectivity to the shaping of plot, we see that Flaubert and Tolstoy both attend to the impossible bind of their heroines' being a mother in one frame and a lover in another. Emma's daughter, Berthe, is deliberately kept before us as a reminder of her mother's illusory schemes. Conceived when Emma has stopped loving Charles, named in honor of a fantasy lover, farmed out for care as part of Emma's strategy for meeting Rodolphe, forgotten when her mother plans to flee with her lover, summoned to see her mother spit up poison and die, abandoned by both parents to idleness and ignorance—Berthe seems merely to be a semiotic pointer to her mother's disastrous life, with no narrative reality of her own. Tolstoy's investment in the sanctity of motherhood, however, goes further.

Anna is inescapably a mother. She first appears in the novel accompanied by Vronsky's mother on the train to Moscow, and this scene of the two mothers seems constructed to suggest that Anna will never shed her son, no matter how ardently she takes on a lover. It suggests as well that she and Vronsky are at socially incompatible stages of their lives. Figuratively in the same position as his mother, Anna has already made her choices, married, had a child. These deeds can be neither undone nor—in the Tolstoyan scheme of things—transformed.

Further, she swiftly becomes a mother again; Tolstoy unwaveringly equates intercourse with the production of children. (Flaubert's text separates the issues of desire and procreation. Children come, all too predictably, from marriage; no reader imagines that Rodolphe's or Léon's lovemaking might beget a child.) Anna not only becomes pregnant but almost dies on delivery of her daughter. Thereafter, Tolstoy stresses her inability to care for this second child and remain bonded with her first one. One of the most poignant moments of the book occurs just before the suicide, when a distraught Anna has her little girl brought to her and then looks at this child blankly: ''How is this? That's not it—this is not he!

Where are his blue eyes and his sweet timid smile?'' (682). The moment is psychotic (Emma too becomes psychotic, but through desire betrayed, not motherhood); Anna can mother only her husband's child. Under duress, the only child she can see is her abandoned Serezha.

Divorce is out of the question in *Madame Bovary*—lovers are sought, not another husband—but in the plot of *Anna Karenina* it is curiously deployed. Tolstoy makes it available to Anna when not wanted, and he has Karenin refuse to offer it whenever Anna is psychologically in a position to accept it. Moreover, the divorce lawyer is a strikingly un-Tolstoyan character. Insolent, catching moths with his fingers during Karenin's interview with him, he can barely restrain his glee over his client's distress. When we consider that the only other grotesque figure in this hugely peopled novel is a peasant seeking to buy off forest land at a cheap price, a certain representational logic emerges. Tolstoy cannot present as normal—as shaped by credible norms—those men who most threaten his aristocratic scripts: the divorce lawyer who would rupture the sacred institution of the family; the peasant who would strip the forests and sell the timber at a profit.

Further, Tolstoy delineates in Levin what Flaubert withholds: the sustained example of how, despite endless problems, to do it right. Unlike Anna, Levin has his own land, his own work, his own ideas. When Kitty first rejects him, he turns to his land and his work to hold him up, and they do. Levin seeks to write a treatise on the dilemma of Russian agriculture in the late nineteenth century, and Tolstoy allows him to probe these matters as far as Tolstoy himself could probe them. In other words, Levin is endowed by his creator with a rich intellectual life. *He* is permitted to call into question some of his culture's most traditional practices. The male and female protagonists of this novel are thus inserted into different emotional, territorial, and intellectual domains. These differences all work toward Anna's destruction and Levin's survival.

Finally, Tolstoy (insistently) and Flaubert (overwhelmingly) sexualize their heroines. Emma and Anna as characters are created through their hair, their eyes, their beauty, their desire, their shame. Levin is also created through his muscular body, but more essentially through his ideas, his land, his love, his aspirations. The difference between these two lists—and between the narratives each inspires—comprises, in little, the representational history of Western gender distinctions. Not surprisingly, the measure in which Henry James refrains from insisting on his heroines' sexuality is also the measure in which he refreshingly escapes from this history. It is time now to visit *The Golden Bowl*, at the scene that concludes in Amerigo and Charlotte's embrace.

"Well then, there it is [Charlotte is speaking]. I can't put myself into Maggie's skin— I can't, as I say. It's not my fit—I shouldn't be able, as I see it, to breathe in it. But I can feel that I'd do anything to shield it from a bruise. Tender as I am for her too," she went on, "I think I'm still more so for my husband. *He*'s in truth of a sweet simplicity—!''

The Prince turned over a while the sweet simplicity of Mr. Verver. "Well, I don't know that I can choose. At night all cats are grey. I only see how, for so many reasons, we ought to stand toward them—and how, to do ourselves justice, we do. It represents for us a conscious care—"

"Of every hour, literally," said Charlotte. She could rise to the highest measure of the facts. "And for which we must trust each other—!"

"Oh, as we trust the saints in glory. Fortunately," the Prince hastened to add, "we can." With which, as for the full assurance and the pledge it involved, their hands instinctively found their hands. "It's all too wonderful."

Firmly and gravely she kept his hand. "It's too beautiful." . . .

They were silent at first, only facing and faced, only grasping and grasped, only meeting and met. "It's sacred," he said at last.

"It's sacred," she breathed back to him. They vowed it, gave it out and took it in, drawn, by their intensity, more closely together. Then of a sudden, through this tightened circle, as at the issue of a narrow strait into the sea beyond, everything broke up, broke down, gave way, melted and mingled. Their lips sought their lips, their pressure their response and their response their pressure; with a violence that had sighed itself the next moment to the longest and deepest of stillnesses they passionately sealed their pledge. (*NY* XXIII, 316–17)

James's lovers' language contrasts vividly with the language that Flaubert and Tolstoy provide their heroines to think through their adulterous experience: for Emma, the sentimental clichés of romance; for Anna, the guilt-inducing discourse of her patriarchal society. In both cases, the provenance of such language is clear. We glimpse the institutions behind their words, and we register the unsurpassable limitations thus imposed. Adulterous projects conceived within these discourses must collapse, either through the unreality of expectations or through the intolerableness of indictment. The language game in force ensures disaster.

James, by contrast, sharing his own verbal resources with his protagonists, seeks to liberate. *The Golden Bowl* ponders liberation from conventional constraints on an unprecedented scale—a novelistic world in which characters as capacious as the language they live in might be equal to every nonverbal crisis they encounter.[11] Seeking to fuse psychic and syntactic flexibility, the late-Jamesian text is tenderly complicit with its protagonists' projects, interested in the production of mutually sustaining verbal surfaces rather than the jagged exposure of inadequate rhetorics, ideological dead ends.

Thus Charlotte and Amerigo talk exquisitely to each other, transforming—through their verbal/conceptual resources—the coming adultery into the vigilance of "a conscious care." Their talk, like Maggie's later, has a quasi-magical quality; it does not merely formulate its object but begins to bring it into being. Yet such talk is labor as well. Jamesian conversations enact an unpredictable dialectic; they do not play out—as Emma's and Anna's conversations tend to—the givens of a known language game. Charlotte and the prince's verbal elasticity makes its way deftly past the moral obstacle of adultery (no characters in literature are better at the grace of nonencounter than James's), issuing into a realm of

tenderness, conscious care, trust, beauty, and sanctity; on the aroused charge of
these felt virtues they seal their "pledge." The embrace that crowns this verbal
foreplay achieves a perfected contradictoriness of meanings: at once a betrayal
of their talk and its culmination, at once a betrayal of the Ververs and the seal
of their protection. Unlike Emma and Rodolphe, unlike Anna and Vronsky,
Charlotte and Amerigo share a discursive audacity that—rather than subvert or
submit—aesthetically reconceives public norms in the light of private capacities.
Exploiting their art of "caring" for others, they would generate a personal, unco-
opted space of fulfillment while scrupulously maintaining their already contracted
social commitments, thus making honor compatible with deceit. This private
realm would remain finely free—a dared and achieved oasis of individual value—
despite its immersion within a wider social network of incompatible constraints.
In this scene James registers the provocative charm and chill of their enterprise.

Their genial claim of mutual beneficence requires, though, a systematic manipulation of the roles of subject and object. Paul Armstrong and Mark Seltzer,
among others, have recently explored the strategies of perception in *The Golden
Bowl*, the ways in which love relationships are structured as power relationships.[12] In the quoted scene, Charlotte maneuvers Maggie into the role of object—
"I can't put myself into Maggie's skin—I can't, as I say"—so as to enable her
own free-moving subjective response. Charlotte further requires the fiction of
herself as previously objectified by the Ververs ("I'm placed—I can't imagine
any one *more* placed" [*NY* XXIII, 258], she tells Fanny) in order to justify her
first liberating countermoves. Not only does the inaugural gesture of a free subject
depend on the opposing notion of a fixed object, but such a subject is also
released into action by the perception that she has been herself a fixed object
for others. The shorthand figure for this double perception is the performer (the
actor, the circus acrobat, the mistress of shades), and the performance that is
*The Golden Bowl* masterfully unfolds as a dizzying ballet of subjects who were
once objects moving around objects who were once subjects.

The surface of this dance yields great beauty, yet its lifeblood is the differential
flow of power. As Leo Bersani writes, "A Jamesian dialogue is almost an abstract
diagram of political processes from beginning to end; . . . it maps out the intim-
idations and negotiated concessions which come into play as a result of the
imbalances and inequalities immediately produced by a relation between two
. . . human subjects" ("Subject of Power" 10). Despite claims of mutual care
(the nurturing of each of the four principal subjects *as* subjects), the narrative
logic of *The Golden Bowl* can develop the subject in Maggie-as-object only by
exploiting the object in Charlotte-as-subject. The jockeying for power—the sub-
ject/object differential—is the enabling dynamic of Jamesian plot structure. And
Charlotte becomes its primary victim.

The point is less the language Charlotte uses to think through her experience
than the compositional fact that, of the four protagonists in this novel, she is
the most severely positioned. Charlotte enters the text sharply placed as the
prince's object of desire, her gender role as a woman who can make men desire

her both accepted and displayed. Her strength is the obverse of her gender rigidity. As J. A. Boone notes, "Charlotte's victimization is inevitable, given her acceptance of societal definitions of her options; all the roles she has occupied—'old maid,' 'adulteress,' 'wife'—are grounded in assumptions of female inferiority or capitulation" (381).

Charlotte's role as gender-defined object subtly coerces Maggie's as subject, and in one sense *The Golden Bowl* can be said to offer the unedifying spectacle of two mystified women identifying each other as the enemy, wounding each other as they fight it out over their men, working to sustain relationships they cannot afford to call into question. The men tend to watch from afar. "Lying like gods" (*NY* XXIV, 94), semisupine, they assist "at the recurrent, the predestined phenomenon . . . the doing by the woman" (*NY* XXIII, 51) of the requisite work. Their value as the reward that justifies the women's struggle seems to go without saying.

I know of no other novel that so teases the reader through selective representation of its characters' subjectivity. What does Maggie think during the first half of the book? What does Charlotte think at any time? What is each woman's relation to herself, as opposed to others' objectifying or strategic sense of her? And what is the bearing of these withheld perspectives on *The Golden Bowl*'s representation of marriage, adultery, and the subject?

Our lack of access to Maggie's subjectivity in volume one prevents us from knowing why her marriage fails. To what degree is it because she remains a daughter and fails to become a wife? To what degree is it because Charlotte intervenes as her husband's mistress? When does her marriage start to go off? As for our near total lack of access to Charlotte's subjectivity, it ensures that we remain ignorant about why her marriage fails as well. To what degree is it because she has all along remained in love with the prince? To what degree is it because Adam has never yielded himself as a husband, preferring to remain his daughter's father? When does that marriage go off?

James's compositional strategy both presses us to raise these vulgar questions and keeps us from answering them. This novel, at first entitled "The Marriages," emerges as only oddly about marriage at all. Its primary relations are, arguably, those between a daughter and her father and between a lover and his mistress. The only substantially married couple here is the Assinghams (a relationship on whose cozy normality James depends greatly—much more than the critical literature is prepared to concede). The prince and Maggie, like Adam and Charlotte, are most massively represented less in marriage than in the insistently subject-object counterpoise of courtship, on the eve of marriage.[13] The only child produced by all three of these marriages is (from an affective view) a cipher—shown in no dramatized relation with his mother and in but a minimal one with his father and his grandfather. The novel opens and closes with the possibility of Maggie's marriage. Its last image recalls the closing embrace of the typical courtship novel: the marriage is yet to be realized.

As for adultery as marriage's other, it lacks here the disturbing force of its role in *Madame Bovary* and *Anna Karenina*. Its intercourse neither begets bastards nor damages legitimate children, interrupts no credibly established marital patterns, leads to no ravage on the part of anyone except (probably) Charlotte. The psychic fluency of the four principals prevents anything gross from happening. Freed thus from the specificity of what might be called its scar value, adultery aligns itself with the epistemological issue of abstract trust, crazily oscillating between polarized aesthetic and moral valuations—"the vigilance of care," on the one hand, and the intrusion of "what's called Evil—with a very big E," on the other.[14] Its representation may certainly be enlisted by critics in behalf of the status quo, since *The Golden Bowl* ends by shoring up social norms, meeting and defeating the eccentric temptations of incest and adultery. But it may be equally enlisted in behalf of social reform, the novel on this view proposing "a critique that reveals the popularly understood ideal of wedlock to be a state of impasse, of irresolvable tensions and conflicts" (Boone 374).

Both views are accurate. Marriage and adultery are represented with their conventional valuation intact and at the same time disconcertingly deconstructed. Indeed, the novel, incoherently, both assuages and disturbs.[15] It seeks to make judgment impossible even as it arouses in the reader the desire for the finest discriminations. Its impenetrable aesthetic surface sustains with civility the traffic it is required to bear yet intimates at the same time the nearness (just below) of unspeakable things. The novel ends without tears, its two marriages positively rerouted, yet with the haunting suggestion that its social engineering has exacted a more than human price, one inseparable from "the shriek of a soul in pain" (*NY* XXIV, 300)—pain caused less by a violation of norms than by a sort of hemorrhage within the norms themselves.

Unlike *Madame Bovary* and *Anna Karenina*, *The Golden Bowl* requires no death to resolve the central crisis of social form and subjective feeling, yet it resolves the crisis in such a way as, uncannily, to undo the differences between form and feeling, crisis and resolution, on which the coherence of each of these terms depends. If we say that *Madame Bovary* sees through Emma's project and *Anna Karenina* sees beyond Anna's, then *The Golden Bowl* seems to call into question the subject-object axis that grounds seeing itself.

With this move, all acts of knowing become radically problematic. I have spoken above of the representational consequences of not knowing; I speculate now on why this text resists being authoritatively known. By undermining any subject's secure grasp on any object, by blurring any reader's interpretive "take" on its various transactions, *The Golden Bowl*—parting company from *Madame Bovary* and *Anna Karenina*—enacts its pervasive rhetorical ambition: to intimate without ratifying and thus to escape the culture's conventional pegs of authoritative predication (and the vulgar assessments—moral, intellectual, emotional—that go with such predications). This is the novel's undeclared romance, its way of discursively abetting its protagonists in their search for virgin space within an already heavily contracted terrain. It is against just such an ungrounding aim that we best measure the novel's ubiquitous countermove: its ceaseless whisper of economic exploitation, its confessional intimation of its determinate insertion within the money terms and power practices of Western capitalism.

In the three analyses above I have examined a common thematic—adultery—and pursued a cluster of interrelated questions, all of them bearing on the representation of the gendered subject within a larger ideological field. In each text the protagonist moves—whatever her sense of private motive—within a network of socially furnished terms and practices that impede (even when they invite) individual mastery. A measure of James's likeness and difference emerges in these comparisons, yet not at the expense of flattening his peers so as to make him round.

The following three analyses—involving *The Brothers Karamazov, The Golden Bowl* again, and Proust's *Recherche*—operate according to similar assumptions and procedures. Here the common element is structural: the penchant of each text for a round of staged, almost ritualistic "visits"—"visits" that seem to typify the way that each text constructs the subject's encounter with the social world as such. I attend to the focal character's relation (manifest and latent) to the experience under observation, the reasons for the staginess of the event, and the ideological reverberations of these scenes elsewhere in the text.

In book 3, chapter 10, of *The Brothers Karamazov*, Alyosha hurries from his father's house to Katerina Ivanovna's. A scene of great violence has just taken place (Dmitri's attack on his father), but Alyosha is now about to enter on a subtler kind of violence, between women. Going up the stairs, he hears "flying footsteps and rustling skirts" (132), but on entrance he finds only Katerina. The scene soon loses its veneer as a decorous visit.

Asking for Alyosha's coarsest impressions of his brother ("oh as coarsely as you like!" [133–34])—which she would respond to with godlike acceptance—Katerina hears of Dmitri's explicit instruction that Alyosha bow to her: "He told me to bow to you—and to say that he would never come again—but to bow to you" (134). This gesture, as Edward Wasiolek has shown, is eloquent with disturbing meanings. It recapitulates the inaugural scene of Dmitri and Katerina's passion—his bowing down before her rather than accept her offer of herself in exchange for the money he has brought to clear her father—and it is precisely this gesture of sublime self-effacing that Katerina's own pride cannot bear. His nobility makes her feel intolerably small, and her subsequent project is to recover the higher moral ground by abasing herself anew, by making him betray her. The bow alludes as well to Father Zosima's earlier bow toward Dmitri—in recognition of Dmitri's suffering and perhaps also in silent apology for Zosima's inability to prevent the gestating murder he all but sees before him. This context of pious gestures flecked with ambiguous motives serves as the cue for Katerina to summon Grushenka out of hiding and onto the scene.

Insistently described as sweet, with her drawling voice and her sensuous catlike movements, Grushenka seems at first to play her scripted role within Katerina's salvational melodrama. Entranced by such submission, Katerina embraces the purring Grushenka—"Here I must kiss your lower lip once more. It looks as though it were swollen, and now it will be more so'' (137)—and then enters on a breathless narrative of Grushenka's former misadventures and present reform, all this told through a first-person plural pronoun that reveals how she has co-opted her rival's story. Alyosha becomes uneasy; "faint, imperceptible shivers kept running down him" (137). Katerina waxes hotter, kissing Grushenka's hand on both sides, and suddenly the performance moves out of her control.

Grushenka turns from passive object to directing subject; we realize there are (there have been from the beginning) two scripts at work here. Describing herself as an indolent "silly creature," without character, Grushenka now solicits Katerina's hand in return. Verbally caressing Katerina ("You sweet young lady, you incredible beauty!"), she holds the hand before her contemplatively.

"Do you know, angel lady," she suddenly drawled in an even more soft and sugary voice, "do you know, after all, I think I won't kiss your hand?" And she laughed a little merry laugh.

"As you please. What's the matter with you?" said Katerina Ivanovna, starting suddenly.

"So that you may be left to remember that you kissed my hand, but I didn't kiss yours." There was a sudden gleam in her eyes. She looked with awful intentness at Katerina Ivanovna.

"Insolent creature!" cried Katerina Ivanovna, as though suddenly grasping something. She flushed all over and leaped up from her seat. Grushenka too got up, but without haste.

"So I shall tell Mitya how you kissed my hand, but I didn't kiss yours at all. And how he will laugh!"

"Slut! Go away!"

"Ah, for shame, young lady! Ah, for shame! That's unbecoming for you, dear young lady, a word like that."

"Go away! You're a creature for sale!" screamed Katerina Ivanovna. Every feature was working in her utterly distorted face.

"For sale indeed! You used to visit gentlemen in the dusk for money once; you brought your beauty for sale. You see, I know."

Katerina Ivanovna shrieked. (139)

The encounter concludes with Grushenka telling Alyosha as she leaves: "I got up this scene for your benefit. . . . See me home, dear, you'll be glad of it afterwards" (139). Each woman has sought to manipulate the other into performing in her little spectacle; each, it turns out, has moved from a prior humiliation into her directorial scenario. Grushenka wins easily because she at least knows the game she is playing and knows how to play both of its roles. Katerina, for her part, once she has been humiliated by Dmitri, never escapes from the ritual of unconscious laceration: damaging oneself so as to inflict damage on the other.

The Russian word for this activity is *nadryv*, glossed by Wasiolek as "to strain or hurt oneself by lifting something beyond one's strength" (160). *Nadryv*, Wasiolek continues, is "a purposeful and pleasurable self-hurt. . . . It is . . . the impulse we all have to make the world over into the image of our wills'' (160). Exploited by another—Katerina by Dmitri, Grushenka by a former lover—each woman has been reduced to the impotence of a mere object, and each now engages in abusive scenarios of revenge. The social world no longer appears as an interactive realm of mutual subjects. Rather it becomes an arrested stage with a single drama on it—the drama, as Freud might put it, of ''someone being beaten,'' with self and other alternating between the two fixed roles.[16] The ideological resonance of this lacerating encounter is best measured if we move briefly to the two pivotal scenes to which it is keyed: the legend of the Grand Inquisitor, on the one hand, and Alyosha's later visit to Grushenka, on the other.

''The Grand Inquisitor'' spells out on a cosmic scale the implications of *nadryv*, its central role in a Christian drama of rebellion and return. With his creaturely status no longer bearable, his interrelatedness a continuous affront, his will and pride humiliated for the last time, the Inquisitor formulates his rebellion in the name of God's unjust world and Christ's impossible demand. The unpredictable interplay among vulnerable subjects must be henceforth banished; the Inquisitor freezes the social scene before him into a posture of permanent abuse, so as to cure it. He directs humanity into their objectified, alien roles. Christ's kiss (so unlike the staged kisses between Katerina and Grushenka) is the free, unplanned, subjective gesture—transforming the subject-object ritual into a subject-subject encounter—that the Inquisitor's architected world cannot accommodate.

The scene of Alyosha's visit to Grushenka begins exactly like the other two. A humiliation has occurred (Zosima's stinking death) that cannot be borne, and—goaded by the resentful Rakitin—Alyosha turns toward Grushenka to complete his abasement. He will make love to her, thus getting his revenge on God's unjust world by conceding and enacting its sordid motives. As for Grushenka, by seducing him, she will prove to them both that his spirituality is a sham; meanwhile, the watching Rakitin will receive payment from Grushenka and enjoy the spectacle of their baseness. All three imagine themselves directing this little piece of theater.

It turns out otherwise for them all. Filled with grief over Zosima's death, Alyosha feels no lust but only ''the intensest and purest interest'' (327) as Grushenka sits on his knees and speaks of the man who had earlier abused her. Alyosha glimpses the pain within her, and at Rakitin's brutal announcement about Zosima, she glimpses the pain within Alyosha. Her piety rushes on her; she crosses herself and begs Alyosha's forgiveness, since, though evil, she did at least once ''give away an onion.'' There follows the parable of the onion— the story of the evil woman whose single good deed was sufficient for God's angel to hold out an onion to her in the lake of fire in order to pull her out if the onion held firm. Other sinners in the burning lake noticed, of course, and tried to climb out by holding onto the woman, who kicked them off and, in so doing, broke the onion. Alyosha's kindness to Grushenka further releases her own narrative of betrayal and revenge—she sees deeply into her mixed motives for the first time—and Alyosha likewise discovers what he has been trying to do and why. When she tearfully thanks him, he replies that all he has done is give her an onion.

Alyosha returns to the monastery and, falling asleep, dreams of the feast of Cana of Galilee. In his vision Father Zosima appears, joining in the celebration of wine replacing water, onions being given to beggars, loving fathers coming back to their rebellious and bereft sons. Alyosha awakens and weeps with joy. This sequence, then, echoes and transforms the staged rituals of the other scenes. Christ asks for only an onion, and even wounded subjects (those most abused, most intent on revenge) may give this involuntarily, unthinkingly, to other subjects. Despite frozen game-plans and fixed social postures, the human subject remains radically unpredictable, open to Satanic rebellion or Christlike charity, capable of astounding. Mikhail Bakhtin rightly calls Dostoevsky the great novelist of surprise: he "always represents a person *on the threshold* of a final decision, at a moment of *crisis*, at an unfinalizable—and *unpredeterminable*—turning point for his soul" (*Problems* 61).

It remains but to shadow slightly this paradigm of ideological coherence, of subjective freedom taking the form of involuntary Christian community. Such a paradigm, we must notice, operates best within the novel's male relationships. The "temptation scene" we have just examined is structured so that sexual desire cannot enter it; its male-female axis gives way at the last to the more crucial axis of two males: Alyosha and his beloved Father Zosima. Sons' relations with siblings and with fathers reveal Dostoevsky's surest ideological orientation; Alyosha would have to be invented if he did not exist.

The sexually charged arena of the female is less coherent. We may remember that strange lovemaking between Katerina and Grushenka, its physical detail in excess of any thematic use Dostoevsky can make of it. We may remember as well the most disturbing character in the novel—Lise—last seen moaning in an ecstasy of *nadryv*, her finger deliberately slammed in a door, her mind revolving about the image of dismembered children. Finally, we may remember that the text's last deployment of Dmitri places him between Katerina and Grushenka and that, despite Dostoevsky's need for plot resolution at this juncture, his wheels merely spin. The women end up snarling at each other, and the chapter closes with Katerina snapping, "Leave me, please!" (727). On such a note we take our own leave of *The Brothers Karamazov*, its capacity for surprise intact, its subject-to-subject sublimity still vulnerable to the play of uncontrolled, unregenerate forces.

From Dostoevsky to James is a big step under any circumstances. When the James in mind is *The Golden Bowl*, it risks seeming an incoherent step. I want to foreground the differences by examining book 5, chapter 2, of the *Bowl*—the scene enclosing the bridge game—in part because Jamesian social structure within this last novel resembles the strategic opacity of shiftingly paired and opposed bridge players more than it does the potential transparency of Christian community. I begin with some reflections on the game of cards itself (an activity that appears in Dostoevsky never as strategy but in the un-Jamesian register of obsession, as in *The Gambler*).

Bridge is first of all a game, one of relatively high leisure. To enter into its precincts is to enter into a rule-governed, social activity. The greatest pleasures in the game come from the stimulation of the greatest tensions, followed by their successful release. These tensions, though, are themselves artificially created, generated by partners and opponents who are only—for the purposes of the game—in league or in opposition. In addition, the game (though its aesthetic dimension never disappears) is sometimes enmeshed within an economic context in which the rewarding of prizes to the most skillful player(s) can generate an atmosphere of motionless intensity. Such a testing of one's intelligence through one's capacity to master a language and attend to the display and withholding of signals can be exhausting.

Finally, the language of bridge is so richly encoded that its practitioners (despite their skills) often fail to decode flawlessly. A coded signal may, given the complexity of the developing context, be susceptible to undecidable interpretations. Yet there can be no question of recourse to another, more clarifying language: only the authorized code is permissible, and to stray from the rules is (among serious players) to be ejected from the game. The ideal bridge-speech would be one that serves as communication to one's partner yet is either a spoken silence or an achieved deception to one's opponents (despite their equal proximity). Were everyone to show his or her cards, this exquisite design of partial knowledge and artful barriers, of subjects and objects straining to decipher each other's concealed and intimated secrets, would come undone; and the game would disappear. It all happens in a very small space.

The bridge game in the novel is briefly set up and never subjected to such allegorical analysis; yet certain procedures of *The Golden Bowl* do seem to align themselves accordingly. The novel's flaunted artifice—its narrational fidelity to epistemological uncertainty, its desire for maximum complexities within a minimum of materials, its focus on coded secrets either concealed or revealed, its delight in symmetrical complications, its penchant for turning the banality of "natural" situations into the intrigue of "artful" contests, its implicit commentary on its own procedures—rarely fails to strike the reader. Maggie compares the bridge game openly to her own controlling activity (as though she were "consciously, as might be said, holding them in her hand" [*NY* XXIV, 239]) and indirectly to that of her creator ("they might have been figures rehearsing some play of which she herself was the author" [*NY* XXIV, 242]). The allegorical impulse may after all be less mine than James's.

The bridge game serves mainly to frame Maggie's strange encounter with Charlotte. Preparing for this encounter, Maggie insistently characterizes herself as the victim: with "her heart in her hands" (*NY* XXIV, 248), "her head . . . on the block" (*NY* XXIV, 249), "her neck . . . half broken and her helpless face staring up" (*NY* XXIV, 249). Such helplessness joins with Maggie's other arresting figure for herself: "the scapegoat of old" (*NY* XXIV, 241), charged with others' sins and expelled into the desert to die (though she imagines her finer punishment will be to remain in place, "somehow for their benefit . . . to keep proving to them they had truly escaped and that she was still there to simplify" [*NY* XXIV, 241]).

It is hard not to recast these roles (and hard not to speculate that James is inviting us to do so). Maggie's humiliation is as exaggeratedly staged as Charlotte's pride. Charlotte is the trapped one, the "creature . . . out of the cage" (*NY* XXIV, 245), who will be—precisely in this scene—recontained and made to serve. Not Maggie but Charlotte must remain there to simplify, to prove to the others the reality of their escape; when the time comes, she will be the scapegoat exiled to American City. Charlotte may point to the others sitting at the table as the price Maggie must pay, yet the very sentence in which she does so strays to "the several great portraits . . . that awaited on the walls of Fawns their final far migration" (*NY* XXIV, 253)—portraits that allude to Charlotte's similar doom, that mutely testify by their object-status to the object Charlotte must inevitably consent to be, whatever her subjective performance here.

Maggie fears most in this encounter that Charlotte will draw on a greater intimacy with Adam than her own, just as later she exults most in her discovery that the prince is hers, not Charlotte's. "They were together thus, he and she, close, close together—whereas Charlotte, though rising there radiantly before her, was really off in some darkness of space that would steep her in solitude and harass her with care" (*NY* XXIV, 257). The effect of her performance— and one wonders if this is not also its motive—is to denature the subject-subject relationships between Charlotte and her husband, Charlotte and her lover. Within these potentially intimate pairings, the princess has invisibly inserted herself, managing to triangulate them in such a way that she and each of the men become the subjects, working together, while Charlotte becomes the object, worked against.

The scene closes in a Judas kiss, though Maggie's concealed plotting makes her join Charlotte as a candidate for that role. "Conscious perjury" on both their parts, the kiss is deliberately watched—absorbed—by all the other principals. It is a kiss for them all, a kiss as pure surface spectacle, revealing little about the subjects (as subjects) engaged in it, intimating a great deal about the fictions they perform within a shared space. No one there takes the kiss as other than a strategic lie. It is nicely emblematic of *The Golden Bowl*'s polished veneer, its crafting and recrafting of the wayward materials of human desire, its deliberate display of design at all costs.

The violence that punctuates the plot of *The Brothers Karamazov* has been repressed to the texture of consciousness in *The Golden Bowl*. James's novel imposes such discipline on actual utterance—those sheer duets that seem the product of years of linguistic practice—that his center of consciousness, Maggie, would probably explode if she was not permitted other outlets. Fortunately she is, and I have counted in volume 2 as many as fifteen fantasized speeches, some of these quite memorable. Consider what we would miss if we did not hear resonating in our heads the following: "Oh yes, I'm *here* all the while; I'm also in my way a solid little fact and I cost originally a great deal of money" (*NY* XXIV, 53) or "You've such a dread of my possibly complaining to you that you keep pealing all the bells to drown my voice; but don't cry out, my dear, till you're hurt" (*NY* XXIV, 108) or "Yes, look, look. . . . Look at the possibility that, since I *am* different, there may still be something in it for you—if you're capable of working with me to get that out" (*NY* XXIV, 195) or "Yes, you see—I lead her now by the neck, I lead her to her doom, and she doesn't so much as know what it is, though she has a fear in her heart which, if you had the chances to apply your ear there that I, as a husband, have, you would hear thump and thump and thump" (*NY* XXIV, 296) or "You don't know what it is to have been loved and broken with. You haven't been broken with, because in *your* relation what can there have been, worth speaking of, to break?" (*NY* XXIV, 338).

All these saucy utterances come from Maggie's imagining her own or others' voices, for once uncensored. What we would miss without them is the charged venom that flavors this novel with a bitterness all its own. Like the governess in *The Turn of the Screw*, Maggie leads an interior life that is manic, that absorbs fully ("oh as coarsely as you like") the thrust and parry of her existence. These interior monologues are saturated in sarcasm and insult; they register her consciousness as something like a mined and detonating battleground. What does it mean, for the representation of subjectivity and social life, that Dostoevsky's and James's tensions are played out in such antithetical spaces?

In his last novel, Dostoevsky's people—though unpredictable—are potentially transparent to each other, momentarily capable of uninhibited verbal delivery of their souls. Speech wounds in *The Brothers Karamazov* (the text is full of "tragic phrases [that] comfort the heart" [338]), but speech may also heal. Alyosha's main function is—by tendering to his interlocutor an uncritical frame of Christlike charity—to stimulate and receive the balm of uncensored speech. Silence can be more expressive than speech in Dostoevsky's world—one thinks of those eloquent gestures like the bow and the kiss—but silence is rarely a sustained practice.[17] *The Golden Bowl*, by contrast, understands speech as essentially strategic and heuristic. It encloses speech within the pregnant ambience of silence, just as Dostoevsky's novel encloses silence within the confrontational domain of speech. James's text, in other words, registers dialogue not as a medium in which conflict oscillates between staged exacerbations and intimate resolutions but rather as a performative activity undertaken by two subjects who enter and exit from dissimilar positions. No wonder silence is safer.

Gesture and speech in *The Golden Bowl* originate in the consciousness of difference itself—the sense that social life is a differential space shared by subjects in some ineradicable measure opaque to each other. The kiss we have glanced at is no aberration but a gesture artfully performed by two such subjects, watched by three others. When we consider that each of the four principal performers (omitting the Assinghams for simplicity) engages simultaneously in relationships that are self-reflexive, paired, triangulated, and quadrilateral, we arrive at some twenty-eight relationships (many of them unrepresented, none of them irrelevant): how could such characters' moves not seem strategic?

*The Brothers Karamazov* yearns for (and memorably produces) encounters in which individual difference—after blazing out—becomes contained (however briefly) within a communal gesture of Christlike love or understanding. *Nadryv* is for Dostoevsky's characters an ineradicable illness—a condition of their ungovernable selfhood—yet at moments they overcome themselves and speak to each other transparently as subject to subject. James's text, by contrast, most memorably produces encounters in which difference neither blazes out nor becomes extinguished—encounters in which intimacy and separateness uneasily coexist, such as Maggie and Adam's last long talk, Maggie and Amerigo's ultimate approaching embrace.

We approach a difference between these two novels that cannot be formulated within a phenomenological model. The subject-object model of phenomenology, privileging consciousness as it does, appeals greatly to literary criticism; yet, as John Rowe has argued, its premises conceal a problematic.[18] The problematic has to do with the socially produced nature—the alterity—of consciousness itself, with its incapacity to possess itself fully, in the form either of self-reflexivity or of entry into another's subjectivity. Dostoevsky's rare scenes of intimacy momentarily transcend this problematic by their access to a subjectively shared discourse of Christian charity, and in this they differ crucially from James's in *The Golden Bowl*.

Here no one becomes fully conscious either of the subjective project of another or of the ramifications of his or her own. The novel appears as a sort of supreme phenomenological effort—for the tracking of such projects is its major concern—yet there remains an unaccountable supplement. One might say, drawing on critics who have examined the economic language and transactions of the novel, that consciousness generated by the binary articulations of this discourse is born repressed, self-protectively blind to its own procedures.[19] Maggie and Adam seem noncoincident with themselves, moving within a symbolic field that imposes a sort of cognitive dissonance as the price of its empowerment. Unlike Christian community, economic appropriation is a shared frame that functions best through mystification. Thus Maggie and Adam keep at bay the exploitative implications of their performance and their language for it. James's *Bowl* is most interestingly fissued, then, in the intimation that consciousness—the keynote of his entire novelistic enterprise—is not given but socially produced, and therefore decentered, its intentional acts as frighteningly wayward as they are admirably deliberate. Is this why the text's most resonant phrase, cited by everyone but never stilled, is "pity and dread"?

The scene to which I turn in Proust's *Recherche* likewise focuses on the ritualized behavior of a self alienated from its own springs of thought and feeling. Mlle Vinteuil's triangulated relationship with her present lesbian lover and her absent father achieves transparency only through the diagnostic lens of a retrospective narrator. The doubled narratorial role of an experiencing child and a remembering adult is unique to Proust's narrative. No character or narrator in James enjoys temporal privilege on such a scale, and the Dostoevsky world of temporal immediacy constructs clarification otherwise than through sifting the passage of time.

In the scene in question, the Proustean narrator exploits, precisely, his temporal overview. "It is perhaps from another impression which I received at Montjouvain, some years later, an impression which at the time remained obscure to me, that there arose, long afterwards, the notion I was to form . . . " (I, 173).[20] I shall return to the problematic concealed within the narrator's project of recuperation. For the moment I want to note some of the suggestive elements in the immediate context of the child Marcel's stumbling upon Mlle Vinteuil. First, this scene (occurring late in "Combray") follows hard on his desire to come upon some sensual peasant-girl within the Roussainville woods, a girl who would incarnate the enchanting spirit of the place and who—in yielding herself to him—would confirm his capacity for complete merger with the Other. Such a girl fails to materialize, of course, and in half-hidden compensation for her absence, Marcel engages in his first hesitant masturbation—an early illicit attempt to find within what remains withheld outside. A page later, and not unrelated to this desire and its frustration, he chances on Mlle Vinteuil in mourning at Montjouvain.

The scene is situated, further, within a bristling parental context. Marcel's parents not only refused to visit this tabooed site but are now absent for the day and have allowed him to "stay out as late as I pleased" (I, 174). Released from their supervision, he finds his way to the locus of transgression and there encounters his first genuine scandal. The earlier Combray disturbances, represented by Françoise's domestic brutality and by Legrandin's snobbism, pale before this strange scene of sexual deviancy. With Mlle Vinteuil's father likewise absent (he "had but lately died" [I, 174]), she is also for the first time free to transgress. The scene thus unfolds—for both the subject watching and the subject acting—as shaped in every way by the departure of parents, and this means, of course, that for both of these truant children, the parents are still oppressively there.

Mlle Vinteuil's physical movements are observed with a slow-motion deliberateness that has no counterpart in Dostoevsky or James. Narrative attention is so patient as to suggest that the nuances of gesture are keyed to abysmal mysteries. Nuances thus lingered over keep suggesting that merely cursory attention to them—attention limited to the passing time of the present—would miss their charge of meaning. She carefully places the photograph of her father on a nearby table (as he had placed his music so that visitors would notice it on entry), and then her friend appears. From this point on, Mlle Vinteuil never ceases to send double signals. Her invitation to the friend to join her on the sofa, her yawn, and her attempt to close the shutters are all programmed moves, signs meant either to underline her depraved role or to show her resistance to it, signs in continual conflict.

But then she must have guessed that her friend would think that she had uttered these words ["People will see us"] simply in order to provoke a reply in certain other words, which she did indeed wish to hear but, from discretion, would have preferred her friend to be the first to speak. . . . "When I say 'see us' [she went on] I mean, of course, see us reading. It's so tiresome to think that whatever trivial little thing you do someone may be overlooking you."

With an instinctive rectitude and a gentility beyond her control, she refrained from uttering the premeditated words which she had felt to be indispensable for the full realisation of her desire. And perpetually, in the depths of her being, a shy and suppliant maiden entreated and reined back a rough and swaggering trooper. (I, 176)[21]

Someone may be overlooking indeed: her father's portrait is positioned so as to overlook, Marcel is there overlooking for all he is worth, Mlle Vinteuil is a perpetual prisoner of her own surveillance, and the narrator overlooks them all. (Where would this huge text be without the premise of a life overlooked?) The "rough and swaggering trooper" who would get free, who seeks sensual release, cannot extricate herself (himself?) from the "shy and suppliant maiden." The text insists on such moralized cliché to polarize this interior gender conflict: the "maiden" houses Mlle Vinteuil's "true nature" (I, 176), whereas the "trooper" appears as an eccentric and dissolute bad actor.[22] The maiden's "scrupulous heart" remains ignorant of the obscene script required to produce "the scene for which her eager senses clamoured" (I, 176), and her words ring false, revealing their strain of self-consciousness.

Eventually she elicits her friend's sudden stinging kiss on her breast, they chase each other "like a pair of amorous fowls" (I, 177), Mlle Vinteuil calls attention to the "inexplicable" presence of her father's picture looking at them, and the "ritual profanations" (I, 177) move into their final phase. Half-encouraged, half-reproached by Mlle Vinteuil—who now springs to her friend's lap and holds out her "chaste brow to be kissed precisely as a daughter would have done" (I, 178)—the friend takes up the photograph and murmurs to Mlle Vinteuil that she intends to spit on it. This rehearsed gesture leads to a closing of the shutters and the end of Marcel's eavesdropping.

The psychological analysis that accompanies and follows this scene—drawing for its authority on the passage of time between the eavesdropping child and the reflecting adult—emerges as masterful. Mlle Vinteuil appears as a "sadist," that is, "an artist in evil" (I, 179); her desire for melodramatic effect and her insistence on role-playing testify to the unnaturalness of this invasion of the trooper within the maiden. "Naturally virtuous," she assesses all sensual pleasure itself as evil, and sadists such as she act out the clichéd scripts of evil "in order to gain the momentary illusion of having escaped beyond the control of their own gentle and scrupulous natures into the inhuman world of pleasure" (I, 179).[23] What she would—yet cannot—eradicate by her ritual is her father's bequeathed presence in her body (his face, his family's blue eyes) and in her mind (his courtesy and gentleness, his virtue). In other words she would, by retreating into the immediacy of her body's urgency, eradicate her inheritance itself: the intricate history that has produced her. Marcel concludes that she would never have imagined evil to inhere in such exotic and strenuous role-playing if she had discerned its true status, in herself as in others, as "indifference to the sufferings one causes [others]" (I, 180).

This final phrase is decisive, and the narrative moves on to other matters, Mlle Vinteuil's "case" being finally explained. Yet it seems to me that "in-difference-as-evil" reopens everything it is meant to close: it breaks down the simplistic relations between the maiden and the trooper, the father and the daughter. After all, the virtuous father is also the egotist whose pride in his musical compositions requires devious rituals for being stroked. Has he not passed this on as well? In other words, the narrator's elaborate interpretation seeks to shore up, beneath the daughter's histrionic ritual of abuse, the underlying paradigm of her natural devotion: a devotion that means that the time separating parent and child is not (as it might appear) the lost time of defection but is rather time retraced, made whole again. The narrator can read her thus only by sim-plifying (in his retrospective summary) her inheritance from her father and by registering her attempted move away from filial fidelity—like her move away from gender norms—in the unnatural terms of self-abuse. Such terms do not invite further reflection. We are meant to accept this "case history"; the very crispness of the analysis separates the authoritative analyst from the plumbed and moralized object of his thoughts.

The episode, if lingered on rather than "understood," bristles with unresolved tensions. The young woman seeking to escape becomes, through the narrator's recuperative retrospect, more than ever bonded with her father, further than ever from her goal of liberation—kept away from growth in time even as her interpreter has used the passing time to learn to read her. This objectifying lens only increases her self-alienation; the shadow of the third figure (the absent father, the invisible watcher, the musing narrator) falls decisively on the scene.[24] Under such a shadow, the figure acting out the moves of a contradictory script must appear inherently mystified—always self-deceived because in thrall to absent others and to conflicted motives generated over time, always alienated because shown spin-ning within the blinded present moment, always grasped authoritatively by a narrator-subject whose own vision has been freed from such temporal tyranny. As we must now explore, the vignette of the mystified Mlle Vinteuil may be most suggestive not thematically—in her open connection with the child Mar-cel—but procedurally: as a revealing index of the narrator's epistemological project.

The child Marcel may resemble Mlle Vinteuil in his mystification and truancy, but the adult narrator Marcel does not. The latter's self-possession is in fact constructed through scenes like this one, emerging unanswerably in his authority achieved over the span of time and in his capacity to analyze others. The re-cuperative project of the *Recherche* is nourished, precisely, by the narrator's desire to capture the otherness of the world within the restorative terms of his own discourse. Contemporary Proustean criticism problematizes just this goal, however; we are now beginning to wonder to what extent the novel's central conception of an all-fathoming narrator is the fantasy-creation of an arrested child. Unmediated communicability, possession of others' interior being, attained self-knowledge—the Proustean narrator-subject would, in recuperating time, achieve retrospective self-transparency through the triumphantly purgative ordeal of writing itself.

A poststructuralist perspective highlights the contradiction at work here between a project based on language as an impersonal medium unamenable to any subject's total control, on the one hand, and the Proustean goal of self-knowledge through the mastery of a perfected subjective discourse, on the other.[25] So long as the text is conceived "as the expression of desire and not the desire of expression," Samuel Weber has written, it remains "dominated by the very [Idealist] tradition it so powerfully solicits and subverts" (923–24). The text, then, as a desire-permeated, never stabilized web, is the conceptual frame that allows us to return to our focal scene, to probe the strategic distinction between the displayed (mystified) Mlle Vinteuil and the concealed (authoritative) narrator and to identify the elusive desire fueling that distinction.

We might best chart this narrative desire by observing how cunningly the text deploys homosexual desire. It highlights homosexual desire within certain probed characters as adeptly as it shrouds it within certain others. Eve Sedgwick has recently discussed this strategy of display and concealment, focusing on Charlus as the legible character (just as Mlle Vinteuil is legible) and Albertine as the illegible one.

It is exactly in their relation to visibility that the two erotic loci are so violently incommensurable. Charlus' closet is spectacularized so that the erotics around Albertine (which is to say, around the narrator) may continue to resist visualization; it is from the inchoate space that will include Albertine, and to guarantee its privileged exemption from sight, that the narrator stages the presentation of Charlus; it is around the perceptual axis between a closet viewed and a closet inhabited that a discourse of the world takes shape. (Sedgwick, "Closet II" 110)

Let us now draw these threads together. Mlle Vinteuil's deliberately espied and anatomized psyche—with its comfortable terms of a natural identity and an unnatural invader, of parental love deeply responded to (despite death) by filial love, masking as sadism—certainly emerges as what the text wants us to see. Her self-alienating ritual is fully yielded up to us as the closet viewed. The question then arises: What is the closet inhabited? Is it that "indifference to the sufferings one causes" others (even one's children, even one's parents)—a sort of incorrigible penchant for betrayal, a fickleness that is associated with bodily life in the present moment and that the text mentions here but cannot incorporate into its portrait? Is it thus an irremovable residue of subjective narcissism, an unknowable supplement that contaminates even the narrator, that would call into question (if admitted) his project of undeviating self-possession and achieved penance? Is it the repressed awareness that sexual identity is not a matter of natural (family-descended) norms violated by artificial invaders, that parental-filial relations do not simply take the pattern of selfless generosity bestowed, abused, and retrospectively repaired, that parents suffocate as well as nourish, that departure from them (as from our own lost selves) is not merely the pretext for a later and all-recuperating return but instead a genuine departure, an unredeemable loss? These questions swarm about a common concern: that the *Recherche* project—like all essays in writing—embodies a search in time and language and not a mastery of either, that the searching subject at its center achieves selfhood only through a process that calls into question the meanings of subject, self, and center.

As we have seen in these analyses, subject, self, and center are specular and affiliatory terms; they have no intrinsic meanings. The center is a function, not an absolute; it grounds nothing but instead shifts according to fluctuating definitions of the larger field. Likewise, subject and self mean only with respect to object and other; they are conceptually interdependent notions. Louis Althusser, seeking to define the larger structural activity within which this dynamic operates, claims, "The category of the subject is the constitutive category of all ideology . . . insofar as all ideology has the function (which defines it) of 'constituting' concrete individuals as subjects" (171). We obtain our sense of uncoerced, unpredictable inwardness—our sense of ourselves as centered—through spontaneous assent to and adjustment of the social scripts that solicit us. Identity is not an inborn property; we go to culture to construct it. We enter social networks to take on personhood; we must become Other to become Self.

Identity is decentered, then, a something generated through the personal activation of scripts and roles provided by culture. In the first set of discussions, I sought to indicate the contours of the larger ideological economies within which the subject lives out her sexual identity. Emma's and Anna's adulteries are conceptualized within a linguistic medium whose vocabulary condemns these acts to fantasy-expectations or suicidal guilt. Charlotte's, by contrast, is at first enabled by James's discourse of aesthetic sufficiency—of so refining the surfaces of one's shared life that the interior is freed to go its own way—yet *The Golden Bowl* intimates that this liberating project is based on (and eventually undermined by) a subject-object dynamics of power that pays for the engorgement of the subject with an equivalent exploitation of the object.

In the second set of discussions, I sought to analyze the scripts that nourish (openly or latently) the subject-object ritual that punctuates selected social encounters. Dostoevskyan *nadryv* underwrites the master-slave dynamic between Grushenka and Katerina, but Grushenka's later reconciliation with Alyosha transcends the defensive barriers of *nadryv*, arriving at a Christ-modeled subject-to-subject openness. In *The Golden Bowl* the strategic orientation seems unremovable, as though the economic system within which motive and assumption are scripted in this text ensured a certain supplemental strand of unknowing subject-object exploitation interwoven within subject-subject care, of behavior in disturbing excess of anyone's self-knowledge. Finally, Proust's *Recherche* unfolds a temporal drama in which the protagonist-narrator's epistemological moves—his strategic analysis of Mlle Vinteuil's ritualistic behavior—hint as well at the simplifications he requires, the blindness he must disown, to authorize his fragile identity by appropriating hers.

In these instances, desire for mastery does not mean its attainment—the subject remains incompletely self-knowing, caught up within uncontained systems—and this is true for authors as well as characters. Thus, to return to my choice of novelists in this essay, James's own crucial distinction between his kind of fiction and that of Tolstoy and Dostoevsky opens up to question. "Large loose baggy monsters, with their queer elements of the accidental and the arbitrary" (*AN* 84), he called such inartistic works in his preface to *The Tragic Muse*; and his four or five other comments on the wilder Russians sound the same note of lack of judicious mastery.[26] Such novels are "uncomposed," and by that James means unselective, unfocalized through a commanding center of consciousness. Once this privileged concept loses its privilege, though, once "center" and "consciousness" appear as produced by structure(s) and thus dependent on larger economies in order to be thought at all, once they become recontaminated by that which they are meant to hold at bay—then James's fictions begin to share a common problematic (the decentering of subjective consciousness, the problematizing of authorial mastery), and his insertion within this group of European novelists may make more sense.

Readers too are scripted; larger agencies move within their moves, and their encounters with texts are never innocent. In every impression, there is a crossing of boundaries, an impact, a violation.[27] Even the most genial round of visits risks unleashing a disturbance, as poor Mark Montieth discovers. Newton Winch kills himself at the conclusion of Montieth's little social call, unable to bear the clamor within his own identity caused by exposure to one intolerably like him, yet other. "I really think I must practically have caused it" (*CT* XII, 459), Montieth murmurs as the story ends.

Subjective identity is indeed relational, an affair of contrasts and juxtapositions, of images in the mirror. James becomes who he is because of what his culture is and who his peers are, the company he does and does not keep. These groupings are subject to infinite changes (each change brings, knowingly or not, its own determinate agenda), yet James comes into (differential) being only insofar as he is grouped, seen against others, seen by others. This is so because an author is never an entity unto itself but is instead an alterable frame through which we determine—in the uses made and yet to make of the author—how (in John Rowe's words) "literature serves or subverts the culture's complex acts of self-representation and self-preservation" (*Theoretical Dimensions* 28). It is not Henry James, then, but "Henry James"—as he makes his round of visits to "Flaubert," "Tolstoy," "Dostoevsky," and "Proust."

## NOTES

1. Ample bibliographical information on these materials is available elsewhere in this volume. Without citing James's own critical pieces, I mention here only a few basic scholarly texts: Bewley (*Complex Fate*), Matthiessen (*American Renaissance*), and Long, for James's relation to Hawthorne; Lerner, Cargill, and Peterson, for his relation to Turgenev; Leavis and Cargill, for his relation to George Eliot; Peter Brooks and Stowe, for his relation to Balzac. On James in relation to Realism and Naturalism, see Becker, Powers (*Henry James and the Naturalist Movement*), Grover, and Perosa (*Experimental*). On James in relation to Impressionism and Modernism, see Winner, Charles Anderson, Stowell, Kirschke, Rowe (*Henry Adams* and *Theoretical Dimensions*), Carroll, and Donadio.

2. James's most focused commentary on Flaubert appears in his 1876, 1893, and 1902 essays. On Proust he has virtually nothing to say, and according to Edel (*Henry James, The Master* 496), we cannot know whether he read *Swann's Way* (it appeared three years before his death). His commentary on Tolstoy is brief, scattered, and notorious. He mentions only *War and Peace* (which in the preface to *The Tragic Muse* he oddly calls *Peace and War*); he may not have read *Anna Karenina*. I can find no evidence that he read anything by Dostoevsky. There has been very little systematic comparison of James with any of these peers other than Flaubert. For further commentary, see Grover, Gervais, Lubbock (*Craft*), Edel (*Henry James, The Master*), Hardy, Perosa ("James, Tolstoy"), and Bersani (*Astyanax*).

3. Briefly put, I approach the subject by way of Jean-Paul Sartre, Jacques Lacan, and Michel Foucault; gender by way of Gilbert and Gubar, Luce Irigaray, and Jacobus; the text's ideological context by way of Althusser, Pierre Macherey, and Jameson. I have learned the most about a "theoretical Henry James" from Rowe and Seltzer. I wish also to thank my colleague Peter Schmidt for a critical reading of this essay in an earlier draft form.

4. All passages from French texts will be cited in standard English translations; I use de Man's revision of Aveling's translation of *Madame Bovary* and Kilmartin's revision of Scott-Moncrieff's translation of the *Recherche*. Longer passages will also be given in French after the translation when the original wording suggests more than the translation captures.

> Les ombres du soir descendaient; le soleil horizontal, passant entre les branches, lui éblouissait les yeux. Çà et là, tout autour d'elle, dans les feuilles ou par terre, des taches lumineuses tremblaient, comme si des colibris, en volant, eussent éparpillé leurs plumes. Le silence était partout; quelque chose de doux semblait sortir des arbres; elle sentait son coeur, dont les battements recommençaient, et le sang circuler dans sa chair comme un fleuve de lait. Alors, elle entendit au loin, au-delà du bois, sur les autres collines, un cri vague et prolongé, une voix qui se traînait, et elle l'écoutait silencieusement, se mêlant comme une musique aux dernières vibrations de ses nerfs émus . . .
>
> Elle se répétait: "J'ai un amant! un amant!" se délectant à cette idée comme à celle d'une autre puberté qui lui serait survenue. Elle allait donc posséder enfin ces joies de l'amour, cette fièvre du bonheur dont elle avait désespéré. Elle entrait dans quelque chose de merveilleux où tout serait passion, extase, délire. (*Oeuvres* 1:438–39)

5. I am conscious of the sexual tenor of my own language here, and I recognize that male readers may well respond to the eroticized representation of Emma differently than do female readers. Tanner attends at length to Flaubert's "morselization" of Emma (*Adultery* 349–65); all keen readers of the text have noted the author's virtually hypnotic focus on his heroine's embodied career.

6. "il avait l'air aussi calme dans la vie que le chardonneret suspendu au-dessus de sa tête, dans sa cage d'osier" (*Oeuvres* 1:358).

7. "Ils examinèrent ses robes, le linge, le cabinet de toilette; et son existence, jusque dans ses recoins les plus intimes, fut, comme un cadavre que l'on autopsie, étalée tout du long aux regards de ces trois hommes" (*Oeuvres* 1:560).

8. Flaubert's restrained tenderness is inseparable from his sense of universal cliché; I think of his rendering of Frédéric and Mme Arnoux's last meeting, as well as his treatment of Félicité and of Bouvard and Pécuchet. In a different vein—but drawing on the same linguistic awareness—Joyce uses clichés that "finer" writers would have jettisoned or simply mocked, in order to create the mental world of the extraordinarily ordinary Leopold Bloom.

9. I assume that my readers, like myself, do not read Tolstoy and Dostoevsky in Russian. I make use of the Maude translation of *Anna Karenina* here, and later of Matlaw's revision of the Garnett translation of *The Brothers Karamazov*.

10. As John Bayley puts it: "The climax of the seduction is the end of life flowing like a fountain or blazing like a fire: it is like the constriction of the black bag, the confrontation of death. Everything shrinks to one fact" (*Tolstoy* 214).

11. Compare Leo Bersani: "In James's late fiction the narrative surface is never richly menaced by meanings it can't wholly contain. Complexity consists not in mutually subversive motives but rather in the expanding surface itself which, when most successful, finds a place in its intricate design for all the motives imaginable" (*Astyanax* 131).

12. Skeptical commentators on this novel have long recognized—at least since Matthiessen—the exploitation at the heart of these relationships. Paul Armstrong (*Phenomenology*) explores this issue in the subject-object vocabulary of phenomenology, and Mark Seltzer (by way of Foucault) brilliantly reads the twin discourses of love and power as "two ways of saying the same thing" (66).

13. I press this point to make it clear, but I also recognize James's remarkable grasp of the silent struggles that take place within marriage. The subtlety of his achievement here is, so far as I know, unequaled. Yet the absence from both Ververs' unions of so many other dimensions of marriage—what one might call its inertial solidity, its involuntary intimacy achieved over time—imparts a certain weightlessness to James's rendering.

14. Frederick Olafson argues that what is at stake here has less to do with marriage or adultery per se than with the fundamental dissolution of trust itself within personal relationships. "Having been lied to, [Maggie] in effect arranges things in such a way that all the persons concerned are permanently shut up in a system of lies from which there can be no exit" (311).

15. As Gabriel Pearson succinctly puts it, *The Golden Bowl* presents "the surfaces of civilization as complex illusions, out of direct contact with their own illicit depths, yet in secret and fascinated commerce with them. . . . The whole novel . . . is impossibly both an act and refusal of descent into its own depths" (350).

16. In Freud's essay entitled "A Child Is Being Beaten," the roles of subject and

object shift dizzily as Freud interprets in three different ways a dream whose structural focus on desire, guilt, and illicit release never alters.

17. The rare radiance of speech in this last novel is even rarer in Dostoevsky's earlier work. "The Double," *Notes from the Underground*, and *Crime and Punishment* reveal, through their claustrophobic blockages, how far Dostoevsky had to travel to achieve his cathartic moments of community.

18. In his chapter on "The Reader in the Text" (in *Theoretical Dimensions*), John Carlos Rowe speaks of literary phenomenology's striving toward a grasp on unconditional subjective processes, the fantasy—common to all idealisms since Kant—of a shared and universal humanity.

19. Some of the most fruitful recent criticism of *The Golden Bowl* has resisted the blandishments of "Jamesian ambiguity" and pursued this determinate cultural-historical approach. (See commentaries by Agnew, Porter, Seltzer, and Boone.)

20. "C'est peut-être d'une impression ressentie aussi auprès de Montjouvain, quelques années plus tard, impression restée obscure alors, qu'est sortie, bien après, l'idée que je me suis faite du . . ." (*Recherche* I, 159).

21. Mais elle devina sans doute que son amie penserait qu'elle n'avait dit ces mots que pour la provoquer à lui répondre par certains autres, qu'elle avait en effet le désir d'entendre, mais que par discrétion elle voulait lui laisser l'initiative de prononcer. . . .

—Quand je dis nous voir, je veux dire nous voir lire; c'est assommant, quelque chose insignifiante qu'on fasse, de penser que des yeux nous voient.

Par une générosité instinctive et une politesse involontaire elle taisait les mots prémédités qu'elle avait jugés indispensable à la pleine réalisation de son désir. Et à tous moments au fond d'elle-même une vierge timide et suppliante implorait et faisait reculer un soudard fruste et vainqueur. (*Recherche* I, 161)

22. Randolph Splitter speaks of the "simplistic, stereotyped view" (52) at work in the narrator's gender characterizations.

23. "de façon à avoir eu un moment l'illusion de s'être évadés de leur âme scrupuleuse et tendre dans le monde inhumain du plaisir" (*Recherche* I, 164).

24. Not only do the male watcher and narrator (Marcel) banish from readerly attention the role of Mlle Vinteuil's friend in this encounter—she simply drops out of the analysis—but (joining with the watching father) they contain as well the most disturbing lesbian implications of this scene of desire. By emphatically imposing an Oedipal paradigm on this revolt of the daughters, Marcel ensures that no pre-Oedipal alignment (the child in search of the mother rather than in bondage to the father) be allowed, though the acting out of desire between the two women almost begs to be inserted into this other interpretive configuration.

25. Paul de Man and Samuel Weber (drawing on Gerard Genette and Gilles Deleuze) inaugurate this poststructuralist line of demystifying commentary on Proust's *Recherche*. Jeffrey Mehlman, Randolph Splitter, David Ellison, and Vincent Descombes continue to probe the gap between the text's synthetic claims and its differential practice.

26. In his discussion of James's views on Tolstoy, Sergio Perosa ("James, Tolstoy") identifies James's concern about the Russian's "tumultuous reflection of life in its chaotic richness" (368), uncontrolled by an art of selective narrative focus.

27. John Carlos Rowe wrote: "The 'impression' as at once material and immaterial,

as violent act and superficial glance, as fleeting moment and enduring mark (memory trace), as noun that cannot suppress its verbal origin—this impression is the divided present and rhetorical catachresis in which language finds its own origins, even as it preserves this secret beneath the gaze of the eye and the voice of the I'' (*Theoretical Dimensions* 193–94).

# 12
# Closure in James: A Formalist
# Feminist View

## *Mary Doyle Springer*

> The novels of Henry James . . . pose a continual challenge to the masculinist
> bias of American critical theory.
>
> —Nina Baym

Formalism and feminism have usually been treated by feminists as mutually
exclusive, and I shall do my best in this essay to suggest how they can instead
be mutually supportive, and productive of a fuller understanding of complex
works such as the fiction of Henry James.

It is by now obvious that feminist criticism is not a single-minded activity—
its practice insists on not being pegged or categorized. We are at home with,
and even prefer, "a divided and multi-faceted movement," and we find feminist
criticism to be "situated within the exchange that constitutes it, within the
differences which divide it from any self or essence, any unified position"
(Jacobus, xiii and 292). American feminist critics have usually been recognized
for their primarily political approach to a literature that they view as heavily
imbedded in its context of time and society—hence their disdain especially for
the once dominant formalism of the once New Critics. (Toril Moi describes that
battle as a "binary opposition between reductive political readings on the one
hand and rich aesthetic appraisal on the other" [85]). And yet the American
movement also contains critics like Myra Jehlen, with whom I agree when she
states, "If aesthetics raises the question of whether (and how) the text works
effectively with an audience, it obviously is bound up with the political: without
an aesthetic effect there will be no political effect either." Her point is that "we
should begin . . . by acknowledging the separate wholeness of the literary subject,
its distinct vision that need not be ours—what the formalists have told us and

told us about: its integrity.'' Where few feminist critics can agree with Jehlen, however, is when she notes, ''We need to acknowledge, also, that to respect that integrity by not asking questions of the text that it does not ask itself, to ask the text what questions to ask, will produce the fullest, richest reading'' (Jehlen 579). Nothing human is alien to us. We may ask of a text whatever questions we please, so long as we realize that we will get only the answers that the particular questions make possible. We cannot simultaneously raise aesthetic questions and political ones, though we can raise them in the light of each other, as I propose to do. True, some works call up one kind of critical question sooner than another—for example, it is more productive to analyze the treatment of women in James's work than in the works of Herman Melville, where there appear so few women characters.

French feminists—Julia Kristeva, Hélène Cixous, Luce Irigaray—by contrast, show a central interest in what might broadly be termed a new aesthetics when it is not called semiotics, a study of written expression often in the light of psychoanalytic criticism. Though they try to identify a feminine style of writing and thinking, full of unspoken reverberations, they do not necessarily limit it to the writing of women. And they do not turn away (as American ''gynocritics'' do) from the study of male artists, who after all continue to dominate the canons of literature and the visual arts and who continue to construct representations of women that have social and political consequences.

Looking at James through feminist eyeglasses, I hope to explore readings made possible by both the French feminine aesthetic and American feminist politics. As a formalist, I shall avoid the overemphasis on language that characterizes current feminists on both sides of the ocean and that also, ironically, is typical of their declared archenemy, the New Criticism. The more complete formalist aesthetic of Aristotle, which looks not only to language but also to character, plot, point of view, and narrative manner in their effects on the work as a whole, is much closer to James's own aesthetic and its practice. His practice, and that of later authors, make clear an extremely important consideration that feminist disavowal of form has insufficiently taken into account, namely, that form does not mean a set of traditional devices employed for traditional effect by traditional authors. Form is the form employed by the given present work and includes all *its* devices, however traditional or radical. In this regard, lack of closure, the subject of this essay, is just as formal an art as closure—lack of closure is *the* closure by which the given work takes comprehensible form.

James was a conscious formalist who loved ''a handsome wholeness of effect'' because ''the 'importance' of a work of art is wholly dependent on its *being* one: outside of which all prate of its representative character, its meaning and its bearing, its morality and humanity, are an impudent thing. Strong in that character [artistic form], which is the condition of its really bearing witness at all, it is strong every way'' (*AN* 329, 38).

His implicit message to feminists is very clear, and I shall take it centrally to heart in this essay: in fiction, the study of the literary form is our best guide to the practical and social "importance" of the work. To abandon the holistic study of art (in its multitudinous radical as well as traditional forms) is to abandon a major key to "morality and humanity." His art is also the major key to the implied author, to the political aspect of James himself as a presenter of women.

Partly I agree with Hélène Cixous when she says, "Let us not be trapped by an analysis still encumbered with the old automatisms." And she warns that "the demon of interpretation—oblique, decked out in modernity" will sell us "the same old handcuffs, baubles, and chains." What she calls the "New Women," when they "dare to create outside the theoretical," are "called in by the cops of the signifier, fingerprinted, remonstrated, and brought into the line of order they are supposed to know" (Cixous, 887, 892). To be antitheory and antianalysis is to have feminist supporters these days, both in France and in America. But, we may ask, how does that suit Cixous's other admonition: "We have no womanly reason to pledge allegiance to the negative. The feminine (as the poets suspected) affirms" (884)? In my view, the old automatisms—for example, the presumed major villain: Aristotle's theories of plot, character, and diction—*ought* to remain automatic, strict, and also usefully empty, as concepts that each individual work can then be seen partly to depart from in its individuality. If we never theorize, interpret, or extrapolate imaginatively from the theory of others, we shall never "see" or know the political importance of anything we read, for we will have given away our reading glasses. My account of the radical departure of James from "rules" of form depends entirely on knowing what it is he departs *from*. And I am equally indebted to feminist critics who constantly "theorize" (as indeed Cixous does) about the need for departures and change and what they might look like. Like it or not, we think in categories, and the question becomes how to free ourselves by making use of them so that they cannot use and impose on us.[1]

Having employed Wayne Booth's term "implied author" (a term that has crept into critical language so usefully that it is often employed without quotation marks), I shall also compose a central question revised from Booth's current ethical question in *The Company We Keep*. Is the implied author of James's fiction a man whom women can take for a friend? The question is an ethical and political one, but it follows on an aesthetic one, and we may expect the answer to be as complex as friendship itself.

Since the question is worth a book, I have chosen to limit my study to the single aesthetic device of closure, a discussion that Jamesian critics have tended to limit to plot closure alone. In closures not only of his plots but also of his characters and of his famous convoluted language, James is unusual if not strange, and strange in ways that may help us understand his attitudes toward women.

Let us begin with some of his women characters. Though he is a male, and a "canonized" writer, James has until recently been treated gingerly by feminist critics because he has so long been recognized for some unforgettably strong and sympathetic female characters, women who are in keeping with their author's time, place(s), family, and social class and yet startlingly individual. Certainly we cannot blink the fact that "he was temperamentally incapable of admiring or being interested in any but socially aristocratic or respectable bourgeois types," nor the fact that "James really felt that bad manners was worse than murder" (Hays 171).

If hardly a banal Victorian gentleman, as is sometimes loosely claimed, James certainly was to some extent a man of his time and place and to a passionate extent a loyal man of his family. Perhaps no reader of mine can be sure of a balanced feminist perspective on his work without also consulting the family context of his work, especially as it appears in his sister's diary and her biography (Strouse, *Alice James*), and also the extraordinary account of "the lessons of the father" in their complex effect on Henry James as a son (Habegger, "Lessons"). These works, however, seek the man, whereas my limited space and my inclination both lead me to concentrate on the implied author of James's fiction and criticism.

Even if we were to peg James contextually, it would not really make less difficult the task of feminists wishing to place his works ethically or politically, since in his work the social context is paradoxically so pervasive as to be almost unobtrusive. James seems to present his people as affluent members of the upper class not only because that is the class he knew best but also, especially, because that allows them freedom from economic constraints, freedom to think and space in which to act more or less reflectively.

It is also hard to place ethically an author who is rarely directly attitudinal in his fiction.[2] He simply wanted, like his friend Joseph Conrad, to "see" vividly and to make the reader see. When pity is expressed ("the poor girl"), it is usually accompanied ironically by a suspect point of view—for example, when it is Winterbourne expressing pity for Daisy Miller.

Character, not plot, was James's prime emphasis. The widespread feminist suspicion of traditional plot, for its manipulation of women characters and their outcomes, was entirely shared by James, as I shall show. The "germ" of his composition, he tells us, was never plot ("nefarious name") but rather "the sense of a single character," often the "character and aspect of a particular engaging young woman" (*AN* 42).

(James writes that he found himself "fatally incompetent" to present "the *elder* woman," whom he claims to have viewed as unredeemably locked into her role as "the wife and mother, in whom nothing was in eclipse, but everything rather . . . straight in evidence, and to whom therefore any round and complete embodiment had simply been denied" [*AN* 193]. This seems a curious lack of self-knowledge, coming from the same man who had for friends and models such interesting older women as Edith Wharton and from the same author who could tantalize us with such characters as Mrs. Touchett in *The Portrait of a Lady*, Mrs. Gereth in *The Spoils of Poynton*, Miss Tina in *The Aspern Papers*, and others that crowd in for mention. It appears that James could have meant only that he had failed to attempt the "complete embodiment" of older women as protagonists, and that is indeed a serious loss.)

Like his admired Ivan Turgenev, James allowed himself simply to be struck by his character, to watch her, to see her "subject to the chances, the complications of existence." The task of the author was limited: to find for the characters "the right relations, those that would most bring them out," and to "invent and select and piece together the situations most useful and favorable to the sense of the creatures themselves, the complications *they* would be most likely to produce and to feel" (*AN* 42–43, my emphasis).

Thus James saw himself and his plots ("relations") as the servants of his characters, and not the reverse. It is this attitude of service to characters who are in possession of themselves that prevents James's gaze from becoming the "male gaze" so usefully pinpointed by feminist film critics (and about which fiction also deserves scrutiny). Consider the author's famous question to himself at the birth of Isabel Archer: "What will she *do*?" It is acutely up to her to decide, according to the kind of person *she* is at any given point in her "complications." The reader joins the author in watching, and we owe to him not so much a construction of his own but rather an increasingly sharp eye on the situations, actions, and responses of the characters. With the exception of secondary characters who function more as "situations" than prime characters (e.g., Aunt Penniman and Madame Merle), almost no female character is conceived as a finished or closed character, and it follows that we cannot easily test her author against any easy set of feminist principles having to do with the representation of women—with the very notable exception of that principle of representation itself. James's women are not simply presented to us on the author's authority as to their characters but rather come before us in constant movement so natural to them (and yet nature contains its surprises) that they seem to act entirely on their own. If they are judged, it seems to be somehow *our* judgment, even though the author can be said to have selected every word, every action. If there is morality, we are rarely or never told what the moral is, and there is also that "perfect dependence of the 'moral' sense of a work of art on the amount of felt life concerned in producing it" (*AN* 45).

Paradoxes abound. If James's characters are not presented as characters—that is, if they are not (at least not rhetorically) an Aristotelean set of habits by which we can recognize them, if they are not finished either in themselves or usually in their endings—why are they so unforgettable, as though they had changed our lives? And if James simply lets them take their head in action while he watches them, how can one speak of his sympathy for them and for their often conspicuous bravery? I hope I shall be able to show that the task of making up our minds is not impossible, even if never finished.

Though he was actually making judgments every minute, as we all are forced to do, James's reluctance to promulgate ideas is James's one great idea. (One defers, of course, to T. S. Eliot's famous dictum.) He trusts human beings, and women even more than men, to find their way no matter how headstrong that way may be, and the story of their search is all. We forget by now just how radically feminist is the desire simply to tell such a story, but Richard Chase suggests that no American novelist until the time of Henry James and Edith Wharton had the imagination to present a "fully developed woman of sexual age" (quoted in Baym, "Melodramas" 73). To the extent that this is so, it is a further radical grace of their author that we find those female characters to be of ongoing complexity and frequently find the irony of open-ended closures as to who they are and how their stories will end.[3] A flash portrait of Fleda Vetch rises to my mind—what will *she* do, now that the treasure house of Poynton has burned down? Who, really, *is* she?

Otto Friedrich, writing "Of Apple Trees and Roses," could as well have been writing of James and fiction when he said: "I decided to let nature take its course, which is a political act . . . for nature as such is a constant state of aggression and destruction. . . . Weeding is what we call our choices" (71). By analogy, James can be said to commit a political act when he stands back to observe rather than govern his characters, when their main activities are seen to be learning and change (Isabel Archer, Maggie Verver, Strether, Maisie, Fleda Vetch), and when the main choice he makes is *not* to weed out but to exploit the mistakes made by "clumsy Life, at her stupid work" (*AN* 121). It is instructive to compare James with Dickens the didact or with the great satirists whose gardens, out of generic rhetorical necessity, are steadily weeded in the hope of directing life toward new and neater conclusions. James has a far less authoritative inclination. Though he is a constant ironist, it is notable how rarely he is moved toward either satire or apologue and how relatively thin the results are in his works in those forms, such as "The Death of the Lion" and "Benvolio."

In those occasional main characters that are closed characters, James finds tragedy. The governess in *The Turn of the Screw* is such a one. At twenty, she is inspired by a lone and authoritative sense of herself. Employed by a man who shifts his semipaternal responsibilities to her, she correctly sees herself as "obsessed." She rests at Bly in the "great state bed, as I almost felt it," and to "watch, teach, 'form' " her pupils is all her desire (*NY* XII, 159–60). It is already clear that the world she inhabits is what some French feminists would call masculine and what all would call symbolic, a world that adopts paternal metaphors and mirrors the male. She sees no irony in speaking of the "horrid unclean school-world" with its "stupid sordid head-masters," from which, however, Miles has returned only to be subjugated to her own obsessive will and vision. The author's irony shines when the governess articulates herself as a mirror to her male employer: "It was a pleasure . . . to feel myself tranquil and justified, doubtless perhaps also to reflect that by my discretion, my quiet good sense and general high propriety, I was giving pleasure—if he ever thought of it!—to the person to whose pressure I had yielded. What I was doing was what he had earnestly hoped and directly asked of me" (*NY* XII, 174).[4]

The governess lacks, as the children initially do not, almost all of what Julia Kristeva would call a feminine sense of "*jouissance*," of the "carnivalistic" play of life, a playfulness that attempts to fool us out of what is often our insane rationality—including perhaps our excesses of critical rationality. Is there a possibility that her critics have all aped the governess in her dangerous desire to control all mysterious matters? Is there a possibility that too much ink (including my own) has been spilled on *The Turn of the Screw* in our attempts to resolve the question of whether the ghosts are real or the governess mad?[5] By very reason of her superrationality she may be mad, and feminists might applaud the madness as at least a positive release from the superrationality. When James said he was setting "a trap for the unwary" and then said no more, he was obviously willing to leave the world without providing a dictated closure either for the character or for the story. Perhaps exactly there was his chosen "closure"—to leave us alone forever with our doubts about this woman and about this kind of woman. What, after all, is the worth of closing down a ghost story such as this with a cheap, tight ending that allows us to sleep more easily? Poor Miles may in fact be said to have paid with his life for the governess's insistence on making real the ghost that appears in perhaps every one of our windows if we stare as hard as she does.

Virginia Woolf understood very well James's refusal invariably to close on, to define clearly, the situation in a story, and we begin to see in her remarks a connection between his interest in ghost stories and the lack of deterministic closure that carries him so close to feminist interests. In fact, he seems to use ghosts here to point toward the great pity we ought to feel for a mind like that of the governess's as it strives for dominance and closure. In an essay on James's ghost stories, Woolf wrote, "The stories in which Henry James uses the supernatural effectively are . . . those where some quality in a character or in a situation can only be given its fullest meaning by being cut free from facts" ("Henry James's Ghost Stories" 291). If so, James is positing the same obscure "unseen world" whereon the psychoanalytic feminists set great value—the world from which Spencer Brydon profits so greatly in "The Jolly Corner." Woolf is then only partially right when she says, "The horror of the story comes from the force with which it makes us realize the power that our minds possess for such excursions into the darkness; when certain lights sink or certain barriers are lowered, the ghosts of the mind, untracked desires, indistinct intimations, are seen to be a large company" ("The Supernatural in Fiction" 295). Woolf's personal fears to the contrary notwithstanding, James may be suggesting (as his feminist allies would) that perhaps we ought to be on more peaceable terms with that "large company." Woolf speaks of the silence in nature that precedes the governess's visions and quotes James's description of it: "The rooks stopped cawing in the golden sky, and the friendly evening hour lost for the unspeakable minute all its voice" (*NY* XII, 176).

It seems to me that there is another Jamesian irony here. For him the hour *is* "golden" and "friendly," silent, simply not prone to speech. The horror is that for the governess (in whose point of view we get the scene), the moment is "unspeakable" in the sinister, rationalist meaning of the word, and our fear is borne out for one who cannot sustain "excursions into the darkness." The governess achieves a dangerous symbolic order by all her later moves to make visible, and thus controllable, figures of ghosts that would have been better left to the silence. James, in a significant simile in his preface, says clearly that Peter Quint and Miss Jessel "are not 'ghosts' at all, as we now know the ghost, but . . . demons as loosely constructed *as those of the old trials for witchcraft*"— that is, constructed out of someone's political need for them—and he goes on to speak of the inartistry of "the limited deplorable presentable instance" of ghosts made real. His purpose was all aesthetic—"to express my subject all directly and intensely"—but the implications of this expression are well worth the thought of feminists (*AN* 175).

If my reading is taken as plausible, then the children are James's heroes for their ability to move equally freely in the darkness and the light. And Flora is a kind of feminist hero of the story when she literally turns her back on the symbolic order by which tangible ghosts are summoned out of the silence, a summoning that ultimately kills her brother, whose only weapon is his "absolute intelligence." Flora writes her little life with what French critics would call an "*écriture féminine*," characterized by what the story calls "increase of movement . . . intensity of play, the singing and gabbling of nonsense, and the invitation to romp" (*NY* XII, 211), qualities that the "eternal governess" finds deeply suspect. Miles too has his moments of "*jouissance*," in the garden at night and even at moments with his sister in the classroom, until the "eternal" teacher is finally left alone with him to exert her fatal control.

I have spoken of the governess as a maker of controllable figures and of "masculine" metaphors that represent a closed, didactic mind, a syndrome that is anathema to feminists (and presumably to the implied author). But I believe it is unwise to carry to extremes a gendered identification of these qualities.[6] Hierarchical closure of many kinds is traditionally male, but not *necessarily* male, as the governess proves. And her view of the world is not *ipso facto* suspect for being symbolic and metaphoric or even for participating in the dominant symbolism of male traditions. Her view of the world is suspect primarily because both she and Miles become locked by her will into that world, at peril because they less and less have the playful sensibility of a "baby girl" like Flora. What we are teaching each other, as feminist critics, about the dangers of metaphor as traditionally employed is important in reading for closure of mind in both male and female characters as well as their authors; but there is no reason to expand our suspicions into an antisymbolic principle.

Aristotle, seeking clarity as a value for poetry, opposed "metaphors, foreign words," and the like, but only when used "unfittingly" as against "suitably" for the intended effect. And surely he was not wrong to say also that the making of metaphors is the mark of the "well-endowed" poet in that it calls for imagination and reveals resemblances (Aristotle 43–44). To say "suitably" is to speak about the formal effect of a given metaphor. What feminists help us recognize additionally is that the resemblances may sometimes be a matter either of a questionable perspective (as in the governess's metaphorically enjoying her "state bed") or of an oppressive convention that has escaped the sensitivity of the author but not that of his critics. Nothing of the potential good and evil of metaphor escapes James in his stories. He clearly delights in metaphors (the "bench of desolation," the flawed "golden bowl," the "sacred fount," etc.), but they produce resemblances that liberate our thoughts and feelings about characters and their actions.

Thus metaphors, like all closures, are subject to verdict first, sentence later, and a formal judgment must precede the verdict. Metaphor is as metaphor does, when it contributes to the *dynamis* of the story, the effect of it as a whole. The "sacred fount" is an ugly metaphor in the novel of that name, a fount of life that feeds vampirism. The story takes advantage, at the start, of an expectation that the vampire is female. And then the whole play of the metaphor by a turn of the screw, so to speak, opens out into a wholly human and androgynous concern: a fear that either person in a close relationship of two may "eat" and deplete the other. Metaphor, one of the most closed devices of language, has been employed to make this expansive, androgynous point.

In regard to plot, canonical decision-making has tended to valorize traditional generic structures and their kinds of plots, and they are therefore being reexamined in the light of feminism (see Froula). James seems to cut the ideal figure of a canonical author, belonging as he did to an upper-class, male-dominated society and family ("a society of women in a world of men," he called it) and presenting in his fiction the women that he found there. Usually he left them where he found them—betrayed and trapped by the men they love and on whom they depend, truly "a world of men" that includes not only fathers, husbands, and male friends but also their doting, treacherous female appendages—witness the tales of Isabel Archer, Fleda Vetch, Milly Theale, Catherine Sloper, and Maggie Verver. As Maggie herself finally says, "I see it's *always* terrible for women" (*NY* XXIV, 348–49). Yet with rare exceptions (and the exceptions, again, are tragic), James brings the plots of his stories to an end that we do not experience as artificial closure but that is nevertheless not a random selection of events. James fully understood the ethical implications attendant on plot selection and development. For him, the artist's "prime sensibility" to life is a "soil," and "the quality and capacity of that soil, its ability to 'grow' with due freshness and straightness any vision of life, represents, strongly or weakly, the projected morality" (*AN* 45).

We note an insistence on the female metaphors of "growth" and nutrition and a gentle suggestivity, carried out in so many of his plots, that is entirely the reverse of the conventional authoritative type of closure, of both action and thought, that we have come to deprecate in male authors of James's period. Like Emily Dickinson, he knew to "tell all the truth" about life in his fiction but to "tell it slant" and not doctrinaire. He would have understood perfectly what one of Virginia Woolf's characters says in *The Waves*: "Let a man get up and say, 'Behold, this is the truth,' and instantly I perceive a sandy cat filching a piece of fish in the background. Look, you have forgotten the cat, I say" (203).

James never forgot the cat, often enough a creature who sneaks up on us so darkly in his work that we tend to miss or back away from the almost casual horror. I think of some of his endings: the quiet and unprotesting death of May Bartram that prepares the final agony in "The Beast in the Jungle," the silence that surrounds Catherine Sloper quite meaninglessly in *Washington Square*, the fearful price, in wasted lives, that lies underneath the muted happy ending of "The Bench of Desolation," the calmly retaliatory ruthlessness of Madame de Mauves that issues in the impossibly possible sudden suicide of her husband, the wife in "The Author of 'Beltraffio' " who would prefer to let a child die rather than let it be raised by the father the wife disapproves of. If these are products of a "growth," they are strange and grotesque fruits, and the "projected morality," though full of pity, could never be stated in finished aphorisms. It is finally not a wonder that Gertrude Stein saw James as a "precursor" of her kind of fiction—that is, of a formally determinate kind of ambiguity.[7]

James was suitably indeterminate in his plots, we can begin to see, when he so often left his women where he found them. I suggest that he did so because of his feeling for the lives they were actually leading, his respect for them, and his unwillingness to impose on them what he might think they should do. He left them alone in the most positive sense, to watch them work things out. Thus he thought the finest section of *The Portrait of a Lady* was the nighttime scene of Isabel sitting alone in silent reflection. And thus also the ending of the novel (which, in the olden days, was complained about for not having tied up the plot ends) is conclusively inconclusive in its closure. Why does Isabel not leave her supersubtle rotter of a husband? Because she is not ready to, until she figures out what to do with the complex situation in which she finds herself. By hard experience she is now fully capable of figuring it out, and James knows this and leaves her to her task, refusing to impose his view of what she ought to do, refusing even to have a view.

It is not that her story has no plot, in the much-abused Aristotelean meaning of that term, but that James has systematically, *plottedly*, represented her growth from the beginning and through the middle of the action in such a way that plot closure belongs to her and to her alone. I feel moved to say, in the light of such plots as James's, that the feminist suspicion of plot—what Julia Kristeva calls "the arbitrary completion" that "murders" speech (55–59) in a "bounded text" (38)—may be too sweeping. But I should like to think that her key word is *arbitrary*, since it is not a word we are tempted to apply to James.

James himself, writing on George Eliot's *Adam Bede*, sounds like a feminist critic of the 1980s when he says that the rather stiff marriage that ends that novel is "an evidence of artistic weakness," resulting from the view "that the story must have marriages and rescues in the nick of time, as a matter of course" (Donoghue 8). James knew very well, as the numerous recent studies of his "failed-marriage plots" have shown, that marriage is often "the situation that generates the complications . . . instead of being the means whereby complications are resolved" (Hinz 903).[8] Where James differs from some of the feminist antiplot critics, however, is in his manifest understanding that it is the subject matter and effect of closure that are our concern and not formal closure itself. It is simply too tidy, reactionary, and unlikely of Adam Bede to marry the prim Dinah when all through the book he was drawn to the wilder Hetty Sorrel. By contrast, the most revolutionary ending *Washington Square* could have is the truthful, "bounded" ending it does have: the dreadful confinement of Catherine within her small, square space, which "ossifies, petrifies, and blocks" (Kristeva 58). It is from our sense that her situation is impossible of rescue that our sense of moral outrage will arise. It is not the plot imposed by the writer that is at fault but the plot that real-life social conditions impose on women. Women like Catherine will arise and go not when plot as a formal element is hounded out of fiction writing but when opportunities are forced open for such women in the actual world outside the book.

In James's house of fiction, there are many plots and many subject matters, not all dealing with defeat and constraint. When Maggie Verver welcomes back from adultery her rather unprincely prince at the end of the book, it is not a defeat but an ambiguously open victory that implies what Joseph Boone calls "James's double-barreled critique of the social institution of marriage," a critique that breaks up "ideologies of gender and genre" (374). Again, in all that Maisie comes to know the hard way in *What Maisie Knew* (with an angrily ironic narrator backing her up, as happens also in *Washington Square*), we have the small-girl version of all that Isabel Archer knows by the end of her story—that point where I have noted that James refuses to impose a view of what she should do next. Greater respect has no man for a woman—and it is a respect so great that he tacitly ignores any claim that she is, after all, his creation. All women are created, but it does not follow from this that they are the playthings of their creator.

That he does not play with them does not mean that James is not responsible to his own sense of things. When he approaches a feminist subject matter directly, as in *The Bostonians*, he is not afraid to confront the militant feminist, Olive Chancellor, with her own excesses. Nor, on the other hand, does he spare his pity for Verena, who allows herself to be "wrenched" (*BO* 448) away from her feminist connections by her lover, so ironically named Ransom. What the narrator-author sees is that beneath the hood that Ransom has draped over her "to conceal her face with her identity," Verena is in tears. The author is far from indifferent as he comments, on the last page, that in the union she is about to make with this kind of man, "these were not the last tears she was destined to shed" (*BO* 449).

"Every narration," announces Julia Kristeva, "is made up, nourished by time, finality, history, and God," the author who is engaged in a "nonalternating negation" of lifelikeness and flux (48). Though James saw himself as a historian, "hugging the shore of the real" and recording it, his "real" was customarily ambiguous, full of its semiotic undertow, dramatic in the telling, but constantly reflective and often uncertain in many of his conclusions. He knew a story when he saw one, but he told it mainly for its drama and not for the sake of his godlike power over it. Kristeva believes (similarly to Bakhtin) that it is a mark of all novels, as against other genres, that "explicit completion is often lacking, ambiguous, or assumed in the text of the novel. This incompletion nevertheless underlines the text's structural finitude" (55). This ambiguity and lack of explicit completion in James seem to me greater than in most novelists of his century, part of his greatness as a novelist and as a person. Of course, there is structural finitude in James's works. "Looseness," he tells us, was "never much my affair" (*AN* 320). We begin his stories with expectations, and by the time we close the book, we "see" where those expectations have brought us, though often there is the sense of what Aristotle would call an impossibility rendered probable. The "Princess" (in all her subterranean meaning as the adjunct of the prince) of the first half of *The Golden Bowl* has become by the end the recognizable yet very different "Maggie" of the second part.

Luce Irigaray has said that there can be no relationship between the sexes until men have recognized women as Other rather than as mirror images of themselves. In Maggie Verver's case, she is not throwing out an image of Woman to the prince but is producing an-Other image of herself. Only in that assurance do we feel a measure of closure. A major plot "loop" has come to a resolution with the departure of the Ververs, but the ambiguity of the embrace that draws in the prince on the last page is merely "finitude" and not "completion" of these complex lives. What Elizabeth Berg calls "the contradictions of the affirmative woman" are in sway. Berg warns, with great perspicacity, against any plan of women to "brace women's mobility [as an indicator of Woman] against the fixity of petrified man." To refuse to be essentialist Woman is to swim out into the unknown, but it also prevents a kind of false "security in the perpetuation of our own expression." Berg could be speaking of Maggie at the end of the novel when she says, "The assumption of our complicity in the masculine universe requires that we rethink the forms of that complicity; that we take the responsibility of trying to make sure that our complicities are genuinely strategic" (20). That James understood so delicate a matter as the strategic complicities that women undertake in order to survive in a "masculine universe," and that he gave imaginative form to them, imply a recognition of the painfully labyrinthine ways of that universe, if not an overt protest against it. His recognition makes him not father but friend to Maggie, and to her parallels in the real world.

For someone who was early placed on the defensive about his style, James takes surprisingly little critical interest in language, usually preferring to develop his theoretical ideas about character and plot. He thought highly of language when it was "developed, delicate, flexible, rich" speech. "The more it suggests and expresses the more we live by it—the more it promotes and enhances life" (James Miller 289). (A feminist semiotician could hardly put it better.) In a review of a certain Miss Prescott's novel, he roundly objected to language used for "puppet-fingering" physical description, for two reasons. One was that it interfered with the freedom of the characters: " 'Good heavens, Madam!' we are forever on the point of exclaiming, 'let the poor things speak for themselves. What? Are you afraid they can't stand alone?' . . . Imagine Thackeray forever pulling Rebecca's curls and settling the folds of her dress.'' Tellingly, he also makes an ethical connection between ''puppet-fingering'' kinds of artifice and more natural presentations of both sexes: ''This bad habit of Miss Prescott's is more than an offence against art. Nature herself resents it. It is an injustice to men and women to assume that the fleshly element carries such weight. In the history of a loving and breaking heart, is that the only thing worth noticing? . . . What do we care about the beauty of a man or woman in comparison to their humanity?'' (James Miller 210).

James's use of language is only just now beginning to be discussed in feminist political terms, and with far less sophistication than the discussions of character and plot. Dorothy Richardson was no doubt making irresponsible fun when she characterized James's style as ''a non-stop waggling of the backside,'' taking place ''where no star shines and no bird sings''—but Richardson has her adherents, early and late.[9] William James, in a 1907 letter to his brother, was only a little more appreciative when he wrote that for ''gleams and innuendos and felicitous verbal insinuations you are unapproachable.'' But, he continued, ''the bare perfume of things will not support existence, and the effect of solidity you reach is but perfume and simulacrum'' (Matthiessen, *James Family* 342). (What a difference the passage of eight decades can make is apparent when we stop to think that these remarks might well be taken for praise among our feminist and other contemporary critics who believe that to strive for anything more than ''gleams and innuendos'' in the use of language is to achieve a false solidity in the presentation of human affairs.)

Viewing the matter from both an immediately rhetorical and political point of view, Darshan Singh Maini says James's style contains the ''sexual and intellectual idiom of the upper classes'' and is chiefly a device of their dialogue, ''though in its own way it does suggest their fecklessness, emotional aridity, and spiritual erosion.'' ''Here the language, removed from the heat and din and dust of the street and pub, tends to become autotelic and circular, turning viciously on its own limited axis.'' Such a discussion turns us to what we should be looking at, but it tends to portray an author not in control of his medium, a hopeless aristocrat prone to ''strange spiritual hungers towards the end [that] could hint at the unconscious radical impulses in him'' (Maini, ''Politics'' 168).

Here we need to raise again the question of artistic closure, a formal device that not only suggests the personal style and needs of the author but also helps him convey an intentional rhetorical effect. A few years ago, my husband and I undertook what may be a historical first: to read aloud to each other the entirety of *The Golden Bowl*. At times we gasped and laughed out loud (''Come *on*, Henry!'') at those ''circular, turning'' sentences that never end. But as our formalist feminist consciousness grew with the reading, it began to seem that the complexity of the story and of its ending was properly reflected in those unending sentences. ''The strange spiritual hungers'' that are at stake seem to belong primarily to Maggie's shaky hopes rather than her author's. The recent studies of the marriages in both *The Golden Bowl* and *The Bostonians* suggest that James had made up his mind at least to marital ambiguity and that he chose, however consciously or unconsciously, to reflect it in his syntax as well as his plot closures.

In this connection it is useful to compare actual late style with what has been loosely called "late style" by looking at the concluding language of *The Ambassadors*. We are closely in Strether's consciousness in the last pages as he makes a decision to be "deterrent and conclusive" in his final interview with Maria Gostrey. With her, as with Mrs. Newsome, "there's nothing anyone can do. It's over. Over for both of us." This leaves his own life conclusively inconclusive: " 'To what do you go home?' 'I don't know. There will always be something' " (*NY* XXII, 323–25). Most of the last few pages that express this conclusiveness are almost stichomythic in the abrupt closure of their sentences. But there is an exception. It lies at the moment when what might be called Strether's "masculine" firmness melts at the pain of what he is losing in losing Maria. Appropriately, convoluted language marks convoluted feelings: "He took a minute to say, for really and truly, what stood about him there in her offer—which was as the offer of exquisite service, of lightened care, for the rest of his days—might well have tempted. It built him softly round, it roofed him warmly over, it rested, all so firm, on selection" (*NY* XXII, 324).

It is worth noting that the convolution of feeling and expression here has to do with Strether's painful refusal to allow Miss Gostrey to take on the prescribed and traditional caretaking role of the female—a role that Julia Kristeva would call an "official law" of society. Though it may at first seem bizarre to adopt a notion of James's diction as "marginal" and even "carnivalesque" in the passage just quoted, still it is full of breaks, of semiotic music, of qualifications. Strether's stammering thought seems to me not to defy Kristeva's notion that "carnivalesque discourse breaks through the laws of language censored by grammar and semantics and, at the same time, is a social and political protest. There is no equivalence, but rather, identity, between challenging official linguistic codes and challenging official law" (65).

In this light, James can be looked at, from early to late, as a developing linguistic revolutionary, and it is we, his critics, who are the traditionalists. (A carnival indeed!) Why are we still so reactionary and resistant to odd language, in these times when feminism and deconstruction have so shaken the boundaries in linguistics? Mikhail Bakhtin suggests, "What is realized in the novel is the process of coming to know one's own language as it is perceived in someone else's language, coming to know one's own belief system in someone else's system" (*Dialogic Imagination* 282). If so very much as that is available—that we should get to know better both ourselves and Henry James as we compare our feeble, careful syntaxes against his expansive strangeness—we ought not to deprive ourselves by simply making mock, as his lessers have done for too long.

My own point about James's diction and syntax is simply my usual formalist one: that convoluted language is as it does and that though it is a feature of "late James," as some sounds are a feature of late Beethoven, it can also be seen to work for the effect of the given piece, as well as letting us know the depths of our implied author.

It is worth pausing for a moment to note that James is not unique among great artists, those whose greatness is in fact rather often expressed (once our consciousness is alerted) in subtle-minded, odd closures. James achieved closure, as all art must, but as we look to see how he did it, we find radical disruptions of our usual expectations of forms. I am prepared to argue that the fulfillment of "usual expectations" may belong to lesser artists, and often lesser ethical and philosophical characters among artists. If one looks, for a change, at visual artists of the most famous periods in art, one sees, as W. H. Auden did, that the old masters understood that suffering occurs "while someone else is eating or opening a window or just walking dully along" ("Musée des Beaux Arts"). Not only suffering but all the moving events of life can and do happen off to the side, producing extremely odd closures to our vision, as Brueghel did with the drowning of Icarus.

In the Correr gallery in Venice is another Brueghel—framed, coherent, a work of art—but with similarly disruptive "closure." Entitled *Adoration of the Magi*, it indeed shows a parade of the kings' rich camels, interestingly through a *Flemish* street. But the most prominent activities are those of the townspeople absorbed in coping with winter weather: they cut holes in the icy river to get water, and there is a strong detail of a child sledding. The weakest detail, at the extreme left corner of the painting, is the cave containing the holy family. The implied painter, as Auden understood, was a thinker subtle-minded enough to know that ignorant life always disrupts the nostalgic plots of Scripture. Similarly, in Tintoretto's *The Last Supper* in San Giorgio Maggiore, Christ and his apostles are at the table at left in the painting. Though they are marked somewhat vaguely by halos, by far the most prominent figure in the painting is a maid handling dishes at center front. Her curious cat climbs up the dish basket to have a look— at the dishes, not at the Lord. Virginia Woolf would be content—not only do we have here an artist who has not "forgotten the cat" but one who has awarded her centrality.

Julia Kristeva has noted another such disruption, in the eyes of Bellini's madonnas—the most traditionally composed of all painting "plots" (Kristeva, 237–69). She provokes us to think hard about the relation of such compositions to the character, feminist or otherwise, of the implied painter or writer or musical composer. I am drawn to Arnold Schoenberg's idea, in his *Harmonielehre*, that dissonances differ from consonances only in degree and that dissonances are perhaps nothing more than remoter consonances. They may be nothing more than that technically, but in their effects they may be deeply subversive, though we need new eyeglasses to look at the old forms and see what has happened. Remoter consonances are new perspectives on truth.

If I am right in drawing these connections, James belongs to a company of

major artists in various media to whom it was manifest that art gains in truth as
well as beauty when its forms ("consonances") balk at a misrepresentative
formality. James speaks for the whole company when he says that closure is not
a matter of "dessert and ices" that finish off the dinner (James Miller 32, 33).
When closure consists neither in sweetness, nor in icily constrained forms, nor
in traditional emphases, it remains open to the feats of genuine art.

By now I hope to have made clear that I believe that both James's theory and
James's fiction stand up well under contemporary feminist scrutiny, aesthetic as
well as ethical—two terms for which feminists do not allow divorcement. We
believe, with Wallace Stevens, that "aesthetic creeds, like other creeds, are the
certain evidence of exertions to find the truth" (Stevens 169), and some feminist
ideas about closure and style seem already to have been lodged in James's creative
intuition.

There is little in his work to suggest that he was a self-conscious feminist—
he limited his métier to Art and let everything follow from that. We cannot even
lay it to his feminism that he chose so many women characters, though we may
admire the results, an extraordinarily lively and sympathetic account of unusual
women of his class. He was perfectly frank about his having chosen women
primarily for their artistic interest.

It is easy to object of course "Why the deuce then Fleda Vetch, why a mere little flurried
bundle of petticoats, why not Hamlet or Milton's Satan at once, if you're going in for a
superior display of 'mind'?" To which I fear I can only reply that in pedestrian prose,
and in the "short Story," one is, for the best reasons, no less on one's guard than on
the stretch; and also that I have ever recognized, even in the midst of the curiosity such
displays may quicken, the rule of an exquisite economy. The thing is to lodge somewhere
at the heart of one's complexity an irrepressible *appreciation*, but where a light lamp
will carry all the flame I incline to look askance at a heavy. (*AN* 129)

The truth is out: women are "light lamps," and the superior act of artistic
ingenuity is to get them to "carry all the flame." Thus his women are of use-
value to him—but do we not sense also his commitment and affection for them
as he reviews them each by each? Light lamps though they may be, they are
"affected with a certain high lucidity," these "very young women," and they
"thereby become characters." They share "acuteness and intensity, reflexion
and passion," and like Fleda Vetch, each one has "a contributive and participant
view of her situation." And (nonessentialist in gender as James is) if men can
offer similar traits, they too may capture the top role. "They are thus of a
family—which shall have also for us, we seem forewarned, more members, and
of each sex" (*AN* 130).

Yet choosing women subjects was not for James solely a "charming" artistic
problem—he also complains, on grounds of truth slighting, of other great authors
who left the "task unattempted"": "There are in fact writers as to whom we
make out that their refuge from this [representation of women as main characters]

is to assume it to be not worth their attempting; *by which pusillanimity in truth their honor is scantly saved"* (*AN* 49, emphasis added). He complains further that even when women are "main," they are never "suffered to be sole ministers ... but have their inadequacy eked out with comic relief and underplots ... when not with murders and battles and the great mutations of the world"—and by their authors' surrounding them "with a hundred other persons, made of much stouter stuff [presumably male]" (*AN* 50). Conversely, James suggests that we are made to care about Bassanio's predicament with Shylock only because the extremity of it "matters to Portia" and because "Portia matters to us." Thus he credits Shakespeare for a "deep difficulty braved," that of making a young female character, "if not the all-in-all for our attention, at least the clearest of the call" (*AN* 50). To make a woman "the clearest of the call" is, then, not just an interesting artistic problem. Rather, never to do so is a sign of scant honor and low-grade respect for the truth.

We may pause to ask what other male author, before or after James, has shown so androgynous a sense of truth and of conscious obligation toward it. By contrast, James Joyce seems almost a father-protector whose understanding of women is exploited for his own ends. We may apply a litmus test: can we imagine Joyce standing by Molly Bloom's bedside and asking modestly, "What will she *do*"? None of Joyce's female characters, represented with full sympathy and almost uncanny knowledge, hold any secrets or "mystification" for him— in his often satiric distance, they are somehow possessions of his in a way that is not true of James. It is curious to reread James's *The Art of the Novel*. To do so is to watch a man eagerly and respectfully revisiting his characters as old friends, looking to see if they have changed since he last met them, reviving his old affection for them. Though he saw faults in the novels with great clarity, they tended to be, once he released them, the habitations of characters with a permanent life of their own.

By the measure of authors capable of assessing the use-value of women to art, capable entirely *because* of a deep understanding of women's lives and needs, Henry James seems to me to belong among the larger, more open, and loving spirits that art can lay claim to. His very dark vision of a morally tangled world arose without doubt from his profound understanding, and that vision, not his "patrician" place in society, is surely the reason for his mistrust of political movements. We were so long blinded by the patrician notion of James that it has taken us a long time to see how passionately his dark vision has involved us and propelled us toward truth in all its complexity. Yet it has already been fifty years since Glenway Wescott began the proper tribute to our desperate involvement: " ... Jamesian teas in one's own head, in the sleepless nights, or coincident with the mechanics of the day; jabbering in one's broken heart. In rehash of the plotting and planning, the much ado about everything, in hypothesis and hair-splitting fairness, the brain may break like the heart" (184 [1971]).

Two difficult decades of polishing the feminist eyeglasses to their present acuteness and sophistication have allowed us to begin to recapture that involvement with what James *actually does*, in a perspective unbiased by his top hat. The feminist theorists and critics with whom I have surrounded myself in this essay are those who have seen that the best theoretical questions are the ones most open to unexpected answers, the feminist commentators dialogic in their approach to ethics and politics, those who are the least bigoted and complacent about the role of the author's personal history in his work, those who understand that literary form, far from being itself a falsifying closure, is, as James believed, our best eyeglass on life. With their help, we are only just beginning to understand the relation of Henry James to women as well as men.

## NOTES

1. See M. H. Abrams for a valuable discussion about extrapolation from seemingly deterministic theories like Aristotle's. He believes with Ludwig Wittgenstein that the validity of theory, like that of language, "consists in the way it is in fact used to some purpose, rather than its accordance with models of how it should be used" (12).

2. Clifton Fadiman was probably the first critic of James to observe: "You cannot pin him down to an attitude. For him an attitude and analysis are uncompromisingly in opposition" (Fadiman 485). James would have agreed: "Nothing is my last word about anything. I am interminably super-subtle and analytic" (*SL* 76). Our poststructuralist era alerts us to differentiate these terms carefully. James adopted a perspective on his subjects, a lookout point from which to analyze his characters, but not in order to strike attitudes toward them. So eager was he to avoid what he called the "mere muffled majesty of irresponsible 'authorship' " (*AN* 328) that he frequently surrendered narrative point of view to a *ficelle* character within the story (*AN* 322–23).

3. In connection with my previous remarks on lack of closure as one kind of positive form, we need also to see that "open-endedness" is not an accurate enough term. As David Gordon aptly notes, "In a novel closure is not only possible but inevitable, for what is called open-endedness in fiction is only an ironic form of closure." Gordon goes on to quote H. Porter Abbott, who says that "because it is made up, a story ends where it ends" (112). To mistrust that fact is to mistrust fiction altogether. Closure is as closure does, as I suggest in regard to James's variety of open and closed endings.

4. On irony, Julia Kristeva speaks of the "linguistic episteme, which . . . has taken upon itself to oversee all thinking, although, in fact, it is merely a symptom of the drama experienced by the Western subject as it attempts to master and structure not only the logos but also its pre- and trans-logical breakouts. *Irony* alone . . . is the timid witness to this drama" (27). Translating this into the pitiful human terms of James's story, we see that the governess, in this and many other passages, is trying to control any "trans-logical breakouts." James lets us know this through her very words, which belong to her point of view but betray to us a terrible innocence. Alas, for her, the whole story is a "trans-logical breakout."

5. See Springer 89–115. My account there expands on the fatal role of the governess as teacher and former of young minds. In general, I agree with Leon Edel when he says, "Always in the Jamesian tale there is not so much the haunting ghost as the haunted human" (*Ghostly Tales* vii). "This was James's great discovery—that certain people who see ghosts . . . become as it were contagious. They are not only haunted—they haunt" (*Ghostly Tales* viii).

6. Though French writers like Julia Kristeva are sometimes viewed with alarm as essentialists, Toril Moi valuably points out that Kristeva's semiotic approach is "not exclusively or essentially feminist, but it is one in which the hierarchical closure imposed on meaning and language has been opened up to the free play of the signifier. Applied to the field of sexual identity and difference, this becomes a feminist vision of a society in which the sexual signifier would be free to move" (172). This is the "French connection" I see in James's fictions: they originate in a heavily gendered society, and yet his closures often leave the "sexual signifier" strangely free to move, ambiguous and open to change.

7. Janice Doane speaks usefully of James's reliance on silence, of his pushing "traditional narrative to its limit" (17). But I doubt he did so, as Shoshana Felman suggests (quoted by Doane), in order to reinforce "the indecision which inhabits meaning" (17). Closer to James, I think, is Ralph Rader's concept of determinate or "unambiguous ambiguity." Rader introduced the concept in an essay entitled "The Unambiguous Ambiguity of Conrad's *Lord Jim*," presented at an International Narrative Conference at Ohio State University. In an expanded, published version of the essay, "*Lord Jim* and the Formal Development of the English Novel," the phrase was lost but the valuable concept is discussed.

8. One of the current riches of James criticism, and of plot theory, is the proliferation of essays on marriage and family plots in general and on James's plots in particular, especially those of *The Golden Bowl*, *The Bostonians*, and *The Portrait of a Lady*. I call special attention to the excellence of the commentaries by Baym ("Melodramas" and "Revision"), Boone, Hinz, Jonnes, Maxwell, Niemtzow, and Yeazell (*Language and Knowledge*) and also to the more complete bibliography provided by Boone.

9. Sandra Gilbert and Susan Gubar quote Richardson approvingly and uncritically.

*Lucrezia Pantiatichi* by Bronzino, Galleria degli Uffizi Firenze, Florence. In 1953, Miriam Allott showed that this painting seemed to be the source for the Bronzino that Milly Theale resembles in *The Wings of the Dove* (1902).

# 13
# The Art in the Fiction of Henry James

*Adeline R. Tintner*

James paid attention to art all his life, and he used it continually as a fruitful strategy for the construction of his fiction. The masterpieces of the great museums found their way into his tales, as did the painting and sculpture in the possession of the wealthy collectors of upper-middle-class society. To comprehend the vast number of references, each with its different function in furthering the meaning and advancement of James's novels and tales, I am taking the liberty of arranging my essay as if it were a museum tour, for that is virtually what a trip through James's fiction turns out to be.[1] Sometimes, to keep to this basic but not inflexible plan, I have ignored the chronology, but generally James's early stories favor the art of Renaissance Italy and ancient Rome, consonant with his early museum trotting, followed then by his familiarity with the Louvre, whose masterpieces he was exposed to both early and late. In the work of his last period, the life he led in country houses and his visits to various museums in England manifest themselves in the metaphoric transmutation of much of the art he saw into analogies for the purpose of clarifying the unknown by the known.

Not only was he exposed to the art made by the eminent painters and sculptors of his father's circle and to the experience of trying to be an artist himself, but he was encouraged by his father to translate his impressions of art into art criticism. In the 1870s, in his late twenties and thirties, he wrote a number of reviews of art exhibitions for American periodicals. Among these, he distinguished himself as the first critic in English to appreciate the work of Edward Burne-Jones, soon after to become one of the most famous of the pre-Raphaelite school. In his late autobiography, *A Small Boy and Others*, he tells us of his first exposure to art at the age of thirteen when he, with his brother William, wandered into the Galerie d'Apollon of the Louvre, where he got its message of "beauty and art and supreme design . . . , history, fame and power." It acted on his imagination in a way that "no other 'intellectual experience' of our youth . . . could pretend . . . to rival." The Delacroix ceiling there, portraying *Apollo Overcoming the Python*, had such a great effect on him that we seem to find elements deriving from the great ceiling painting lodged within "The Sweetheart of M. Briseux" (1873) and modifying the texture of James's first published novel, *Roderick Hudson*.

James's early work shows how he built certain stories around the vision of a single artist. He was interested from an early age in engravings found in books, and one of his first tales demonstrates his use of Gustave Doré's illustrations for Perrault's *Contes*. In "Gabrielle de Bergerac" (1869), the legend of the Sleeping Beauty as illustrated by Doré is actually brought into the tale of prerevolutionary France, for the old Chevalier who tells the story alludes to one of Doré's plates for Perrault's version of the fairy tale. "Do you remember in Doré's illustrations to Perrault's tales, the picture of the enchanted castle of the Sleeping Beauty?" He then gives a detailed description of the actual plate so that we know James must have had it under his hand. Next, in "A Landscape Painter" (1866), James makes clear that he was aware of the scandalous *Déjeuner sur l'Herbe* by Manet in the hero's plan for painting a "Rural Festival," a double of Manet's picture. Other tales of the time refer to equally well-known paintings of the time— Moreau's *Oedipus and the Sphinx* in "A Day of Days," for instance.

Once James gets to Europe on his own, the result of exposure to so much art finds its way in a true Baedeker tale, "Traveling Companions," where, with guidebook in hand, James's young hero picks his way from museum to museum, from Milan to Rome, with many stops on the way, a journey that parallels his feelings for Charlotte Evans, a young woman who is also engaged in seeing the masterpieces of art. We begin with Leonardo and end with Titian, going from religious to secular art, from *The Last Supper* to *Sacred and Profane Love*, from friendship to marriage. It is, in fact, James's museum catalogue story. What "Traveling Companions" did for Italy, "A Passionate Pilgrim" did for England, and there we go from Hampton Court to Oxford to James's first country house with its wonderful and eclectic collection of museum-type masterpieces.

But the stories of the middle and later seventies show a concentration on single artists. "The Madonna of the Future" is a Raphael story with a hero whose failure depends on his confusing himself with that Italian genius. "The Diary of a Man of Fifty" is an Andrea del Sarto story, where the hero is cursed by the same weakness that the painter was afflicted with, extreme jealousy of his wife, and whose ruined life and ruinous attitude to it cannot, fortunately, ruin in turn the life of a young man whom the man of fifty thinks he is steering away from marrying the daughter of the woman whom he thinks betrayed him. In 1874 Madame de Mauves had been attached to a configuration of Hans Memling or Van Eyck, a cold frigid type of northern Madonna with no blood in her veins and from whom, finally, the hero detaches himself.

A classical wing is included in James's gallery, and "The Last of the Valerii" is a Vatican story. The figure of his main character, Count Valerius, is compared to the "famous bust of the Emperor Caracalla," and his head is covered with the same dense crop of curls. Named after a Roman emperor, he resembled "a statue of the Decadence" of the Roman Silver Age. His confessor told him he was a "good boy but a *pagan!*" The rest of the story includes what amounts to a catalogue of the Vatican collection: they are all Roman gods and constitute a Pantheon of their own. The great statue of Hera is involved in the invention of the recently excavated Juno, for like it, she wears a "long fluted peplum." Since the young Count is a Pagan, he visits the Pantheon and contemplates the bull's eye in the roof "through which the pagan gods and goddesses used to come sailing." The myth of the return of the pagan gods and goddesses has been adroitly placed right in the heart of Christianity, where the church preserved the pagan deities as harmless relics of the pagan past. Fifteen years later James did another story, "The Solution," tied to Roman sculpture, only now it is that of the Republic, not the Empire's Silver Age. It concerns the standards of behavior of young Americans of the period of Republican glory in the generation of the 1830s, set in opposition to the lax standards of moral behavior in the international colony in Rome just before the liberation of Italy. In this tale the young American attaché, supposedly a barbarian, has a greater sense of honor than his sophisticated colleagues. As a joke they convince him that he has put a young woman in a compromising position. The Roman lawgivers presented in statues of the Republican leaders are seen as analogues to American representatives of state, for the American minister in Rome appears "like a sitting Cicero."

In spite of his early conditioning for the neoclassical, James favored the Romantic movement in French painting. Led by Eugène Delacroix during the 1860s, the Romantics won the battle against Ingres and the Classicists. We see that battle itself in "The Sweetheart of M. Briseux," in which James inaugurates in 1873 a series of stories evoking, in this instance, the spirit of a school of painting as well as individual masterpieces of art. The small museum in the province is filled with dull neoclassical paintings, the school to which Harold Staines, the fiancé of the young woman, is committed. He paints her as if she were the Mona Lisa and fails, but an unknown young man—whose name, Briseux, means stone breaker—makes a brilliant Romantic portrait of the young woman, a portrait that later gains him success at the salon.

In the British wing of James's museum, the Romantic character reveals itself in an early story, "The Author of 'Beltraffio' " (1884). The aura of pre-Raphaelitism in which James had steeped himself in his first years in England dominates this tale. James had met the chief exponents of pre-Raphaelite painting through Charles Eliot Norton. Here the art-for-art's-sake represented by this movement takes a beating, though presumably the tale is written from the point of view of a young writer who accepts it. James sees, though, that the tendency of the writer (so engulfed in his commitment to art) antagonizes his wife. She is compared to a portrait of a past and conservative school of art, that of Sir Joshua Reynolds, with a mind-set to match, for she lets her son die rather than see him grow up corrupted by his father's writing. Distinctions between her beauty and that of her sister-in-law, who conforms in a superficially imitative way to the appearance of a Rossetti, continue to show how art of opposite intentions makes concrete the narrative tensions of the plot. Both an investigation of the tenets of the art-for-art's-sake of John Addington Symonds, who is the acknowledged model behind Mark Ambient, and a criticism of its effect are skillfully managed in this perhaps most brilliant example of James's *nouvelles* of the early 1880s. The pre-Raphaelites, seen as attempting to reform all forms of life—clothing, furniture, manners, landscape—are here resisted, with tragic results, by a rigid opponent of an opposing point of view.

In the short stories of the period from 1875 to 1881, James plants the work of art as an object worthy of possession, a symbol standing for a character, and an index pointing to part of the plot. This is more easily done in the short span, but for a novel such as *The Portrait of a Lady* the problem of the priority of the human being over the work of art is resolved by Ralph Touchett, who sees in Isabel's character "the finest thing in nature. It is finer than the finest work of art, than a Greek bas relief, than a Titian, than a Gothic cathedral." Here he raises her above the best in ancient, medieval, and Venetian Renaissance art. But although a fine human being wins out over art, there are still pieces of fine art that act as analogies for the self-images of the characters. Ralph, who will die early, is like a Watteau painting, where death lives with pleasure. Lord Warburton has his artistic equivalent in *The Dying Gladiator*. The Correggio, Henrietta Stackpole's favorite picture, stands for the life, ironically, she will end up having, the life of a wife and mother, in spite of all her early protestations to the contrary. St. Peter's is the third named work of art of museum quality in this novel, and it serves as an emblem of Isabel's sense of freedom. In it, "her conception of greatness never lacked space to soar. She gazed and wondered . . . and paid her silent tribute to visible grandeur." The museum piece now has a talismanic role; it tells us something important about a character or plays a vital role in furthering a theme.

## THE STARRED MASTERPIECE

Around this time the starred masterpiece in the museum or outside the museum, especially in the short tales, creates a nimble bit of narrative strategy for James. Pater wrote of the Mona Lisa that if she were set "beside one of those Greek goddesses or beautiful women of antiquity," they would be "troubled by this beauty, into which the soul with all its maladies has passed." Taking up this statement in his novel *Confidence*, James has put his Mona Lisa beside a Greek goddess, where, next to "the embodiment of the old fancy," she might stand as "the symbol of the modern idea." The Houdon statue of Voltaire in "The Conquest of London" is used as the physical focus and the model for the witty and ambitious American adventuress who breaks through certain social taboos and conquers London in the same way that James did Paris. In "The Aspern

Papers,'' Verrocchio's statue of Bartolommeo Colleoni, the soldier of fortune and the most famous of the Venetian *condottieri*, is introduced just after Tita has propositioned the narrator, thus justifying itself as a pivotal icon of the tale. The narrator's reflections on the character of Colleoni, combined with his desire to find help through contemplation of the statue, introduce the question the reader must answer for himself: who after all are the real *condottieri* of this story? The statue appears at the crisis when Tita makes her offer of the papers in exchange for marriage between her and the "publishing scoundrel." "That was the price— that was the price!" We relate Tita's character to Colleoni's; as a soldier of fortune, he had his price and sold his favors to the highest bidder, whether Venice or Milan. This parallel between Tita and Colleoni raises other questions about whether or not any papers did exist and about the amount of money that Tita actually gouged out of the narrator without giving evidence that there were any documents worth the narrator's financial support.

In *The Princess Casamassima* (1886) we see a further development in James's use of the work of art. There is an extension in the definition of what a work of art is, even though the works included are simply one or two. Included are beautiful examples of the art of bookbinding, for James himself owned examples of Robert Rivière, one of the great bookbinders of the nineteenth century, and James's protagonist, Hyacinth, is himself an artist of the craft. The two great works of plastic art that both the princess and Hyacinth have admired are Titian's *Bacchus and Ariadne* and the Elgin Marbles, classed by Richard Monckton Miles as the chief influences on the imagination of John Keats, with whom James identifies Hyacinth. Throughout the novels there are icons of Keats and his circle, and James continues to make associations between Titian and the Elgin Marbles, or at least Greek bas-reliefs, as early as *The Portrait of a Lady* and as late as "The Velvet Glove."

*The Bostonians* (1886) displays James's increasing tendency to use the specified museum work of art only once even in a long novel. In this case it is *The Sistine Madonna* by Raphael, and like *The Madonna of the Chair*, which was the starred masterpiece of "The Madonna of the Future," it appears again in *The Ivory Tower*. In fact, in the first appearance, there are "two photographs of the Sistine Madonna," two because in the conversation between Verena and Olive in the small house in Marmion, where the photographs are pinned on the wall of the room, each woman is going to consider herself a martyr—Verena, a martyr to Olive, and Olive, a martyr both to Verena and to Basil Ransom, who is threatening to take away Verena and thus destroy Olive's emotional investment in her. James might have been drawn to use this painting by Raphael after his review of Turgenev's *Virgin Soil*, in which he noticed Mme. Sipiagin's "resemblence to Raphael's Dresden Madonna"; there is also a clue in his insistence on the German books in Olive's library, for Goethe wrote some famous lines to the Sistine Madonna. Within the Impressionist scenes in *What Maisie Knew* there is one work of art that helps Maisie find her "moral sense," the colossal gilded Virgin at the top of the Cathedral of Notre Dame. It represents values of stability to the child. It is not that Maisie is sensitive to all religious art, for she had not liked the ugly, primitive madonnas in the National Gallery, but the great golden Madonna is the comforting mother she never had.

It is not accidental or without meaning that the word *innocent* occurs as a pictorial and verbal pun in the critical scene of *Daisy Miller* (1878). It takes place when we are under Velázquez's portrait of Innocent X (see Figure 1); the pope's name is the tenth time we meet the word *innocent*. Since all the others have led up to this one, the reader knows it is crucial in the story, or the reader ought to know. A friend tells Winterbourne that he saw Daisy sitting, unchaperoned, in a secluded nook with an Italian. Puns occur often in this story, and by putting the prettiest girl in Rome under the most beautiful picture (in which the name of the pope is that of the characteristic of the young girl), James creates another, more complex pun. After nine variations of Winterbourne's mention of Daisy's innocence, the tenth coincides with her sitting under the Velázquez portrait, and the number ten is used to make puns on Pope Innocent the Tenth. After that conjunction, all the contraries, philosophical and active, that coexist in Winterbourne's mind are set in motion. The convergence and confrontation between Daisy and Innocent the Tenth are an especially fine example of how James's experience as an art critic and viewer of pictures in the great museums of the world contributed to his technique as a storyteller.

At the beginning of the 1880s, having successfully experimented with using the single work of art as a symbolic focus in *Daisy Miller*, James varies his dependence on the starred masterpieces. In *Confidence*, the Venus de Milo (the "Venus who has lost her arms") stands thus as the goddess of love who has lost her powers of embracing and of establishing the power of touch between lovers. And that is what has happened to Blanche and Gordon Wright, lovers who have lost contact with each other. In its silent armlessness at the Louvre, the Venus confronts the glum Gordon, who in his silence seems to receive the message. He is sitting with Angela, who is likened to the *Mona Lisa*, and she shares honors with the other most famous work of art in the Louvre. We see her with "hands crossed in her lap" and with her "inscrutable smile"; she is presented against a fantastic background resembling that of the *Mona Lisa*.

## THE PORTRAIT GALLERY

James wrote, "There is no greater work of art than a great portrait." We are not surprised that a writer of such humanistic concerns and such researches into the human heart would put a high value on depictions of persons. Lyon, the portrait painter in "The Liar" (1888), aspired to add his own work to the exemplary group of "half a dozen portraits in Europe" that he "rated as supreme" and that he saw as "immortal." By this date, six of this group of portraits had already been hung in the museum world of James's stories. There are three of them in "The Sweetheart of M. Briseux" (1875): *Mona Lisa*, which the bad painter wants to copy; Titian's *Man with the Glove*, which will reappear

1. *Pope Innocent X* (1650) by Velázquez, Palazzo Doria-Pamphili, Rome.

in *The Ambassadors* (probably very interesting to James personally because his brother William had been photographed in the same pose as a young man); and Rubens's *Chapeau de Paille* in the National Gallery. The other three are Raphael's *Cardinal Inghirami*, which the two spectators in the Pitti Palace compare to *The Madonna in the Chair* in "The Madonna of the Future"; Velázquez's *Innocent X*, which acts so wittily and focally as a foil for Daisy Miller's behavior; and, finally, Moroni's *Tailor*. Lyon tells us that this last portrait, one "of the productions that helped to compose the immortal six," was the picture on which he modeled his own work. The six portraits come from the four great repositories of masterworks in Paris, London, Florence, and Rome, and they sum up in cosmopolitan fashion the very essence of great portraiture. The artist in "The Liar" is the first of a long line of artists in the later fiction whose aim is to expose character in the painted portrait. The world of the studio creeps into the metaphors of this tale. One woman has "a sort of appearance of fresh varnish . . . so that one felt she ought to sit in a gilt frame." Colonel Capadose, the liar in the tale, looks like "a Venetian of the sixteenth century." The lying colonel is seen by the painter as an artist in his own line. "He paints, as it were, and so do I!" "The Lesson of the Master," which follows this tale, bridges the two worlds. The country house is seen as a "cheerful upholstered avenue into the other century" and is actually based on Osterley House, an Adam house belonging to the Earl of Jersey. It is now viewed as a private museum with an outstanding Gainsborough, which Osterley actually had on its walls. James then changes this setting to the suburban house of a successful author with a workroom constructed like a painter's studio, "a room without windows . . . like a place of exhibition." The characters next meet in a gallery of contemporary paintings, and the atmosphere of the "doing" of art takes over, for even the young heroine exhibited on the artsy-craftsy walls of her rooms "many water-colours" from her own hand.

Once embarked on this theme, James extends it in *The Tragic Muse*, where the great portraits of the National Gallery convince the hero (who has given up a political career to become a portrait painter) of the worth of trying to add to their accumulated treasures. The opening scene is at the Paris salon, and the climactic scene of the first volume is in the green room of the Comédie Française, where Miriam Rooth, the girl who becomes a great actress, is convinced of her métier by identifying with the great Rachel in Gérôme's masterpiece, her portrait, exhibited on the walls. Miriam herself is painted by Nick Dormer as "The Tragic Muse," which in 1890 would mean to every English reader Sir Joshua Reynolds's title for his portrait of Mrs. Siddons, the English equivalent of Rachel. James's connection with Mrs. Siddons was through his close friend Fanny Kemble, her great-niece, who fed him stories of her illustrious family. James extends his museum world in this novel through the presentation of two architectural monuments—Notre Dame Cathedral, which Nick and Gabriel Nash visit on their trip to Paris, and the English ruined Abbey of Beauclere, on the estate of Nick's political sponsor, Mr. Carteret. In a neoclassic imitation of the temple of Vesta on the Dallow property, Nick sees that his fiancée does not know the difference between the collector of art and the man who makes art, which Nick aspires to be. The second volume of the novel involves Nick's starting on his career as such a man by his painting of the now successful Miriam. Miriam's choice, similar to Nick's, is between being a committed artist and being an ambassador's wife.

To James, Sir Joshua Reynolds represented the height of British portraiture, as one can see from his comments on art, and he had read Sir Joshua's *Discourses*. James had read the following dictum by Reynolds:

He who borrows from an ancient . . . and so accommodates it to his own work . . . can hardly be charged with plagiarism: poets practice this kind of borrowing, without reserve. But an artist . . . should enter into a competition with his original, and endeavor to improve what he is appropriating to his own work. Such imitation . . . is a perpetual exercise of the mind, a continual invention. Borrowing or stealing with such art and caution, will have a right to the same lenity as was used by the Lacedaemonians, who did not punish theft, but the want of artifice to conceal it.

In his *Autobiography*, James repeats almost the same words about his "borrowing" from other writers. Van Dyck, Reynolds, and Romney are referred to as the classifications of the physical types of other characters in *The Tragic Muse*, but for Nick Dormer, the modern artist, there is the well-known contemporary artist and friend of James, John Singer Sargent, whose *Ellen Terry as Lady Macbeth* was "the most discussed picture of the year" and was exhibited at the New Gallery just about the time *The Tragic Muse* began to appear serially. The second portrait of Miriam Rooth that Nick Dormer paints is not suggestive of Reynolds's *Mrs. Siddons as the Tragic Muse* but rather of many portraits of women by Sargent. In the novel, the analogy between Nick's work and the work of well-known artists works two ways—backward, between Nick Dormer and his actress model, and forward, between John Singer Sargent and his actress model, which establishes a contemporary model for presenting a contemporary actress of distinction.

But this is just the beginning of the presence of Sargent in James's fiction. As we read in "The Beldonald Holbein," a clever tale of 1901, a lady at a dinner party defines the geographical boundaries of a set of London society thus, "Oh, it's bounded on the north by Ibsen and on the south by Sargent!" This area occupies a large part of James's fiction at the turn of the century, and Sargent provided both the model and the standard for James's growing interest in the making of art. Even as early as 1884, when James met Sargent, he represented for James the ruthless portrayer of what he saw as the truth on the surfaces of his models; Sargent's influence lasts up through *The Sense of the Past*, one of James's two uncompleted novels. Sargent painted a well-known portrait of James and did three drawings of him, two of which survive. James wrote only one essay on the painter, but Sargent lives for the reader in James's fiction. Charles

Waterlow, a "rising Impressionist" portrait painter in the short novel *The Reverberator* (1888), has worked with Carolus (Duran), as Sargent had; Waterlow makes two trips to Spain, as Sargent had with Helleu, and he has a Paris studio that resembles Sargent's Paris studio. "The Aspern Papers" (also 1888) is linked to Sargent, for Sargent provided James with the germ of the story. That year also saw the appearance of "The Liar," a tale about a painter who has the ability to reveal his model's lying tendency; it was well-known that Sargent had "unmasked a woman who was a inveterate liar." In "Glasses," the narrator is a painter who has a cool, ironic point of view and who, like Sargent, also has many commissions in the United States. James also arranges Flora Saunt to resemble closely a brilliant picture by Sargent of Mrs. Henry White, for both the heroine of the tale and the lady in the portrait wear shimmering white and pearls. They both hold opera glasses. What makes the resemblance more a matter of fact than conjecture is that in the summer of 1895, a week before James began to think about the story, he took Mrs. White to the theater and probably saw the portrait hanging in the White home.

The portrait painter as narrator or as the point-of-view character appears in two more stories in 1900, "The Special Type" and "The Tone of Time." In the first, the painter tells the reader that he knew from the model's expression that he was not very charitable or courtly and that he, as a painter, would make these unpleasant characteristics "cross, at any cost, the footlights . . . of my frame." One can even see that Sargent's portrait of *Mrs. Carl Meyer and Her Children* (which James had praised highly in print in 1897) influences the description of Milly Theale's pearls, which suited her "down to the ground," because Mrs. Meyer's string of pearls, as James wrote, was "ineffably painted" and "hangs down to her shoes." The museum masterpiece now has retreated, and the natural masterpiece, like Mrs. Brash, who appears to be a walking Holbein portrait, occupies the center of the imaginative stage in "The Beldonald Holbein." Milly Theale, too, is a walking Bronzino, and the museum masterpiece pops up once more in *The Ivory Tower* when we sit among Veroneses and Correggios in the Dresden Museum. But for the most part at this time, portraits are now alive in the flesh or are invented pictures by great masters. Titian's *Man with the Torn Glove* appears for a brief moment when Strether and Bilham tour the Louvre, and the reference again is to the flesh-and-blood gentleman, Chad Newsome, whose parallel to the Titian is obvious. As for the enigmatic picture in *The Sacred Fount*, there is no well-known painter invoked, nor is the picture other than one imagined by James himself, who, with his "painter's eye," could create an original to contribute the "torch of analogy" to his intentions. The poster in "The Real Right Thing" resembles one by Toulouse-Lautrec or Beardsley, though it is a generalization of a type, not a specific reference. Lawrence's painting of Lady Sandgate's great-grandmother in *The Outcry* and Reynolds's *Duchess of Waterbridge* are examples of the retention of a real master as the painter of imagined masterpieces. People are compared to ambiguously identified masterpieces like Spencer Brydon's *alter ego*, who, in "The Jolly Corner," appears with as great an "intensity" as a modern portrait. Though James wrote that "art makes life," life can be art when we refer and relate it to art.

## THE MUSEUM OUTSIDE THE MUSEUM

James's interest in landscape was confined, usually, to the park of a gentleman or to the kind of limited, worked-on plot of nature, such as the garden at Wadham College, "the sweetest of all the bosky resorts in Oxford." Nature artifacted is what charms James's imagination, as we see in the deformed garden of the deforming personality of Mrs. Ambient in "The Author of 'Beltraffio.' " Since Impressionism had altered the taste for landscape, James, in a sense, expands his estate parks, and in "Lord Beaupré" (1892), the territory of a landed seat is more vast and grand because it belongs to a hereditary nobleman and the garden is a lure for mothers of debutantes who want to catch the "rose," the *grand parti*. The garden enters James's fictional world with this story. Since the theme is the natural as opposed to the artificial in nature, the property is the real hero or heroine. But in the next story, "The Visits," we confront a tale of topiary art. It tells how formal French gardens based on Le Nôtre's gardens at Versailles and exported to English estates can affect a sensitive young girl and how her natural instincts are crushed by the rigid formality of such an environment. Louisa Chantry confesses her love for him to a young man whom she barely knows, in one of the small enclosed rooms created from topiary rooms developed from the green maze of the formal gardens of a horticultural showplace where everyone misses the way, including the girl. She is so ashamed of her behavior that she finally dies from the stress. She had been lost in the confusing artificial garden; she returns to die in her own home, which is the very opposite of the showplace, for it is natural, farm-like, and healthy. The garden in which she was tempted to speak her feelings was purposely misleading, designed for the artificial seventeenth-century amatory games the French delighted in. The vocabulary and images of the tale are constantly being directed to the out-of-doors, not to the interiors of the houses. Four years later, James has moved from gardens to houses and their furnishings in two novels, *The Spoils of Poynton* and *The Other House* (both 1896), but then he finishes his interest in nature by creating, in "In the Cage" (1898), a milieu in which arranging cut flowers for the dinner tables of the aristocracy becomes in itself an art form. Mrs. Jordan, the artist in this case, is so devoted to her task that to the lords and ladies she serves, her bouquets look to come "not from a florist, but from one of themselves." She views the success of the dinner party as determined by her arrangements. "They simply give me the table—the rest, all the other effects, come afterwards." The vocabulary again is thick with horticultural terms, and Mrs. Jordan's escape from the dreary reality of her life is situated in the creation of her own art form of flower arrangements.

In contrast to a rather contemptuous portrait of a silly and pretentious Impressionist painter in "A New England Winter" (1884), James takes Impressionism much more seriously when he reaches *The Ambassadors*. It is more or less assumed by critics that the point of view in *The Ambassadors* is that taken by Impressionist painters—the outdoor scenes, the Parisian cityscape, and the discovery scene in the French countryside where Chad and Marie de Vionnet are revealed to be lovers in the technical sense to Strether (who had believed in their "virtuous" relationship). Actually, James is Impressionist only in the sense that he uses the same field of vision as the Impressionists do; unlike the Impressionists, he was not satisfied with only a retinal vision. It is James's interpretation of the retinal vision, through Strether's consciousness, that makes the book, not the retinal vision itself. The scene of Marie and Chad in the boat has been called a typical Impressionist scene or, rather, an imitation of a typical Impressionist picture. But far from seeing the couple as a picture, Strether now sees them at this point as a play: "the picture and the play seemed to melt together," and when they arrive it is the play that dominates. James never was enthusiastic about any Impressionist painter of the top rank, and the only one he could absorb was Sargent, whose Impressionism was a personal style more closely related to Manet than to Monet, and to the brilliant brushstroke of a painter like Hals. Sargent never accepted the Impressionists' principles, nor did he show with them (his métier was that of portraiture), and basically, he would be fitted by their judgment of his work into the framework of an academician.

The museum elements in *The Ambassadors* are there as part of James's intent to make the novel a statement of praise of Paris and an exploration of what the city was giving to civilization. He presents a series of objects, ranging from Miss Gostrey's collection of "things" in her flat, a collection that constituted a "little museum of bargains," to the Louvre itself. The assimilation of Chad to the Titian portrait of the *Man with the Torn Glove* becomes meaningful when Chad gives to Mamie Pocock a copy of Fromentin's *Les Maîtres d'autrefois*, which, among other things, is a guide to the paintings of the Netherlands in the Louvre. In spite of the atmosphere of Impressionism and its point of view in the novel, Strether's hold on his identity is tethered to his museum view of Europe. His trip to Notre Dame Cathedral has the effect of a museum, for "the mighty monument laid upon him its spell," and he sits under it as if "under the charm of a museum." It is important that the discovery scene should come through the deconstruction of Strether's view of French landscape as something seen "through the little oblong of the picture frame," for before he sees the two people in their incriminating setting, the view "fell into composition, full of felicity. . . . It was Tremont Street, it was France, it was Lambinet." Then suddenly everything changes, and the Lambinet landscape, which is not an Impressionist picture but a proto-Impressionist one, changes to a play, and the scene is transformed into a scene at the theater, with Madame de Vionnet engaging in theatrics "solely in French." It is, therefore, a French play about a "bad" woman, recapitulating the first play Strether and Maria Gostrey had seen in London.

*The Ambassadors* is a long novel, and many strains can be found in it. An important one is the Arcadian strain. The Arcadian theme is embodied in a phrase, "high melancholy and sweet," and derives from museum sources, which in turn have their origins in Latin poetry. Erwin Panofsky tells us that Arcady was an imaginary golden realm invented by Virgil and that it was unlike the Theocritan idylls. In Arcady are both human suffering and frustrated love, which cause a dissonance, something to be found and spread through the Western world from Virgil's *Eclogues*. There the dissonance is shown in the "vespertinal mixture of sadness and tranquility" resulting from our knowledge that death and loss of love go hand in hand in Arcady, whose climate and landscape are situated in evening time, lighted by the evening star and darkened by lengthening shadows. As Panofsky sums it up, the Arcadian dream is "incarnate of ineffable happiness surrounded with a halo of 'sweetly sad' melancholy," of which James's phrase "high melancholy and sweet" is a distillation and which is not to be confused with the pastoral. In the seventeenth century, the Arcadian concept spread through the agency of Guercino's painting based on the inscription "Et in Arcado ego," in which a skull says to a group of shepherds, "Even in Arcady I (Death) am." Poussin painted one picture with a skull and the same inscription, which here means what it meant in the Guercino. But Poussin also painted a second picture, in which there is no skull and in which the inscription is now translated differently, since Death no longer is the speaker. The *ego* now refers to the voice of the occupant of the tomb, a dead Arcadian, addressing a mortal as follows: "I, too, even the dead and buried, once lived in Arcadia, the realm of bliss." This change in meaning was recognized in the next century when Diderot translated it as "Je vivais aussi dans la délicieuse Arcadie." This new translation, as Panofsky has pointed out, is really a mistranslation, but it has become the one we all use, and soon the word order was changed by Goethe and Balzac to fit the change in meaning. It becomes "Et ego in Arcadia" in Balzac's "Madame Firmiani," which may have served as one of the sources for *The Ambassadors*, and it is the way James translates it in his short story "Brooksmith."

For James, the channel was both pictorial and literary. Watteau gave him the props of the Arcadian stage set, all rococo items—statuary, fountains, and pavilions bathed in a melancholy sweetness—and Balzac's *Comédie Humaine* provided James with such Arcadian scenes as those from *Les Paysans*, which animate *The Europeans*, where "the *ton* of the Golden Age" is penetrated by the lies of the countess, Felix's sister. The country house of Les Aigues in *Les Paysans* ("Arcadie est aux Aigues, et non ailleurs!") is penetrated by the destructive aims of the peasants. Balzac even uses the Poussin painting, "Et Ego in Arcadia," to make his point clearer. James thus was surrounded by the Arcadian tradition. Though it appears in his novels before *The Ambassadors*, it is there he allows it to blossom forth and to create the prevailing tone. It is the evening time of Chad and Marie de Vionnet's love affair, and for the woman there is only frustration and the death of love. A building up of certain rococo details, with Miss Barrace as an eighteenth-century *commedia del' arte* figure and with the artifacts of Gloriani's garden supporting this Arcadian mood, creates a background for the passage of time reflected in Strether's *carpe diem* speech to Bilham. Even Watteau's *Embarcation for Cythera* in the Louvre, the perfect pictorialization of couples joining in a dance-like walk, may have provided James with the coupling of his characters, a coupling that breaks the ritual of the marriage couple in an *école galante* ritual and that is not to be confused with the wooing-coupling of the pastoral. Even the scene that reveals the adultery behind Chad and Marie's relationship is placed in Virgilian time: "not a breath of the cooler evening that wasn't somehow a syllable of the text," for it is "towards six o'clock" when Strether arrives at the inn. When he visits Mme. de Vionnet, it is always in the evening, and he is aware that her home is filled with "relics" that recall the Virgilian presence of death. The past is contained in her things, her future is at stake, and her present, surely in Woollett's judgment, is questionable. Looking back through her suite of rooms, Strether is aware that "the whole thing made a vista, which he found high melancholy and sweet." The Arcadian dusk is emphasized by "clusters of candles" and by "the small plash of the fountain," that ubiquitous rococo decor that is symbolic of vanishing time and of the act of love. Marie's future is not to be happy. But we also know that Chad will be saved from the Arcadian trap by his practical American business sense. The last Arcadian scene treated by James appears in *The Wings of the Dove*; the climactic middle takes place at the great house Matcham, which had, "for Milly . . . as the centre of an almost extravagantly Watteau-composition, a tone as of old gold" that prefigures Milly's death. In volume two, the mood changes to that of redemption, and sacred love now banishes the presences of Watteau and the rococo. "Et ego in Arcadia" has run its course.

At the end of the century, those masters of art looked at diligently in James's early heroes and heroines return. The late novels concentrate on the splendid Venetians who painted so much of the luxurious life around them. Veronese's *Marriage at Cana* in the Louvre pictorially dominates *The Wings of the Dove*. But of all the masters in James's museum, Titian is perhaps the most celebrated. In "Traveling Companions" and in "The Sweetheart of M. Briseux," where the *Man with the Torn Glove* first appears before it becomes so important an icon in *The Ambassadors*, we prepare for *The Wings of the Dove*, where Titian represents the entire spectrum of the colorist tradition for the South and for the Renaissance and where Turner does the same for the North and Modernism. Both artists are so filled with life that the moribund Milly must opt for the lesser talents. And for his tired characters James chooses the English watercolorists, men of lesser plastic stretch. We find Cotman in the gentle Mr. Longdon's home in *The Awkward Age*, and poor devitalized Sidney Traffle of "Mora Montravers" has his "precious little old Copley Fielding." However, one watercolorist, Hercules Brabazon, a gentleman painter who had his first show at the age of seventy and who knew both Sargent and James, was a much stronger painter, closer to the kind of talent for dramatic contrasts of light and shade that distinguishes Turner. James includes both Brabazon and Sargent in the list of British painters whom he calls "some of the loveliest flowers" grown by native Britishers. "Great Gainsboroughs and Sir Joshuas and Romneys and Sargents, great Turners and Constables and old Cromes and Brabazons form . . . a vast garden in themselves." But now James's museum contains pictures of his own invention, and we are not surprised that some of them are landscapes. In *The Golden Bowl*, the prince conceives of a metaphor to describe his appreciation of the lovely day, "just as if the whole place and time had been a great picture from the hand of genius," and the landscape he looks at presents itself as a masterpiece. He sees the cathedral he will visit later with Charlotte as part of his vision, for both he and we are reminded, undoubtedly, of the Gloucester in that vision, of the true "hand of genius," that of Turner, who has made watercolors of that cathedral. James's interest in landscape seems to have stemmed from his appreciation of both Cotman and Turner and emerges chiefly in his late work, though there are random landscape scenes in the earlier work, as in *Confidence* and "A New England Winter."

## THE GALLERY OF THE *FIN DE SIÈCLE*

If most of the nineteenth-century art movements James played with—Realism, Naturalism, and Impressionism—are lightly touched on, so are the paintings of the dreamers, the pre-Raphaelites and the Symbolists. They appear in his work first in the 1890s and are developed later. A typical example of how the legend of Salomé, beloved of the Symbolist poets and painters, penetrated James's late work is the revision he made in a scene of *Roderick Hudson*. The 1905 additions to the 1875 novel show his interests in the work of Gustave Moreau, work that he had anonymously enjoyed as early as 1875 but that he felt secure enough to reveal only years later. In the dozen lines he inserts in the revision of the novel that refer to the plastic vision of Christina in the mind of Gloriani, the sophisticated sculptor, James develops what the character had said to Roderick in 1875, "She would make a magnificent Herodias." In 1905 he substitutes "Salomé" for "Herodias," and in the fuller paragraph devoted to the expansion of this notion, he shifts his emphasis from the head of Christina to the head of Roderick on "a great gold tray." This revision coincides with the 1905 popularity of Salomé in contemporary art and music. The year 1905 saw the first performance of Richard Strauss's opera *Salomé*, dedicated to Sir Eugene Speyer, in whose home Strauss, Sargent, and James were frequent visitors. The New Stage Club had performed Wilde's *Salomé*, the basis for the opera, in London in the same year, and that year the young Picasso made two drypoints of Salomé. In Gloriani's expanded 1905 paragraph there are elements seemingly suggested by Oscar Wilde's play, and we know that James owned a signed copy of the first edition of his *Salomé*. Even with its ironic overtones, the merging of Christina with Salomé in such detail shows James's continued preoccupation with the destructive influence of Christina, who in *Roderick Hudson* will be the cause of death for Roderick and who in *The Princess Casamassima*, if not the actual cause of death for Hyacinth Robinson, will be at least the cause of his disillusion with revolution and of his conflict that could be resolved only by his suicide.

We proceed to other Symbolists who influenced James, for only certain aspects of this complicated movement that followed Impressionism in both art and literature can explain certain parts of a tale like "The Altar of the Dead." In it we see reflected the Symbolist predilection for a personal, secularized religion that Khnopff, the Anglophile Belgian Symbolist and editor of the *Studio*, publicized by photographing his own personal altar. Mary Antrim and Stransom, who join in a personal altar, also have Symbolist tastes, for they listen to "Beethoven and Schumann," the two musical heroes of the Symbolists. In the summer of 1899, during a trip to Paris, James wrote how that city seemed a "monstrous massive flower of national decadence," though he eagerly absorbed its sights and, since it was the height of the craze for billboard posters, appropriately wrote a poster story, "The Real Right Thing," during that year. The story appeared before the last year of the old century. It is printed as a picture in itself, topped by Howard Pyle's strange drawing. Its three columns of print occupy two pages and create a design, and it becomes both "picture and text." Even more important, the main character, the somewhat shady widow of the dead writer, is a *fin-de-siècle* poster come alive. "Her effect there—fantastic black, plumed, and extravagant, upon deep pink—was that of some 'decadent' coloured print, some poster of the newest school."

We might even shed some light on the murky text of *The Sacred Fount* if we view the narrator as Pierrot, and even if the narrator is called both Harlequin and Pantaloon, Arthur Symons, the critical spokesman for the Symbolists, interpreted Beardsley's Pierrot as one who takes on the masks of others. Symons described this Pierrot as a "type of our century" for whom "Simplicity" is "the most laughable thing in the world," noteworthy for "intellectualizing his pleasures, brutalizing his intellect." The narrator of *The Sacred Fount* is thus precisely described. The mask being held by the Old-World painted character in the room at Newmarch suggests not only this Pierrot, who takes on the masks of others, but also the painters Ensor and Redon, who used masks; and the landscape of the grounds of Newmarch suggests the decaying parks of the Belgian Symbolists. So penetrated by the aesthetics of the Symbolists is *The Wings of the Dove* of the following year (1902) that it could be called the Symbolist novel of James par excellence. First, we see the strain in the biblical title, revealing the late nineteenth-century interest in religions of personal kinds. Then we are aware of the *fin de siècle* sick, redheaded heroine, of the interest in Byzantine things, of the chimera, with which the descriptions of Mrs. Lowder show kinship. To these is added a reference to Maurice Maeterlinck, not only as a writer but as a force behind the creation of a Symbolist theatrical *mise-en-scène*. Figures of speech and scenes seem to stem from those plays that James saw, especially from *Aglavaine and Sélysette* and *The Princess Maleine*. Byzantinism was also the rage of Paris. Byzantine designs were used to advertise even baby food and soap. Thus James becomes topical when he identifies Milly with Theodora's

-court and introduces Gibbon, from whose great work we learn so much about life in imperial circles. Another Symbolist icon is the sphinx; pictorializations of that Egyptian *femme fatale* by Gustave Moreau and Elihu Vedder, the American Symbolist painter, are behind James's sphinx, May Bartram ("the impenetrable sphinx"), confronting John Marcher in "The Beast in the Jungle" (1903). James may have been prompted to adapt their confrontation from Moreau's remarkable picture *Oedipus and the Sphinx*, now in the Metropolitan Museum, which shows how horrified the sphinx is by what she sees in Oedipus's face and how he, in turn, is horrified by the truth he sees in hers. Because the tale by James is about knowledge and the act of knowing (these two words in some form occur about sixty times), the Oedipus-and-sphinx image is the appropriate Symbolist icon. This use of Symbolist visual structures does not mean a similarity in intention: it points to another example of James's lifelong penchant for redoing and correcting works of art for his own purposes. Since he was not sympathetic to the sensualism and eroticism of the Decadents, his remodeling of their icons is really a form of criticism, for he pointed out in his preface to *What Maisie Knew* that the appropriation of works of art, either visual or literary, was the most telling form of appreciation as well as of criticism.

The dreamer, however, who did not set up any anxieties, the English painter who may be considered a father of continental Symbolism, was Burne-Jones, whose version of a dream world was asexual and literary, filled with reflection and a monkish atmosphere, all congenial to James, who was also a good friend of the artist. James's essay of 1877 on the pre-Raphaelite artist's seven works exhibited at the Grosvenor Gallery was one of the first published appreciations in English of that painter. James's enthusiasm for Burne-Jones's work diminished when Sargent's work, a kind of personal Impressionism, began to impress the writer, even though the friendship with Burne-Jones grew deeper. Yet the "*studio* existence, with doors and windows closed, and no search for impressions outside," as he wrote in a letter, put James off now, and though he conceded that there "remains, however, a beautiful poetry," painting itself "is with him, more and more 'out of it.' " Given this change of taste, it seems paradoxical that at the same time that he disavows the painter, there begin to appear in James's fiction definite signs of an adaptation of Burne-Jones's vision. James's viewing of a private showing with Sargent of *King Cophetua and the Beggar Maid* had its effect on the trance-like oratory of the poor girl Verena in *The Bostonians* (1886). When Burne-Jones died in 1898 during James's writing of the tale "The Great Good Place," the author filled *his* dream world with images based on Burne-Jones's canvases. He had written ecstatically of *The Mill* as a picture of "extraordinary sweetness" and a depiction of "the hour of revery." As in his critical passages on the picture, so in his tale there is the same inability to define, in terms of place or time, the mood or atmosphere, with the exception of the Italian landscape characteristic of both tale and picture. There are "little green gardens" in both and a "high dry loggia." Both tale and picture recall Italian locations, what George Dane in the tale had "seen in old cities, old convents, old villas." In both there are monks and in both the feeling of happiness. Just as *The Mill* was the model for "The Great Good Place," so a later series of pictures by Burne-Jones became the model for "Flickerbridge" (1902). This is another story of a retreat from the world, but it is not a dream, only an area tucked away from the world, an area that has to be vacated by the hero because it is about to be ruined by publicity. The visual model behind it is now no longer Doré's version but Burne-Jones's *Briar Rose* panels of the Sleeping Beauty, shown in 1890 and 1891, in which the princess is kept sleeping and is not to be awakened. James follows his friend's version of the story. Frank Granger, an Impressionist painter, is taking refuge in a small town after a severe case of the flu and a severe case of being fed up with *pleinairisme* and the modern world. He escapes back to pre-Raphaelite traditions. When asked why he did not wake up the princess, Burne-Jones replied that he wanted to "stop with the Princess asleep and to tell them no more." In the tale, Granger admits that he has "found . . . just the thing that one has ever heard of that you most resemble. You're the Sleeping Beauty in the Wood." The language and the metaphors in the story perpetuate the medieval aspects that are part of Burne-Jones's imaginative world. James's twist is that the sleeping beauty, who lives in a private enclave safe from publicity, is an elderly spinster, not a young beauty.

## THE GALLERY OF ACADEMIC AND GENRE PICTURES

There is a whole category of objects in James's museum that are not to be included among masterpieces of painting or sculpture but that sometimes are beautiful, often unique, and sometimes distinguished only for their curious nature; in any case, they are there to serve a symbolic or technical function in the complicated world of James's fiction. Often they are academic or genre paintings. James has written on his early susceptibility to literary painting, so it is not surprising that a pictorial representation of Milton dictating to his daughters, seen and reviewed when James was thirty-two, should play an important part in his literary reconstruction of Milton's *L'Allegro* and *Il Penseroso* in his tale "Benvolio" (1875). He invokes Milton's two poems to illustrate the theme of the only allegory he ever wrote, to show the contrast between the life of social activity and the life of scholarly seclusion necessary for the writer. In 1874, a bicentenary of Milton's death engaged James's interest, as did the exhibition of Eastman Johnson's "Milton Dictating *Paradise Lost* to his Daughters," which James reviewed. Anyone who has seen either the painting or a reproduction of it will recognize the professor's study in "Benvolio": "Everything else was ancient and brown; the walls were covered with tiers on tiers of books." The professor "made his daughter his reader and his secretary," for he was blind, as Milton had been.

Even the slave paintings for which Jean-Léon Gérôme was known appear in *Roderick Hudson*. "Rowland had never been in the East, but if he had attempted to make a sketch of an old slave-merchant, calling attention to the points of

Circassian beauty, he would have depicted such a smile as Mrs. Light's'' as she lets Christina's hair "fall through her fingers, glancing at her visitor with a significant smile." Such pictures were very popular with American collectors. James had also written art pieces on Gérôme and had commented on his "cold literalness." Fifteen years later, James would come on Gérôme's *Rachel* in the green room of the Theatre Français, a painting in a totally different dimension that, as we have seen, became the pictorial focus of the end of the first part of *The Tragic Muse*.

## THE GALLERY OF GENRE PAINTING AND POPULAR PRINTS

After the turn of the century, James became more attached to the art he had enjoyed when young. "The Birthplace" (1903) contains a reminder of a sentimental print of his youth, brought in as a metaphor when Morris Gedge's job as the curator of the birthplace of "the supreme poet," Shakespeare, is threatened. When Gedge triumphs and turns to tell his friends the good news, they suggest to him "some picture, a sentimental print, seen and admired in his youth, a 'waiting for the verdict,' a Counting the Hours." This print is based on a famous pair by Abraham Solomon, an English genre painter of the period: *Waiting for the Verdict* and its sequel, *Not Guilty* or *The Aquittal*. James may have seen the first when he was in Europe with his parents, or he may have seen the prints in reproduction. His susceptibility to genre pictures is recorded in his *Autobiography*, where he mentions Delaroche's *The Young Princes in the Tower* and Maclise's *The Play Scene in Hamlet*. *Not Guilty* was not exhibited until two years later, in 1859, but James probably experienced the prints as a duet, as most prints of "before and after" were shown. The doubleness of the prints seems to have been copied in the double crisis of Morris Gedge, for his life divides itself into two important scenes. In the first one he expects to be fired because he is too recondite in his talk; in the second he expects to be fired because he feels he has gone too far in dramatizing the purely speculative aspects of the poet's birthplace. The halves of Gedge's personality are joined by being presented to another young couple, of a higher class, who are visiting from America, and he realizes that his power was "to show as in a picture the attitude of others"; the picture that has been built up by language, position, and forms of gesture depends on the duet of genre prints that so well express not only Gedge's dilemmas but also his abilities.

## THE CABINET OF CURIOSITIES

In addition to the art of the museums, there is the material culture that consists of the curious and the freakish elements of one's environment. There is a whole company from the circus gamboling through "The Death of the Lion" (1895), where the language of the sawdust is carried throughout the story. There is a "bearded lady" in "Dora Forbes," the male writer impersonating a woman. The artist of the story has his sitters "leap through the hoops of his showy frames." There is a young man in another story who is in love with a hairdresser's dummy. We encounter in another a mesmerist. A desk that sends messages to a sensitive lady composer, and a young man convinced by doting parents that he has married their dead daughter, are the eccentric curiosities of "Sir Dominick Ferrand" (1892) and "Maud Evelyn" (1900). In *The Spoils of Poynton*, ugly things are described more carefully than are the beautiful things, and they are more specified; they are easier to do than the desirable "things" that have been left to the reader's imagination, for James also delighted in the grotesqueries of the familiar. The ugly things owned by the Brigstocks and the pen wipers collected by Mr. Vetch suggest the everyday world from which Poynton is spiritually and materially removed, for in their vague generality they partake of the ideal, not the real. We find in "The Solution" (1889) a red "Cardinalesque" carriage that lights up a whole chapter on the old papal Rome and pricks the pretensions of the honourable Blanche, who, like the churchmen of the time, will stop at nothing to marry off her three daughters. This tale is matched by another, later tale, "The Velvet Glove" (1909), in which "the old Cardinalesque chariot" is replaced by "a chariot of fire," one of the early automobiles, giving those riding in it the freedom of a goddess who grants magical favors or who would like to have them granted to her. Edith Wharton's car, a Panhard, gave James material for this story, which is an Edith story disguised as a mock epic. We are not surprised to find that a phrenological plaster head figures in "The Figure in the Carpet" (1896). Vereker mentions "the organ of life" as the key to the figure in the carpet of his own work, and "organ" was the designating term used by the phrenologists. The attention to this inserted icon is productive of rather startling speculations as to what organ the "organ of life" points to, especially since the capital letter *P* is punned on for clearly designated reasons.

## THE GALLERY OF EASTERN ART

Exotic decorative objects occur late in James's fiction: the pagoda figures in *The Golden Bowl* (1904) as Maggie Verver's predicament in sensing that something has gone wrong in her marriage, and the ivory tower from India figures importantly in the unfinished late novel *The Ivory Tower* (1917). The first is actually a description of something not so extraordinarily exotic. Since the eighteenth century, imitations of the pagoda had existed all over England on the grounds of country houses that had any pretensions to gardens also large enough to boast horticultural divertisements and exotic buildings. In *The Ivory Tower*, we find the most carefully spelled out single objet d'art in all of James's fiction and the virtual center of the novel. Minutely described, "the high curiosity of the thing was in the fine work required for making and keeping it perfectly circular; an effect arrived at by the fitting together, apparently by tiny golden rivets, of numerous small curved plates of the rare substance . . . contributing to the artful, the total rotundity.'' To prevent this ''wonder'' from being ''wasted,'' as indeed it is not, we must keep our eye on its congruity with the plot itself, for the tower plays a critical part in the confrontation between Gray Fielder and Horton Vint, who will be his chief despoiler. As Gray speaks of the premium he will give Horton for the care of his fortune, he keeps touching his ivory tower. The fact behind his trust in Vint consists of his having remembered that Vint saved his life as a child. Horton twits Gray as being ''insanely romantic'' to be so affected by that childhood incident. The great fortune is deeply involved with the letter that Gray hides in the drawer of the ivory tower, and he justifies his romanticism as being actually reasonable: ''I'm never so reasonable . . . as when I'm most romantic.'' In his notes, James refers to his narrative devices in the terms of the tower: ''my right firm *joints*, each working on its own hinge, and forming together the play of my machine . . . when each of them is settled and determined it will work as I want it.'' The word *joint* is repeated innumerable times to define a bend in the plot. The notes James made indicate that the story will be composed of ten books, from early summer to Indian summer. ''That brings me round and makes the circle whole,'' just as the tower is ''perfectly circular,'' containing what we are led to believe is Mr. Gaw's exposé of the corruption in the American financial world.

## THE AMERICAN WING

There is also an American wing to James's museum, and it appears most strongly in his late work, as part of his nostalgia for the lost world of his youth. In ''Fordham Castle'' (1904), most of the references are to death-in-life, a state in which two characters have been placed by their socially ambitious relations. We see in the hair of a lady a reminder of ''the old fashioned 'work', the weeping willows and mortuary urns represented by . . . the capillary flowers that he had admired in the days of his innocence.'' These lines refer to the ''mourning pictures'' that, in his youth, James had seen on the walls of his relations. If we go back to *The Portrait of a Lady*, we see another kind of American popular art, that of the caricature Ralph makes of Isabel dressed in the American flag as Columbia, an icon that appeared most frequently during 1876, the year of the Centennial and the only date mentioned in the novel. We jump ahead to the early 1900s once more with ''Julia Bride'' (1908), located in the new Metropolitan Museum with the surrounding atmosphere of works of art, with petty chicanery going on among the personalities involved in the betrayal of the young woman. And if we examine what James thought of the policy of acquisition of art by the Metropolitan Museum at this time, we find he wrote it was a shame that because the men who had amassed great fortunes and who determined the museum's policy were now intent on acquiring only the most desirable art, ''acres of canvas and tons of marble'' would be ''turned out into the cold world as the penalty of old error.'' Julia, like the art no longer desirable, is also to be ''turned out into the cold world.'' Like it, she is to be deacquisitioned. In ''Crapy

Cornelia'' (1909) and ''A Round of Visits'' (1910), James turns his attention
to the new skyscraper architecture burgeoning in New York at the turn of the
century, a phenomenon he experienced to his wonder and horror during his
American trip of 1904–5. James constructed the first of the two stories just
mentioned out of his experience of primitive movies, many of which he witnessed
in London; these movies were produced by the Biograph Company from 1897
on, especially the Enoch C. Rector film of the Corbett-Fitzsimmons world cham-
pionship prize fight in Carson City, Nevada, on March 17, 1897. We find this
experience entering ''Crapy Cornelia'.' in a metaphor describing the appearance
of Cornelia's head, an image that ''grew and grew, that came nearer and nearer
. . . after the manner of the image in the cinematograph.'' Given this image, the
reader should be prepared to recognize a group of other images in the story
derived from the iconography of early movies. The source of the bright light
that streamed from the projector of the new invention pertains to the overlighted
world of the rich widow who wants to marry the hero of the tale, and the
competition for White-Mason's hand is between her world, corresponding to the
glaring exposure of the movie light that ''assaults'' the hero, and the dim world
of Cornelia, identified with the faded shadows of early photographs. Boxing
images refer to the overlighted and overexposed world of Mrs. Worthingham,
whose home has a ''glare'' and lack of ''the associational charm.'' Thus the
hero finds in Cornelia's home, filled with old carte-de-visite photographs, memories of his past.

## THE MUSEUM OF LIFE: THINGS AND PEOPLE

By the time we get to *The Sacred Fount* (1901), the museum talks. The
narrator refers to his ''little gallery—the small collection represented by'' the
main characters—a ''museum of those who put to me with such intensity the
question of what had happened to them.'' They are a collection of types fit for
a social museum, waiting to be sorted out. In this ''museum of those who'' ask
the narrator to guess their secrets, there is a real portrait gallery, with a picture
as baffling as the secrets of the living persons themselves. The museum in this
novel is not a Uffizi but a museum of life, and from now on, after 1901, James
is concerned with what is manageable and unmanageable in human beings. In
*The Sacred Fount*, the narrator-spectator has lost the catalogue for his museum;
he is in the dark about the exhibits. He guesses but he never knows, and we
follow him in his ''obscurely specific'' quest. We are finished with the kind of
collector we found earlier in James: Sanguinetti (in ''Rose-Agathe,'' first published in 1878 as ''Théodolinde''), who collected a hairdresser's dummy; Rosier
(in *The Portrait of a Lady*), who collected china; Mrs. Gereth (in *The Spoils of
Poynton*), who collected furniture. After 1901, either collectors have their things
passed down to them, as does Marie de Vionnet in *The Ambassadors*, or, like
Adam Verver and Maggie in *The Golden Bowl*, they must give up the most
precious of their human furniture. In *The Golden Bowl*, Damascene tiles and

three precious vases are the only specific collectibles on view at Fawns, though there is a valuable Florentine picture in Maggie's townhouse. By the time we reach *The Outcry* (1909, 1911), the owners are getting rid of their great art, either by threatening to sell to rich Americans or finally by donation to the National Gallery. James's museum in this, his last completed novel, is emptied of its treasures, and the best is bequeathed to the public museums where the author first enjoyed great art; the art finally belongs to the people. The only collectors who can keep their works of art without guilt are those who collect their impressions of art, not the actual works themselves. And they are the richest of all because their art dwells in their consciousness. In *The Spoils of Poynton*, Fleda Vetch remembers Poynton after it burns, and in *The Golden Bowl*, Amerigo imagines his own Turneresque watercolor of the landscape at Matcham without having to buy it.

At the same time that the equation between art and people is being rewritten by James in *The Sacred Fount*, he varies it in "The Beldonald Holbein" (1903), where a woman becomes a celebrity because she is seen as a Holbein masterpiece. The tale is based on a true story, for James recorded in one of his notebooks that Julia Ward Howe was "thought *the* most picturesque . . , 'Holbein', etc. that ever was . . . *Revanche*—at 75!" The tale is about a plain, elderly relative of a vain and aging beauty, Lady Beldonald, who imports the former to act as her foil. The result is that the artists whom Lady Beldonald had wanted to paint her are interested only in her old attendant, who seems to be a Holbein portrait brought to life. In the end the Holbein is sent back to America, where she perishes for want of appreciation. The tale is also based on the actual purchase by Isabella Gardner, at this time, of Holbein's twin portraits of Sir William and Lady Butts (see Figure 2). She was accustomed to telling James about such purchases for her collection and to showing or sending him photographs. The elderly Mrs. Brash is described as wearing very much the same kind of severe black-and-white costume as Lady Butts. At the top of Mrs. Gardner's real Holbein portrait, we read *Anno Aetatis Sue LVII* ("In the Fifty-seventh Year of her Life"). Instead of keeping the age of Julia Ward Howe, seventy-five years, when her success as a Holbein took place, James has deliberately changed the age to fifty-seven. "Here was a benighted being to whom it was to be disclosed in her fifty-seventh year (I was to make that out) that she had something that might pass for a face."

James found his real models for the things in *The Spoils of Poynton* in a real place, and for the frontispiece to that novel in the New York Edition, he wrote to the director of the Wallace collection and asked permission to have photographed a few of the museum's precious objects to illustrate the book. He had seen there "a divine little chimney-piece with all its wondrous garniture, a couple of chairs beside it, and a piece on either side of the pale green figured damask of the wall, which struck me on the spot . . . as representing . . . exactly the 'subject' I want for *The Spoils of Poynton*." He was trying to get rid of the "too marked museum-quality," and, detached, this selection of objects "might per-

2. *Lady Butts* (ca. 1543) by Hans Holbein the Younger, Isabella Stewart Gardner Museum, Boston.

fectly refer itself to some country-house possessed of rare treasures.'' This quality, that of the museum, was one he tried to avoid in his late stories, and as early as ''The Lesson of the Master'' (1892), he had furnished his country house with the treasures of Osterley, a real country house, perhaps the greatest of Robert Adams's houses. It is the model for ''Summersoft,'' the house in the tale, as James acknowledges in a letter to the owner, Lady Jersey, and he uses actual elements of the house itself in his description of Summersoft, even to the mention of the great Gainsborough in the long gallery.

Two Rothschild houses appear as models. The first, Mentmore Towers, is the product of Mayer de Rothschild's fortune and imagination, aided by Sir Joseph Paxton's architectural genius, and the second is Waddesdon Manor, the home of Ferdinand de Rothschild, built in imitation of a French chateau and containing a collection of superb eighteenth-century pieces, most of which were made for French pre-Revolutionary royalty. After visiting Waddesdon in 1885, James wrote to Grace Norton that ''the gilded bondage of that gorgeous palace will last me for a long time,'' and it surely did, for in an amazing way, though the Verver house, ''Fawns,'' in *The Golden Bowl* is an eighteenth-century house with the date 1713 set into the wall and not a modern approximation of a French royal palace, Waddesdon operates in that novel as a kind of metamuseum. A number of precious objects from Waddesdon Manor seem to have crept into metaphors that reveal the characters' states of feeling and their awareness of their dilemmas. Two large Guardis and three ship vases made for Marie Antoinette seem to be behind the many ship images in *The Golden Bowl*. Though rare, the ship vases are not unique, but a south German eighteenth-century table whose top illustrates a city square dominated by a public square in which a Palladian building occupies the center of attention is definitely one of a kind. This appears to have influenced the figure of speech in which Adam compares Amerigo's union with Maggie to a public square in which his son-in-law had, like a ''great Palladian church . . . suddenly been dropped.'' An automaton of German make of the mid-eighteenth century, an environment of figures and theatrical scenes that have to be wound up by a key to work, seems to be behind Maggie's metaphor while watching her family play bridge. There are many more figures of speech that connect up with exhibits at Waddesdon, like the marble vases that flank the terrace steps and that tell the fables of Jupiter and Io and of Ariadne, mythological references made by Maggie as she watches Charlotte descend similar garden steps.

The great change after 1900 in the use James makes of the work of art is that the museum has yielded its place to the private home of the very rich. The appropriation of art changes from submission to the visual stimulation of great art, which we found in James's early fiction, to the art metaphor that stems from a character's consciousness. This becomes especially true in the last four novels. In *The Golden Bowl*, the impulse that operates in a collector of beautiful objects must be carefully guided so as not to deform life itself. In *The Outcry*, works of art do not automatically confer love and a sense of responsibility on the people who have inherited them. An interloper from the middle class, the young art expert Hugh Crimble, has to teach these aristocrats their duties to art and to England. The pictures at Dedborough, the aristocratic home with the emblematic name, will come to life only when they have been transferred to the National Gallery, for their habitual environment has lost its vitality. The appreciation of those who love art will restore meaning to them, for appropriation can be done only through appreciation. Ownership through inheritance is meaningless.

In the last two incomplete novels, works of art have lost their museum classifications. They operate now with a "mystic meaning proper to themselves to give out." *The Ivory Tower* gives its name to a curious object of utility made at a time and in a place remote from the America of 1910. It shares with the golden bowl ingenuity and skill in its construction, together with a capacity for a symbolic as well as a utilitarian role. *The Sense of the Past* (1917) deprives the portrait (which in the 1890s and the early 1900s was as charged with relational connections as a living character itself) of its museum status, for the portrait in the unfinished novel is by an unknown artist. But its power lies in its capacity to act as if it *were* a person and to summon up the past for the American historian, Ralph Pendrel, who is as responsive to his picture as Lord Theign in *The Outcry* was not. Aurora Coyne, the rich American heroine, is compared to a Venetian portrait of the Renaissance, but her ability to pull her fiancé back into the present depends not on her resemblance to art but on her healthy actuality as a strong specimen of the twentieth century.

James's museum was created by him to provide scenery, variety, and appropriate analogues designed to clarify the human drama that was his chief concern. For that reason, no art object was introduced unless it was organically related to the fiction, and no art object was the result of the author's mere whim. If, as we read, we cannot find a rationale for the appearance of a piece of artistic material culture, the failure is ours and not Henry James's.

## NOTE

1. For a fuller treatment of this essay, see my *The Museum World of Henry James*, especially the index, which guides the reader to multiple references for a given work of art, and the notes, which locate all quotations.

# 14
## James's Revisions

### Anthony J. Mazzella

With his 20 completed novels and 112 short stories it may be said that Henry James was never entirely satisfied, for like his fictional creation, the writer Dencombe in "The Middle Years," James was "a passionate corrector, a fingerer of style; the last thing he ever arrived at was a form final for himself" (*NY* XVI, 90).

James's fiction tended to appear serially, in book form, and in one or several collected editions, frequently in both England and America; and each new publication of the same work demonstrates a revised work, with, occasionally, more than six different published versions of a single text. For example, S. P. Rosenbaum tells us that for *Roderick Hudson* there are "seven editions and three sets of revisions" and that for *The Spoils of Poynton* there are four different texts (Rosenbaum, "*Spoils*" 162, 163). A collation of these different versions can provide an illuminating reading experience, especially if a generation has elapsed between major reworkings of the text, as is the case with *The Portrait of a Lady* between 1881 and 1908, when the New York Edition version was published.

The thorny issue for a student of James is how to understand these texts: As variations on a theme but the same symphony? As the same recitative but with new embellishments? As an entirely new composition, but one having the same name? James speaks of his fictional ideas, their sources and development, in his notebooks; he continues this discussion in his prefaces to specific volumes in the New York Edition, where he also discusses his revisions; and he comments again on the revisions, as the occasion warrants, in his letters. The authority of James in these sources (and the subsequent challenge to this authority) have tended to establish the direction taken by scholarship devoted to James's revisions. The story of James's fiction is also the story of his revisions, a journey begun by Clara F. McIntyre in *PMLA* in 1912.

James inveterately revised his novels, tales, and travel writings with each reissue, but his revisions for the New York Edition provide the principal focus for most discussions of his revisionary art. James held that these novels and tales constituted "nothing but fine gold" (*HJL* IV, 403). They were intended to be of "benefit not only for myself, but for the public at large" (*HJL* IV, 408). Nevertheless, there was a concern, initially voiced by Charles Scribner, that the revised early works would disappoint "owing to loss of freshness" (*HJL* IV, 409). James, however, insisted that his revised works for the New York Edition were the only form that mattered, as he indicated in a September 14, 1913, letter to Fanny Prothero (a friend and neighbor of James who lived in London and at Dial Cottage in Rye). The letter included reading lists of works for a "delightful young man from Texas [Stark Young, later drama editor of *The New Republic*]," works that, James stressed, "are all on the basis of the Scribner's (or Macmillan's) collective and revised and prefaced edition of my things, and . . . if he is not minded somehow to obtain access to *that* form of them, ignoring any others, he forfeits half, or much more than half, my confidence" (*HJL* IV, 683). Later editors were not always to agree with James, especially regarding *The American*, whose revised New York Edition text they have tended not to reprint.

James's principal comments on this and other revisions appear in his prefaces to the early and the penultimate volumes in this edition. In his preface to *Roderick Hudson*, which serves as an introduction to the whole of the New York Edition, James speaks of revision in the context of "reading over, for revision, correction and republication, the volumes here in hand" (*AN* 4); he speaks of "re-perusal" (*AN* 8), a recurring term in the prefaces, and of "patch[ing] up one's superstructure" (*AN* 17), "structure" being another recurring term. Thus revision, in part, means correction.

It is also in this preface that James introduces the metaphor of the painter's sponge and varnish bottle in an attempt to describe the act of revising: "I have felt myself then, on looking over past productions, the painter making use again and again of the tentative wet sponge. . . . The simplest figure for my revision of this present array of earlier, later, larger, smaller, canvases, is to say that I have achieved it by the very aid of the varnish bottle" (*AN* 11–12). In this preface, James also quotes himself, "I have 'nowhere scrupled to rewrite a sentence or a passage on judging it susceptible of a better turn' " (*AN* 12). Added to revising to correct, then, is revising to rewrite (a sentence), to amend, to enhance so as to realize "the buried secrets, the intentions," and to improve the work.

James's discussion of two problems he encountered with the original text of *Roderick Hudson* sheds light on another aspect of his concept of revision. Revision did not mean to change the structure of a work: James would not alter the plot or introduce or remove characters or reverse what had happened in the original. For example, James considered "the time-scheme of the story [to be] quite inadequate"; that is, "at the rate at which [Roderick] falls to pieces, he seems to place himself beyond our understanding and our sympathy" (*AN* 12). For James, the problem here is that "the damage to verisimilitude is deep" (*AN* 18), and in keeping with his view of inviolable structure, he left the damage in its irreparable state.

Similarly, in his preface to *The American*, James remarks another "affront to verisimilitude" (*AN* 37), the "queer falsity" (*AN* 35) of the novel and its serious flaw—the conduct of the Bellegardes. "They would positively have jumped . . . at my rich and easy American and not have 'minded' in the least any drawback" (*AN* 35). As with *Roderick Hudson*, James believed that in the revision, the solution lay in having the novel reside effectively in one consciousness—Mallet's in the former and Newman's here. But James had his doubts: "I was perhaps wrong in thinking that Newman by himself . . . would see me through the wood" (*AN* 39). James's decision, again, not to alter the plot of the novel implies that to revise does not mean to change the structure.

Nowhere in the next preface, the one to *The Portrait of a Lady* (nor for that matter in the preface to *The Princess Casamassima*), does James discuss the revisions apart from invoking the familiar term of "re-perusal" (*AN* 52). The *Portrait* preface contains his famous "house of fiction" metaphor and his continued emphasis on structuring his works around a center of consciousness, this time that of Isabel Archer. But this preface does highlight something new, something that was introduced in his very first preface, the terminology of anxiety. James speaks of "the fruitless fidget of composition" (*AN* 40) and "the divided, frustrated mind" (*AN* 41) as he sought, with his original production, "some right suggestion," "some better phrase," "the next happy twist of my subject, the next true touch for my canvas" (*AN* 40).

The note of terror James speaks of in the preface to *Roderick Hudson* (*AN* 5) is also sounded in his letters. To his nephew, Henry James, Jr., James wrote on April 3, 1908, of "the Nightmare of the Edition . . . my terror of not keeping sufficiently ahead in doing my part of it (all the revising, rewriting, retouching, Preface-making and proof correcting) has so paralysed me—as a panic fear— that I have let other decencies go to the wall. . . . Fortunately I have kept at it so that I am almost out of the wood, and the next very few weeks or so will completely lay the spectre" (*LHJ* II, 96).

The ambivalence James felt—the joy in his monument to his art and the "panic fear"—is evident, though masked, in his magisterial preface to *The Golden Bowl*, the one preface that Jean Kimball identifies as containing James's most extended discussion of the act and substance of revision (Kimball 131). With a sense of wonder, James describes how his revisions come into existence. "The term that . . . finally 'renders,' is a flower that blooms by a beautiful law of its own . . . in the very heart of the gathered sheaf; it is *there* already, at any moment, almost before one can either miss or suspect it—so that in short we shall never guess, I think, the working secret of the revisionist" (*AN* 342).

Finally, James equates revising with a moral act and with his very being. "I have found revision intensify at every step my impulse intimately to answer, by my light, to those conditions [of life]'' (*AN* 347). Further, "as the whole conduct of life consists of things done, which do other things in their turn, . . . so, among our innumerable acts, are no arbitrary, no senseless separations. . . . We recognise . . . that to 'put' things is very exactly and responsibly and interminably to do them. . . . These things yield in fact some of its most exquisite material to the religion of doing'' (*AN* 347).

Within this religion of doing, James identified "the incomparable luxury of the artist. It rests altogether with himself not to break with his values, not to 'give away' his importances. . . . Thus if he is always doing he can scarce, by his own measure, ever have done'' (*AN* 348). James's perpetual revising, thus, has a richer core.

All of which means for him [the artist] conduct with a vengeance, since it is conduct minutely and publicly attested. Our noted behavior at large may show for ragged. . . . But on all the ground to which the pretension of performance by a series of exquisite laws may apply there reigns one sovereign truth—which decrees that, as art is nothing if not exemplary, care nothing if not active, finish nothing if not consistent, [then] the proved error is the base apologetic deed, the helpless regret is the barren commentary, and "connexions" are employable for finer purposes than mere gaping contrition. (*AN* 348)

For James, revision is the "religion of doing"; it is art, it is life, it is necessity. Yet also present is James's tremor in the face of his revisions, which is openly acknowledged in the preface to *The Golden Bowl* so as to be displaced. "The question of the 'revision' of existing work had loomed large for me, had seemed even at moments to bristle with difficulties; but that phase of anxiety, I was rejoicingly to learn, belonged to the [past]'' (*AN* 337). James admits that once he began the act of rereading his early works, he felt "purged of every doubt." He attributed his fears to his "too abject acceptance of the grand air with which the term Revision had somehow, to my imagination, carried itself—and from my frivolous failure to analyse the content of the word'' (*AN* 338).

But even his definitions of *revision* communicate a duality, as if he had to avoid the term *rewrite* (except for a sentence) at all costs. "To revise is to see, or to look over, again—which means in the case of a written thing neither more nor less than to re-read it'' (*AN* 338–39). For James, revising the early works was an "*act* of re-appropriation'' (*AN* 336), with the difference between the revision and its predecessor being simply that "the 'old' matter is there, re-accepted, re-tasted, exquisitely re-assimilated and re-enjoyed'' (*AN* 339). But not rewritten. At this stage, he expressly excludes rewriting from his definition. "Re-writing . . . , for my *conscious* play of mind, [has] almost nothing in common [with revising]'' (*AN* 339). James regarded "re-writing as so difficult, and even so absurd, as to be impossible'' (*AN* 339). He added, "What re-writing might be was to remain—it has remained for me to this hour—a mystery'' (*AN* 339).

Yet James, in a March 5, 1907, letter to Grace Norton, did acknowledge (if only parenthetically) that the early works were, indeed, rewritten. He considered the New York Edition, on which he had "been very busy these last months," to be "a 'handsome' . . . array . . . owing much to close amendment (and even 'rewriting') of the four earliest novels" (*LHJ* II, 70).

On New Year's Eve 1907, James, having received *Roderick Hudson* and *The American*, the first two volumes of the New York Edition, dictated to Charles Scribner's Sons a heartfelt expression of his emotion. "I am serenely content. The whole is a perfect felicity, so let us go on rejoicing" (*HJL* IV, 484). Within eight years, though, James was to see the joy destroyed. In his August 25, 1915, letter to Edmund Gosse, James considered the New York Edition, "from the point of view of profit either to the publishers or to myself, [as] practically a complete failure. . . . I remain at my age . . . , and after my long career, utterly, unsurmountably, unsaleable." Worse, for James, was the fact that the edition had "never had the least critical attention at all paid it" (*LHJ* II, 497–98).

This absence was rectified with a vengeance in the decades following James's death in 1916. From the 1920s onward, James's revisions have been subjected to intense scrutiny. This "critical attention," more often than not, has been illuminating.

Even so, one should frankly introduce an issue perhaps best phrased, though in a different context, by E. A. Sheppard, who underscores the ambivalence that scholars feel about the whole question of James's revisions. "That any author should spend months over an improvement (as he considered it) in the mere *wording* of his novels and stories, is a procedure incomprehensible, it seems, to critics [and students] of the present day" (253–54).

Nevertheless, the revisions do exist, and dozens of commentators have thought the study worth investigating. An overview of the various studies of James's revisions reveals a number of favored capitals, with *The American* and *The Portrait of a Lady* topping the list. Also popular subjects of study are *Roderick Hudson* and *The Ambassadors* (though the visitors to the latter disembarked largely at the site of the misplaced chapters). A smaller number of visits were accorded *The Turn of the Screw*, *Daisy Miller*, "Four Meetings," *The Spoils of Poynton*, and even *Watch and Ward*, a novel James disavowed and excluded from the New York Edition. Only brief stopovers were given to *The Awkward Age*, *The Golden Bowl*, "Pandora," "A Passionate Pilgrim," "The Pension Beaurepas," *The Princess Casamassima*, *The Reverberator*, "The Siege of London," *The Tragic Muse*, *What Maisie Knew*, *The Wings of the Dove*, and *The Bostonians*. The last was also omitted from the New York Edition, though James regretted its absence ("I feel . . . how the series suffers commercially from its having dropped completely out" [*LHJ* II, 100]) just as he bemoaned the loss of its preface ("I should have liked to write that Preface to the Bostonians—which will never be written now. . . . *that* is a thing that has perished!" [*LHJ* II, 499]). Several intrepid guests remarked on the New York Edition as a whole, and one pugnacious traveler roundly criticized nearly all the other visitants—

twice. Some unpublished dissertations visited individual works, the New York Edition generally, and the tales included therein.

But even before Helene Harvitt produced the first study devoted to James's revisions of a single work, even before there was a New York Edition, J. C. Heywood, as Clara F. McIntyre reported, was publishing what may very well be the earliest comment in connection with criticism of James's revisions. Heywood, writing on *The Passionate Pilgrim* and *Transatlantic Sketches* in *How They Strike Me, These Authors* (Philadelphia, 1877), declared, "Ambiguities and obscurities, as well as inadequacies of expression, are so uncommon in these books that those which appear are all the more displeasing and inexcusable, since the writer has plainly shown that they might have been avoided" (McIntyre 354). Thus, according to Heywood, there was a time when "ambiguities and obscurities" were viewed as so "uncommon" in James that any such appearance in the period of *Daisy Miller* was cause for complaint.

Indeed, the history of critical analysis of James's revisions is one of complaints, defenses, illumination, and controversy. Generally, some scholars have criticized James for revising the early works and spoiling their spontaneity, whereas others, taking their cues from James, have argued that he was using the "painter's sponge and varnish bottle" to fully realize earlier intentions. Still others have concluded that some of the revised works, especially *The Portrait of a Lady*, were so substantially altered from the original that each constitutes a discrete entity. And recent criticism has sought to place the revised works for the New York Edition in the context of the daily events in James's life, citing notebook entries, appropriate letters, and the sequence of composition of the prefaces and of fictional revision to see how their interaction may shed light on textual study.

The study of James's revisions began three years after the publication of the New York Edition was completed and has been represented in nearly every decade thereafter and with increasing frequency, especially with the advent of the *Henry James Review* in 1979. Clara F. McIntyre produced the first academic analysis of James's revisions. Writing in *PMLA* in 1912, she noted that because we "have to work at times to grasp [James's] meaning," she sought "to discover . . . some of the causes for this loss of clearness" (354, 355). To this end, she contrasted early and revised texts of *Roderick Hudson*, *The Portrait of a Lady*, *The Awkward Age*, and *The Golden Bowl*. In comparing James to Shakespeare, she introduces a common criticism. McIntyre thought that, like Shakespeare in the later plays, James "might have had too much thought for his expression, have tried to pack too much in a single sentence. But [James] . . . has more frequently *thinned* a passage than enriched it; he has packed in more expression rather than more thought" (368). She concludes ruefully: "The question may well arise whether a mode of writing which so constantly distracts attention from the substance to the form of expression is still to be called *style* . . . [James] 'require[s] a second reading, not . . . for the discovery of new beauties or the savoring again of old ones, but to be understood at all' " (371).

During the subsequent course of studies of the revisions, the distinction between style and substance was quickly to fade (and as quickly to return), so that, eventually, style came to be viewed *as* substance, the manner in which James wrote as indicating the meaning, and the revised work as constituting a new one.

Within six years of McIntyre's study, Theodora Bosanquet, who took James's dictation, published an insider's account of the revisions. Bosanquet regards the New York Edition as having "greater elegance" than the earlier texts (which she characterizes as "simple . . . smooth . . . [and] pretty" [59]) and as being "nearly always richer and more alive." She sees the revisions as trying to secure "emotional tension[,] . . . [t]ruth . . . and accurate registration of each perceived tone" (59). She recommends, at the close, to "anyone who wants to discover for himself the mode of growth of a great artist's sensibility," the revised texts of *The American, The Portrait of a Lady, The Princess Casamassima*, and the shorter tales of the 1870s and 1880s.

Such an adventurer will be . . . well qualified . . . for judging between a provocative young critic's verdict that "all the early works have been subjected to a revision which in several cases, notably *Daisy Miller* and *Four Meetings*, amounts to their ruin," and [James's] confident hope that he "shouldn't have breathed upon the old catastrophes and accidents . . . wholly in vain. . . . I have prayed that the finer air of the better form may sufficiently seem to hang about them and gild them over—at least for readers, however few, at all *curious* of questions of air and form." (Bosanquet 62)

The year 1923 saw commentary by a fellow author, Robert Herrick, who first met Henry James in 1905 when James was revisiting America. Herrick gave James a tour of Chicago. James also invited him to Lamb House in the summer of 1907. In recalling the Rye visit, Herrick wrote, "It was on what Henry James himself might have called, in the earlier days, a suave English summer afternoon that the complete heinousness, from my point of view, of the contemplated undertaking against those youthful writings was revealed to me" (733). Herrick makes it clear he objected to the revision. Although as "a young novice I was considerably in awe of my host, the respected Master of my craft; nevertheless, I ventured after a while (as the effects of his 're-touching' became more and more painfully evident) to remonstrate—to say something about the respect one owed to one's past, living or buried, and the impossibility of this sort of resurrection by breathing the breath of one's present life into what for good or ill had been done and finished under another inspiration." According to Herrick, James defended the revisions by saying, "I could never allow such bad writing in a definitive edition!" (734). Herrick's letter of gratitude for the Lamb House visit elicited a reply from James, dated August 7, 1907, in which James discusses the revisions. "All thanks . . . for your so curious & urgent remarks on the matter of my revisions. . . . The re-touching with any insistence will *in fact* bear but on one book (*The American*—on *R. Hudson* and the *P. of a Lady* very much less) but in essence I shouldn't have planned the edition at all unless I had felt close revision . . . to be an indispensable part of it. . . . You also will be ravished! Trust me & I shall be justified'' (Herrick 735–36). Herrick's next comments are crucial for their marking none of the earlier dichotomy between form and content; he felt that William James's ''philosophy should have convinced the novelist of the impossibility—above all in his peculiar case—of making a 'mere revision of surface and expression' without inevitably affecting 'substance,' where the two are so inextricably fused as Henry James under other circumstances would be only too delighted to admit that they are fused in his own work'' (736–37).

The following year marked the appearance of the first study, in *PMLA*, of James's revisions devoted to a single work, one that again separated form and content: Helene Harvitt's ''How Henry James Revised *Roderick Hudson*: A Study in Style,'' and the next year, very quickly, marked the appearance of a correction, also in *PMLA*, by Raymond D. Havens.

Harvitt indicates that her source for the first (1875) appearance is that of 1883 and that for the New York Edition she used the 1921 Macmillan edition. Her purpose is to study ''the nature of the revisions'' and to ''classify them . . . with the idea of throwing more light on Jamesean style'' (203). She notes that though ''there is barely a sentence in *Roderick Hudson* which has remained unchanged,'' James ''never altered the order of a paragraph'' (203). Her general view is that only ''in a few cases [is] the second version an improvement on the first'' (225). She concludes that ''in revising *Roderick Hudson*, Henry James made very few radical changes, . . . he in no way altered the story, but . . . he made a most minute revision of his style,'' and she adds that he included ''a great tendency to analyze; . . . in the final version this tendency became a habit, an affectation, if you will. The effect of that introspective, analytical trait is an obscuring of spontaneous, natural passages, making them labored, heavy, ambiguous, and sometimes almost impenetrable'' (227).

Havens's first point is that Harvitt, working in Paris, did not realize that ''the text which she quotes throughout her article as from the first edition, comes in reality from a thoroughly revised later version,'' adding that if Harvitt ''had been able to refer to an American edition published after 1882, she would have noticed the two copyrights (one issued to the publishers in 1875, and one to the author in 1882) and the 'Note' (which has a page to itself): '*Roderick Hudson* was originally published in 1875. It has now been minutely revised, and has received a large number of verbal alterations. Several passages have been rewritten' '' (433). Havens argues that a comparison of ''this previous revision [with that of the 1875 text] . . . will show that minute and fastidious correction was an early habit with Henry James, but it will not . . . reveal any evidence of the growth of 'that introspective, analytical trait,' or much 'obscuring of spontaneous, natural passages. . . . ' On the contrary, the changes were made in the interest of greater clarity and definiteness, of euphony, and of fresher, less hackneyed phrasing'' (433). Havens concludes, ''The changes made in the 1882 edition . . . are of considerable interest, not alone because they correct the impression that all of Henry James's revisions were towards the more involved and less effective, but because they reveal a great artist at work in the period just before he reached the zenith of his powers" (434).

In 1927, Pelham Edgar touches on the revisions for the New York Edition in his chapter on *The American*. His interest, like that of Harvitt and Havens, is "the processes of James's style" (241). Edgar considers the changes to constitute "a rigorous verbal revision" (237). Edgar's conclusions are that "James, as time went on, required more words to express his meaning . . . [and] that in his eagerness to escape banality he . . . sometimes [paid] the penalty in an unponderable ponderosity of phrase" (241).

During the 1930s and early 1940s, very little was published on James's revisions. Indeed, F. O. Matthiessen in 1944 would complain, "One sign of how little technical analysis James has received is the virtual neglect of his revisions." In his own study, Matthiessen focuses on *The Portrait of a Lady* because "it is a much richer book than either of the two others [*Roderick Hudson* and *The American*]" ("Painter's Sponge" 49). Matthiessen stresses the major changes in the novel, including the new ending of the novel itself, which he asserts did not mean James intended to suggest that Isabel Archer would eventually leave Rome for Caspar Goodwood but that Henrietta Stackpole would be optimistic about this possibility.

In the following year, Royal Gettmann produced a detailed study of Henry James's revision of one of the "less rich" novels, *The American*. The purpose of Gettmann's study is "to compare the first and final editions of *The American* with respect to prose style, characters, and plot" so as "to deduce from the differences and from the Prefaces James's general theory of revision." His position is to challenge the "notion that the later James was unable or unwilling to ask a plain question or give a direct answer," though he does remind us of "Edith Wharton's amusing story of how, on an automobile trip, James asked a direction of an old pedestrian and completely befuddled him. Mrs. Wharton came to the rescue with the simple words, 'Where is King's Road?' " (279). For Gettmann, "the key to James's theory of revision" is evident in his treatment of Newman; James "looked upon Newman as a conscientious biographer looks upon his subject: he had no right to change in 1907 what Newman said and did in 1877, but he could speculate about the states of mind back of those deeds and words" (290). Gettmann concludes that "the changes which James made . . . square exactly with his general statements on the subject of revision" (293) and that "it is wrong . . . to assume that James the Reviser mercilessly manhandled the works of James the First" (295).

Interest in the revised *American* was to resurface a decade later in at least four studies before interest shifted again to *The Portrait of a Lady*. Leon Edel, in his editor's commentary in *The Ghostly Tales of Henry James* (1948), examined not *The American* or *The Portrait* but *The Turn of the Screw*. By 1955 Edel reaffirmed his earlier view that "in his revision of the story for the New York Edition [James] altered his text again and again to put the story in the realm of the governess's feelings" (Edel, *Psychological Novel* 45).

Ten years later, Thomas M. Cranfill and Robert L. Clark reasserted Edel's view. Robert Kimbrough, the following year, in his Norton Critical Edition of the tale, concurred in the views of Edel, and of Cranfill and Clark. In the New York Edition, "James seemed intent on shifting the center of attention away from the details of action observed by the governess to the reactions felt by the governess" (Kimbrough 91).

Disagreement with this widely shared view followed within a half dozen years. E. A. Sheppard was the first to object; in her 1974 book, devoted entirely to *The Turn of the Screw*, Edel, Cranfill and Clark, and Kimbrough are criticized for participating in "a 'chain of error' " (253). On the basis of a line-by-line collation of the 1898 Heinemann edition and the 1908 New York Edition, Sheppard asserts "categorically that, with a single exception, James's revisions in *The Turn of the Screw* not only were stylistic, and merely stylistic, in intention but also, as regards character and incident, effect no change whatever in the impression conveyed to the reader" (253). Reaffirming this view in 1972 was David Timms, who commented in detail on the removal of commas, on stream of consciousness, and on the "feelings" of the governess.

The decade of the fifties opened with a major controversy. Robert E. Young, then an undergraduate at Stanford University, discovered that chapters 28 and 29 in the New York Edition of *The Ambassadors* were in the wrong order, "a mishap," according to Young, "particularly ironic," since James considered the work to be his most perfectly constructed novel. Young concluded, "There must be something radically wrong with a writing style that has managed to obscure an error of this magnitude for so many years from the probing eyes of innumerable readers, publishers, editors, critics, and even the author himself" ("Error" 253). A contretemps then ensued between Edel and Young, with Edel declaring that the reversal does not occur in "the first edition, published by Methuen, in England, two months before the defective American edition" (Edel, "Further Note" 128). The error, according to Edel, is in the American editions and is one of publishing, not authorship. A year later, Young challenged the view that James is absolved from blame because Harper's introduced the error in the first American edition ("Final Note" 489). Young believes James reread *The Ambassadors* for his revisions for the New York Edition and thus "had several opportunities to detect the error, but never did so" ("Final Note" 490). Edel's letter to the editor of *American Literature* continued the debate, with Edel observing that "to argue, as Mr. Young has done, that because an error was made, and the readers have not discovered it, *ergo*: something is wrong with James as a writer, is to make an assumption as ill-founded as it is illogical" ("Letter" 371–72).

Apart from the fireworks over *The Ambassadors*, the 1950s produced studies of the revisions of *Daisy Miller*, "A Passionate Pilgrim," *Watch and Ward*, *What Maisie Knew*, and *The American*. There was another brief flap over *The Ambassadors*; the end of the decade, however, marked the beginning of the ascendancy of *The Portrait of a Lady*, an interest to be resumed at the end of the sixties and to intensify in the early seventies with the publication of the final volume of Edel's biography.

The 1960s produced more than a dozen articles on James's revisions, covering a wide range of works, including "Four Meetings," *The Reverberator*, a reissue of the New York Edition, *The Ambassadors, Daisy Miller, The American, The Spoils of Poynton, Watch and Ward*, "Pandora," *The Portrait of a Lady, The Bostonians*, and *Roderick Hudson*. Three studies closed out the decade of the sixties, all published in 1969. Dominic J. Bazzanella examined the conclusion of *The Portrait of a Lady*, Herbert F. Smith and Michael Peinovich focused on *The Bostonians*, and Sacvan Bercovitch considered the revision of Rowland Mallet in *The American*.

The decade of the 1970s opened with an expression of what has become the continuing central controversy in James's revisions: whether the revised works are new works. In 1972 Edel published the final volume of his five-volume *Life of Henry James*. In discussing James's revisions of *The Portrait of a Lady* for the New York Edition, Edel asserts, "The later Isabel Archer is so altered as to be almost a new personage" (*The Master* 326). Moreover, "the net effect of James's revision . . . and particularly in *The Portrait*, is to enhance the text, and in this instance the rewriting has been so subtle and skillful as to create a new novel." Indeed, "James created a situation in which the early text must be regarded as having its own validity quite distinct from that of the late text. The New York Edition becomes a separate and unique entity" (Edel, *The Master* 329). By 1985, however, with the publication of his one-volume *Henry James: A Life*, Edel had modified—and qualified—his view. "The net effect of James's revisions, and particularly in the *Portrait*, is to enhance the text, and in that instance, the rewriting has been so subtle and skillful as to create *almost* a new novel" (Edel, *A Life* 626, emphasis added).

The rest of the seventies, however, in addition to producing articles asserting the "separate . . . entity" (Edel, *The Master* 329) of the revised *Portrait*, was concerned with a variety of works for a variety of purposes; one essay, on *The Wings of the Dove*, was to be cited in the eighties, in another controversy, as "an epochal article" (Parker, *Flawed Texts* 104).

In 1973, for instance, Adeline R. Tintner referred to Gettmann's observation that "in James's 1907 revision of *The American* the old Marquis's confessional paper included an additional motive for Madame de Bellegarde's murder of her husband and the marrying off of her daughter to M. de Cintré": that Madame de Bellegarde may have committed adultery with M. de Cintré. It is Tintner's view that "a close reading of chapter eight of the early versions of *The American* (1877 and 1879) answers the question." Here she finds Valentin comparing himself and Claire to Orestes and Electra. As Tintner observes, the mother of Orestes and Electra is Clytemnestra, "not only the murderer of their father and her husband, King Agamemnon, but also the lover of Aegisthus, whom she set on her murdered husband's throne. The implication is clear that Mme. de Bellegarde, Claire's and Valentin's mother, is an adulteress as well as a murderess. This appears to have been James's intention from the start'' (''Atreus'' 98–99).

Also in 1973, Maqbool Aziz revisited ''The Pension Beaurepas.'' The first publication of the tale was in the *Atlantic Monthly* for April 1879. Aziz argues that the story (dealing with the international theme) employs satire ''to reflect the currents and cross-currents of individual behaviour'' (''Pension'' 268). James revised the tale for the 1881 two-volume collection *Washington Square, The Pension Beaurepas, A Bundle of Letters* and used the 1881 version as his copy text for the New York Edition. Aziz uses the original version because ''there is little textual difference between the original and the text of 1881'' (''Pension'' 282 n. 2). Aziz argues that James revised ''with [the] definite aim . . . of reviving the notes of irony and satire in his conception and portrayal of the characters'' and that ''in the revisions [the satiric intention] has been recharged and reinforced'' (''Pension'' 268, 271). He holds that '' 'retouching' is the best word which describes James's principle of revision'' and that James is ''reseeing'' (''Pension'' 273). Aziz feels that in the early version ''James failed to produce'' ''the [satiric] effect [he] must have intended . . . in the original'' and concludes that ''by using a variety of the right 'brush strokes,' '' the revision ''brings the final version closer to the archetype of the intention in the author's mind'' (''Pension'' 273, 281).

Additionally in 1973, but on a wholly new subject, Kermit Vanderbilt studied notes, largely musical, regarding James's ''Four Meetings.'' His thesis is that ''the musical side of James's creativity has been slighted in favor of the presumably stronger influence of the pictorial arts.'' It is Vanderbilt's contention that in the frequent revisions, ''James was continually heightening the dynamic structural effects of musical composition in his work,'' a thesis that Vanderbilt feels the three texts of ''Four Meetings'' help to develop (739).

In 1975, Anthony J. Mazzella's ''The New Isabel'' appeared in the Norton Critical Edition of *The Portrait of a Lady* and reintroduced the idea of discrete texts. Mazzella begins his analysis by announcing that the first (American) edition of 1881 and its revised text for the New York Edition ''are two *Portraits*, not one, and . . . each is a different literary experience,'' that ''the new *Portrait of a Lady* published in 1908 was now a changed *Portrait*,'' and that ''the original characters [especially Isabel] exist differently in the revision. And we are responding in a new way to new characters in a new work'' (''Isabel'' 597, 598). To support this thesis, Mazzella evokes, among other items, the famous kiss:

The kiss is a sudden explosion for the early Isabel, nothing more: ''His kiss was like a flash of lightning; when it was dark again she was free.'' But the kiss is so much more for the later Isabel, for in the revised version we finally begin to see *why* Isabel is afraid of the erotic: ''His kiss was like white lightning, a flash that spread, and spread again, and stayed; and it was extraordinarily as if, while she took it, she felt each thing in his hard manhood that had least pleased her, each aggressive fact of his face, his figure, his presence, justified of its intense identity and made one with this act of possession. So had she heard of those wrecked and under water following a train of images before they sink. But when darkness returned she was free." ("Isabel" 610)

Mazzella concludes: "James suggests that, at heart, what Isabel fears is a loss through the erotic of . . . the freedom of the mind to function unimpeded. And he suggests that it is essentially for this reason that she must return to Rome" ("Isabel" 610–11). Robert D. Bamberg, in his Norton Critical Edition "Textual Appendix," adds, "James believed that he had not only 'revised' the [*Portrait* for the New York Edition] but had literally rewritten it" (493).

The following year, Nina Baym's "Revisions and Thematic Change in *The Portrait of a Lady*" also asserts that "the version of 1881 is a different work" (184). In 1978, James W. Tuttleton edited the Norton Critical Edition of *The American*. In "A Note on the Text," Tuttleton, who "prefer[s] the directness and immediacy of the early version of the novel," argues, as do Mazzella and Baym in the case of the *Portrait*, for the existence of two discrete works: "Whatever one may think of James's revisions for the 'New York Edition,' it is clear that the 1907 edition of *The American* is so extensively revised that it is a substantially different book from the novel James composed in the mid–1870s" (*American* 315). Earlier, in 1975, H. K. Girling "collat[ed] a single paragraph of the [holograph] manuscript [at Harvard's Houghton Library] of Henry James's *The Princess Casamassima* with the editions of the novel published in [his] lifetime" to determine the difficulties inherent in a variorum edition ("On Editing" 243).

Sister Stephanie Vincec's 1976 study, " 'Poor Flopping *Wings*': The Making of Henry James's *The Wings of the Dove*," is for a later commentator the single most important article on James's revisions. Its context is Vincec's attempt to read the novel within the New Critical tradition of paying "close attention to the work of art but very little to peripheral information or established critical opinion" (60). When she lost her way with the second volume, where James "seemed to ignore [the connections established in the first] and, without any guidance for the reader, to arrange his elements in a quite different manner" (60), Vincec examined the "peripheral information" of letters, notebook entries, and preface. But since neither notes nor preface "explain[ed] the subtle connections of the double subject," and the "letters neither mention the *Notebooks* nor prepare for the late Preface" (61–62), Vincec investigated the unpublished sources. The result was that these "filled the gaps in the factual history of the making of *The Wings of the Dove*" and "also put the published primary sources into clearer perspective. Finally, they answered, in a way, my questions about the structure of the novel" (63). Vincec concludes: "James's failure to re-read the entire novel before publication or to apply . . . compression left on his hands a too-lengthy novel with structural imbalances that no mere verbal revision could correct. One thing is clear. The author's subtlety has no bearing on the structure of this novel" (93). Moreover, any analysis of the novel "is mistaken which attempts to evaluate this work (perhaps it is unique in this respect) without the benefit of the peripheral information contained in the historical record'' (93).

The 1980s witnessed an explosion in studies of James's revisions, a burst of activity coinciding with the establishment of the *Henry James Review*. James W. Tuttleton, in the premiere volume, devoted an article to rereading *The American*. He points out, ''There has been little discussion, in a century of criticism, over whether it is necessary to choose between [the original and the revision].'' But he does criticize the final text. ''In my judgment, the *doubtful* retouchings constitute a distinctive irritant to readers who are familiar with both texts'' (''Rereading'' 139). Nevertheless, for Tuttleton, ''the revisions [of *The American*] are so extensive [that] no mere emendation of the original, incorporating the changes, is possible'' (''Rereading'' 140). The problem in James's revisions, as formulated by Tuttleton, always comes down to the question of which text to choose, for by choosing any given text, one eliminates all the others. Tuttleton explicitly declares his preference for ''the early version of the novel, the book as young James essentially wrote it in Paris in the mid–1870s. In this regard, I concur with Leon Edel, who has observed that the New York Edition of *The American* 'is almost another book' which 'lacks the pristine qualities, the visual sharpness, and the intensity with which Henry, feeling himself as good as the Europeans, wrote this tale in a Paris that kept him at arm's length' '' (''Rereading'' 140).

In 1980, Richard A. Hocks took *Daisy Miller* on a journey backward into the past. Though the article is not concerned with James's revisions per se, Hocks does bring them up when he states that ''the *Daisy Miller* text that eventually came out of James's revision for his New York Edition'' reflects a paradox. ''The American Daisy-figure underwent an idealized transformation, while the cultural ambience associated with her became, for James's sensibility, part of a poetic past subject to the ravages of the present'' (Hocks, ''*Daisy Miller*'' 169). He reminds us of the consensus that James's revisions give a poetic patina to the earlier comedy of manners. Then Hocks focuses on a feature he sees as ''crucial in interpreting the text'': ''the emphasis on James's 'middle point of view' in the conflict he portrays, and . . . the importance to the story of Winterbourne, who is, after all, our narrative register rather than Daisy'' (''*Daisy Miller*'' 170). But Hocks closes his essay by asserting: ''At best [Daisy and Winterbourne] were perhaps complementary figures. Daisy's enthusiasm and spontaneity needed to be tempered by . . . the critical faculty, whereas Winterbourne . . . was not spontaneous enough. . . . And so the story does remain a true dialectical inquiry, as well as an unforgettable early success of James and American Realism'' (''*Daisy Miller*'' 178). Hocks's essay, by ranging among the different texts to make its points rather than dealing with a single text, an approach practiced by Tintner and others, enhances the argument for a variorum edition.

William T. Stafford, the following year, speculated on future criticism of *The Portrait of a Lady*. He comments on the revisions, speaking of ''the 'two' *Portraits of a Lady*,'' of ''the two Isabel Archers,'' and of ''the strange truth, sort of known by most Jamesians but still somehow not quite worked out, that the early text has a validity . . . [separate] from the later text." Thus, "as [his] first prophecy," Stafford anticipates that "more awareness, more attention, more critical feeding off the disparities and similarities between the *two* versions of the novel is likely to be one major direction . . . which . . . criticism of *The Portrait of a Lady* is to take during its second hundred years" (*"Portrait"* 93).

Also in 1981, Adeline R. Tintner gave *Roderick Hudson* a centennial reading, discussing, among other issues in her wide-ranging essay, the revisions for the New York Edition. Her guiding principle is "to try to figure out what has intervened for James to make [the revision]." She reminds us: "James did his revision on shipboard as he left the United States in 1905 for London. *Roderick* had lost its original chapter headings, which were a hang-over from Hawthorne, in its 1879 revision, when its thirteen original chapters were doubled to twenty-six" (*"Roderick Hudson"* 189). Tintner then considers revisions more or less sequentially as they occur in the novel. For example, she sees many of the additions in the first few chapters emphasizing American details "under the stimulus of the 1904–05 trip" (*"Roderick Hudson"* 189). Later on, the addition of a simile for the Cavaliere's smile ("like the red tip of a cigar seen for a few seconds in the dark") she traces to Joseph Conrad's Marlow through James's close contact with Conrad from 1897 on. In 1902 James had supported a grant for Conrad, "Conrad [had] sent James all his books," and James "concealed a tribute to Conrad's *Heart of Darkness*" in his chapter for *The Whole Family* written in 1906 (*"Roderick Hudson"* 194). In the last section, Tintner discusses "The Third Incarnation of Christina Light," giving us another term to use to try to define a revised text by James.

Thomas M. Leitch, also in 1981, examines Henry James as the hero of the New York Edition. Leitch states, "Because the greater sensitivity James imputes to the consciousness of his central reflectors tends to privilege imaginative over social reality, the New York Edition becomes, as a whole, a parable about the sovereign power of the imagination" (25). Leitch provides another definition of Jamesian revision: "The most vital imaginative activity of all, according to the prefaces, is . . . criticism or revision" (32).

In contrast to Leitch's approach regarding James as hero is Michael Anesko's 1983 article " 'Friction with the Market': The Publication of Henry James's New York Edition," a prelude to his book-length study, which traces James's experiences in trying to assemble the New York Edition. Anesko holds that the critical factor in selecting the short novels and tales was space and that, through the changing evaluation of the New York Edition's design, James "had no preconceived notions about its ultimate arrangement" (*"Publication"* 374). Anesko asserts that James had intended to group his works not chronologically (as Scribner's preferred) but artistically, "to class [his] reprintable productions," in James's own words, "as far as possible according to their kinds" (*AN* 130). Nevertheless, when the edition spilled over into a twenty-fourth volume, James surrendered to the judgment of his editor, W. C. Brownell, arguing that "I feel at last, over the whole business of the preparation and putting-through of the Edition, rather completely *Spent!*" and adding that his own judgment about what to subdivide and expand "refuses, verily, to give another kick!" (Anesko, "Publication" 375 n. 53).

In 1982, Frederick Newberry published "A Note on the Horror in James's Revision of *Daisy Miller.*" Though acknowledging studies by Viola Dunbar in the fifties and Carol Ohmann in the sixties, Newberry asserts, "There remains at least one as yet unnoticed and particularly crucial [revision]—and it involves just a singe word: horror" (229). Newberry argues, "One of the graceful secrets sounded in *Daisy Miller* involves what Winterbourne hears—'whore'—as opposed or in addition to what we see he ought to hear—'horror.'" Newberry concludes, "When Mrs. Costello . . . calls Daisy a 'horror,' . . . there are adequate contextual reasons to suppose that Winterbourne hears 'whore'—a word his aunt would surely never use, a word, indeed not homonymous with 'horror,' but all the same a word so similar in sound to it that rather exacting enunciation is required to prevent the two from sounding alike" (231).

Newberry's article underscores what is emerging as a common chord of consideration involving studies of James's revisions; that is, the interpretive conclusions reached come about only because one *is* doing a study of the revisions. These interpretive conclusions would not result if one were reading any of the texts singly. Because of the shuttle process of going back and forth from one text to another *simultaneously*, we see details that we would otherwise miss. A study of the revisions, then, does not illuminate any one text but, rather, the process itself of studying the revisions.

The following year, George Monteiro used the revisions to examine geography in "The Siege of London," pointing out that the text, in its original 1883 book form, contains "embarrassing errors of geography" involving the American West (144). Also in 1983, B. Richards, using early and revised versions of both *Roderick Hudson* and *The Princess Casamassima*, discovered another model for Christina Light: Eleanor Strong, "another American expatriate of James's Roman years" ("Another Model" 60). Again in 1983, Adeline R. Tintner, examining the revisions for the New York Edition, found a textual error in a sentence in *The Spoils of Poynton* on page 71 of volume 10, a sentence that is correct in the 1897 English and American editions.

By 1984, Hershel Parker tried to apply the brakes to the majority of revision studies. In a polemical chapter, "The Authority of the Revised Text and the Disappearance of the Author: What Critics of Henry James Did with Textual Evidence in the Heyday of the New Criticism," in his book *Flawed Texts and Verbal Icons: Literary Authority in American Fiction*, Parker states that he reviewed "some ninety literary critics" by assembling a "hundred or so items . . . from standard sources" in order to learn what they "had to say about Henry James's revisions of his fiction" (*Flawed Texts* 85). What he found was that they "were mainly critics who remained critics, manifesting no ambition to retool themselves as identifiable textual critics or textual bibliographers and never

claiming to be operating under an editorial theory . . . or a critical theory. . . .
They focused briefly upon the process of composition and revision only as a
means for celebrating one or another finished (or re-finished) product. They
were, to judge from their words, practitioners of the New Criticism without
knowing it" (*Flawed Texts* 86). Parker criticized these critics for "not perform[ing] the basic chores of scholarship," for not relating biography to composition and attendant circumstance to the revisions for the New York Edition.
Parker also challenged the idea that the revisions produced a new work. What
Parker ultimately insists on is that certain "unasked questions" be answered.
"What does it take, the critics might have wondered, for revisions to constitute
a different 'version,' and then what more does it take for revision to push a text
beyond the status of a new version into the status of a different literary work,
'a new work'?" (*Flawed Texts* 107). For Parker, "The critics had . . . succeeded
in converting an essentially extrinsic kind of study into a near-intrinsic kind by
ignoring the way the part and the whole of the literary work functioned as it
was first written" (*Flawed Texts* 101). Nevertheless, Parker cites one "major
exception to all these generalizations": Sister Vincec's article on *The Wings of
the Dove*. "Vincec's is an epochal article . . . an absolutely essential document
in the understanding of late James. Yet she does not tie the whole problem up,
does not fully justify her impressions about the crucial flaw [the split structure]
. . . by internal evidence matched to the brilliantly assembled external evidence.
She names the problem but does not fully analyze it by a 'reading' of the novel"
(*Flawed Texts* 104). In a parting salvo, Parker characterizes most of the commentators on James's revisions as "the pack of academics whom the New
Criticism loosed upon the words of the disembodied Master" (114).

Also in 1984, Parker published a companion piece to the *Flawed Texts* chapter.
In "Henry James 'In the Wood': Sequence and Significance of His Literary
Labors, 1905–1907," he produced "a literary log of the most difficult phase of
James's work on the New York Edition, the period when he was 'retouching'
the first three novels in the series, *Roderick Hudson*, *The American*, and *The
Portrait of a Lady*" (495). At the end of the "literary log," Parker summarizes
how he thinks critics should approach the New York Edition: it is a mistake to
think of James as having completed the revision of one work and its preface
before starting another. Parker then repeats his views on the interrelationships
of the prefaces and other work James was writing—including fiction and nonfiction—to the process of revision. In closing, Parker remarks, "Conscientious
study of Henry James as composer and reviser has hardly begun" ("Henry
James" 513).

The criticism in the years to follow appears to have taken some of its cues
from Parker's strictures, though perhaps not immediately. For example, W. R.
Macnaughton, in a 1985 defense of *The Tragic Muse*, discusses the revisions
only toward the end of the article. It is Macnaughton's view that "James has
improved an extremely impressive 1890 version of [the novel] through the revisions he made for the New York Edition" ("In Defense" 9). Cheryl B. Torsney

in 1986 considered primarily the political context of *The Portrait of a Lady* and
secondarily the revisions. Her thesis is that the *Portrait* is "a novel concerned
obviously with marital confusion and discord caused by distorted expectations
but less obviously with political relationships" (86). When she discusses the
revisions, Torsney finds that "James's distaste for imperialist politics had grown
between 1880, when he began *The Portrait*, and 1906, when he began to revise
it: his hero Gladstone had proven ineffective in dealing with the foreign policy
issue of Irish Home Rule, his friends had formed anti-imperialist leagues, and
he had been exposed during his American tour to the leaders of the American
imperial endeavor" (98). She concludes: "The novel, in both the 1881 and the
1908 editions, is James's indictment of the aggressive imperialist mentality,
based on merely material acquisition, which absorbs not just art and form but
also entire personalities in its quest for quantitative expansion. In retrospect it
is a sad, prophetic novel. . . . By 1881 and certainly by 1908 James sensed an
impending world conflict, the promise of which is implied in the political theme
of *The Portrait of a Lady*" (101).

In his detailed 1986 article "Visions and Revisions: The Past Rewritten,"
Lyall H. Powers investigates "the 'moment' in which the task [of revising *The
Portrait of a Lady*] was undertaken: James's return to America, in August, 1904
(after an absence of two decades), and the importance of Newport, Rhode Island,
for its associations with Minny Temple and as James's 'metaphor of ideal compromise' " (109). Powers sees these events as providing "the ambience and
atmosphere for James's revisions of *The Portrait of a Lady* . . . [leading to] the
increased importance given to Isabel's mind (or consciousness or moral imagination); the augmented theme of the erotic—focused on Caspar's kissing Isabel;
and the deepened emotional appeal of Ralph Touchett." For Powers, "the string
of associations that had kept Minny vivid in his mind . . . all contained an element
that served to distinguish Minny from them. Minny alone had been freed by her
early death, freed from 'this base ignoble world' (as Ralph Touchett is in *The
Portrait*), and thus spared what all the others had to know—the tragedy of love
touched with deep sorrow." The suicides of James's friends Mrs. Henry Adams
and Constance Fenimore Woolson "suggested that 'the great relation of men
and women, the constant world renewal' was perhaps not so great after all. And
James's 'great relation' with [Hendrik] Andersen [the Norwegian-born sculptor]
would soon enough prove unsatisfactory—because, one must assume, of its very
palpable quality" ("Visions" 111). Powers sees the "augmented kiss" in the
novel as having been influenced by James's experience with Andersen; nevertheless, the central influence is Minny Temple's, and "it is clear that Minny
Temple's most important contribution to *The Portrait of a Lady* is to be found
in the character of Ralph Touchett" (112). Powers concludes:

Like James himself following his experience with Hendrik Andersen, Isabel knows now
what the physical offering promises and entails. Where compromise between physical
and spiritual is possible—as James may have sought it in his return to Newport, accom-

panied by Andersen—it can be made; but where choice between them is obliged, as it evidently was for both James and Isabel, there need be no hesitation: devotion to the spirit, to the ghost, must be maintained that its promise be fulfilled: [as Ralph tells Isabel] "You won't lose me—you'll keep me. Keep me in your heart; I shall be nearer to you than I've ever been." ("Visions" 114)

About the early and late texts, Powers concludes: "Each is a distinct and discrete item in the canon. If one seeks to understand the early flowering of James's talent, one will turn to the early version of *The Portrait*. If one seeks an example of that talent at the height of its power, one will turn to the revised version. But truly to appreciate the development and achievement of Henry James as master craftsman and moralist, one must have both—each in its ordered place" ("Visions" 114).

Also in 1986, Adeline R. Tintner published another study of sources, now in the context of icons. Tintner argues, "Since the very name of *The Portrait of a Lady* designates it as a work of art, the novel receives from the first an iconic emphasis" ("Dusky" 140). In the course of her study, she asserts: "The revision for the New York Edition offers us in many ways another novel. The plot has not changed, but certain insertions have been made that alter the sensibility of Isabel Archer and bring her consciousness and imagination up to the expanded imagination of her author" ("Dusky" 146). Later in her article, Tintner explains what she means by "another novel." "It is the intrusion of . . . signs of the new century that makes the revised novel different" ("Dusky" 152).

Among the more recent articles examined in this overview of scholarship on the revisions is Gordon Hutner's 1987 "Goodwood's Lie in *The Portrait of a Lady*." Though Hutner uses the New York Edition text in the Bamberg Critical Edition, he does allude to the revisions. His thesis is communicated in the title: when Goodwood tells Isabel in 1881 that Ralph Touchett "had 'explained everything' and had implored the earnest lover to 'Do everything you can for her; do everything she'll let you,' " he is not telling the truth. He tells Isabel that "Ralph's injunction came at their last conversation," but James makes clear that no such injunction passed during that last conversation in chapter 48 of both the first edition and the New York Edition. Hutner believes that the reason James had Goodwood lie and Isabel deceived once again was to help "clarify the notoriously unsatisfying conclusion of the novel." For "if her earnest suitor is really lying, then her decision [to return to Rome] may be still more acute, from James's perspective, even if Isabel does not know the details of Caspar's deceit. Having seen the ghost of Gardencourt, Isabel knows that this tempting lie in the garden is but the 'next best thing to her dying,' whereas she must choose life as 'her business for a long time to come' " ("Lie" 143). Since proof is not absolute about whether Goodwood did or did not lie, Hutner believes that "in either case, these details of Goodwood's exhortation recall to readers how lies operate throughout the novel to create difficult ambiguities for Isabel, as if characters were insidiously assuming the novelist's desire to see what a young girl would make of herself in a fictionalized set of circumstances. In this Countess Gemini speaks for all, as James represents the case and as Goodwood misrepresents it, when she announces of the scenario she sketches concerning Isabel's antagonists, 'Let us assume that I've invented it!' " " ("Lie" 143–44).

In the last year of the decade of the 1980s, Susan L. Marshall examined James's fragmentary novel in " 'Framed in Death': *The Sense of the Past* and the Limits of Revision," arguing that James was "losing faith in art's ability to structure life" (197). In using terms like *process* and in linking "James and the reader," she anticipates an approach that ushered in the last decade of the twentieth century. Her focus, however, is on the fact that James "began [the novel] in 1899, put it away in 1900 . . . , and came back to his unfinished manuscript in 1914"—especially on "some minor but interesting revisions in the earlier typescript, handwritten by James when he took up his novel again" (198). These revisions concern "a spacious house" becoming an "animated home," and the character Aurora Coyne; simply expressed, "a woman becomes an image, and her image becomes her presence" (200). Marshall sees this "double impression of Aurora" as foreshadowing "Ralph [Pendrel]'s doubling with the [strange] portrait [secreted alone in a small back parlor]" (200). When the portrait figure comes to life and recognizes Ralph, Marshall believes, the novel becomes stillborn. "Ralph was unable to calculate or imagine beforehand how others in the past would respond to him, and the experience of improvising becomes too much for him." She speculates, "Apparently, James was not willing or able to create an artist in precarious control of his material" (205). For Marshall, James put "the troublesome work aside" as a way of resolving the "dilemma" of "objectifying characters . . . [by] subjecting them to his will and [thereby] robbing them of the vitality which inspired his creation" (207). Despite the abortive nature of the work, she believes that "it suggests a step forward in [James's] exploration of the limits of creation" (207).

The decade of the 1990s opened with further exploration of the process of artistic creation and a potentially fruitful direction in the study of James's revisions: Dana J. Ringuette's "The Self-Forming Subject: Henry James's Pragmatistic Revision." Ringuette argues that the critical approach to James's revisions, an approach that compares texts, "misses the mark when it comes to an accounting for James's sense of revision" because "comparison, in this context, presupposes a static sense of similarity and difference which either unites or disunites early and late editions" (117)—a presupposition that is not valid. Citing James's comments on revision in the preface to *The Golden Bowl*, the final preface for the New York Edition, Ringuette asserts that he aims "to examine the concept of revision in [the following] light: to re-see its place in the theoretical paradigm of literary authority and in the critical register of commentary on and by James, and to re-see it within the context of its philosophical counterpart—specifically the 'pragmatism' of Charles Sanders Peirce" (115). Ringuette stresses that his subject is not "variant editions, emendations and particular textual changes and histories.'' Rather, his objective is ''to investigate what sense of artistic agency or authority . . . is yielded by James's notion of 're-seeing,' and to suggest what ramifications such agency would have for readers (including editors) of his works, as well as for his protagonists.'' His principal aim is to show that ''the creative process, for James, simply is revision'' (116). Seizing on James's formulation in the prefaces of one aspect of his creative process as ''an unforeseen principle of growth'' (*AN* 98), Ringuette sees in it ''a decidedly pragmatistic aspect'' (116); for Ringuette, the elements that go into producing a fictional work by James ''exert an influence beyond what the artist wills into them'' and seem to constitute what ''he cannot predict or entirely determine'' (117). According to Ringuette, this ''unforeseen principle of growth'' relates to ''a revised sense of self'' for both the author and the reader. Essentially, ''revision [in James] . . . is a developmental principle revealing an expanding consciousness, constantly realizing growing relations'' (119). Revision, then, is simply the latest manifestation of new awareness. In this principle of revision, which challenges ''fundamental assumptions concerning the nature of self and assumptions about the agency of author, reader and work,'' Ringuette finds a parallel in the philosopher Charles Sanders Peirce's work on ''analytic categories, and his understanding of Doubt and the struggle of inquiry toward Belief'' (121). Ringuette links Peirce's theory of signs, his ''guiding or leading principles of inference,'' with James's ''unforeseen principle of growth'' (122), in which both are ''a nexus of relations which yields a subject''—a self or a ''text'' (123). Self—or ''text''—is knowable only in a ''triadic relation with community and consciousness.'' Ringuette sees consciousness in James as ''a focus within a context of attaching concerns'' and uses *The Portrait of a Lady* as illustration, wherein the subject is ''the intervening ground between [Isabel Archer's] consciousness and community; the subject is the formation—that is, revision—of self'' (125). When Isabel discovers the intimacy between Gilbert Osmond and Serena Merle, Isabel ''has attained an addition to her beliefs and in this sense has reformed her self . . . and has shown that one is in the continual reformation of self'' (127). Ringuette concludes by examining the role of the narrator in James, arguing that the narrator participates in revision, ''finding his own sense of agency processive rather than stable.'' That is, the narrator changes as Isabel changes; because both ''are involved in this process of reforming, the reader's awareness and self-consciousness must undergo a similar process'' (128). Ringuette's contribution to a promising direction in the study of James's revisions is his linking of author, character, and reader in the act of ''continual renewal, reperusal and revision'' and his demonstrating that the ''continuity in life and art . . . is a continuity of contingency and change'' (129). Nevertheless, this approach does not appear to account for the interpretive consequences of why revisions in James occur where they do, with one specific set of words rather than another.

These articles on James's revisions culminated in 1990 with the first book-length study, Philip Horne's *Henry James and Revision*. Horne presents a richly documented argument for the effective power of James's conscious art of revision and for the superiority, in the main, of the later versions over the earlier ones.

In brief, these studies of James's revisions have demonstrated that though the emphasis has been on the revisions for the New York Edition and the approach has been largely interpretive, a number of essays have considered the earliest James novels, those omitted from the New York Edition, and the intermediate stages of revisions. At least two articles have criticized most of the previous studies for neglecting the biographical context, whereas others have consulted not only the texts but also the notebooks, letters, prefaces, and biographies. The conclusions drawn about James's revisions have been equally diverse—ranging from those that contend that James is finally realizing unrealized intentions, is introducing changes anachronistically, and is producing a different work, to those that assert that James is a compulsive reviser, engaging in criticism that constitutes a moral imperative, is the hero of his New York Edition, and is a partner with the reader in expressing continually evolving awareness and growth.

Perhaps one more stop is permissible before journey's end, this time at a work heretofore largely neglected, James's last great novel, *The Golden Bowl*, one of those works that is only briefly but perhaps tellingly revised. It shares revisions with many of the works in the New York Edition: an increase in contractions and a reduction in commas; a loss of relative pronouns in a number of instances; certain Anglicized spellings, like *connexion* for *connection* (*GB* I, 4; *NY* XXIII, 4) and *aesthetically* for *esthetically* (*GB* II, 368; *NY* XXIV, 360); and a number of word reversals, such as "There was no point, visibly" (*GB* II, 369) and "There was visibly no point" (*NY* XXIV, 361). More interestingly, the big scenes are scarcely touched. But when they are, the results are worth noting. For example, "The Princess," the chapter that opens the second volume and that contains Maggie Verver's famous pagoda image "represent[ing] our young woman's consciousness of a recent change in her life" (*NY* XXIV, 4), has except for spelling changes only one substantive revision that may be described as telling. Meditating in retrospect on her decision to meet her husband at home at Portland Place instead of at Eaton Square, Maggie thinks again of his tardy arrival for dinner, in the first text described as "the final lateness of Amerigo's own advent" (*GB* II, 4) and in the New York Edition as "Amerigo's own irruption" (*NY* XXIV, 11). In this novel, with its "hieratic" overtones and its clandestine meeting in a cathedral, *advent* would communicate, perhaps, an unintended annunciation, whereas *irruption* strikes both the impending note of upheaval in Maggie's relation to the prince and her ever present sense of his physical presence, his beauty, and his erotic power over her.

Sometimes the revisions are less successful. In his consistent practice to introduce contractions in the New York Edition, James altered the following pronouncement by Charlotte about Adam Verver's love for his daughter: from "The greatest affection of which he is capable" (*GB* I, 263) to "The greatest affection of which he's capable" (*NY* XXIII, 262). Surely, Charlotte's recognition of "her place'' in Adam Verver's affections requires that every syllable of every word be enunciated, and the deepened quality of her estrangement is lost by this contracted revision in the New York Edition.

This journey through James's and the critics' discussions of his revisions (including on average in recent years almost an annual dissertation on the subject) leaves us, I think, with a clear sense that when the texts are revised, the meanings change, and that there is a demonstrable need for a variorum edition of James's fiction. James may very well have anticipated just such a need, for he has Maggie Verver, in both texts, speak of ''an intelligent comparison, a definite collation positively''! (*GB* II, 330; *NY* XXIV, 322).

# III
# HENRY JAMES'S NONFICTION

# 15

# On the Use of James's Notebooks

*Lyall H. Powers*

Behind my simple title lies a mild ambiguity, for there are really two questions to be addressed under this heading: what use did James make of the notebooks and of what use are they to us, more or less scholarly critical readers at the end of the twentieth century? Evidently the two categories of "use" overlap and to some extent virtually coincide. First of all, however, it should be understood that the term *notebooks* here covers the variety of material included in *The Complete Notebooks of Henry James*: the nine scribblers of handwritten notes, with the earliest entry November 7, 1878, and the latest May 10, 1911; the seven pocket diaries, with the earliest entry May 6, 1909, and the latest October 26, 1915; handwritten notes for the play *The Chaperon*, for the unfinished novel *The Ivory Tower*, and for the unfinished tale "The E.P.D. Subject"; and typescript notes from James's dictation for a number of works—his "Project" for *The Ambassadors*, both unfinished novels *The Ivory Tower* and *The Sense of the Past*, his unfinished story "Hugh Merrow," and so on. Six of those scribblers were useful to James chiefly for recording his ideas for novels and tales and plays and for the development (to a greater or lesser extent) of the ideas; two of them (the American Journals, 1881–82 and 1904–5) were useful as autobiographical reminiscences of his life in the United States and as an occasion for justifying to himself his decision to become an expatriate; and the ninth (August 22, 1907, to October 10, 1909, the "little red book") he used for notes on "London Town"—not just the city proper but the whole metropolis that is officially Westminster.

Taking notes was always an important part of Henry James's career, evidently from the earliest years. The text of the second book he published, *Transatlantic Sketches* (1875), is just a step away from the notes on which the various essays were based; many of the constituent pieces still frankly indicate this in their titles—"Swiss Notes" (1872), "Florentine Notes" (1874)—and several of them remain in diary form. But the practice of regularly noting down impressions, ideas, phenomena—the actual forming of a habit of note-taking—was later in coming. The earliest note we have is dated November 7, 1878; three years later, however, James is still acutely aware that he hasn't yet got into the habit. His first American Journal begins (Brunswick Hotel, Boston, November 25, 1881):

> If I should write here all that I might write, I should speedily fill this as yet unspotted blank-book, bought in London six months ago, but hitherto unopened. It is so long since I have kept any notes, taken any memoranda, written down my current reflections, taken a sheet of paper, as it were, into my confidence. Meanwhile so much has come and gone, so much that it is now too late to catch, to reproduce, to preserve. I have lost too much by losing, or rather by not having acquired, the note-taking habit. . . . I ought to endeavour to keep, to a certain extent, a record of passing impressions, of all that comes, that goes, that I see, and feel, and observe. (*NO* 213–14)

We recognize here the voice of the novelist for whom experience consisted of impressions and whose art was increasingly devoted to the effective conveying of the importance of impressions as experience. James would soon enough (September 1884), in "The Art of Fiction," declare, "A novel is in its broadest definition, a direct impression of life; that, to begin with, constitutes its value, which is greater or less according to the intensity of the impression." To that he adds the equally familiar insistence on "the importance of exactness—of truth of detail": "the air of reality (solidity of specification) seems to me to be the supreme virtue of a novel . . . it is here that [the author] competes with his brother the painter in *his* attempt to render the look of things" (*LC*-I, 50, 53). The emphasis is on catching the very note and trick of life, and the usefulness of the notebook in recording the catch is clearly implied. James remained faithful to the idea; he repeated it with even sharper emphasis a quarter of a century later in the preface to *The Ambassadors* (1909): "Art deals with what we see, it must first contribute full-handed that ingredient; it plucks its material, otherwise expressed, in the garden of life—which material elsewhere grown is stale and uneatable. But it has no sooner done this than it has to take account of a *process*— . . . . The process, that of the expression, the literal squeezing-out, of value is another affair—with which the happy luck of mere finding has little to do" (*LC*-II, 1308).

The notebooks, especially the six scribblers, were used as repositories of James's impressions of life, "the look of things"; and of particular interest is the caught kernel of an idea that seemed to promise fruitful development—what he called a "germ" or "*donnée*." These scribblers are full of such germs. Perhaps the most familiar is in the entry dated October 31, 1895, in which James notes what young Jonathan Sturges had told him of the advice given him by a sad William Dean Howells, "in the evening, as it were, of life": "Live all you can: it's a mistake not to. It doesn't so much matter what you do—but live"

(*NO* 140–41). James adds this comment: "It touches me. . . . Immediately, of course—as everything, thank God, does—it suggests a little situation" (*NO* 141). And so the note continues, developing the idea of the figure of an elderly man, who turns out to be Lewis Lambert Strether of *The Ambassadors* (1903), and his involvement in the career of Chad Newsome; and the little situation burgeons into a substantial novel. In fact, James often conceived of the given germ as likely to develop into something small and neat, yet he always had to fight his tendency to expand and expand. That he often lost the fight is a fact for which we must be grateful. Another such example, noted under November 28, 1892, "about a simultaneous marriage, in Paris (or only 'engagement' as yet, I believe), of a father and a daughter," is clearly a preliminary sketch—as James develops it for a page and a half—of Adam and Maggie Verver for *The Golden Bowl* (1904) and also of the other two marriage partners, not quite yet unmistakably Charlotte and Amerigo, but the relationship itself is fixed. James observes, "I see a little tale, *n'est-ce pas?*" (*NO* 74). An interesting coincidence is that further development of this germ shares the entry of February 14, 1895, with further development of the germ of "the dying girl who wants to live," which is, of course, *The Wings of the Dove* (1902).

The scribblers are, as I say, full of these kernels to be fostered and carefully tended. James would occasionally gather them into lists—and the tendency increased as he approached the new century, the twentieth. See, for example, December 21, 1895:

. . . provisional labels of the *sujets de roman* . . .

1° *La Mourante*: the girl who is dying, the young man and the girl he is engaged to. [*The Wings of The Dove*]

2° *The Marriages* (what a pity I've used that name!): the Father and Daughter, with the husband of the one and the wife of the other entangled in a mutual passion, an intrigue. [*The Golden Bowl*]

3° *The Promise*: the *donnée* that I sketched (I have it all), as a three-act play for poor E. C. [*The Other House*, for Edward Compton; see December 26, 1893] (*NO* 146)

A variation of this kind of list is to be found under the date February 15, 1899; it is a more fully annotated list and the beginning, thus, of actual development.

Development does not always, as we have seen, accompany the noting of the *donnée* or germ; sometimes it is simply postponed and sometimes then extended over several subsequent entries—and not always in the same scribbler. He was not regular in his use of the scribblers but tended to work on whatever blank pages presented themselves. But his technique of development resembles nothing so much as a discussion. He uses the pages of the notebooks to talk things over with himself, explaining what he sees as the interesting possibilities of a germ—what facet might be turned toward the audience, how he will manage that, and (most important) to what end or what point. The discussion is often quite formal; it sometimes seems like a distinct performance intended for the public eye. In fact, however, all that was quite a private affair, as can easily be seen by comparing the scribbler notes with those definitely intended for a kind of publication—the "Project for Novel," for example, sent to Harper, publisher of *The Ambassadors*—or the typed notes taken at his dictation.

When "writer's cramp" struck James during the winter of 1896–97 and he had to resort to secretarial aid, his manner of "discussion" changed; for one thing, it was no longer *private* dialogue. Yet he did cling to something like a talk with himself as preliminary to actual development; Theodora Bosanquet, his last amanuensis, called the performance "jawbation"—a vocal equivalent. Occasionally such activity intruded on the actual dictation; the rough-copy typescript of his essay "Mr. and Mrs. Fields" (intended for the *Cornhill Magazine* and the *Atlantic Monthly* in 1915) contains two passages illustrative of such intrusion. These lack the *brio*, the very performance quality of James writing to James; it is as though he was intimidated by the ear of Miss Bosanquet (see *NO* 536–58).

At the other end of the spectrum of James's self-communion as illustrated by the scribblers is the cluster of impassioned invocations and appeals "to all the powers, forces, and divinities to whom I've ever been loyal and who haven't failed me yet—after all: never, never yet!" (January 4, 1910, *NO* 260). These calls for succor—inescapably private, personal, and on a few occasions ecstatic—are typically addressed to his muse, usually called "*mon bon*." (He often lapses into French at charged moments of dialogue with himself or the muse—or *daimon*—as though he felt it a tongue more appropriate for intimate intercourse.) These appeals occur at moments of evident stress, of particular excitement, of barely controlled rapture. The earliest I have found of instances of this kind of dramatic monologue occurs in the first American Journal, under the date December 26, 1881; James is there enthusiastically anticipating the opportunity of writing for the theater—"the most cherished of all my projects . . . one of my earliest. . . . None has given me sweeter emotions" (*NO* 226). He then reviews his experience of the French stage, the work of Alexander Dumas fils, Victorien Sardou, Émile Augier; the direct vocative intrudes: "No, my dear friend, nothing of all that is lost. *Ces émotions-la ne se perdent pas; elles rentrent dans le fonds même de notre nature; elles font partie de notre volonté.* The *volonté* has not expired; it is only perfect today" (*NO* 227). Some further light on the identity of that friend, *mon bon*, is afforded by a passage in "The Art of Fiction" (which he began some sixteen months after the entry just quoted). Commenting on Walter Besant's exhortation that the writer make his characters "clear in outline," James observes, "how he shall make them so is a secret between his good angel and himself" (*LC*-I, 54).

James's running dialogue with himself and especially his communion with his good angel, "*mon bon [ange]*," will be of interest to anyone who cares how a literary artist's mind works—what factual data strike the sensitive soul as promising, how the artist then stirs them about and frets over their possibilities and seeks the means of realizing their potential artistically. What helps us to know the artist and aids our understanding of the artistic process contributes to our appreciation of the end product, the literary text.

The notebooks are useful to us as a source of information about James, in a variety of ways: to begin with, two of the scribblers are quite specifically and intentionally autobiographical. The American Journal I, beginning with an entry for November 25, 1881, and ending with an entry for November 11, 1882, records James's thoughts and feelings at the moment of repatriation after an absence of half a dozen years—an absence he originally intended to be much longer. This journal gives James the opportunity to justify his commitment to living abroad; that is the note sounded early: "I have made my choice, and God knows that I have now no time to waste. My choice is the old world—my choice, my need, my life. . . . it is an inestimable blessing to me . . . My work is there— and with this vast new world, *je n'ai que faire.* . . . My impressions of America . . . I don't need to write them (at least not *à propos* of Boston)" (*NO* 214). He adds, a year later, "Boston is absolutely nothing to me—I don't even dislike it" (*NO* 232).

His reminiscences of the preceding five years give a capsule summary of his removal to France (October 20, 1875) and setting up in Paris "with the idea that I should spend several years there" (*NO* 215), his meeting with the French writers, the grandsons of Balzac, his dissatisfaction with "the little American 'set' . . . ineffably tiresome and unprofitable" (*NO* 216), his happy move to London and gradual entry into London society and his election to the cherished Reform Club, and finally his getting down to serious work on *The Portrait of a Lady* in Italy. The American Journal I is a helpful supplement to his autobio- graphical volumes written a generation later and especially to *Notes of a Son and Brother*. An interesting feature of this journal specifically anticipates that volume of 1914 and casts additional light on James's lifelong love-hate rela- tionship with his native land. In a late entry, when he was back in Cambridge for Christmas 1881, he records the visit of his brother Wilky, whom he has not seen for eleven years, and emphasizes the effect of that reunion: "The long interval of years drops away. . . . The feeling of that younger time comes back to me in which I sat here scribbling, dreaming, planning, gazing out upon the world in which my fortune was to seek. . . . But all that is sacred; it is idle to write of it today. XXXXX" (*NO* 224–25). Yet he does resume writing of it: "What comes back to me freely, delightfully, is the vision of those untried years. . . . I knew at least what I wanted then . . . I wanted to do very much what I have done, and success, if I may say so, now stretches back a tender hand to its younger brother, desire" (*NO* 225).

Home as found awakens homesickness for the cordial English fireside in Piccadilly, homesickness aggravated by his exasperation at the imperfect America he has had to meet; yet beyond and beneath that is the strangely touching nostalgia for an earlier good time, a good *American* time—very much like Mark Twain's nostalgia for the good old times on the Mississippi "when I was a boy." This nostalgic tone nicely harmonizes with that of the last quarter of *Notes of a Son and Brother*, where James rehearses his experience of Cambridge and Harvard Law School. Chapter 9 begins, "I went up from Newport to Cambridge early in the autumn of '62 and on one of the oddest errands . . . I could possibly have undertaken" (*NS* 270). Two chapters later the inveterate expatriate focuses on the mid-sixties, the end of the Civil War and the death of Nathaniel Hawthorne. The nostalgia, the oddly patriotic theme, emerges as he dwells on the essence of Hawthorne's art:

His work was all charged with a *tone*, a full and rare tone of prose. . . . And the tone had been, in its beauty—for me at least—ever so appreciably American; which proved to what a use American matter could be put by an American hand: a consummation involving, it appeared, the happiest moral. For the moral was that an American could be an artist, one of the finest, without "going outside" about it, . . . quite in fact as if Hawthorne had become one just by being American *enough*, by the felicity of how the artist in him missed nothing, suspected nothing, that the ambient air didn't affect him as containing. (*NS* 383–84)

The American Journal II further fleshes out this aspect of Henry James's view of his native land. The earliest dated note is for December 11, 1904; it is preceded by a brief, incomplete note, undated but clearly just a few days earlier. The last entry is dated March 30, 1905. James is back in America after an absence of more than twenty years to pursue a transcontinental lecture tour and arrange for publication of the collective edition of his fiction by Scribner. On the whole, he did not at all like what he found: his impressions are recorded in a series of articles gathered together in *The American Scene* (1907). But the notes dwell on and linger over the very years nostalgically caressed in American Journal I and fondly recalled in the last quarter of *Notes of a Son and Brother*—the sixties. These two journals—anticipating and supplementing the later volumes I indicate—help us to understand the meaning of that decade in James's life. He hovers over and ponders Cambridge and Harvard; the present impression propels him inescapably into the past. "I seem to myself to hang over 2 other interwoven strands—my own little personal harking back to the small old superceded Law-School (in presence of the actual—the big new *modern*); and some sort of glance at one's old vision of Memorial Hall" (*NO* 236–37). Three months later, when he is at the midpoint of his lecture tour and finds himself at the southern tip of California, his mind harks back to Cambridge, and again the nostalgic demon is insistent. "I feel as if I could *spread* on C[ambridge], and that is my danger. . . . For *my* poor little personal C. of the far-off unspeakable past years, hangs there behind, fixing me with tender, pleading eyes, eyes of such exquisite pathetic appeal and holding up the silver mirror, just faintly dim, that is like a sphere peopled with the old ghosts" (*NO* 238). He identifies many of the ghosts by name; then comes the clear, frank explanation of the nostalgia: "The point for me . . . is that I knew there, *had* there, in the ghostly old C. that I sit and write of here by the strange Pacific on the other side of the continent, *l'initiation première* (the divine, the unique), there and in Ashburton Place'' (*NO* 238). He mentions "The 'epoch-making' weeks of the spring of 1865!'' and the summer at Newport and North Conway, "the following summer at Swampscott—'66 . . . the unforgettable groupings and findings and sufferings and strivings and play of sensibility and of inward passion there'' (*NO* 238).

The further he gets from the 1860s, the more significant, the more important those years seem to him, and it is hard to escape the sense that for him they were the crucial moment of his life. There is, in fact, a brief dictated note (1900–1901) that really clinches the matter; it is called, significantly, "The Turning Point of My Life'' and was evidently the response to a request from W. D. Howells. James locates the point early in the decade of the sixties, the academic year 1862–63 spent at Harvard Law School, Dane Hall; there, at that time, he seems to have made his definite commitment to the profession of writer.

I brought away with me certain rolls of manuscript that were quite shamelessly not so many bundles of notes on the perusal of so many calfskin volumes [of the Law]. These were notes of quite another sort, small sickly seed enough, no doubt, but to be sown and to sprout . . . in a much less trimmed and ordered garden than that of the law. . . . I must there, in the cold shade of queer little old Dane Hall, have stood at the parting of my ways. (*NO* 437–38)[1]

The first blossom to sprout from "this soil that so little favored it'' (*NO* 438) appeared in 1864—the year of James's majority, the year of Hawthorne's death—and led to further groupings, sufferings, and strivings of the nascent artist.

The "play of sensitivity and of inward passion'' is a further reference, of course, to the young artist's endeavors, but they refer as well to another facet of the dearly remembered decade, to another kind of passion, surely. For there is a name lurking between the lines of American Journal II that rapturously recall Newport, North Conway, and Swampscott, the name Mary "Minny'' Temple. She was surely the deepest love of Henry James's life, his constant guiding spirit, the sweetest of the ghosts of his past. He said his final farewell to Minny Temple (unaware that it would be so) in 1869, when he embarked on his first journey abroad alone. The fact of her persistent presence in his life is made quite explicit in *Notes of a Son and Brother*, and it is with his vivid memories of Minny Temple that the volume closes.

I was in the far-off aftertime to seek to lay the ghost by wrapping it . . . in the beauty and dignity of art. The figure that was to hover as the ghost has at any rate been of an extreme pertinence, I feel, to my doubtless too loose and confused general picture. . . . Much as this cherished companion's presence among us had represented for William and myself . . . her death made a mark that must stand here for a too waiting conclusion. We felt it together as the end of our youth. (*NS* 479)

The passage alludes specifically enough to Milly Theale, heroine of *The Wings of the Dove*, but *The Portrait of a Lady* was much in James's mind and expressly in his notes during the writing of the passages in American Journal I: the novel had just been published (1880–81). Negotiations for the New York Edition and the consequent reviewing and revising of his earliest works were near the front of James's mind during the closing months of American Journal II—not least, revision of *The Portrait*. The very language of those final lines of *Notes of a Son and Brother* blatantly echoes the language that recounts Isabel Archer's sense of the death of Ralph Touchett and the fulfillment of his prophecy that she might—if she lived to suffer enough—be able to see the ghost of Gardencourt, as it is presented at the opening of the final chapter of the novel. Ralph had promised her, "You won't lose me—you'll keep me. Keep me in your heart; I shall be nearer to you than I've ever been."[2]

Six of the other seven scribblers (the seventh contains preparatory notes for the unfinished "London Town" project) are devoted principally to James's concerns as an artist, but they contain a good deal of biographical information—his whereabouts on a given date, what he has been reading, whom he has visited, who have been his guests, and which of these have been the sources of which possible ideas for stories. The seven pocket diaries, which cover the period from February 1909 to October 1915, are a rich resource of quotidian biographical information; they are mainly appointment books and provide many more specific details of his social activities and visits (both as guest and host)—giving date, even hour, and address—than one finds in the scribblers. The information is, unfortunately, not entirely reliable. It is quite clear that James often used the diaries to record social events after the fact rather than just to remind him of appointments to be kept; and his memory occasionally played him false. An early example is the last entry for August 1909:

*30 August 1909 Monday*
Go to Mrs. D'Almeida-Corey 4. [James crosses out "Go up to see Mrs. Curtis (?) (or next day.)"] (*NO* 307)

The diaries contain not only many items crossed out as erroneous but also more than a few others that are erroneous but *not* crossed out. The diary entries need the reliable confirmation of other resources (e.g., letters sent and—such as escaped his bonfires—received).

In spite of these features, the list of James's social contacts noted laconically in the diaries, both people and milieus, provides a rather full account of the setting in which the social drama of Edwardian and Georgian England (and to some extent of contemporary Paris as well) was staged; and the list indicates, furthermore, the eclectic and catholic quality of that society in which an easy mingling of individuals from various walks of life—the ambassadorial, political, literary, and artistic—was to be found. With that we find a perhaps surprising mixture of English and American, aristocrats and commoners, in the social gatherings—surprising until we recall that many of these English aristocrats were originally American and hence commoners. We might look, for example, at the last few entires before Christmas 1909:

*7 December 1909 Tuesday*
Went afternoon theatre with Eliz Robins—in her box. Bariatinsky in Hedda Gabler. [Lydia Yavorska, wife of the Russian Prince Bariatinsky.]
*9 December 1909 Thursday*
Went to tea Lady Lovelace and John Buchan. Stayed dinner, but came away early to go Haymarket to 1st performance *Blue Bird* in Mme Maeterlinck's box. Went with her and Mrs. Sutro afterwards to supper at Sutro's—Maeterlinck with S. (*NO* 311)

Or we might look at the bustle of entries for November 1911: November 16, "Dined Mrs. Waldorf Astor's, 4 St. James's Square, Prince Arthur, Lord Curzon, Lady Essex etc."; November 18, "Lady Jekyll 5:30"; November 19, "Lady D. Nevill"; November 21, "Lady Mond"; November 24, "Ethel Sands"; November 26, "Hill Hall: Helleu and daughter, Sargent, Percy Grainger, etc." Or we might note the tantalizingly brief string of entries recounting his visit with Edith Wharton to the Astors' Cliveden on the Thames, from July 27 to August 2, 1912, interrupted by tea with the Ranee of Sarawak at Ascot ("Vernon Lee was there") and by James's severe "pectoral attack!" I especially like the little account of tea (September 1, 1912) at the Protheros' Dial Cottage in Rye's High Street—"where came Violet Markham and one *King*, young Canadian 'statesman,' whom I brought round to garden here etc." (*NO* 367). Said King was William Lyon Mackenzie King (1874–1950), who was to be Canada's longest-serving prime minister, 1921–30 and 1935–48.

The diaries record, accurately, James's sitting for his portrait, during his last visit to the United States, for his nephew Billy James, beginning March 4, 1911, for four consecutive days, and then for Cecilia Beaux (whose name he regularly spelled "Baux") just twice in April after Helena Gilder's arrangements with the painter on April 5. Less than a year later they record his sitting three times for John Singer Sargent (January 24, February 1, March 13, 1912) for a charcoal drawing commissioned by Edith Wharton. Finally we find the record of his sitting, as part of the celebration of his seventieth birthday, for Sargent in his Chelsea studio (again) ten times between May 18 and June 24, 1913 (the famous portrait now hangs in the National Portrait Gallery in London) and for the young sculptor Derwent Wood (for a bust) on seven consecutive days, July 9–15, after Sargent had introduced them on June 30.

The diary entries for the year of his final visit to his native land, returning with his dying brother William and his wife, that is from the end of August 1910 to the beginning of August 1911, constitute a useful supplement to the American Journals as an autobiographical account of James's American years—as well as of nagging ill health and his various attempts at a cure. Indeed, the diaries keep fairly close track of the state of James's health in these later years and indicate at the same time a somewhat surprising stamina in the old gentleman:

he always managed to maintain a pretty full social schedule in spite of all. The entries for the early months of 1914 include a relentless regimen of dental attention following the "momentous interview" of February 2 with his dentist, Dr. George Field; the next several pages are dotted with mention of his visits—six weeks' worth—during which most of his teeth were extracted, and he was fitted with replacement "machinery." Another example of that surprising stamina—surprising especially to one who knows London—is contained in the account of one of James's long walks (he was properly convinced of the virtue of walking for one's health); the date is April 3, 1914, some two weeks after the last of his bouts with the dentist: "Long resolute walk from Piccadilly Circus down to Westminster and thence all along the Embankment to the corner of Chelsea Hospital Road. I was more than 3 hours—nearer 4—on foot—the length of the effort was the effective benefit—and this benefit was signal. I broke the hideous spell of settled *sickness*" (*NO* 395).

A further biographical supplement, appearing to the unpracticed eye to be as dull as dishwater, is provided by James's cash accounts and his list of addresses. The accounts offer a useful insight into James's financial activities, both income and disbursements. He usually kept track of these items in the appropriate pages at the end of each annual diary—"Financial Records" or "Memoranda"—although he sometimes included them in the dated sections. We find the record of royalties from his agent Pinker, from the various houses (Harper, Heinemann, Houghton Mifflin, Macmillan, Scribner), and sometimes both—January 5, 1909, "From Pinker Scribner Royalties £10.0.0." Very often the individual source is specified—for June 17, 1909, "From Harper and Bros for 'Crapy Cornelia' less J.B.P.'s commission 92.3.6," or later that year, November 4, "From Pinker as Harper's advance on *Julia Bride* 180.0.0." The saddest of these give the depressing account of returns on the New York Edition—see, for example, the entry for January 2, 1914.

James also kept fairly regular records of income generated by real estate in Syracuse, New York, which he and his brother William inherited from their father and which was managed by William's son Harry. Initially, monthly payments are noted at £51 (with the January sum always notably larger, ca. £82) or at $250 when he was in the United States (1910–11); subsequently, irregular payments were evidently controlled by Harry at his uncle's instructions. Syracuse income alone gave James over $3,000 a year; it is instructive to compare that sum with the annual rent for his flat in Chelsea, about $850—see the disbursement for March 24, 1913, "Paid 1st quarter rent Carlyle Mansions £42.7.0" (the exchange rate was about £1 to $5). There is also James's record of taxable income and taxes paid as well as of his life insurance premiums and dividends for these years of his life.

The lists of addresses give just about what one would expect, with a few surprises. Bruce Porter of San Francisco, listed in 1909 and also in 1910, is mildly interesting as an acquaintance James made during his 1904–5 American lecture tour but is more important as the future husband of Henry's niece Margaret

Mary "Peggy" James; and the 1911 listing of Edward Sheldon, N.Y.—American dramatist (1886–1946)—gains luster from the diary entries that record James's attendance at the premiere of Sheldon's play *The Boss* in New York on January 30, 1911, and Sheldon's visit to Lamb House on July 28, 1914. Most surprising, maybe, is another item for 1911: "Francis Viélé-Griffin, 16 Quai de Passy, Paris." James's connection with this Franco-American Symbolist poet (a confrère of Stuart Merrill) remains something of a mystery, but given James's association with Charles Du Bos, André Gide (see diaries for New Year's Eve 1912 and New Year's Day 1913), Maurice Maeterlinck, and others, it is not altogether incredible. The addresses give us a glimpse into private household matters, James's complacencies of the peignoir, with the listing of two Swedish masseurs (seemingly distinct but suspiciously near neighbors—one in Carlyle Place, Victoria St. S.W., and the other in Carlyle Mansions, Victoria, S.W.); a barber in Kensington (Maison Jean Strobeau); and an "Aurist," Harold Barwell F.R.C.S., in Queen Anne Street. James often jotted down in his scribblers little utterances that struck him as typical of this or that sort of speaker—for August 22, 1885: "Phrases of the people . . . a young man, of his *patron*, in a shop . . . 'he cuts it very fine.' . . . ''Ere today, somewhere else tomorrow: that's 'is motto.' '' There is a gentle ironic echo of one of these in an address for 1914; for April 8, 1883, "A good (American) comparison: 'As . . . and as silent as a chiropodist" (*NO* 20); the echoing address—"Benjamin May, Chiropodist, 13 King's Road," etc.

In the eyes of many Jamesians, the most genial use of the notebooks is to be found in what they tell us, more or less directly, about the stories themselves— from the original germ to the penultimate, immediately prepublication phase. It is instructive, certainly, to pay attention to the kinds of ideas that recommended themselves to James and so became actual novels and tales; it might also be a fruitful pursuit to ponder those accepted *données* that never did benefit from his fructifying artistic care. There are lists of undeveloped germs, gathered up and fondled devotedly and repeatedly—ideas that one might expect would have *demanded* his artistic treatment but did not (and often to one's chagrin). See, for example, the lists for December 21, 1895, for May 7, 1898, and for May 10, 1899 (and see also, of course, the footnotes provided for those lists). Then there remains the intermediary group, the half-developed germs—the stories left incomplete. The most famous and best known of these, because they are the most substantial and (perhaps) furthest developed, are *The Ivory Tower* and *The Sense of the Past*. For both of these we have various stages of development; for *Tower*, the germinal note of February 10, 1909, the sketch "The K. B. Case and Mrs. Max" (1909–10), and the full-blown "Notes for *The Ivory Tower*" (1914); for *Sense*, the germinal note of August 9, 1900, the "First Statement" (1914), and "Notes for *The Sense of the Past*" (1914–15). There are two partially completed tales. The first, barely a fragment two pages in length, is called "The E.P.D. Subject (Summer of 1893, June)"; it is tantalizingly supported by the fairly substantial notes of February 28, 1892, and of June 15, 1901 (*NO* 65, 196). It looks promising; it is based on a *crime passionel*—Edward Parker

Deacon's murder of his wife's lover. Deacon's daughter Gladys became the second wife of the ninth Duke of Marlborough (her predecessor was Consuelo Vanderbilt); it is an international episode—doubly so, in fact! The second tale, "Hugh Merrow," is a twenty-three-page typescript that looks impressively finished—as far as it goes. Difficult to date accurately, it was possibly dictated between September 11, 1900, and June 12, 1901: a note under the earlier date is still anticipatory, whereas that under the latter strongly suggests that at least a good start has been made. Hugh Merrow is a portraitist to whom a childless couple come to ask that he do a portrait of a child—theirs, the one they have never had and will never have. James got the idea from Paul and Minnie Bourget when they visited with him at Torquay in September 1895; they presented the idea as a story by the Italian novelist Luigi Gualdi—or at least as his idea for a story. James did nothing with it, evidently because he was discouraged by the belief that the story was someone else's; but the general idea haunted him, that of painting the portrait of someone who never in fact existed. One version of the idea, "Gualdo's story of the child *retournée*," is given sketchy development on May 7, 1898 (*NO* 169); it became the tale "Maud-Evelyn" (1900). But that note is followed by another version, a woman who wants to create a respectable past via the portrait of a deceased husband she has never had—"The Tone of Time" (1900)—which adds another ironic wrinkle. On February 16, 1899, James looks again at the "idea of the portrait *à la* Gualdo" and confesses "it haunts me" (*NO* 179). Then, on September 11, 1900, he reveals that another word from the Bourgets has enabled him to deal freely with the haunting idea. What he says there is particularly useful in offering a couple of glimpses into the working of the artist's mind. First, "I learned last month from P. B. what makes the little 'Gualdo' notion of 'The Child' really . . . quite *disponible* to me on my own lines. They know nothing of his ever having *written or published* such a tale." He continues, helpfully: "it is moreover a question for me of a mere *point de départ*: that a young childless couple comes to a painter and asks him to *paint* them a little girl (or a child *quelconque*) whom they can have as their own—since they so want one and can't come by it otherwise. My subject is what I can get out of *that*. . . . *Me voilà donc libre. Bon!* XXXXX" (*NO* 192). That observation ought to recall the little development of the May 7, 1898, note on the Gualdo story *retournée* that became "Maud-Evelyn"—especially the ending: "35 pages. (Subject—subject)." In each case, he has hold of his *story*; he has yet to discover what it is truly "all about"—its *point*, its subject. To put it another way, he has the wherewithal to convey "the look of things"—the childless couple, the husbandless dead girl—but has yet to decide what *meaning* that "look" shall be arranged to convey. There they remain, as if waiting for another Ivy Compton-Burnett to happen along and awaken them into quasi-Jamesian life.

A related phenomenon is the set of notes for a play to be made from the short story "The Chaperon"; we have the germinal notes for the tale (July 13, 21, 1891), a pair of notes for a play by that name (1893), and finally the "Rough

Statement for *The Chaperon*'' (1907), which runs to twenty-five pages in *The Complete Notebooks* and is composed of substantial snatches of dialogue and of substantial chunks of explanatory and exploratory prose.

The case of *The Chaperon* as a prose-fiction derivative rather than a literary work left incomplete leads us to another Jamesian phenomenon well documented by the notebooks—the realized adaptation of one genre into another. The longest interval between original and reprisal, almost two decades, is marked by the tale "Owen Wingrave" (1892; see notes of March 26 and May 8, 1892) and the play *The Saloon* (January 1911 opening; see note of November 15, 1910). The most complex affair begins with the one-act play for Ellen Terry, *Summersoft* (never produced; see notes of November 24, 1892, and February 6, 1895), becomes the tale "Covering End" (1898), and is staged in 1908 as the three-act *The High Bid*. Then there is the play *The Other House* (originally thought of as *The Promise*; see notes of December 26, 1893, and January 23, 1894), which was laid aside, resumed, published as a novel of that title (1896), and finally readied for production (1909), which it never achieved. *The Outcry*, intended for a repertory series that was cancelled because of the death of Edward VII (1910), became a surprisingly successful novel (1911; see James's dust-jacket blurb, probably of July of that year).

It is, however, hardly surprising at all that every one of these cases except the last has its roots in the 1890s—the "dramatic years"—for the call of the theater was then sounding strongly and insistently in James's ear. But the point not to be missed is that we touch here on the very core of James's career, notebooks, and artistic being. We find at that core his realization that as far as he was concerned, entrance to the dramatic chamber and to the narrative was to be achieved by the one "open Sesame," that a single key would unlock both doors—with a little help from his friend.[3]

Most satisfying for the student of James's method of artistic creation, however, are probably those instances that allow us to follow the stages of development of the enticing germ all the way to fruition; and a general rule might be that the more pages of development, the more satisfaction to the curious critic. *The Ambassadors* offers a singular example: we have the substantial initial note of October 31, 1895—Howells's advice to young Jonathan Sturges, "Live all you can . . . " (*NO* 140–42)—but we also have the lengthy "Project of Novel" (September 1, 1900) that James prepared for Harper. That formal intermediate step is, strictly speaking, an anomaly: no other examples of that "step"—except the fragments used as jacket material for *The Finer Grain* (1910) and for *The Outcry* (1911; mentioned above)—remain "in any form in which they can be imparted," as James told H. G. Wells in November 1902, and to that he added, "I shall not again draw up detailed and explicit plans for unconvinced and ungracious editors" (Edel and Ray 85).

Nevertheless, two generous approximations to that project are to be found within the scribblers, and they enjoy the additional advantage of being *in*formal, private developments of genial ideas. There are many pages of developmental notes for *What Maisie Knew* after the recording of the seminal germ on November 12, 1892, as there are for *The Spoils of Poynton* (originally conceived of under the title *The House Beautiful* and published serially as *The Old Things* in 1896) after the initial note set down on Christmas Eve 1893. The lengthy series of notes are given alternately as though the two novels were being developed in tandem, and the two books were published some months apart in 1897. It is important to remember that the two germs in question begin to be developed in 1895—*after* the collapse of James's five-year experiment in writing for the theater, in trying to work expressly in the dramatic form; and both works are themselves experiments in dramatic narrative. James's first note after the crucial failure of *Guy Domville* on its opening, January 5, 1895, has served as something of a red herring: "I take up my own old pen again—the pen of all my old unforgettable efforts and sacred struggles. . . . It is now indeed that I may do the work of my life" (January 23, 1895). He seems there to be making a distinction between the pen used for the drama and that, "my own old pen," used for narrative and seems to be uttering a sigh of relief at being able at last to turn away from the pen of drama. The truth is, it turns out, that his relief comes from a turning away from the theater, not from the dramatic form but from the theatric form—a crucial distinction, and so it has ever been for James. That distinction is clearly specified in his letter to Henrietta Reubell on Christmas Eve 1894: "I may have been meant for the Drama—God knows!—but I certainly wasn't meant for the Theatre" (*LHJ* I, 226).

The notebooks are particularly useful, in fact, in illustrating James's working out of the relations among drama, theater, narrative, and picture—distinguishing drama from theater, establishing the connection between drama and narrative, and associating picture with drama (and therefore with narrative). In a note for October 22, 1891, James grasps an opportunity to escape "the *déboires* and distresses consequent on the production of *The American*" (*NO* 61), to turn over the germ for a short story that he calls "my little drama." The distinction between theatrical drudgery and rewarding dramatic creativity is clear. Just three months later he pens a note that further clarifies that distinction and also intimately associates the dramatic and the narrative; but that association itself includes a distinction as well: "It is all one quest—in the way of subject—the play and the tale. It is not one *choice*—it is two deeply distinct ones; but it's the same general *enquête*, the same attitude and *regard*. The large, sincere, attentive, constant quest would be a net hauling in—with its close meshes—the two kinds" (*NO* 62).

It becomes apparent that "*choice*" refers to the actual textual handling—preparing a script for the stage or creating a prose-fictional narrative. Clarification results from pondering the third major novel of the 1890s, *The Awkward Age* (1899; see entry of November 18, 1894 for initial "germ")—not only the rich genial ambience of the first developmental note and its subsequent echoes later among his dictated notes (*NO* 469; and see below) but also the preface James wrote for the novel.[4] The choice in question here is inescapably fiction, yet the style is very close (James points out) to that of a theatrical script; his preface acknowledges his indebtedness to the French novelist Gyp (Comtesse Martel de Janville)—"mistress, in her levity, of one of the happiest of forms . . . 'dialogue' " (*LC*-II, 1127). It is not the theatrical, however, but the dramatic mode that James adopted for treatment of his subject. The preface then details the familiar plan of a circle consisting of "small rounds" arranged to illuminate the several aspects of "my situation, my subject in itself"; then James adds: "The beauty of the conception was in this approximation of the respective divisions of my form to the successive Acts of a Play. . . . The divine distinction of the act of a play . . . was, I reasoned, in its special, its guarded objectivity" (*LC*-II, 1131).

A note of May 7, 1893, seems, initially, to blur the distinction again—"I have been worrying at the dramatic, the unspeakably theatric form" (*NO* 76)— and to revive the option of "my own old pen" as a soothing alternative. "I should like to dip my pen into the *other* ink—the sacred fluid of fiction." The next sentence, however, clarifies James's intention that the phrase "the . . . theatric form" be a correction of, rather than an appositive to, "the dramatic." "Among all the delays, the disappointments, the *déboires* of the horrid theatric trade nothing is so soothing as to remember that literature sits patient at my door" (*NO* 76–77). Repetition of "*déboires*" from the note on his distress over preparing *The American* for stage production helps confirm the intention (see *NO* 61).

Everyone remotely familiar with James's career knows of his recognition, after the failure of *Guy Domville*, of a cherished compensation for that disappointment, compensation in the form of "the precious lesson" (which can perhaps stand to be quoted just once more), "*of the singular value for a narrative plan too* of the . . . divine principle of the Scenario . . . a key that, working in the same *general* way fits the complicated chambers of *both* the dramatic and the narrative lock" (*NO* 115; entry for February 14, 1895). Two notes, later in the year, resume the idea of compensation and add illumination to the distinctions in question; both appear in the midst of James's extensive development of the idea for *The Spoils of Poynton*—or *The House Beautiful*, as he is still calling it. The earlier note, August 11, 1895, ponders what he "has to show" for his "wasted years . . . of theatrical experiment" and finds the answer to be "fundamental mastery of statement—of the art and secret of it, of expression, of the sacred mystery of structure" (*NO* 127). The later, October 15, 1895, tells of his pleasure at discovering "the little practical form" for *Spoils*; and the discovery "brings back to me all the strange sacred time of my thinkings-out, this way, pen in hand, of the stuff of my little theatrical trials." Then, revealingly, he specifies: "the old problems and dimnesses—the old solutions and little findings of light. Is the beauty of all that effort—of all those unutterable hours—lost forever? Lost, lost, lost? It will take a greater patience than all the others to see!—My new little notion was to represent Fleda as committing—for drama's sake—some broad effective stroke of her own" (*NO* 134). He has the dual-purpose "key" firmly in hand.

We must return to this passage in a moment to look at another instructive comment and also to follow the lead of the demand for patience—to the serious matter of the little help from his friend, his "demon of patience," whom he called "*mon bon*." One of the early occasions of his invoking the aid of his good angel (April 29, 1894; he is working out "The Coxon Fund") introduces another association among those that signally characterize this important decade in his career. "*Voyons un peu, mon bon*," he writes as he develops the plan of dividing the tale into "numbered sections," and he then adds the significant combination—"each one a fine dramatic and pictorial step" (*NO* 96). Notice "and," not "or."

The same combination of features is proposed again as James begins developing his idea for *The Awkward Age* (March 4, 1895); that long note is in turn followed by his first development of the germ for *The Spoils of Poynton*, in terms of a play—"I seem to see the thing in three chapters, like 3 little acts [etc.]" (*NO* 122). This note for *The Awkward Age* concludes, "Make the conflict, in other words, a little drama—or make it so perhaps by thickening the situation, interweaving with it pictorially the other element" (*NO* 121). Twenty years later, the idea expressed here and in connection with "The Coxon Fund" has been raised to the status of a governing law. About halfway through the long fourth paragraph of the "Notes for *The Ivory Tower*" James explains, "By the blest operation this time of my Dramatic principle, my law of successive Aspects, each treated from its own centre, as, though with qualifications, The Awkward Age, I have the great help of flexibility and variety; my persons in turn, or at least the three or four foremost, having control, as it were, of the Act and Aspect, and so making it *his* or making it *hers*" (*NO* 469).

Such notes are useful in suggesting the kind of result James sought—whatever his raw material. It is also interesting to see how often he calls, at critical moments, for the aid of his guardian angel to promote the dramatic rendering. The last developmental note for *Spoils* (February 19, 1896) begins by quietly observing, "It must be unmitigated objective narration—unarrested drama." But soon James rises to the emotional exclamation: "IT MUST BE AS STRAIGHT AS A PLAY—that is the only way to do. Ah, *mon bon*, make *this*, *here*, justify, crown . . . the acquired mastery of scenic presentation" (*NO* 159). Indeed, as time goes on, the requests for aid become increasingly urgent and unabashedly passionate. One of the most impressive is the late example from "The K. B. Case" (January 4, 1910), a preparatory note for *The Ivory Tower*. "I come back yet again and again, to my only seeing it in the dramatic way . . . I come back, as I say, I all throbbingly and yearningly and passionately, oh, *mon bon*, come back to this way that is clearly the only one in which I can do anything now" (*NO* 260–61). The passion is not surprising; it is appropriate to the poet wooing his muse. Somewhat surprising, perhaps, is that this is evidently a masculine muse—

whether *male* or not—and not simply according to the French *mon bon*, or, once (August 9, 1900; see *NO* 190), the Italian *caro mio*, but clearly in English as well. For in the note of March 29, 1905 (the work in question is not prose fiction but material for *The American Scene*), James seeks the aid of his "familiar demon of patience, who always comes, doesn't he?, when I call. He is here with me in front of this green Pacific—he sits close and I feel his soft breath, which cools and steadies and inspires, on my cheek" (*NO* 237). Yet in function this good angel is at least androgynous and thus capable of fulfilling the muse's traditional role. An early note, the first for "The Coxon Fund" (April 17, 1894), makes the point sharply: "It is just this story . . . that I must shut myself up with in the sacredest and divinest of all private commerces. Live with it a little, *mon bon*, and the happy child will be born" (*NO* 90).

A last glimpse at James's system of artistic fructification reveals him again and again fondling his *données*, turning each hopeful seed over and back to discover what is to be done, talking to himself, invoking his good angel. And we see that what happens, when it fortunately does, is a kind of magic—always with "dramatic" results. There are two examples, the first coming at the end of a note for October 22, 1891. "I interrupt myself, because suddenly, in my imagination the clearing process takes place—the little click that often occurs when I begin to straighten things out pen in hand, . . . I catch hold of the slip of a tail of my action—I see my little drama" (*NO* 62). The second, on October 15, 1895, occurs amid the development of *Spoils*—and again the click: "Well, eureka! . . . How a little click of perception, of this sort, brings back to me all the strange sacred time of my thinkings-out, this way, pen in hand" (*NO* 134). When the click occurs, when the magic works—as so often happened in James's career, especially from the 1890s onward—he is able, *mon bon* aiding, to achieve dramatic narration, to make his novels and tales demonstrative rather than explanatory. The notebooks are useful in helping us to understand James's increasingly confirmed desire to *show* via his fiction rather than *tell*; he would show by making his narrative dramatic, like a play, or pictorial, like a painting, or scenic, like a play or a painting. Then, theoretically, his readers could *see* the point of his fiction, see for themselves rather than having it explained to them.

A danger that constantly haunted James—a danger that threatened to make the magic "click" inaudible, perhaps—was that of being overwhelmed by his very data, by a superabundance of the raw material on which his novels and tales were to be based. That is the dilemma of the painter in his tale "The Real Thing." The Major and Mrs. Monarch are simply too much of the real thing to allow any scope for the artistic imagination; using them as models, the painter creates monsters. James had carefully qualified his theory of "realism" in 1884, when he maintained that the business of the artist in fiction was not to render simply "the look of things" but especially "the look that conveys their meaning." A couple of passages form his prefaces to the New York Edition are in this matter helpful supplements to the notebooks. Of the source of *The Spoils of Poynton*, he recalls, "There had been but ten words, yet I had recognized in them . . . all the possibilities of the little drama of my 'Spoils' " (*LC*-II, 1141). But his informant persisted and continued beyond the ten words, supplying more and more facts. James explains: "I saw clumsy Life again at her stupid work. . . . I didn't of course stay her [the informant's] hand—there never *is* in such cases 'time'; I had once more the full demonstration of the fatal futility of Fact." Perhaps the most effective expression of the artistic *process*—to which he refers in the preface to *The Ambassadors*, quoted earlier ("Art deals with what we see. . . . But it has no sooner done this than it has to take account of a *process*")— is that found in the culinary metaphor that appears at the close of the preface to Volume 15, the first volume of tales of artists: "We can surely account for nothing in the novelist's work that hasn't passed through the crucible of his imagination, hasn't, in that perpetually simmering cauldron his intellectual *pot-au-feu*, been reduced to savoury fusion. . . . Its final savour has been constituted, but its prime identity destroyed. . . . If it persists as the impression not artistically dealt with, it . . . can only be spoken of as having ceased to be a thing of fact and not yet become a thing of truth" (*LC*-II, 1236–37).

These passages from the prefaces simply make explicit what is everywhere implicit in the notebooks. The notebooks are (to resume James's culinary metaphor) not so much recipe books as they are the accounts of the master chef's discovering how to prepare his succulent and sustaining dishes—and how to entice us to sup without extending a blatant invitation. Those accounts of discovery constantly indicate also the need to distinguish carefully between the raw material—the "real" ingredients dropped into the *pot-au-feu*—and the finished product, the true potage.

As a last word on the use of the notebooks in aiding our appreciation of what James was all about (especially as a master in fiction)—his associating the dramatic, the pictorial, and the scenic with the narrative, his caution with the fatal futility of Fact, his desire to render the *real* so as to make it *true*—we might choose a line from his development of the idea for "The Real Thing" (February 22, 1891): "I saw a subject for very brief treatment in this *donnée*. . . . It must be a picture; it must illustrate something" (*NO* 55). Again we note: the look of things, yes, but the look that conveys their meaning.

The notebooks are indeed engrossing and their uses almost endless . . . but the whole of anything is never told. One can take only . . . so much. *Basta—basta cosi!*

## NOTES

1. It is surprising that R.W.B. Lewis, in *The Jameses*, locates the turning point of Henry James's life at the moment in "the late fall of 1860" (111) when Henry decided that painting (which he was pursuing with William James and John LaFarge under William Morris Hunt) was not to be his métier—and this in spite of the evidence of James's two American Journals and *Notes of a Son and Brother*. Yet Lewis does quote at length from

the earlier American Journal, including the familiar "untried years" passage that I quote above (see *The Jameses* 328). Lewis seems to have been unfamiliar with "The Turning Point of My Life," perhaps because he relies, in *The Jameses*, on the 1947 edition of James's notebooks—which does not contain that dictated piece.

2. Every Jamesian scholar recalls James's response to Grace Norton's telling him that she recognized Minny Temple in Isabel Archer; his gentle "You are both right and wrong" allows, if it does not absolutely encourage, recognition of Minny Temple in Ralph Touchett—and certainly of James himself in Isabel.

3. I do not even mention here the very familiar cases of *Daisy Miller* and *The American*, in their twin generic versions.

4. The important developmental note of March 4, 1895, is immediately preceded by the second of two notes for February 27, 1895—a reference to Brada's *Notes sur Londres* that aroused James's interest in "the picture of contemporary manners . . . in this country." "Brada speaks of . . . *Primo*, The masculinization of the women, and *Secondo*, The demoralization of the aristocracy . . . their general vulgarization" (*NO* 117). The developmental note is followed—under the same date, March 4, 1895—by (1) a long passage copied from *Notes sur Londres* and (2) a substantial paragraph connecting Brada's remarks with the *Awkward Age* idea; James makes out there "a little drama" (*NO* 121) (see below).

# 16
# The Epistolary Art of Henry James

## Darshan Singh Maini

He was a letter-writer if you liked—natural, witty, various, vivid, playing, with the idlest, lightest hand, up and down the whole scale. His easy power—his easy power: everything that brought him back brought him that.
—"The Abasement of the Northmores"

Though the high value of Henry James's letters was quite clear to his correspondents and compeers well before the great James revival around the early forties, and though the critics did extensively and incisively use the available epistolarium to light up the mysteries and the mystique of his craft, there has hardly been any major effort to bring into focus all the energies of personality and imagination that these letters embody in order to give them at once a sovereign, sui generis character in terms of epistolary aesthetic and an inner, emphatic aspect in relation to James's work as novelist and critic.[1] Leon Edel's brief but insightful commentaries, which he places at the head of each volume of *Henry James Letters*, offer some rare peeps into the mind of "the Master" and, taken together, do constitute a kind of linked story—the grandest of its kind. But it was not Edel's aim, in terms of his extended and high engagement, to view that vast imperium from so many angles that suggest themselves the moment one begins to have a measure of the flood and the tide in sight. For to immerse oneself in that element is to be drawn into some of the deepest currents of the human imagination, as also into strange vortexes of winding, unwinding thought. But, of course, the Edel odyssey is the inevitable takeoff for anyone wanting to close with the text and the texture of the letters in an inclusive and overarching manner. Depending on how one responds to the music of the Jamesian mind in labor for over half a century or so in a genre he continued to love, refine, and extend till the end, it should be possible for an involved reader to recognize its tone and timbre, its signature and style. The effort here, then, is to milk an aesthetic out of the mechanics James employed to preserve the high form of things even in his letters. And though there are, to be sure, some other great letter writers in the English tongue, there is something in the aspect and ambience of James's letters that suggests a rare and rich experience and that makes an attentive reader return from these arbors with "a lapful of roses," to recall a metaphor from *The Portrait of a Lady*. It is a quiddity that at its best has a noble air and that even when it degenerates into dramatics or hysterics never quite loses the mark of distinction. To deal, then, with James the epistolary artist is to extend the area of Jamesian studies as we have come to see them over the years.

However, to define this aesthetic is to ask at the outset some general questions regarding the rationale and the "metaphysic" of letter writing as such. For it is one art that even the humblest of imaginations have sought to cultivate after their own fashion. At bottom, a letter is an extension of the self in its most immediate and intimate form. In short, unless it happens to be a purely business or formal affair, it is a song of sorts. It is the closest disposition of personality in word and image. And this aspect comes out even in letters that are destined to join the wastepaper basket immediately after receipt and perusal. Where a personality as rich and complex and coercive as James's is concerned, the writing of letters rises quite above the hum of greetings and salutations and civilities even when those be the putative signs or signals. Perhaps one wandering phrase moving wraithlike in a fog of words may redeem a whole blankness, or one witty comment may alter the balance of interest. And again, it is the reading between the lines and the subtext of discourse that may eventually create an aesthetic of absence in a very special manner. James's letters, as we shall see, were written in full awareness of their purpose and potential. And it should be helpful to start with some observations on the question and exercise of writing letters.

That James regarded his epistolary industry as part of his vocation as writer, subject almost to the same canons of conduct, would be easily seen even after a brush with a few random specimens. For he displayed from the beginning, when he set pen to paper at the age of seventeen or so, a certain regard for the composition of letters and a sense of enjoyment that later developed into an aesthetic concern with the genius of this genre. As his imagination of observation and evocation grew with each passing year, the business of letters emerged as a parallel attraction, comparable in its own way to the arcana of fiction. There is not only the same quality of engagement but also a similar search for the right phrase and the right tone of things. Even when he knew he was writing for a pair of private eyes—loved friend or relation or writer—James could seldom lay aside his *literary self*. It would perhaps be truer to say that he had virtually no other self or, to put it differently, that this self subsumed almost all the energies of his psyche and all the visions of his "transcendent" eye. To write, then, was to incur a priestlike obligation and put the muses at the services of a dream. Thus, even when he turned out trivia with an air of solemnity, he was somewhere, at the back of his mind, struggling to cope with the imperatives of his literary self. In almost anything he wrote, he was highly self-conscious, as if some ideal, normative reader were looking over his shoulder. The mask of the artist always abides.

That James at the outset considered letter writing high "fun," a unique form of intellectual gaiety and a play of the imagination and of the spirit at ease, is clear enough. There is, therefore, a certain kind of relaxed lyricism that inheres in these letters till the end. But more importantly, he also preserves the Arnoldian "high seriousness" at the same time, a concern for the moral quality of the muses at work. And, I believe, it is this nexus between high fun and high seriousness that constitutes the appeal of the epistolary form for him. No wonder that he was inclined to "give it the glory of the greatest literature" (HJL IV, 123), as he affirmed it. And in his own reviews of the volumes of published letters by his contemporaries, James displays an envious and affectionate regard for those who could take this art form to its highest reach. For example, though not a great admirer of Thomas Carlyle otherwise, James is overawed by the imperiousness of the English writer's epistolary talent.[2] And he is prepared to give him a seat on the Parnassus. Letter-writing, then, was not for him a casual affair despite its casual airs; it was a dialogue of the self with "jocund" spirits of "the great good place," on the one hand, and with one's own *daimon*, on the other.

And yet James also entertained a peculiar aesthetic of ambivalence in regard to the whole question of publishing letters. As a private document carrying a freight of intimacies and endearments, a letter ideally would be the last thing to be aired in the open and to solicit attention. Such soliciting would almost amount to a whoredom of the mind, a sort of intellectual obscenity. And we know James's dread of anything that suggests a fall from form, style, and grace in life. Perhaps it is this moral diffidence (which, at times, looks queasy and finical) that also prevented him from peering into the bedrooms of his protagonists and that turned him into a voyeur in his later fiction. That is to say, though there is a keen desire to preserve the privacy of letters, there is an equally strong desire to share their sweetness and tang and bite with those who could savor the spread and the aroma with something amounting to epistolary taste. When, therefore, Percy Lubbock says that James "seems to have taken pains to leave nothing behind him that should reveal his privacy," (LHJ I, xvii), he has not quite noticed that the intimacies or the privacies in such cases get converted into transparent themes and images nonetheless. This kind of ambivalence is, in fact, part of James's general aesthetic as well and governs the dialectic of form and theme in his novels and tales.

The question of publishing letters as a matter of high literary duty, where such a traffic of minds or such a compact of imaginations is seen as a dialogue of great ideas or even as an incisive commentary on the events and personages of the day, is something that James could not but view with understanding and admiration. For there runs through all his extended correspondence so great a relish of great letters. He read with avidity all such volumes, and he treated the select few with a rare degree of respect. Clearly his objection to the publishing of a certain type of private letter was a different matter altogether. For there he seemed to draw the line. No such intimacies that a later "scoundrelly publisher" or a reckless biographer could *use* to establish *his* thesis would be left in the drawer. That kind of inquest amounted to bad taste and even degenerated, at times, into a ghoulish exercise. The writer of the letters was not there to respond, to rebut, or to dispute. His image, postmortem, could be vandalized by the breed of literary gravediggers and bodysnatchers that one could easily see emerging on the scene in James's own time. So when he, one day late in life, decided to make a bonfire of those huge stacks of letters he had received from scores of acolytes and admirers, from numerous adventurous females, and from the golden boys of his Freudian years, it was something of a sacrificial act, a ceremony of offerings at the altar of the deity of letters. Indeed, one can imagine him seated of an evening in the green room at Lamb House tossing those cherished sheets, one by one, into the log fire at his feet, musing over their strange, unhappy fate and pondering to "burn, burn" *his* letters; he must have meant only such letters as could possibly compromise his position or image or perhaps lend themselves to a doubtful interpretation. In a letter to Mrs. J. T. Fields, dated January 2, 1910, James talks of "the law of not leaving personal and private documents at the mercy of any accidents," (*HJL* IV, 541), and I take this to mean that he could have had no objection to the papers and epistles that belonged to the category of public or historic documents. And rightly, I think, his correspondents did not heed his overt warning and, in fact, went on to preserve whatever they received from that memorable and felicitious pen. It is, therefore, almost impossible to think that he wished all his letters to be destroyed or that he did not hope the best of the kind to be salted away for the future reader. It could even be argued that he in fact would have immensely liked to see his name blazoned as a letter writer of great weight and charm. Perhaps those who held these precious goods knew not only their high value but also the coded message of the master. They had to exercise their judgment, their taste, and their discretion in the matter. I would even go on to aver that the whole tone and style of his letters suggests a posited literary life for them, a posthumous existence as the handiwork of a conscious craftsman. For there is no doubt that he did not scribble even the meanest note without an eye on posterity, as it were. He could not, therefore, have contemplated a fiery fate for his own letters despite his rhetorical and putative concern to the contrary. And, again, I take his advice to his nephew Harry James, regarding the Shakespearian "curse" on the future movers of his "bones" (his *literary body* embalmed in his letters), as only a Joycean joke, though a joke that cloaked an anxiety and an appeal.[3] For if the visionary uncle thus sought to guard against snooping and unsparing, hard-nosed literary sleuths, he had surely sent the message across to the right heir. It is no wonder that it was finally William James's eldest son who, overcoming the fears and scruples and hesitations of his mother, decided to commission Percy Lubbock for the job of editing selected letters. Harry James realized their high destiny, though understandably he was keen to present only that side of his uncle's life that was in conformity with the novelist's message, as also with the norms and values of the society he moved in. Harry James wrote to his sister apropos of the preserved, recovered, and reprieved correspondence, "For it's full of literature as well as character. In fact I suspect that these letters will become, in the history of English literature, not only one of the half dozen greatest epistolary classics, but a sort of milestone" (*HJL* I, xxvii). And the novelist's nephew could not have uttered a truer word. As Leon Edel rightly observes, James's "correspondence constitutes one of the greatest self-portraits in all literature" (*HJL* I, xv). In any case, just as no one else in the world could have written some of the novels and tales and prefaces that define the Jamesian oeuvre, no one else could have written this order of letters. They remain an astounding monument of an "unaging intellect."

The issue of burning such letters turns up, as Edel has observed, in James's fiction also; the examples of *The Aspern Papers*, "Sir Dominick Ferrand," and "The Abasement of the Northmores" come to mind. And though the hazards of leaving one's intimate letters around could be a sufficient reason for their destruction, there is little to suggest that indeed it was an "act of sadism on posterity" (*HJL* I, xiii). It is easier, however, to agree with Edel that the letters of the great man's friend and schoolmate in "The Abasement" described quite accurately James's own view on the matter. Thus, "if many pages were too intimate to publish, most others were too rare to suppress" (*CT* XI, 12). Between these two positions or parameters, then, we must seek to understand the compulsion of his epistolary muses.

One could go on to construct a fairly plausible mystique of letter writing. For James was conscious not only of the ceremony of such an exercise but also of the refinements that went with it. And this ceremoniousness is clearly observable in his mode of address, openings, and endings. There is a distinct air of gallantry and gaiety in the letters that do not carry sad tidings or James's response to some death. And even there a certain kind of playfulness of the bereaved imagination may be discovered in the midst of much solemnity. That some of his most moving letters relate to the demise of his friends and relations is, again, quite natural. There was a strong elegiac strain in his writings even otherwise, and the passing away of a dear one, or even of an admired and loved writer, almost always touched the deepest chords in him and brought out his poetry, his humanity, and his nobility. Thus the vein of ceremoniousness and tenderness in his letters is something innate to his nature. That he should be using "heavy mourning stationery, with a half-inch black border" (*HJL* III, 380 n.1) at the time of his stricken sister's death is wholly in keeping with his concern for the form of things, and this concern, in other and lighter situations, could turn into a Freudian playfulness.[4]

Thus, in an 1893 letter to Francis Boott, James wrote: "I have one of your gentle gossamer screeds again to thank you for. I enjoy the Tuscan tradition of letter-paper a shade less painfully as a reader than as a writer" (*HJL* III, 436). That's the Jamesian way of stating that even the rustle of fine tissue paper and the color, virginal white or girlish pink, had for him its own lyric charm. He had a lover's feel for the *romance* of letter writing. And one can well imagine the old man caressing and fondling the parchment when the missives from an adoring female, or from a Fullerton later, produced in return a Freudian *frisson*. If his fiction was the sacred fount in a deeper sense, renewing the wells of sexuality, his letters in the end did the same duty for him. The ceremony of epistolary consummation completes the case, so to speak.

That even the hours spent writing letters meant something of a ceremony for James would again indicate the high place such an exercise had in his writing regimen. For instance, writing to Sir John Clark from Washington in 1882, he observes, "In the good old world one's mornings are sacred—that is my letter-writing time" (*HJL* II, 366). In the years at Lamb House later, the morning hours generally were given to those fabulous novels and tales that eventually capped his long and sustained labors, but the business of letter writing retained its high ceremonial aspect. And when the typewriter and Theodora Bosanquet or Mary Weld were on hand, he had a new freedom of form, and even a new idiom. He begins a letter to Grace Norton, "Here goes again—I am letting my Remington loose at you" (*HJL* IV, 91).

Another thing to remember about this kind of epistolarium is the place of letter writing in one's life when it was almost the only means of reaching out to those one loved or cared for. In the absence of the telephone and of other swifter modes of communication, letters alone could carry a whole register of news and views, of dreams and desires. In other words, the expansiveness and the avidity of such outpourings could well be understood in terms of the ethos and requirements of the age. It is no wonder that Victorian and Edwardian epistles tended to extravagance, wit, eloquence, and elegance. They were, in part, a substitute for the newspaper and the media, and they often served as chronicles of the times. That is why the subjects ranged from kings and queens, from dynasties and empires, to cabbages and cauliflowers and kitchens.[5] In high hands such as those of a Henry James or a William Dean Howells, the letters were capable of subsuming both public and private areas of experience in a unique kind of symbiosis. This larger aspect of the business of letter writing again accounts for the form and the spirit of the letters written at once as intimate sallies of the heart and the imagination and as philosophic notations on God, on the mystery of human life, and on the affairs of the wide world. For a writer like James, the letter form would, then, be continually seeking a larger canvas, a larger theme, and a larger treatment. If, indeed, it is possible to use the dramatic analogy of his later tales, where the themes stretch out in wondrous fashion and find their "redemptive form," one may say of his finest letters that they too are dramatic poems of an imagination under press of events and circumstance, an imagination that branches out into all manner of extremities and yet retains its aesthetic form. The explosive principle of expansion and containment that the critics have noticed in the dialectic of his fabulation may well be seen at work in such specimens. For, as I have argued so far, his letters were but a spillover of a novelist's fabulous industry. And they had the same problematics. Setting down his thoughts and emotions in letters involved an inner drama of confessions and candid utterances, on the one hand, and of reticences, avoidances, and retractions, on the other. And in this interplay of the contraries lay the charm, the difficulty, and the challenge. It constituted a kind of epistolary poetics. All the fevers of his emotionally attenuated and vacant life had to be worked out of the system, and saturations had to be obtained through the prodigality of art. And in this hunt, the letters, in particular, assumed an iconographic importance. As early as 1886, in a letter to Elizabeth Boott, James refers to the "horrible despotism of circumstances" and to the need for ways to meet the assault of contingencies. He adds, "My correspondence is the struggle of my life" (*HJL* III, 135).

This brings us to the question of the link between James's letters and his novels and tales. Apart from the theory of the novel that we may glean from the letters (a theory that is duplicated in his criticism, in the prefaces, in the notebooks, and in the autobiographies in a more formal and sustained manner), it is interesting to see how his primary experiences or impressions of persons and places first enliven his letters and then feed his muses in the tales that follow. Indeed, the "germ" or the "seed" of many a story or tale could be traced in the letters, in those sheltered passages where the hints suggest a whole hum of possibilities. If one reads the letters conjointly with the tales, the meanings of those highly complex and involved fictions become clearer, at least in some cases. It is not within the scope of this essay to go into illustrative details, but anyone willing to track down the quarry in those little sanctuaries would not, I guess, return unrewarded. For at times the line from source to letter to story almost becomes visible. And the letters, in any case, are understandably a rich hunting ground for certain types of characters in James's fiction. Leon Edel has, of course, done an impressive amount of insightful literary sleuthing in this regard in his five biographical volumes, but the James territory is so large, so mysterious, and so mystifying as to keep teasing the reader of the novels and the tales into the arcana of the correspondence for some other possible clues. And that vast allegory of life and letters that Edel so heroically hoisted, dredging out details in plausible theses (James's geminian rivalry with William James, Minny Temple's death, the tragic and hopeless figure of Constance Fenimore Woolson, the theme of wasted passion and nostalgia, etc.), is authenticated, time and again, in those little chinks James permits himself to leave open in his communications to some select correspondents. That James, despite the impression of having dreamt up a whole gallery of characters from nowhere, still took quite a few from life is no longer disputed. A fairly large list could be easily drawn up. Whether that would help us in any significant way to understand fictional characters and whether the Jamesian theory of art and hermeneutics suggested by his tales of writers and artists permits us to do so are other matters. It would, however, tell us one thing about his method. He had an artful way of disguising his originals, masking them in so many costumes and involving them in so many dodges as to seem to leave little trace behind, therefore making the job of the critical tracker a stupendous affair. And even when the readers of his own day were able to identify the "victim" (in his satirical and ironic tales, above all), as, for instance, in the case of Miss Birdseye in *The Bostonians*, we learn from his letter of self-defense to William of how such Peabodys were no more than simple notations in the complex algebra of his compositions and how they were evolved from his own "moral consciousness" (*HJL* III, 68) in the final analysis. And the more exciting game, of course, is the one Edel above all has set into motion. It is fascinating to see the master erecting a whole series of screens in the novels and tales only to give the game away in the letters when he is not wearing the top hat and the tailcoat. Even then he is generally cautious enough to plant red herrings along the route of his argument, though there are some moments when he lowers the guard and lets himself go. The security of the letter form permits indulgences and certain wildnesses. Will it, therefore, be too fanciful to suggest that his letter writing constituted, in a crucial sense, his emotional therapy and that it provided an aesthetic of its own kind?

The place or value of letters in James's life and art couldn't perhaps be more forcefully brought home to the James reader than in the meaning—and perhaps the moral—to be read in those two fantastic letters that he dictated from his deathbed to his brother and sister, speaking as *Napolean Bonaparte* and signing those notes in Corsican spelling, *Napoleane*. As he realizes the hour of "the Distinguished Thing" and scuffles with the fact in an ebbing consciousness, the Jamesian unconscious erupts in one last heave of the will to register a strange, obscure urge. What visions of life and power cross the fading mind, what empires and dynasties of dreams, is difficult to tell. All we know from those gathered around at the deathbed is that as he finally lay dead in state, his face reportedly assumed a remarkable resemblance to the face of the French emperor! If, then, these letters are to be taken in the Freudian sense as the signatures of his spirit at the time of the great departure, or as a testament of his hidden self, we may ponder endlessly the mystery of the master's complex personality. That the last act of the dying artist happens to be an epistolary flourish may not permit us to suggest a theory of sorts, but there is little doubt about the high solemn ceremony of the act in question.

The chronological history of James's letters as presented or preserved in Edel's volumes is so rich and varied and extended as to suggest some palpable perspectives of development and a whole of range of possibilities en route. To discern, then, certain patterns of personality and disposition, of thought and values, of idiom and style, patterns that seem to emerge from this epistolarium, is to see a twin portrait of fused form and color—the artist as letter writer, and the letter writer as artist. It has been noted by some James critics that the novelist's cherished protagonists, such as Isabel Archer and Lambert Strether (his spiritual surrogates and androgynous halves), are almost painfully at work to achieve an aesthetic destiny of high moral tone, suggestive of a Venetian Renaissance painting.[6] That is to say, amid all the goings-on and the noise of disparate news, amid the daily hum and traffic of trifles, amid the sounds of the small change of life—the pitiful royalties, the agents and the publishers, and a whole lot of diurnal transactions—there is yet one's "persistent self" (of which George Eliot speaks so eloquently in *Middlemarch*) that endures and abides and that seeks a persona in tune with its deeper rhythms. It is this complex portrait, a product as much of nervous energies as of moral vision, that James seems to be painting, a suggestive self-portrait somewhat in the style of a Rembrandt. Undoubtedly, in the thick of composition when a letter is on the easel, so to speak, he cannot fully see the brushwork, stroke by stroke, but the striving for a particular kind of effect is unmistakable. There is a distinct desire to project an image of the self in its sombre intensity and in its spiritual form. And this, indeed, is the cumulative impression when one has turned over these letters by the hundreds and savored their riches. There is a presence, a seated majesty, and yet an illusiveness withal, a nimbus of notations, a chiaroscuro of flitting images, memories, and reflections. The observant side of James's societal self and the creative side of his poetic self combine to create an image of a visionary of detail and a historian of cultures and civilizations. The letters in such an extended aspect become an aid to the understanding of a spacious and vanished era. It is in the archives of such minds that the history of a race or a people finds its truest expression.

Such a reading of the freewheeling letters suggests an epistolary phenomenology, the sort of phenomenology that becomes particularly noticeable in James's novels and tales of the final phase. As in the case of his fiction, his correspondence shows him as a person inclined to saturate his sensibility with direct impressions and then to distill them into memorable images. The immediacy of the moment and the warmth of the sensuous apprehension of reality are not rendered, as a rule, without the mediating power of the emplastic imagination, but there is no doubt James had almost the same kind of reverence for the energies of experience and for their voluntary, epiphanic ethic as had William James.[7] And in this sense he was a pragmatist of a rare kind. Whereas in the novels or tales he could organize the changing arc of experience, vision, and values, as in the case of a Strether or a Milly Theale, in his letters, as we group them into periods and phases (as Leon Edel has done), or into issues and areas of interest (cultures and the international theme, politics and war, death and religion, marriage, love and sex), or into his aesthetic concerns (theory of the novel, questions of form and fabulation and of narrative strategy and style), or into his views of writers and artists, of his compeers and contemporaries, or, finally, into his comments on cities, country houses, and cathedrals, we watch the making of a literary personality—a whole graph of emerging, evolving, transforming perceptions. To be sure, we do not have in these letters a reeking smell of life, of the kitchen, the toilet, the bedroom, and the basement, for James's "indirect vision" worked in its own way, but how a ravaging imagination gets soaked in sights and sounds and how it is shaped by the dialectic of experience may well be seen from phase to phase. The objection that this experience remains chiefly cerebral, vicarious, and voyeuristic, as critics like Maxwell Geismar and Leslie Fiedler have argued, is true enough up to a point, for James's predatory and "grasping" imagination had a tendency to follow the quarry to the lairs, where the animal simply disappeared and the hunter was left to hoist a doubtful metaphysic of red herrings. This applies to some of his complex later novels and tales, which often tease us eventually into despair and even distaste. But then experience in James always meant experience *above* a level and the appropriation of things through the imagination of empathy, which is finally what any kind of aesthetic or creative imagination amounts to. In the letters, however, a certain kind of Keatsian sensuousness inheres, particularly in those long missives where James seeks to bring out the poetry of place and mansion. Here the painterly style is achieved as a visual alignment of impressions and attitudes. It is the sensory impression become word.

The earliest letters Leon Edel has been able to locate were written by the young James to his Newport friend Thomas Sergeant Perry, first from Geneva and later from New York, when James was beginning to savor the thrill of letter writing. There are, to be sure, no inklings as yet of the direction his epistolary muses are to take, and there are few observations of any notable substance, but it is already clear that the new occupation is going to be a delectable exercise of the imagination. In January 1860, he wrote, "Please also keep my letters, and I will yours for I think it will be fun reading them over when we meet again" (*HJL* I, 14). This relish of what he wrote was to remain with him till the end, when he was advising the receivers of the letters to consign them to the flames. A certain talent for parody and raillery is evident even at the outset. And he is equally playful in his letters to his mother. An early example of the style he was to cultivate with care may be seen in an 1863 letter to Perry. James is talking here of the kind of Presbyterian divines under whom "his mother sat in youth" and of the impression they made. "The brimstone," he wrote, "fizzles up in the pulpit but fades away into musk and cologne-water in the pews." And he adds in parenthesis, "Don't it strike you that I am very epigrammatic?" And a month later he begins thus, "Dear Sarge: I drop you a line out of the fulness of my heart and the emptiness of my head." Clearly, James seeks to create effect through a certain amount of verbal cunning. Again he writes to Perry, in another letter: "Some folks excel in letterwriting—others in other departments of literature. I doubt not but Shakespeare and de Musset were very poor fists at a letter" (*HJL* I, 44, 48, 52). The reference to Shakespeare is intriguing; it can only be a ploy of the mind, a youthful sally perhaps unrelated to fact or knowledge.

Around this time, when James was in his early twenties, he begins to see himself vaguely as an American St. Beuve in the days to come, for it is as a reviewer and critic that he wishes to shine. He is, of course, unhappy with the state of American letters, but he has, as he affirms in a letter to Perry, great faith in the energies of the American race and in its "moral consciousness" and "spiritual lightness and vigour" (*HJL*, I, 77).[8] And with that end in view, he is keen at the start to bring a degree of French intellectual energy and daring and finesse to the business of criticism. In this context, he uses a metaphor that is to become central later when he takes up the question of cosmopolitan culture in his international tales. "I feel," he wrote to Perry, "that my only chance for success as a critic is to let all the breezes of the west blow through me at their will" (*HJL* I, 77). In other words, the reflexive but rigorous theory of the novel that is to emerge later in his critical writings and that is, of course, to inform his better fiction is already present in embryonic form. These early letters present the problems of an imagination on a leash in the midst of a largesse of ideas and impressions. This intellectual magnanimity is to abide till the end, even when his letters become more and more fantastic and more and more arcane in the manner of his later fiction. Indeed, as the prodigality of thought draws James into a fantasia of criticism, he struggles to retain a reverence for the principle of proportion in the same measure.

The letters to Perry are a prelude to the story of the "passionate pilgrim" and, in themselves, do not have a touch of greatness. John Keats, for instance, had, at a corresponding age, already gone so far into the mysteries and meaning of art as to leave the reader of his letters with an impression of Shakespearian insights. There is little of such power and such spiritual magnificence in James's earliest epistolary sallies. At best, they are clever and breezy, showing no deeper engagement of the mind or imagination. However, by the time he undertakes his first "grand tour" of Europe (1869–70), James begins to organize his perceptions and views into an aesthetic gestalt. No theory is yet visible, either of art or of life and society, but James's descriptive powers do suggest a search for the grid of the energies animating the landscape, the peoples, and the cultures he seeks to memorialize.

These letters, written chiefly to members of his family in America, are the outpourings of a son and brother discovering new allegiances and fraternities, new areas of interest and involvement. The English countryside with its lyric, nostalgic charm, the humming and buzzing city of London, its clubs and great houses, its cathedrals and art galleries, its salons and literary circles—all these sirens of the eye and the mind are sought to saturate a sensibility engaged in the adventure of faith and experience. There is a proper degree of awe and reverence in invoking the romance of the Old World, and the youthful "pilgrim" is, on the whole, in a delirium of discoveries and delights. The meetings with John Ruskin, Dante Gabriel Rossetti, William Morris, Leslie Stephen, and George Eliot, among others, show that James is almost already close enough to the magic circle of writers and artists, though his "scribblements" as such do not yet amount to anything of real value. Most of these letters are rich in the poetry of detail; they have a sprawling and discursive charm of their own. The underlying aesthetic has the same force and fecundity we are soon to find in his literary letters for the *Nation* and the *Tribune*.

Though ultimately it is the English race, culture, and soil that are destined to shape James's finest aesthetic and moral perceptions, as the later letters would show, in the impressionistic years of his youth he seems to have pawned his imagination to the countries of the Continent, particularly to Italy. As he moves through this sunlit land of high history, high art, and high dream, James is in a state of intense intellectual stir, and the gathering notations are converted into letters of observation, discovery, and report. The seeds of many a Jamesian idea on the subjects of civilization, art, ancestral houses, and the like lie scattered in these early missives, written in an idiom that is basically to stay with him as tender of treatment. It is a language of the mind as it roams over time and space, subjecting sensory impressions to scrutiny and creating a collage of adoration and comment. James is a revelling and revering acolyte serving his time in the temple of Italian art. And some of his comments on the great painters, such as Tintoretto, Bellini, Raphael, and Michelangelo, are penetrating enough to present the lineaments of an aesthetic sensibility in the making. In a long letter to William James from Venice, he put Tintoretto in the class of the highest geniuses, such as Shakespeare, and talks of the artist's great "prodigality" and spiritual depth. But the important points to notice refer to the facticity of the scene or of the figure and to the concreteness of the process. A Tintoretto, says James, is "a great fragment wrenched out of life and history, with all its natural details clinging to it and testifying to its reality. You seem not only to look *at* his pictures, but *into* them." James wishes that he could "fling down a dozen of his pictures into prose of corresponding force and color" (*HJL* I, 39–40). James himself comes close enough to such an ideal of expression in his later fiction, and there is no doubt that the mannerist style, the spiritual wrenchings, and the baroque effects in some ways go back to the "Italian hours" of his youth. Indeed, the marriage of poetry and power that Tintoretto represents in the highest degree becomes the American novelist's dream of fiction. Several James critics have referred to his fondness for that supreme painter and have even traced the sources of the text here and there. What remains to be emphasized more vigorously, however, is the nature of the aesthetic connection, along with the Jamesian hunger for isolating moments of experience into ensembles of fictive reality much in the manner of the Italian "master." These letters, tossed off in the fullness of aesthetic faith, bring out the burgeoning contours of James's religion of art. It is this type of realism that he perceives as a distinctive mark of the tribe of Tintoretto—a realism in which the surface begins to glow with an inner energy, suggesting a spiritual engagement of the imagination. He is equally responsive to the "unspeakable purity" of Bellini's "drawing" and to Raphael's spiritual ease, which he describes almost in accents of biblical prose. Writing to his mother from Florence in 1869, he observes, "To Rafael apparently, the world was clear, tranquil and serene—he looked at things and they pleased him"

(*HJL* I, 151). But clearly his own muses sought the more mysterious, complex, and ambivalent forms of art, setting up in the process a dichotomy of social vision and aesthetic necessity and a corresponding dialectic of energies.

The Italian adventure takes the tourist James to the cities for which his eager imagination is already primed; they speak to it as to a native come home. Though Florence has a lyric charm for him and "seems to be colored with a mild violet, like diluted wine," Rome, "the Eternal City," so overtops his imagination as to throw him into an apperceptive state of mind (*HJL* I, 155, 159).[9] In a letter to William dated October 30, 1869, he goes wild with the awe and majesty of the experience. "At last—for the first time—I live! It makes Venice—Florence— Oxford—London—seem like little cities of pasteboard. I went reeling and moaning thro' the streets in a fever of enjoyment" (*HJL* I, 160). He is later to be more understanding of the eternal charm of London, that Babylonian city to which his whoring imagination inevitably returned, but right now it is Rome and Rome all the way, and all his youthful passion centers around the city of the Caesars. "It makes," he wrote to his mother, "all this modern ecclesiasticism, to my perception, seem sadly hollow and vulgar" (*HJL* I, 174). And it is important to note that it is this Rome that gets translated into images of great beauty and power in *Roderick Hudson*, *Daisy Miller*, and *The Portrait of a Lady*. James did not have a historical imagination such as Shakespeare possessed, but he had a powerful sense of history and a tremendous sentiment. These Roman letters help locate the roots and the foci of that affair with Rome that an indulgent imagination, even when distanced from it in time and place, evokes as a metaphor for one aspect of history or another. The Jamesian prose, becoming more and more impressionistic in color and detail, seeks, then, to capture the historical ambience as much as the inner, nervous life of Rome—the flutter of things, the poetry of place and person. This way of rendering the spiritual side of a city is to become a settled practice in the middle years of James's life. And we see this richly in his naturalistic novels such as *The Bostonians* and *The Princess Casamassima*, where the French form is extended to include the romance of the city along with its transparent ironies and poetic paradoxes. As James tells William, the "animal heat" of the moment cannot last beyond an hour or so, and "the great thing" is "to soak" oneself "in the various scenes and phenonmena" (*HJL* I, 179). It is this concept of "soaking" and saturation that we find hoisted as a part of the Jamesian theory of the novel in his critical essays and prefaces. To be sure, there are some awkward inconsistencies in the impressions he conveys back home. Though he calls Florence a "pasteboard" city in a letter to William, in a letter to his father ten weeks later it turns into a "spiritual city" with an "immortal soul" (*HJL* I, 189).

Most of these letters are addressed to his family—a family of minds and imaginations unique in American annals—and one notices a pattern in James's long missives home. Starting on a note of concern for health or weather or the state of his purse and the like, he soon enlarges the area of interest to include scenery, local color, the social hubbub, the American tourists (whom he treats with condescending disdain and amusement, on the whole), and other such marginalia. And when he is comfortably launched into the enterprise in front of him, he brings out his guns to signal the real hunt. That hunt is for Italian treasures of art and for the spirit that threw up such rare and splendid works in such lavish quantities out of some obscure churnings in, and wrenchings of, the Renaissance mind. James seldom, at this stage, goes farther afield, and he is generally content to savor the riches and to record some hints regarding the key to the mystery and beauty of the achieved artifacts and products. In short, the Italian cities and palaces, galleries and churches, still brought out for him the poetry of a vanished civilization. The darker and murkier side of the Roman tide seems not to have significantly touched the pilgrim spirit whose surrender to the Italian gods, it appears, would brook no doubts or questions at this point in its voyage of discovery. Later, in a long letter to William from Rome, he wrote, "I have been taking a deep delicious bath of medievalism"; in another letter, he refers to "the unanalysable *loveableness* of Italy" (*HJL* I, 182, 366).

It is no wonder that when he returns to England, James strikes a melancholy note, and "the beastly London" appears so meager after the Italian repast, or even after Paris, "the New Jerusalem" (*HJL* I, 194). It appears that the London of his mellower and riper sentiment is still years away. However, the English countryside is enough to delight the eye and appease the imagination. Talking of its cows and sheep, inter alia, the novelist uses a gourmet's grammar. He wrote to William, "The beef varies—it has degrees, but the mutton is absolute, infallible, impeccable" (*HJL*, I, 205).

Around this time a personal tragedy—the death of his beloved cousin Minny Temple—draws out the elegiac note of great beauty, delicacy, sentiment, and lyricism that we are to witness in the notes of bereavement James always wrote at the demise of a dear relation, friend, or figure. The mystery and the meaning of death profoundly affected his mind, and he often let his imagination of grief explore, somewhat gingerly, the dark territory far and beyond. He had no great metaphysical interest in this matter, but the brutal fact, with its stubborn refractoriness, did bring out his poetry and his pain. When Leslie Fiedler, therefore, talks of *thanatos* in James, one is obliged to repair to the letters for an authentic peep into the nature of this crush on death. And it is in this first such letter—the one written to his mother from Great Malvern—that we see the ravishing power of death. Remembering her as a person of great spiritual charm and "ethereal brightness," he adds that Minny "will survive in the unspeakably tender memory of her friends. . . . Twenty years hence what a pure eloquent vision she will be. Let me think that her eyes are resting on greener pastures than even England's" (*HJL*, I, 219–227). To Grace Norton, James wrote that "her life was a strenuous, almost passionate *question*, which *my* mind, at least, lacked the energy to offer the elements of an answer for" (*HJL* I, 232). That Minny Temple is destined to shine as a pure flame later in his fiction and to become a memorable metaphor for the novelist's search for transcendence shows how, in James, the energies of art operate. Milly Theale emerges as *avatara* in

*The Wings of the Dove*, the archetypal "heiress of all the ages" (*AN* 292) and arguably the unravished bride of the Jamesian imagination. Whether he was in love with his beautiful cousin or not makes little difference to her potential as a most potent symbol in his work. Perhaps she was not a fever in his blood— no woman, as we see in his later letters, ever brought James to the boil—but the form of her *image*, and idea, could conceivably suggest the nature of Jamesian aesthetics. But for these letters of great and beautiful grief, we would not be in possession of a serviceable key to his skill of transmuting experience and reality into figures of art.

The Jamesian high tour is thus brought to an end for the nonce by the tragic death of Minny Temple. A part of life is gone, and gone too is a phase—the pilgrim years and the plums of European soil and airs. A more experienced and critical James is soon to return to Europe, but a certain splendor is over and a certain spirit vanished. He is ready for a sustained encounter with the American reality, which, despite its meagerness, baits his imagination. No doubt the return home is "a kind of death," as Leon Edel puts it, but James appears to be conscious of the need for "a really *grasping* imagination" to do duty to a new civilization (*HJL* I, 237, 252). And it is at this time that he talks of "a complex fate, being an American" (*HJL* I, 274). This expressive phrase defines, as perhaps nothing else does, James's subtle and ambivalent relationship with the country of his origin. The whole historical situation and all the attendant contradictions, challenges, and dreams are summed up in it.

The European tour of 1872–74 produces another crop of letters, but now the accent falls on politics, society, dinners, and the ever enlarging circle of acquaintances, friends, and writers. The admiring aesthete of the earlier years yields place to the social historian, though, to be sure, his observations on societal issues are not yet ripe enough to be translated into art. But certain other clues to his strategies of garnering material for his tales become apparent. The first fruits of his labor—*Roderick Hudson*, "Madame de Mauves," *Daisy Miller*— are taking shape from the "seeds" embedded in the letters home. Later, in the prefaces, he would develop a whole theory of the novel in relation to the disposition of the "seeds" and the "germs" in the dark dialectic of development, but even at this stage one can see at work the methods of converting into a memorable tale or novella a mere rumor, a hint, a salacious piece of gossip, or a little story going the rounds of the salon and the country house. The letters help connect the clues to at least some of the complexities that one encounters even in the James of this period. Out of a great quantity of social trivia and twaddle, James, it appears, is able to retrieve certain moments and details to enshrine in his fiction. The letters thus become a proving ground in the first instance, apart from serving as a storehouse for those stray impressions and airs. He himself is beginning to realize the virtue of the process. Writing to William from Rome in 1873, he comments, "From all my letters as they come, you get, I suppose, a certain impression of my life, if not of my soul." He adds in parenthesis, "By soul, here, I mean especially brain" (*HJL* I, 364).

James's fiction often leads some of his readers to think he was deficient in human sentiments and warmth, chiefly because his way of rendering high emotion in art has a peculiar air of detachment and indirection, if not of chilliness and attenuation. One has only to read some of the letters to see the kind of family feeling that envelops them. There is a high sense of involvement in the daily lives and fortunes of his friends and relations. There is a generosity of mind, spirit, and temperament that in the novels and the tales often gets lost in the master's subtleties and complexities. Here the immediacy of the moment admits of a more direct response, though it must be admitted that even then James is not above adding a clause or a codicil to throw the proceedings, at times, into a certain amount of confusion. For instance, he talks about running into some women of great charm and beauty, but to avoid the impression of any real involvement, he is quick to throw in a light phrase or two to take the heat out of his description. A certain playfulness is almost always visible—and also a certain ache.

In an 1874 letter to his mother from Florence, he makes a statement that some thirty years later will become the theme of a celebrated short story, "The Beast in the Jungle." "Absolutely nothing has befallen me," he tells her (*HJL* I, 453). Obviously John Marcher's fate, when James came to write that tale in 1903, could not have even remotely reminded him of what he had casually scribbled in a tone of sweet amusement, so characteristic of his letters to his mother, years ago. Clearly, James's emotionally thin life, which was to trigger the Freudian fuses in the tales of the final phase, must have been all along a nodule of pain in his consciousness. One could easily set these words to his mother as an epigraph at the head of his late tales of spiritual torment, of depletion and deprivation, of vacancies and vapidities. This great theme of his advanced years had thus made its first innocent appearance in a letter in which he also, among other things, makes fun of the business of marriage. Responding to his mother's suggestion that he take a wife, he quips, "I will bore a hole in my nose and keep it down with a string, and if you will provide the wife, the fortune and the 'inclination,' I will take them all" (*HJL* I, 454). The buried sexual life of James, of course, finds its authentic and agonized expression in his later works, but the letters do give the game away, here and there, despite James's scruples, hesitancies, and reluctances. We will see more of this when we come to the letters written to friends and "lovers" in the winter of his dismay.

The letters that now follow (in Edel's second volume, covering the years 1875–83) become an epistolary tide carrying James, an emerging artist conscious of his talent and eager to exploit his cunning and quiddity, over the stiles of society and into the homes of the nobility and the haunts of bohemia. He is on the threshold of a great career, and there is a sense of intellectual thrill. His American sensibility seeks to connect with the dominant European, particularly British, paradigms of perceptions and values. And as he explores, more and more, the structure of European society and takes down notes to be communicated back home in the form of letters, he begins to find the lineaments of the international theme. The tragedy of manners and morals we find dramatized in such early novels as *Roderick Hudson*, *The American*, and *Daisy Miller* is seen struggling to be born in these letters of insightful information on the emerging imbroglio. The questions of cultures, civilizations, and societies are aired with a view to defining his own situation in countries that at once charm and intrigue his imagination. This period of letter writing is crowded with observations of a general nature. Somewhere at the back of his mind, James is beginning to realize the sociology of the novel per se. One could almost say that he saw the great European novel figuratively unfolding itself before his amused eye. The Roman ruins, the Parisian purlieus, and gray, Babylonian London are turning into chapters for the vast enterprise now under way. There is, as Leon Edel puts it, "an almost Balzacian prodigality and fertility" in the long, expansive missives James regularly sends across the Atlantic, to the delight and wonder of his correspondents (*HJL* I, xii). The mind and the machinery involved in the gathering of impressions are now well attuned to the requirements of the imagination, and his "possession of the old world" is bruited about with a certain kind of intellectual sangfroid or what Edel chooses to call "swagger" (*HJL* I, 206). His role as a keen observer of the European scene is quite in keeping with his evolving view of the novel as an organic mesh of individual, society, and state. The letters are true indices of the Jamesian insight into the genius of the bourgeois art form, though, like Balzac, whom he admired more than any other novelist, he could not rise above the world view that lay beneath the surface.

The starting point of the second round is Paris again, and the American James is determined to find the terms on which this city of the senses and the imagination is going to receive him. Since Paris meant, more than anything else, the world of art, literature, and thought, the letters now dwell more on French writers than on the sights and sounds of the great courtesan city. The earlier letters from Italy, as we have seen, were a feast for the eye even when the subject was a painter and not some place or object of interest. There is a scenic quality about those letters, as though the splendor of what the eye saw had somehow passed on into their frame. But in the Parisian letters, the accent shifts to art and the problematics of art. Not the eye, which still roves over the boulevards, gardens, and galleries with loving interest, but the intelligence is engaged. Or perhaps it would be truer to say that the mind's eye is now fully roused, and the physical aspects of Paris are being stored in memory for later use or evocation in his productions. The tourist has already folded up; the man of letters has arrived.

Also, James's interest in politics, seldom seen in proper perspective, moves fitfully to the fore. Paris, as we know, is not only the Mecca of art but also the center of political thought, movements, and revolutions. Its hoary history is a strong stimulant to the mind, and living in the midst of its marks and memorials, its cobbled streets and pavements redolent of radical airs, is likely to cause such a history to grow on the imagination. It does not turn James into a radical thinker, but the residues of Parisian radicalism would hence be seen in strange ways in the naturalist novels that follow some years later. I have argued elsewhere that there is almost a "Freudian" side to his politics and that the repressed radical is not altogether a fanciful figure.[10] Right now, however, his politics are fairly straight and simple. Writing to his father in 1875, he says: "I find the political situation here very interesting and devour the newspapers. The left has carried through the whole thing with great skill and good sense" (*HJL* II, 15). Addressing his sister, Alice, a couple of months later, he observes, "I see none but ardent monarchists and hear everything vile said about the Republic but I incline to believe in it, nevertheless" (*HJL* II, 30). That James moved in Royalist circles at this time is well known, but it is only in such asides in his letters that we get a glimpse of his latent political sympathies. An American republican is talking to a sister known for her radical views on society, state, and politics.

And now ensues a new phase in James's literary career. He is beginning to take serious notice of contemporary publications, and though the formal critical essays on the French, Russian, and English writers are yet to come, in the letters to William Dean Howells and to some members of his family, James offers views with his characteristic charm, candidness, and consistency. For instance, Ivan Turgenev is seen as a person of rare "angelic" charm and as a novelist of novelists, fully in control of his material and highly conscious of craftsmanship. The kind of poetic realism and impressionistic prose that characterized James's own best fiction are, above all, the elements in the Russian master that appear to have enthralled him. More interesting and revealing is a statement he makes on the subject of Turgenev's mode of storytelling and on the manner in which tales originated for Turgenev. James tells William that Turgenev "had never *invented* anything or any one. Everything in his stories comes from some figure he has seen. To his sense all the interest, the beauty, the poetry, the strangeness, etc., are there, *in* the people and things . . . in much larger measure than he can get out" (*HJL* II, 26). This is almost what James was to say of his own method when he elaborated his ideas on "the germs" and "seeds" of his stories. In the preface to *The Portrait of a Lady*, he wrote, "I might envy, though I couldn't emulate, the imaginative writer so constituted as to see his fable first and to make out its agents afterwards: I could think so little of any fable that it didn't need its agents positively to launch it" (*AN* 44). That appears to have been the "lesson" of Turgenev, though to be sure James, despite his avowed preferences, fairly frequently abstracted a particular experience in such a manner as to make it a passage from ideas to figures and story. His inveterate mode of perception often complicated the matter for him and rendered him liable to inverting the Turgenev process. But he strenuously promoted the virtues of concreteness, vividness, and facticity, at least in theory.

The French writers who draw James out early enough include Renan ("has a perfume of the highest intelligence"), Flaubert ("wonderfully simple, honest, kindly"), and Gautier ("extreme perfection") (*HJL* II, 33–38). The death of George Sand around this time results in a long critical article studded with rare insights, though his letters show no particular fondness for her work. However, before the French interlude is over, James, the literary journalist, is abroad. He has been writing his Paris "letter" for the American *Tribune* and enjoying himself broadly in the exercise of his wit and intelligence. By this time, he has evolved a prose style of great charm and complexity, and for all his desire to remain readable, he cannot help making the *Tribune* pieces "literary" enough to trouble the editor. To his suggestion that James make the "letter" more "newsy" and "gossipy," the novelist responds: "I am too finical a writer and I should be constantly becoming more 'literary' than is desirable. To resist this tendency would be rowing upstream. I had better, therefore, suspend them altogether. I have enjoyed writing them, however, and if the *Tribune* has not been the better for them I hope it has not been too much the worse" (*HJL* II, 64). He tells his father that he has had to stop the "letter" because he could not make them "a flimsier sort," and he adds wryly, "I thought in all conscience they had been flimsy enough" (*HJL* II, 66). I have quoted the letters concerning the *Tribune* at some length in order to point out James's diffidence in regard to the whole sad business of art and popularity and the price to be paid. As we know, this issue was to be a perpetual problem with him, and eventually he even makes it a thematic concern in his later fiction. In the tales of writers and artists, it becomes central enough to make James explore the "aesthetic" of literary fame and popularity. In "The Next Time" (1895), the protagonist, Ray Limbert, is a novelist who agonizes over his inability to propitiate "the bitch goddess" of success, for "the purity of his gift" would not stand abridgment beyond a point or a level. As the narrator ruefully notes: "You can't make a sow's ear of a silk purse! It's grievous indeed—if you like—there are people who can't be vulgar for trying" (*CT* IX, 220). The language almost recalls the letter to his father written some nineteen years earlier. The sentiment in that regard has not changed. If anything, it is turning into a theory.

And thus he returns to England. James writes to William from Etretat on July 29, 1876: "I desire only to feed on English life and the contact of English minds. I have got nothing important out of Paris nor am likely to" (*HJL* II, 58–59). And if this is James's own view of his Parisian apprenticeship, obviously the French novelists, on the whole, do not cut as deep into his imagination as is often assumed. His admiration for Flaubert and for Balzac in particular did eventually become something of a passion, and his high regard for the French notion of form and style in art did remain the guiding principle of his own craft, but it is clear that his spiritual nourishment as a writer needed a life of ethical affirmations and continuities. And this he found not among the French people but among the English, a people whose moral life, on the whole, constituted for the American James one of the great glories of the Western world.[11] He tells Charles Eliot Norton that his "dream" is to be the "moral portrait-painter" of this "strongest and richest race in the world" (*HJL* II, 197). What compels attention and admiration is "the magnificent temperament of the race" (*HJL* II, 118).

"The bachelor of Bolton Street," as the letters of the next few years show, is now well set on the social course, and the daily round of dinners, clubs, and country houses throws him into a state of excitement that is at once emotional and intellectual. "The wheel of London life," he tells William, now holds him bound to the great metropolis, which administers to his senses and to his imagination as the more glittering and brilliant Paris never did (*HJL* II, 100). The city begins to grow on James in the manner of a well-nourished creeper and, in the end, has a steadier hold on his heart than any other city in the world. Even "the Eternal Rome" has to make room for the grey Philistine London in his affections. Yes, the club-haunting, salon-happy James—the up-and-coming literary lion out on the conquest of London—is not a fanciful image, and it is not surprising to see him making much of his membership of the exclusive Athenaeum Club, which, as he tells William, "transfigures the face of material existence" for him (*HJL* II, 102). It is as an insider that he finally gets under the skin, so to speak, and unmasks the hidden brutalities and vulgarities of the upper set. The London-based novels and tales are his gleanings from these outings, and much as he shares the world view of the British upper class, James ultimately manages to hoist his own order of aesthetic aristocracy.

Now that his early novels are beginning to be noticed, and reviews and commentaries are making their mark, James starts reacting to some of the reviews in his letters. These stray observations have led later critics to see these books from a different perspective. In two successive letters to Howells, for instance, he spiritedly defends the ending of *The American*, which involves the sacrifice of Madame de Cintré by Newman. A happy conclusion would, James argued, destroy the dialectic of the story. "The whole point of the *dénoument* was, in the conception of the tale, in his losing her," he tells Howells (*HJL* II, 70). Continuing the argument some months later, he comments on the "inevitability" of the tragic ending, and he adds: "We are each the product of circumstances and there are tall stone walls which fatally divide us. I have written my story from Newman's side of the wall, and I understand so well how Mme de Cintré couldn't really scramble over from *her* side. I suspect it is the tragedies in life that arrest my attention more than the other things and say more to my imagination; but, on the other hand, if I fix my eyes on a sun-spot I think I am able to see the prismatic colors in it. I agree to squeeze my buxom muse. The merit [of *The Europeans*] would be in the amount of *color* I should be able to infuse into it" (*HJL* II, 105–6). The reference to *The Europeans* helps one to see that light and gay book as an impressionist tale of great charm. There is a touch of Constable and Turner in the sketch, and its soft chromatic quality is the effect James is hinting at. It is James himself who confirms that Mr. Wentworth in *The Europeans* "*was* a reminiscence of Mr. Frank Loring" (*HJL* II, 189). Writing to William, who has a rather low view of *The Europeans*, James is stung into a quick rejoinder: "I think you take these things too rigidly and unimaginatively. You're quite right in pronouncing the book 'thin' and empty." And he goes on to defend *Daisy Miller* and its last paragraph. "I don't trust your judgment altogether," he tells him. "I have a constant impulse to try experiments of form" (*HJL* II, 193). He'll again write in defense of *Daisy Miller* a couple of years later to a "Victorian bluestocking," Eliza Lynn Linton. "The whole idea of the story," he tells her, "is the little tragedy of a light, thin, natural, unsuspecting creature being sacrificed as it were to a social rumpus that went on quite over her head and to which she stood in no measurable relation. To deepen the effect I have made it go over her mother's head as well" (*HJL* II, 304). Similarly, when *The Portrait of a Lady* is in the public gaze and Isabel Archer is much talked about, James writes about her to Howells as well as to Grace Norton. He tells the former that "the girl is over-analysed . . . in the early part of the book," and he notes to the latter that she is "both right and wrong about Minny Temple" as the original of Isabel Archer. "I had her in mind and there is in the heroine a considerable infusion of my impression of her remarkable nature. But the thing is not a portrait. Poor Minny was essentially *incomplete* and I have attempted to make my young woman more rounded, more finished" (*HJL* II, 321, 324). All these impressions coming from the master make such letters significant signals. Later we are to hear his own words on many a controversial novel and story, on many a scene and character, and the use of the letters for the purpose of lighting up certain complexities and obscurities thus becomes an early habit with James.

A careful study of the letters of this period—one of the fullest and richest in this regard—shows that James is picking up some correspondents, such as Howells, Adams, and Grace Norton, for more intimate, expansive, and thoughtful letters. In long letters that show great quantities of knowledge and great exertions of the spirit, one has the impression of watching magnanimities of mind and word. There is a certain prodigality about this prose, and a certain splendor. It is in some of these letters that we may look for the Jamesian statement on "the mystery of our hearts and our experience" (*HJL*, II, 133).

By the time James is set to write *The Portrait of a Lady*, the magnum opus of his middle years, and the naturalist novels, he is already turning over in his mind problems of state and society in relation to individual lives. His interest in British politics, in the energies of the Empire, and in its fate is strong enough to dispel the popular view about his concern with politics per se.[12] And this "spiritual" involvement in the fortunes of the English race and in its institutions and instrumentalities of power and governance may best be seen in the interstitial spaces of the novels to come; the letters around this time, however, carry a discernible pattern of thought on the subject. For all his conservatism of taste and temperament, James remains out of sympathy with the very class that seems to define the limits of his "dream." For there is one side of this class that shows a peculiar order of inhumanity and a special kind of spiritual sickness. At its best and highest, it throws up the finest flowers of human civilization, but its very excellence breeds, ironically and inevitably, a lower species of the "lords" of life whose moral shabbiness does not bear looking into. "The creature most odious to me in the world," James wrote to Grace Norton, "is the English narrow middle-class Tory. . . . To tell the truth I find myself a good deal more of a *cosmopolitan*" (*HJL* II, 134–35).[13] Though the ambiguities of dramatization may at times lend a text more than one meaning and thus confuse the message, the letters speaking in the novelist's own voice leave little doubt. It is the comelier side of conservatism, then, that James cherishes above all, and it is a politics of the imagination, not of the purse and position alone. He is horrified, for instance, at the thought that England would enter a war for the sake of "prestige." He wrote to William on January 28, 1878: "An *empire so artificial* as that of Great Britain must be vigilant and jealous, not to begin to crack and crumble. . . . At any rate, I believe England will keep out of war . . . for the sake of her 'prestige' . . . the mere prestige is not sufficient ground for a huge amount of bloodshed. This seems to me to indicate a high pitch of civilization—a pitch which England alone, of all the European nations, has reached . . . the defense of prestige being a perfectly valid *casus belli* to the French mind" (*HJL* II, 152–53, emphasis added). He repeats the expression "artificial empire" when writing to Grace Norton on December 21, 1879, and he mourns the passing away of "the spirit that created this Empire" (*HJL* II, 261). He has also no good words for "the class of young doctrinaire Radicals . . . all tainted with priggishness" (*HJL* II, 218). And he is aware of the danger of "sinking into dull British acceptance and conformity" (*HJL* II, 239).

Meanwhile, as his fame spreads and his name is beginning to be associated with imaginative art of a rare kind, James is becoming more and more conscious of the business side of his life. *Daisy Miller*, in particular, has sent his stock soaring, and he feels less and less obliged to depend on his father's purse. His tales are being commissioned and his projected novels listed for serialization. The Hawthorne biography (1879) helped stabilize his reputation as a critic and biographer despite some harsh notices in America. And even as he keeps a vigilant eye on his productions, he also watches the flow of royalties with care and concern. As the Pope of fiction, James is apt to be talked of as a person least interested in small and sordid transactions. But no: the letters unmistakably show that typical Irish-American strain in him that requires a judicious husbanding of resources. There is never a hint of parsimoniousness though, and he could never be meanspirited in matters of money. Still, the pursuit of money and the sound of gold do please him. Perhaps his attitude in this regard is best summed up a little later in the pronouncements of the two opposed characters, each an aesthete, in *The Portrait of a Lady*. Whereas Ralph Touchett calls people rich "when they're able to meet the requirements of their imagination," it is the snobbish and refined Osmond who comes close enough to the Jamesian view of the matter when he observes that it is not the *possession* of money but the *pursuit* that is really offensive. So in the letters, the pecuniary or commercial side of things is, on the whole, seen to his advantage. And though he wails over his lack of talent for striking bargains, he isn't as naive as he sounds in a letter to Howells. "My fame," he tells him, "indeed seems to do very well everywhere— . . . it is only my fortune that leaves to be desired. . . . The truth is I am a very bad bargainer and I was born to be victimized by the pitiless race of publishers" (*HJL* II, 243). Much as he later laments also the ethics of "the publishing scoundrels,'' they give a theme for some of the tales, including that subtle drama "The Aspern Papers." But again, it is typical of James to worry more over the printer's devil than the publisher's royalties. He could lose his sleep and his temper over the issue.

All in all, the London debut has been successful beyond his dreams, and the letters, full of high gossip and U-slang, show that despite his occasional frettings and fumings over the ways of the upper world, James is fairly immersed in the tide of entertainments flowing freely for him at this hour. He has, we find, a good nose for scandals (which he is going to turn into tales) and an eye for effects. At least in the letters, he is not above tweaking a lordly nose or two. To ruffle the feathers of this fashionable fraternity and send up some dust and stink is an exercise that his amused and playful imagination does not shrink from.

Lionized by London society, James is ready for an "affair" with the American upper classes, and the opportunity turns up in the person of Isabella Stewart Gardner, a Boston socialite of great wealth, charm, and position. She represents a type that nineteenth-century America threw up in some quantity to prove its credentials in the world of art: the American art collector in Europe taking home "the spoils" to set up galleries and museums. And what's more, these fabulously rich collectors also collect literary lions, painters, and sculptors as trophies of the drawing room. Mrs. Gardner's eye and imagination pick up James for a very special relationship, and the American writer is quick to respond. Writing to her on January 29, 1880, he says: "I have a happy faith that we shall Europeanize together again, in the future. But doubtless we shall, before that, Americanize; as I hold fast to my design of going home." He adds, "Look out for my next novel, it will immortalize me" (*HJL* II, 265). And it is not an empty boast or prophecy, for *The Portrait of a Lady* was destined to become a classic while the master was still around. By playing "courtier" to Mrs. Gardner, who, as Edel tells us, ordered James's century of letters to her to be preserved in the Gardner Museum in Boston as a special gift, James plays a troubadour role in keeping with the requirements of a playful and indulgent imagination. It is in such aesthetic and indirect liaisons that he is to sustain his romantic passion. Art and the votaries and vessels of art thus become a substitute for his erotic impulses.

The American connection, however, still remains tenuous at this stage. His famous lament over the absence of a usable culture for the novel in America, a lament that he aired so rhetorically in *Hawthorne*, also finds an echo in a letter to Howells. "I sympathize even less," he wrote, "with your protest against the idea that it takes an old civilization to set a novelist in motion—a proposition that seems to me so true as to be a truism. It is on manners, customs, usages, habits, forms, upon all these things matured and established, that a novelist lives . . . which I enumerate as being wanting in American society." But he adds an attractive sop and tells Howells, "You will be the American Balzac" (*HJL* II, 267). This is perhaps the most definitive statement by James on the nature and state of the novel as he saw it. It is in the lap of a complex culture such as he saw in France and in England that he could see this art form rising fully to its aesthetic pitch and destiny. He admired in his own way the Hawthornian romance, but he could not vote for it against the novel, which to his mind represented a higher order of imaginative engagement or, at any rate, a more representative register. All such statements made in the letters with a sense of understanding and responsibility help bring into focus the informing aesthetic of the Jamesian novel.

James is at this time greatly worried about the Irish problem, and he wrote to his mother: "The political atmosphere is red-hot: there is one word in Society— the abominable Irish. They are, I think, abominable . . . the Irish belong to the category of the impossible." But he wouldn't go in for repression and "a reign of terror." He concludes, "In short the politics of middle-class Toryism and the *Daily Telegraph*, mixed up with a queer, musty Swedenborgianism: an unsavoury compound" (*HJL* II, 339). "It is the age," he wrote to Thomas Perry, "of Panama Canals, of Sarah Bernhardt, of Western wheat-raising, of merely material expansion" (*HJL* II, 341–42). In general, James appears to feel the force of the Industrial Revolution, which was then entering the classical phase of capitalism. Broadly speaking, he distrusts its mechanics and its philosophy, somewhat in the manner of the old aristocrat. He senses the vulgarities, obscenities, and inhumanities of the system, but there is no sign that he has the intellectual courage and insight to meet the challenge at this stage. A world of refinements is vanishing, and that is all he seems to care for.

Thus, the death of George Eliot moves him profoundly, and all his earlier admiration for her is summed up in a letter to Alice James. "She was," he observes, "surely an extraordinary woman—her intellectual force and activity have, I suspect, never been equalled in any woman. . . . She led a wonderfully *large* intellectual life" (*HJL* II, 337). And when death strikes in the family and his mother is gone, James writes to Mrs. Gardner about that "pure and exquisite soul." He adds, "I thank heaven that one can lose a mother but *once* in one's life" (*HJL* II, 377). And then his father dies. In a deeply moving letter to William, who was sojourning abroad, he talks of the union of his beloved parents beyond the grave. But the letter to Grace Norton in her hour of desolation and grief is perhaps "the noblest" letter he ever wrote, to recall Edel's beautiful comment (*HJL* II, 329). There is about this letter a certain spiritual strength and serenity that comes from the deepest springs of one's being. And it is a letter that deserves to be quoted at some length. "The gift of life," wrote James, "comes to us from I don't know what source or for what purpose; . . . it is . . . a great mistake to surrender it while there is any yet left in the cup. In other words consciousness is an illimitable power, and though at times it may seem to be all consciousness of misery, yet in the way it propagates itself from wave to wave, so that we can never cease to feel . . . there is something that holds one in one's place" (*HJL* II, 424).

Edel's third volume (1883–95) carries a great variety of letters in the same

vein. Death, religion, the declining health of the arts, the state of his diminishing
royalties, the state of British politics, London society, contemporary writers and
their books—all these and related issues keep turning up again and again. However, two new themes for his epistolary muses—the trauma of James's defeat
in the theater and the misery of a life that is beginning to show the ravages of
an unspent sexuality—add a fresh dimension to the range of his correspondence.
On the subject of the theater and the stage, we have in some of these letters a
few of his profoundest utterances and also a bewildering variety of poses, subterfuges, and rationalizations. At the same time, we do see the emerging lineaments of the dramatic novel that he was destined to evolve out of his defeat and
that he made a uniquely Shakespearian experience. The letters of the period
show how after a high literary season lasting many a summer, James's fortunes
are faltering and he is clutching at many a straw to save his position. His literary
friendships—with Stevenson and Conrad, in particular—show a degree of high-
mindedness and sincerity rarely seen among peers and rivals, though the complicated masonry of James's tributes does suggest, here and there, the master's
sly wit and reservations. The twin horrors of literary decline and emotional
erosion are seen lurking in the letters he writes after the suicide of his friend
Constance Fenimore Woolson and the *Guy Domville* debacle. And some of his
most harrowing and symbolic tales are written during this period. The emblematic
James of the final years is seen lurking in the wings.

With *The Portrait of a Lady* behind him, James is primed for the big three
naturalistic novels that are not to advance his fortunes but that will consolidate
his reputation nonetheless. He now talks of "the torment of style," and he tells
Howells how his effort to analyze inevitably results in putting the structure of
the story under severe strain. "It is always the fault of my things," he wrote,
"that the head and the trunk are too big and the legs too short. . . . My tendency
to this disproportion remains incorrigible" (*HJL* III, 26–27). This is the kind of
criticism that he will make later about *The Wings of the Dove* when he comes
to write the celebrated prefaces. There is, indeed, hardly a Jamesian fault of
technique or form that the master himself did not realize. If his letters to knowledgeable correspondents are written to defend his style and narrational techniques, they are also written to acknowledge the limitations of his experiments
and productions. There is about his genius a certain integrity of statement that
is hard to come across in the highly conceited world of literary lions.

Apropos of other writers, James is pretty free in his letters, and he subjects
their books to an engaging scrutiny. For instance, Anthony Trollope's autobiography is described as "one of the most curious and amazing books in all
literature, for its density, blockishness and general thickness and soddenness"
(*HJL* III, 14). The "little group" of Daudet, Zola, and the Goncourts is summed
up as a fraternity "with its truly infernal intelligence of art, form, manner—its
intense artistic life" (*HJL* III, 28). And he is hard on Hardy's *Tess*. Writing to
Stevenson, he makes one of his most prejudiced and unfair statements. "But
oh, yes dear Louis," he pontificates, "she is vile. The pretence of 'sexuality'

is only equalled by the absence of it, and the abomination of the language by the author's reputation for style" (*HJL* III, 406). Perhaps this kind of crass comment, rare in James, is occasioned by his own declining reputation and by the desire to please Stevenson in this indirect but unwarranted manner.

Of course, James is more circumspect when he is responding to the writers themselves regarding their late productions. He is particularly wary when writing to women novelists such as Mrs. Humphry Ward or Violet Paget (Vernon Lee). And when he wants to be critical without appearing to do so offensively, as in a letter to Paget, James can use his style for the purpose. In such cases, he resorts to roundabout apologetics, after drawing some private mirth from the exercise. He has been abominably remiss in acknowledging Lee's dedication to him of the novel *Miss Brown*, and thus he interlards criticism: "There is a certain want of perspective and proportion. You are really too savage with your painters and poets and dilettanti; *life* is less criminal, less obnoxious, less objectionable . . . more *pardonable*. . . . And then you have impregnated all those people too much with the sexual, the basely erotic preoccupation: your hand has been violent, the touch of life is lighter." But even in such letters he can let slip in a valuable comment. Continuing, he adds: "Cool first—write afterwards. Morality is hot—but art is icy! . . . Be in it, more piously plastic, more devoted to *composition*—and less moral" (*HJL* III, 86–87). Later James himself is to write novels and stories of evil, abomination, and terror—the tales of "the pit," so to speak, and the advice to Lee about life being shades lighter in reality might strike one as highly ironical, but the theory of art and composition briefly aired in the letter is to assume, in the prefaces, a definitive form.

Letters to Stevenson (as later to H. G. Wells) constitute a special category in James's correspondence and reveal a peculiar kind of chink in the master's psychic defences. The desire to please rising and popular writers may even be viewed in the case of the younger Wells as an aspect of intellectual flunkyism, and a James admirer is somewhat embarrassed. Of course, he had a genuine respect for Stevenson's prose style and a genuine regard for Wells's enormous intellectual energies and bounce, but these facts do not hide his own abasement now and then. At any rate, the language becomes at times inflated and purple and lacks the power of true rhetoric. And this kind of adoration can even lead him to pronounce their minor books works of genius and art and what not. It is a curious mix-up of insights and ironies.

Leon Edel views the Stevenson adoration as James's "search for an anchorage." This is a happy phrase, though it hides a whole lot of Jamesian anxieties, insecurities, and uncertainties. The correspondence begins in December 1884 and continues till Stevenson's death in 1894. James is full of admiration for Stevenson's "gaiety" in the midst of his protracted ill health, for it is this quality that gives the tough Scotsman's work a spiritual dimension. And James's manner of addressing him becomes more and more informal as the letters between them multiply. However, for all his kowtowing to Stevenson, he is prepared to defend his own form and style of fiction when it is under assault. He is mortified that such a sensitive reader as Stevenson should fail to understand the multiple beauties of a book like *The Portrait of a Lady*. "Upon my word," he wrote him, "you are unfair to it—and I scratch my head bewildered. 'Tis surely a graceful, ingenious, elaborate work" (*HJL* III, 206). But Stevenson's harsh criticism notwithstanding, James continues to pay court to him in his absolute trust. James tells him in a letter that *The Master of Ballantrae* is an achieved work of craftsmanship, "a pure hard crystal, my boy, a work of ineffable and exquisite art" (*HJL* III, 273).

To be sure, it is as prose stylists of rare charm and reach that James and Stevenson set up a correspondence of minds. Presumably, Stevenson too was eager to please the master, and his letters must have been partly a matter of showmanship. At any rate, James's letters are, and he gives one the impression of being continually in search of both expressive and sparkling phrases. In his letter of April 28, 1890, he wrote, "Roast yourself, I beseech you, on the sharp spit of perfection, that you may give out your aromas and essence!" (*HJL* III, 280). However, even as he sings out praises for Stevenson's *Catriona*, he does air his own theory of the novel. "The one thing I miss in the book is the note of *visibility*—it subjects my visual sense, my *seeing* imagination, to an almost painful underfeeding. The *hearing* imagination, as it were, is nourished like an alderman, and the loud audibility seems a slight the more on the baffled lust of the eyes" (*HJL* III, 438). This is a theory that Joseph Conrad was also to voice in the celebrated preface to *Typhoon*.

It appears to me, then, that whereas James's views on art and on the theory and business of the novel have a high level of penetration and engagement, his comments on individual works of fiction, poetry, or drama are not always worthy of trust. His critical imagination in such cases is often tangled up with the requirements of his own confused urges. The letters, somehow, give the game away.

To return, then, to the troubled tide of James's letters around this time, we find him struggling to cope with the ghosts of *Guy Domville* and Constance Fenimore Woolson, on the one hand, and with the whole question of an emerging new aesthetic, on the other. And to complicate matters, his politics too are in a state of turmoil. As we enter this dark phase, we see the letters becoming more and more plaintive and more and more aggressive at the same time. The storm of gathering misfortunes—the *Guy Domville* defeat, the Woolson suicide, the declining sales, the rejection of his tales—so overwhelmed him as to bring out at once the best and the worst in him. When he does finally wrest an aesthetic victory out of a literary defeat and go on to write the prodigious novels and tales of the final phase, he has visibly paid an excruciatingly painful price. The letters to his trusted friends have, at times, a harrowing, lacerating tone, and one can see an exquisite sensibility in full battle with "the assault of reality." The marks of "the beast" are there for anyone to see. The civilities and the graces are not gone, but the tone becomes increasingly histrionic.

James's "dramatic years" begin on a positive and promising note. His novel

*The American* has a measure of success on the stage, and having "tasted blood," he is encouraged to think that at last an Ibsenian turn in his fortunes is at hand. He even fools himself into believing that he has, indeed, missed his métier and that "the pale little art of fiction" cannot match the power and glory of drama, his "*real* form," his "characteristic form" (*HJL* III, 329). James was dying to score a resounding victory on the stage, and the orgiastic dream of footlights, ceremonial bows, thunderous applause, money and fame, has become a fever and a torment. He perhaps never had such a passion for any woman in any case, and it may not be too fanciful to suggest this thing as a case of displaced sexuality. For soon enough, when the sirens of the stage desert him, he will pronounce the theater a vile "pit" and a soulless decoy. In either case, one can see James constructing a doubtful, untenable aesthetic out of psychological fears and compulsions, and it is not till the Ibsenian ghosts are exorcised and the aesthetic lessons are learned that he begins to come out of the trauma and evolve the theory and practice of the dramatic novel. With the ignominious treatment of *Guy Domville* by the theater audience, and with the failure of the three-act comedy *Mrs. Jasper* to make it to the stage, James begins "to *hate* the whole theatrical subject" (*HJL* III, 452).

At this stage of his nervous exhaustion and spiritual depletion, an event of a shattering nature darkens his days. For Woolson's suicide is, as he darkly understands, to be laid partly at his door. As her four surviving letters to James indicate between the lines, the master was not altogether impervious to the overtures of a sincere, sensitive, and intelligent woman who also happened to be a passable novelist and who regarded him as a supreme artist of his type.[14] We will never know the full story, but it is possible to construct a fractured scenario of vague declarations and designs, of retreats and retrievals, of understandings and misunderstandings. The typical Jamesian feints, fears, and frolics, coupled with the idiom of ironies and ambiguities, could exasperate even an angel, and perhaps poor Woolson felt she had been led down a garden path and then abandoned. Alternatively, she might have exonerated James altogether for the confusion and misery of her own heart, and she might have taken her own life to end a long ache and a long wait. All these, at best, are speculations or surmises. Still, James's spirit is in great torment in the letters he writes soon after her death. Writing to John Hay, he moans: "Before the horror and pity of it I have utterly collapsed. . . . She had always been, to my sense . . . a woman so little formed for positive happiness that half one's affection for her was, in its essence, a kind of anxiety; but the worst sensibility to suffering or exposure to disaster that I have ever apprehended for her was far enough from this brutal summarized tragedy" (*HJL* III, 459–60). And he speaks to Dr. W. W. Baldwin in a somewhat similar tone: "A beneficent providence seemed to have constructed her—pitilessly—for the express purpose of suffering. . . . Half of my friendship for her was a deep solicitude, a deep compassion, a vigilant precaution" (*HJL* III, 464). On the same day, he also wrote to Katherine De Kay Bronson, "But it was all reduced to ashes by the fact that a beneficent providence had elaborately constructed her to suffer'' (*HJL* III, 467). What one needs to notice is James's inability to understand that such a pity could lead to the feeling of love in Woolson's heart and that, as Elizabeth Barrett Browning put it in a memorable sonnet, pity alone is an insufficient emotion, unable to sustain itself. It is, then, the pity of pity that sums up this unconsummated, unacknowledged story of love. One thing more: that James could repeat a striking phrase (and he does that fairly frequently when writing to different friends around the same time) is understandable, but that he should do so even in letters of such profound grief and feeling is disturbing. The stylist in James, it appears, is seldom given a holiday.

James's sexual troubles are soon to begin when his relationships with a series of young men complicate the issue for him. There is little to suggest that James has turned gay in the evening of his life, though as we'll soon see, the pathos of old age and loneliness and the ache for some human warmth or for the company of youth after a whole life of abstinence and emotional asceticism cannot but stir some doubts. On the subject of homosexuality, however, he wrote to Edmund Gosse, about J. A. Symond's pamphlet ''A Problem in Modern Ethics'': ''I think one ought to wish him more *humour*—it is really *the* saving salt. But the great reformers never have it—and he is the Gladstone of the affair'' (*HJL* III, 398).

As we go over the letters collected in Edel's volume 4—the concluding bunch—we soon see James locked up in the most bewildering and baffling combats of his life. Even as the fantastic and fabulous tales of the Edwardian years, quite a few of which are but allegories of his own agonized state of mind, issue from a bruised and baited imagination, the letters become more and more daring, more and more open. There is a keen sense of loss, regrets, and nostalgia and a great urge to close the gap between dream and desire. The consciousness of age and the approaching end, though seldom voiced directly or loudly, seems to have triggered his quest for a kind of permanence in art. And this metaphysical James erupts as much in the letters of this period as in the novels and the tales. Without doubt, it is not a hunt for God; despite his vague yearnings and musings in some of his elegiac letters, it is largely a secular heaven that James craves, a "great good place" where the imagination of loving may revel in condign company. Since all the "lovers" of the closing years are young men of considerable physical and intellectual charm, one is likely to think of the master in terms of late homoeroticism. And the language of the letters certainly is a lover's language and displays a certain amount of freedom and playfulness along with a deep current of anxiety. But as I have maintained elsewhere at some length, the signs of dark sexuality in late James—the Lolita complex, voyeurism, necrophilia, and other Freudian eruptions—do not necessarily add up to homosexual experience.[15] More likely, these are the ravages of unconsummated heterosexual love, and the need for the golden boys is a compensatory exercise. It is simply an ache for "a touch of June" in November, to recall a phrase from an obscure little poem.

That attractive ladies, chiefly socialites and novelists, still figure as part of the high fun in James's letters is evident enough. There is little evidence, however, of any degree of passional or spiritual involvement. At times, the letters almost amount to epistolary romance. He is content to be courted, to be desired, to be adored. And, indeed, one cannot imagine him in the role of a great lover. He couldn't have, for instance, staked his life, his happiness, or his fame on any woman on earth. He couldn't freeze or burn for any beauty. There are within his inner defenses strange and complicated barriers that are hard to cross. He could create adorable young heroines of great spiritual charm, but no such woman, it appears, was able to breach his battlements. He would not lower the drawbridge if he felt an invasion of his sanctuary was intended.

The subject of marriage turns up now in some letters, but as in his younger days, James often makes light of it, treating the whole thing with amused interest. Somehow he cannot see himself as a husband and a father, and he feels exempt from a state of marital life. There are several little statements to this effect. However, even if marriage is not for him, or he for marriage, he fully understands the spiritual side and the erosive side of its condition. Writing as early as 1884 concerning a rumor of his marriage, he told Grace Norton, who received some of his longest and most thoughtful letters, "There are all sorts of things to be said about it; mainly this, that if marriage is *perfectly* successful it is the highest human state; and that if it fails of this it is an awful grind, an ignoble, unworthy condition" (*HJL* III, 54). And since there is scarcely a happy marriage in his entire corpus of fiction, one is driven to the conclusion that James could not really think of a marriage that somehow didn't lead to, or end up in, a waste of the human spirit.

The letters to Edith Wharton, who sought the master's attention more than his love, display a high level of wit and intellectual gaiety, and James uses her partially for a couple of his short stories, "The Velvet Glove" being a more direct example. As their friendship grows and as Wharton's fame and fortunes become an object of interest and admiration, their relationship assumes a complex psychological character. She is certainly, to begin with, in awe of James's genius, and she possibly seeks, as a much younger woman, to rouse his libidinal level without a distinct idea of the direction. In her autobiography, *A Backward Glance* (1934), she recalls how he remained curiously insensitive to her charms when they first met at several dinner parties in the days of her frocks and frills and plumed hats. As she archly put it, he "noticed neither the hat nor the wearer" (172). However, when we examine the letters and some of the symbolic tales, we discover a delightful, warm relationship but also, here and there, a touch of muffled envy, perhaps even malice, in the master and an urge to disown the debt and twist the great lion's tail in the "pupil." No wonder James refers to her as the "Angel of Devastation" in a letter to Walter Berry (possibly her lover) and as the "Firebird" in a letter to Howard Sturgis.

With James finally moving into Lamb House at Rye, away from the social whirl and hubbub of London, he gets into the age of the typewriter and the dictated letter. A new sense of space and of release and a new colloquial style marked by intellectual slang and energy begin to shape his correspondence. The idiom acquires, at times, a sexual freedom, and the prohibited words sneak into some of the letters written to his younger friends and "lovers"—W. Morton Fullerton, Hendrick C. Andersen, and Dudley Joycelyn Persse. He speaks to Fullerton of "the *essential loneliness*" of his life, and to Andersen he wrote: "My dear, dear, dearest Hendrick . . . I return . . . to put my arm around you and *make you* lean on me as on a brother and a lover" (*HJL* IV, 170, 225–26). Soon it is Persse who sends James into raptures of love. If one carefully examines the psychological base or context of these letters, it is possible to see James not as a dirty old man tailing one boy after another but as a lonely person in search of a vanished energy, an elixir to revive his spirits. These letters may even be seen as man's eternal longing for youth and beauty and immortality. In short, they may be seen as a mythical quest, a "sacred fount" to appease the hungers of the spirit.

The letters of the later years continue, all the same, to show James's eagerness to pursue the Muses with courage and conviction despite the general indifference and even hostility to his new productions. It is the dream of fiction that propels his pen now, and he appears to be in search of the Holy Grail of the novel.[16] The letters can give only a dim picture of the vast project forming in his mind. Oddly enough, as his lean life struggles for a touch of warmth, his imagination becomes, in that proportion, more and more gorgeous. That's the paradox of art; it feeds ravenously on the wants and wastes of life!

If James's relationships with his young men seem not to prosper much, his literary friendships, except for the H. G. Wells episode, show a measure of ripeness. Grace Norton and Charles Eliot Norton, Edith Wharton, Leslie Stephen, Joseph Conrad, Rudyard Kipling, Hugh Walpole, and scores of other writers included in his epistolarium receive his respectful attention—and, of course, a few sly strokes. On the up-and-coming Kipling, James has some very unpleasant things to say to Grace Norton in a Christmas Day letter of 1897. He admires Kipling's "great talent" but sees no psychological "*shades*" and depths in him. James wittily put it, "In his earliest time I thought he perhaps contained the seeds of an English Balzac; but I have quite given that up in proportion as he has come steadily from the less simple in subject to the more simple—from the Anglo-Indians to the natives, from the natives to the Tommies, from the Tommies to the quadrupeds, from the quadrupeds to the fish, and from the fish to the engines and screws" (*HJL* IV, 70). And yet nearly four years later, James writes to Kipling on *Kim* in a language of utmost adoration: "You are too sublime— you are too big and there is too much of you. . . . What a luxury to *possess* a big subject as you possess India" (*HJL* IV, 210). What is one to make of the turnabout? Is it a sincerely felt and altered view of the writer or an example of James's increasing tendency to court the rising new stars?

And this brings us briefly to the celebrated and controversial letters between James and Wells. This correspondence has received enough critical attention to obviate the necessity for any detailed comment. The letters show, in sum, the perennial clash of two opposed temperaments and two opposed modes of perception in relation to art *qua* art. Though the younger novelist was essentially right to treat art as an aid to life and not as an autotelic exercise, unanswerable to moral or social challenges, Wells, like so many other readers of James, hugely misunderstood the Jamesian aesthetic of the novel. The mystique of the novel James sought to construct apparently does send out negative messages, and some of his own lamentable lapses in the later tales do tend to show up the master as a supersubtle aesthete lost in the cobwebs of his own theory and complicated craftsmanship. But this view of James, as any sensitive reading would show, runs counter to his essential *vision* of the novel. What he wanted was to make the novel a work of art so fine and full as to render the social reality, with all its ambiguities, in a finished form. And the dialectic of form that we see enunciated in his critical essays and hoisted in his fiction in no way militates against the view of the novel as an instrument of sociological perceptions. It is precisely the social energies of Wells's Dickensian novels that James admires most. As he wrote elsewhere, "The particular intentions of such matters as *Kipps*, as *Tono-Bungay*, as *Ann Veronica* so swarmed about us, in their blinding, bluffing vivacity that the mere sum of them might have been taken for a sense over and above which it was graceless to inquire" (*FN* 273). And yet James was apt to be misunderstood when he wrote to Wells thus, "It's art that *makes* life, makes interest, makes importance, for our consideration and application of these things, and I know of no substitute whatever for the force and beauty of its process" (*HJL* IV, 770). Obviously, what he means is that the ideal possibilities offered by art to fine consciousness constitute the only type of life worth caring for. And art makes life in the sense that it returns its debt to life in the form of higher and enriched perceptions. However, it is not this controversy that disturbs a James admirer but rather the master's strange desire to please Wells at all costs, even as Wells betrays a typical brashness and insensitivity and even ridicules James's work in his own novel *Boon*.

On his own late novels, James makes some marginal comments that help give a peep into the working of his mind. He knows exactly why these books baffle the common reader and why a James reader has to be broken to the kind of brew that works its way in a slow, measured manner. Writing, for instance, to the Duchess of Sutherland on December 23, 1903, he says: "Take, meanwhile pray, the *Ambassadors* very easily and gently: read five pages a day—be even as deliberate as that—but *don't break the thread*. The thread is really stretched quite scientifically tight. Keep along with it step by step—and then the full charm will come out" (*JHL* IV, 302). It is undoubtedly the kind of response that Conrad's novels of psychological and moral complexities also demanded in a different way, which is why Conrad commanded James's great respect. James wrote to him, "I read you as I listen to rare music—with deepest depths of surrender" (*HJL* IV, 418).

At this time James is writing *The American Scene* and the New York Edition, with its great prefaces. In the prefaces James develops a theory of the imagination (best defined in the preface to *The American*) that fitfully finds expression even in his letters. When James's one-act play *The Saloon* is rejected by George Bernard Shaw's Acting Stage Society, James tells Shaw, among other things about the nature of art, that the imagination has a "life of its own" (*HJL* IV, 512). One wonders, finally, if the two fantastic letters James dictated from his deathbed, with their Napoleonic mystique, did not in some way relate to the sovereignty of the imagination and if "the balloon" cut off from the earth wasn't floating in some haze of vision. The wheel of the Jamesian imagination has perhaps come full circle.

Considering that James wrote letters in such quantity and in such high spirits, it is somewhat intriguing to find his fiction fairly free of epistolary intrusions. To be sure, letters as a thematic nucleus do generate, among other things, an aesthetic of ethics in such tales and novellas as "A Bundle of Letters," "Sir Dominick Ferrand," "The Abasement of the Northmores" and "The Aspern Papers," but except for "A Bundle of Letters," written wholly in epistolary form, the fiction does not show in any significant degree the Jamesian style in epistolary action. In the novels, above all, there is a peculiar meagerness, if not absence, of letters as such. Of course, letters are frequently mentioned or cited in paraphrase within the dialogues of the dramatis personae, but for some reason James is simply content, on the whole, to keep them out of our sight. One possible reason could be that the familiar, overused, sentimental love letter of the Victorian novel distressed his aesthetic sensibility, but I think the deeper reason perhaps lay in his instinctive reticence in regard to such matters. A few business letters are there but then the characters are not generally permitted to unbutton their authentic selves in this manner. That aesthetic privilege remains with the novelist, who may use other narrational devices to illumine the interior landscapes. An earlier example should suffice. In *Washington Square*, letters between the two lovers, Catherine Sloper and Morris Townsend, and those between the comic aunt and her niece's impecunious and importunate suitor, are frequently the subject of discussion, but there is no signed missive with its text in the entire volume. One can see how the comic imagination of James might have reveled in the penmanship of Mrs. Penniman, at any rate, but no, the novelist eschews even that little Dickensian luxury. And this is true for most of his major representative novels. Obviously, James kept his epistolary muses apart, in readiness for the real engagements of life. His fiction, he felt, could feed itself on many a subtler brew and bone.

And, finally, there is the question of his epistolary style, which, as we have seen, keeps subtly acquiring fresh dimensions as the engaged imagination enlarges the area of interests. The epistolary impulse never deserts him or weakens till the end. On the contrary, it exhibits itself in fantastic new forms. Basically, of course, the style here is an extension of the style evolved in his novels and tales, a style honed in obedience to the imperatives of a radical imagination that is at once aesthetic and humanist. It is even a succession of styles, and the development has a dialectical character. However, in all essentials, the *nuclear* Jamesian style inheres and abides from phase to phase, as in the novels. And it is a style of intelligence and wit in high tide and in high tone, incorporating a patina of art and culture. There is an air of ease and civility linked to poetic energies, insights, and epiphanies. In the process, the style develops a complexity of thought and statement and, ultimately, a metaphysical dimension of the type we meet in John Donne's verse. The thought becomes image through a sensuous rendering of reality, a process T. S. Eliot described so unerringly in his critical essays. No doubt Eliot's great regard for the later James lay in, among other factors, the novelist's complete mastery of the art of aesthetic conversion. The engineering of an organic style, then, was ultimately a question of husbanding all the resources of the mind, the imagination, and the spirit in fit and proper proportion. Its vintage character betokens a gradual ripening of rhetoric.

However, within this general Jamesian style there are certain feisty flourishes and dandyish exertions that are more peculiar to the letters than to his other productions. Perhaps the intimacy of the letter form permitted, within its confined parameters, such salacious sallies and intellectual gaieties. In any case, style as the *other* man is more appropriately to be seen at work here, though as I have said earlier, even then some part of the Jamesian psyche remains teasingly draped, out of our reach and ken. The high-spiritedness of the letters is still a form of cabala and codes. Thus we watch "the evolution of a personal style," as Edel puts it, much in the manner of the ceremonious, ambassadorial prose of the novels. A signature is sealed in style. And the handwriting, as Edel affirms, increasingly becomes "larger, more regal, more indecipherable" (*HJL* III, xv).

Is there also a *family* style or, if you like, a *house* style in these letters? For if one examines the letters of the James family—an epistolary family of conscious cut and class—one begins to see a certain pattern of expression. It is not quite easy to define, and there are, in addition, certain angularities *within* the matrix of the family correspondence that resist a clear statement. Yet the pattern does exist, if only to suggest a code of language, a turn of word and phrase, a mode of perception. This idiom and the quiddity seem to stem from Henry James Senior's Emersonian eloquence, combined with a dash of *brahmanical* wit and Yankee humor. There is the same kind of metaphorical freedom here that one notices in the father's philosophical variations and linguistic extensions. And though William James frequently showed annoyance with the pleated prose and narrational intricacies of his brother's fiction, his own letters to Henry and to his sister, Alice, have a *familial* complexity. Above all, there is in William's letters, and more so in those of Henry and Alice, a keen desire to psychologize things, to draw out the energies of events or the buried essence of things and to strike out for freshness of thought and expression. The result is an ingenious or artful integrity of statement that, though honoring limits and reticences, is still brimful of meanings and suggestions. The style is lambent, with controlled luxuriance and coiled, sinewy strength uniquely bound in an armature of expressive words. The imagery, in particular, tends toward a Shakespearian aspect, which is to say that the reiterative and obsessive images form a visionary grid. This is as true of James's style as of Alice's. Ironies, mirth, and "intellectual larking" create an ambience of ingrown ease and lend this style a familiar bite and tang. This phenomenon is more pronounced in the letters of Henry and Alice, who seem eventually to form a consanguinity of character, both in regard to cognition and trick of phrase. As Alice's biographer Jean Strouse puts it, there is "the notion of a shared identity across the boundaries of gender" (*Alice James* 251). And in her diary, Alice refers to "the exquisite *family* perfume of the days gone by," a perfume that also seems to envelop the family rhetoric, if one may say so (quoted in Strouse, 285).

That James was conscious of the "Paterization" of his prose apart from the "Paterization" of his aesthetic, which Adeline R. Tintner has examined in rich detail, could perhaps be adduced from some stray hints in his letters.[17] However, there is no doubt he still aimed at that kind of luminous, stately, and dramatic prose that he admired in Pater. No wonder that in a letter to Edmund Gosse, James sums up the spirit of Pater's style in a kind of *Paterese*. That celebrated passage deserves to be quoted at some length.

I think he has had—will have had—the most exquisite literary fortune: i.e. to have taken it out all, wholly, exclusively, with the pen (the style, the genius) and absolutely not at all with the person. He is the mask without the face, and there isn't in his total superficies a tiny point of vantage for the newspaper to flap its wings on. . . . Well, faint, pale, embarrassed, exquisite Pater! He reminds me, in the disturbed midnight of our actual literature, of one of those lucent matchboxes which you place, on going to bed, near the candle, to show you, in the darkness, where you can strike a light: he shines in the uneasy gloom—vaguely, and has a phosphoresence, not a flame. (*HJL* III, 492)

James's style has all the frills, and not a few of the frivolities, of the aesthetic prose associated with Pater, but it differs radically from Paterism in its larger ethical reverberations, or "in the wider sphere of reference," if I may recall the words of another Alice, William's wife, uttered in another context.[18] For in the final analysis, the Jamesian style, whether in his fiction, in his letters, or in his other writings, has a certain visionary dimension that lifts it quite beyond the Pateresque horizons.

And, finally, I like to imagine the master in his epistolary labors, bent over a spread of elegant white, ivory, or gray sheets, absorbed to his intellectual gills in the sacred business of letter writing, humming to himself as the words rise to the surface of the imagination and take off in schools of fantastic form and color. And when the typewriter arrives some years later, we can see him in our mind's eye pacing the floor of his spacious study and dictating letters as though they had descended full-blown from a *Shiva*'s head, words cascading down the line of the argument in natural grace and beauty and power. The ceremony of letter writing is apotheosized. It is a visionary industry that finds him, like John Keats, a "sleepless eremite" watching "priestlike" the story of "earth's human shores" from the vantage point of age and achieved art.

## NOTES

1. Percey Lubbock was commissioned soon after the death of James to edit the mass of letters then available from different sources, and he performed that job with skill and insight, on the whole. But the two volumes of Lubbock's edition of *The Letters of Henry James* do not carry a fairly large body of important letters that have since come to light and also leave out some crucial letters, as Leon Edel was quick to perceive when, some years later, he sat down to spend almost his entire scholarly life in the employ of "the Master," consummating his long and worshipful labors in his four definitive volumes of the letters. These volumes carry letters selected out of some 15,000 extant. Edel's earlier volume, *The Selected Letters of Henry James* (1956), consisting of 120 letters, had both the flavor of an epistolary aperitif and the promise of a fabulous spread. It may be remembered that whereas Lubbock had generally the copies to work on, Edel used holographs as far as possible. He did not resort to "truncation" and even retained some misspellings "for flavor." It is also Edel's view that several letters still remain out of public sight. All references in this essay are to Edel's four-volume edition (*HJL*), except those pertaining to the unpublished letters used by Adeline R. Tintner in an article in the *Henry James Review*. Other collections of James's letters are by the actress Elizabeth Robins and the writer E. F. Benson. These letters were addressed to Robins and Benson, and not many deserve to be reprieved. Two recent volumes are *The Selected Letters of Henry James to Edmund Gosse, 1882–1915*, edited by Rayburn S. Moore, and *Henry James and Edith Wharton: Letters, 1900–1915*, edited by Lyall H. Powers. Of course, the best of the Gosse letters are already in Edel's volumes. Volume 11 of the *Henry James Review* includes Stephen H. Jobe's two-part list of all of Henry James's published letters, printed in well over one hundred books and periodicals.

2. Reviewing Froude's biography of Carlyle, James observes, "He appears to have been no more of a thinker than my blotting paper, but absorbent like that to a tremendous degree, of life, a prodigious *feeler*, and painter, as a painter indeed, one of the very first of all" (*HJL* III, 51).

3. For a detailed and penetrating treatment of this aspect, see the first two chapters of Daniel Mark Fogel's *Covert Relations*.

4. James was quite clear in matters such as the "mourning stationery" and took care to observe the form of things. Even otherwise, the stationery used by him had a certain style about it, as I had occasion to notice when I examined some of the letters at the Houghton Library, Harvard University.

5. This was a common feature of Victorian and Edwardian letter writers. For instance, Gertrude Bell's *Letters* give a detailed and graphic picture of the British politics of hegemony in Iraq, which she watched and helped promote during her years in England.

6. See Fogel, "Framing James's Portrait," and Maini, "Isabel Archer."

7. For a detailed study, see Hocks, *Henry James and Pragmatistic Thought*.

8. In a letter to Perry (August 15, 1867) commenting on the Harvard faculty and students, among other things, James concludes: "American Literature is at a dreadful pass.—Nothing decent comes to the light" (*HJL* I, 72).

9. James is not consistent in the manner of dating his letters. In the same month, for instance, he uses the day both before the month ("26 Oct. 1869") and after ("Oct. 30th 1869"). Also, in the earlier letters, he sometimes puts "th" after the date and sometimes does not, though in his later letters the former practice almost stabilizes and becomes his routine.

10. See "The Politics of the Master" in my *Henry James: The Indirect Vision.*

11. In his letter of September 19, 1877, to his father, James wrote that the French are "an awfully ugly and bilious little race. But France is certainly in a hundred respects a more civilized country" (*HJL* II, 139–40).

12. See my essay "The Politics of the Master" in *Henry James: The Indirect Vision* 175–77.

13. See Edel's "Henry James and the Cosmopolitan Imagination."

14. The third volume of Edel's *Henry James Letters* carries, in the form of an appendix, Woolson's four letters of indirect but eloquent expression. These are the surviving embers of a love that turned into a flame in the privacy of her heart. Otherwise, as Edel puts it, "the two destroyed each other's letters by mutual agreement" (*HJL* III, 524). A fourteen-year-old correspondence goes up in flames. I may add in parenthesis that Woolson's love comes out on each page in a suppressed, strangulated cry. The letters (at the Houghton Library) show a very neat, small, compact handwriting.

15. See my essay "Aspects of Love and Sex" in *Henry James: The Indirect Vision* 163–73.

16. See my "Henry James and the Dream of Fiction" 48–55.

17. See Tintner's "Pater in *The Portrait of a Lady.*"

18. It may be pertinent to record here that James's letters to his Lamb House servants are in a fairly simple, functional style. His delicious ironies and witticism, his idiomatic daring and dramatics, his Latinisms, Gallicisms, and U-slang are clearly reserved for his compeers and equals. There is, of course, a class character to his correspondence. He also varies his openings and endings from correspondent to correspondent. Most letters begin with an elaborate apologia in new, expressive phrases, and they end here and there, with a flourish of fun and highly self-conscious sentimental strokes.

# 17

# Henry James's *English Hours*: Private Spaces and the Aesthetics of Enclosure

## *Bonney MacDonald*

By the time James began his expatriate life at 3 Bolton Street, Picadilly, in 1876, his affection for London and the whole of England had been long established. Before his first visit to his London tailor and before he declared his well-known "possession of the old world" from Story's Hotel, James had already immersed himself in foggy, Dickensian London and roamed the verdant English countryside in search of historic, telling details. Indeed, by 1870, James had toured the Continent with his family during his early "sensuous education" and—after a quiet decade in New England—had longed to embark on his own Grand Tour. On February 17, 1869, James sailed to England to begin his first unaccompanied tour of Europe. His departure marked the beginning of a journey that would structure his life abroad and animate his fiction, and his arrival in Liverpool teemed with a long-awaited and long-remembered sense of destiny. "I found myself," as he recalled in *The Middle Years*, "from the first day . . . in the face of an opportunity that affected me then and there as the happiest, the most interesting, and the most alluring and beguiling that could ever have opened before a somewhat disabled man who was about to complete his twenty-sixth year" (*AU* 548). Moreover, the arrival on that windy and "overwhelmingly English morning" became a standard of measurement in the years to come. On arrival, he wrote, "I took up the gage, and . . . never, in common honor, let it drop again" (*AU* 548).

The England that James discovered and embraced in the 1870s is recorded and—to use James's term—"appropriated" in his 1905 *English Hours*. Through these sketches of city and country, James takes part in cultural rituals of late-nineteenth-century England. Like many other American writers—among them Norton, Fuller, Hawthorne, Howells, and Twain—he followed the prescribed route of the Grand Tour with Baedekker, Murray, and Ruskin in hand and published his impressions in increasingly popular essays on travel. James's tour, his impressions of England, and more specifically, his recorded impressions of England's cities and country sights, represent, however, more than his participation in literary and cultural customs. James's *English Hours* (composed primarily of essays written in the 1870s) constitutes a means by which James began indirectly to describe a style and an artistic stance. For James, the English travel sketch offered an accessible and established vehicle through which he could articulate new ideas on aesthetics. Through his portrait of England as an enclosed and overcrowded territory, James uses his observations to develop his emerging craft. In response to an overpopulated and public landscape, James finds comfort in the English idea of domestic and social privacy. More important, however, he uses these expressed preferences—for the shadowy landscapes of hidden glens, private country houses, and dimly lit chapels—as a means of discussing the aesthetic dimensions and consequences of privacy. In his preference for the shaded and enclosed spaces of English landscape and interior, James finds a means for developing an aesthetic of indirectness, enclosure, and compressed power that would influence his writings in the years to come. Moreover, in advancing his preference for the enclosed, the limited, and the withheld, James suggests that limitation and restriction encourage their opposites—that enclosure actually opens up a more expansive literary geography and that restriction generates freedom.

Initially, James encounters a nation saturated with a sense of history. In the countryside, James discovers what he triumphantly labels the "headwaters of his own loyalties" (*EH* 170), and in Chester he strolls along the ancient wall that belongs to "a class of things fondly remembered" (*EH* 65). In England, "history appear[s] to live again" (*EH* 5)—so much so that while James contemplates a medieval stone structure at Exeter Cathedral, the past literally comes to audible life. Gazing at the "broken-visaged effigies of saints and kings" along the dark wall, James fancies that "they are broodingly conscious of their names, and histories and misfortunes; that . . . they feel the loss of their noses, the long June twilight turns . . . they begin to peer sidewise . . . and converse in some strange form of early English" (*EH* 96). For James, the English past comes alive for his claiming; the past is "always seen, [and it always] . . . presents a full face" (*EH* 200).

James departs from an expressed appreciation for the past as he moves on to more complex social and aesthetic issues of public and private spheres in British life. Throughout the sketches, he approaches his ideal of privacy after confronting the overly public and often crowded texture of British life. In medieval Chester, for instance, he notes that "the population has overflowed . . . and you hardly find elbow-room," not to mention solitude. Like many American tourists accustomed to the more open landscapes of their New World, James discovers that the "English landscape is always a 'landscape with figures.' And everywhere you go you are accompanied by a vague consciousness of the British child hovering about your knees and coat skirts" (*EH* 40). In London, James confronts much the same British "hub-bub" as he walks eagerly through Green Park and St. James Park on his way to Westminster. Having made his way clear of the "shufflers" and "little smutty children sprawling on the damp turf" of the parks, James reaches the abbey entrance to find yet another "dense group of people" (and perhaps a chance for wordplay, as well). The American innocent abroad shows his American roots, here, with a touch of bawdy humor worthy of Twain, as James quips: "Beyond this [group] it was impossible to advance. . . . I put my nose in the church and promptly withdrew it. The crowd was terribly compact, and beneath the Gothic arches the odour was not of incense." Faced with overcrowded sights and landscapes, James reluctantly submits at every point to "being crowded out of a place. . . . [T]here are, selfishly speaking, too many people" (*EH* 135).

Having established England as an overly peopled landscape, *English Hours* registers two categories of response or, even, defense: that of the English and that of James. The British, James notes, defend themselves against their overly crowded surroundings first through an expressed love of manners and adherence to public convention. England is startlingly practiced at "squaring itself with fashion and custom. In no other country . . . are so many people to be found doing the same thing at the same time—using the same slang, wearing the same hats and neckties, collecting the same china plates" (*EH* 22). These observations on convention, however, only contribute to the foundation of what most interests James in the British respect for conformity. Though the British are conformists, he observes, they are also noted for a particular brand of eccentricity that gives their conformity an edge. The monotony of their conventionality would "become oppressive," James remarks, "if the foreign observer were not conscious of [a] latent capacity . . . for a great freedom of action" (*EH* 122). Here James is working toward an aesthetic of contrast and creative opposition as he tries to understand how British conformity joins with a prickly eccentricity. He is on his way to suggesting that freedom is encouraged, if not generated, by restriction. More specifically, he is working toward an aesthetic of opposition by which convention and restriction generate their opposite. James's comments on England's cohesiveness and its contrasting eccentricity thus take on interesting connotations. In England "[e]veryone is free and everyone is responsible. . . . With [Americans] there is infinitely less responsibility; but there is also, I think, less freedom" (*EH* 125). In exploring this mix of outer conformity and inner license, James wants to know how the English "reconcile the traditional to [conventional] usage" (*EH* 122). Throughout *English Hours*, James wants to uncover their social "secret"; that is, he wants to learn "what becomes of that explosive personal force in the English character which is compressed and corked down by social [and public] conformity" (*EH* 123).

Working his way from the social to the aesthetic, James finds that, in addition to using convention as a defense against an overly peopled landscape, the British are also accomplished at something seemingly much different—at the occasional art of "letting loose" and of taking a holiday for "a little change." Attempting to answer the question of what becomes of British "personal force" when it is held in by conformity, James turns to the festivities on Derby Day. In contrast to the Americans, who are "sadly inexpert" at the *real* art of leisure, the English—of all classes—have "a large appetite for holidays [and] the ability . . . to know what to do with them when taken" (*EH* 128). At Epsom Downs, under a sky sprinkled with "little idle-looking, loafing, irresponsible clouds," James relishes the spectacle of England "off its guard" (*EH* 182): "The people that of all peoples is habitually most governed by decencies, proprieties, rigidities of conduct, was for one happy day, unbuttoning its respectable straight-jacket and affirming its large and simple sense of the joy of life" (*EH* 181). Characteristically, James is initially drawn to the festivities of his own class. His gaze falls on the elegant and costumed picnics on top of the shiny coaches. With the handsome thoroughbreds and colorful jockeys whizzing by in the background, however, James finds himself more fascinated by the bawdy and congenial pedestrians than by the opulent spectators who are lunching on champagne and lobster salad.

Perching on his own coach, James focuses on a group of gypsies that "had been drinking deep." In the tradition of the Hawthorne voyeur (Coverdale peering down through the trees from a topmost branch at Blithedale, or Clifford Pyncheon eyeing the townsfolk on parade from his gabled window, for instance), James uncharacteristically takes delight in a scene of merry, working-class debauchery. A young man of twenty has "staggered as best he could to the ground, [where] his cups proved too many for him, and he collapsed and rolled over." James explains with a degree of exuberance and fascination, "In plain English, he was beastly drunk." James's attention and pleasure continue as the young man's equally disabled friends try to place him into a nearby carriage. Their task, of course, is made difficult by their collectively drunken state and by their "package," who, James gleefully remarks, remains unmanageable for being "a mere bag of liquor. . . . He lay in a helpless heap—the best intoxicated young man in England" (*EH* 185).

The observed revelry at Epsom in *English Hours* offers an unusual portrait of life among the less-than-privileged classes. In this Derby Day scene, moreover, James works his way toward a better grasp of the English opposition between conformity and release and—in James's above-cited terms—"[private] insularity and [public] usage." Similarly, he also works his way toward the lingering question of how the "explosive personal force in the English character" expresses itself when it is "compressed and corked down by social conformity." The whole scene at the Derby was "not brilliant nor subtle nor especially graceful, . . . but as an expression of that unbuttoning of the popular straight-jacket it [gave] meaning to the old description of England as merry" (*EH* 188). James partially answers his question on the tension between public and private by observing a long-held preconception of "merry" England; he locates England's ability to maintain convention in its ability to enjoy occasional release and tipsy revelry.

Shifting from England's response to its crowded cities and landscapes to James's own responses—and from social to aesthetic issues—*English Hours* articulates an emerging aesthetic preference for scenes that are domestic, subtle, private, shadowy, and often obscured by twilight's dim glow. This preference is most pronounced in James's accounts of the "well-appointed, well-filled country house." In its private and charming details, it is the most memorable of "all the great things that the English have invented." It stands handsomely as "delightful proof of English domestic virtue, [and] of the sanctity of the British home" (*EH* 273). The details of James's accounts, however, are more telling than his general praises. In the sketches of country house architecture and setting, James expresses an aesthetic preference for privacy that not only structures the English travel pieces but also influences his writings to come. Whether in the small cottages of Chester or in the massive stone mansions of the country, James relishes the chiaroscuro of "a perfect feast of crookedness, . . . random corners, projections and recesses, [and] odd domestic interspaces." Approaching an estate called Compton Wyniates in Warwickshire, he is sure that he has "arrived at the farthest limits of what ivy-smothered brickwork and weather-beaten gables can accomplish for the eye." For James, it offers charm and comfort through its domestic seclusion and by virtue of "being shut off from the world" (*EH* 221).

In keeping with his preferences for secluded English domesticity, James moves further toward his preferred visual stance in his insistence on the inaccessibility of England's beauty. In contrast to Italy's immediate appeal, for instance, England's is subtle and often difficult to discern. On first glance, for instance, English cathedrals appear "pale and naked." To catch the awaiting loveliness, the gazer must wait patiently. "After a while, . . . when you perceive the light beating softly down . . . and your eye measures [the columns] caressingly . . . and lingers on the old genteel inscriptions . . . [and] when you become conscious of that sweet, cool mustiness in the air," you witness the haunted charm of the church (*EH* 72–73). Just as Spencer Brydon would later intuit during the pursuit of his alter ego, and as Maggie Verver would unswervingly know in her efforts to regain the prince, so James's "imported consciousness" here realizes that desired beauty must be approached tentatively. "To walk in quest of any [desired] object," as James wrote of the Litchfield Cathedral, "to find your way, to steal upon it softly, to see at last, . . . [and finally] to push forward with a rush, and emerge and pause and draw that first long breath . . . is a pleasure left to the tourist even after the broad glare of photography has dissipated so many of the sweet mysteries of travel" (*EH* 83).

Not unlike earlier American writers—Hawthorne and Dickinson, for instance—James is drawn to hidden and shaded settings whose beauty is subtle, and difficult to articulate. Like the dim and shaded forest glen in *The Scarlet Letter*, or the equally obscured "slant of light" in Dickinson, James's realm of subtle English beauty is not easily seen with a direct glance, nor readily described by direct prose. Like Dickinson, who preferred to "dwell in Possibility—A fairer house than Prose," James articulates his preference for the delicate scene that shows itself to be far superior to any directly visible object in the glare of broad daylight. The endearing and earnest sweetness of the English girl, for instance, is "far too soft and shy a thing to talk about. The face of this fair creature ha[s] a pure oval, . . . and she smile[s] in a way that [makes] any other [smile] seem a mere creaking of facial muscles" (*EH* 207).

The colors of James's England are muted and blended shades of gray and green. On a country walk in North Devon, he savors the tones of "unpolished silver" that color the "stony backs and foundations and over-clambering garden verdure of certain little gray houses" that merge with the nearby "tender green of scrub oak and fern" (*EH* 102). Similarly, the *real* beauty of Wells Cathedral is not its accessible "wealth of detail" but its subtle, "even, sober, mouse-colored gray" (*EH* 110). James is enchanted by the "sweet accord" between "all stony surfaces covered with . . . the living green of the strong ivy which seems to feed on their decay" (*EH* 186). In this gray-green contrast between dusky, inanimate stonework and verdant, living ivy, James approaches an aesthetic of contrast that characterizes much of *English Hours*. On a dark and gray day in Monmouthshire, the primroses stand out more than they would in bright sunshine. And although the day is dimly lit and drenched by rain, "there are intervals of light and warmth, and in England a couple hours of brightness *islanded* in moisture . . . leaves an uncompromised memory" (*EH* 246). The scene is more memorable not in spite of, but because of, the *partial* and thus contrasting shades of light and dark that provide an aesthetic medium for James's ideas on openness and closure.

Visually, the shadowy interiors and gray-green landscapes exude a haunting and subtle sense of mystery. And, as with other scenes of travel, James not only gazes at the outer contours but also internalizes the mystery-laden scenery and uses it as a means of articulating an artistic stance. James begins with the directly seen landscape or object and proceeds to comment on the psychology of his recorded preference. Observing the "black-coated" and "bonneted" congregation at Wells Cathedral, for instance, James imagines a haunted and enigmatic medieval climate inside the cathedral. The setting is mysterious, and James wants to keep it that way. The scene therefore remains in the "shadows" visually as well as psychologically. Gazing fixedly at a row of young men "clad in black gowns and wearing . . . long hoods trimmed with fur," James prefers to remain in the dark. "Who and what they were I knew not, for I preferred not to learn, lest by chance they should not be so medieval as they looked" (*EH* 111–12).

If James relishes England's shadowed scenes, he is even more effusive when those scenes are enhanced by the dim glow of an "interminable English twilight" (*EH* 83). English cathedrals and landscapes always come out best "when the day begins to fail" and direct vision is even more limited (*EH* 147). On the long summer days in England, the afternoon light has a way of "lingering on until within a couple hours before midnight" (*EH* 108). Gathering material for the "eternity of pleasure," and relishing the long shadows and the ebbing flood of summer light that would constitute the memorable opening of *The Portrait of a Lady*, James seeks out scenes of English twilight: he sees Canterbury in the fading light; All Souls College when "the afternoon light was fading in the stillness" (*EH* 195); Warwickshire when the town displayed Claude-like "purple shadows and slowly shifting lights" (*EH* 198); Stratford as the "twilight was still mildly brilliant" (*EH* 203); and Wroxton Abbey in the "thickening twilight." Similarly, at Wroxton, James wanders through countless dim halls "while the twilight darkens the corners of the expressive rooms and the victim of the scene, pausing at the window, turns his glance and sees . . . the great soft billows of the lawn melt away into the park" (*EH* 223).

If James, like England itself, sought refuge from an overly crowded and public landscape through the secluded subtleties of the English country house, he further endorses England in his insistence on the social value of privacy. On arrival in England, James is impressed by the "admirable English practice of letting people alone" (*EH* 141). The beauty and luxury of English comfort, he adds, is that it is a "limited and restricted, an essentially private affair" (*EH* 156). Here James begins on the level of social observation, moves on briefly to examine the social consequences, and then uses that social commentary as a means of further articulating his emerging artistic stance.

England's national life depends on a split between public and private spheres in a way that is foreign to both Americans and Europeans. England's "machinery of ease," as James calls it, thoroughly depends on a commonly held distinction between public and private relations. This hierarchical plan is the "ever-present fact to . . . a stranger" (*EH* 158). Indeed, it is based on the unspoken English assumption that there *is* such a thing as a stranger (a problematic term in an American democracy) who, necessarily, dwells permanently outside private comforts and thereby provides definition by contrast. Pleasure, in short, is a private and not a public affair. This fact of British life first strikes James in London, where he compares the French or Italian cafe to the equivalent British offering. In London there is simply no " '*public* fund' of amusement": "You must give up the idea of going to sit somewhere in the open air, to eat an ice and listen to a band of music. You will find neither the seat, the ice, nor the band. . . . An Englishman who should propose to sit down, in his own country, at a cafe door would find himself remembering that he is pretending to participations, contacts, fellowships the absolute impracticality of which is expressed in all the rest of his doings" (*EH* 159). The French and Italians prefer their pleasure in public, strolling forth under brightly decorated arcades and among festive crowds. The British, however, prefer to "sit on a terrace overlooking gardens and have [their] *cafe noir* handed to [them] in old Worcester cups by servants who are models of consideration" (*EH* 159).

Continuing his social observation, James is prepared to comment only partially on the consequences of the British penchant for privacy. The genteel privacy that allows for *cafe noir* to be served by private servants, of course, may be preferred by the entire nation, but it is available to only a select few. Initially,

James offers neither critical approval or disapproval but discusses the issue solely on aesthetic terms. He finds himself drawn to the "broad prosperity and pastoral expanse" of Blenheim and is convinced, by the paintings displayed at Warwick Castle, that "good pictures" do not belong on crowded museum walls but should be hung in "largely spaced half-dozens on the walls of fine houses" (*EH* 90).

Of course, privacy on this scale is possible only for the upper classes, and James thus comes to understand all scenic beauty in England as essentially conservative in nature. Moreover, James not only finds himself (quite easily) adopting a conservative outlook on the link between aesthetic pleasure and social caste, but he also suggests that social conservatism itself—with its love of privacy and restraint—offers a useful guide to English society and landscape. The visitor need not be *told* about England's conservatism, for the fact is "written in the hedgerows and in the verdant acres." Strolling in Warwickshire, James senses "some very ancient and curious opinions still comfortably domiciled in fine old houses . . . [and] ornamental woods." And though it excludes many—or, perhaps, *because* it does—this atmosphere of Toryism colors the air and characterizes the very "style of the landscape" (*EH* 210). To emphasize his aesthetic— and *nearly* social—claim, James fills in the remaining gaps. Conservatism itself, he suggests, is a necessary condition for beauty in England. An Episcopal service provides him with his needed effects. With its "magnificent intonations [and] pompous effects," the church displays a spectacular but still understated and exclusive beauty. Its ritual and music "suggested too what is suggested in England at every turn; that conservatism has all the charm and leaves dissent and democracy . . . nothing but their bald logic" (*EH* 73). As if anticipating the famous list of qualities missing in America recorded in James's 1879 Hawthorne biography, this 1877 essay similarly insists that conservatism and accrued history alone can produce culture and beauty. Conservatism (and here we sense no regret on James's part) has "the cathedrals, the castles, the gardens, the traditions, the associations, the fine names, the better manners, the poetry. Dissent has the dusky brick chapels in provincial by-streets, the names out of Dickens, the uncertain tenure of the *h*, and the poor *mens sibi conscia recti*" (*EH* 73–74).

That James observes and concurs with the exclusive tastes and preferences of Victorian upper-class standards comes as no surprise. Like many Americans of the late nineteenth century, James traveled to England and the Continent in search of a source for culture; and like many, he located that source in the fastidious and urbane charms of aristocratic convention. My point here, however, is not to locate the well-known social biases of a young author in his travel sketches but to suggest how those expressed preferences function as a vehicle for developing an emerging aesthetic stance and style. With a temporary shift from social observation back to material sights, I want to move toward an unexpressed but telling link between James's appreciation of England and his experiments in style.

As suggested by James's preference for hidden country houses, shadowed gray-green and wooded landscapes, and twilight scenes, James is fond of the private and enclosed dimensions of English beauty. In the essays on Wells and Salisbury, James's penchant for domestic privacy and for dimly lit interiors becomes especially pronounced. Throughout, James praises not only the private and the enclosed but also the quaint, crooked, and nearly *diminutive* proportions of English scenes and objects. At the Abbey of Glastonbury, he finds historical continuity in the "little street [and] little inn." And, similarly, he finds that the Vicar's Close near Wells Cathedral "consists of a *narrow* oblong court, bordered on each side with thirteen *small* dwellings and terminat[es] in a ruinous *little* chapel. The little houses are very much modernized but they retain . . . their *compactness* and neatness, and a certain *little* sanctified air as of cells in a *cloister*. The place is *adorably* of another world and time" (*EH* 112, emphasis added). In descriptive accounts that seem to recall Beatrix Potter's Keswick in the Lake District more than a noble stone abbey in Wells, James's preference for the tiny, diminutively scaled scene carries him even further into a realm of obscured and entangled landscapes and interiors. At Canterbury, he admires the cathedral's mute but conveyed "desire . . . to be shut up to itself" (*EH* 147). And at Rochester, the haunted-looking cathedral is "small and plain, hidden away in rather an awkward corner. . . . It is dwarfed and effaced by . . . the adjacent castle" (*EH* 145).

Marked by privacy and narrow dimensions, James's favored interiors are not only (socially) unavailable to the lower classes but (aesthetically) nearly inaccessible to any viewing at all. In Devonshire, James approaches a cottage that stands securely hidden by hedges. Behind "huge embankments of moss and turf . . . [and] smothered in wildflowers, . . . grand ivy, . . . flowering thorn [and] golden broom . . . that toss their blooming tangle to the sky" stands a small thatched dwelling. And if the landscape is an intricate web of brush, the cottage itself—"crushed beneath its burden of thatch [and] coated with a rough white stucco" (*EH* 94)—reinforces the impenetrability of the scene. James's English interiors, scaled by a preference for the private, the dimly lit, the diminutive, and the entangled, recall the intricacy of the Chinese puzzle box. They contain, in other words, an exponential number of crannies and spaces that, in turn, lead to more of the same. At Wells, for instance, James approaches the Church of St. Cuthbert in the dim glow of "eventide." He begins by observing the human scene, but his eye is quickly drawn to the *contained* architectural space and crannies of the structure. On the edge of the churchyard, "four old men" sit gossiping in front of a "low gabled house." The scene's enclosure increases when James describes these "extraordinary specimens of decrepitude" as seated not only under the low gables but also inside a dark "antique alcove" that, in turn, is further subdivided into "three shallow little seats" (*EH* 115).

As noted above, one of England's great "facts" is its equation of privacy and beauty. In England, beauty and accessibility are mutually exclusive. "If you therefore talk of anything beautiful in England, the presumption will be that it is private; and . . . if you talk of anything private the presumption will be that it is beautiful. This is something of a dilemma" (*EH* 226). Through James's prose, the reader receives only a partial explanation of that "dilemma." James indeed insists on the inaccessible charm of England. It is hidden away behind hedgerows and garden walls and inside dark stone churches and country houses. For James, however, this inaccessibility is the least of the dilemma—indeed, it adds to his pleasure. In fact the "dilemma" that excites James's appreciation of England's hidden and shadowed landscape is not so different from the dilemma of Maggie Verver, of *The Golden Bowl*, who must strike a balance between accomplishing her private task (of regaining the prince's love) and submitting to a public and self-defeating "outbreak of the definite." Maggie must strike a balance between what she *privately* knows and sees on the one hand and what she *publicly* says and reveals on the other. And in contemplating English scenery, James finds a vehicle for articulating an early version of this same tension between the unsaid and the said, between private and public. As a travel writer, he explains, he can either publicly describe England's hidden charms and risk violating the very privacy that makes the scene beautiful, or he can withhold his account (*his* "outbreak of the definite") and thereby forfeit his expression and the public dimension of his art. Thus, he continues, when "the observer permits himself to commemorate [and describe] charming impressions, he is in danger of *giving* [away] to the world the fruits of friendship and hospitality. When on the other hand he *withholds* his impression he lets something admirable slip away without having done it proper honour" (*EH* 226, emphasis added).

Like Maggie, who, in the evening carriage scene, must "keep up" the tension between giving in to her immediate longings for the prince and withholding her expression in the interest of her envisioned goal (*NY* XXIV, 55–61), James similarly searches for a productive balance by delicately "mingling discretion with enthusiasm" (*EH* 226). In the opposition between private and public in English society and landscape, James finds a vehicle for his thoughts on the aesthetic tension between private and public—between the unsaid and the expressed.

The question of how private and public dimensions of English society and landscape blend together, however, remains far from settled. For throughout *English Hours*, James returns indirectly to the (above-noted) questions of what becomes of private eccentricity and license in the face of Britain's public conformity and convention. As *English Hours* moves from scenic observation to social commentary and aesthetic inquiry, James begins to equate England's private and inaccessible charms not only with hidden landscapes and cramped interiors but also with imaginative license and increased artistic freedom. If, on a social level, England's conformity, overpeopled landscape, and constant reference to a public dimension generate occasional bawdy merriment (as on Derby Day) and an insistence on privacy as a prerequisite for pleasure, then something similar, James ventures, may happen on an artistic level.

Roaming through England in the 1870s, James both concurs with the English on the value of privacy and instinctively *claims* the power of that privacy as a force for his emerging art—the private and enclosed aesthetics of England's landscape and the restricted pleasures of English society structure an emerging aesthetic of privacy and enclosure. Approaching a sixteenth-century country house in Warwickshire, James finds precisely the constricting dimensions he seeks. The cobbled footpath "admits [him] into the small, quaint inner court. From this court, [he is] at *liberty* to pass through the crookedest series of oaken halls and chambers" (*EH* 221, emphasis added). James's sketches of English nooks and hidden interiors increasingly articulate an aesthetic that equates enclosure and restriction with opportunity and "liberty."

Through the English sketches from the 1870s, James locates a wealth of suggestion in England's landscape of enclosure and privacy. Like the thatched cottages he enjoys, England's scenery, its interiors, and its society seem "small, but . . . one could perceive nowhere any limit" (*EH* 230). Containment and restriction (be it social or physical) are desirable and to be coveted. In Chester, for example, the medieval wall creates a restricting, "stony girdle. [But] through it, surely, [its citizens] may *know* their city more intimately than their untucked neighbors" (*EH* 63). Compared with the American, who "seem[s] loosely hung together," every Englishman "is a tight fit in his place" (*EH* 70). In Chester's shops along the arcade created by the wall, the cramped rooms would seem to restrict life under their low ceilings and behind their impenetrable "lattices of lead and bottle glass." Instead, within their cramped contours, "human life . . . expanded into scant freedom and bloomed into small sweetness" (*EH* 69).

American literature is filled with the often problematic discovery that social and imaginative freedoms flourish best in restriction—if indeed they flourish at all. Hester Prynne reluctantly but instinctively returns to the limits of her native Boston; Huck's river adventures and moral discoveries are themselves framed by the restricting shores of the Mississippi; and in his later years, even the self-reliant Emerson grants that "we can afford to allow limitation if we know it is the meter of the *growing* man" (*Selections* 343). Along with Hawthorne and Dickinson, as well as Twain, Henry James understood how—to cite Emerson's admission in "Fate"—"necessity comports with liberty." When recalling his first impressions of a dim hotel room in London, James argues that because its winter light *restricts* vision, it also *encourages* imagination. On his first wintry visit, James discovers his Dickensian London in the parlor fires of the "lone twilights of the clubs, . . . the afternoon tea and toast, and the torpid old gentleman who wakes up from a doze to order potash water." James provides the organizing and telling note, however, when he uses the enclosed geography of the English interior as the ideal set for the writer. Describing the sparsely lit room in the center of the darkening city (and perhaps echoing Hawthorne's account of a Moonlit Room), James suggests that, for the author at least, "this is the best time [and setting] for writing, and that during the lamplit days the white page he tries to blacken becomes, on his table, in the circle of his lamp, with the screen folding him in, more vivid and more absorbent. . . . The [gray] weather makes a kind of sedentary midnight and muffles the possible interruption. It is bad for the eyesight, but *excellent for the image*" (*EH* 35–36, emphasis added).

In the English travel sketches from the 1870s, then, James records his instinctive preference for the domestic privacy, subtlety, and enclosed atmosphere of English society, landscape, and interiors. In these preferred customs and scenes, however, James has also located a Romance medium for working out not only his affection for England's private spaces but also an aesthetic of enclosure as well. As he wrote of his 1869 arrival in England, "I took up the gage, and . . . I have never, in common faith, let it drop again" (*AU* 548). In England, James picked up his "gage" so that his resulting aesthetic pleasure indeed became (in one definition of "gage") a *pledge* or a deposit from which he would draw for a lifetime. But in echoing Emerson's sometimes reluctant praise of limitation and its causal connection with liberty, James also adopted a standard of measurement—a "gage" or gauge—and a growing sense of the artistic value of *necessary* limitation and restriction. In the enclosed and measured charm of England, James discovered the aesthetic dimension of Emerson's late account of how necessity and limitation "comport with liberty." Through the tension between public and private realms of English life, James comes to understand how (on a social and artistic level) restriction and containment generate their opposite. In the English travel sketches, James's initial fondness for British privacy and restriction becomes a vehicle for articulating a literary aesthetic of enclosure and limitation. "Captivity," as Dickinson once suggested, "is Consciousness—[but] So's Liberty."

# 18
# Henry James the Dramatist

*Susan Carlson*

The full flowering of Henry James's career as a dramatist is almost always overlooked. In both *The High Bid* and *The Outcry*, two of his four Edwardian plays, James displays his greatest skills in successfully bringing to the stage the fusions of American and British perspectives, art and life, and morality and manners, fusions that also power his late fiction. In his defense of a third Edwardian play, *The Saloon*, James extols (to no less an audience than G. B. Shaw) his late theater as a viable, even realistic, approach to presenting life on stage:

And if you waylay me here, as I infer you would be disposed to, on the ground that we "don't want works of art," ah then, my dear Bernard Shaw, I think I take such issue with you that—if we didn't both *like* to talk—there would be scarce use in our talking at all. I think, frankly, even that we scarce want anything else at all. They are capable of saying more things to man about himself than any other "works" whatever are capable of doing—and it's only by thus saying as much to him as possible, by saying, as nearly as we can, all there is, and in as many ways and on as many sides, and with a vividness of presentation that "art," and art alone, is an adequate mistress of, that we enable him to pick and choose and compare and know, enable him to arrive at any sort of synthesis that isn't, through all its superficialities and vacancies, a base and illusive humbug. (Letter to Shaw, January 20, 1909, in *CP* 645)

In the volley of letters James and Shaw exchanged over *The Saloon* and the theatrical issues it raises, James did not win Shaw's approbation. Similarly, with his now century-long following of readers, reviewers, and critics, James has been infrequently remembered for his drama. But as I will detail below, his lifelong involvement with the theater should be remembered, ultimately, as a valiant, laudable, and competent effort to purify and preserve for live performance the nuances of his singular social milieu.

Though there have been some recent reevaluations of James's late drama (Carlson, Brenda Murphy), most study of James's theater remains focused on "the dramatic years" and on *Guy Domville* in particular, as Leon Edel prescribes in his incisive introduction to *The Complete Plays*. We have Edel to thank not only for his rescue and preservation of the plays but also for the way he has encouraged all students of Henry James to reconsider the plays, especially as they relate to the development of James's fiction. Now it is rare for a Jamesian scholar looking at James's late fiction, James's work in the nineties, or James's relationship to his audience to overlook the plays. Few quarrel with the importance Edel attaches to what James called "the divine principle of the Scenario" (*NB* 188). Yet, ironically, James's drama and his theatrical career remain threatening to the critical community, perhaps because acknowledging James as a playwright means acknowledging some plodding, even some embarrassingly bad, work. More painfully, it means listening to a James uncharacteristically drawn to prescribed attitudes and limited structures: "The five-act drama—serious or humorous, poetic or prosaic—is like a box of fixed dimensions and inelastic material, into which a mass of precious things are to be packed away. It is a problem in ingenuity and a problem of the most interesting kind" ("Tennyson's Drama" 98). Not surprisingly, then, very little has been written about James's drama. In the pages that follow, I want to suggest both why the drama is overlooked and how it can be appreciated as the product of James's participation in the transformations of the turn-of-the-century British stage. After a general overview of all of James's plays and the primary critical issues they raise, I will consider four plays that represent the evolution of James's theater: *The American*, *The Reprobate*, *Guy Domville*, and *The High Bid*.

## OVERVIEW

As Edel suggests on the contents page for *The Complete Plays*, James's dramas fall into three clearly defined time periods. First, there are the "Beginnings," which include *Pyramus and Thisbe* (1869), *Still Waters* (1871), *A Change of Heart* (1872), and *Daisy Miller* (1882). Second, there is the work of the years Edel has memorialized as "The Dramatic Years": *The American* (1890), *Tenants* (1890), *Disengaged* (1892?), *The Album* (1891), *The Reprobate* (1891), *Guy Domville* (1893), and *Summersoft* (1895). Finally, there are the dramas that Edel categorizes as "The Later Plays" but that seem to be more accurately thought of as "The Mature Plays": *The High Bid* (1907), *The Chaperon* (1893, 1907, never completed), *The Saloon* (1908), *The Other House* (1908), *The Outcry* (1909), and *The Monologue Written for Ruth Draper* (1913).[1] Other nonchronological groupings of the plays begin to suggest the variations in James's approach to and success with his lifelong drama work. Those plays that developed as theatrical adaptations of James's fiction are *Daisy Miller*, *The American*, *The*

*Chaperon*, and *The Saloon* ("Owen Wingrave"). With *Summersoft*, the play preceded the story ("Covering End"); and with *The Other House*, the scenario for the play preceded the novel, which preceded the full play version. The majority of the plays are full-length, three-act plays (*The American* is unique with its four acts), though James also penned one-acts in *Pyramus and Thisbe*, *Still Waters*, *A Change of Heart*, *Summersoft*, *The Saloon*, and *The Monologue Written for Ruth Draper*. Only a fraction of the plays were professionally produced in James's lifetime, including *The American*, *Guy Domville*, *The High Bid*, and *The Saloon*. With the publication of his plays, James was more fortunate. *Pyramus and Thisbe* appeared in the *Galaxy* in April 1869, *Still Waters* in the *Balloon Post* on April 12, 1871, *A Change of Heart* in the January 1872 *Atlantic Monthly*, and *Daisy Miller* both in the *Atlantic Monthly* and in book form. Additionally, four of the plays written in the "dramatic years" of the nineties appeared in James's two volumes entitled *Theatricals* (*Tenants* and *Disengaged* in the first volume and *The Album* and *The Reprobate* in the second). Ironically, James published none of the plays he saw produced. Besides the plays Edel was able to collect for *The Complete Plays*, James appears to have written segments of several others, but these and many notebook references to the plays did not survive James.

James's connection to the theater did not begin and does not end with his plays, however. Edel explains in *The Complete Plays* that James developed his passion for the theater from childhood and that theater-going remained a vital part of his cultural agenda throughout his life. In addition, James's journalistic writing includes exhaustive considerations of the artistic merit to be found in the French and British theaters of the 1870s and 1880s. Later writings, as well as correspondence with Elizabeth Robins and William Heinemann, indicate his careful readings of Ibsen.[2] Throughout his life, James also developed an extensive network of friendships and acquaintances with actresses, playwrights, actor-managers, and others at the forefront of both popular and avant-garde theater, predominantly British theater. His connections included Elizabeth Robins, Ellen Terry, Fanny Kemble, G. B. Shaw, A. W. Pinero, William Archer, George Alexander, Johnston Forbes-Robertson, Edward Compton, Augustin Daly, and Harley Granville-Barker. Finally, James's nontheater writings have been successfully rewritten by others not only for the theater but also for television and the movies. The 1980s, for example, saw the major movie adaptations of *The Bostonians* and *The Europeans*. (See Edel, "Why the Dramatic Arts Embrace Henry James.")

Curiously, the critical evaluations of this man steeped in the theater have been directed away from the theater. Francis Fergusson, in his important analysis of Jamesian technique, goes so far as to erase the drama altogether by devising his analysis of James's "Dramatic Form" solely from James's fiction. Even among those more attentive to the plays themselves, the tendency continues to accept the judgments—of Edel, Walter Isle, Michael Egan, Leo Levy, and others—that the drama is best appreciated as a corollary to James's fiction. Indeed, such critics have relied on their study of James's plays to extend our understanding of the complexities of James's fiction. But they have discouraged close study of the plays as plays. There remain only two book-length studies (Carlson, Kossman) and a handful of essays focusing primarily on the plays.

The eclectic group of critical discussions of the plays often concentrate on two central issues: (1) James's attitude to drama and to the theater and (2) James's relationship to his audience. James's attitude to the theater was always based on excitement; even speculating about theater work brought James an energy unmatched in his other endeavors. Several often-cited passages from James's public and private writings capture the electric mood. Reviewing the Parisian stage in 1872, for example, James glories in the unmatchable brilliance to be found at the Théâtre Français:

The stage throws into relief the best gifts of the French mind, and the Théâtre Français is not only the most amiable but the most characteristic of French institutions. I often think of the inevitable first sensations there of the "cultivated foreigner," let him be as stuffed with hostile prejudice as you please. He leaves the theatre an ardent Gallomaniac. This, he cries, is the civilized nation, *par excellence*. Such art, such finish, such grace, such taste, such a marvellous exhibition of applied science, are the mark of a chosen people, and these delightful talents imply the existence of every virtue. ("The Parisian Stage" 1872, in *The Scenic Art* 3–4)

The enthusiasm infuses James's private writings too, where he credits the French stage with enabling his dramatic voice. "The French stage I have mastered; I say that without hesitation. I have it in my pocket, and it seems to me clear that this is the light by which one must work today" (December 26, 1881, in *NO* 226–27). But it is in his responses to the theatrical production of his own work where James is most undeniably ecstatic. He writes to his brother William after the successful opening of *The American*:

Now that I have tasted blood, *c'est une rage* (of determination to *do*, and triumph, on my part), for I feel at last as if I had found my *real* form, which I am capable of carrying far, and for which the pale little art of fiction, as I have practised it, has been, for me, but a limited and restricted substitute. The strange thing is that I always, innermostly, knew *this* was my more characteristic form—but was kept away from it by a half-modest half-exaggerated sense of the difficulty (that is, I mean the practical odiousness) of the conditions. (February 6, 1891, in *HJL* III, 329)

As James encountered difficulties in his own theater ventures, however, this unalloyed joy gave way to the ambivalence that would mark his dealings with the theater from the early nineties onward. Even before the debacle of *Guy Domville* in 1895, James was confiding to William and William's wife his mixed response to theatrical life, distinguishing between the drama he continued to treasure and the theater he was weary of.

I mean to wage this war ferociously for one year more—1894—and then (unless the victory and the spoils have by that become more proportionate than hitherto to the humiliations and vulgarities and disgusts, all the dishonour and chronic insult incurred) to "chuck" the whole intolerable experiment and return to more elevated and more independent courses. The whole odiousness of the thing lies in the connection between the drama and the theatre. The one is admirable in its interest and difficulty, the other loathsome in its conditions. If the drama could only be theoretically or hypothetically acted, the fascination resident in its all but unconquerable (*circumspice!*) form would be unimpaired, and one would be able to have the exquisite exercises without the horrid sacrifice. (December 29, 1893, in *HJL* III, 452)

After the public humiliation of *Guy Domville*, James made the drama-theater distinction central to his thinking, repeatedly writing to his friends, "I *may* be meant for the Drama—God knows!—but I certainly wasn't meant for the Theatre" (Letter to Elizabeth Lewis, December 15?, 1894, in *HJL* III, 496; see also Letter to Elizabeth Robins, December 31, 1894, in *HJL* III, 503). In later years, James continued to judge his experiences through this bifurcating distinction, but he never lost the attraction to the experience of the theater. Even during his long absence from the theater, from 1895 to 1907, theater ventures could tempt him as nothing else could.

But I've also said I *would* do him [George Alexander] a *fresh* one-act thing; and it's strange how this little renewal of contact with the vulgar theatre stirs again, in a manner, and moves me. Or rather, it isn't at all the contact with the theatre—still as ever, strangely odious; it's the contact with the DRAMA, with the divine little difficult, artistic, ingenious, architectual FORM that makes old pulses throb and old tears rise again. The blended anguish and amusement again touch me with their breath. (January 22, 1899, in *NO* 171)

James's familiarity with the drama of several nations also contributes to his ambivalent, complicated relationship with the theater. Edel and Rudolph Kossman have insisted on privileging the French theater as James's primary model, taking their cue from James's own valorization of the French. Elsewhere I have argued for a closer analysis of James's work in its British theatrical context, specifically in the realm of the British comedy of manners, where James proved himself a master. But Ibsen's influence on James has been most prominently urged, perhaps because in connecting James with Ibsen, critics can avoid comparisons between James's work and the questionable drama of the nineteenth-century French and British theaters (Cromer, Egan, King). Anne Margolis has written about James's similarly plural response to the internal distinctions of British drama. The vast differences between the traditional popular theater of actor-managers and the avant-garde theater that championed Ibsen, Shaw, and others occasioned contradictory responses from James. Just as James insisted on separating his ideas of drama and theater, Margolis notes, so also did he split his theatrical allegiances; his desire to reform and remake the British stage conflicted with his desire for money and theatrical success (77–79).

The divided allegiances that stem from James's energetic though ambivalent attitude to the theater account also for his fractured response to theatrical audiences. On the one hand, James desired the money and fame that he saw Henry Arthur Jones, Arthur Wing Pinero, and other playwrights exacting for successful London runs. Margolis speculates further that James envisioned using the power to be gained from on-stage success to dictate his own terms in all his publishing concerns (75). On the other hand, James had a strong scorn for the theatrical audience he planned to lure. In his 1870s and 1880s pieces about the London stage, he finds the theater at best a place for the fashionably well-dressed to parade their clothes and at worst an institution that would always be held back by English "hypocrisy and prudery" ("The London Theatres" 1877, in *The Scenic Art* 96). Several recent analyses of James's relationships to his audiences, his marketplace, and his readers have expanded our understanding of this internal antagonism. Michael Anesko, Marcia Jacobson, and Margolis use their reading of "the dramatic years" to help explain James's lifelong ambivalence toward all aspects of the production and reception of his work. As we will see below in a closer view of four plays, James's ambivalent attitudes to drama, theater, and audience led to an emotionally charged but uneven dramatic canon.

Unfortunately, discussions of James's complicated relationship to drama and theater have frequently displaced close consideration of the plays themselves. So my summary of the critical issues connected with James's drama brings me only belatedly to the plays. To suggest the sophisticated approach James brought to his drama, I will detail just one of his main theatrical concerns—his women.

Since Howells, readers of James's work have noted his special affinity for women. Critics have always paid close attention to James's sympathetic portraits of women, and in the last decade, feminist critics have mapped out their own version of the terrain James's women occupy. The relationship between James and women is not, however, an easy one.[3] Sandra Gilbert and Susan Gubar have recently documented the pressing nature of "the woman question" during the years of James's authorship (133–37). With James in particular, they note his manifestation of the fears male writers of his generation expressed toward women writers (James was in the first generation of male writers to cope with successful and powerful women predecessors). Virginia Fowler notes similarly that though James identified his art with women, he feared a too predominantly female world. His observations in *The American Scene* as well as his 1906–7 discourses on the manners and speech of American women suggest the great extent of those fears at the end of his career. Yet such fears did not prevent James from making some rare, extraordinary attempts to bring his women to subjectivity (see Fowler 32 and Habegger, "Lessons of the Father"). Though there is not unanimity, there is some general agreement that James identified and sympathized with his women even though he could rarely project for them a world in which they would be free from patriarchal constraints. In James's plays, the extent of women's powers and limitations is additionally conditioned by the demands of the genre.

Most of James's plays are comedies.[4] In drawing particularly from the British and French comedies of manners he was so familiar with, James inherited a genre with conflicting attitudes toward women. On the one hand, such social dramas set women in powerful positions and allow them a range of behaviors not usually sanctioned. James was adept at giving life and depth to such women, as his plays *Tenants, Disengaged, The Album, The Reprobate, The High Bid,* and *The Outcry* attest. On the other hand, comedies—especially comedies of manners—almost invariably counteract such female freedom with an ending in marriage. Though marriage is joyously promised at the end of each of the six comedies listed above, James clearly understood the impositions of marriage, especially for women. That he also understood the imposition of marriage on his art is clear from a letter to William. When, during the run of *The American,* James rewrote act four to clarify Claire and Newman's decision to marry, he acceded to the demands of stage and genre but only, as he tells William, at the price of compromising himself. "So the fourth is now *another* fourth which will basely gratify their [the audience's] artless instincts and British thick-wittedness, and thanks to it the poor old play will completely save one's *honour* (which is all I care for) as a *permanent* and regular thing. It will be much for it to 'keep the stage' " (November 15, 1892, in *HJL* III, 397). The world James created for his dramatic women was paradoxical. Yet within its confines and restrictions, James worked to perfect a stage version of his novelistic melding of manners, morals, and social salvation. John Carlos Rowe suggests that sacrificing is one of the main actions Jamesian women can undertake (*Theoretical Dimensions* 92). Yet in James's plays, as in his fiction, he elevates sacrifice into salvation. And as his women set out on missions of salvation, their manners become their armor and their weapons as they circumspectly battle to bring morality to the lives of those around them. In the plays, it is through their battles to reform the moral lives of those around them that women move toward subjectivity and selfhood.

James is not a major dramatist and is often not even a good one. But he brings to the stage a unique blend of comedy and culture, conditioned always by his concern for making the stage his own territory.

## THE PLAYS

Whereas *Pyramus and Thisbe, Still Waters, A Change of Heart,* and *Daisy Miller* show James exploring the possibilities of dramatic form, his stage version of *The American* best represents the difficulties he had in his early writing for the theater. James's artistic problems with the play have many sources. It was still, of course, early in his career, and he had not yet enjoyed the advantage of seeing his work performed. But James's skill in and attachment to fiction writing constituted a more debilitating handicap. James was unable to translate his fictive concerns into theatrically viable language as he deliberately resisted the alterations playwriting seemed to require. Envisioning the transformation of his novel

*The American* into a play, James in fact looks for the result to be nothing but "bad": "I must extract the simplest, strongest, baldest, most rudimentary, at once most humorous and most touching one [play], in a form whose main *souci* shall be pure situation and pure point combined with pure brevity. Oh, how it must not be too good and how very bad it must be!" (May 12, 1889, in *NO* 53). The result is, in fact, a tedious play that maintains a troubled double identity—as drama and as fiction. When James simplifies and shortens in his attempt to give his audience what he thinks it wants, he produces drama full of broad intrigue and laughable melodrama. Christopher Newman himself is often no more than a parody of his novelistic self. Noémie Nioche's role is enlarged so that her flirtations trivialize more than their share of the play. It is only fair to note that James's efforts to make *The American* into popular theater result in a product not that dissimilar from the more successful plays of his contemporaries Jones and Pinero. But by drawing on the sophistication of his fiction, James presents his own demanding internal measure of these broad theatrical effects. And the melodramatic effects clearly seem inadequate. The "bad" moments seem so "bad" not because they are part of a play but because James also has moments in which his characters engage in clever, meaningful banter. Even in *The American*, James's theater is not always "bad"; he shows some promise as a playwright.

With Claire de Cintré especially, James creates a stage presence fit to convey the complex and valuable mannered life that he so often studies and that was to become the hallmark of his best plays. Before he meets Claire, Newman describes to Valentin the sort of woman he seeks as his wife: "I want a *first-class* woman, and I don't care what she is, so long as she's only perfect; beautiful, amiable, clever, good, the product of a long civilization and a great cultivation! I shall expect her to have everything the world can give—except a fortune" (*CP* 198). And as Newman later informs her, Claire indeed comes "up to the mark" (*CP* 207). As James's primary vessel in the play for what is valuable in culture and manners, Claire is not easily diminished by the melodrama and intrigue of the play. Yet Claire is only a shadow of the culturally conscious characters James would learn to position believably at the center of his plays. From his experience with *The American*, however, James clearly learned that his best theater would not grow from his fiction. To both W. D. Howells and Robert Louis Stevenson, he acknowledged that the play "suffers damnably from the straight-jacket of the unscenic book" (Letter to Stevenson, October 30, 1891, in *HJL* III, 361).

*The American*'s hybrid of fictive and dramatic techniques displays both James's inadequacies and his strengths as a young playwright. But more instructive than James's journeyman-like work on the play is his response to its theatrical environment. At the threshold of James's "dramatic years," the play is most significant for the several kinds of public encouragement it brought James. His letters from the many months of the play's writing and production convey James's sustained, high-pitched joy. In preparation for the London premiere, James even made arrangements for costumes and stage furniture. Most charmingly of all, he attended London rehearsals, playing the role of benevolent host. Elizabeth Robins, James's friend who played Claire in London, remembers his supplying the cast with sandwiches. "He was like a man 'at home' in his new house, accepting naturally his office of host" (Robins 53). But a still more important mark of James's fervid involvement in *The American* is his response to the public attention paid to his work.

Written for Edward Compton, the play opened first in Southport in January 1891, and after several months of provincial touring it premiered in London's Opera Comique in September. This double production allowed James multiple opportunities to interact with theater people and operations. Most thrilling for James was the ovation he earned from the fifteen hundred attendees at Southport's opening night. In his report to his sister, Alice, he is glowing with pride:

It was really *beautiful*—the splendid success of the whole thing, reflected as large as the surface presented by a Southport audience (and the audience was very big indeed) could permit. The attention, the interest, the outbursts of applause and appreciation hushed quickly for fear of losing (especially with the very bad acoustic properties of the house) what was to follow, the final plaudits, and recalls (I mean after each act) and the big universal outbreak at the end for "author, author!" in duly *delayed* response to which, with the whole company grinning in delight and sympathy (behind the curtain) I was led before by Compton to receive the first "ovation," but I trust not the last, of my life. (January 4, 1891, in *HJL* III, 320)

James appeared to ovations on the first night in London also. The reception was not quite as enthusiastic but perhaps more respectable, for the audience boasted the likes of George Meredith, John Singer Sargent, George du Maurier, Arthur Pinero, and Augustin Daly. The reviews of both openings by preeminent critics offered qualified praise, which also encouraged James. Though behind the scenes at Southport, William Archer warned James that his play would not succeed in London as it had in the provinces, Archer's review in the *World* praised a play "full of alert and telling dialogue and incidents which show a keen eye for stage effect." Clement Scott's encouragement came with his instruction that James the master of fiction should develop his budding dramatic talents: "I think that the idea underlying 'The American' is as admirable a dramatic idea as an author could well devise. The contrast between the new world and the old, the battle between wealth and pride, with love in the balance, is exactly the germ that in experienced hands should make a brilliant comedy of manners." As he wrote to William in the following month (see above), James thrived on such attention and found the response gratifying enough to launch himself on four more years of theater work. As a look at *The Reprobate* and *Guy Domville* will show, these were years in which James became more adept at the games of theater production and fairly skillful in writing drama.

*The Reprobate* is the best of the four theatricals James published in 1894 and 1895. Egan, Levy, and F. W. Dupee have all remarked on its merit. And though it remained unproduced in James's lifetime, the play demonstrates the skill that

James was gaining during the "dramatic years." As James himself counsels, such "rejected addresses" as this play, when "given to the light," can teach us much about the theater ("Note" to *Theatricals: Second Series*, in *CP* 350).

James's long "Note" that prefaces the published versions of both *The Reprobate* and *The Album* has received as much, if not more, attention than the play because in this public forum James displays his conflicting desires about the theater, conflicts that his private correspondents were familiar with. The theater audience is, once again, blamed for giving "the taint of the perfunctory even to the cleverest play" (*CP* 348). And though drama is an "insufferable little art" (*CP* 351), demanding inconsequential subjects from any writer who tries on "the theatrical strait-jacket" (*CP* 348), the challenge of it privileges drama above "any other aesthetic errand" (*CP* 351). Reviewers of *Theatricals: Second Series* tied this display of James's tortured relationship with drama to his continuing inability to write for theater in his own voice. The reviewer in the *Critic* notes that James would have improved his work "had he allowed himself to be guided by his own instincts": "The literary and dramatic qualities of the works have been affected injuriously by a too conscientious effort to comply with them [the conditions of the theater] literally" ("Mr. Henry James's 'Theatricals' ").

Despite its deflating preface and some qualified literary reviews, the play itself is good, with surprisingly few hints of James's earlier struggle to define his dramatic voice. Most of the play is carried by its quick action and delightful dialogue. The two main characters, Mrs. Freshville and Paul Doubleday, are former lovers who meet by chance at the Hampton Court villa of Mr. Bonsor. Mrs. Freshville is there clandestinely, chasing a new love, Captain Chanter. She eventually ends up with a third man, Pitt Brunt. Doubleday is there as a semi-imprisoned, thirty-year-old ward of Mr. Bonsor. As the "reprobate" of the title, Paul is under tight moral guard because of past indiscretions (especially his time with Mrs. Freshville). As the action moves all the characters toward the predictable comic pairings and marriage, we follow a series of events in which characters "save" one another. The well-made play form, which disrupted some of James's early efforts like *The American*, becomes his tool here. For example, bold, climactic act endings function as comedy, not melodrama. Dialogues that include melodramatic moments are usually parodic; for example, Mrs. Doubleday's tale of her "hard" past is meant not to elicit pity but to expose her weak character. And Mrs. Freshville's end-of-play pairing with Pitt Brunt makes ironic reference to the happy ending of marriage. Only in the third act is there an indication of James's artificial manipulation of characters and plot. The generally comfortable feeling in James's plot is complemented by clever and appropriate wordplay, a far cry from the heavy-handed dialogue of *Daisy Miller* and *The American*. For example, Paul's reference to the "railroad of social intercourse" expands along with his growing social confidence: "You *can* go a certain length, Mamma, you can achieve certain runs—but you can't make the time you did! A road may be well kept up, but if you go in for heavy traffic you must lay your account with a smash. Don't therefore, as I say, don't magnify small accidents. Don't cry out about a collision when there has only been a casual bump!'' (CP 448).

Supporting this bright action are a handful of familiar Jamesian ideas, salvation primary among them, as I mentioned above. Paul, who has accepted his wardens' judgment that he is morally bruised (he tells Blanche Amber [Mr. Bonsor's niece] that he is a "moral leper" [CP 434]), learns through the tutelage of Mrs. Freshville, Blanche, and Captain Chanter that his moral behavior is as healthy as anyone's. In recognizable Jamesian fashion, he acknowledges the vicissitudes of moral life. And his loving acceptance by Blanche at the end of the play certifies his internalization of a civilized code. Interestingly, though his education points him toward recognition of himself, he applies his education by saving two of his principal instructors, Captain Chanter and Mrs. Freshville, neither of whom is as worthy as Paul but both of whom benefit from Paul's integrity. The correspondence shows that as late as 1908, James saw Paul as the key to *The Reprobate*. I find, however, that his treatment of the two main women is more instructive about James's developing theater. With Paul, James refines the broad strokes of *The American*: with Mrs. Freshville and Blanche, he looks forward to the subtleties of *The High Bid*.

As the only uninvited guest at Mr. Bonsor's villa, Mrs. Freshville squeezes her clandestine appearances on stage in between the other inhabitants' interactions. She is isolated, interacting only with one other character at a time. But whether she is ingratiating herself with the butler Cubit, chiding the runaway Chanter, flirting with Brunt, or reminiscing with Paul, she displays many of the qualities James demands from his leading ladies: she is clever, charming, quick, and insightful. However, she is distinguishable from many of James's other central women because of her questionable past. Her Parisian liaison with Paul, her affair with Chanter, and her ambiguous marital status go hand in hand with her frequently fickle behavior in the play. In addition, our knowledge of her past prepares us for the laughable couple she and Brunt present at the end of the play. This figure of the older, more experienced, more worldly woman will become the successful and powerful center of James's best plays. But here James exposes the fine line he is able to draw between a woman whose experience increases her moral value and one whose experience tarnishes her worth. This woman-with-a-past is not redeemed; ånd though she does help bring Paul to his moral enlightenment, she is kept from Blanche Amber. In later plays James will bring his experienced woman to the social and cultural aid of a needy young woman (like Blanche) just entering the social scene, but in *The Reprobate*, James does not allow Mrs. Freshville a single moment of access to Blanche Amber. His portrait of Mrs. Freshville, in other words, reveals how James's glorification of women in his best plays has developed out of a less praiseworthy, clearly patriarchal categorization of women. Blanche, then, more than Mrs. Freshville, prefigures the Jamesian dramatic heroine of his later drama. She is young and unmarried but as sharp as anyone else in the play and almost as savvy as Mrs. Freshville. In her very first appearance, when she cleverly establishes a connection with Paul against the frantic counterefforts of her guardian, we are alerted to her as the best representative in the play of an approach to life that is open yet thoughtful, moral yet accepting. The scenes in which she appears are among the best because melodrama cannot attach to her clear-eyed attitudes.

The effect of both Mrs. Freshville and Blanche is muted because James does not put the two women in league, as he would so successfully in *The High Bid*. The clumsiness of the denouement also diminishes the women's ascendancy. Nevertheless, in *The Reprobate*, James demonstrates a developing sense of theatrical exigencies and exercises his skills at dramatic dialogue and characterization.

*The Reprobate* was not staged until after James's death.[5] Thus it is by *Guy Domville*, which *was* so memorably staged, that James's dramatic skills of the nineties are almost exclusively examined. Most students of James are at least vaguely familiar with *Guy Domville* as the "dramatic" end of "the dramatic years." Yet in studying James's drama, one would be more accurate to think of the events surrounding *Guy Domville* as a turning point—not the ending point—to James's career as a playwright. To suggest how the play figures in James's dramatic life, I will look first at the play itself, so often overlooked in the recounting of its reception. Then I will summarize the public life of the play, which too neatly has come to be the hallmark of James's theater career.

James eagerly offered the idea for *Guy Domville* to the popular actor-manager George Alexander after Alexander had produced Pinero's *The Second Mrs. Tanqueray* and thus demonstrated his commitment to serious drama. Though Pinero's play was one of the best of the many nineties plays about women-with-pasts, James's play offered a less familiar, more intellectual, focus on Jamesian staples—renunciation and salvation. Guy Domville, on the eve of his entry into the Catholic church in 1780, is called on, as the last of the Domvilles, to preserve the family by renouncing his religious vows and marrying. Not only does Guy unexpectedly find himself torn between his commitments to family and to religion, but he also must negotiate the delicacies of his platonic love relationship with the widow Mrs. Peverel and his encumbered friendship to Frank Humber. The play is atypical of Jamesian drama in that it is not comic or woman-centered. It is, however, the first of his plays in which the central character is portrayed as a social "artist" who masters the "art" of living.

The opening act is among James's best. The dialogue is a model of delicate, revealing, mannered banter, full of subtle Jamesian conflict. During what are supposed to be Guy's last hours out of the church, he and Mrs. Peverel find their conversation about duty and "helping" also unavoidably about their unexpressed love.

*Mrs. Peverel*: You have indeed the vocation, Mr. Domville.

*Guy*: I have the opportunity. I've lived with my eyes on it, and I'm not afraid. The relinquished ease—the definite duties—the service of the Church—the praise of God: these things seem to wait for me! And then there are people everywhere to help.

*Mrs. Peverel*: If you help others as you've helped me, your comfort will indeed be great!

*Guy*: I *have* my comfort, for under your roof I've found—my only way, my deepest need. I've learned here what I am—I've learned here what I'm not. Just now, as I went from place to place with the child, certain moments, certain memories came back to me. I took him the round of all our rambles, yours and mine—I talked to him prodigiously of his mother.

*Mrs. Peverel*: *I* shall talk to him of his absent tutor. (*CP* 489–90)

Reviewers and commentators alike have noted, however, that in act two, James abandons this effective balancing of commentary, emotion, and action. When the scene shifts from Mrs. Peverel's rural retreat at Porches to the Domville estate at Richmond, James overplays the connivings and evil of the decadent social world of Lord Devenish and Mrs. Domville (Guy's cousin). As Margolis suggests, James may have been hoping to appeal to the coarser tastes of his audience by offering a reconstituted Guy enthralled by his high-flying social life and even by offering a drinking match between Guy and George Round (91). For whatever reasons, in act two James undermines the grace and charm of the first act as he exaggerates the moral dilemmas Guy faces. Ironically, the Guy of act two retains the smooth language of act one to describe his observations. For instance, he says to Mrs. Domville in discussing his lost innocence: "It goes down like an ebbing tide! I pick up fresh feelings as you gather pink shells; and when I hold these shells to my ear I find in each the mysterious murmur of the world!" (*CP* 498). But Guy's decision to marry a woman he hardly knows seems wildly out of character.

In act three, when James returns the action to Porches, he recaptures the measured, somber mood of act one. As act two ends, Guy makes his first renunciation in refusing his arranged marriage. In act three, he matches that with a second renunciation—he must give up Mrs. Peverel to her more constant lover, Frank. Irrevocably this time, Guy dedicates himself to the Catholic church. The shadings of meaning that James easily conveys with Guy, Frank, and Mrs. Peverel on stage reappear in this final act. And though James does not prevent Guy's renunciation of Mrs. Peverel from seeming somewhat perverse, James's refusal to offer what would have been a popular, romantic tie suggests the originality in his portrait of mannered nuances. Several years later, in remembering James's dramatic career, his friend Edmund Gosse accurately described the effect of James's bold conclusion: "The only disadvantage that I could discover was that instead of having a last scene which tied up all the threads in a neat conclusion, it left all those threads loose as they would be in life" (430).

The play itself, then, remains valuable for its generally successful portraiture of the fragile realm of renunciation and of religious and familial duty. James knew, as he wrote William, "it's altogether the best thing I've done" (January 9, 1895, in *HJL* III, 509). I would add that in underusing Mrs. Peverel, one of his most interesting characters, James invites speculation about what more the play could have been. Mrs. Peverel's story of renunciation parallels Guy's, but whereas Guy's retreat to the church seems appropriate, she is strangely rewarded with a connection to Frank Humber, a connection she is clearly ambivalent about. Edel notes that during production, the audience's sympathies were with her, *not* Guy, and proposes that James could have better explained in fiction Guy's rejection of her love, as well as her acceptance of Guy's decision. Yet James the playwright would also find a way of fully considering such a complex woman when, in his Edwardian drama, he made his female characters his central characters. Before we consider that mature work, however, we need to review the ugly public scar that *Guy Domville* so prominently seared on James's theatrical career.

In both *The Complete Plays* and his biography of James, Edel recounts the events surrounding the opening night of *Guy Domville*, January 5, 1895. St. James's Theatre in London was packed, above, with the fashionable supporters of intellectual drama and loaded, below, with loyal George Alexander fans. Act one came off beautifully. But when act two disappointed both audiences, act three became a battleground between those above, determined to support James's heroic effort, and those below, set on registering their complaints to Alexander. When James arrived at the theater near the end of the play (he had spent the evening watching Oscar Wilde's *An Ideal Husband* in a vain attempt to calm his nerves), he had no idea of the battle in progress. So when Alexander ill-advisedly brought James on stage to the audience's calls for the author, James faced one of the worst moments of his life. The actor Frank Dyall reported that James was "green with dismay" (*CP* 477), and H. G. Wells, who was present to review the play for the *Pall Mall Gazette*, detailed the debilitating moment:

Disaster was too much for Alexander that night. A spasm of hate for the writer of those fatal lines must surely have seized him. With incredible cruelty he led the doomed James, still not understanding clearly how things were with him, to the middle of the stage, and there the pit and gallery had him. James bowed; he knew it was the proper thing to bow. Perhaps he had selected a few words to say, but if so they went unsaid. I have never heard any sound more devastating than the crescendo of booing that ensued. The gentle applause of the stalls was altogether overwhelmed. For a moment or so James faced the storm, his round face white, his mouth opening and shutting and then Alexander, I hope in a contrite mood, snatched him back into the wings. (*Experiment* 64)

When James recounts his perspective on the bleak event, he describes an "abominable quarter of an hour during which all the forces of civilization in the house waged a battle of the most gallant, prolonged and sustained applause with the hoots and jeers and catcalls of the roughs" (January 9, 1895, in *HJL* III, 508). To this opening-night scene, as melodramatic as any climactic moment in a third-rate drama, James responded by denying the theater, which had consumed his energy for five years. He returned to fiction, noting defiantly in his notebooks, "I take up my old pen again" (January 23, 1895, in *NO* 109).

Most critics have chosen to read *Guy Domville* as the end to James's infatuation with the theater. But for this pivotal moment in James's life there are variant readings.[6] Guy Domville did not close on its eventful first night. On its second night, which James attended, the play was performed to what the reviewer G. W. Smalley reported as "a perfect storm of applause" (*CP* 480). Subsequently, the production ran for an honorable five weeks (though James himself reported that his friends were swelling the ranks with multiple visits). In addition, the critical reception of the play was positive, much more encouraging than the response to *The American* had been. Shaw, Wells, and A. B. Walkley were among those eager to credit the delicate differences of this play even while acknowledging the difficulties of act two. Yet despite such support, as a direct result of his experiences with *Guy Domville*, James retreated almost completely from active participation in the theater for over ten years.

He did not forget the theater, however. Almost immediately he reconsidered his rejection of the stage, writing the one-act *Summersoft* at Ellen Terry's invitation. Nothing came of the project, and for the next few years James turned down several other offers for him to return to playwriting. But James did return to the theater in the late Edwardian years, when he finished five more theater pieces. In each of them, he extends the grace of *Guy Domville* and the theater competency of *The Reprobate*. However, it is with *The High Bid*, the first of his Edwardian efforts, that he produces his best play.

By 1907, when James wrote the play, the world that conditioned his drama and his theater was much changed. The drawing-room society he had championed in his nineties drama was now self-consciously aware of living out its twilight years. A theater that was before bulwarked against thinkers like Ibsen and Shaw now welcomed discussion and experimentation.[7] In this altered climate, James felt free to return, in a new and relaxed way, to the international-manners drama he had abandoned with his theatrical adaptations of *Daisy Miller* and *The American*. As he worked up the initial ideas for *The High Bid* way back in 1892, James foresaw that the salvation of British culture, which would be the core of this play, had to draw from an American temperament.

What my American woman must represent, at any rate, is the idea of attachment to the past, of romance, of history, continuity and conservatism. She represents it from a fresh sense, from an individual conviction, but she represents it none the less—and the action must be something in which she represents it effectively—with a power to save and preserve. In other words, she, intensely American in temperament—with her freedoms, her immunity from traditions, superstitions, fears and *riguardi*, but with an imagination kindling with her new contact with the presence of a *past*, a continuity, etc., represents the conservative element among a cluster of persons ... already in course of becoming demoralized, vulgarized, and (from their own point of view), Americanized. She "steps in," in a word, with a certain beautiful beneficence and passion. *How* she steps in, how she arrests and redeems and retrieves and appeals and clears up and *saves*—it is in the determination of this that must reside the *action* of my play. (November 24, 1892, in *NO* 72–73)

He first developed his American savior in the one-act *Summersoft*, written for Terry in 1895. This version of the play was never produced, but in 1907 James was convinced by the actor-manager Johnston Forbes-Robertson not only that the play should be produced but also that it should see public life in three acts.[8] At Forbes-Robertson's urgings, James expanded *Summersoft* into three acts at breakneck pace (in twenty days) and produced *The High Bid*, a script that combined clean dramatic lines and mature cultural insight. James's American woman, the widow Mrs. Gracedew, comes to Covering End, the family home of Captain Yule, merely to visit and admire. But finding the house endangered by Mr. Prodmore's greed, she positions herself to save the house by enabling Cora, Prodmore's daughter, to marry her clandestine lover, Hall Pegg, and by keeping Cora's intended, Yule, for herself.

Whereas James's previous social wizards like Mrs. Freshville, Mrs. Vibert (*Tenants*), and Mrs. Jasper (*Disengaged*) had been separate from his moral aestheticians like Guy Domville, Paul Doubleday, and Grace Jesmond (*The Album*), in Mrs. Gracedew, James brings together his moral voice and his social artist. And salvation is, if anything, more central than in any previous play. For Mrs. Gracedew saves the whole of British mannered society along with the particular inhabitants of Covering End. To help us appreciate these acts of salvation, James encourages our scrutiny of each character's social and cultural aptitude. We measure the worthiness of the inhabitants of James's rarefied world against the extremes he offers in the butler Chivers and in Prodmore. Chivers, with "perfect manner and tone" (*CP* 555), is a human symbol of social decorum. He borders on being an artifact of past glory. Prodmore, with his graceless mimicking of manners, can muster but an artificial imitation of social response. Of all those who fall between these poles of behavior, in Mrs. Gracedew, James offers the golden mean, a character whose words and actions bring the natural and the social comfortably together. Throughout the play she and Yule engage the others in some of James's most graceful, scintillating, and meaningful dialogues.

As I have hinted several times in discussing James's earlier plays, his success in *The High Bid* is directly linked to his placement of Mrs. Gracedew at the center of the play. Yet as I have also forewarned, this woman is the culmination of James's ambivalent attitude toward the women of his plays. Behind Mrs. Gracedew stand less reputable figures like Mrs. Freshville, for example. We have no indication that Mrs. Gracedew has committed moral indiscretions, as Mrs. Freshville has, but we feel the shadow of such secrets, since Mrs. Gracedew's social vivaciousness closely parallels Mrs. Freshville's. In addition, Mrs. Gracedew produces in the male characters the unsettling emotions and responses a powerful woman can set off; and James most clearly counteracts the discomfort she produces by marrying Mrs. Gracedew to Yule at the end of the play. But James also offers his sympathy toward Mrs. Gracedew and the women she represents by making clear the link between her extraordinary social skills and her second-rate social position. Though Mrs. Gracedew is clearly the most powerful person in the play, she has had to gain her power by magnificent and constant efforts. She risks everything—her money, her happiness, her future.

She must control everyone—the butler, the ingenue, the manipulative father, her potential lover. In addition, she cannot operate directly but must win her way through backhanded, underhanded, and convoluted language and actions. For example, when Yule realizes that he will no longer be forced to marry Cora to save his house from Mr. Prodmore, Mrs. Gracedew does not (and cannot) simply suggest that he marry her instead. In her indirect way, she must let him feel he has come to that decision on his own.

*Yule*: (Taking it in further, making it out, staring before him; but then wincing, pulling himself up, clouded again.) Oh I see—I lose my House!

*Mrs. Gracedew*: (Shocked at his simplifications.) *Dear* no—*that* doesn't follow! (After an instant.) You simply arrange with *me* to keep it.

*Yule*: (Sincerely wondering.) "Simply"? (Not making it out.) How do I arrange?

*Mrs. Gracedew*: (As cheerfully, sociably preaching patience.) Well, we must *think*. We must wait. (As if it's a mere detail, only the principle granted; fairly talking as if to a reasonable child.) We'll find some way all right!

*Yule*: (Quite willing to hope so, yet failing completely to see; and with an awkward nervous laugh for it.) Yes—but what way *shall* we find? (Then as if he can think only of the impossible ways, the ways that don't fit now.) With Prodmore, you see, (with a still greater awkwardness for his having even thus indirectly to refer to it) it was—as you say—"simple" enough.

*Mrs. Gracedew*: (Thinking, demurring, downright.) I never called *that* simple!

*Yule*: (As wondering what, and how much, she knows; defining, however ruefully, his relation to the Prodmore terms.) It was at any rate clear. (After an instant.) I could marry his Daughter.

*Mrs. Gracedew*: (As in slow, conscious amazement, pointed irony, long-drawn and fine.) *Could* you?

*Yule*: He put it in such a way that I had to—a—(then rapid short) pretend to think of it. (Then as she takes this from him, in all its dreadfulness, as it were, only with the silence of her so feeling for him; sociably.) You didn't *suspect* that?

*Mrs. Gracedew*: (As if these personal appeals from him really touch her too much; breaking off from him as by the effect on her nerves of her positive excess of interest.) Don't ask me too many questions! (*CP* 597–98)

And finally, to underline the complex roots of women's social power, James intensifies his scrutiny of the connections between women. James makes clearer in this play than in any of his others that women maintain their strength by passing on their skills from generation to generation. As Mrs. Gracedew sets an example of the female tradition of "creative living" for Cora, James reaffirms the delicate, central place of women in society.

In placing this complicated woman at the center of his tale of salvation, James offers an expansive theatrical investigation of a changing Edwardian society. An outsider by virtue of nationality as well as sex, Mrs. Gracedew possesses a unique vision and skill. Though some historians of the English country home

424

Henry James's Nonfiction

blame rich Americans like Mrs. Gracedew for the demise of the system, James offers her as its savior. As an American from Missoura Top, she knows the sad results of having no culture to filter down from the upper class. At home, she must actually *teach* "taste." Since she so acutely feels the absence of mannered society, she alone can show the English—Yule in particular—why traditions, codes, and manners are sacred. When Mrs. Gracedew defends Yule's past and traditions to him against his more modern plea for directly helping the poor, her attempt to save Covering End best exemplifies James's thinly disguised call for saving an endangered British mannered society.

*Yule*: One's "human home" is all very well—but the rest of one's humanity is better! (She gives at this a charming wail of protest; she turns impatiently away.) I see you're disgusted with me, and I'm sorry; but it's not my fault, you know, if circumstances and experience have made me a very modern man. I see something else in the world than the beauty of old show-houses and the glory of old show-families. There are thousands of people in England who can show no houses *at all* and (with the emphasis of sincerity) I don't feel it utterly shameful to share their poor *fate*.

*Mrs. Gracedew*: (Roused at this, but unwilling to lose ground, and moved to use, with a sad and beautiful headshake, an eloquence at least equal to his own.) We share the poor fate of humanity whatever we do, and we do much to help and console when we've something precious to *show*. (Then warming, with all charm, to her work.) What on earth is more precious than what the Ages have slowly *wrought*? (Specious, ingenious.) They've trusted us—the grave centuries—to *keep* it; to do something, in our turn, for them. (Then in earnest, tender, pleading possession of her idea.) It's such a virtue, in anything, to have lasted; it's such an honour, for anything, to have been *spared.* . . . You *must* have beauty in your life, don't you see?—that's the only way to make sure of it for the lives of others. Keep leaving it to *them*, to all the poor others, and heaven only knows what will *become* of it! Does it take one of *us* to feel that?—to preach you the *truth*? Then it's good, Captain Yule, we come right over—just to see, you know, what you may happen to be "up to." (*CP* 581–82)

As James's American spokesperson for tradition, Mrs. Gracedew is James's most articulate and believable champion of the mannered world he created in his plays. But she is not as successful as James intends because Yule's well-argued position has gained extra force with each passing year. Gertrude Elliott, the actress who originally played Mrs. Gracedew, pleaded with James to tone down Mrs. Gracedew's zeal, since audiences were often compelled to side with Yule in part to escape her excess. James defended his character and her central role most reasonably to Elliott, but he must have sensed that in Yule he had created a popular hero whose belief's closely paralleled those of much of his audience.[9] James attempted to solve the difficulty Yule presents by having him renege on his liberal politics and marry Mrs. Gracedew (and her social conservatism). The fact that Yule's role in the play has occasioned such troubled response indicates, however, how seriously James's play has been treated, both by critics and by the theater public.

Forbes-Robertson opened the play in Edinburgh on March 26, 1908, and though the critical reception favored a London opening, Forbes-Robertson's involvement in the huge success of Jerome K. Jerome's *The Passing of the Third Floor Back* meant that London exposure for James's play was limited to five matinee performances at Herbert Beerbohm Tree's Afternoon Theatre. The very favorable press reviews focused on the likeable character of Mrs. Gracedew and the rare creation on stage of a believable mannered milieu. Max Beerbohm is representative in his ecstasy over Forbes-Robertson's performance of the line "I mean to whom do you beautifully *belong*?" Beerbohm wrote: "In his [Forbes-Robertson's] eyes, as he surveyed the old butler, and in his smile, and in the groping hesitancy before the adverb was found, and in the sinking of the tone at the verb, there was a whole world of good feeling, good manners, and humour. It was love seeing the fun of the thing. It was irony kneeling in awe" (266). Perhaps appropriately, the performances marked a quiet end to the public moments in James's dramatic career.

To study James's mature drama is to see James as a very minor and moderately successful playwright of the British stage. In *The High Bid* most prominently, but also in *The Outcry* and the more melodramatic *The Saloon*, he reaches the "standard of maturity" that L. C. Knights located in James's drama ("Restoration Comedy"). *The High Bid* and *The Outcry* have stood even the stiffest of dramatic tests; both were revived on the London stage in the 1960s and earned some favorable reviews. In sum, James's strengths as a dramatist are most visible in his last plays. As *The High Bid* demonstrates, he learned to make drama an arena for his exceptional women, his showdowns in international manners, and his delicately crafted social milieux. In addition, in his Edwardian theater, James claims almost exclusive rights to theatrical considerations of personal sacrifice and cultural salvation. Clearly, his best theater is more similar to than different from his best fiction.

To study James's earlier drama is to discover a writer more often than not producing weak work. In James's dedication to the theater during the 1890s and before, he confuses the fictive and the dramatic, he enslaves himself to dramatic conventions even when they do not suit his needs, he overstates his melodrama, and he too often deliberately avoids important "issues."

But, finally, I would return to *Guy Domville* as the single play most representative of all James's theater work. I do not nominate *Guy Domville*, as others have, because of its devastating opening night and its symbolic value as a turning point. I choose it, rather, because it combines the best and the worst of Jamesian drama. Against the subtle exchanges of Guy and Mrs. Peverel, James sets the melodramatic drinking match of the second act. Against the self-effacing sacrifices of Mrs. Peverel, James sets the boisterous intrusions of the Domvilles into Guy's life. James's drama does not expose him as a failure but as a writer who made his theatrical life one of his most public displays of conflicting needs and desires.

## NOTES

1. I have followed Edel in the datings for the plays. The dates indicate the time of a play's writing and not necessarily its production or publication. *Disengaged* was probably written late in 1891 or early in 1892 (*CP* 295).

2. In *The Scenic Art*, Allan Wade has collected most of James's writings on the theater and drama from 1872 to 1901.

3. John Carlos Rowe notes the difficulty feminist critics have had in coming to terms with James. He suggests that James's portraits of socially imprisoned women have offered such critics too little hope (*Theoretical Dimensions* 87–88).

4. *The Other House* and *The Saloon* are clearly not comedies. And though *Guy Domville* emulates comedy in its pacing and characters, its mood and actions are less joyous than those usual in comedy.

5. Allan Wade staged it quite successfully in 1919, as Edel reports (*CP* 402–3).

6. William Macnaughton (*Henry James* 41) and Margolis (94) are among those who have most recently found that *Guy Domville* did not constitute such a drastic turning point.

7. In her analysis of James's mature drama, Brenda Murphy overstates the case for connecting James's work to the new voices urged on by Ibsen and Shaw. These writers certainly made it easier for audiences to appreciate plays like James's. However, even James's Edwardian work is more in the tradition of Congreve and Pinero than that of Ibsen and Strindberg.

8. Ironically, George Alexander was also interested in the play, having read "Covering End," the fictive version of *Summersoft*. Edel and Babette Levy argue that Forbes-Robertson's more artistic temperament probably inclined James toward him.

9. In his letter to Elliott, he states, "My small comedy treats its subject—and its subject is Mrs. Gracedew's appeal and adventure—on Mrs. Gracedew's grounds and in Mrs. Gracedew's spirit, and any deflection from these and that logic and that consistency would send the whole action off into a whirlwind of incoherence" (October 22, 1908, in *HJL* IV, 496).

# 19
# The Autobiographies: A History of Readings

*Carol Holly*

Henry James began his career with a profound distrust of the autobiographical form. It is "a form foredoomed to looseness," to the "terrible *fluidity* of self-revelation"; and "looseness," says James, was "never much my affair" (*AN* 320–21). Toward the end of his life, however, James produced volume after volume of autobiographical prose, first the first-person biography of William Wetmore Story (1903), then the travel book *The American Scene* (1907), then the prefaces to the New York Edition of his novels and tales (1907–9). Several years later he recounted the "personal history" of his "imaginative faculty under cultivation" in two and a half volumes of autobiography: *A Small Boy and Others* (1913), *Notes of a Son and Brother* (1914), and *The Middle Years* (1917). James claims that this history is "as fine a thing as possible to represent," and as such, the autobiographies constitute both the climax and the capstone not only to a decade of experimentation with autobiographical form but also to the whole of his artistic career (*AU* 454–55). Because he wrote the autobiographies after several years of professional discouragement, emotional illness, and personal loss, this history of the imagination also reflects both the conscious needs and the unconscious conflicts of the elderly, ailing man.

It is possible to offer this reading of the autobiographies only because, over a period of many years, critics have revolutionized our theoretical assumptions about autobiography as a genre. We have gone from understanding autobiography as a species of history to considering it as a literary text. We have gone from assuming that autobiography refers to the autobiographer's past to considering the ways in which the story of the past reflects his priorities, both conscious and unconscious, in the present. We have posited that autobiography is integral rather than peripheral to a writer's career. As the following discussion demonstrates, this theoretical shift has shaped and reshaped our thinking about Henry James and his autobiographies throughout this century. It also continues to suggest new directions for James studies in the century ahead.

Published in 1913 and 1914, *A Small Boy and Others* and *Notes of a Son and Brother* appeared at a time when, as William Spengemann observes, "the idea of individuality and the writing of autobiography became sufficiently widespread to generate the kind, if not the degree, of popular, critical, and scholarly interest" in the genre "that we take for granted today" (177). This broad-based cultural interest may partially account for James's decision to experiment with autobiographical form in the last years of his life. So too might it account for the fact that a number of contemporary reviewers were interested in treating *A Small Boy* and *Notes* as belonging to what "literary journalists" then defined as "a more or less distinct literary form" (Spengemann 190). Read as literature, the autobiographies not only were appraised for their self-conscious artistry, their informing aims and designs, but also were compared with autobiographical narratives like Wordsworth's and Proust's, which similarly portrayed the workings of memory and the education of the artist. But the reviews also suggest that there was no consensus in 1913–14 on how to approach *A Small Boy* and *Notes*. Were they to be read as literary narratives, the most recent and perhaps most experimental of James's career? Or were they to be viewed as historical documents, replete with information about the origins of James's identity as an artist? Spengemann notes that the "predominately anecdotal character of the myriad autobiographies published during the first half of this century and the historiographical bias of literary scholarship in the same period conspired to place autobiography in the general category of biographical literature, where it served mainly as a source of gossipy entertainment for the common reader and of documentary data for biographers and historians" (190). And most of James's reviewers complied with this view when they approached the autobiographies as historically informative accounts of James's past.[1]

James died in 1916, and in the years following his death, critics began the difficult task of documenting his life, evaluating his fiction, and assessing the overall direction of his career. William Cain argues (163–64) that the burgeoning "critical and scholarly interest" in the novelist's work, an interest that we call the Henry James revival, "dates from the mid–1930's" and the Henry James issue of the avant-garde magazine *Hound and Horn*. But in the years preceding the revival, Rebecca West (1916), J. W. Beach (1918), Van Wyck Brooks (1925), Pelham Edgar (1927), and Cornelia Kelley (1930) studied James's fiction in book-length works that, in some cases, were prefaced by brief biographical sketches of James's early years. Given the absence of the family letters and other documents later made available to Leon Edel, the autobiographies became in these studies the primary, if not the only, source of material on James's early years. Given too what Spengemann suggests were the prevailing assumptions about the historical status of autobiography, the literary valuation of the autobiographies that appeared in some of the contemporary reviews was now replaced by the implicit understanding that *A Small Boy* and *Notes* were transparent records of James's past. Indeed, most of these critics rely extensively on the autobiographies for their sketches of James's past by providing a substantially greater proportion of paraphrase or direct quotation than of biographical analysis, and they do so, in two cases, without acknowledging the autobiographies as sources. And they give little attention to the autobiographies as texts written by the elderly author in the last years of his life.

This reliance on the autobiographies for insight into James's early years became, if anything, more deeply entrenched in the thirties and forties when several commentators turned to the autobiographies for passages that seemed particularly suggestive on the subject of James's sexuality and deeper psychology. The influence of Freudianism had by this time become pervasive enough to inform cultural assumptions about human personality and to encourage critics and biographers to speak out on matters that had previously been considered improper to discuss in biographical studies. Such speculation on James begins with Glenway Wescott's claim, in *Hound and Horn*, that the novelist, "it is rumored, could not have had a child" (523 [1934]). Building on this rumor, as well as on Wescott's pairing of the themes of "expatriation and castration" in James's life, Stephen Spender suggests, in *The Destructive Element*, that James was either castrated or otherwise seriously injured—the "rumor of castration seems exaggerated and improbable"—when "he was called on as a volunteer to help with a fire engine to put out a bad fire" (36–37 [1936]). The incident to which Spender refers is described by James in what we now refer to as the "obscure hurt" passage in *Notes of a Son and Brother* (ch. 9). But Spender learned about it from Rebecca West, who, without mentioning the autobiographies, merely states in her book that James "sustained an injury" while fighting a fire around the time of the outbreak of the Civil War (20).

Then in 1944, the psychiatrist Saul Rosenzweig turned directly to the "obscure hurt" passage itself to posit an interpretation that would significantly influence the biographers who emerged a decade later. Spender had previously hinted at a connection between castration or "fear of castration" in James and in his characters' "preoccupation with death" (37 [1936]). In a somewhat similar fashion, but with the depth and detail lacking in Spender, Rosenzweig argues for a link between "castration anxiety" in James's early life—his essential sense of "inadequacy" or "impotence"—and the recurring attention to death and ghostly appearances in James's fiction (453–54).[2] It is curious that Rosenzweig overlooked the other autobiographical passage that seems particularly pertinent to his interpretation: James's description of his dream of the Louvre in chapter 25 of *A Small Boy and Others*. But several years later, Lionel Trilling set a precedent for much future criticism of the fiction by making the dream of the Louvre passage central to his analysis of *The Princess Casamassima*.

The interpretations advanced by these early critics, and especially their interest in the Louvre and "obscure hurt" passages as privileged sources of psychological insight, significantly influenced the three full-scale biographies produced in the wake of the James revival: F. W. Dupee's *Henry James* (1951), Leon Edel's

*Henry James: The Untried Years* (1953), and Robert LeClair's *Young Henry James* (1955). Both Dupee and Edel, for example, use the dream of the Louvre passage to structure large portions of their biographies, Dupee his first chapter (appropriately entitled "The Dream of the Louvre") and Edel the "Notes on a Nightmare" section of book one. Building on Rosenzweig's theory of "castration anxiety," Edel also mines the passage for evidence of what he believes to be James's most fundamental psychological conflict, the "fears and terrors of a 'mere junior' threatened by elders and largely by his older brother" (*Henry James: The Untried Years* 75). So too does the "obscure hurt" material in *Notes* now occupy a central place in biographers' discussions of James's youthful development and essential psychology. By accurately dating the injury and, like F. O. Matthiessen and Dupee, identifying it as a strain to the back, Edel puts to rest previous conjectures that James may have been castrated in his efforts to fight a fire in Newport in 1861. But both Edel and Dupee draw on Rosenzweig's interpretation of the passage to posit not only the injury's confirmation of James's deep-seated sense of physical and emotional inadequacy, a helplessness possibly inherited from his lame father, but also James's ability to use the injury to set a course for his future. Says Dupee: "He writes of the injury and its aftermath as if he were aware of their climactic position in an order of events reaching back to the small outsider of his New York childhood. Owing to his invalid state he now at last actually *is* 'other'; and having, as it were, established his difference on a simple palpable physical basis, he is free—indeed by the rule of conversion he is *obligated*—to try to compensate for it in appropriate ways and to return to life by means of his art" (49–50 [1951]). Both Dupee and LeClair, moreover, link James's youthful invalidism as a result of the accident to "some fear of, or scruple against" romantic involvement with his cousin Minnie Temple (Dupee 45 [1951]; see also Edel, *Henry James: The Untried Years* 226–38).

The use of these passages, however, is but one of the ways in which the biographers of the 1950s relied on the autobiographies for their studies of James's early years. A few years before, Matthiessen, in *The James Family*, had traced James's boyhood development in large part by quoting lengthy passages from *A Small Boy*, *Notes*, and *The Middle Years*. Dupee suggests the affinities between Matthiessen's approach and the biographies of the fifties when, in *Henry James*, he insists, "Any account of Henry's youthful mind must lean heavily on *A Small Boy and Others* and *Notes of a Son and Brother*" (27 [1951]). Fortunately, Dupee is unwilling to claim, in the manner of LeClair, that "the extensive use" made of the autobiographies "is justified . . . because of the amazing accuracy" of James's recollections (8 [1951]). He describes the autobiographies as an "organized reverie" that subordinates "detail and chronology" to the "emotional essence" of James's early life (28 [1951]). And Edel follows his lead both by calling attention to the mediating power of James's memory in the autobiographies (see, for example, 82) and by providing valuable correctives to James's chronological distortion of specific events.[3] Edel even goes so far as to insist that a biographer must never "abdicate in favor of autobiography," as Percy Lubbock said he should (*Henry James: The Untried Years* 14). Yet Dupee and Edel share with LeClair the fact that they not only structure major portions of their biographies on James's narratives but also, with the exception of their psychoanalytic speculations, rely primarily on James for information on and insight into his early life and mind.

Take the definitive version of James's youth, *The Untried Years*, for example. A survey of the volume reveals that in some cases, entire chapters and sections of chapters reproduce through quotation or paraphrase the contents of passages in *A Small Boy* and *Notes*. Edel also follows James's lead in establishing some basic tenets of James's personality: his sense of youthful detachment, his imaginative relationship with others, and so on. As Alfred Habegger observes of Edel's recent one-volume *Henry James*, moreover, Edel models his account of James's movement from America to Europe and his development thereby from provincial to cosmopolite directly on James's retrospective view in the autobiographies. Habegger notes: "The dubious Place Vendome memory, the Galerie d'Apollon dream, the sight of a peasant woman near a ruined castle . . . all contribute to the view that James's great formative encounters were with European and not American civilization. In developing this interpretation, which clearly has a great deal to say for it, Edel follows the writer's own lead in *A Small Boy and Others*, where the second half's Europe forms a rich antiphonal response to the first half's America." What is more, Habegger explains, Edel "too often settles" for the autobiography's impressions of James's early American milieu instead of undertaking the scholarship necessary for "some critical, *external* understanding of it" ("Review-Essay" 205).

There is perhaps no final way out of a biographer's dependence on James's extensive recreation of the world of his youth. Paul John Eakin appropriately asks, "Where would LeClair, where would Edel, where would anyone be with regard to the matter of James's early years without the testimony of the autobiographies?" ("Obscure Hurt" 676–77). But it is difficult to reconcile Edel's awareness of the fictive nature of the autobiographies with his extensive reliance on the volumes for the purpose of biography. And it is unsettling to realize how indebted to James are the interpretations we inherit from his definitive biographer. Perhaps it is time, as Habegger suggests, "for other biographers to have a go at all the unpublished materials and see what they can make of them" ("Review-Essay" 208). Perhaps it is time to set clearer limits on the biographical uses of the autobiographies and also, in future work, to reach a more complex understanding of the role of the autobiographies in James's life and career. Jean Strouse's discussion ("Real Reasons") of the autobiographies as a version of the James family myth suggests one of the options open to the biographer of the future.

The 1950s was the decade when the biographical uses of the autobiographies were at their height. It was also the decade when critics began to recover the sense of the texts that prevailed in some contemporary reviews and to read them as a distinct literary form. Central to this process, curiously enough, was F. W.

Dupee, the biographer who acknowledged his need to "lean heavily" on the autobiographies for his account of James's youthful mind. "Lean heavily" is exactly what Dupee did, but in *Henry James* he incorporated something that we miss in Edel and LeClair: a brief discussion of the autobiographies as literature. Noting that they "are perfectly distinct as to purpose, method, and theme," Dupee compared *A Small Boy* and *Notes* with James's other studies of the "artistic personality," his biographies of Hawthorne and Story, for example, and also with Marcel Proust's autobiographical novel, *A la recherche du temps perdu*, and with Henry Adams's "history of an American mind," *The Education of Henry Adams* (28 [1951]).

Perhaps it was this brief analysis that quickened Dupee's desire to make the autobiographies more widely available. Perhaps it was his desire to say more about their distinctness as literary texts. Whatever the reason, Dupee published in 1956 the first edition of the autobiographies to appear in forty years, his one-volume *Autobiography*. And he wrote a critical introduction that extended his consideration of both the "purpose, method, and theme" of the autobiographies and the tradition of modern autobiographies and autobiographical novels (Proust's, Joyce's, Yeats's) to which they belong. Here Dupee also defined more fully than before the role of the autobiographies in James's career: "The autobiography is definitely a part of his major work, and to this fact it owes its character of finality. In particular, it completes the task of summing-up which he began with *The American Scene* (1907), his most elaborate essay on American culture, and continued with the prefaces he wrote for the 'New York Edition' of his novels and tales (1907–1909)" (*AU* xi). It is noteworthy that, as a biographer, Dupee refers to *A Small Boy* and *Notes* as James's memoirs, perhaps to justify the documentary use to which he puts them. As a literary critic, however, he declares the term *autobiography* as central to our understanding of the texts. "Neither 'Memoirs' nor 'Reminiscences' will do for a work which is so subjective, so purposeful, and so well-organized as this one is. On the other hand, like any first-rate autobiography, the work is given momentum and meaning by the recorded development—moral and professional—of the individual who is both its subject and its author" (*AU* x).[4]

Dupee published the *Autobiography* at the very point at which, according to James Olney, the academic world began to undergo a major shift in its thinking about autobiography as a genre. Beginning in 1956 with the publication of Georges Gusdorf's "The Conditions and Limits of Autobiography," this shift entailed a reaction against the "naive threefold assumption" about autobiography that, to a greater or lesser degree, informs all the biographies of Henry James: "first, that the *bios* of autobiography could only signify 'the course of a lifetime' or at least a significant portion of a lifetime; second, that the autobiographer could narrate his life in a manner at least approaching an objective historical account and make of that internal subject a text existing in the external world; and third, that there was nothing problematical about the *autos*, no agonizing questions of identity, self-definition, self-existence, or self-deception—at least none the reader need attend to.'' Olney goes on to say that it was this sudden attention to the *autos* of autobiography, to the shaping, creating ''I'' of the autobiographical narrator, that ''opened up the subject of autobiography specifically for literary discussion'' (20–21).

Why this turn to the autobiographical ''I'' should have occurred in the fifties is a question that has occupied a number of critics, Olney among them. Perhaps critics had begun to exhaust the interpretive possibilities of other, more traditionally defined genres. Perhaps they had grown impatient with the New Critical emphasis on the self-contained work and yearned for attention to the historical dimension of literature.[5] Perhaps it was the ''fascination with the self and its profound, its endless mysteries''—perhaps too ''an anxiety about the self''— that drew an increasing number of literary critics to a consideration of the genre (Olney 23). Certainly, in the case of Henry James, both the trajectory of the career and the similarities between the autobiographies and the novels seem to have made natural or inevitable the emergence of the literary criticism on the autobiographies that began with Dupee.

This criticism was strengthened when, in his classic study *Design and Truth in Autobiography* (1960), Roy Pascal included James in a chapter devoted to literary autobiography or, as the chapter title suggests, ''The Autobiography of the Poet.'' But it was with Robert Sayre's *The Examined Self* (1964) that literary criticism of the autobiographies really began to come into its own. A study of the autobiographical inquiry into the American experience, *The Examined Self* describes, among other things, how the autobiographies of Henry Adams and Henry James give form and meaning to modern American life. Though Sayre does not say so, his pairing of Adams and James is not especially new: both Dupee and Pascal recognized the connection between *The Education of Henry Adams* and James's autobiographies, and Sayre may well be indebted to this recognition for his book. But Sayre nevertheless felt that most readers believed that the autobiographies ''are inferior work and not worthy of . . . [the] extended treatment'' that *The Education* deserves (ix). Accordingly, he had to convince his readers that James's autobiographies ''are an entirely different kind of autobiography from the *Education*, but just as good, in their way, and therefore just as important to the subject'' (ix). This project necessitated a close detailed reading of *A Small Boy* and *Notes* (with brief attention to *The Middle Years*) in order to illuminate what Sayre saw as their unity of form. It also necessitated a deliberate, self-conscious attack on the critical establishment.

Sayre takes on, for one thing, the Jamesians and other readers who have sought in the autobiographies ''only background for James's love of the theater and painting, information about William James or Henry Senior.'' They have done a ''disservice'' to the autobiographies in being indifferent to their ''intricate unity'' or valuable social commentary (138). Then he criticizes both of his predecessors for reading the autobiographies too narrowly, Dupee for relegating them to James's period of ''summing up,'' thus defining them as ''side lights to the greater action,'' and Pascal for categorizing them as autobiographies of "the poet," thus limiting them to stories of the writer's trade (168–69). In his preface, however, Sayre makes it clear that it is not just the Jamesians (and Roy Pascal) who are at fault for these limited critical approaches. It is the academic world overall that, among other things, regards autobiography as "pedestrian truth and therefore not art." He adds, "These errors of the tribe have had a wider-than-ever circulation, I feel, because of a number of modern academic errors: excessive reaction against the nineteenth-century emphasis on personality, overemphasis on internal structure in art (removed from its reasons and wider consequences), a decline of biographical criticism, and a scorn for biographical elements" (x).

What most concerns me about Sayre's thinking here—and the reason I discuss him at length—is not only his elaborate defense of the autobiographies as literature but also his complex assumptions about referentiality and criticism. In the biographies, the autobiographies were read as transparent reflectors of James's past even when the biographer—Dupee in particular—interpreted the autobiographies as mediated or literary texts. Thus Sayre castigates the academic "tribe" for both its neglect of the fictive dimensions of autobiography and its New Critical emphasis on the "internal structure in art." But he in turn makes excellent use of the analytical methods of New Criticism to support his vision of the "intricate unity" of the autobiographies. And though he attacks James's biographers for excessive valuation of the "biographical elements" of autobiography, elsewhere in *The Examined Self* Sayre recognizes a relationship between James's autobiographical act and the biographical circumstances of James's late years. He suggests, that is, that the autobiographies functioned as "therapy of a kind" for the writer, who was mourning his brother William and doubting his creative powers (146). What Sayre has done here is define a critical methodology that privileges the autobiographies as reflective of James's personal concerns and literary techniques during the period in which they were written. In doing so, he has anticipated the theoretical orientation toward the autobiographies that was developed by a burgeoning number of critics in the decades to come.

When in 1969 William Hoffa continued the efforts of Dupee, Pascal, and Sayre to define the autobiographies as "significant literary document[s]" (293), he ushered in a new and important phase in the history of criticism on *A Small Boy* and *Notes*. To be sure, the growing number of critics who in the 1970s and 1980s approached the autobiographies as literature attend to the matters of autobiographical form and tradition discussed by their predecessors. But the need to defend the literary value of the autobiographies, and thereby to justify one's critical project, gradually disappears from the criticism altogether.[6] And close readings of the text become an accepted and ever more popular critical practice. Some Jamesians, of course, continue to ignore the literary nature of the texts, and some, like Richard Hall, persist in mining significant passages for insight into James's early life or essential psychology. Both the "obscure hurt" and dream of the Louvre passages, moreover, continue to be used to illuminate concerns central to texts other than the autobiographies themselves.[7] Nevertheless, throughout the last two decades, the growing critical preoccupation with autobiography as a genre in general and with the fictive dimensions of James's autobiographies in particular has enriched our understanding of the autobiographies as texts worthy of discussion in their own right.

One of the concerns that dominates these recent discussions of the autobiographies—the role of autobiographical narrator—can be addressed by looking first at Hoffa's essay. Hoffa identifies as the real subject of the autobiographies not the artistic education of the young Henry James but the mature James's "own dramatized consciousness of the past as it lived in the present" (282). This observation is related to several key points in his argument—the idea, for example, that the autobiographies share "many of the themes and techniques of his 'Major Phase' novels" and the notion that they thus become "in a sense, the 'American novel' he had hoped to write after his trip to the United States in 1904–5" (278). What interests me here, however, is the way in which Hoffa's attention to the "dramatized consciousness" enables him to comment on James's self-reflexive process of selecting and shaping his materials. "What 'framing' and 'encircling' he gave his memories," says Hoffa, "was apparently not done in an attempt to distort the truth, but to give perspective and dimension to his own development as an artist" (281). Several years earlier, Dupee, Pascal, and Sayre had identified the various "strands" or "themes" that, woven throughout the autobiographies, gave them the kind of unity that critics had previously discerned in James's fictions, and Sayre had also addressed the framing devices by which James focused his memories and charged them with meaning. Let us look now at the numerous ways in which, according to more recent critics, James gave focus, unity, and what he calls "rightness" and "beauty" to A Small Boy and Notes (HJL IV, 803).

The first critic to follow Hoffa, David Kirby, highlights James's tendency to give shape to potentially formless memories by remembering them "in terms of the books he has read and the plays and objets d'art he has viewed" (639). A few years later in 1976, Thomas Cooley likewise addressed the artistic composition of specific memories in A Small Boy, and Alfred Habegger has recently shown how James's commitment to creative revision of the past affected James's presentation of the letters of Minnie Temple ("Henry James's Rewriting"). Other critics, Cooley included, are concerned with the form of the narratives overall. Millicent Bell suggests that James's autobiographical form "denies plot, action, visible progression in time and space, reducing all to the now of consciousness" or the "wandering awareness that composes by chance association." Even individual chapters contain "many elements differing not only in date but differing also in narrative status—remembered scenes or episodes, miniature biographies of others, present philosophical reflections, all connected by apparent accident in the mind of the narrating consciousness" ("Henry James" 470, 472). By looking specifically at chapter one in A Small Boy, however, Bell discovers on the level of chapter and sentence a unity to this seemingly "wandering" or "webbed" form ("Henry James" 477). All the themes present in the narrative are contained within individual chapters, indeed within individual sentences, and any particular sentence builds by accretion or "agglutinating association" that with "its resonances of meaning, miniaturizes the structure of *The Autobiography* as a whole, or of any of its chapters" ("Henry James" 478–79). Adeline Tintner also discerns a pattern to James's associative method of narrative when she says of *A Small Boy and Others*, "Each chapter leads on from the preceding one, usually by the repetition of the last sentence or thought" ("Autobiography as Fiction" 245). A closer reading shows, moreover, that James will often drop one "thread" of association within a chapter in order to pursue another, then return in the following chapter to recover the thread he had previously dropped.[8]

It may appear from these remarks that the autobiographies altogether defy the linear or chronological model of much autobiography written before the twentieth century. But many critics, both old and new, recognized that the autobiographies are nonetheless structured, as James himself explains, on the story of developing consciousness or the "personal history" of his "imagination" (*AU* 454). *A Small Boy and Others* begins, for example, with the time in Albany, New York, when James first woke to "the wonder of consciousness in everything" (*AU* 4). It goes on to trace the development of that consciousness through the family's subsequent residence in New York City and their departure for Europe in 1855, and it ends with the "lapse of consciousness" James experienced when, at age fourteen, he contracted typhus in Boulogne (*AU* 236). James deliberately, if loosely, structured this story of developing consciousness by recovering the myriad impressions absorbed by the small, gaping boy who represents James's youthful self. "He is a convenient little image or warning of all that was to be for him, . . . of all he was to demand: just to *be* somewhere—almost anywhere would do—and somehow receive an impression or an accession, feel a relation or a vibration" (*AU* 17). Many critics have noted, moreover, that James intentionally shaped this story of artistic education to conform to his mature sense of personal and artistic priorities.

Cooley and Tintner argue, for one thing, that the general movement in *A Small Boy* goes from the isolated images that appear to the small, gaping boy of his earliest childhood to the complex clusters of images absorbed by the youth who, arriving in Europe in 1855, is more equipped to see unity and meaning in his heretofore random impressions. Cooley similarly shows how James manipulated chronology throughout the narrative to make his initiation into European culture appear to have been more consistent and dramatic than it was in his youth. We know from Edel's *Henry James: The Untried Years* that James combined into one unbroken sojourn the family's two trips to Europe in the 1850s (1855–58, 1859–60). He also changed the order of events toward the end of the book so that his story of developing consciousness comes to a climax with the vision of "history and fame and power" he encountered in the Louvre (*AU* 196).

In this chapter, Cooley notes, James "combined impressions from three widely different periods of his life": the period in which he first visited the Louvre, the period in which he dreamt the Galerie d'Apollon nightmare, and the autobiographical present in which he recalls both the visit and the nightmare to produce this climactic moment in the text (113–14). Of course, no two readers agree on the significance of the nightmare in James's story of the past. Tintner believes it demonstrates the "tremendous effect" of the Louvre on the "consciousness" of the older James ("Autobiography as Fiction" 247). Cooley believes it suggests that "impulses deep within him had irrepressibly asserted James's right to a central place not only in the temple of art and culture but of 'history and fame and power, the world in fine raised to the richest and noblest expression' " (112). And Paul John Eakin highlights the relationship between the dream and James's autobiographical act (*Fictions* 76–86). But for all their differences, these critics share one trait: unwilling to read the dream out of context to support readings of James's youthful mind or his fiction, they interpret the Louvre passage as an integral part of James's story of his past, or as a symbol of James's autobiographical act, or as both. The point of most of such analyses of *A Small Boy*, in fact, is to demonstrate how each of the significant passages in *A Small Boy and Others* fits into the pattern of autobiographical discourse or the overall narrative design.

*Notes of a Son and Brother* figures much less prominently than *A Small Boy* in the predominately formalist readings given to the autobiographies in recent decades. Both Cooley's and Sayre's chapters on the autobiographies are largely devoted to *A Small Boy and Others*, and *Notes* does not figure at all in John Pilling's chapter on James in *Autobiography and Imagination*. In fact, until the appearance of Eakin's lengthy piece on the autobiographies in the 1984 issue of *Prospects* (reprinted in *Fictions*), critical attention to *Notes* was limited to remarks in the briefer, article-length discussions by Bell ("Henry James"), Tintner ("Autobiography as Fiction"), and Jane Tompkins ("Redemption").

Critics have been divided, moreover, on how to approach the volume. Because James devotes more attention to family in *Notes* than he does in *A Small Boy*, Tompkins declares that the "nature" of this largely commemorative "relation" with others is "the main issue for the critics of the autobiography" ("Redemption" 682). Yet Tompkins ignores the fact that, as Tintner claims, the "main thrust of *Notes of a Son and Brother* exhibits James's growing authorhood" ("Autobiography as Fiction" 249). Tintner leans toward Tompkins's view when she suggests that James's story of authorhood is nonetheless "interrupted by the introduction of letters written by his father and his brother"—an interruption that parallels the "interruptions of Proust's 'I' story by the story of Swann's love affair" ("Autobiography as Fiction" 248). But Eakin's careful reading of the chapters on William and Henry Sr. reveals that "most of the material about others in *Notes*—and William's case is no exception—develops the themes of James's story of himself" (*Fictions* 90).

In short, this story portrays "the conflict and drama" in James's struggle to be "just *literary*" in a world in which "a decent respect for the standard hadn't yet made my approach so straight that there weren't still difficulties that might seem to meet it, questions it would have to depend on" (*AU* 255, 413). Not only did American society in general regard as something of a failure a man who was not engaged in business or some other respectable vocation, but Henry James, Sr., had also declared to his children that any profession, even that of the writer, was too "narrowing" (*AU* 269). An additional obstacle to James's vocational development was the sense of inferiority experienced throughout most of his boyhood and youth. In *A Small Boy and Others*, he continually emphasized the sense of shame, ineptness, and failure he felt in relation to William and other boys who performed knowingly and successfully both in school and out. And he portrays himself as a "deeply hushed failure" at the beginning of *Notes of a Son and Brother* as well (*AU* 241). Here James's sense of inferiority is also shown to have become a major obstacle for the young man who, now in his teens, is beginning to consider his vocation. What could he do, he wonders in chapter two, with the impressions that had begun "to scratch quite audibly at the door of liberation, of extension, of projection" when he was ashamed to confess that he "really lived by them" (*AU* 253–54)? James then goes on to write the chapters on William (3–5) and Henry Sr. (6–8)—chapters that either reflect his current vocational uncertainties or "prefigure the problems of vocation that he would face" when he too began to write (Eakin, *Fictions* 91).

Critics interested in the narrative structure of *Notes* interpret the four chapters that follow the material on William and Henry Sr.—chapters that describe his "obscure hurt," his visit to the wounded soldiers at Portsmouth Grove, and his subsequent efforts to become a writer—as the climax and resolution to this prolonged struggle for selfhood and vocation. Bell argues that the "injury, physical or psychic, gave him warrant for that substitution of imaginative for active doing for which, as we have seen, his whole life had been preparing" ("Henry James" 474). Having previously discussed the beneficial role that illness plays in *A Small Boy*, Eakin similarly suggests that his "apparently disabling injury is presented, paradoxically, as an enabling event, associated with health and growth, and forming 'a cover for every sort of intensity' " (*Fictions* 106–7). Of course, a Boston physician's unwillingness to take seriously the idea that James was injured at all was "a devastating setback to the young man's quest for a serviceable contemporary identity" (Eakin, *Fictions* 109). But in his description of a subsequent visit to wounded soldiers at Portsmouth Grove—what Eakin calls the "affective center of James's narrative" (*Fictions* 112) and what Bell calls the "moment of crisis and reconstitution" ("Henry James" 474)— James portrays his younger self as experiencing a "triumphant affirmation" of both his own wounded condition and his inactive way of life (Eakin, *Fictions* 112). Bell suggests that it "is surely significant that it is precisely now, in the year of the war that he spent in Cambridge, only half-pretending to be a law student, that he began to write." The young James, she believes, had been able to convert the guilt he felt for the real wounds received by his biological and generational brothers into the "totality of non-participating participation through art" ("Henry James" 475). Eakin, however, emphasizes the beneficial effects James experienced through the "public assertion of his identity as an artist."

On the pretense of studying law at Harvard, James began to write the stories and criticism that were soon to be published in the leading periodicals of the day. And "the small boy, son, and brother had something to show" for himself at last (Eakin, *Fictions* 119).

Eakin suggests that it "seems likely that James originally intended to conclude *Notes*" with the story of his coming of age during the war years, but when he was "3 quarters" done with the volume he received from his sister-in-law, Alice, the packet of letters that his cousin Minnie Temple had written to John Chipman Gray in 1869, the last year of her life (*Fictions* 120). Rounding off the narrative with a tribute to Minnie, James thus gave the volume a distinct sense of finality. For it marked not only the occasion of her death and, as James says, "the end of our youth" (*AU* 544) but also, through attention to Minnie's very different fate, the new life that James experienced in becoming a writer.

To trace the story of James's growth as an artist in *A Small Boy* and *Notes* is, as many critics recognize, to identify but one source of unity in the volumes. There is unity as well in the shared identity between the character of James's younger self and the mature artist who creates him. Indeed, many are the passages where James as autobiographical narrator merges with the consciousness of his creation, experiencing the past through his eyes, or otherwise calls attention to the "drama of his own 'registering' intelligence" as he recalls and recreates the past (Hoffa 285). The narrative is thus structured so that the teleological relationship between character and narrator implicit in any autobiography—the boy is father to the man, the girl mother to the woman—is self-consciously displayed, even celebrated, in *A Small Boy*, *Notes*, and *The Middle Years*. Hoffa insists, moreover, that "the unity of the *Autobiography* comes from James's awareness that the process of writing his autobiography is itself an experience of the same nature as the process of growing into manhood and artistic maturity" (283–84). James's youthful discovery of his identity as an artist is thus paralleled by his reaffirmation of this identity in the act of remembering and recreating the past. As he says in his famous 1914 letter to Henry Adams, written in response to Adams's apparently pessimistic reading of *Notes*, "You see I still, in presence of life (or what you deny to be such), have reactions—as many as possible—and the book I sent you is proof of them" (*HJL* IV, 706).

For many critics, the affirmation of artistic identity, both in the autobiographies and in the letter to Adams, is intimately related to the fact that in 1910 James had suffered a debilitating nervous illness as the result of a series of professional disappointments.[9] Some of these critics have merely observed that James used the autobiographies to recover his artistic powers and renew his faith in life. Others have attempted to describe the specific role the autobiographies played in James's recovery. For Robert Sayre, the autobiographies functioned as a "therapy of a kind," as we have seen (146). In his final volume of biography, *Henry James: The Master*, Leon Edel similarly argues that James cured himself by returning to childhood in the autobiographies and thereby working off or releasing his "discouragement and depression" (455). When these Jamesians discuss the autobiographies as therapy rather than as literature, they have, of course, significantly expanded the theoretical orientation we encounter in Hoffa, Tintner, and Bell. For they suggest, however implicitly, that the autobiographies do not simply reflect James's priorities as an artist who is building "rightness" and "beauty," "conflict and drama," into his story of the past. The autobiographies also reflect the psychological struggles James was experiencing just before and during the time he was writing the story.

Paul John Eakin discusses this relationship between the autobiographical text and the life of its creator in his recent essay in *New Literary History*. Eakin recognizes that it has "become commonplace for students of autobiography to assert that the past, the ostensible primary reference" of autobiographical texts, "is a fiction" ("Obscure Hurt" 675) and to treat as a literary fiction the text that purports to be about that past. Eakin believes, however, that critics are mistaken in their attempts to force the distinction between the fiction of autobiography and "the experiential reality" that the autobiographer lived. "Autobiography, for all the manifold fictions in which it is implicated, is nothing if not a referential art" ("Obscure Hurt" 675–76), he maintains, and by carefully analyzing the "obscure hurt" episode in *Notes*, Eakin demonstrates how James's historically inaccurate, but nonetheless highly suggestive, description of his injury in 1861 serves "as the missing verifiable" referent for the painful "inner truth" of James's experience in the past, "the inner truth that had left no trace" ("Obscure Hurt" 689–90). But the capacity of autobiographical discourse to refer, however mysteriously, to material from the past does not erase its capacity to refer as well to the life of the autobiographer who writes it. Autobiography is "a major event in the life of the biographical subject," Eakin maintains. It is in fact a major "biographical event" ("Obscure Hurt" 676, 679).

The implications of Eakin's theory for future work on James are, of course, exciting and profound. Imagine, if we can, a study of James's life and work in which an entire chapter—not a smattering of pages, as we have in Edel's *The Master*—is devoted to the role of the autobiographies in the life of an older James. Not only does Eakin suggest a direction for such a biographical account when he addresses "the importance of a *contextual* understanding of autobiography's recreation of biographical fact," both for the time written about and for the time of the writing ("Obscure Hurt" 679). But in his James chapter in *Fictions*, Eakin also provides a detailed reading of the "autobiographical act" as "biographical event" in the life of the aging James. Central to Eakin's argument is the belief that "autobiographical truth is not a fixed but an evolving content in an intricate process of self-discovery and self-creation" (*Fictions* 3). This process is particularly apparent in the case of *A Small Boy* and *Notes*, where "James's emphasis on the performative value of his undertaking" is best understood "as a manifestation of some imperative drama of consciousness going forward in the present" (*Fictions* 57). To trace that "drama of consciousness" through both narratives is, for Eakin, to demonstrate in detail how the autobiographies actually functioned as therapy for James. Here Eakin focuses on the relationships among the themes of "sickness, solitude, and confinement" that are the "enabling conditions" for identity formation not only in James's small boy but also in the autobiographical narrator, who, himself suffering from illness and depression, continually probes the identity of the boy and the meaning of his painful experience (*Fictions* 71). Eakin traces James's searching encounter with the past through several key passages in each volume, including the dream of the Louvre in *A Small Boy* and the portraits of William and Henry Sr. in *Notes*. But as we have seen, the climax of and resolution to this process occur in the famous Civil War chapters in *Notes*, in which "James derived strength for the present from the insight he acquired into the resources of his ego in meeting a life crisis during the Civil War so long ago" (*Fictions* 124).

Three critics since Eakin have provided readings that, directly or indirectly, either expand on or challenge this thesis. My article " 'Absolutely Acclaimed': The Cure for Depression in James's Final Phase," for example, argues that "the confidence in artistic power James enjoyed in the spring of 1914"—just after *Notes of a Son and Brother* was published—was due not only to "the therapeutic benefits of the autobiographical act" but also to the enthusiastic reception that both autobiographies received from the British Press ("Cure" 127). However, Donna Przybylowicz's attention, in *Desire and Repression*, to the repressed content of the autobiographies fundamentally challenges the notion that self-analysis in the autobiographies could have therapeutic power at all. Przybylowicz reads the "gaps, omissions, condensations, and displacements" in the autobiographies as evidence not of the successful resolution of material from the past but of "the disguised message of the unconscious" (204–5). James M. Cox also challenges Eakin's reading of the autobiographies by questioning in particular the idea that "the experience at Portsmouth Grove successfully integrates James's sense of separation between himself and American life into the resolved unity of the life of art" ("Memoirs" 249). But to mention these alternate readings is not to diminish the importance of Eakin's ambitious and original contribution to James studies. Rather it is to suggest the possibility that, in sorting out these approaches, the biographer of the future might bring to a reading of James's late years some of their complexity, richness, and detail.

Central to our expanded understanding of the significance of the autobiographical act to the late years of Henry James are the contributions of several critics who address the role of the autobiographies in James's development as a writer. John Pilling notes that in the past, almost "all studies of James elect to treat his writing career as if it ended with 'The Golden Bowl', and as if the two unfinished novels ('The Sense of the Past' and 'The Ivory Tower'), the book of memoirs ('William Wetmore Story and His Friends'), the travel book ('The American Scene') and the three volumes of autobiographical writing . . . were plainly inferior to what had preceded them" (23). This trend is changing now that critics have begun to treat as worthy of discussion in their own right not only the autobiographies but also *The American Scene*, the prefaces, and other late works as well. A good deal of generic confusion has, of course, resulted from the concerted effort to restore these texts to their rightful place in the oeuvre. Hoffa, Tintner, and Bell attempt to legitimate the autobiographies by defining them as novels, for example, whereas Gordon Taylor and Mutlu Blasing attempt the same for *The American Scene* and the prefaces by defining them as autobiography. Nevertheless, the increased attention given to each of these texts has resulted in a new vision of James's late career; critics now see these texts as related works that have previously been treated as distinct—or altogether ignored—and James's late nonfiction accordingly provides a more complete picture of James's efforts in his final years.

Many critics base their reassessment of the late years on James's characterization of the autobiographical act in chapter 11 of *Notes of a Son and Brother*. Here, Eakin observes, James casts himself ''as the artist, the 'teller of tales,' who has found in the story of his own life the 'long sought occasion' for the working out of a peculiarly challenging aesthetic 'task,' the presentation of the 'personal history . . . of an imagination' '' (*Fictions* 60). And here, as early as 1973, Charles Feidelson found a textual ground for his pioneering discussion of James's preoccupation with the character of the ''man of imagination'' in the last years of his life. To be sure, Feidelson is primarily concerned with James as novelist, not autobiographer. He is interested first in identifying James's ''man of imagination'' as the Romantic hero familiar to us from Blake and Wordsworth and then in discussing the ''problematic interplay between these Romantic premises and the premises of a 'realistic' social novelist'' (336). But Feidelson is nonetheless instrumental both in identifying the commonality among several major works of James's late career—*The Ambassadors*, the prefaces, and the autobiographies—and in seeing James's autobiographies as the culmination of a lifelong preoccupation with the figure of the imaginative man.

Since Feidelson, other critics have speculated further about the shape and significance of James's late career. For one thing, they have considered the various traditions to which the autobiographies belong: the tradition of the ''education'' that Cooley sees in Twain, Adams, and Howells; the tradition of the ''creative autobiography'' that Tintner sees in Joyce and Proust; the tradition of the modern autobiography or autobiographical novel that Bell sees in Conrad and Proust and that Pilling sees in, among others, Adams, Yeats, Sartre, and Nabokov. These connections between the autobiographies and a variety of late-nineteenth- and twentieth-century texts tend to confirm the view of James as modernist, a view that, according to Richard Hocks (Review of Przybylowicz), has emerged in James studies in the past ten years. But even as they look beyond James to writers who experiment in similar ways with autobiographical form, critics have begun to follow Feidelson's example and consider in some detail the specific works in James's oeuvre that prefigure or anticipate the autobiographies. Tintner sees a link between the autobiographies and James's contribution to the collaborative novel *The Whole Family*, for example, and in the *Harvard Library Bulletin*, I trace a connection among the autobiographies, the prefaces, and the autobiographical fragment ''The Turning Point of My Life'' (1910). But perhaps the fullest treatment of the place of the autobiographies in James's late writing appears in Przybylowicz's *Desire and Repression: The Dialectic of Self and Other in the Late Works of Henry James.*

In a book heavily laden with terminology, Przybylowicz employs Marxist and poststructuralist methodologies to illuminate the decenteredness—and thereby the essential modernism—of most of James's writings after the late 1890s. The "protagonist or autobiographical persona in the late works," she maintains, "does not manifest a unified sensibility, an integrated ego ideal that is the focus of the nineteenth-century bourgeois novel but is dominated by the irruption of discontinuous unconscious impulses onto the controlled conscious level, which is most clearly evidenced in the aggressivity between self and other. The autonomy of the subject is lost under the effects of psychic disintegration and fragmentation—he is decentered" (2–3).[10] Particularly useful to our understanding of the autobiographies is both Przybylowicz's detailed attention to the textual gaps and omissions that reveal James's highly ambivalent feelings toward his father and brother and her understanding of James's attempt to compensate for these feelings by creating a "plenitude of being" in his autobiographical discourse and vision of the past (204). Useful too is her sense that the post–major phase period reflects a significant development in James's career. This sense enables her to suggest connections among James's autobiographical writings—*William Wetmore Story*, *The American Scene*, the prefaces, and the autobiographies—and also to trace the affinities among the autobiographical texts, the essays of World War I ("Within the Rim" and "Refugees in Chelsea," among others), and much of the fiction of the period, including the unfinished novels *The Ivory Tower* and *The Sense of the Past.*

A similarly ambitious study of the late years appears in William Goetz's *Henry James and the Darkest Abyss of Romance.* Clearly indebted to Feidelson, Goetz is concerned with the "paradox" that "the work of Henry James, though famous for its dramatic and objective qualities and for a reticence of the author that is one source of the ambiguity of much modern literature, is in fact deeply concerned with the question of the presence of the author in his works" (ix). Goetz is not interested in denying the referential capacity of *A Small Boy* and *Notes* and thus, like Przybylowicz, in illustrating "their strategies of condensation and displacement" (202). Rather he is "interested in the formal or technical question of the ways in which James will admit the signs of the author's self into his writing," not only in his novels and other fiction but also in his criticism, his prefaces, and his autobiographies (ix). This project enables Goetz to discuss the ways in which James handled the formal problems that the use of the first person posed for his autobiographies and thereby to provide useful close readings of the texts. It also allows him to make a major claim for the role of the autobiographies in James's career. Not only, he says, do the prefaces and the autobiographies form a "diptych, together claiming to furnish a complete history of the development of James's imagination," but there is "a fundamental continuity" as well "between James's fiction, which already contains an autobiography *in potentia*, and

Henry James's Nonfiction

the explicitly autobiographical works that capped his career in the twentieth century'' (6). In his late fiction, James allows ''the characters' minds increasingly to approximate the magisterial intelligence and sensitivity of that of their creator'' (7). Then, when he discovers his ideal subject in himself—''What was *I* thus, within and essentially, what had I ever been and could I ever be but a man of imagination at the active pitch?'' (*AU* 455)—James fulfills his greatest ambition as an artist. Goetz notes:

The insistence on the long period of waiting and gestation that preceded the novelist's discovery of his ultimate theme shows the autobiography to be in a sense the culmination of James's entire career. It shows the continuity, too, between his fictional representation of a consciousness like Strether's and his final representation of himself in the mode of nonfictive autobiography. Whereas Strether was still a ''comparative case,'' James himself presumably furnished something closer to that absolute case of an imagination in ''*supreme command*'' that had always been his ideal. (10)

In spite of his belief that the autobiographies are the culmination of James's career, Goetz organizes his book so as to privilege his analysis not of the autobiographies, the subject of his initial chapters, but of *The Ambassadors*, the subject of his final chapter. Thus he reflects a trend in James studies that, for all our efforts to reevaluate the autobiographies, nonetheless continues to ascribe greater value to James's work in the novel. This trend is reflected nowhere more clearly than in the brief critical discussions of *The Middle Years*.

Left unfinished at James's death, *The Middle Years* begins in 1869 with James's first independent trip to Europe and, in a little more than six chapters, continues the history of James's artistic development throughout his early years in London. The few critics who consider the narrative tend to use the fact that it is incomplete to confirm their view that, as Hoffa suggests, James had nothing left to say autobiographically by the summer of 1914. The ''real conclusion to James's *Autobiography* is to be found in his novels and stories'' (Hoffa 290).[11] It is true that, in a letter written to his nephew in 1913, James vowed that ''never again shall I stray from my proper work'' in the novel (*HJL* IV, 803). But that letter was written in the midst of a misunderstanding between James and his nephew over the uncle's presentation of family documents in *Notes of a Son and Brother*. This incident—an episode in a history of subdued conflict with Harry, a history I touch on in ''Absolutely Acclaimed''—understandably left James frustrated with the peculiar demands of autobiographical art. But later, once *Notes* was published and the British press was giving it highly favorable reviews, James seems to have felt a renewed enthusiasm for the genre. In a letter written to Harry on April 7, 1914, he notes that the ''two books together appear to have made me (vulgarly speaking) famous, and to be greeted as a new departure, a new form and manner struck out in my 70th year.'' Several pages later he claims that he ''probably *shall* perpetrate a certain number more passages of retrospect and reminiscence,'' if he is ''able to live on and work a while longer''; he then begins to consider the various projects he might undertake. One of these—the history of "the period from 1869 to the beginning of my life in London"— becomes *The Middle Years* (quoted in Holly, "Absolutely Acclaimed" 132– 33).

Our understanding of the autobiographies has been significantly complicated and enriched in the past several decades by critics who have proclaimed the importance of James's autobiographical act, both to his life and to his career. Perhaps it is time to consider the possibility that James was no more finished as an autobiographer than he was as a novelist when, in the summer of 1914, he abandoned all his writing projects and focused his attention on the war.[12] Perhaps it is time to consider the possibility that, as his contemporary critics believed, autobiography had become the "new form and manner" of his final years.

## NOTES

1. For further discussion of the contemporary critical reception of the autobiographies, see Holly's "British Reception."

2. Leon Edel provides further reference to early theories of the "obscure hurt" in *Henry James: The Untried Years* 176.

3. Edel not only identifies the date of the "obscure hurt" as six months later than James positions it in *Notes* but also specifies the reasons why James obscured the chronology of the family's travels in the 1850s; see *Henry James: The Untried Years* 137– 38, 175–79.

4. This inconsistency between Dupee's labels for the autobiographies becomes even more striking when one considers that he continues to use the term *memoirs* in the revised edition of *Henry James* that came out the same year as *Autobiography*.

5. See also Cox, "Recovering Literature's Lost Ground."

6. William Spengemann observes that autobiography "may be said to have arrived at its present critical status with the publication [in 1970] of Francis R. Hart's very business-like and unpretentious essay, 'Notes for an Anatomy of Modern Autobiography.' " Although several critics throughout the late 1960s had "pleaded for the recognition of autobiography as literature," it was Hart's essay that "reflected a general acceptance of the genre by literary critics as a form worthy of systematic analysis" (183– 84). Clearly the work of Hart and other autobiography theorists during the late 1960s and early 1970s also affected the climate of critical opinion toward James's autobiographies.

7. Too numerous to list here are the many critics who have made either of these psychologically suggestive passages central to their theories of James's art. Among some of the most recent, however, are Donadio 254–58; Rowe, *Henry Adams and Henry James* 136–44; Schneider, *The Crystal Cage* 32–37; and Strout, "Dream of the Louvre," and *Veracious Imagination* 275–81.

8. For further discussion of the organization of the autobiographies, see Goetz, chs. 2 and 3; and Pilling, ch. 2.

9. For interpretations of James's nervous breakdown, see Edel, *Henry James: The Master* 443–47; Holly, "Absolutely Acclaimed" 126; and Strout, *Veracious Imagination* 279.

10. As Avrom Fleishman puts it, poststructuralist theory has called into doubt "the capacity of any language to order decisively, to represent adequately, and to embody symbolically. . . . Just as language displaces any subject, when the subject is, as in the case of autobiography, the self, language becomes the model of the self's inclinations toward self-alienation—toward the evasion of identity and the responsibilities of identification with/as oneself that has been widely observed in contemporary culture" (32).

11. For similar interpretations of *The Middle Years*, see Eakin, *Fictions* 122–23; and Goetz 79–80.

12. For a reading of *The Middle Years* that indirectly supports this view, see Babin.

# 20
# The Duality of
# *The American Scene*

## *Charles Caramello*

Following an absence of twenty years, Henry James revisited the United States in 1904–5 to gather material for a new novel and to glean "impressions" for several papers on American manners—the latter soon collected and published as *The American Scene* (1907).[1] James's sharp critique of a transient and materialist society, *The American Scene* also comprises, in its second and complexly related aspect, his portrait of himself as an expatriate who had returned home and become that society's harsh critic. James jointed that critique and self-portrait at the theme of dispossession. He depicted the "ubiquitous alien" (*AS* 87), the immigrant masses flooding into urban America to perform its labor, as the dispossessors of James and his kind and as the new possessors of America; but he also depicted them, in a striking turn, as merely repeating his *own* forebears' dispossession of Native Americans and possession of *their* land.

Stunningly experimental in type and technique, *The American Scene* belongs simultaneously to the large body of travel literature that James produced throughout his career and to the sequence of highly variegated autobiographical writings that occupied him, following the "third manner" novels, between 1902 and 1914. It reflects, moreover, James's late turn toward romantic representation and first-person narration, modes he had disparaged in his literary criticism and theory but had revived in his own last phase. Not surprisingly, then, *The American Scene* has enjoyed a distinguished history of commentary that has persistently held the book's dual aspects in tension, finding it a book equally about America and about the Jamesian perspective on America. And, not surprisingly, the book has figured centrally in the debate, now over a century old, about the nature and degree of James's "Americanness."

## A HOWLING HOMESICKNESS

In January 1902, James wrote Grace Norton of his desire to revisit the United States: "The idea of *seeing* American life again and tasting the American air, that is a vision, a possibility, an impossibility, positively romantic" (Edel, *Henry James: The Master* 227–28). The impossible came to seem increasingly possible in subsequent months, and he wrote his brother William, in May 1903, of his desire "to return to my birthplace" before advancing age precluded such travels. Though he twice begged off, detailing all his reasons, he did note that he was in search of "experience" he might convert into *"material"*; elaborating, he made a nice point that he would repeat to other correspondents and would repeat in *The American Scene* itself: time, absence, and change, to paraphrase his terms, had made his "native land" as "romantic" to him now as "Europe" had been to him when he was a young man. Travel there, consequently, would provide an opportunity to mine rare material for "the production of prose" (*HJL* IV, 270–75; and see *HJL* IV, 259, 329).

To others, however, James specified more private reasons. Writing to Sarah Butler Wister in December 1902, for example, he referred to the recent death of Wister's mother, the actress Fanny Kemble, and then characterized "the tramping *ghosts* of other years" as now his "principal company," as more numerous than "the present and the palpable." Haunted, James thought "to come home again before the 'romance' of Charleston and the like completely departs," thought to "go home for six months." He feared, however, being " 'too late'; not yet too late for Charleston, etc., but too late for myself," too late for "repatriation." He remained, nonetheless, still "romantically" with her (*HJL* IV, 259). Two years later, he struck the same morbid note. Having just disembarked in the United States, he wrote his brother Robertson in September 1904, "The Dead we cannot have, but I feel as if they would be, will be, a little less dead if we three living can only for a week or two close in together here." He had "come home at last" (*HJL* IV, 320).

Given such tensions between professional and personal motive, James not surprisingly found himself, once launched, in conflict. At first romantically enthralled with "this mighty land," with the "so visible and observable world that stretches before one," he was soon complaining constantly of its vast emptiness, of the American simplicity he long ago had depicted in *Hawthorne* (1879). "I seem to see patria nostra *simplify* as I go," he now wrote Edith Wharton, "see that the *main* impressions only count, and that these can be numbered on the fingers" (*HJL* IV, 329, 331, 342).[2] He had wanted, impossibly, to rediscover an old America and to discover a new one; but he found the old one had become new in ways he had not romantically foreseen. Moreover, the returnee who had "come home" repeatedly complained to his English correspondents of his "constant homesickness," his being "transcendentally homesick," his *"howling homesickness,"* and ultimately, his "nostalgic *rage"*—not for America but for England (*HJL* IV, 329, 331, 340, 356). Disconnected by time from his past

American home, by space from his present English home, James felt the romance go sour, became "tired of my adventure" and, especially, "weary . . . of the perpetual effort of trying to 'do justice' to what one doesn't like" (*HJL* IV, 348, 355).

Unfortunately, he had contracted to do justice to America. Besides collecting impressions for use in fiction, he had agreed to a series of Impressions to be published in the *North American Review* and, later, in a volume.[3] Intending to write them while on the move, he soon found, as he wrote his editor George Harvey, that "seeing, observing, noting, visiting, moving etc." left no time for writing and that the "formidable process" of seeing, etc., was "of the essence" (*HJL* IV, 327).[4] He waited until he had returned to England, then, before writing what he called his "American Book"—his initial plan calling for two separately titled, complementary volumes.[5] Repeating to several correspondents his earlier dismay at having discovered he could not write it *en plein air* (*LHJ* II, 45–46; *HJL* IV, 397), he told others that the writing now, though challenging, was again proving more difficult than he had expected.[6] Comparing his project at different points to Hippolyte Taine's *Voyage en Italie* (1866) and to Paul Bourget's *Sensations d'Italie* (1891), he also raised the two sources of the difficulty he was facing: subject and medium.[7]

James's subject, America, posed the first difficulty. As he wrote to Bourget, he "came back . . . victim in all ways to the immense incoherence of American things." He had "found the country formidable and fatiguing," and as he had earlier complained to Wharton, he had "failed to arrive at a single conclusion, or to find myself entertaining a single *opinion*" (*HJL* IV, 388). He wrote to Paul Harvey, similarly, that he had found America "an extraordinary world, an altogether huge 'proposition,' . . . giving one . . . an immense impression of material and political power; but almost cruelly charmless" (*HJL* IV, 397). And having just read H. G. Wells's recent *The Future in America*, James chastised Wells for oversimplifying America and confessing that he, James, "accursedly" complicated things. With a "passion for the idea" and with a "wealth of ideas," Wells had written a yelling book. But James added defensively, "It's a yelling country, and the voice must pierce or dominate; and *my* semitones . . . will never be heard" (*HJL* IV, 421–22).

James's medium, memory, posed the second difficulty. He wrote variously to Wharton, W. E. Norris, and others that his "impressions" had begun to "melt and fade and pass away," that his documents, his memoranda, were failing him, and he could only "run a race with an illusion, the illusion of still *seeing* [his book]" as it "recedes . . . ahead of me" (*HJL* IV, 375; *LHJ* II, 46). Though he had expressed to William James and to Howells in his early letters his special desire to see "the Middle and Far West and California and the South" (*HJL* IV, 273; and see *LHJ* II, 9), he would explain to Morton Fullerton, after publication of *The American Scene*, that "there won't and can't be, *à l'heure qu'il est*, any second or 'Californian' volume of the American stuff." And he gave Fullerton, as he would William James, four key reasons: (1) too much time had elapsed; (2) "Europe" had intervened on his memories; (3) his "meagre documentation" lacked adequacy; and (4) he had to contend with the "dire *thinness* of the picture *là-bas*," a thinness that was causing the picture to fade (*HJL* IV, 454, and see 465–70).[8]

James had come to America, in short, without an idea or ideas with which to frame its vastness and to organize its variousness, without a conceptual point of view from which to see his subject; and he had returned from America, it follows, with a plethora of impressions but still no such principle of selection and arrangement, still no such point of view—he had only his desire to simplify and a swarm of rapidly "melting" impressions. He still had the intention, moreover, that he had first expressed to his brother William and to Howells and that he now repeated to Wharton and to others: he wanted "to clear the ground of [*The American Scene*] to be free for more inspiring work." As he explained, "The threshing out [of] my American matter in this form will really enable me to use some of it . . . in the fictive form better" (*HJL* IV, 387). From *Hawthorne*, to *William Wetmore Story and His Friends* (1903), to *The American Scene*, James habitually deprecated large commissions for nonfiction as financial necessities that delayed the writing of novels, his real work; but he had contracted to cover the American scene, and good professional that he was, he met the terms of his contract.

## THE AMERICAN SCENE

In *Democratic Vistas* (1870), Whitman argued that American society had first secured political rights and next secured material prosperity but, following the trauma of the Civil War, needed to secure an informing ethos, a moral and spiritual center. Otherwise, he warned, the nation would fail to evolve into a true culture and, instead, would devolve back through its prior gains. Some three decades later, James landed in America and found himself "up to his neck" in his subject (*AS* 5). The American "*donnée*," his "subject," lay in "the great adventure of a society reaching out into the apparent void for the amenities, the consummations, after having earnestly gathered in so many of the preparations and necessities" (*AS* 12). Though characteristically Jamesian in its abstract diction and its focus on manners, the point accords in substance with Whitman's. James had seen "the monstrous form of Democracy" at work (*AS* 54) and had found that "the interest of the American scene [was], beyond any other, the show, on so immense a scale, of what Democracy . . . is making of things" (*AS* 323). It was making, he clearly believed, a botch.

Antebellum America had lacked history, traditions, and institutions, James had argued in *Hawthorne*, and modern America had exacerbated that lack. At once the effects and the continuing causes of that lack, three forces dominated the new American scene: wealth ("the expensive as a power by itself"), publicity ("the air of unmitigated publicity, publicity as a condition, as a doom, from which there could be no appeal"), and transience ("to move, move, move, as an end in itself, an appetite at any price'') (*AS* 9, 84). Money, its acquisition and expenditure, fueled them. With money in place of tradition, for example, wages had to take the place of manners. "Wages, in the country at large, *are* largely manners—the only manners . . . one mostly encounters" (*AS* 197). More important, with the reforms of the Progressive Era barely under way, money had produced a class stratification so extreme that even James, studiously avoiding such matters, could not ignore it. Nonetheless, he focused not on the wealthy becoming wealthier or on the poor becoming poorer but on an emerging middle class becoming increasingly trapped between circumstance and desire.[9]

Indeed, James focused throughout more on social effects than on economic causes, and he found his themes in money and motion. He elaborated "the expensively provisional" (*AS* 77)—articulated wealth, publicity, and transience—through an analysis of two new "institutions": the hotel and the Pullman car. First considering the Waldorf-Astoria, he concluded that the "American spirit" had made the hotel its "social" and "aesthetic" ideal, had so considered it, indeed, "a synonym for civilization . . . that one is verily tempted to ask if the hotel-spirit may not just *be* the American spirit most seeking and most finding itself" (*AS* 102). He felt so certain that it was, in fact, that he later reverted in his "Charleston" paper to the idea that the hotel constitutes "for vast numbers of people the richest form of existence" (*AS* 406), and he centered his "Florida" paper, his last, on the apotheosis of the hotel spirit in the mammoth pair of The Royal Poinciana and The Breakers. He had found "hotel-civilization" ubiquitous, had found "the hotel-spirit . . . an omniscient genius, while the character of the tributary nation is still but struggling into relatively dim self-knowledge" (*AS* 438–39); and he saw, ultimately, the end of "one's pilgrimage [in Florida] but to find the hotel-spirit in sole *articulate* possession" of the scene (*AS* 442).

James explicitly bound the hotel with the Pullman car—the railroad sleeping car—when he astutely equated "the Pullmans that are like rushing hotels and the hotels that are like stationary Pullmans" (*AS* 408). He was arguing, in effect, that Americans lacked the history and traditions requisite for the construction and transference of great private houses but that they had the vast spaces that required rapid public transportation; as a result, they developed a hotel culture that they also took on the road. He was depicting a dystopia in which "bagmen"—commercial travelers—shuttled between rented public habitations via rented public conveyance, these "bagmen" and their manners—expensive, public, and transient—being emblematic of all Americans. The vision prompted the vestigial democrat in even James to concede an animating genius—"the American genius for organization" (*AS* 105) or, more elaborately, "the universal organizing passion, the native aptitude for putting affairs 'through' " (*AS* 445). But the vision remained an aristocrat's nightmare.

America, again, had simply lacked time to become a true culture, and it continued to try to gainsay a "golden truth . . . the truth that production takes time, and that the production of interest, in particular, takes *most* time" (*AS* 153). America, in effect, could produce only the "interest" entailed in watching its own kinetic, democratic forces at work, and as a result, it continued to reenact collectively the acute self-consciousness that James, from *Hawthorne* through the New York Edition prefaces, depicted as *the* salient trait of postbellum America: "a society trying to build itself . . . into some coherent sense *of* itself" and "reaching out . . . for some measure and some test of its success" (*AS* 159). Deftly transposing a temporal metaphor into a spatial one, James himself textually reenacted how America's lack of history, with self-consciousness as a consequence, had produced a lack of depth. In the "American alignment," he wrote, nothing is "behind" anything because "so many things affirm themselves as preponderantly before" (*AS* 294); able to produce "duration" only by making "the decades count as centuries and the centuries as aeons" (*AS* 315), America could produce density only in the same way: by illusion. As a result, it could make only spectacle, show, "scene."

And James used the nation's capital, appropriately, to emblematize this essential quality. In his "Washington" paper, he depicted the eponymous city as an illusory capital for a still emerging nation, depicted it as stage set, as painted backdrop, "painted once for all in clear, bright, fresh tones, but never emerging from its flatness, after the fashion of other capitals, into the truly, the variously, modelled and rounded state" (*AS* 339). Placing a small group on stage, conversing against that backdrop, James developed his conceit of Washington as a doubled *City of Conversation*. Washington, that is, "talks about herself, and about almost nothing else" (*AS* 342–43), but she talks about herself as, precisely, the City of Conversation—hers is the tone of "*conscious* self-consciousness" (*AS* 344). Washington, moreover, was the only American city in which men existed socially, and that gave James, by negative example, "the key to everything" (*AS* 345), revealed to him, to mix a metaphor, "the sentence written largest in the American sky": American society comprised only women (*AS* 346). And that, in turn, had led James to wonder if American men would ever catch up socially with American women, a question he could not answer, though he found it "*the* most oddly interesting [inquiry] that the American spectacle proposes to us" (*AS* 350).

Evidently James was proposing that the Civil War had literal effects on gender, and he was then using gender to figure a sexual allegory of sectional difference, with masculine North and feminine South coming together in a marital—or perhaps androgynous—mid-Atlantic federal city. The men who had gone off to war in James's youth, that is, had since gone off to business; they had created modern New York with its raw, economic power, a power manifest, appropriately, in the ubiquitous phallic skyscraper. They had also defeated and militarily occupied the South; and this new South had undergone a "strange feminization"—"whereas the ancient order was masculine, fierce and moustachioed, the present [South] is at the most a sort of sick lioness" (*AS* 417). But James again reconverted those tropes into literal effects, for he also was arguing that postbellum democracy had made something new, something public and transient, not just of habitation and transportation but also of familial and "intersexual" relations.[10]

James had found and then depicted the United States, in sum, as a democracy in critical motion—as a nation in critical motion, indeed, precisely because it was a democracy. Money fueled the engines of motion, of change, produced hotels that blighted urban areas, railroads that blighted rural areas, hotels and railroads that together destroyed privacy and leisure, that fostered publicity and haste. Brutal vulgarity marked its North, frailty its South, acute self-consciousness its capital. Hardly flattering, the depiction also seems hardly disinterested, as we shall see. As James did throughout *The American Scene*, that is, he had projected his psychic map onto the landscape, had moved geographically from that which he personally most admired but feared, a vital but brutal masculinity, to that which he found neither admirable nor fearsome but romantic, a frail femininity. And what he did here with the sexes, moreover, he would also do with the classes and, especially, races.

## THE UBIQUITOUS ALIEN

In the first of four New York papers, "New York Revisited," James recounts his earlier visit to Ellis Island. When there, he had adopted the point of view of the native, the native who, seeing the arriving aliens, would experience a Fall, would eat of the Tree of Knowledge, would know that "it is his American fate to share the sanctity of his American consciousness, the intimacy of his American patriotism, with the inconceivable alien" (*AS* 85). The native had to share, less abstractly put, his home, and so must a repatriated native: the aliens "were *at home*" in his New York, James discovered, but "*he* was at home too," and "it was this very equality of condition that . . . made the whole medium so strange" (*AS* 124–25). James used that strangeness to focus his response to "the great 'ethnic' question" (*AS* 120); he proposed that the forces of transience and publicity, working through demography, had replaced the antebellum homogeneity with a fearsome heterogeneity. Having failed to find that homogeneity when traveling in America, he now addresses the presence of the Jew in New York, the Italian in Boston, and the African in the South.

He sets the tone with his headlines for "New York and the Hudson": as he approached The Aliens at Home, he had found The New York Ghetto to have become The New Jerusalem.[11] He had found the alien an invader "already in possession of the field" (*AS* 123), had found himself witness to "the Hebrew conquest of New York" (*AS* 132). Though he could not foresee the full effect of that conquest on his native land, he could forbear, as it were, its effect on his native tongue. Pondering The Accent of the Future, his phrase nicely ambiguous, James concludes that "the 'ethnic' synthesis" will produce some accent, perhaps a very beautiful one, but it will not be English—"in any sense for which there is an existing literary measure" (*AS* 139). Extending this motif through the next two papers, he observes that in his childhood the "foreign note" was Irish (*AS* 196), now it is Jewish, and he eventually closes out the question where he began it. He recalls an "exotic boss"—the status is telling—who spoke "fluent East-side New Yorkese," and considering "*his* inward assimilation of our heritage and point of view," James asks, "What, oh, what again, were he and his going to make of us?" (*AS* 207).

He later replays the scenario in "Boston," recounting under the headline The New Bostonians how a group of Italians, again militarily, advanced on the position he had taken on Beacon Hill. They were "gross aliens to a man, and they were in serene and triumphant possession"; they brought home how far off was " 'my' small homogeneous Boston of the more interesting time" (*AS* 231). Gross aliens en masse, they had conquered and displaced exemplary, individuated Brahmins. James's Boston, "exempt as yet from the Irish yoke," had been "the concentrated Boston of history, the Boston of Emerson, Thoreau, Hawthorne, Longfellow, Lowell, Holmes, Ticknor, Motley, Prescott, Parkman, and the rest" (*AS* 245). Just as the Irish and then the Jews, in short, had taken James's New York, so had the Irish and then the Italians taken his Boston. And James knew perfectly well, of course, that the New Jerusalem had been a name for Boston, City on a Hill, since its founding.

James starts his final variation on this theme in his "Richmond" paper. He recalls "an African type or two [previously] encountered in Washington" and proceeds to limn that "group of tatterdemalion darkies [who had] lounged and sunned themselves" at the railway station, who had represented for him the Southern Black as the Northerner had never known him, "all portentous and 'in possession of his rights as a man' " (*AS* 375). Soon after, in Richmond, he had encountered more active "black teamsters who now emphasized for me with every degree of violence that already-apprehended note of the negro really at home" (*AS* 378). Continuing this variation in "Charleston," he ponders The Negro as Servant, deplores the indifference and ineptitude of a "negro porter" who had put James's bag in the mud, laments "the apparently deep-seated inaptitude of the negro race at large for any alertness of personal service," laments the passing of "the old Southern tradition, the house alive with the scramble of young darkies for the honour of fetching and carrying," and deplores a complementary "negro waiter," not indifferent but, in his overzealousness to please, equally inapt and inept (*AS* 423–24).[12]

Patently racist and offensive, this is tricky material that James's apologists still might seek to recover. After all, they might say, James seems to blame the diaspora, the forced migration of the Jews, for their loss of their own culture and their assimilation of his; indeed, he attributes real vitality to the Jewish immigrants. Similarly, he may criticize a group of Italian diggers and ditchers who had not engaged him in conversation, observing that, in *their* native land, he could expect "a social relation with any encountered type"; but he blames their sullen unapproachability, precisely and ironically, on their having migrated to "the land of universal brotherhood" (*AS* 118–20). And, finally, he notes how his "African type" must "loom" and "count" in a community—the South—so lacking in other features, but he turns that looming against the South: in effect, the African now looms for the Southerner because he reminds the Southerner of the folly of slavery and of the rebellion fought to protect it, the folly of "a cause that could never have been gained" (*AS* 394).[13] In short, an apologist might argue that James depicts the alien and African as victims of historical forces set in play by others—as unwilling exiles from their lands who appear as aliens only from the perspective of the natives who fearfully imagine being displaced by them.

One inclined to disagree, however, might reply that James adverts to unsavory metaphors when he argues that displaced Jews do manage to maintain some sense of their cultural identity: they are like "snakes or worms" who, chopped up, "wriggle away contentedly and live in the snippet as completely as in the whole"; they are like "the splinters on the table of a glass-blower," each of which—of whom—keeps "his or her individual share of the whole hard glitter of Israel" (*AS* 132). In addition, James fails to see that his own archaic paternalism, not the Italians' putative lack of fraternalism, caused his problems in that encounter. And, most egregiously, James weaves a nasty subtext through his commentary on the African: he first shows Africans having obtained their civil rights and, moreover, their masculine rights ("his rights as a man")—the latter meaning not inconsequential given his "strangely feminized" South; he next shows Africans taking possession of that South for their home, and his metaphors here transform Africans from docile and apparently nonhuman creatures, sunning themselves, into active human beings driving animals; perhaps not surprisingly, then, he finally gives us Africans as railroad porters and hotel waiters—depicts them as servants to other men in surrogate places for the latter's homes.

Apologists might rejoin, of course, that James is depicting *America* as having turned immigrant Jews into mere worms or glass slivers, *America* as having made immigrant Italians "crude" (*AS* 270), *America*—the Union—as having kept emancipated Africans docile creatures, *America*, finally, as having kept everyone—aliens, Africans, and natives—in the same state of alienated transience. But one might again counter that James portrays himself as having adopted the native point of view only to find that the alien had already adopted it, had made it his own, and had extended it, assimilated, into the future—just as the alien had the native tongue. And when James reminds himself not to preach "a sweet reasonableness" about the African to the Southerner, admonishes himself that the "non-resident" ought to demure, he is admonishing himself, in effect, not to behave like an antebellum abolitionist or a postbellum reconstructionist (*AS* 375–76). In the North, James found that the alien had become the new American, and he, James, had become the dispossessed, the new alien; but he apparently decided that, as such, as "non-resident," he had no business preaching reasonableness about the alien to the native either.

One certainly can grant that James was astute to conclude that America offered

its poor the "freedom to grow up to be blighted, and it may be the only freedom
in store for the smaller fry of future generation" (*AS* 137). But *James* too was
blighting the poor—the alien and the African—through his metaphors and his
typologies. He could conceive the alien, in fact, only as a mass, with national
or racial type marking the limits of individuation; and this contrasts strikingly
with his litany of proper Bostonians by proper name, his distinguishing individuals from the New England homogeneity. Similarly, he could conceive the
African only as an "alien," no matter how native-born that African or his
forebears. Those blindnesses are striking, and apologists could only offer, as an
unpersuasive last defense, that James so destabilized the terms *native* and *alien*
by making them relative to perspective that we cannot be sure, finally, what he
had in mind.

## THE RETURN OF THE NATIVE

Thomas Hardy had already used the title *The Return of the Native*, James
noted; otherwise, he would have liked it for his "series of papers" (*HJL* IV,
328). It fits their complexity as well. At one level, the American nativism, long
suppressed by the Europeanized James, had returned to his consciousness and
enabled the perspective of "returning absentee." At a second level, James the
American native had then returned to America while, simultaneously, the native
land, America, had returned from the depths of memory to meet him. And at a
third level, finally, the American native James, in the strange *tour de force* that
concludes *The American Scene*, conjures a Native American, the dispossessed
American Indian, who returns to address America through a mediumistic James.
Specifically, this hypothetical returning native indicts the America that had be-
fouled nature and that had dispossessed the Indian as the Natural Man, and, in
effect, he indicts James and James's "race" and generation for their complicity
in the befouling and dispossession. Simultaneously if surreptitiously, then, this
native imagined by James is also warning the alien to avoid committing the same
crimes of rapacious materialism and cruel dispossession against James and *his*
"native" generation.

That sociological theme of public American waste and dispossession corresponds to, and interacts with, a psychological theme of private Jamesian loss
and dispossession. As we have seen, James as generic "returning absentee" had
taken up the perspective of the "native" only to find that the alien had already
assimilated it—taken it and converted it into his own; James could take, then,
only the uneasy, almost oxymoronic, perspective of a repatriated expatriate,
could find no native perspective to take. As an elderly "returning absentee,"
however, one with a private past and "a horrible, hateful sense of personal
antiquity" (*AS* 80), James also had to contend with the loss of his past and with
the barriers to its memorial return. In fact, James notes that he had attempted
through "excursions of memory" to effect "an artful evasion of the actual" but
had found that he could escape "the ubiquitous alien" neither into the future

nor into the present but only into the past (*AS* 87). When he had attempted to do so, however, he also found that his past had been amputated. Hoping that America would return to him, he had discovered, instead, an abyss both social and psychic.

In the crucial passage, James recounts his visit to Washington Place to view his "birth-house": he found that a skyscraper "so block[ed] . . . the view of the past, that the effect for me, in Washington Place, was of having been amputated of half my history" (*AS* 91). The house, literally, had been demolished. He later recounts his return to Ashburton Place, on Beacon Hill, to a home of his youth. He found there not a blocked view but, rather, an open vista that "had begun to yawn into space," into the modern urban space of street grids and skyscrapers. The two "ancient houses" he sought, however, still "kept their tryst," and James occupied himself with "reading into one of them . . . the history of two years of far-away youth spent there at a period—the closing-time of the War—full both of public and of intimate vibrations." The shock came, though, when he returned a month later to find "but a gaping void, the brutal effacement, at a stroke, of every related object, of the whole precious past." The houses gone, "it was as if the bottom had fallen out of one's own biography, and one plunged backward into space without meeting anything." The incident figured to James "a connection that had been sharp, in spite of brevity, and then had broken short off," figured "the sense of the rupture" that he would "carry with me" (*AS* 228–30).

Recounting the first scene, James may have slid, unconsciously, from his father's amputated leg, across severance from his birthplace, to his own amputated past; and then, in a reprise of the scene, through his own back injury in Newport to his period of recovery in Boston during the war. He was already associating, doubtless, the injury to the body politic with that to his body, public trauma with private, and associating both with his vocation as a writer and, as such, an alien in society—precisely the nexus he would construct in his *Notes of a Son and Brother* (1914).[14] In any case, he seems to have been equating the public past with his private past and to have been suggesting, as in *Hawthorne*, that the Civil War had been the event severing early nineteenth-century America from late. Now though, as Peter Buitenhuis has suggested, he was portraying as well the great waves of foreign immigration to American cities as a parallel event severing late-nineteenth-century America from twentieth-century modern America—severing James's America from the alien's (189).

That powerful sense of violent disconnection gives added point to James's comment that public "commemorative mural tablet[s]" are "unthinkable" in future-oriented New York but that he had erected a private, mental memorial in Washington Place (*AS* 91–92), a notion he reiterates when he recounts his visit to Salem on his "pilgrimage . . . for the New England homogeneous." He had encountered there "a remorseless Italian" and "a civil Englishman," neither of whom could point the way to "the Seven Gables" or to "the birth-house of their chronicler." Only a small boy, "a dear little harsh, intelligent, sympathetic American boy," a "master of his subject," knew the location of the latter (*AS*

265–70). James himself, of course, was producing in *The American Scene* the memorial tablet for his birth house, just as he was commemorating in it, by enumerating their names, the homogeneous New England intellectuals—most of them, in a nice irony, historians. But James's dear little surrogate for the memorial function of his book, his small boy, would give way, ultimately, to James's much harsher surrogate for its didactic function, the returning Native American.

Before turning to that concluding passage, we must first recall that James ordered his papers in *The American Scene* straightforwardly; he followed the eastern seaboard strictly north to south. More subtly, however, he was framing twelve papers named for cities with a first paper whose title designates a region and a last whose title designates a state; in effect, he was framing his fundamentally urban book with papers devoted to nonurban environments—respectively, rural New England and primordial Florida.[15] He was framing the city, then—etymologically, the site of civilization—between the rural conditions that preceded it and, in a twist, the primordial conditions that preceded them. The great champion of culture was rewinding history toward nature with the same blend of arcadian nostalgia and romantic apocalyptism that one can find in Whitman.[16] And he concluded that rewinding by calling Florida, in an odd trope, a greater antiquity than the Nile because of "the antiquity of the infinite *previous* . . . when everything was still to come"; it gave him a "foretaste," moreover, of the sense he would have of California as a "primitive *plate*, in perfect condition, but with the impression of History all yet to be made" (*AS* 462).

We must also recall, second, that James characterized the railroad as an agent of blight that he had used, a point he makes explicit twice, in both cases mentioning the romance of the landscape now blighted and in one case analogizing the blighting of it with the banishing of the Indian to the reservation.[17] And we must finally recall, in relation to that analogy, that James ended his "Washington" paper with extended reference to the Indian. Standing before the Capitol, James had met "a trio of Indian braves, braves dispossessed of forest and prairie, but as free of the builded labyrinth as they had ever been of these." They projected an immense image, one "reducing to a single smooth stride the bloody footsteps of time. [There] . . . shining in the beautiful day, was the brazen face of history, and there, all about one, immaculate, the printless pavements of the State" (*AS* 363–64). As difficult to "read" as any of the oblique images in James's last manner, the scene juxtaposes the bloody history of extermination with the bland face of the Capitol and, even more specifically, appears to juxtapose the bronze statue *Freedom* (1863), surmounting the Capitol dome and wearing a helmet "topped by an eagle's head and flowing plumage reminiscent of an American Indian headdress" (James Goode 60), with the bronze-complexioned trio of braves, the promise cast in metal with the reality endured in flesh.

With those motifs, James set up the final passage of *The American Scene*, one his American publishers excised for its harshness.[18] Having earlier spoken of "the great moving proscenium of the Pullman" (*AS* 433)—its plate window framing at once a tableau and a moving picture—James now seems to hear the train saying, as he had earlier heard Democracy say, "See what I'm making of all this—see what I'm making, what I'm making!" James responds in the subjunctive, responds as "if I were one of the painted savages you have dispossessed," responds that the Pullman with all it symbolizes has ravaged everything, has destroyed the land and, even worse, has prompted a "pretended message of civilization" that is, instead, "but a colossal recipe for the *creation* of arrears." But he then must return to the indicative, for were he a "beautiful red man with a tomahawk," he precisely would not be what he is, a white man with a train ticket—he would not "have been seated by the great square of plate-glass" that had afforded him the vantage for criticism but that, simultaneously, had implicated him in what he was criticizing (*AS* 463–65).[19]

Ultimately, then, James had enacted on his trip and was now reenacting in his text the conflict built into his initial motives for his return. He had wanted to come back to America a disinterested observer of manners, but he could come back, of course, only a highly interested returnee—his sociological observations obviously colored by his psychological state. And inevitably, perhaps, he had enacted on his trip the very behavior he was criticizing. He had come to America to glean impressions, capital he could spend in his Impressions and bank for later fiction; he had sponsored his trip in part by giving public lectures; he had stayed for the most part in hotels and had traveled almost exclusively by Pullman. He had become a literary "bagman," in short, and one engaged, moreover, less in the "masculine" adventure of business than in the "feminine" business of letters. It is no wonder that James conjured a Native American to attack *him* as an invader—but also no wonder that James, dispossessed, hurtling through a biographical abyss, simultaneously attacked the immigrant as invader. He may have felt vulnerable, certainly culpable, when traveling in his American Pullman, but he also seems to have become more secure, certainly more critical, when writing from the safe distance of his English home.

## ASPECTS AND PROSPECTS

To accomplish the goals of that writing, James had to adopt a complex narratorial stance. Though he uses the first person in *The American Scene* sometimes for himself as writer in 1905–6 and sometimes for himself as traveler in 1904–5, he most often uses the first person to refer to himself as writer and the third person, nominally and pronominally, to refer to himself as traveler. In the latter case, he usually calls himself as traveler "the restless analyst," but he also employs a plethora of other nominal epithets that tend to stress either the restless analyst's functional role as observer and critic or his autobiographical status as returning absentee.[20] That split, in turn, reflects the comment on "the Author's point of view and his relation to his subject" with which James opened the dense preface to *The American Scene* by stating, "If I had had time to become almost as 'fresh' as an inquiring stranger, I had not on the other hand had enough to cease to be, or at least to feel, as acute as an initiated native" (*AS* xxv). Because James had been poised at that precise moment, he now claims unique status for his impressions of America.

As he goes on to explain how he had formed and would now express his sense of American "aspects and prospects" (*AS* xxvi), he notes that he once had "confidence in the objective reality of impressions" (*AS* 6) but that he now frets over the "romantic, if not the pathetic, circumstance of one's having had to wait till now to read even . . . meagre meanings" into the American scene (*AS* 7). Waiting years to revisit America had affected what he was then and is even now "reading into the picture" (*AS* 15). His confidence in the objectivity of impressions, in a sense, had already been compromised by the delay that, in turn, had poised him at his privileged moment for observation. On this note, James introduces the central tension that informed his interpretation of America and now informs his representation of it—the tension that also forms the subject of a metadiscursive thematics of interpretation and representation in *The American Scene*: things have essential meanings that they project *and* perceived meanings that are projected on them; correspondingly, perceivers read out meanings proper to things and read in meanings that accrue to things. And those, however troubling, are the epistemological facts of life.[21]

Forced to operate within those facts, the Jamesian observer still had to interpret and then represent, had to make sense of what he saw and make a sense of his subject.[22] The observer and analyst trying to do so, however, soon discovers another problem: "for the restless analyst, there is no such thing as an unrelated fact, no such thing as a break in the chain of relations"; not only must he "discover connections," but he cannot not discover them. And the observer and analyst of America then discovers yet another problem: the "living fact, in the United States, *will* stand . . . for almost anything you may ask of it" (*AS* 321–22). Ideologically complicit in the America he sought to observe, as we have seen, the returning absentee also found himself epistemologically complicit in the America he had then sought to represent. He either had seen relations that existed to be found or had found relations that did not exist—either had seen them objectively or, more likely, had constructed them subjectively; and not only had he altered facts to fit those relations, it follows, but he could also construct any relation between always alterable facts.

As an observer, seeking to represent America, then, James would also, inevitably, *mis*represent it. To take one example, he had found Richmond "simply blank and void," lacking all reference, so he had made that its reference (*AS* 370). Later, observing the statue of General Lee and adhering to his "desperate practice, . . . the subtle effort to 'read' a sense into the senseless appearances about me" (*AS* 392), James had returned to and solved "the riddle of the historic poverty of Richmond. It is the poverty that *is*, exactly, historic: once take it for that and it puts on vividness" (*AS* 394). But James also came to believe that "the South is in the predicament of having to be tragic, as it were, in order to beguile'' (*AS* 420), to be interesting; and he makes it tragic, in effect, by converting blankness into poverty and poverty into the vividly historic. He cannot say, of course, whether the South yielded that interest or whether his own investment in his sense of the South, as it were, had returned it.[23] But he seems to have done something, in any case, for which he later scolds American magazine illustrators: ''when you haven't what you like you must perforce like, and above all misrepresent, what you have'' (*AS* 457).

James refuses to represent some things, however, precisely because his principles of representation entail such misrepresentation. Having found the present marked by public and by private loss, he guards the past by setting limits on criticism, guarding the war, particularly, with a tactical nostalgia.[24] And having found the present marked above all by shameless publicity and lack of privacy, he also uses romance to color, and to cover, certain realities of the past. In the most passionate passage in his notebooks, James confessed that he had discovered, at the ''unspeakable group of [his family's] graves'' in Cambridge Cemetery, ''why I had done this; . . . why I had come'' to America—and confessed that he had broken down emotionally at the site (*NB* 320–21). Impersonalizing and generalizing the incident in *The American Scene*, he figures ''a builded breakwater against the assault of matters demanding a *literal* notation'' and figures himself ''on the breakwater—looking down, if one would, over the flood of the real, but much more occupied with the sight of the old Cambridge ghosts''—not only those of his family but also those of Lowell and Howells (*AS* 68). He prefers the company of those ghosts to the importunities of the real, but he also chooses not to represent clearly the identity of those ghosts or, especially, their power over him.

Not only did a ''romantic circumstance,'' then, affect what James eventually read into America, but romance also informed his view of America and his mode of representing it. He conceded to being ''a lover, always of romantic phenomena, and an inveterate seeker for them'' (*AS* 285); he acknowledged that rejecting the ''statistical'' as his basis for analytical reportage had put his ''record'' in danger of accounting for things that speak ''but of the personal adventure—in other words but of one's luck and of one's sensibility'' (*AS* 297). And he repeated what he had said privately to William James about his predisposition, ''Europe had been romantic years before, because she was different from America; wherefore America would now be romantic because she was different from Europe'' (*AS* 366). He was well on his way toward the definition of romantic experience that he would develop in the New York Edition prefaces—''the things that can reach us only through the beautiful circuit and subterfuge of our thought and our desire'' (*AN* 32). And such things, for James the late Impressionist, included virtually everything.

James had elaborated, in sum, how ''reading into the picture'' had both benefits and dangers, and he attached its inevitability, moreover, to ''the human, the social question'' that made the observer and analyst, ''before each scene, wish really to get *into* the picture, to cross, as it were, the threshold of the frame''

(*AS* 35). Not convertible acts, reading into and getting into are, rather, circularly entailing acts; "foredoomed . . . to 'put in' a certain quantity of emotion and reflection" (*AS* 331), the observer discovers that he then, by virtue of that reading in, gets into the picture, enters it, and must then again, circularly, read his own emotional projections, signs of his presence, as part of that picture. The Jamesian observer was so foredoomed, moreover, because he had come to America already an interested observer, had brought with him vast reservoirs of emotion sprung from both his nostalgia for the past and his quickly developing sense of alienation from the present. He had put that emotion, read that emotion, into the American scene; and he then had to read, in *The American Scene*, his presence there.

America itself, of course, was a blank page that had required this kind of active reading: Soldier's Field is "like some flat memorial slab that wants to be inscribed" (*AS* 69); New York Bay is like "the vast white page that awaits . . . the black overscoring of science" (*AS* 75); the "American street-page" is a blank (*AS* 244); the Museum of the Confederacy "was a pale page into which he might read what he liked" (*AS* 384); and so on. If history, as James argued, "is never, in any rich sense, the immediate crudity of what 'happens,' but the much finer complexity of what we read into it" (*AS* 182), then American history lacks doubly: nothing has happened, *and* no one has read complexity into that lack of event. James the traveler had to enrich American history by reading complexity into the scene, and James the writer has to enrich it yet again by reading complexity into the "meagre" documentation of his travels. James's reader, in turn, must enrich that history yet again by reading complexity into *The American Scene*. James says as much in an autoreferential titular allusion characteristic of his late manner: "the American scene" will hold little for an observer "unless he be ready, anywhere, everywhere, to read 'into' it as much as he reads out" (*AS* 291).

## THE FOURTH MANNER

From the time he first told Grace Norton of his hopefully "*seeing* American life again," to his description to Edmund Gosse, midway through his trip, of "this extraordinary process of 'seeing' my native country" (*HJL* IV, 350), James had implied an equal interest in the American scene and in his perspective on it. He had told his brother Robertson that "for such a sodden absentee as I have long been, the *point of view* requires a good deal of taking" (*HJL* IV, 320); and he explained to George Harvey which point of view he would take. He would write "the best book (of social and pictorial and, as it were, human observation) ever devoted to this country," but, he added, "it *must* be absolutely personal to myself and proper to my situation." Having coveted the title *The Return of the Native*, he continued, he might use *The Return of the Novelist*. It "*describes* really my point of view . . . I'm so very much more of a Novelist than of anything else and see all things *as* such" (*HJL* IV, 327–28). He would write, then, from a perspective at once personal and novelistic; and if his final title—to borrow terms from his prefaces—stressed the dramatic scene, his working titles had stressed the fine central intelligence focusing it. Paradoxically, he would use his novelistic techniques to write a non-novel about novelistic perceptions of America.

With respect to genre, *The American Scene* belongs most obviously to the long line of travel literature that James published throughout his career, especially as that line converged with the shorter line of autobiographical writings that he produced between 1902 and 1914—each of the latter, incidentally, stressing almost equally place and person.[25] Adeline Tintner has reminded us that James characterized his other "tour" book, *A Little Tour in France* (1884, 1900), as written from notes "altogether governed by the pictorial spirit," notes that "are impressions, immediate, easy and consciously limited"; Tintner notes that James specified that one must choose, in fact, between "the perception of surface" and "the perception of very complex underlying matters" ("Photo Album" 4258). Tintner has also shown that James consistently regarded Impressionism, as he said of Sargent in 1893, as "an enormous 'note' or memorandum rather than a representation." Using the artist-tale "John Delavoy" (1898) as a further reference, Tintner has added that James contrasted two types of point of view: an Impressionistic point of view that precludes depth and an interpretative, novelistic point of view that produces depth ("Two Ways of Seeing" 363).

We can begin to approach the intergeneric tensions of *The American Scene* if we coordinate Tintner's first opposition between subject as the surface of things versus subject as their underlying causes and effects with her second opposition between Impressionistic perspective on subject as retinal and diffused versus novelistic perspective on subject as cerebral and focused. James certainly was gathering impressions, quick views of the American spectacle, the American scene; and though he did not examine "matters already the theme of prodigious reports and statistics," as he says in his preface, he did analyze "features of the human scene, . . . properties of the social air" (*AS* xxvi). As traveler, in sum, he had perceived surface *and* underlying matters, had assumed a point of view at once retinal *and* interpretative; and as writer, he would do the same—but he also would analyze himself as traveler, as both a surface and a depth, would view and interpret himself as the previous viewer and interpreter of the scene, with that previous viewer's memories and desires subject to scrutiny.

We should recall, in this context, that as a reader and professional reviewer, James had long been attracted to travel literature and to autobiographical forms such as the memoir; as a young reviewer, particularly, he had addressed not only many travelogues but also several personal memoirs of expeditions and of religious missions. We also should recall, moreover, that James would have known the conventions of the anthropological field report, well established by the turn of the century; they dictated not only statistics and analysis but also an account, in a real sense autobiographical, of the credentials and procedures of the anthropologist. And we should finally recall that James had practiced a high degree of autoreference, in two senses, in his late-phase novels: he thematized in them not only the procedures of interpretation and representation that he was employing but also the perspective from which he was employing them.[26] While traveling in America, he had observed and analyzed as a novelist; and in *The American Scene*, he thematized the ramifications of his novelistic procedures and perspective.

Though we cannot pause here to consider at length two pertinent aspects of James's elaborated theory of the novel, we must recall them briefly. First, James repeatedly worried the problem of differentiating between novelistic romance and realism, a differentiation that finds its central formulations in *Hawthorne*, "The Art of Fiction" (1884, 1888), and, especially, the prefaces to *The American* and *The Portrait of a Lady*. As the young champion of the realistic novel, James had had little trouble, in *Hawthorne*, enumerating the salient features of Hawthornian romance and thus, by indirection, the features of a proper realism. By the mid-1880s, however, he was declaring "an old fashioned distinction between the novel of character and the novel of incident . . . as little to the point as the equally celebrated distinction between the novel and the romance" and, moreover, "to answer as little to any reality" (*LC*-I, 54–55). And ultimately, as elderly prefacer, he found the only possible distinction to lie in the kind of experience represented, with romantic experience being that mediated, as we have seen, by thought and desire. Second, James consistently disapproved the autobiographical, or first-person, form of the novel, a disapproval he sustained from one of his earliest reviews in the 1860s through his central formulation of the problem in the preface to *The Ambassadors*.[27]

In that preface, composed soon after *The American Scene*, James conflated the two issues, taking up the choice he had made not to construct his protagonist Strether as "at once hero and historian," not to endow "him with the romantic privilege of the 'first person'—the darkest abyss of romance this, inveterately, when enjoyed on the grand scale." Though not without value, "the first person, in the long piece," James declared, "is a form foredoomed to looseness," never much his affair. Both as a character and as a compositional element, Strether has to observe stiffer proprieties, "has exhibitional conditions to meet, in a word, that forbid the terrible *fluidity* of self-revelation" (*AN* 320–21). But by this time, again, James had come to see that virtually everything reaches us through the circuits of thought and desire, that virtually all experience, perforce, partakes of the romantic and that the self experiencing the world, no less than the self representing his or her own story, always teetered on the edge of an abyss, external reality only tenuously arresting the plunge. In his only novelistic venture into the first person "in the long piece," *The Sacred Fount* (1901), the narrator, in fact, took that plunge.

William James had read his brother's last great novel, *The Golden Bowl* (1904), when Henry was still in America. Criticizing it as the epitome of his brother's musty "third manner," William urged Henry "to embark on a 'fourth manner' " of straightforward writing (Matthiessen, *James Family* 339). With that, William set the stage for his response, in May 1907, to *The American Scene*. It was, he said, *"supremely great"* but purely "third manner"; Henry had produced "the illusion of a solid object": "your account of America is largely one of its omissions, silences, vacancies. You work them up like solids." Though William agreed that absences marked America, he felt that his brother could have suggested them while stressing American presences. In effect, he accused Henry of being a successful, though false, conjurer, manipulating absences in America *and* in his writing to produce the illusion of presences in both; and in effect, William exhorted Henry to work, instead, like a sculptor, exhorted him to use positive mass to define negative space, to use strong and clear writing to reveal, and to treat analytically, American absences (Matthiessen, *James Family* 431–42; *Letters of William James* II, 277–80).

Though James had gleaned impressions while on tour, he had handled them differently than most Impressionists would have. He reshaped them in the studio, that is, slowly, laboriously, after the fact, from a personal point of view and toward a novelistic end, an end that included an autoreferential thematizing of the point of view itself. Though such a treatment of subject follows perfectly from the aesthetic principles that had informed the great "third manner" novels— *The Ambassadors*, *The Wings of the Dove*, and *The Golden Bowl*—James had to make two almost paradoxical modifications of those principles in his last nonfictional writings. First, he was working with "real" materials, often archival materials, but made their reality meaningful, sensible, by circuiting them through his point of view—the point of view of an incorrigible novelist. And second, he was working with generic conventions that demanded the use of the first person; and those demands propelled him, as he knew they would, toward "the darkest abyss of romance" and toward its corollary, "the terrible *fluidity* of self-revelation."[28] James had embarked decisively on a "fourth manner," but it hardly matched William's specifications.

## A BOOK NO SERIOUS AMERICAN WILL NEGLECT

James had opened his *Hawthorne* with the proposition "that it takes a great deal of history to produce a little literature, that it needs a complex social machinery to set a writer in motion" (*HA* 3); and he then elaborated at length on why antebellum America could produce only romance and, the genius of romance, Hawthorne. Giving a social turn to this literary formula in *The American Scene*, James there proposed "that it takes an endless amount of history to make even a little tradition, and an endless amount of tradition to make even a little taste, and an endless amount of taste, by the same token, to make even a little tranquillity" (*AS* 169). By 1905, obviously, the United States had produced more than a little literature, though it had not produced that of the expatriate James—leading him, perhaps, just after his visit, to choose to name his collected works "The New York Edition."[29] In any case, the United States had not produced, and James could not produce for it, civility.

The American press had gone after *Hawthorne*, though with less rancor than legend suggests.[30] By 1905, however, reviewers had in James a figure to be reckoned with, and they approached *The American Scene* with due respect.[31] As Rosalie Hewitt has superbly shown, moreover, those early reviewers also established terms that critical commentary would elaborate, often repetitively, for the next seventy years. She sees those reviewers as having tended either to denounce the work as a "negative assessment of modern America" by an aristocratic expatriate or to praise it as "a probing study by a native son." Whatever the case, Hewitt adds, most of them commented on James's point of view, and those who did so largely "agreed that James's subject was not really America, but rather his *impressions* of America" (179, 193). I would slightly revise Hewitt's insight, for James, I would say, had sought to complicate such binaries as expatriate/native and subject/perspective ("America"/"impressions"), and his later commentators, I would also say, followed his lead.

In 1918, for example, in his famous "Baedecker" to the "continent" of James's oeuvre, Ezra Pound argued that "there was emotional greatness in Henry James's hatred of tyranny" and that "there was titanic volume, weight, in the masses he sets in opposition within his work" ("Henry James" 297). No casual recognition of ethical rigor being manifested in aesthetic rigor, Pound's comment specifically cast James as a Prometheus, a titan, and thereby links a politics of liberating power with a poetics of commensurate purpose and force. Pound found James "the triumphant stylist" in *The American Scene*, moreover, and proceeded to describe the book as the "triumph of the author's long practice. A creation of America. A book no 'serious American' will neglect." It is a "grave record," a "faithful portrayal" that "any American with pretences to an intellectual life" must peruse: "It is not enough to have perused 'The Constitution' and to have 'heerd tell' of the national founders" ("Henry James" 327). With characteristic bombast, Pound had accorded *The American Scene* the prestige of the founding documents; but his having done so suggests the degree to which the debate over James's Americanness, since *Hawthorne*, had been a debate over James's moral authority as a critic of America. It would continue to be so.

In fact, one of the central forums of the later James revival, the April-May 1934 number of *Hound and Horn*, "Homage to Henry James," opened with Marianne Moore's "James as a Characteristic American" and contained two complementary essays on *The American Scene*, Lawrence Leighton's "Armor against Time" and John Wheelwright's more striking "Henry James and Stanford White." Suggesting the degree to which James's "nostalgia" had become a critical *donnée* in the debate, these latter essays also suggest how commentators of the moment were turning that nostalgia toward differing polemical ends. Leighton and Wheelwright, that is, each offered James's romanticizing of America in his defense, arguing that his romantic nostalgia had caused him to dislike not America but modernism in America. Leighton, however, tamed James's criticism by making it personal: America "held [for James] the romance of the unexplored," of the road he had not taken, and James directed his nostalgia, elegiacally, to those unrealized possibilities (383). But Wheelwright, by contrast, found James's criticism compromised by his nostalgia, the latter part and parcel of his aestheticizing; correct to appreciate the romantic "archeological architecture" of the century's first decade and to distrust the modernist skyscraper, James nonetheless, according to Wheelwright, had framed his analysis in aesthetic rather than in socioeconomic terms and had failed, as a result, to develop a cogent critique.[32]

Commentators after the Second World War continued to focus on James's expatriation and nativism, but from even sharper angles of vision. In a well-known and somewhat self-serving introduction to a new edition of *The American Scene* (1946), W. H. Auden—himself an expatriate to America in 1939 and a naturalized citizen in 1946—praised James the expatriate for holding an ethos of *romanitas*, in which "virtue is prior to liberty," while Auden quietly reproached an America that "has come, symbolically, to stand [for the premise] that liberty is prior to virtue" (xv). James's European ethos had made him, in Auden's view, not only an alien in America but also the proper moral instructor for America. The American novelist-critic Wright Morris, by contrast, loudly beat James's nativist drum in *The Territory Ahead* (1957). He located the source of James's moral authority not in his foreignness but in his nativism, in the submerged nativism that James had brought to the surface while in America. James was no "victim of nostalgia" in Morris's view (190), and his *American Scene* "puts in question the very reason for [the contemporary American novelist's] existence—his contemporaneity." That writer had yet to call back the truly—that is, the truly forward-looking—native perspective; and wherever he looks, as a result, he finds "that James, like Kilroy, was already there" (197).

In the late 1960s, two important scholars reshifted focus and revisited, with sharp differences, the question of James's nostalgia. Introducing new editions of *The American Scene* in 1967 and 1968 respectively, Irving Howe and Leon Edel took virtually opposite tacks on that nostalgia. Pulling the punches that he had to while introducing a lavishly illustrated edition of a famous work, Howe nonetheless characterized *The American Scene* as "a conservative book," an "often elegiac" book, in which James had avoided "the center of American society—its economic arrangements and structure, its offices and factories" (Introduction, *Scene* vii, ix); whatever William James may have thought, *The Golden Bowl* was the truly powerful instance of James's moral force.[33] Introducing what would become the standard edition of *The American Scene*, by contrast, Edel chose for his leitmotif James's self-characterization as "the restless analyst"; he presented a James, like Morris's, not nostalgic but, precisely, analytical. Edel concluded, indeed, on the stirring note that James's closing pages, spoken "before the era of polluted air and polluted rivers, before the audio-visual saturation, before the landscape laced with asphalt ribbons," should challenge us still with their anger (Introduction, *Scene* xxiii).

In more recent years, scholars have revisited nearly all the central questions raised by *The American Scene*—aesthetic, ideological, epistemological—from sophisticated theoretical positions. Setting out "to interpret James's America in the light of James's act of representing it" (412 [1982]) and arguing that James used his techniques of representation not just to depict America but simultaneously to enact the creative myth of American redemptiveness, Laurence Holland elaborated perhaps the best formalistic analysis of *The American Scene* we are likely to get.[34] Countering Holland, in turn, from ideological and epistemological vantages respectively, Mark Seltzer and John Carlos Rowe have brought us to state-of-the-art commentary, if not to the final word.[35] In an explicitly Foucaldian critique, Seltzer saw *The American Scene* as "James's most extensive account of the links between forms of discourse and the structures of power" in the world but, nonetheless, as a book in which "James's tactics of representation reproduce the very tactics of power that he ostensibly resists and disavows" (19, 100). And in an implicitly Derridean analysis, Rowe saw *The American Scene* as enacting not American redemptiveness but American self-consciousness, as a book neither reflecting nor constituting a cohesive vision of America but, rather, replaying the temporalities and differences, aporia intact, of America's envisioning itself (*Theoretical Dimensions*).

*The American Scene*, indeed, remains a book through which, by the history of its reception, we can gauge broader shifts in visions of America, for regardless of what James had taken as his subject, his commentators have taken James's America, not America's James, as theirs—and they have remade that America, repeatedly, in the image of their own historical moments. That has a nice appropriateness, for James himself had always promoted the American subject. After the publication of *Hawthorne*, he had encouraged Howells to "be the American Balzac. That's a great mission—go in for it!" (*HJL* II, 268). And in 1902 he had admonished Edith Wharton "in favour of the *American Subject*. . . . Take hold of it and keep hold and let it pull you where it will. . . . Profit, be warned, by my awful example of exile and ignorance" (*HJL* IV, 235–36). He greatly feared, of course, that he had lost that subject, that "the mixture of Europe and America which you see in me," as he apparently told Hamlin Garland, "has . . . made of me a man who is neither American nor European. I have lost touch with my own people" (Babiiha 13). With that, he voiced the fear hidden within the very claim he had made for *The American Scene*: rather than being both European and American, he might well have become neither.

James argued in *William Wetmore Story and His Friends* (1903) that "a man always pays, in one way or another, for expatriation, for detachment from his plain primary heritage" (*WW* I, 333); and he then drew from Story's case— "the case of the permanent absentee or exile"—the "general lesson" it taught: "in the long run, Story *paid*—paid for having sought his development [as an artist] even among the circumstances that at the time of his choice appeared not alone the only propitious, but the only possible" (*WW* II, 223). He later came to see, moreover, in *Notes of a Son and Brother* (1914), "to what a use American matter could be put by an American hand." He now drew from Hawthorne's case the lesson that "an American could be an artist, one of the finest, without 'going outside' about it" (*NS* 411). James had gone outside to live, and outside for his material, and coming home in 1904–5, "*seeing* American life again and tasting the American air," he never quite came inside. Yet he had remained "American enough" perhaps—to adapt his last comment on Hawthorne (*NS* 411)—to match the greatest stranger's book on the United States, Tocqueville's *Democracy in America*, with the greatest expatriate's book, *The American Scene*.

## NOTES

1. For Leon Edel's chronology and itinerary of James's visit, see *AS* 479–82.

2. James had spoken pleasantly of "this New England rural vastness," but he soon came to disparage "all the millions of square miles that spread vacantly about me here," to disparage more contemptuously—and contemptibly—the "irretrievable niggery wilderness," the "vast niggery wilderness," he found North Carolina to be. He noted pleasantly the "blandness in nature" of Florida but complained of the "overwhelming *Muchness* of space and distance and time" of his journey through the "looming largeness" of the Middle West, and he even complained when the magnificence of nature in Southern California "completely bowled me over . . . ; for there is absolutely nothing else, and the sense of the shining social and human inane is utter" (*HJL* IV, 332, 340, 344, 346, 351, 355, 356–57).

3. In January 1904, James asked Howells, "Will you kindly say to [George] Harvey for me that I shall have much pleasure in talking with him here of the question of something serialistic in the North American, and will broach the matter of an 'American' novel in *no* other way until I see him." James was "hungry for Material, whatever I may be moved to do with it." He apparently had planned to do a novel, since he repeated some months later, "I should greatly like before I chuck up the game to write (another!!) American novel or two—putting the thing *in* the country; which would take, God knows— I mean would require—some impressions" (*LHJ* II, 8–9; Edel, *Henry James: The Master* 229). James eventually used his material in "The Jolly Corner" (1909) and in the two unfinished, posthumous novels, *The Ivory Tower* and *The Sense of the Past* (both 1917).

4. James had written his agent, James B. Pinker, that his "book of Impressions" would give him "plenty to do" while traveling, but once actually traveling, he had found writing it impossible. In autumn 1904, he wrote Edmund Gosse that "the blot on my vision and the shadow on my path is that I have contracted to write a book of Notes," that seeing and writing were in conflict, that he already had found "my *Tone*," but that he would return to England "as a saturated sponge and wring myself out there"—a metaphor he would repeat to the same correspondent four months later (*HJL* IV, 323, 332–33, 351–52).

5. James wrote Peggy James in November 1905 that he might need "two distinct volumes instead of one," and a few days later, he wrote Edith Wharton, "it looks as if it would take me perhaps *two* (separate) volumes (*of* Impressions, pure and simple) to do" (*LHJ* II, 36: *HJL* IV, 375). He explained to William James in the same month that he envisioned "two moderately-long books (separate, of course, not two vols . . . but a sort of First and Second Series, with an interval between, the first winding up with Philadelphia and Washington and the second beginning with two papers on the South and going on . . . )"; he had "practically *done* the first" (*HJL* IV, 381). In December, he spoke again to Paul Bourget of "my probable two volumes" and, two days later, to W. E. Norris of his plan for "two [volumes], separate and differently-titled" (*HJL* IV,

388; *LHJ* II, 46). By March 1906, however, James was writing to Paul Harvey of his forthcoming "book," his forthcoming "volume" (*HJL* IV, 397).

6. James wrote Edith Wharton in November 1905, "Though I *shall* rejoice when it is over, I meanwhile quite like doing it." And he wrote W. W. Norris in December, "And yet the thing interests me to do, though at the same time appalling me by its difficulty" (*HJL* IV, 375; *LHJ* II, 46).

7. James had expressed to William in 1903 his desire "to see the Country . . . in *cadres* as complete, and immeasurably more mature than those of the celebrated Taine when he went, early in the sixties, to Italy, for six weeks, in order to write his big book [*Voyage en Italie*]" (*HJL* IV, 273). Two years later, he wrote Wharton that he was busy "trying to make my ten months in America, the subject of as many *Sensations d'Italie* as possible and finding, strangely, that I have more impressions than I know what to do with or can account for" (*HJL* IV, 375).

8. James wrote William: "The fates have been all against . . . my having been able to carry out my plan and do a second instalment, embodying more and complementary impressions. Of course I *had* a plan—and the second volume would have attacked the subject (and my general mass of impression) at various *other* angles, thrown off various other pictures, in short *contributed* much more. But the thing was not to be." He felt the book "a mere rather melancholy lopsided fragment, infinitely awkward without its mate," but he also felt "frustrated and fragmentary" his "American time." As a result, he was "in possession of unused and yet usable material from it still" (*HJL* IV, 465–70).

9. "To make so much money that you won't, that you don't 'mind,' don't mind anything—that is absolutely, I think, the main American formula" (*AS* 237), James argued. But that formula, he also saw, condemns a middle class to frustration. "The frustrated American . . . is the American who 'makes' too little for the castle and yet 'minds' too much for the hustled herd" (*AS* 238).

10. Just as the hotel took the role of the private house on the American scene, and the Pullman that of private car, so had a public notion of family replaced the private family. American manners, James argued, register "the apotheosis of the Family" (*AS* 325); and this conception of family—related to that of the democratic people—gave rise, in turn, to "ubiquitous children" in public (*AS* 251), including the spectacle of "the little pale, carnivorous, coffee-drinking ogre or ogress who prowls down in advance of its elders, engages a table—dread vision!—and has the 'run' of the bill of fare" (*AS* 425)—who breakfasts alone.

11. The opening headlines in the first New York paper may strike the modern reader, indeed, like titles for a series of horror films—complete with the paranoiac tone proper to that genre: The Obsession of the Alien, The Ubiquity of the Alien, The Scale of the Infusion, The Effect of the Infusion, and so on.

12. Given James's predilection for the left-handed compliment, moreover, one cannot automatically assume flattering his well-known remark: "How can everything so have gone [in Southern society] that the only 'Southern' book of any distinction published for many a year is *The Souls of Black Folk*, by that most accomplished of members of the negro race, Mr. W.E.B. Du Bois?" (*AS* 418).

13. James speaks of "the immense, grotesque, defeated project—the project, extravagant, fantastic, and to-day pathetic in its folly, of a vast Slave State (as the old term ran) artfully, savingly isolated in the world that was to contain it and trade with it" (*AS* 371). *That* delusion, hopelessly provincial, had marked "the eternal 'false position' of

the afflicted South" (*AS* 376) and had led, inevitably, to its present state. In an often cited passage, moreover, James notes of a young, moustachioed, and patriotic Virginian encountered at the pathetic Museum of the Confederacy that the latter perhaps "wouldn't have hurt a Northern fly, [but] there were things . . . that . . . he would have done to a Southern negro" (*AS* 388–89).

14. For the most thorough elaboration of this nexus, see the chapter on James in Eakin (*Fictions*).

15. James began with a long paper on New England, proceeded through four papers on New York, added one each on Newport, Boston, and (together) Concord and Salem and one each on the coastal cities Philadelphia, Baltimore, Washington, Richmond, and Charleston, and concluded with a paper on Florida.

16. Using that arrangement, moreover, James could place the brief paper, "The Sense of Newport," near the hinge of the sequence. Anomalous, its title not only refers to the meaning of Newport—the *sense* of Newport gleaned by the observer—but also suggests that Newport once had *sense*—had values, taste—that it now lacks. Specifically, the antebellum and wartime Newport of James's youth had the good sense evidenced by its lovely cottages, testaments to a taste that could accommodate culture to a picturesque nature; but the Newport of the modern moment, lacking that sense, erects mammoth cliffside houses, monuments to the ostentation of new and vast wealth, obliterating natural beauty—the same "white elephants," as James calls them, that he first had seen on the New Jersey shore and whose public, hotel versions he last would see in Palm Beach. Newport, then, epitomizes something central to the American scene: a nation without history but with wealth blights nature rather than accommodates culture to it, builds cities but not civilization.

17. Approaching the Hudson by train, looking "as through the glaze of all-but filial tears," James saw "the River shine . . . as a great romantic stream" but also saw that "to use the train at all had been to put one's self, for any proper justice to the scenery, in a false position." He had been complicit in the loss "of the rights of contemplation; rights as reduced, in the United States, to-day, and by quite the same argument, as those of the noble savage whom we have banished to his narrowing reservation" (*AS* 148–49). He later recalls "another occasion on which the romantic note sounded for me with the last intensity" (*AS* 152), a stop at Washington Irving's home "Sunnyside." "It has taken *our* ugly era to thrust in the railroad . . . the railroad that is part, exactly, of the pomp and circumstance, the quickened pace, the heightened fever, the narrow margin expressed within the very frame of the present picture" (*AS* 156). Were it not for the railroad, of course, he could not now be framing that picture.

18. James seemed more angry, however, over Harpers' elimination of his page headlines (see *HJL* IV, 448).

19. This final passage evidently inspired Donald Barthelme's witty visual collage *Henry James, Chief* (1977). For a reproduction and a shrewd discussion of it, see Rowe, "Who'se Henry James?"

20. James calls himself, on the one hand, the student of manners, the cold-blooded critic, the systematic story-seeker, the ancient contemplative person, the maker of these reflections, the observer, the fond critic, the most restless of analysts, the brooding analyst, the observer like a fond investor, the musing moralist, the ruthless analyst, and so on, and on the other hand, the returning absentee, the revisiting spirit, the restored absentee, the palpitating pilgrim, our anxious explorer, the observer from without, the repatriated absentee, the unappeased visitor, the freshly repatriated, the strayed amateur, and so on.

In a further complication, James sometimes employs those epithets particularly and indicatively (the restless analyst thought . . . ), sometimes generally and subjunctively (were a restless analyst to think . . . ). For an interesting and pertinent discussion of James's self-designations in his travel writing about Italy, see Edel, "Three Travelers."

21. James "remember[s]," for example, that "the imaginative response to the conditions here presented [in New York Bay] may just happen to proceed from the intellectual extravagance of the given observer" (AS 74); worries if a particular response to New York had simply "testified to the enjoyment of a real relation with the subject" (AS 116–27); worries if his tendency to find each successive impression of New York the strongest one was "a sign of the city itself, or only another perversity on the part of a visitor apt to press a little too hard, everywhere, on the spring of the show" (AS 194); and warns himself, ultimately, to beware "the vice of reading too much meaning into simple intentions" (AS 328).

22. Nature, for example, had placed Newport as a "touchstone of taste—with a beautiful little sense to be read into it by a few persons with the critical, the tender spirit" (210–11). In every case, though, the critically minded person will believe that "objects and places . . . must have a sense of their own, a mystic meaning proper to themselves to give out," and that "the prime business and the high honour of the painter of life [is] always to *make* a sense—and to make it most in proportion as the immediate aspects are loose or confused" (AS 273).

23. That James needed to find the South beautiful, as he notes, raises for him again "the quantity to be 'read into' the American view . . . before it gives out an interest" to the observer, to the "fond investor" (AS 372). As several commentators have observed, James was particularly drawn to financial and military metaphors.

24. James wrote that "criticism has no close concern with Alumni Hall," the Harvard memorial to the Union Dead—"it is as if that grim visitor found the approaches closed to him" (AS 61); and he notes that Civil War commemoratives in the Boston Public Library and, especially, the Saint-Gaudens memorial on Boston Commons to Robert Gould Shaw and the Fifty-fourth Massachusetts exemplify "works of memorial art that may suddenly place themselves . . . outside articulate criticism" (AS 250). Similarly, Concord, with its Revolutionary and its literary associations, has "something in the air which makes us tender, keeps us respectful; meets, in the general interest, waving it vaguely away, any closer assault of criticism" (AS 263–64). As he would say in his critical prefaces, "to criticise is to appreciate, to appropriate, to take intellectual possession" (AN 155); and as he says here, "there is in all contemplation, there is even in any clear appreciation, an element of the cruel" (AS 411).

25. James's travel literature includes *Transatlantic Sketches* (1875), *Portraits of Places* (1883), *A Little Tour in France* (1884), *Essays in London and Elsewhere* (1893), *English Hours* (1905), *The American Scene* (1907), *Italian Hours* (1909), and though not usually included, the posthumous fragment *The Middle Years* (1917)—this last, in fact, making use of material that James, while he was writing *The American Scene*, collected for a projected book on London (see *LHJ* II, 36–37, and *NB*, notebooks VI and VIII). James's later works of nonfiction include *William Wetmore Story and His Friends* (1903), *The American Scene*, the prefaces to the New York Edition (1907–9), *A Small Boy and Others* (1913), *Notes of a Son and Brother* (1914), and, again, *The Middle Years*. Each pays considerable attention to site—whether Rome, America, New York, Newport, Cambridge, London, or, in the prefaces, "the country of the blue," James's literary imagination; and each is, of course, autobiographical.

26. See, for example, Stowe's analysis of "systematic realism" in James.

27. See James's posthumous review of Bayard Taylor's *John Godfrey's Fortunes: Related by Himself; A Story of American Life* (1865) (*LC*-I, 621–25).

28. Several scholars have discussed the fusion of romance and first-person narration in James's fiction and in his late nonfiction; see Auerbach, Goetz, Przybylowicz.

29. James wrote to Scribners that the chosen name "refers the whole enterprise explicitly to my native city—to which I have had no great opportunity of rendering that sort of homage" (*HJL* IV, 365). At the same time, of course, the name refers New York to James's enterprise and makes that enterprise "American."

30. Most reviewers found James condescending or patronizing—the recurring terms—toward American life, American literature, and Hawthorne as American writer; they found the book written from a variously named French, English, or more generally "foreign" point of view and found it written toward an English audience—a point not only obvious but, in fact, acknowledged by James. At the same time, most found it more criticism than biography—also a point acknowledged by James—and, on the whole, praised it as criticism—praised James's analytical powers in general, his analysis of Hawthorne's works in particular, and, indeed, his clarity of style. In short, the reviewers found James the cultural critic at worst offensive and at best negligible, but they found James the literary critic fair and astute (see Linda Taylor 38–59).

31. Most reviewers treated the book as "difficult" but "honest," and most treated James's alleged "foreign" point of view rather positively. They divided over the question of the genre and focus of the book, though they saw it, by and large, as about America *and* about James—one called it "only superficially a book of travel." Though one reviewer found James "overbearingly egotistical" and another found his book "too personal, too microscopic," most, as with *Hawthorne*, praised its analytical force. Whether favorable or unfavorable, however, virtually every reviewer seemed to have remarked on the difficulty, complexity, or sheer complication of James's thought and, particularly, his syntax (see Linda Taylor 390–404).

32. Specifically, Wheelwright found James "one of those reactionary socialists who see Waste not Exploitation as the oberse [*sic*] of the medal of Profit, and, however inadequate this may be [as basis for social critique], it equipped him, or perhaps followed from his temperamental equipment, as an aesthete" (491).

33. Sounding much like Wheelwright, Howe found James "an impressionist painter of secondary social effects, and in that role, unsurpassed" (Introduction, *Scene* ix). In Howe's view, James's nature as "*a writer*" (xii)—James had said "Novelist," Wheelwright "aesthete"—prevented his seeing economic base structure as cause of superstructural social effects and, therefore, as the proper site for analysis.

34. For Holland, *The American Scene* accrued an importance comparable to Whitman's *Democratic Vistas* "in redefining the myth of America and channeling it into the twentieth century" (412 [1982]).

35. At this writing, that word belongs to Cameron.

# Appendix 1: An Annotated Chronology of Henry James's Principal Publications in Book Form

This lightly annotated chronological list of Henry James's principal publications in book form extends to 1917, the year after James's death. It does not, therefore, include several major posthumous publications, most notably *The Notebooks of Henry James*, ed. F. O. Matthiessen and Kenneth B. Murdock (1947), *The Complete Plays of Henry James*, ed. Leon Edel (1949), and the two-volume Library of America edition, *Henry James, Literary Criticism*, ed. Leon Edel, which contains James's complete literary essays and reviews, nearly a thousand pages of which appear for the first time in book form (1984). Such works are listed, however, in Appendix 2, Landmarks of Henry James Criticism, where each such edition is marked with a dagger (†) to distinguish it from purely secondary studies of James. Data in the following list of James's books are drawn from Leon Edel and Dan H. Laurence, *A Bibliography of Henry James*, 3d ed., rev. with the assistance of James Rambeau (Oxford: Clarendon Press, 1982).

## 1875

*A Passionate Pilgrim and Other Tales*. Boston: James R. Osgood. Short stories: "A Passionate Pilgrim," "The Last of the Valerii," "Eugene Pickering," "The Madonna of the Future," "The Romance of Certain Old Clothes," "Madame de Mauves."

*Transatlantic Sketches*. Boston: James R. Osgood. Travel writings, chiefly on England and Italy, with essays also on Switzerland, France, Germany, and Holland.

*Roderick Hudson*. Boston: James R. Osgood. First appeared in *Atlantic Monthly*, January–December 1875. James later would call *Roderick Hudson* his first novel, in effect disavowing the earlier *Watch and Ward*, published serially in *Atlantic Monthly* in 1871 and in book form in 1878.

## 1877

*The American*. Boston: James R. Osgood. First appeared in *Atlantic Monthly*, June 1876–May 1877.

## 1878

*French Poets and Novelists*. London: Macmillan. Essays on, among others, Baudelaire, Balzac, and Turgenev (whom James had befriended in Paris and whom he read in French translations).

*Watch and Ward*. Boston: Houghton, Osgood. First appeared in *Atlantic Monthly*, August-December 1871. James's first novel, but see the note on *Roderick Hudson* (1875).

*The Europeans: A Sketch*. London: Macmillan. First appeared in *Atlantic Monthly*, July-October 1878.

*Daisy Miller: A Study*. New York: Harper and Brothers. A best seller in England and America, this novella was James's greatest popular success. Rejected by the editor of *Lippincott's Magazine*, the story was first published by Leslie Stephen in *Cornhill Magazine*, June-July 1878.

## 1879

*An International Episode*. New York: Harper and Brothers. First appeared in *Cornhill Magazine*, December 1878–January 1879.

*The Madonna of the Future and Other Tales*. 2 vols. London: Macmillan. Short stories: "The Madonna of the Future," "Longstaff's Marriage," "Madame de Mauves," "Eugene Pickering," "The Diary of a Man of Fifty," "Benvolio."

*Confidence*. London: Chatto and Windus. James considered this comparatively unsuccessful novel a "pot-boiler." First appeared in *Scribner's Monthly*, August 1879–January 1880.

*Hawthorne*. London: Macmillan. Written by James for Macmillan's English Men of Letters series, this was the first book-length critical study of an American author.

## 1880

*A Bundle of Letters*. Boston: Loring. A short story published without authorization in a slim, small-format book. First appeared in the *Parisian*, December 18, 1879.

*The Diary of a Man of Fifty and A Bundle of Letters*. New York: Harper and Brothers. Contains two previously published short stories.

*Washington Square*. New York: Harper and Brothers. This volume bears the date 1881 but was published on December 1, 1880. First appeared in *Cornhill Magazine*, June-November 1880 and was also serialized almost simultaneously in *Harper's New Monthly Magazine*, July-December 1880.

## 1881

*The Portrait of a Lady*. 3 vols. London: Macmillan. The masterpiece crowning the first phase of James's long career, this novel first appeared in *Macmillan's Magazine*, October 1880–November 1881 and was serialized almost simultaneously in *Atlantic Monthly*, November 1880–December 1881.

## 1883

*Daisy Miller: A Comedy in Three Acts*. Boston: James R. Osgood. James gave his novella a different, happy ending in this dramatic adaptation.

*The Siege of London, The Pension Beaurepas, and The Point of View*. Boston: James R. Osgood. The novella "The Siege of London" first appeared in *Cornhill Mag-*

*azine*, January-February 1883. "The Point of View" first appeared in *Century Magazine*, December 1882.

*Collective Edition of 1883*. London: Macmillan. Includes *The Portrait of a Lady* (3 vols.), *Roderick Hudson* (2 vols.), *The American* (2 vols.), *Washington Square*, *The Europeans*, *Confidence*, and four volumes of novellas and short stories.

*Portraits of Places*. London: Macmillan. Travel essays on Italy, France, England, and America.

## 1884

*A Little Tour in France*. Boston: James R. Osgood. Travel writing. First appeared under the title "En Province" in *Atlantic Monthly*, July-November 1883 and February, April, and May 1884.

*Tales of Three Cities*. Boston: James R. Osgood. Short stories: "The Impressions of a Cousin," "Lady Barberina," "A New England Winter."

*The Art of Fiction*. Boston: Cupples, Upham. The cover of this volume was lettered "Walter Besant and Henry James, The Art of Fiction." The volume includes Besant's essay "The Art of Fiction" (first published by Cupples, Upham in August 1884) and, without authorization, Henry James's manifesto of the same title, published in *Longman's Magazine* in September 1884. James's essay, pp. 51–85, is one of the great critical documents of fictional realism.

## 1885

*The Author of Beltraffio, Pandora, Georgina's Reasons, The Path of Duty, Four Meetings*. Boston: James R. Osgood. The first four stories in this collection first appeared in 1884; "Four Meetings" was first published in 1877.

*Stories Revived*. 3 vols. London: Macmillan. Fourteen short stories in three volumes, including six that had not appeared earlier in book form: "A Day of Days" (1866), "A Landscape-Painter" (1866), "Rose-Agathe" (1878 under the title "Théodolinde"), "Poor Richard" (1867), "Master Eustace" (1871), and "A Most Extraordinary Case" (1868).

## 1886

*The Bostonians*. 3 vols. London: Macmillan. First appeared in *Century Magazine*, February 1885–February 1886.

*The Princess Casamassima*. London: Macmillan. First appeared in *Atlantic Monthly*, September 1885–October 1886.

## 1888

*Partial Portraits*. London: Macmillan. Literary reviews and essays on American, English, and French writers, as well as on Turgenev, and including "The Art of Fiction" in its first authorized book publication.

*The Reverberator*. 2 vols. London: Macmillan. First appeared in *Macmillan's Magazine*, February-July 1888.

*The Aspern Papers, Louisa Pallant, The Modern Warning*. 2 vols. London: Macmillan. All three pieces, including the important novella *The Aspern Papers*, had first appeared in magazines in 1888.

## 1889

*A London Life, The Patagonia, The Liar, Mrs. Temperly.* 2 vols. London: Macmillan. The novella *A London Life* and the tales "The Patagonia" and "The Liar" had been serialized in 1888, "Mrs. Temperly" in 1887 (under the title "Cousin Maria").

## 1890

*The Tragic Muse.* 2 vols. Boston: Houghton Mifflin. First appeared in *Atlantic Monthly*, January 1889–May 1890.

## 1892

*The Lesson of the Master, The Marriages, The Pupil, Brooksmith, The Solution, Sir Edmund Orme.* New York: Macmillan. Six short stories, all first published in magazines, 1888–91.

## 1893

*The Real Thing and Other Tales.* New York: Macmillan. Short stories: "The Real Thing," "Sir Dominick Ferrand," "Nona Vincent," "The Chaperon," "Greville Fane."

*Picture and Text.* New York: Harper and Brothers. Essays on artists, including John Singer Sargent and Honoré Daumier.

*The Private Life, The Wheel of Time, Lord Beaupré, The Visits, Collaboration, Owen Wingrave.* London: James R. Osgood. A collection of recent short stories. In America, the six tales appeared in two uniform volumes, *The Private Life* and *The Wheel of Time.*

*Essays in London and Elsewhere.* London: James R. Osgood. Includes essays on Flaubert and Ibsen.

## 1894

*Theatricals, Two Comedies: Tenants, Disengaged.* London: Osgood, McIlvaine. Neither play was produced.

*Theatricals, Second Series: The Album, The Reprobate.* London: Osgood, McIlvaine. Two more unproduced plays.

## 1895

*Terminations: The Death of the Lion, The Coxon Fund, The Middle Years, The Altar of the Dead.* London: William Heinemann. The first three titles were published in magazines in 1893 and 1894; this was the first appearance of "The Altar of the Dead."

## 1896

*Embarrassments: The Figure in the Carpet, Glasses, The Next Time, The Way It Came.* London: William Heinemann. Short stories first published in magazines in 1895 and 1896.

*The Other House.* 2 vols. London: William Heinemann. James's first novel after the "dramatic years," first published in the *Illustrated London News*, July 4–September 26, 1896.

## 1897

*The Spoils of Poynton*. London: William Heinemann. This short novel, or novella, first appeared as *The Old Things* in *Atlantic Monthly*, April-October 1896.

*What Maisie Knew*. London: William Heinemann. First appeared in *Chap Book*, January 15–August 1, 1897.

## 1898

*In the Cage*. London: Duckworth. This novella first appeared in this edition, with no prior serialization.

*The Two Magics: The Turn of the Screw, Covering End*. London: William Heinemann. *The Turn of the Screw* first appeared in *Collier's Weekly*, January 27–April 16, 1898; *Covering End* was first published in this edition.

## 1899

*The Awkward Age*. London: William Heinemann. This experimental novel, in which James largely eschewed narratorial "going behind" in favor of dialogue, first appeared in *Harper's Weekly*, October 1, 1898–January 7, 1899.

## 1900

*The Soft Side*. London: Methuen. Short stories: "The Great Good Place," "Europe," "Paste," "The Real Right Thing," "The Great Condition," "The Tree of Knowledge," "The Abasement of the Northmores," "The Given Case," "John Delavoy," "The Third Person," "Maud-Evelyn," "Miss Gunton of Poughkeepsie."

## 1901

*The Sacred Fount*. New York: C. Scribner's Sons. This novel first appeared in book form, without prior serialization.

## 1902

*The Wings of the Dove*. 2 vols. New York: Charles Scribner's Sons. Of the three great "major phase" novels, this was the first published but the second in order of composition, having been written between *The Ambassadors* and *The Golden Bowl*; there was no prior serialization.

## 1903

*The Better Sort*. London: Methuen. Short stories: "Broken Wings," "The Beldonald Holbein," "The Two Faces," "The Tone of Time," "The Special Type," "Mrs. Medwin," "Flickerbridge," "The Story in It," "The Beast in the Jungle," "The Birthplace," "The Papers"; all of these tales were published in magazines between December 1900 and January 1902 except the last three, which had their first appearance in this volume.

*The Ambassadors*. London: Methuen. James called *The Ambassadors* his favorite "all round" of his novels. It first appeared serially in *North American Review*, January-December 1903.

*William Wetmore Story and His Friends*. 2 vols. Edinburgh: William Blackwood and

Sons. James wrote this biographical account of the American sculptor and his circle at the request of Story's family.

## 1904

*The Golden Bowl*. 2 vols. New York: C. Scribner's. This climactic novel of the "major phase" had no prior serialization.

## 1905

*The Question of Our Speech, The Lesson of Balzac: Two Lectures*. Boston: Houghton Mifflin. Both lectures, delivered by James during his American tour of 1904–5, had prior magazine publication.
*English Hours*. London: William Heinemann. All but two of these essays on English topics had been published earlier in book form.

## 1907

*The American Scene*. London: Chapman and Hall. Many of the chapters in James's great, challenging account of his recent American tour were published first in magazines.

## 1907–1909

*The Novels and Tales of Henry James*. New York Edition. 24 [26] volumes. New York: Charles Scribner's Sons. This highly selective edition, with James's acclaimed critical prefaces (collected in 1934 in *The Art of the Novel*), was published two volumes at a time between December 1907 and July 1909 in twenty-four volumes. In 1917, after James's death, Scribner's issued the unfinished novels *The Ivory Tower* and *The Sense of the Past* in volumes uniform with the original twenty-four and thereafter advertised the New York Edition as being in twenty-six volumes. Vol. I, *Roderick Hudson*; vol. II, *The American*; vols. III–IV, *The Portrait of a Lady*; vols. V–VI, *The Princess Casamassima*; vols. VII–VIII, *The Tragic Muse*; vol. IX, *The Awkward Age*; vol. X, *The Spoils of Poynton*; vol. XI, *What Maisie Knew, In the Cage, "The Pupil"*; vol. XII, *The Aspern Papers, The Turn of the Screw, "The Liar," "The Two Faces"*; vol. XIII, *The Reverberator, "Madame de Mauves," "A Passionate Pilgrim," "The Madonna of the Future," "Louisa Pallant"*; vol. XIV, *"Lady Barbarina," The Siege of London, "An International Episode," "The Pension Beaurepas," "A Bundle of Letters," "The Point of View"*; vol. XV, *"The Lesson of the Master," "The Death of the Lion," "The Next Time," "The Figure in the Carpet," The Coxon Fund*; vol. XVI, *"The Author of Beltraffio," "The Middle Years," "Greville Fane," "Broken Wings," "The Tree of Knowledge," "The Abasement of the Northmores," "The Great Good Place," "Four Meetings," "Paste," "Europe," "Miss Gunton of Poughkeepsie," "Fordham Castle"*; vol. XVII, *"The Altar of the Dead," "The Beast in the Jungle," "The Birthplace," "The Private Life," "Owen Wingrave," "The Friends of the Friends," "Sir Edmund Orme," "The Real Right Thing," "The Jolly Corner," "Julia Bride"* ["The Friends of the Friends" had previously appeared as "The Way It Came"]; vol. XVIII, *Daisy Miller, "Pandora," "The Marriages," "The Real Thing," "Brooksmith," "The Beldonald Holbein," "The Story in It," "Flickerbridge," "Mrs. Medwin"*; vols. XIX–XX, *The Wings of* the *Dove*; vols. XXI–XXII, *The Ambassadors*; vols. XXIII–XXIV, *The Golden Bowl*; vol. XXV, *The Ivory Tower*; vol. XXVI, *The Sense of the Past*.

## 1908

*Views and Reviews*. Boston: Ball Publishing. Essays and reviews on English and American writers, edited by Le Roy Phillips, James's first bibliographer.

## 1909

*Italian Hours*. London: William Heinemann. A large volume of James's writings on Italy, some writings going back to the 1870s, others more recent or written expressly for this volume.

## 1910

*The Finer Grain*. New York: Charles Scribner's Sons. Short Stories: "The Velvet Glove," "Mora Montravers," "A Round of Visits," "Crapy Cornelia," "The Bench of Desolation." All were published in 1909 and 1910; "A Round of Visits" was James's last story, published in *English Review*, April-May 1910.

## 1911

*The Outcry*. London: Methuen. James's last novel, a novelization of his play of the same title (written in play form in late 1909 and revised in 1910).

## 1913

*A Small Boy and Others*. New York: Charles Scribner's Sons. The first volume of James's autobiography.

## 1914

*Notes of a Son and Brother*. New York: Scribner. The second volume of James's autobiography.

*Notes on Novelists*. London: J. M. Dent. Chiefly essays on English, French, and Italian novelists, this volume also includes the text of James's lecture on Browning, "The Novel in 'The Ring and the Book,' " and four of James's magazine essays on London, reprinted from 1897 issues of *Harper's Weekly*.

## 1917

*The Ivory Tower*. London: W. Collins Sons. See also the entry on the New York Edition, under 1907–1909, above.

*The Sense of the Past*. London: W. Collins Sons. See also the entry on the New York Edition, under 1907–1909, above.

*The Middle Years*. London: W. Collins Sons. Seven chapters of what was to have been the third volume of James's autobiography, *The Middle Years* was first published in *Scribner's Magazine*, October-November 1917.

# Appendix 2: Landmarks of Henry James Criticism

This lightly annotated list of landmarks of Henry James criticism is for the most part restricted to books and to major posthumous editions of James's nonfiction; each of the latter is marked with a dagger (†) to distinguish it from secondary works.

## 1905

Cary, Elisabeth Luther. *The Novels of Henry James: A Study*. The first book-length study of James's novels.

## 1913

Hueffer (Ford), Ford Madox. *Henry James: A Critical Study*. A critical appraisal by one of James's younger disciples.

## 1916

West, Rebecca. *Henry James*. Another critical study by a practicing novelist of the rising generation.

## 1918

Beach, Joseph Warren. *The Method of Henry James*. An influential systematic attempt to study James's technique and to assert its continuity with James's ethical concerns. Beach published a revised, expanded version in 1954.

Pound, Ezra. *Little Review* (August 1918), special Henry James Number. Essays from this historic number, which Pound organized, interrupted the serialization of James Joyce's *Ulysses* and spilled over into the September issue. Pound contributed three essays, and the issue also includes important essays by T. S. Eliot and A. R. Orage.

## 1920

†*The Letters of Henry James.* 2 vols. Ed. Percy Lubbock. Despite the high selectivity, the deletion of putatively embarrassing or compromising material by the editor, and the chronological imbalance in favor of the late James, this first major edition of James's letters remains valuable and includes material not included in Leon Edel's four-volume *Henry James Letters* (1975–84).

## 1921

Lubbock, Percy. *The Craft of Fiction.* Lubbock codified (and in the process rigidified) the principles set forth by James in the New York Edition prefaces.

†*The Works of Henry James.* 1921–23. 35 vols. Ed. Percy Lubbock. Unlike the quite selective New York Edition arranged by James himself, this collection includes all of the novels and tales published in book form by James (except three works adapted by James from his own plays—*The Other House*, "Covering End," and *The Outcry*—and also except the two posthumous, unfinished novels). This collection also includes the New York Edition prefaces.

## 1925

Brooks, Van Wyck. *The Pilgrimage of Henry James.* A sustained attack on James as an American aesthete who abandoned his country and its native realism.

## 1927

Edgar, Pelham. *Henry James: Man and Author.* The first book-length biography.

## 1930

Kelley, Cornelia Pulsifer. *The Early Development of Henry James.* In this pioneering critical study, Kelley emphasizes the moral seriousness James derived from Goethe and George Eliot.

Phillips, Le Roy. *A Bibliography of the Writings of Henry James.* An important source for the definitive modern bibliography compiled by Leon Edel, Dan H. Laurence, and James Rambeau.

## 1931

Rourke, Constance. *American Humor: A Study of the National Character.* Rourke emphasizes James's native American comedic dimensions and his originality as an American humorist and satirist.

## 1934

†*The Art of the Novel: Critical Prefaces by Henry James.* Introduction by Richard P. Blackmur. Valuable not only as a one-volume compilation of James's New York Edition prefaces but also for Blackmur's acute analytic introduction.

"Homage to Henry James." A special number of *Hound and Horn*. Ed. Lincoln Kirstein, Yvor Winters, and Allen Tate. Includes important essays by Newton Arvin, Stephen Spender, Marianne Moore, Edna Kenton, and most important, Edmund Wilson (the original version of his Freudian reading of *The Turn of the Screw*, "The Ambiguity of Henry James").

## 1935

Spender, Stephen. *The Destructive Element: A Study of Modern Writers and Beliefs.* Spender establishes James's focus on the political and moral corruption of society as the master paradigm for his study of modern literature; the first American edition was published in 1936.

## 1938

Knights, L. C. "Henry James and the Trapped Spectator." This essay, in the original series of the *Southern Review*, set the tone for four decades of James criticism concerned preponderantly with the fusion between moral and technical concerns in James's fiction.

## 1943

Henry James Number. *Kenyon Review.* Ed. Robert Penn Warren. Includes important essays by Katherine Anne Porter, Francis Fergusson, Jacques Barzun, Austin Warren, David Daiches, R. P. Blackmur, and F. O. Matthiessen.

## 1944

Matthiessen, F. O. *Henry James: The Major Phase.* Matthiessen's great critical study of the "major phase" novels includes, in an appendix, his important essay on James's revisions.
Rosenzweig, Saul. "The Ghost of Henry James." Published in *Partisan Review*, this pioneering essay, a psychoanalytic interpretation of James's life and fiction, was an important precursor to Leon Edel's biography of James.

## 1945

Dupee, F. W., ed. *The Question of Henry James: A Collection of Critical Essays.* This important collection has been seen in retrospect as one of the principal manifestations and vehicles of the so-called James revival of the 1940s.

## 1947

†*The Notebooks of Henry James.* Ed. F. O. Matthiessen and Kenneth B. Murdock. This edition of the notebooks, though in many respects superseded as well as augmented by *The Complete Notebooks* (ed. Edel and Powers, 1987), contains valuable, occasionally misleading interpretive commentary by the editors.

## 1948

Leavis, F. R. *The Great Tradition: George Eliot, Henry James, Joseph Conrad.* Leavis enshrines James—particularly the early James—in the tradition of passionately moralizing realism described and celebrated in this influential study.
†*The Scenic Art: Notes on Acting and the Drama, 1872–1901.* Ed. Allan Wade. A collection of James's theatrical reviews and essays.
Trilling, Lionel. "*The Princess Casamassima*: An Introductory Essay." This eloquent, unprecedented argument that James wrote an engagé, well-informed political novel in *The Princess Casamassima* was published in the journal *Horizon* and was later reprinted, with revisions, in *The Liberal Imagination*.

## 1949

†*The Complete Plays of Henry James*. Ed. Leon Edel. Edel's monograph-length introduction is a précis of his 1931 Sorbonne dissertation, "Henry James: Les Années
Dramatiques."

## 1951

Canby, Henry Seidel. *Turn West, Turn East: Mark Twain and Henry James*. As the title
suggests, this is a comparative study.
Dupee, F. W. *Henry James*. A slim, one-volume, widely admired critical biography.

## 1952

Bewley, Marius. *The Complex Fate: Hawthorne, Henry James, and Some Other American
Writers*. Bewley explores various parallels between James and Hawthorne.

## 1953

Edel, Leon. *Henry James: The Untried Years, 1843–1870*. The first volume of Edel's
monumental five-volume biography, introducing the biographer's key themes.

## 1956

†*The Painter's Eye: Notes and Essays on the Pictorial Arts by Henry James*. Ed. John
L. Sweeney. A selection of James's reviews and essays on painters and painting.

## 1957

Anderson, Quentin. *The American Henry James*. A provocative study of James's fiction
as allegorizing his father's religious philosophy.
Crews, Frederick C. *The Tragedy of Manners: Moral Drama in the Later Novels of
Henry James*. A brilliant study, the author's Yale honors thesis.
Edel, Leon, and Dan H. Laurence. *A Bibliography of Henry James*. The definitive
bibliography of James's works, with sections on books, contributions to books,
letters, contributions to periodicals, translations, and miscellanea. Revised editions
were published in 1961 and (with the assistance of James Rambeau) 1982.

## 1958

Wegelin, Christof. *The Image of Europe in Henry James*. A comprehensive, still indispensable discussion of the international theme in James's novels and tales.

## 1960

Poirier, Richard. *The Comic Sense of Henry James: A Study of the Early Novels*. Poirier
examines the moral and thematic bearings of James's comic sense in such early
works as *The American*, *The Europeans*, and *Washington Square*.

## 1961

Booth, Wayne C. *The Rhetoric of Fiction*. Includes an influential critique of what Booth
argues is a gap between James's intentions and his achieved fiction with respect
to point of view and rhetorical ambiguity.

Cargill, Oscar. *The Novels of Henry James*. A big book covering most of the major novels, devoting substantial chapters to each and including an extensive review and critique of scholarship to date.

Ward, J. A. *The Imagination of Disaster: Evil in the Fiction of Henry James*. A study of evil in James's fiction and necessarily, therefore, of good, expanding on Graham Greene's view that James had a sense of evil "almost religious in its intensity."

## 1962

†*The Complete Tales of Henry James*. 1962–64. 12 vols. Ed. Leon Edel. Includes a brief introduction to each volume by Edel.

Edel, Leon. *Henry James: The Conquest of London, 1870–1881*. Vol. 2 of *The Life of Henry James*.

———. *Henry James: The Middle Years, 1882–1895*. Vol. 3 of *The Life of Henry James*.

Geismar, Maxwell. *Henry James and the Jacobites*. A sustained attack on James and on his supposed "cult" among academic critics—written by an important American Marxian critic.

Krook, Dorothea. *The Ordeal of Consciousness in Henry James*. One of the most important of all critical studies of James, Krook's penetrating discussion of the philosophical dimensions of James's fiction blazed the trail for later critics who pay close attention to Jamesian epistemology (e.g., Paul Armstrong, Sharon Cameron, Laurence Holland, John Carlos Rowe, Mark Seltzer, and Ruth Bernard Yeazell, among others).

## 1963

Sharp, Sister M. Corona. *The Confidante in Henry James: Evolution and Moral Value of a Fictive Character*.

Wiesenfarth, Joseph. *Henry James and the Dramatic Analogy: A Study of the Major Novels of the Middle Period*.

## 1964

Gale, Robert L. *The Caught Image: Figurative Language in the Fiction of Henry James*. A detailed study of patterns of imagery in James's fiction.

Holland, Laurence. *The Expense of Vision: Essays on the Craft of Henry James*. A sophisticated, subtly nuanced, important study of James's epistemology; Holland works back and forth between the New York Edition prefaces and the novels to show how formal matters embody broad historical and cultural issues.

Vaid, Krishna Baldev. *Technique in the Tales of Henry James*. The first major study devoted to James's short fiction.

## 1965

Blackall, Jean Frantz. *Jamesian Ambiguity and The Sacred Fount*. A pioneering study of a novel that has figured more and more importantly in studies of James's ambiguity.

## 1966

Putt, S. Gorley. *Henry James: A Reader's Guide*. This volume is distinguished by being the first—and to date the only—critical study to discuss every single one of James's tales along with all of his longer fictions.

## 1967

Ward, J. A. *The Search for Form: Studies in the Structure of James's Fiction*. Explores Jamesian structural paradigms, showing that James blends Romantic, organic notions of form with formalist, neoclassical principles.

## 1968

Isle, Walter. *Experiments in Form: Henry James's Novels, 1896–1901*. Shows James's progress toward a protomodernist experimentalism in the fiction written between the failure of his play *Guy Domville* (1895) and the "major phase" novels of 1902–4.

Sears, Sallie. *The Negative Imagination: Form and Perspective in the Novels of Henry James*. Investigates unresolved tensions in James's fiction, excavating James's skepticism and presenting antiaffirmative readings of the major novels.

## 1969

Edel, Leon. *Henry James: The Treacherous Years, 1895–1901*. Vol. 4 of *The Life of Henry James*.

Segal, Ora. *The Lucid Reflector: The Observer in Henry James's Fiction*. A study of the Jamesian "central intelligence."

## 1970

Buitenhuis, Peter. *The Grasping Imagination: The American Writings of Henry James*. A sensitive, intertextual study of James's fiction set in America and his nonfiction writings on his native country.

Winner, Viola Hopkins. *Henry James and the Visual Arts*. A study of the visual arts and James's pervasive analogies between the art of the writer and of the painter.

## 1971

Powers, Lyall H. *Henry James and the Naturalist Movement*. Focuses on the lessons James learned from the French naturalists with whom he became acquainted in Paris in the late 1870s.

Weinstein, Philip. *Henry James and the Requirements of the Imagination*. A highly intelligent study of the conflict between vision and action in major novels by James, notably *The Portrait of a Lady*, *The Ambassadors*, and *The Golden Bowl*.

## 1972

Banta, Martha. *Henry James and the Occult: The Great Extension*. Banta skillfully examines James's use of the supernatural.

Chatman, Seymour. *The Later Style of Henry James*. An exacting, detailed analysis of James's late style.

Edel, Leon. *Henry James: The Master, 1901–1916*. Vol. 5 of *The Life of Henry James*.

Egan, Michael. *Henry James: The Ibsen Years*.

Goode, John, ed. *The Air of Reality: New Essays on Henry James*. An important collection—challenging, theoretically dense essays, many with a Marxian coloration.

## 1974

†*Henry James Letters.* 1974–1984. 4 vols. Ed. Leon Edel. The best, most complete modern edition of James's correspondence, this edition contains only about 10 percent of James's extant letters.

Hocks, Richard A. *Henry James and Pragmatistic Thought: A Study in the Relationship between the Philosophy of William James and the Literary Art of Henry James.*

## 1975

Veeder, William. *Henry James—The Lessons of the Master: Popular Fiction and Personal Style in the Nineteenth Century.* An always acute analysis of the early fiction, particularly telling on the moral dimensions of the rhetoric of the narrator and of the characters in such works as *Washington Square.*

## 1976

Rowe, John Carlos. *Henry Adams and Henry James: The Emergence of a Modern Consciousness.* Rowe concentrates his analysis of James on the author's philosophical modernism, notably his depiction of character as "fluid and relational" rather than as essential and autonomous.

Yeazell, Ruth Bernard. *Language and Knowledge in the Late Novels of Henry James.* An important, first-rate study of James's style and epistemology, notable for a fine analysis of figuration and of dialogue in the novels, illustrated with lucid close readings.

## 1977

Anderson, Charles R. *Person, Place, and Thing in Henry James's Novels.* An important investigation of James's symbolic use of objects and settings.

Edel, Leon. *The Life of Henry James.* 2 vols. A revised edition of Edel's biography, with some chapters rewritten, others dropped, and new ones added.

Felman, Shoshana. "Turning the Screw of Interpretation." A highly influential application of new French critical theories to an extended reading of *The Turn of the Screw.*

Nettels, Elsa. *James and Conrad.* A sound comparative study.

Purdy, Strother B. *The Hole in the Fabric: Science, Contemporary Literature, and Henry James.* James as a pioneer of the modern and postmodern.

Rimmon (Rimmon-Kenan), Shlomith. *The Concept of Ambiguity: The Example of James.* Uses James as the example and paradigm for a powerful exploration of the nature of ambiguity in literary texts.

## 1978

Donadio, Stephen. *Nietzsche, Henry James, and the Artistic Will.* Donadio explores parallels between James and Nietzsche, focusing on the act of will undergirding James's drive for artistic mastery.

Perosa, Sergio. *Henry James and the Experimental Novel.* A brilliant analysis of James's restless experimentalism—which according to Perosa extends beyond the experimental period of the 1890s through the "major phase" novels—and of James's role as a precursor of modernism and postmodernism.

Schneider, Daniel J. *The Crystal Cage: Adventures of the Imagination in the Fiction of Henry James*. Reads the struggle between the free spirit and an entrapping world as the "figure in the carpet" throughout James's fiction.

Springer, Mary Doyle. *A Rhetoric of Literary Character: Some Women of Henry James*. Intelligent, neo-Aristotelian analysis of genre and character in such tales as "The Beast in the Jungle" and "The Bench of Desolation."

## 1979

Bradbury, Nicola. *Henry James: The Later Novels*. A sophisticated structuralist study of how James's characters and readers attain knowledge and understanding in the middle and late novels.

Long, Robert Emmet. *The Great Succession: Henry James and the Legacy of Hawthorne*. The Hawthorne-James relation in James's fiction through the "middle period."

## 1980

Kappeler, Susanne. *Writing and Reading in Henry James*. A theoretically sophisticated close reading of major and experimental fiction by James, particularly good on *The Sacred Fount*.

Sicker, Philip. *Love and the Quest for Identity in the Fiction of Henry James*. James's changing views of love as the key to the quest for identity in his fiction.

## 1981

Berland, Alwyn. *Culture and Conduct in the Novels of Henry James*. Berland places James in the humanistic tradition of Matthew Arnold.

Daugherty, Sarah B. *The Literary Criticism of Henry James*. A comprehensive account of James's criticism, concentrating on his discussions of major writers and critics (e.g., George Eliot, Honoré de Balzac, Hippolyte Taine, Walter Pater) and excluding his discussion of his own work in the New York Edition prefaces.

Fogel, Daniel Mark. *Henry James and the Structure of the Romantic Imagination*. Close readings of the late novels organized around the thesis that James enacts in his novels the dialectical, spiral ascent described by M. H. Abrams as the paradigmatic narrative and thematic structure of English Romanticism.

White, Allon. *The Uses of Obscurity: The Fiction of Early Modernism*. Seeks to apply poststructuralist notions of indeterminacy to the reading of James's fiction.

Wilson, R.B.J. *Henry James's Ultimate Narrative*: The Golden Bowl.

## 1982

Habegger, Alfred. *Gender, Fantasy, and Realism in American Literature*. Includes an iconclastic attack on James (and Howells).

Norrman, Ralf. *The Insecure World of Henry James's Fiction: Intensity and Ambiguity*. A close study of James's rhetoric and ambiguity.

## 1983

Armstrong, Paul B. *The Phenomenology of Henry James*. A philosophically complex and instructive application of the philosophy of Husserl, Merleau-Ponty, and others in the phenomenological tradition to a close reading of James's novels early and late.

Jacobson, Marcia. *Henry James and the Mass Market*. A study of James's pursuit of popular success, continuing Edel's emphasis in the biography on James's concern with the business of authorship and Veeder's investigation of James's desire to at once master and transcend the popular culture of his time.

Stowe, William W. *Balzac, James, and the Realistic Novel*.

Wagenknecht, Edward. *The Novels of Henry James*. A survey with pungent, often sensible comments on the novels themselves and on other commentaries.

## 1984

Allen, Elizabeth. *A Woman's Place in the Novels of Henry James*. Explores the role of woman as sign and commodity in the society James depicts and in his fictional world.

Fowler, Virginia C. *Henry James's American Girl: The Embroidery on the Canvas*. Traces the evolution of James's heroines from Daisy Miller to Maggie Verver and includes also a fine discussion of gender categories in *The American Scene*.

Kaston, Carren. *Imagination and Desire in the Novels of Henry James*. A powerful feminist reading of renunciation in James's novels.

†*Literary Criticism*. Vol. 1: *Essays on Literature, American Writers, English Writers*; vol. 2: *Literary Criticism: French Writers, Other European Writers, the Prefaces to the New York Edition*. Ed. Leon Edel. A monumental collection of all extant literary criticism by Henry James, nearly three thousand pages in all, about a thousand of which had never been reprinted.

Rowe, John Carlos. *The Theoretical Dimensions of Henry James*. A *tour de force* deconstruction and application of virtually every major contemporary school of critical theory to James's fiction; destined perhaps to remain what it has been thus far, the most influential book of the 1980s on James.

Seltzer, Mark. *Henry James and the Art of Power*. Seltzer combines poststructuralist intertextuality with structuralist Foucauldian analysis to show the intricate entanglement of art and power in works that Seltzer thus reads as highly political: *The Princess Casamassima*, *The Golden Bowl*, and *The American Scene*.

Wagenknecht, Edward. *The Tales of Henry James*. A survey with the same tone and format of Wagenknecht's 1983 volume on the novels.

## 1985

Edel, Leon. *Henry James: A Life*. A revised, one-volume edition of the James biography, including new perspectives on James's sexuality and new material about the imaginative origins of *The Turn of the Screw*.

Margolis, Anne T. *Henry James and the Problem of Audience*. Analyzes James's attempt to woo a popular audience while not compromising his artistic integrity and without disappointing the audience, though few, who appreciated his work in spite of comparative failures with the mass readership.

Posnock, Ross. *Henry James and the Problem of Robert Browning*.

## 1986

Anesko, Michael. *"Friction with the Market": Henry James and the Profession of Authorship*. An investigation of how transactions with publishers, copyright considerations, and presumed market forces shaped the New York Edition.

Auchard, John. *Silence in Henry James: The Heritage of Symbolism and Decadence*. A supple, telling thematic and historical study.

Brodhead, Richard H. *The School of Hawthorne*. The most important of the many studies of James and Hawthorne.

Cowdery, Lauren T. *The Nouvelle of Henry James in Theory and Practice*. A penetrating study, particularly good on "The Coxon Fund" and *Daisy Miller*.

Freadman, Richard. *Eliot, James and the Fictional Self: A Study in Character and Narration*. A subtle comparative study of the two novelists.

Goetz, William R. *Henry James and the Darkest Abyss of Romance*. Explores autobiographical dimensions of James's writing.

Przybylowicz, Donna. *Desire and Repression: The Dialectic of Self and Other in the Late Works of Henry James*. A dense Lacanian-Marxist commentary on the late James.

Tintner, Adeline R. *The Museum World of Henry James*. With chapters organized like the various wings of a great museum, this volume is a summa and compilation of Tintner's voluminous scholarship, published over the course of five decades, on James's fictional use of the visual and plastic arts and of the artifacts of material culture.

## 1987

Banta, Martha, ed. *New Essays on* The American. Includes stimulating essays by Peter Brooks, John Carlos Rowe, Carolyn Porter, Mark Seltzer, and Banta.

†*The Complete Notebooks of Henry James*. Ed. Leon Edel and Lyall H. Powers. To the disappointment of some James scholars, this expanded edition jettisons the commentaries provided by Matthiessen and Murdock, arranges the notebook materials differently than in the earlier edition, and adds James's pocket diaries, his unfinished—and hitherto unknown—short story "Hugh Merrow," and new apparatus provided by Edel and Powers.

Edel, Leon, and Adeline R. Tintner. *The Library of Henry James*. A list of all books known to have been in Henry James's library, this volume is an indispensable research tool, the closest we will ever come to reassembling James's long dispersed personal library.

Gargano, James W., ed. *Critical Essays on Henry James*. Vol. 1: *The Early Novels*; vol. 2: *The Late Novels*. Three new essays appear in these two volumes along with reprints of earlier journal articles and book chapters by various authors.

Tintner, Adeline R. *The Book World of Henry James: Appropriating the Classics*. Tintner takes the reader on a multifaceted tour of James's appropriation of the classics of English, French, and American literature.

## 1988

Mizruchi, Susan L. *The Power of Historical Knowledge: Narrating the Past in Hawthorne, James, and Dreiser*. An intelligent application of new historicism to classic American literature.

†*Selected Letters of Henry James to Edmund Gosse, 1882–1915: A Literary Friendship*. Ed. Rayburn S. Moore. Includes some letters that do not appear in Lubbock's or Edel's editions.

Smit, David W. *The Language of a Master: Theories of Style and the Late Writing of Henry James*. Trenchant, detailed stylistic analysis.

## 1989

Auerbach, Jonathan. *The Romance of Failure: First-Person Fictions of Poe, Hawthorne, and James.*

Beidler, Peter G. *Ghosts, Demons, and Henry James.* The Turn of the Screw *at the Turn of the Century.* A well-researched historical study that supports the supernatural reading of James's most heavily disputed tale.

Borus, Daniel H. *Writing Realism: Howells, James, and Norris in the Mass Market.*

Cameron, Sharon. *Thinking in Henry James.* Philosophically dense and complex, Cameron's argument works against both traditional psychologized views that see Jamesian consciousness as internal, autonomous, and centered and poststructuralist views that either dismiss consciousness or subordinate it to the structure of the sign, which is then deconstructed. Instead, Cameron argues that Jamesian consciousness exists outside the individual, in a transpersonal realm, and that it has an imperial, quasi-magical power to shape reality and even to reverse death.

Gale, Robert L. *A Henry James Encyclopedia.* A handy, wise reference volume to James's personal and fictional worlds.

Greenwald, Elissa. *Realism and the Romance: Nathaniel Hawthorne, Henry James, and American Fiction.*

Habegger, Alfred. *Henry James and the "Woman Business."* A brilliant, provocative study of what Habegger alleges is the subordination of James's imagination, in the fiction through *The Bostonians*, to his father's reactionary, repressive views on women and marriage.

Heller, Terry. The Turn of the Screw: *Bewildered Vision.* Draws on contemporary critical theory for a trenchant exploration of James's ambiguity in a reading radically opposed to that of Beidler's important 1989 study.

McWhirter, David. *Desire and Love in Henry James: A Study of the Late Novels.* In fine close readings of the late novels, correlated with James's autobiographical writings, McWhirter traces an existentialist dialectic of love and desire triumphantly resolved in *The Golden Bowl.*

Tintner, Adeline R. *The Pop World of Henry James: From Fairy Tales to Science Fiction.* Tintner on James's incorporation into his fiction of materials drawn from popular culture.

## 1990

Fogel, Daniel Mark. *Covert Relations: James Joyce, Virginia Woolf, and Henry James.* An argument that the development of both Joyce and Woolf was shaped by the later writers' struggle to absorb and surmount the influence of James, who stands in this study, in Woolf's words, as "the bridge upon which we cross" to "the modern novel."

———. Daisy Miller: *A Dark Comedy of Manners.* Includes an overview of critical comment to date as well as a reading of James's most popular novella.

Freedman, Jonathan. *Professions of Taste: Henry James, British Aestheticism, and Commodity Culture.* A critically sophisticated, rigorous exploration of James's relations with Pater, Wilde, and British aestheticism generally.

†*Henry James and Edith Wharton: Letters, 1900–1915.* Ed. Lyall H. Powers. Includes some letters not included in earlier editions of James's correspondence.

Hocks, Richard A. *Henry James: A Study of the Short Fiction*. A penetrating discussion of James's technique and themes in the tales.

Horne, Philip. *Henry James and Revision: The New York Edition*. An important study that emphasizes the conscious art of James's revisions.

MacDonald, Bonney. *Henry James's Italian Hours: Revelatory and Resistant Impressions*. MacDonald explores the evolution of James's style and of his characteristic modes of perception in his writings about Italy.

Porte, Joel, ed. *New Essays on* The Portrait of a Lady. A fine introduction by the editor and four original essays by, among others, Alfred Habegger and William Veeder.

Tuttleton, James W., and Agostino Lombardo. *"The Sweetest Impression of Life": The James Family and Italy*. New essays by leading Italian and American scholars, including Leon Edel and Sergio Perosa.

## 1991

Bell, Millicent. *Meaning in Henry James*. Explores nuances of meaning and theme in James's major fiction.

Campbell, Jeanne. *American Designs: The Late Novels of James and Faulkner*.

Griffin, Susan M. *The Historical Eye: The Texture of the Visual in Late James*. Correlates James's visual sense in the late novels with contemporary art criticism and with the psychology of William James.

Woolf, Judith. *Henry James: The Major Novels*. An intelligent introduction for students.

# Works Cited

Abrams, M. H. "What's the Use of Theorizing about the Arts." In *In Search of Literary Theory*, ed. Morton W. Bloomfield, 3–54. Ithaca, N.Y.: Cornell U P, 1972.

Agnew, Jean-Christophe. "The Consuming Vision of Henry James." In *The Culture of Consumption: Critical Essays in American History, 1880–1980*, ed. Richard W. Fox and T.J.J. Lears, 65–100. New York: Pantheon, 1983.

Allen, Elizabeth. *A Woman's Place in the Novels of Henry James*. London: Macmillan, 1984.

Allen, Walter. *The English Novel: A Short Critical History*. New York: E. P. Dutton, 1955.

Allott, Miriam. "The Bronzino Portrait in Henry James's *The Wings of the Dove*." *Modern Language Notes* 68(1953): 23–25.

Althusser, Louis. "Ideology and Ideological State Apparatuses." *Lenin and Philosophy, and Other Essays*, 127–86. London: New Left Books, 1971.

Anderson, Charles. *Person, Place, and Thing in Henry James's Novels*. Durham, N.C.: Duke U P, 1977.

Anderson, Quentin. *The American Henry James*. New Brunswick, N.J.: Rutgers U P, 1957.

———. *The Imperial Self: An Essay in American Literary and Cultural History*. New York: Alfred A. Knopf, 1971.

Anesko, Michael. *"Friction with the Market": Henry James and the Profession of Authorship*. New York: Oxford U P, 1986.

———. " 'Friction with the Market': The Publication of Henry James's New York Edition." *New England Quarterly* 56 (1983): 354–81.

Arac, Jonathan, Wlad Godzich, and Wallace Martin, eds. *The Yale Critics: Deconstruction in America*. Minneapolis: U of Minnesota P, 1983.

Archer, William. Review of *The American. World*, January 7, 1891.

Aristotle. *Poetics*. Trans. Kenneth A. Telford. Chicago: Henry Regnery, 1961.

Armstrong, Paul B. *The Challenge of Bewilderment: Understanding and Representation in James, Conrad, and Ford*. Ithaca, N.Y.: Cornell U P, 1987.

————. *The Phenomenology of Henry James*. Chapel Hill: U of North Carolina P, 1983.

Arvin, Newton. "Henry James and the Almighty Dollar." *Hound and Horn* 7 (1934): 434–43.

Aswell, E. Duncan. "James's *In the Cage*: The Telegraphist as Artist." *Texas Studies in Language and Literature* 8 (1966): 375–84.

Auchard, John. *Silence in Henry James: The Heritage of Symbolism and Decadence*. University Park: Pennsylvania State U P, 1986.

Auchincloss, Louis. "The Late Jamesing of Early James." *Life, Law, and Letters: Essays and Sketches*. Boston: Houghton Mifflin, 1979.

Auden, W. H. Introduction to *The American Scene*, by Henry James, v–xxiii. New York: Scribner's, 1946.

Auerbach, Jonathan. *The Romance of Failure: First-Person Fictions of Poe, Hawthorne, and James*. New York: Oxford U P, 1989.

Aziz, Maqbool. " 'Four Meetings': A Caveat for James Critics." *Essays in Criticism* 18 (1968): 258–74.

————. "Mr. Amis's Merchandise: 3 SF-Drinks and Some Shorts." *Literary Review* (May 1981): 10–11.

————. "Revisiting 'The Pension Beaurepas': The Tale and Its Texts." *Essays in Criticism* 23 (1973): 268–82.

————. "Shorts, Knickers, or Novels: Kingsley Amis and David Lodge." *Literary Review* (August 1980): 5–7.

Babiiha, Thaddeo K. *The James-Hawthorne Relation: Bibliographical Essays*. Boston: G. K. Hall, 1980.

Babin, James. "Henry James's 'Middle Years' in Fiction and Autobiography." *Southern Review*, n.s. 13 (1977): 505–17.

Baker, Robert S. "Gabriel Nash's 'House of Strange Idols': Aestheticism in *The Tragic Muse*." *Texas Studies in Language and Literature* 15 (1973): 149–66.

Bakhtin, Mikhail. *The Dialogic Imagination*. Trans. Caryl Emerson. Austin: U of Texas P, 1981.

————. *Problems of Dostoyevsky's Poetics*. Ed. and trans. Caryl Emerson. Minneapolis: U of Minnesota P, 1984.

Bamberg, Robert D., ed. *The Portrait of a Lady*, by Henry James. New York: Norton, 1975.

Banta, Martha. *Henry James and the Occult: The Great Extension*. Bloomington: Indiana U P, 1972.

————, ed. *New Essays on* The American. New York: Cambridge U P, 1987.

Barzun, Jacques. *A Stroll with William James*. New York: Harper and Row, 1983.

Bass, Eben. "Dramatic Scene and *The Awkward Age*." *PMLA* 79 (1964): 148–57.

Baudelaire, Charles. "Madame Bovary, by Gustave Flaubert." In *Madame Bovary*, by Gustave Flaubert. Ed. and trans. Paul de Man, 336–43. New York: Norton, 1965.

————. *Ouevres complètes*. Ed. Y.-G Le Dantec. Paris: Pléiade, 1951.

Bauer, Dale M. *Feminist Dialogics: A Theory of Failed Community*. Albany: State U of New York P, 1988.

Bayley, John. *The Short Story: Henry James to Elizabeth Bowen*. Hertfordshire, England: Harvester, 1988.

————. *Tolstoy and the Novel*. New York: Viking, 1966.

Baym, Nina. "Fleda Vetch and the Plot of *The Spoils of Poynton*." *PMLA* 84 (1969): 102–11.

------. "Melodramas of Beset Manhood." In *The New Feminist Criticism: Essays on Women, Literature, and Theory*, ed. Elaine Showalter, 63–80. New York: Pantheon, 1985.

------. "Revision and Thematic Change in *The Portrait of a Lady*." *Modern Fiction Studies* 22 (1976): 183–200.

Bazzanella, Dominic J. "The Conclusion to *The Portrait of a Lady* Re-examined." *American Literature* 41 (1969): 55–63.

Beach, Joseph Warren. *The Method of Henry James*. New Haven, Conn.: Yale U P, 1918. 2d ed., 1954, Albert Saifer.

------. *The Twentieth-Century Novel: Studies in Technique*. New York: Century, 1932.

Becker, George, ed. *Documents of Modern Literary Realism*. Princeton, N.J.: Princeton U P, 1963.

Beebe, Maurice. *Ivory Towers and Sacred Founts: The Artist as Hero in Fiction from Goethe to Joyce*. New York: New York U P, 1964.

Beerbohm, Max. "Mr. Henry James's Play." Review of *The High Bid*, by Henry James. *Saturday Review*, February 7, 1909, 266–67.

Beidler, Peter G. *Ghosts, Demons, and Henry James*: The Turn of the Screw *at the Turn of the Century*. Columbia: U of Missouri P, 1989.

Bell, Gertrude Lowthian. *The Letters of Gertrude Bell*. 2 vols. New York: Boni and Liveright, 1927.

Bell, Ian F. A., ed. *Henry James: Fiction as History*. London: Vision Press, 1984.

Bell, Millicent. *Edith Wharton and Henry James: The Story of a Friendship*. New York: Braziller, 1965.

------. "Henry James and the Fiction of Autobiography." *Southern Review*, n.s. 18 (1982): 463–79.

------. " 'Les Mots ne sont pas la parole': *What Maisie Knew*." *Revue de Littérature Comparée* 57 (1983): 329–42.

------. *Meaning in Henry James*. Cambridge: Harvard U P, 1991.

Bellringer, Alan W. "*The Sacred Fount*: The Scientific Method." *Essays in Criticism* (Oxford) 22 (1972): 244–64.

------. "*The Spoils of Poynton*: James's Unintended Involvement." *Essays in Criticism* (Oxford) 16 (1966): 185–200.

Benson, E. F., ed. *Henry James: Letters to A. C. Benson and Auguste Monod*. New York: Charles Scribner's Sons, 1930.

Bercovitch, Sacvan. "The Revision of Rowland Mallet." *Nineteenth-Century Fiction* 24 (1969): 210–21.

Berg, Elizabeth. "The Third Woman." *Diacritics* 12 (1982): 11–21.

Berland, Alwyn. *Culture and Conduct in the Novels of Henry James*. Cambridge: Cambridge U P, 1981.

Bersani, Leo. *A Future for Astyanax*. Boston: Little, Brown, 1976.

------. "The Jamesian Lie." *A Future for Astyanax: Character and Desire in Literature*, 128–55. Boston: Little, Brown, 1976.

------. "The Subject of Power." *Diacritics* 7 (1977): 2–21.

Bewley, Marius. *The Complex Fate: Hawthorne, Henry James, and Some Other American Writers*. London: Chatto and Windus, 1952.

------. *The Eccentric Design: Form in the Classic American Novel*. New York: Columbia U P, 1959.

Blackall, Jean Frantz. *Jamesian Ambiguity and* The Sacred Fount. Ithaca, N.Y.: Cornell U P, 1965.

———. "James's *In the Cage*: An Approach through the Figurative Language." *University of Toronto Quarterly* 31 (1962): 164–79.

———. "Moral Geography in *What Maisie Knew*." *University of Toronto Quarterly* 48 (1978/79): 130–48. Reprinted in *Critical Essays on Henry James: The Late Novels*, ed. James W. Gargano, 84–100. Boston: G. K. Hall, 1987.

Blackmur, R. P. "Henry James." In *The Literary History of the United States*, ed. Robert E. Spiller et al., 1039–64. New York: Macmillan, 1948.

———. Introduction to *The Art of the Novel: Critical Prefaces by Henry James*, vii–xxxix. New York: Scribner's, 1934.

———. Introduction to *The Golden Bowl*, by Henry James, v–xxi. New York: Grove Press, 1952.

———. *Studies in Henry James*. Ed. Veronica A. Makowsky. New York: New Directions, 1983.

Blasing, Mutlu Konuk. *The Art of Life: Studies in American Autobiographical Literature*. Austin: U of Texas P, 1977.

Bogardus, Ralph F. *Pictures and Texts: Henry James, A. L. Coburn, and New Ways of Seeing in Literary Culture*. Ann Arbor, Mich.: UMI Research Press, 1984.

Boone, Joseph A. "Modernist Maneuverings in the Marriage Plot: Breaking Ideologies of Gender and Genre in *The Golden Bowl*." *PMLA* 100 (1986): 374–88.

Booth, Wayne. *The Company We Keep: An Ethics of Fiction*. Berkeley: U of California P, 1988.

———. *The Rhetoric of Fiction*. Chicago: U of Chicago P, 1961. Rev. ed., 1983, U of Chicago P.

Boren, Lynda S. *Eurydice Reclaimed: Language, Gender, and Voice in Henry James*. Ann Arbor, Mich.: UMI Research Press, 1989.

Borus, Daniel H. *Writing Realism: Howells, James, and Norris in the Mass Market*. Chapel Hill: U of North Carolina P, 1989.

Bosanquet, Theodora. "The Revised Version." *Little Review* 5 (August 1918): 56–62.

Bouraoui, H. A. "Henry James's *The Sacred Fount*: Nouveau Roman avant la Lettre?" *International Fiction Review* 1 (1974): 96–105.

Bowden, Edwin T. *The Themes of Henry James: A System of Observation through the Visual Arts*. New Haven, Conn.: Yale U P, 1956.

Bradbury, Nicola. *An Annotated Critical Bibliography of Henry James*. New York: St. Martin's Press, 1987.

———. *Henry James: The Later Novels*. New York: Oxford U P, 1979.

Brodhead, Richard H. *The School of Hawthorne*. New York: Oxford U P, 1986.

Brooke-Rose, Christine. "The Squirm of the True." Part 1: "An Essay in Non-Methodology." *PTL* 1 (1976): 265–94. Part 2: "A Structural Analysis of Henry James's *The Turn of the Screw*." *PTL* 1 (1976): 513–46. Part 3: "Surface Structure in Narrative." *PTL* 2 (1977): 517–62.

Brooks, Cleanth, and Robert Penn Warren. *Understanding Fiction*. New York: Appleton, 1943.

Brooks, Peter. *The Melodramatic Imagination: Balzac, Henry James, Melodrama, and the Mode of Excess*. New Haven, Conn.: Yale U P, 1976.

Brooks, Van Wyck. *The Pilgrimage of Henry James*. New York: E. P. Dutton, 1925.

Brown, Margaret Ellen. "The 'Unabashed Memoranda' of the Prefaces: Henry James's Letter to the World." Ph.D. diss., University of Illinois, Urbana, 1987.

Budd, John. *Henry James: A Bibliography of Criticism, 1975–1981*. Westport, Conn.: Greenwood Press, 1983.

———. "*The Spoils of Poynton*: The Revisions and the Critics." *Massachusetts Studies in English* 10 (1985): 1–11.

Buitenhuis, Peter. *The Grasping Imagination: The American Writings of Henry James*. Toronto: U of Toronto P, 1970.

Cain, William. "Criticism and Politics: F. O. Matthiessen and the Making of Henry James." *New England Quarterly* 60 (1987): 163–86.

Cameron, Sharon. *Thinking in Henry James*. Chicago: U of Chicago P, 1989.

Campbell, Jeanne. *American Designs: The Late Novels of James and Faulkner*. Philadelphia: U of Pennsylvania P, 1991.

Canby, Henry Seidel. *Turn West, Turn East: Mark Twain and Henry James*. Boston: Houghton Mifflin, 1951.

Cargill, Oscar. *The Novels of Henry James*. New York: Macmillan, 1961.

Carlson, Susan. *Women of Grace: James's Plays and the Comedy of Manners*. Ann Arbor, Mich.: UMI Research Press, 1985.

Carroll, David. *The Subject in Question: The Language of Theory and the Strategies of Fiction*. Chicago: U of Chicago P, 1982.

Cary, Elizabeth Luther. *The Novels of Henry James: A Study*. New York: Putnam's, 1905.

Chase, Richard. *The American Novel and Its Tradition*. Garden City, N.Y.: Doubleday, 1957.

Chatman, Seymour. *The Later Style of Henry James*. Oxford: Blackwell, 1972. Reprint, 1986, Greenwood Press.

Cixous, Hélène. "The Laugh of the Medusa." Trans. Keith Cohen and Paula Cohen. *Signs* 1 (1976): 875–93.

Cohen, Paula Marantz. "Feats of Heroism in *The Spoils of Poynton*." *Henry James Review* 3 (1981–82): 108–16.

Cook, David A., and Timothy J. Corrigan. "Narrative Structure in *The Turn of the Screw*: A New Approach to Meaning." *Studies in Short Fiction* 17 (1980): 55–65.

Cooley, Thomas. *Educated Lives: The Rise of Modern Autobiography in America*. Columbus: Ohio State U P, 1976.

Cowdery, Lauren T. *The Nouvelle of Henry James in Theory and Practice*. Ann Arbor: UMI Research P, 1986.

Cox, C. B. *The Free Spirit: A Study of Liberal Humanism in the Novels of George Eliot, Henry James, E. M. Forster, Virginia Woolf, and Angus Wilson*. New York: Oxford U P, 1963.

Cox, James M. "The Memoirs of Henry James: Self-Interest as Autobiography." *Southern Review*, n.s. 22 (1986): 231–51.

———. "Recovering Literature's Lost Ground through Autobiography." In *Autobiography: Essays Theoretical and Critical*, ed. James Olney, 123–45. Princeton, N.J.: Princeton U P, 1980.

Craig, Randall. "Reader-Response Criticism and Literary Realism." *Essays in Literature* (Western Illinois U) 11 (1984): 113–26.

———. " 'Read[ing] the unspoken into the spoken': Interpreting *What Maisie Knew*." *Henry James Review* 2 (1980–81): 204–12.

Crane, R. S. "The Concept of Plot and the Plot of *Tom Jones.*" *Critics and Criticism,* 616–47. Chicago: U of Chicago P, 1952.

Cranfill, Thomas Mabry, and Robert Lanier Clark, Jr. *An Anatomy of* The Turn of the Screw. Austin: U of Texas P, 1965.

———. "James's Revisions of 'The Turn of the Screw.' " *Nineteenth-Century Fiction* 19 (1965): 394–98.

Crews, Frederick C. *The Tragedy of Manners: Moral Drama in the Later Novels of Henry James.* New Haven, Conn.: Yale U P, 1957.

Cromer, Viris. "James and Ibsen." *Comparative Literature* 25 (1973): 114–27.

Crowley, Donald J., and Richard A. Hocks, eds. *The Wings of the Dove,* by Henry James. New York: Norton, 1978.

Culver, Stuart. "Censorship and Intimacy: Awkwardness in *The Awkward Age.*" *ELH* 48 (1981): 368–89.

———. "Representing the Author: Henry James, Intellectual Property, and the Work of Writing." In *Henry James: Fiction as History,* ed. Ian F. A. Bell, 114–36. London: Vision Press, 1984.

Daniels, Howells. "Henry James and 'An International Episode.' " *Bulletin of the British Association for American Studies* 1 (1960): 3–35.

Daugherty, Sarah B. *The Literary Criticism of Henry James.* Athens: Ohio U P, 1981.

Davidson, Arnold E. "James's Dramatic Method in *The Awkward Age.*" *Nineteenth-Century Fiction* 29 (1974): 320–35.

de Man, Paul. "Reading (Proust)." *Allegories of Reading: Figural Language in Rousseau, Nietzsche, Rilke, and Proust,* 57–78. New Haven, Conn.: Yale U P, 1979.

Descombes, Vincent. *Proust: Philosophie du roman.* Paris: Edition de minuit, 1987.

Doane, Janice. *Silence and Narrative: The Early Novels of Gertrude Stein.* Westport, Conn.: Greenwood Press, 1986.

Donadio, Stephen. *Nietzsche, Henry James, and the Artistic Will.* New York: Oxford U P, 1978.

Donoghue, Denis. "A Hero of Our Times." Review of *A Man of Letters: Selected Essays,* by V. S. Pritchett. *New York Review of Books* 33.11 (1986): 7–10.

Dostoevsky, Fyodor. *The Brothers Karamazov.* Trans. Constance Garnett. Rev. Ralph E. Matlaw. New York: Norton, 1976.

Dunbar, Viola. "The Revision of 'Daisy Miller.' " *Modern Language Notes* 65 (1950): 311–17.

Dupee, F. W. *Henry James.* New York: William Sloane, 1951. Reprint, 1973, Greenwood Press.

———, ed. *The Question of Henry James: A Collection of Critical Essays.* New York: Henry Holt, 1945.

Durkin, Sister Mary Brian. "Henry James's Revisions of the Style of *The Reverberator.*" *American Literature* 33 (1961): 330–49.

Eakin, Paul John. *Fictions in Autobiography: Studies in the Act of Self-Invention.* Princeton: Princeton U P, 1985.

———. "Henry James's 'Obscure Hurt': Can Autobiography Serve Biography?" *New Literary History* 19 (1988): 675–92.

Edel, Leon. "The Architecture of James's New York Edition." *New England Quarterly* 24 (1951): 169–78.

———. "A Further Note on an Error in *The Ambassadors.*" *American Literature* 23 (1951): 128–31.

————. *Henry James: A Life*. New York: Harper and Row, 1985.

————. "Henry James and the Cosmopolitan Imagination." New York: New York University, 1967.

————. "Henry James's Revisions for *The Ambassadors*." *Notes and Queries* 2 (1955): 37–38.

————. *Henry James: The Conquest of London, 1870–1881*. Vol. 2 of *The Life of Henry James*. Philadelphia: J. B. Lippincott, 1962.

————. *Henry James: The Master, 1901–1916*. Vol. 5 of *The Life of Henry James*. Philadelphia: J. B. Lippincott, 1972.

————. *Henry James: The Middle Years, 1882–1895*. Vol. 3 of *The Life of Henry James*. Philadelphia: J. B. Lippincott, 1962.

————. *Henry James: The Treacherous Years, 1895–1901*. Vol. 4 of *The Life of Henry James*. Philadelphia: J. B. Lippincott, 1969.

————. *Henry James: The Untried Years, 1843–1870*. Vol. 1 of *The Life of Henry James*. Philadelphia: J. B. Lippincott, 1953.

————. Introduction to *The American Scene*, by Henry James, vii–xxiv. Bloomington: Indiana U P, 1968.

————. Introduction to *The Complete Plays of Henry James*, 19–69. Philadelphia: J. B. Lippincott, 1949.

————. Introduction to *The Ghostly Tales of Henry James*, v–viii. New York: Grosset and Dunlap, 1963.

————. Introduction to *The Other House*, by Henry James, vii–xxi. London: New Directions, 1947.

————. Introduction to *The Sacred Fount*, by Henry James, 5–15. London: Rupert Hart-Davis, 1959.

————. Introduction to *Watch and Ward*, by Henry James, 5–18. New York: Grove Press, 1959.

————. "An Introductory Essay." *The Sacred Fount*, by Henry James, v–xxxii. New York: Grove Press, 1953.

————. "A Letter to the Editor." *American Literature* 24 (1952): 370–72.

————. *The Life of Henry James*. 5 vols. Philadelphia: J. B. Lippincott, 1953–72.

————. *The Life of Henry James*. 2 vols. Harmondsworth: Penguin, 1977.

————. "The Point of View." *The Psychological Novel, 1900–1950*, 51–75. New York: J. B. Lippincott, 1955. Excerpted in *Henry James: The Turn of the Screw*, ed. Robert Kimbrough, 228–34. New York: Norton, 1966.

————. *The Prefaces of Henry James*. Paris: Jouve, 1931.

————. *The Psychological Novel, 1900–1950*. Philadelphia: Lippincott, 1955; London: Hart-Davis, 1955.

————. *Stuff of Sleep and Dreams: Experiments in Literary Psychology*. New York: Harper and Row, 1982.

————. "The Text of *The Ambassadors*." *Harvard Library Bulletin* 14 (1960): 453–60.

————. "The Three Travelers in *English Hours*." *Henry James Review* 2 (1980–81): 167–71.

————. "Why the Dramatic Arts Embrace Henry James." *New York Times*, March 4, 1984, 2:1, 23.

————, ed. *The Ghostly Tales of Henry James*. New Brunswick, N.J.: Rutgers U P, 1948.

————, ed. *Henry James: Twentieth-Century Views*. Englewood Cliffs, N.J.: Prentice-Hall, 1963.

Edel, Leon, Dan H. Laurence, and James Rambeau. *A Bibliography of Henry James*. 3d ed., rev. Oxford: Clarendon Press, 1982.

Edel, Leon, and Gordon N. Ray. *Henry James and H. G. Wells: A Record of their Friendship, their Debate on the Art of Fiction, and their Quarrel*. London: Rupert Hart-Davis, 1958.

Edel, Leon, and Adeline R. Tintner. *The Library of Henry James*. Ann Arbor, Mich.: UMI Research Press, 1987.

Edgar, Pelham. *Henry James: Man and Author*. Boston: Houghton Mifflin, 1927.

Egan, Michael. *Henry James: The Ibsen Years*. New York: Barnes and Noble, 1972; London: Vision Press, 1972.

Eliot, T. S. "In Memory" and "The Hawthorne Aspect." *Little Review* 5 (August 1918): 44–53.

————. "A Prediction in Regard to Three English Authors, Writers Who though Masters of Thought, Are likewise Masters of Art" [excerpt]. In *Henry James: A Collection of Critical Essays*, ed. Leon Edel, 55–56. Englewood Cliffs, N.J.: Prentice Hall, 1963.

Ellison, David. *The Reading of Proust*. Baltimore: Johns Hopkins U P, 1984.

Emerson, Ralph Waldo. *Essays: First and Second Series*. Ed. Irwin Edman. New York: Thomas Y. Crowell, 1961.

————. *Selections from Ralph Waldo Emerson*. Ed. Stephen E. Whicher. Boston: Houghton Mifflin, 1957.

Fadiman, Clifton, ed. *The Short Stories of Henry James*. New York: Modern Library, 1945.

Feidelson, Charles. "James and the 'Man of Imagination.' " In *Literary Theory and Structure*, ed. Frank Brady, John Palmer, and Martin Price, 331–52. New Haven, Conn.: Yale U P, 1973.

Felman, Shoshana. "Turning the Screw of Interpretation." *Yale French Studies* 55/56 (1977): 94–207.

Fergusson, Francis. "James's Idea of Dramatic Form." *Kenyon Review* 5 (1943): 495–507.

Fetterley, Judith. *The Resisting Reader: A Feminist Approach to American Fiction*. Bloomington: Indiana U P, 1978.

Fiedler, Leslie A. *Love and Death in the American Novel*. New York: Stein and Day, 1960.

Fish, Charles. "Form and Revision: The Example of *Watch and Ward*." *Nineteenth-Century Fiction* 22 (1967): 173–90.

Flaubert, Gustave. *Madame Bovary*. Vol. 1 of *Oeuvres*. Ed. A. Thibaudet and R. Dumesnil. Paris: Pléiade, 1966.

————. *Madam Bovary*. Ed. and trans. Paul de Man. New York: Norton, 1965.

Fleishman, Avrom. *Figures of Autobiography: The Language of Self-Writing in Victorian and Modern England*. Berkeley: U of California P, 1983.

Fogel, Daniel Mark. *Covert Relations: James Joyce, Virginia Woolf, and Henry James*. Charlottesville: U P of Virginia, 1990.

————. *Daisy Miller: A Dark Comedy of Manners*. Boston: Twayne, 1990.

————. "Framing James's Portrait: An Introduction." *Henry James Review* 7 (1986): 1–6.

————. *Henry James and the Structure of the Romantic Imagination*. Baton Rouge: Louisiana State U P, 1981.

————. "Leon Edel and James Studies: A Survey and Evaluation." *Henry James Review* 4 (1982–83): 3–30.

Follett, Wilson. "Henry James's Portrait of Henry James." *New York Times Book Review* 23 (August 1936): 2, 16.

Forster, E. M. *Aspects of the Novel*. New York: Harcourt, Brace and World, 1927. Reprint, 1954, Harcourt.

Foster, Dennis. "Maisie Supposed to Know: Amo(u)ral Analysis." *Henry James Review* 5 (1983–84): 207–16.

Fowler, Virginia C. *Henry James's American Girl: The Embroidery on the Canvas*. Madison: U of Wisconsin P, 1984.

Freadman, Richard. *Eliot, James, and the Fictional Self: A Study in Character and Narration*. New York: St. Martin's Press, 1986.

Freedman, Jonathan. *Professions of Taste: Henry James, British Aestheticism, and Commodity Culture*. Stanford, Calif.: Stanford U P, 1990.

Freud, Sigmund. "A Child Is Being Beaten." In *The Standard Edition of the Complete Psychological Works of Sigmund Freud*, ed. and trans. James Strachey, 17: 179–204. 24 vols. London: Hogarth, 1953–74.

Freundlieb, Dieter. "Explaining Interpretation: The Case of Henry James's *The Turn of the Screw*." *Poetics Today* 5 (1984): 79–95.

Friedrich, Otto. "Of Apple Trees and Roses." *Time*, June 20, 1988, 70–71.

Friend, Albert C. "A Forgotten Story by Henry James." *South Atlantic Quarterly* 53 (1954): 100–108.

Froula, Christine. "When Eve Reads Milton: Undoing the Canonical Economy." *Critical Inquiry* 9 (1983): 321–47.

Gage, Richard P. *Order and Design: Henry James' Titled Story Sequences*. New York: Peter Lang, 1988.

Gale, Robert L. *The Caught Image: Figurative Language in the Fiction of Henry James*. Chapel Hill: U of North Carolina P, 1964.

————. "Henry James." In *Eight American Authors: A Review of Research and Criticism*, ed. James Woodress, 321–75. Rev. ed. New York: Norton, 1971.

————. *A Henry James Encyclopedia*. Westport, Conn.: Greenwood Press, 1989.

Gard, Roger, ed. *Henry James: The Critical Heritage*. London: Routledge and Kegan Paul, 1968.

Gargano, James W., ed. *Critical Essays on Henry James: The Early Novels*. Boston: G. K. Hall, 1987.

————. *Critical Essays on Henry James: The Late Novels*. Boston: G. K. Hall, 1987.

————. "James's *The Sacred Fount*: The Phantasmagorical Made Evidential." *Henry James Review* 2 (1980–81): 49–60. Reprinted in *Critical Essays on Henry James: The Late Novels*, ed. James W. Gargano, 113–30. Boston: G. K. Hall, 1987.

Garland, Hamlin. " 'I Have Lost Touch with My Own People.' " In *Henry James: Interviews and Recollections*, ed. Norman Page, 91–95. New York: St. Martin's Press, 1984.

Garnett, David. *Great Friends: Portraits of Seventeen Writers*. London: Macmillan, 1979.

Gegenheimer, Albert Frank. "Early and Late Revisions in Henry James's 'A Passionate Pilgrim.' " *American Literature* 23 (1951): 233–42.

Geismar, Maxwell. *Henry James and the Jacobites*. New York: Hill and Wang, 1962.

Gervais, David. *Flaubert and Henry James: A Study in Contrasts*. London: Macmillan, 1978.

Gettmann, Royal A. "Henry James's Revision of *The American*." *American Literature* 16 (1945): 279–95.

Getz, Thomas H. "Henry James: The Novel as Act." *Henry James Review* 4 (1982–83): 207–18.

Gibson, William M. "Metaphor in the Plot of *The Ambassadors*." In *Henry James: Modern Judgements*, ed. Tony Tanner, 304–15. London: Macmillan, 1969.

Gilbert, Sandra, and Susan Gubar. *The War of the Words*. Vol. 1 of *No Man's Land: The Place of the Woman Writer in the Twentieth Century*. New Haven, Conn.: Yale U P, 1988.

Gillen, Francis. "The Dramatist in His Drama: Theory vs. Effect in *The Awkward Age*." *Texas Studies in Literature and Language* 12 (1971): 663–74.

Girling, H. K. "On Editing a Paragraph of *The Princess Casamassima*." *Language and Style* 8 (1975): 243–63.

———. " 'Wonder' and 'Beauty' in *The Awkward Age*." *Essays in Criticism* (Oxford) 8 (1958): 370–80. Reprinted in *Henry James: Modern Judgements*, ed. Tony Tanner, 236–44. Nashville: Aurora, 1970.

Goetz, William R. *Henry James and the Darkest Abyss of Romance*. Baton Rouge: Louisiana State U P, 1986.

Goode, James M. *The Outdoor Sculpture of Washington, D.C.* Washington: Smithsonian Institution Press, 1974.

Goode, John, ed. *The Air of Reality: New Essays on Henry James*. London: Methuen, 1972.

———. "The Pervasive Mystery of Style: *The Wings of the Dove*." In *The Air of Reality: New Essays on Henry James*, ed. John Goode, 244–300. London: Methuen, 1972.

Gordon, D. J., and John Stokes. "The Reference of *The Tragic Muse*." In *The Air of Reality: New Essays on Henry James*, ed. John Goode, 81–167. London: Methuen, 1972.

Gordon, David. "Character and Self in Autobiography." *Journal of Narrative Technique* 18 (1988): 105–19.

Gosse, Edmund. "Henry James." *Scribner's Magazine* 67 (1920): 422–30, 548–57.

Graham, Kenneth. *Henry James, The Drama of Fulfillment: An Approach to the Novels*. Oxford: Clarendon Press, 1975.

Greenblatt, Stephen. "Shakespeare and the Exorcists." In *Contemporary Literary Criticism*, ed. Robert Con Davis and Ronald Schleifer, 428–47. 2d ed. New York: Longman, 1989.

Greene, Graham. *The Lost Childhood and Other Essays*. New York: Viking Press, 1951.

Greene, Philip L. "Point of View in *The Spoils of Poynton*." *Nineteenth-Century Fiction* 21 (1967): 359–68.

Greenwald, Elissa. *Realism and the Romance: Nathaniel Hawthorne, Henry James, and American Fiction*. Ann Arbor, Mich.: UMI Research Press, 1989.

Griffin, Susan M. *The Historical Eye: The Texture of the Visual in Late James*. Boston: Northeastern U P, 1991.

Grover, Philip. *Henry James and the French Novel: A Study in Inspiration*. New York: Barnes and Noble, 1973.

Habegger, Alfred. *Gender, Fantasy, and Realism in American Literature*. New York: Columbia U P, 1982.

———. *Henry James and the "Woman Business."* New York: Cambridge U P, 1989.

———. "Henry James's Rewriting of Minny Temple's Letters." *American Literature* 58 (1986): 159–80.

———. "The Lessons of the Father: Henry James, Sr., on Sex and Marriage." *Henry James Review* 8 (1986–87): 1–35.

———. "Review Essay—Leon Edel, *Henry James: A Life.*" *Henry James Review* 8 (1986–87): 200–208.

Hall, Richard. "An Obscure Hurt: The Sexuality of Henry James." *New Republic*, April 28, 1979, 25–31; May 5, 1979, 25–29.

Hardy, Barbara. *The Appropriate Form: An Essay on the Novel.* London: Athlone, 1964.

Hart, Francis R. "Notes for an Anatomy of Modern Autobiography." *New Literary History* 1 (1970): 485–511.

Harvitt, Helene. "How Henry James Revised *Roderick Hudson*: A Study in Style." *PMLA* 39 (1924): 203–27.

Havens, Raymond D. "The Revision of *Roderick Hudson.*" *PMLA* 40 (1925): 433–34.

Hays, H. R. "Henry James, the Satirist." *Homage to Henry James.* Reprint of Kirstein, Tate, and Winters. Mamaroneck, N.Y.: Paul J. Appel, 1971.

Heilman, Robert. *"The Turn of the Screw* as Poem." *University of Kansas City Review* 14 (1948): 277–89. Reprinted in *A Casebook on Henry James's "The Turn of the Screw,"* ed. Gerald Willen, 174–88. New York: Crowell, 1960. Also reprinted in *Henry James*: The Turn of the Screw, ed. Robert Kimbrough, 214–28. New York: Norton, 1966.

Heller, Terry. The Turn of the Screw: *Bewildered Vision.* Boston: Twayne, 1989.

Hellman, Geoffrey T. "Chairman of the Board." *New Yorker* 47 (March 13, 1971): 44–86.

Herrick, Robert. "A Visit to Henry James." *Yale Review*, n.s. 12 (1923): 724–41.

Hewitt, Rosalie. "Henry James's *The American Scene*: Its Genesis and Its Reception, 1905–1977." *Henry James Review* 1 (1979–80): 179–96.

Hilfer, Anthony Channell. *The Ethics of Intensity in American Fiction.* Austin: U of Texas P, 1981.

Hinz, Evelyn J. "Hierogamy versus Wedlock: Types of Marriage Plot and Their Relationship to Genres of Prose Fiction." *PMLA* 91 (1976): 900–913.

Hocks, Richard A. "*Daisy Miller*, Backward into the Past: A Centennial Essay." *Henry James Review* 1 (1979–80): 164–78.

———. *Henry James and Pragmatistic Thought: A Study in the Relationship between the Philosophy of William James and the Literary Art of Henry James.* Chapel Hill: U of North Carolina P, 1974.

———. *Henry James: A Study of the Short Fiction.* Boston: Twayne, 1990.

———. "James Studies 1981: An Analytic Bibliographical Essay." *Henry James Review* 5 (1983–84): 29–59.

———. Review of *Desire and Repression: The Dialectic of Self and Other in the Late Works of Henry James*, by Donna Przybylowicz. *Nineteenth-Century Literature* 42 (1987): 116–20.

Hoffa, William. "The Final Preface: Henry James's Autobiography." *Sewanee Review* 77 (1969): 277–93.

Holder-Barrell, Alexander. *The Development of Imagery and Its Functional Significance in Henry James's Novels.* Bern: Francke, 1959.

Holland, Laurence. *The Expense of Vision: Essays on the Craft of Henry James*. Princeton, N.J.: Princeton U P, 1964. Rev. ed., 1982, Johns Hopkins U P.

Holly, Carol. " 'Absolutely Acclaimed': The Cure for Depression in James's Final Phase." *Henry James Review* 8 (1986–87): 126–38.

———. "The British Reception of Henry James's Autobiographies." *American Literature* 57 (1985): 570–87.

———. "Henry James's Autobiographical Fragment: 'The Turning Point of My Life.' " *Harvard Library Bulletin* 51 (1983): 40–51.

Horkheimer, Max. *Critical Theory: Selected Essays*. Trans. Matthew J. O'Connell et al. New York: Seabury Press, 1982.

Horne, Philip. *Henry James and Revision: The New York Edition*. Oxford: Clarendon Press, 1990.

Howard, David. *"The Bostonians."* In *The Air of Reality: New Essays on Henry James*, ed. John Goode, 60–80. London: Methuen, 1972.

Howe, Irving. Introduction to *The American Scene*, by Henry James, v–xvi. New York: Horizon Press, 1967.

———. Introduction to *The Bostonians*, by Henry James, v–xxviii. New York: Modern Library, 1968.

Howells, William Dean. "Henry James, Jr." In *William Dean Howells: Representative Selections*, ed. Clara Marburg Kirk and Rudolf Kirk, 345–55. New York: Hill and Wang, 1950.

Hueffer (Ford), Ford Madox. *Henry James: A Critical Study*. London: Martin Secker, 1913.

Humphreys, Susan M. "Henry James's Revisions for *The Ambassadors*." *Notes and Queries* 1 (1954): 397–99.

Hutchinson, Stuart. "James's *In the Cage*: A New Interpretation." *Studies in Short Fiction* 19 (1982): 19–25.

Hutner, Gordon. "Goodwood's Lie in *The Portrait of a Lady*." *Henry James Review* 8 (1986–87): 142–44.

———. *Secrets and Sympathy: Forms of Disclosure in Hawthorne's Novels*. Athens: U of Georgia P, 1988.

Hynes, Joseph. "The Middle Way of Miss Farange." *ELH* 32 (1965): 528–53.

Iser, Wolfgang. *The Act of Reading: A Theory of Aesthetic Response*. Baltimore: Johns Hopkins U P, 1978.

Isle, Walter. *Experiments in Form: Henry James's Novels, 1896–1901*. Cambridge: Harvard U P, 1968.

Izsak, Emily K. "The Composition of *The Spoils of Poynton*." *Texas Studies in Literature and Language* 6 (1965): 460–71.

Jackson, Wendell P. "The Theory of the Creative Process in the 'Prefaces' of Henry James." *Amid Visions and Revisions: Poetry and Criticism on Literature and the Arts*. Baltimore: Morgan State U P, 1985.

Jacobson, Marcia. *Henry James and the Mass Market*. University: U of Alabama P, 1983.

Jacobus, Mary. *Reading Women: Essays in Feminist Criticism*. New York: Columbia U P, 1986.

James, Henry. *The Art of Criticism: Henry James on the Theory and Practice of Fiction*. Ed. William Veeder and Susan M. Griffin. Chicago: U of Chicago P, 1986.

——. *The Art of the Novel: Critical Prefaces by Henry James*. Ed. Richard P. Blackmur. New York: Scribner's 1934.

——. *The Complete Notebooks of Henry James*. Ed. Leon Edel and Lyall H. Powers. New York: Oxford U P, 1987.

——. *Henry James and Edith Wharton: Letters, 1900–1915*. Ed. Lyall H. Powers. New York: Scribner's, 1990.

——. *Henry James, Literary Criticism: Essays on Literature, American Writers, English Writers*. Ed. Leon Edel. New York: Library of America, 1984.

——. *Henry James, Literary Criticism: French Writers, Other European Writers, the Prefaces to the New York Edition*. Ed. Leon Edel. New York: Library of America, 1984.

——. "The Manners of American Women." *Harper's Bazar* 91 (1907): 355–59, 453–58, 537–41, 646–51.

——. *The Notebooks of Henry James*. Ed. F. O. Matthiessen and Kenneth B. Murdock. New York: Oxford U P, 1947.

——. *The Scenic Art: Notes on Acting and the Drama, 1872–1901*. Ed. Allan Wade. New Brunswick, N.J.: Rutgers U P, 1948.

——. *The Selected Letters of Henry James to Edmund Gosse, 1882–1915: A Literary Friendship*. Ed. Rayburn S. Moore. Baton Rouge: Louisiana State U P, 1988.

——. "The Speech of American Women." *Harper's Bazar* 90 (1906): 17–21, 113–17.

——. "Tennyson's Drama." In *Theory of Fiction: Henry James*, ed. James E. Miller, Jr., 97–99. Lincoln: U of Nebraska P, 1972.

——. *Theory of Fiction: Henry James*. Ed. James E. Miller, Jr. Lincoln: U of Nebraska P, 1972.

James, William. "Great Men, Great Thoughts, and the Environment." *Atlantic Monthly* 46 (1880): 441–59.

——. *The Letters of William James*. Ed. Henry James. 2 vols. Boston: Atlantic Monthly Press, 1920.

Jameson, Fredric. *Marxism and Form: Twentieth-Century Dialectical Theories of Literature*. Princeton, N.J.: Princeton U P, 1972.

——. *The Political Unconscious: Narrative as a Socially Symbolic Act*. Ithaca, N.Y.: Cornell U P, 1981.

Jefferson, D. W. *Henry James and the Modern Reader*. Edinburgh: Oliver and Oboyd, 1964.

Jehlen, Myra. "Archimedes and the Paradox of Feminist Criticism." *Signs* 6 (1981): 575–601.

Jobe, Stephen H. "A Calendar of the Published Letters of Henry James." Parts 1, 2. *Henry James Review* 11 (1990): 1–29, 77–100.

Johnson, Courtney, Jr. *Henry James and the Evolution of Consciousness: A Study of* The Ambassadors. East Lansing: Michigan State U P, 1987.

Jones, Granville H. *Henry James's Psychology of Experience: Innocence, Responsibility, and Renunciation in the Fiction of Henry James*. The Hague: Mouton, 1975.

Jones, Vivien. *James the Critic*. New York: St. Martin's Press, 1985.

Jonnes, Denis. "Family Pattern, Critical Method, Narrative Model." *Journal of Narrative Technique* 17 (1987): 12–24.

Kappeler, Susanne. *Writing and Reading in Henry James*. London: Macmillan, 1980; New York: Columbia U P, 1980.

Kaston, Carren. *Imagination and Desire in the Novels of Henry James*. New Brunswick, N.J.: Rutgers U P, 1984.

Kauffman, Linda S. "The Author of Our Woe: Virtue Recorded in *The Turn of the Screw*." *Nineteenth-Century Fiction* 36 (1981): 176–92.

Kaufman, Jule S. "*The Spoils of Poynton*: In Defense of Fleda Vetch." *Arizona Quarterly* 36 (1979): 342–56.

Kelley, Cornelia Pulsifer. *The Early Development of Henry James*. Urbana: U of Illinois P, 1930.

Kermode, Frank. *The Classic*. Cambridge: Harvard U P, 1983.

Kettle, Arnold. *An Introduction to the English Novel*. Vol. 2. London: Hutchinson U Library, 1953.

Keyser, Elizabeth. "Veils and Masks: *The Blithedale Romance* and *The Sacred Fount*." *Henry James Review* 2 (1980–81): 101–10.

Kimball, Jean. "A Classified Subject Index to the New York Edition Prefaces (Collected in *The Art of the Novel*)." *Henry James Review* 6 (1984–85): 89–133.

Kimbrough, Robert, ed. *Henry James:* The Turn of the Screw. New York: Norton, 1966.

King, Kimball. "Theory and Practice in the Plays of Henry James." *Modern Drama* 10 (1967): 24–33.

Kirby, David K. "Henry James: Art and Autobiography." *Dalhousie Review* 52 (1972–73): 637–44.

Kirk, Clara Marburg, and Rudolf Kirk, eds. *William Dean Howells: European and American Masters*. New York: Collier Books, 1963.

Kirschke, James J. *Henry James and Impressionism*. Troy, N.Y.: Whitston Press, 1981.

Kirstein, Lincoln, Yvor Winters, and Allen Tate, eds. Special Issue, "Homage to Henry James." *Hound and Horn* 7 (1934): 361–562.

Knights, L. C. "Henry James and the Trapped Spectator." *Southern Review* 4 (1938): 600–615. (Reprinted in *Explorations*, 174–89. New York: George W. Stewart, 1947; New York: New York U P, 1964; Pittsburgh: U of Pittsburgh P, 1976.)

———. "Restoration Comedy: The Reality and the Myth." In *Restoration Drama: Modern Essays in Criticism*, ed. John Loftis, 3–31. New York: Oxford U P, 1966.

Kossman, Rudolph. *Henry James: Dramatist*. Groningen, Netherlands: Wolters-Noordhoff, 1969.

Kraft, James. *The Early Tales of Henry James*. Carbondale: Southern Illinois U P, 1969.

Krause, Sydney J. "James's Revisions of the Style of *The Portrait of a Lady*." *American Literature* 30 (1958): 67–88.

Kristeva, Julia. *Desire in Language: A Semiotic Approach to Literature and Art*. New York: Columbia U P, 1980.

Krook, Dorothea. *The Ordeal of Consciousness in Henry James*. New York: Cambridge U P, 1962.

Laitinen, Tuomo. *Aspects of Henry James's Style*. Helsinki: Suomalainen Tiedeakatemia, 1975.

Leavis, F. R. *The Great Tradition: George Eliot, Henry James, Joseph Conrad*. New York: G. W. Stewart, 1960. Reprint, 1963, New York U P.

Lebowitz, Naomi. *The Imagination of Loving: Henry James's Legacy to the Novel*. Detroit: Wayne State U P, 1965.

LeClair, Robert. *Young Henry James: 1843–1870*. New York: Bookman, 1955.

Lee, Vernon [Violet Paget]. *The Handling of Words*. New York: Dodd, Mead, 1923.

Leeming, David Adams. "An Interview with James Baldwin on Henry James." *Henry James Review* 8 (1986–87): 47–56.

Leighton, Lawrence. "Armor against Time." *Hound and Horn* 7 (1934): 373–84.

Leitch, Thomas M. "The Editor as Hero: Henry James and the New York Edition." *Henry James Review* 3 (1981–82): 24–32.

Lerner, Daniel. "The Influence of Turgenev on Henry James." *Slavonic and East European Review* 20 (1941): 28–54.

Lerner, Daniel, and Oscar Cargill. "Henry James at the Grecian Urn." *PMLA* 66 (1951): 316–31. Reprinted in *Henry James: Modern Judgements*, ed. Tony Tanner, 166–83. Nashville: Aurora, 1970.

Levy, Babette May. " 'The High Bid' and the Forbes-Robertsons." *College English* 8 (1947): 84–92.

Levy, Leo B. *Versions of Melodrama: A Study of the Fiction and Drama of Henry James, 1865–1897*. Berkeley: U of California P, 1957.

Lewis, R.W.B. *The American Adam: Innocence, Tragedy, and Tradition in the Nineteenth Century*. Chicago: U of Chicago P, 1955.

———. *The Jameses*. New York: Farrar, Straus, and Giroux, 1991.

———. "The Vision of Grace: James's *The Wings of the Dove*." *Modern Fiction Studies* 3 (1957): 33–40.

Leyburn, Ellen Douglass. *Strange Alloy: The Relation of Comedy to Tragedy in the Fiction of Henry James*. Foreword by William T. Stafford. Chapel Hill: U of North Carolina P, 1968.

Lloyd, David. "Arnold, Ferguson, Schiller: Aesthetic Culture and the Politics of Aesthetics." *Cultural Critique* 2 (1977).

Lodge, David. Introduction to *The Spoils of Poynton*, by Henry James, 1–18. Harmondsworth: Penguin, 1987.

Long, Robert Emmet. *The Great Succession: Henry James and the Legacy of Hawthorne*. Pittsburgh: U of Pittsburgh P, 1979.

Lubbock, Percy. *The Craft of Fiction*. New York: Scribner's, 1921. Reprint, 1957, Viking.

———, ed. *The Letters of Henry James*. 2 vols. New York: Scribner's, 1920.

Luecke, Sister Jane Marie. "*The Princess Casamassima*: Hyacinth's Fallible Consciousness." *Modern Philology* 60 (1963): 274–80.

McCarthy, Harold T. *Henry James: The Creative Process*. New York: Thomas Yoseloff, 1958.

MacDonald, Bonney. *Henry James's Italian Hours: Revelatory and Resistant Impressions*. Ann Arbor, Mich.: UMI Research Press, 1990.

McElderry, Bruce R., Jr. "Henry James's Revision of *Watch and Ward*." *Modern Language Notes* 67 (1952): 457–60.

McIntyre, Clara F. "The Later Manner of Mr. Henry James." *PMLA* 27 (1912): 354–71.

McLean, Robert C. "The Subjective Adventure of Fleda Vetch." *American Literature* 36 (1964): 12–30. Reprinted in *Henry James: Modern Judgements*, ed. Tony Tanner, 204–21. Nashville: Aurora, 1970.

Macleod, Norman. "Stylistics and the Ghost Story: Punctuation, Revisions, and Meaning in 'The Turn of the Screw.' " In *Edinburgh Studies in the English Language*, ed. John M. Anderson and Norman Macleod, 133–55. Edinburgh: John Donald, 1988.

McMahan, Elizabeth. "Sexual Desire and Illusion in *The Bostonians*." *Modern Fiction Studies* 25 (1979): 241–51.

McMurray, William. "Pragmatic Realism in *The Bostonians*." *Nineteenth Century Fiction* 16 (1962): 339–44.

Macnaughton, William R. *Henry James: The Later Novels*. Boston: Twayne, 1987.

———. "In Defense of James's *The Tragic Muse*." *Henry James Review* 7 (1985–86): 5–12.

McWhirter, David. *Desire and Love in Henry James: A Study of the Late Novels*. Cambridge: Cambridge U P, 1989.

Maini, Darshan Singh. *Henry James: The Indirect Vision*. Ann Arbor, Mich.: UMI Research Press, 1988.

———. "Henry James and the Dream of Fiction." *The Spirit of American Literature*. New York: Envoy Press, 1988.

———. "Henry James: The Writer as Critic." *Henry James Review* 8 (1986–87): 189–99.

———. "Isabel Archer: A Portrait of a Young Woman as Artist." *The Spirit of American Literature*. New York: Envoy Press, 1988.

———. "The Politics of Henry James." *Henry James Review* 6 (1984–85): 158–71.

Margolis, Anne T. *Henry James and the Problem of Audience*. Ann Arbor, Mich.: UMI Research Press, 1985.

Marotta, Kenny. "*What Maisie Knew*: The Question of Our Speech." *ELH* 46 (1979): 495–508.

Marshall, Susan L. " 'Framed in Death': *The Sense of the Past* and the Limits of Revision." *Henry James Review* 10 (1989): 197–209.

Martin, W. R., and Warren V. Ober. " '5 M.S. Pages': Henry James's Addition to 'A Day of Days.' " *Studies in Short Fiction* 25 (1988): 153–55.

Martin, Wallace. Introduction to *The Yale Critics: Deconstruction in America*, ed. Jonathan Arac, Wlad Godzich, and Wallace Martin, xv–xxxvii. Minneapolis: U of Minnesota P, 1983.

Matthiessen, F. O. *American Renaissance: Art and Expression in the Age of Emerson and Whitman*. New York: Oxford U P, 1941.

———. *Henry James: The Major Phase*. New York: Oxford U P, 1944.

———. *The James Family: Including Selections from the Writings of Henry James, Senior, William, Henry, and Alice James*. New York: Alfred A. Knopf, 1947.

———. "The Painter's Sponge and Varnish Bottle: Henry James' Revision of *The Portrait of a Lady*." *American Bookman* 1 (1944): 49–68.

Maxwell, Joan. "Delighting in a Bite: James's Seduction of His Readers in *The Bostonians*." *Journal of Narrative Technique* 18 (1988): 18–33.

Mazzella, Anthony J. "The New Isabel." In *The Portrait of a Lady*, by Henry James, ed. Robert D. Bamberg, 597–619. New York: Norton, 1975.

———. "The Revised *Portrait of a Lady*." Ph.D. diss., Columbia University, 1970.

Mehlman, Jeffrey. *A Structural Study of Autobiography: Proust, Leiris, Sartre, Lévi-Strauss*. Ithaca, N.Y.: Cornell U P, 1974.

Miller, J. Hillis. *The Ethics of Reading: Kant, de Man, Eliot, Trollope, James, and Benjamin*. New York: Columbia U P, 1987.

Miller, James E., ed. *Theory of Fiction: Henry James*. Lincoln: U of Nebraska P, 1972.

Mitchell, Juliet. "*What Maisie Knew*: Portrait of the Artist as a Young Girl." In *The*

*Air of Reality: New Essays on Henry James*, ed. John Goode, 168–89. London: Methuen, 1972.

Mizruchi, Susan L. *The Power of Historical Knowledge: Narrating the Past in Hawthorne, James, and Dreiser*. Princeton, N.J.: Princeton U P, 1988.

*Modern Language Studies*. Henry James Issue. 13 (1983).

Moi, Toril. *Sexual/Textual Politics: Feminist Literary Theory*. London: Methuen, 1985.

Monteiro, George. "Geography in 'The Siege of London.' " *Henry James Review* 4 (1982–83): 144–45.

Moon, Heath. "More Royalist than the King: The Governess, the Telegraphist, and Mrs. Gracedew." *Criticism* 24 (1982): 16–35.

Mordell, Albert, ed. *Discovery of a Genius: William Dean Howells and Henry James*. New York: Twayne, 1961.

Morris, Wright. *The Territory Ahead*. 1957. Reprint. New York: Atheneum, 1963.

"Mr. Henry James's Theatricals." Review of *Theatricals: Second Series*, by Henry James. *Critic* 29 (November 28, 1896): 340–41.

Mülder-Bach, Inka. "Genealogy und Stil: Henry James's *Prefaces*." *Poetica* 20 (1988): 104–30.

Mull, Donald L. *Henry James's 'Sublime Economy': Money as Symbolic Center in the Fiction*. Middletown, Conn.: Wesleyan U P, 1973.

Murphy, Brenda. "James's Later Plays: A Reconsideration." *Modern Language Studies* 13 (1983): 86–95.

Murphy, Kevin. "The Unfixable Text: Bewilderment of Vision in *The Turn of the Screw*." *Texas Studies in Literature and Language* 20 (1978): 538–51.

Nance, William L. "*What Maisie Knew*: The Myth of the Artist." *Studies in the Novel* (North Texas State) 8 (1976): 88–102.

Nardin, Jane. "*The Turn of the Screw*: The Victorian Background." *Mosaic* 12 (1978): 131–42.

Nathan, Rhoda B. "The Farce That Failed: James's *The Spoils of Poynton*." *Journal of Narrative Technique* 14 (1984): 110–23.

Nettels, Elsa. *James and Conrad*. Athens: U of Georgia P, 1977.

Newberry, Frederick. "A Note on the Horror in James's Revision of *Daisy Miller*." *Henry James Review* 3 (1981–82): 229–32.

Niemtzow, Annette. "Marriage and the New Woman in *The Portrait of a Lady*." *American Literature* 47 (1975–76): 377–95.

Norrman, Ralf. *The Insecure World of Henry James's Fiction: Intensity and Ambiguity*. London: Macmillan, 1982.

———. *Techniques of Ambiguity in the Fiction of Henry James: With Special Reference to* In the Cage *and* The Turn of the Screw. Abo, Finland: Abo Akademi, 1977.

Ohmann, Carol. "*Daisy Miller*: A Study of Changing Intentions." *American Literature* 36 (1964): 1–11.

Olafson, Frederick A. "Moral Relationships in the Fiction of Henry James." *Ethics* 98 (1988): 294–312.

Olney, James. "Autobiography and the Cultural Moment: A Thematic, Historical, and Bibliographical Introduction." *Autobiography: Essays Theoretical and Critical*, 3–27. Princeton, N.J.: Princeton U P, 1980.

O'Neill, John P. *Workable Design: Action and Situation in the Fiction of Henry James*. Port Washington, N.Y.: Kennikat Press, 1973.

Palliser, Charles. " 'A Conscious Prize': Moral and Aesthetic Value in *The Spoils of Poynton.*" *Modern Language Quarterly* 40 (1979): 37–52.

Parker, Hershel. "The Authority of the Revised Text and the Disappearance of the Author: What Critics of Henry James Did with Textual Evidence in the Heyday of the New Criticism." *Flawed Texts and Verbal Icons: Literary Authority in American Fiction*, 85–144. Evanston, Ill.: Northwestern U P, 1984.

———. "An Error in the Text of James's *The American.*" *American Literature* 37 (1965): 316–18.

———. "Henry James 'In the Wood': Sequence and Significance of His Literary Labors, 1905–1907." *Nineteenth-Century Fiction* 38 (1984): 492–513.

Parrington, Vernon Louis. *The Beginnings of Critical Realism in America: 1860–1920.* New York: Harcourt, Brace and World, 1930.

Pascal, Roy. *Design and Truth in Autobiography.* Cambridge: Harvard U P, 1960.

Peacock, Ronald. "Henry James and the Drama." *The Poet in the Theatre*, 26–46. New York: Harcourt, Brace, 1946. Reprint, 1960, Hill and Wang.

Pearson, Gabriel. "The Novel to End All Novels: *The Golden Bowl.*" In *The Air of Reality: New Essays on Henry James*, ed. John Goode, 301–62. London: Methuen, 1972.

Perkins, David. *A History of Modern Poetry: From the 1890s to Pound, Eliot, and Yeats.* Cambridge: Harvard U P, 1976.

Perosa, Sergio. *Henry James and the Experimental Novel.* Charlottesville: U P of Virginia, 1978. Reprint, 1983, New York U P.

———. "James, Tolstoy, and the Novel." *Revue de littérature comparée* 57 (1983): 359–68.

Peterson, Dale. *The Clement Vision: Poetic Realism in Turgenev and James.* Port Washington, N.Y.: Kennikat Press, 1975.

Pilling, John. *Autobiography and Imagination: Studies in Self-Scrutiny.* London: Routledge and Kegan Paul, 1981.

Poirier, Richard. *The Comic Sense of Henry James: A Study of the Early Novels.* New York: Oxford U P, 1960.

———. "Visionary to Voyeur: Hawthorne and James." *A World Elsewhere: The Place of Style in American Literature*, 93–143. New York: Oxford U P, 1966.

Porte, Joel. *New Essays on* The Portrait of a Lady. Cambridge: Cambridge U P, 1990.

———, ed. *The Romance in America: Studies in Cooper, Poe, Hawthorne, Melville, and James.* Middletown, Conn.: Wesleyan U P, 1969.

Porter, Carolyn. *Seeing and Being: The Plight of the Participant Observer in Emerson, James, Adams, and Faulkner.* Middletown, Conn.: Wesleyan U P, 1981.

Posnock, Ross. *Henry James and the Problem of Robert Browning.* Athens: U of Georgia P, 1985.

Pound, Ezra. "Brief Note." *Little Review* 5 (August 1918): 6–9.

———. "Henry James." *Literary Essays of Ezra Pound*, ed. T. S. Eliot, 295–338. New York: New Directions, 1968.

Powers, Lyall H. *Henry James and the Naturalist Movement.* East Lansing: Michigan State U P, 1971.

———. "Visions and Revisions: The Past Rewritten." *Henry James Review* 7.2–3 (1985–86): 105–16.

———, ed. *Henry James's Major Novels: Essays in Criticism.* East Lansing: Michigan State U P, 1973.

Proust, Marcel. *A la recherche du temps perdu.* Ed. Pierre Clarac and Andre Ferré. 3 vols. Paris: Pléiade, 1954.

———. *Remembrance of Things Past.* Trans. C. K. Scott-Moncrieff and Terence Kilmartin. 3 vols. New York: Random, 1981.

Przybylowicz, Donna. *Desire and Repression: The Dialectic of Self and Other in the Late Works of Henry James.* University: U of Alabama P, 1986.

Purdy, Strother B. *The Hole in the Fabric: Science, Contemporary Literature, and Henry James.*

Putt, S. Gorley. *Henry James: A Reader's Guide.* Introd. Arthur Mizener. Ithaca, N.Y.: Cornell U P, 1966.

Rader, Ralph. "*Lord Jim* and the Formal Development of the English Novel." In *Reading Narrative: Form, Ethics, Ideology,* ed. James Phelan, 220–35. Columbus: Ohio State U P, 1989.

Ranald, Ralph A. "*The Sacred Fount*: James's Portrait of the Artist *Manqué.*" *Nineteenth-Century Fiction* 15 (1960): 239–48.

Ray, Gordon N. "The Importance of Original Editions." In *Nineteenth-Century English Books,* ed. Gordon N. Ray, Carl Weber, and John Carter. Urbana: U of Illinois P, 1952.

Reilly, Robert J. "Henry James and the Morality of Fiction." *American Literature* 39 (1967): 1–30.

Richards, Bernard. "*The Ambassadors* and *The Sacred Fount*: The Artist *Manqué.*" In *The Air of Reality: New Essays on Henry James,* ed. John Goode, 219–43. London: Methuen, 1972.

———. "Another Model for Christina Light." *Henry James Review* 5 (1983–84): 60–65.

———. Introduction to *The Spoils of Poynton,* by Henry James. Oxford: Oxford U P, 1982.

Rimmon (Rimmon-Kenan), Shlomith. *The Concept of Ambiguity: The Example of James.* Chicago: U of Chicago P, 1977.

Ringuette, Dana J. "The Self-Forming Subject: Henry James's Pragmatistic Revision." *Mosaic: A Journal for the Interdisciplinary Study of Literature* 23 (1990): 115–30.

Robbins, Bruce. "Shooting Off James's Blanks: Theory, Politics, and *The Turn of the Screw.*" *Henry James Review* 5 (1983–84): 192–99.

Robins, Elizabeth. *Theatre and Friendship: Some Henry James Letters.* New York: G. P. Putnam's Sons, 1932.

Rosenbaum, S. P. "*Aspects of the Novel* and Literary History." In *E. M. Forster: Centenary Revaluations,* ed. Judith Scherer Herz and Robert K. Martin, 55–83. London: Macmillan, 1982.

———. "*The Spoils of Poynton*: Revisions and Editions." *Studies in Bibliography* 19 (1966): 161–74.

———, ed. *The Ambassadors,* by Henry James. New York: Norton, 1964.

Rosenzweig, Saul. "The Ghost of Henry James." *Partisan Review* 11 (1944): 436–55.

Rourke, Constance. *Native American Humor: A Study of the National Character.* New York: Harcourt Brace Jovanovich, 1931.

Rowe, John Carlos. *Henry Adams and Henry James: The Emergence of a Modern Consciousness.* Ithaca, N.Y.: Cornell U P, 1976.

————. "Modern Art and the Invention of Postmodern Capital." *American Quarterly* 39 (1987): 155–73.

————. Review of *Writing and Reading in Henry James*, by Susanne Kappeler. *Henry James Review* 3 (1981–82): 67–69.

————. *The Theoretical Dimensions of Henry James*. Madison: U of Wisconsin P, 1984.

————. "Who'se Henry James? Further Lessons of the Master." *Henry James Review* 2 (1980–81): 2–11.

Ruland, Richard. "Beyond Harsh Inquiry: The Hawthorne of Henry James." *ESQ: A Journal of the American Renaissance* 25 (1979): 95–117.

Salzberg, Joel. "Mr. Mudge as Redemptive Fate: Juxtaposition in James's *In the Cage*." *Studies in the Novel* (North Texas State) 11 (1979): 63–76.

Samuels, Charles Thomas. *The Ambiguity of Henry James*. Urbana: U of Illinois P, 1971.

Sayre, Robert. *The Examined Self: Benjamin Franklin, Henry Adams, Henry James*. Princeton, N.J.: Princeton U P, 1964.

Schneider, Daniel J. *The Crystal Cage: Adventures of the Imagination in the Fiction of Henry James*. Lawrence: Regents Press of Kansas, 1978.

————. "James's *The Awkward Age*: A Reading and an Evaluation." *Henry James Review* 1 (1979–80): 219–27.

Schoenberg, Arnold. *Harmonielehre*, N.p.: Universal Edition, 1949.

Schor, Naomi. "Fiction as Interpretation/Interpretation as Fiction." In *The Reader in the Text: Essays on Audience and Interpretation*, ed. Susan R. Suleiman and Inge Crosman, 165–82. Princeton, N.J.: Princeton U P, 1980.

Schorer, Mark. Foreword to *The Craft of Fiction*, by Percy Lubbock. 1921. Reprint. New York: Viking, 1957.

————. "Technique as Discovery." *Hudson Review* 1 (1948): 67–87.

Schrero, Elliot M. "Exposure in *The Turn of the Screw*." *Modern Philology* 78 (1981): 261–74.

Schulz, Max F. "The Bellegardes' Feud with Christopher Newman: A Study of Henry James' Revision of *The American*." *American Literature* 27 (1955): 42–55.

Schwarz, Daniel R. *The Humanistic Heritage: Critical Theories of the English Novel from James to Hillis Miller*. Philadelphia: U of Pennsylvania P, 1986.

Scott, Clement. "The Playhouses." Review of *The American*, by Henry James. *Illustrated London News* 99 (October 3, 1891): 435.

Scura, Dorothy McInnis. *Henry James, 1960–1974: A Reference Guide*. Boston: G. K. Hall, 1979.

Sears, Sallie. *The Negative Imagination: Form and Perspective in the Novels of Henry James*. Ithaca: Cornell U P, 1968.

Sedgwick, Eve Kosofsky. "Epistemology of the Closet I." *Raritan* 7 (1988): 36–69.

————. Epistemology of the Closet II." *Raritan* 8 (1988): 102–30.

————. *Epistemology of the Closet*. Berkeley: U of California P, 1990.

See, Fred G. "Henry James and the Art of Possession." In *American Realism: New Essays*, ed. Eric J. Sundquist, 119–37. Baltimore: Johns Hopkins U P, 1982.

Segal, Ora. *The Lucid Reflector: The Observer in Henry James's Fiction*. New Haven, Conn.: Yale U P, 1969.

Seltzer, Mark. *Henry James and the Art of Power*. Ithaca, N.Y.: Cornell U P, 1984.

Sharp, Sister M. Corona. *The Confidante in Henry James: Evolution and Moral Value of a Fictive Character*. Notre Dame, Ind.: Notre Dame U P, 1963.

Sheldon, Frederick [I. M.] "The American Colony in France." *Nation* 26 (April 18, 1878): 256–58.

Sheppard, E. A. *Henry James and* The Turn of the Screw. Bungay, New Zealand: Auckland U P and Oxford U P, 1974.

Sherbo, Arthur. "Still More on James." *Henry James Review* 12 (1991): 101–16.

Shine, Muriel G. *The Fictional Children of Henry James*. Chapel Hill: U of North Carolina P, 1969.

Shinn, Thelma J. "A Question of Survival: An Analysis of 'The Treacherous Years' of Henry James." *Literature and Psychology* 23 (1973): 135–48.

Short, R. W. "The Sentence Structure of Henry James." *American Literature* 18 (1946): 71–88.

Shumsky, Allison. "James Again: The New York Edition." *Sewanee Review* 70 (1962): 522–25.

Sicker, Philip. *Love and the Quest for Identity in the Fiction of Henry James*. Princeton, N.J.: Princeton U P, 1980.

Siebers, Tobin. "Hesitation, History, and Reading: Henry James's *The Turn of the Screw*." *Texas Studies in Literature and Language* 25 (1983): 558–73.

Singh, Amritjit, and K. Ayyappa Paniker, eds. *The Magic Circle of Henry James: Essays in Honour of Darshan Singh Maini*. New York: Envoy Press, 1989.

Sklenicka, Carol J. "Henry James's Evasion of Ending in *The Golden Bowl*." *Henry James Review* 4 (1982–83): 50–60.

Sklepowich, E. A. "Gilded Bondage: Games and Gamesplaying in *The Awkward Age*." *Essays in Literature* (Western Illinois University) 5 (1978): 187–93.

———. "Gossip and Gothicism in *The Sacred Fount*." *Henry James Review* 2 (1980–81): 112–15.

Smit, David W. *The Language of a Master: Theories of Style and the Late Writing of Henry James*. Carbondale: Southern Illinois U P, 1988.

Smith, Geoffrey D. "How Maisie Knows: The Behavioral Path to Knowledge." *Studies in the Novel* (North Texas State) 15 (1983): 224–36.

Smith, Herbert F., and Michael Peinovich. "*The Bostonians*: Creation and Revision." *Bulletin of the New York Public Library* 73 (1969): 298–308.

Spacks, Patricia Meyer. *Gossip*. New York: Alfred A. Knopf, 1985.

Spender, Stephen. *The Destructive Element: A Study of Modern Writers and Beliefs*. London: Jonathan Cape, 1935; Boston: Houghton Mifflin, 1936.

Spengemann, William. *The Forms of Autobiography: Episodes in the History of a Literary Genre*. New Haven, Conn.: Yale U P, 1980.

Splitter, Randolph. *Proust's Recherche: A Psycho-analytic Interpretation*. London: Routledge and Kegan Paul, 1981.

Springer, Mary Doyle. *A Rhetoric of Literary Character: Some Women of Henry James*. Chicago: U of Chicago P, 1978.

Stafford, William T. "The Ending of James's *The American*: A Defense of the Early Version." *Nineteenth-Century Fiction* 18 (1963): 86–89.

———. "*The Portrait of a Lady*: The Second Hundred Years." *Henry James Review* 2 (1980–81): 91–100.

Stein, William Bysshe. "The Method at the Heart of Madness: *The Spoils of Poynton*." *Modern Fiction Studies* 14 (1968): 187–202.

———. "*The Portrait of a Lady*: Vis Inertiae." *Western Humanities Review* 13 (1959): 177–90.

Stevens, Wallace. *The Necessary Angel: Essays on Reality and the Imagination*. New York: Vintage, 1951.

Stowe, William W. *Balzac, James, and the Realistic Novel*. Princeton, N.J.: Princeton U P, 1983.

Stowell, H. Peter. *Literary Impressionism: James and Chekhov*. Athens: U of Georgia P, 1980.

Strouse, Jean. *Alice James: A Biography*. Boston: Houghton Mifflin, 1980.

———. "The Real Reasons." In *Extraordinary Lives: The Art and Craft of American Biography*, ed. William Zinsser, 163–95. New York: American Heritage, 1986.

Strout, S. Cushing. "Henry James's Dream of the Louvre: 'The Jolly Corner' and Psychological Interpretation." *Psychohistory Review* 8 (1979): 47–52.

———. *The Veracious Imagination: Essays on American History, Literature, and Biography*. Middletown, Conn.: Wesleyan U P, 1981.

Sussman, Henry. *The Hegelian Aftermath: Readings in Hegel, Kierkegaard, Freud, Proust, and James*. Baltimore: Johns Hopkins U P, 1982.

Swan, Michael. *Henry James*. London: Arthur Barker, 1952.

Sweeney, Gerard M. "The Curious Disappearance of Mrs. Beever: The Ending of *The Other House*." *Journal of Narrative Technique* 11 (1981): 216–28.

Taine, Hippolyte Adolphe. *Balzac, A Critical Study*. Trans. Lorenzo O'Rourke. New York: Haskell House, 1973.

———. *Philosophie de l'Art*. 9th ed. 2 vols. Paris: Hachette, 1901.

Tanner, Tony. *Adultery in the Novel: Contract and Transgression*. Baltimore: Johns Hopkins U P, 1979.

———. "The Fearful Self: Henry James's *The Portrait of a Lady*." *Critical Quarterly* 7 (1965): 205–19.

———. "Henry James's Subjective Adventure: 'The Sacred Fount.' " *Essays and Studies* 16 (1963): 37–55. (Reprinted in *Henry James's Major Novels*, ed. Lyall H. Powers, 224–40. East Lansing: Michigan State U P, 1973. Also in Tanner's *Reign of Wonder* in modified form, 319–35.)

———. *Henry James: The Writer and His Work*. Amherst: U of Massachusetts P, 1985.

———. *The Reign of Wonder: Naivety and Reality in American Literature*. Cambridge: Cambridge U P, 1965.

———, ed. *Henry James: Modern Judgements*. Nashville: Aurora, 1970.

Tartella, Vincent. "James's 'Four Meetings': Two Texts Compared," *Nineteenth-Century Fiction* 15 (1960): 17–28.

Taylor, Gordon O. *Chapters of Experience: Studies in Modern American Autobiography*. New York: St. Martin's, 1983.

Taylor, Linda J. *Henry James, 1866–1916: A Reference Guide*. Boston: G. K. Hall, 1982.

Tilley, W. H. *The Background of* The Princess Casamassima." Gainesville: U of Florida P, 1960.

Timms, David. "The Governess's Feelings and the Argument from Textual Revision of *The Turn of the Screw*." *Yearbook of English Studies* 6 (1972): 194–201.

Tintner, Adeline R. "Autobiography as Fiction: 'The Usurping Consciousness' as Hero of James's Memoirs." *Twentieth Century Literature* 23 (1977): 239–60.

———. *The Book World of Henry James: Appropriating the Classics*. Ann Arbor, Mich.: UMI Research Press, 1987.

———. "Henry James's Two Ways of Seeing." *American Bookman*, January 21, 1985, 363–74.

———. "Henry James's Use of 'Jane Eyre' in 'The Turn of the Screw.' " *Brontë Society Transactions* 17 (1976): 42–45.

———. "The House of Atreus and Mme de Bellegarde's Crime." *Notes and Queries*, n.s. 20 (1973): 98–99.

———. " 'In the Dusky, Crowded, Heterogeneous Back-Shop of the Mind': The Iconography of *The Portrait of a Lady*." *Henry James Review* 7.2–3 (1985–86): 140–57.

———. *The Museum World of Henry James*. Ann Arbor, Mich.: UMI Research Press, 1986.

———. "Pater in *The Portrait of a Lady* and *The Golden Bowl*, Including Some Unpublished Letters." *Henry James Review* 3 (1981–82): 80–95.

———. "Photo Album Sheds Light on James' Book." *American Bookman*, May 31, 1982, 4251–64.

———. *The Pop World of Henry James: From Fairy Tales to Science Fiction*. Ann Arbor, Mich.: UMI Research Press, 1989.

———. "*Roderick Hudson*: A Centennial Reading." *Henry James Review* 2 (1980–81): 172–98.

———. "A Textual Error in *The Spoils of Poynton*." *Henry James Review* 5 (1983–84): 65.

Todorov, Tzvetan. *The Fantastic: A Structural Approach to a Literary Genre*. Trans. Richard Howard. Ithaca, N.Y.: Cornell U P, 1975. (Originally published in French under the title *Introduction à la littérature fantastique*. Paris: Editions du Seuil, 1970.)

———. *The Poetics of Prose (Poétique de la Prose)*. Paris: Seuil, 1971. English ed., trans. R. Howard. Oxford: Blackwell, 1977.

———. "The Structural Analysis of Literature: Henry James." In *Structuralism: An Introduction*, ed. David Robey, 73–101. Oxford: Clarendon, 1973.

———. "The Verbal Age." Trans. Patricia Martin Gibby. *Critical Inquiry* 4 (1977): 351–71.

Tolstoy, Leo. *Anna Karenina*. Trans. Louise and Aylmer Maude. Ed. George Gibian. New York: W. W. Norton, 1970.

Tompkins, Jane. "The Redemption of Time in *Notes of a Son and Brother*." *Texas Studies in Literature and Language* 14 (1972–73): 681–90.

———. *Sensational Designs: The Cultural Work of American Fiction, 1790–1860*. New York: Oxford U P, 1985.

Torsney, Cheryl B. "The Political Context of *The Portrait of a Lady*." *Henry James Review* 7.2–3 (1985–86): 86–104.

Traschen, Isadore. "Henry James and the Art of Revision." *Philological Quarterly* 35 (1956): 39–47.

———. "James's Revisions of the Love Affair in *The American*." *New England Quarterly* 29 (1956): 43–62.

Trilling, Lionel. *The Liberal Imagination*. New York: Macmillan, 1948.

———. "*The Princess Casamassima*: An Introductory Essay." *Horizon* 17 (1948): 267–95.

———."The Princess Casamassima." *The Liberal Imagination: Essays on Literature and Society*, 58–92. New York: Viking, 1950.

518                                                                     Works Cited

Tuttleton, James W. *The Novel of Manners in America*. Chapel Hill: U of North Carolina P, 1972.

———. "Rereading *The American*: A Century Since." *Henry James Review* 1 (1979–80): 139–53.

———, ed. *The American*, by Henry James. New York: W. W. Norton, 1972.

Tuttleton, James W., and Agostino Lombardo, eds. *"The Sweetest Impression of Life": The James Family and Italy*. New York: New York U P, 1990.

Vaid, Krishna Baldev. *Technique in the Tales of Henry James*. Cambridge: Harvard U P, 1964.

Vanderbilt, Kermit. "Notes Largely Musical on Henry James's 'Four Meetings.'" *Sewanee Review* 21 (1973): 739–52.

Vandersee, Charles. "James's 'Pandora': The Mixed Consequences of Revision." *Studies in Bibliography* 21 (1968): 93–108.

Van Ghent, Dorothy. *The English Novel: Form and Function*. New York: Rinehart, 1953.

Veeder, William. *Henry James—The Lessons of the Master: Popular Fiction and Personal Style in the Nineteenth Century*. Chicago: U of Chicago P, 1975.

———. "Image as Argument: Henry James and the Style of Criticism." *Henry James Review* 6 (1984–85): 172–81.

Veeder, William, and Susan M. Griffin, eds. *The Art of Criticism: Henry James on the Theory and Practice of Fiction*. Chicago: U of Chicago P, 1986.

Vincec, Sister Stephanie. " 'Poor Flopping *Wings*': The Making of Henry James's *The Wings of the Dove*." *Harvard Library Bulletin* 24 (1976): 60–93.

Wagenknecht, Edward. *Eve and Henry James: Portraits of Women and Girls in His Fiction*. Norman: U of Oklahoma P, 1978.

———. *The Novels of Henry James*. New York: Frederick Ungar, 1983.

———. *The Tales of Henry James*. New York: Frederick Ungar, 1984.

Wallace, Ronald. *Henry James and the Comic Form*. Ann Arbor, Mich.: U of Michigan P, 1975.

Ward, J. A. *The Imagination of Disaster: Evil in the Fiction of Henry James*. Lincoln: U of Nebraska P, 1961.

———. *The Search for Form: Studies in the Structure of James's Fiction*. Chapel Hill: U of North Carolina P, 1967.

Ward, Mrs. Humphry. *A Writer's Recollections*. London: Collins, 1918.

Warren, Robert Penn, ed. *Kenyon Review*. Henry James Number. 5 (1943): 481–623.

Wasiolek, Edward. *Dostoevsky: The Major Fiction*. Cambridge: Massachusetts Institute of Technology Press, 1964.

Watkins, Floyd C. "Christopher Newman's Final Instinct." *Nineteenth-Century Fiction* 12 (1957): 85–88.

Watt, Ian. "The First Paragraph of *The Ambassadors*: An Explication." *Essays in Criticism* 10 (1960): 250–74.

Weber, Samuel. "The Madrepore." *Modern Language Notes* 87 (1972): 915–61.

Wegelin, Christof. *The Image of Europe in Henry James*. Dallas: Southern Methodist U P, 1958.

Weinstein, Philip. *Henry James and the Requirements of the Imagination*. Cambridge: Harvard U P, 1971.

Wellek, René. "Henry James's Literary Theory and Criticism." *American Literature* 30 (1958): 298–321.

Wells, H. G. *Experiment in Autobiography: Discoveries and Conclusions of a Very*

*Ordinary Brain (Since 1866)* [excerpt]. In *Henry James: Interviews and Recollections*, ed. Norman Page, 64–65. London: Macmillan, 1984.

———. "Of Art, of Literature, of Mr. Henry James." 1914. (Reprinted in *Henry James and H. G. Wells: A Record of Their Friendship, Their Debate on the Art of Fiction, and Their Quarrel*, ed. Leon Edel and Gordon N. Ray, 234–60. London: Rupert Hart-Davis, 1958.)

Wescott, Glenway. "A Sentimental Contribution." *Hound and Horn* 7 (1934): 523–34.

———. "A Sentimental Contribution." In *Homage to Henry James*. Reprint of Kirstein, Tate, and Winters. Mamaroneck, N.Y.: Paul J. Appel, 1971.

West, Rebecca. *Henry James*. London: Nisbet, 1916.

Wharton, Edith. *A Backward Glance*. New York: D. Appleton-Century, 1934.

Wheelwright, John. "Henry James and Stanford White." *Hound and Horn* 7 (1934): 480–93.

White, Allon. *The Uses of Obscurity: The Fiction of Early Modernism*. Boston: Routledge and Kegan Paul, 1981.

White, Robert. "Love, Marriage, and Divorce: The Matter of Sexuality in *The Portrait of a Lady*." *Henry James Review* 7.2–3 (1985–86): 59–71.

Wiesenfarth, Joseph. *Henry James and the Dramatic Analogy: A Study of the Major Novels of the Middle Period*. New York: Fordham U P, 1963.

———. "A Woman in *The Portrait of a Lady*." *Henry James Review* 7.2–3 (1985–86): 18–28.

Willen, Gerald, ed. *A Casebook on Henry James's "The Turn of the Screw."* New York: Crowell, 1960.

Williams, M. A. "The Drama of Maisie's Vision." *Henry James Review* 2 (1980–81): 36–48.

Wilson, Edmund. "The Ambiguity of Henry James." *Hound and Horn* 7 (1934): 385–406. (Reprinted with 1938, 1948, and 1959 revisions in *A Casebook on Henry James's "The Turn of the Screw,"* ed. Gerald Willen, 115–53. New York: Crowell, 1960.)

Wilson, R.B.J. *Henry James's Ultimate Narrative*: The Golden Bowl. Brisbane, Australia: U of Queensland P, 1981.

Wimsatt, William K., Jr., and Cleanth Brooks. *Literary Criticism: A Short History*. New York: Vintage, 1967.

Winner, Viola Hopkins. *Henry James and the Visual Arts*. Charlottesville: U P of Virginia, 1970.

Winnett, Susan. "*Mise en Crypte*: The Man and the Mask." *Henry James Review* 5 (1983–84): 220–26.

Winters, Yvor. *In Defense of Reason*. Denver: Alan Swallow, 1937.

Wolk, Merla. "Narration and Nurture in *What Maisie Knew*." *Henry James Review* 4 (1982–83): 196–206.

Woolf, Judith. *Henry James: The Major Novels*. Cambridge: Cambridge U P, 1991.

Woolf, Virginia. "Henry James's Ghost Stories." *Collected Essays*, ed. Leonard Woolf, 1: 286–92. New York: Harcourt Brace and World, 1967.

———. "The Supernatural in Fiction." *Collected Essays*, ed. Leonard Woolf, 1: 293–96. New York: Harcourt Brace and World, 1967.

———. *The Waves*. London: Hogarth Press, 1931.

Worden, Ward S. "A Cut Version of *What Maisie Knew*." *American Literature* 24 (1953): 493–504.

Yeazell, Ruth Bernard. "Henry James." In *Columbia Literary History of the United States*, ed. Emory Elliott et al., 668–89. New York: Columbia U P, 1988.

———. *Language and Knowledge in the Late Novels of Henry James*. Chicago: U Chicago P, 1976.

Young, Robert E. "An Error in *The Ambassadors*." *American Literature* 22 (1950): 245–53.

———. "A Final Note on *The Ambassadors*." *American Literature* 23 (1951): 487–90.

Zabel, Morton Dauwen. Introduction to *In the Cage and Other Tales*, by Henry James, 1–28. Garden City, N.Y.: Doubleday Anchor, 1958.

# Index

Marxist analysis of James, 18

Matisse, Henri, 41–42

Matthiessen, F. O.: on *Confidence*, 118;
*Henry James: The Major Phase*, 7;
*The James Family*, 7, 430; on James's
revisions of *The Portrait of a Lady*,
319; *The Notebooks of Henry James*,
7; and the "obscure hurt," 430

"Maud Evelyn," 304, 348

Maupassant, Guy de, 209–10, 211

Mazzella, Anthony J., on James's
revision of *The Portrait of a Lady*, 322

McCarthy, Harold, *Henry James: The
Creative Process*, 10

McIntyre, Clara F., on James's revisions,
312, 316

McMahan, Elizabeth, on *The Bostonians*,
132

McMurray, William, on James's moral
meaning, 133

McWhirter, David, *Desire and Love in
Henry James*, 23

Memling, Hans, 286

Mentmore Towers, 309

Metaphor: Aristotle's views on, 272–73;
as form of closure in James, 272–73;
in *The Turn of the Screw*, 272

*The Middle Years*, 187, 188, 427; critical
treatment of, 444–45; genre of, 442;
narrative technique in, 439; as source
for biography, 430

Miller, James E., 42, 47, 49

Miller, J. Hillis, 46; critique of James,
75; *The Ethics of Reading*, 92 n.4; and
the "laws" of language, 91–92

Milton, John, 302

Mitchell, Juliet: on *What Maisie Knew*,
165; "*What Maisie Knew*: Portrait of
the Artist as a Young Girl," 76

Mizruchi, Susan, *The Power of Historical
Knowledge: Narrating the Past in
Hawthorne, James, and Dreiser*, 19,
20

*Modern Fiction Studies*, 17

Modernism and James, 27, 261 n.1

Monet, Claude, 296

Money, James's attitude toward, 378–79

Monteiro, George, on James's revision of
*The Siege of London*, 326

Moon, Heath, on *In the Cage*, 166

Moore, Marianne, "James as a
Characteristic American," 466

Moreau, Gustave: influence on James's
fiction, 299, 301; *Oedipus and the
Sphinx*, 301

Moreen, Morgan, 84–85. *See also* "The
Pupil"

Moroni, Giovanni Battista, 292

Morris, William, 367

Morris, Wright, *The Territory Ahead*,
467

Motion pictures, 306

Mull, Donald L., 145 n.2

Muniment, Paul, 137–38. *See also The
Princess Casamassima*

Münster, Eugenia, 113–16. *See also The
Europeans*

Murdock, Kenneth B., on *Confidence*,
118

Murphy, Kevin, on *The Turn of the
Screw*, 169

Nance, William, on *What Maisie Knew*,
164

Nardin, Jane, on *The Turn of the Screw*,
169

Narrative technique, James's comments
on, 26

Narrators, 149

Nash, Gabriel, 142–45, 146 n.8. *See also
The Tragic Muse*

Naturalism: and James, 40, 261;
influence on James, 122; in James's
fiction, 145 n.1; in *The Princess
Casamassima*, 122, 136, 139

Nettels, Elsa, *James and Conrad*, 20

Newberry, Frederick, on James's
revisions of *Daisy Miller*, 326

New Criticism: and feminist criticism of
James, 265–66; and James, 40–41; and
James's autobiographies, 434

"A New England Winter," 295, 299

New Historicist analysis, 93 n.9; of
James, 77–78, 88

Newman, Christopher, 62, 87, 106–7,

# About the Editor
# and Contributors

MAQBOOL AZIZ, Professor of English at McMaster University, is the editor of the Oxford University Press *The Tales of Henry James*.

JEAN FRANTZ BLACKALL, Professor of English at Cornell University, is the author of *Jamesian Ambiguity and* The Sacred Fount (1965) and of numerous essays on Henry James, Edith Wharton, and others. She is a member of the editorial board of the *Henry James Review*.

CHARLES CARAMELLO, Associate Professor of English at the University of Maryland, is the author of *Silverless Mirrors: Book, Self, and Postmodern American Fiction* (1983) and *Henry James, Gertrude Stein, and the Biographical Act* (1993).

SUSAN CARLSON, Professor of English at Iowa State University, is the author of *Women of Grace: James's Plays and the Comedy of Manners* (1985) and *Women and Comedy: Rewriting the British Theatrical Tradition* (1991).

SARAH B. DAUGHERTY, Associate Professor and Graduate Coordinator of English at Wichita State University, is the author of *The Literary Criticism of Henry James* (1981) and a member of the editorial board of the *Henry James Review*.

DANIEL MARK FOGEL, Professor of English, Dean of the Graduate School, and Associate Vice Chancellor for Academic Affairs at Louisiana State University. He is the founding editor of the *Henry James Review*, is the author of *Henry James and the Structure of the Romantic Imagination* (1981), Daisy Miller:

*A Dark Comedy of Manners* (1990), and *Covert Relations: James Joyce, Virginia Woolf, and Henry James* (1990), the coeditor (with J. Gerald Kennedy) of *American Letters and the Historical Consciousness* (1987), and the editor of the Library of America edition of *Henry James Novels, 1886–1890* (1989).

VIRGINIA C. FOWLER, Associate Professor of English at Virginia Polytechnic Institute and State University, is the author of *Henry James's American Girl: The Embroidery on the Canvas* (1984) and *Nikki Giovanni* (1992).

JAMES W. GARGANO, Professor of English Emeritus at Washington and Jefferson College, is the editor of the two-volume collection *Critical Essays on Henry James* (1987).

RICHARD A. HOCKS, Professor of English at the University of Missouri, is the author of *Henry James and Pragmatistic Thought* (1974) and of *Henry James: A Study of the Short Fiction* (1990). He writes the annual reviews of James studies for the *Henry James Review* and, since 1986, the Henry James chapter in the Duke University Press annual *American Literary Scholarship*.

CAROL HOLLY, Professor of English at St. Olaf College, has published essays on James's writing in *American Literature, Harvard Library Bulletin*, and the *Henry James Review*. She is the holder, in 1991, of a National Endowment for the Humanities Fellowship for College Teachers, under which she is working on a book on James's autobiographies.

THOMAS M. LEITCH teaches English and directs the Film Studies Program at the University of Delaware. He is the author of *What Stories Are: Narrative Theory and Discourse* (1986), *Find the Director and Other Hitchcock Games* (1991), and *Lionel Trilling: An Annotated Bibliography* (1992).

BONNEY MACDONALD, Assistant Professor of English at Union College, is the author of *Henry James's Italian Hours: Revelatory and Resistant Impressions* (1990).

DARSHAN SINGH MAINI, Professor Emeritus of English at Punjabi University, is the author of *Henry James: The Indirect Vision* (1988) and of *The Spirit of American Literature* (1988), among many other works.

ANTHONY J. MAZZELLA, Professor of English at the William Paterson College of New Jersey, is the author of "The New Isabel" (first published in the Norton Critical Edition of *The Portrait of a Lady* [1975]) and of several studies of adaptations of James's work to other media, including " 'The Illumination That Was All for the Mind': The BBC Video Production of *The Golden Bowl*."

LYALL H. POWERS, Professor of English at the University of Michigan, is the author of *Henry James and the Naturalist Movement* (1971), the editor of *Henry James's Major Novels: Essays in Criticism* (1973), *Leon Edel and Literary Art* (1988), and *Henry James and Edith Wharton: Letters, 1900–1915* (1990), and the coeditor, with Leon Edel, of *The Complete Notebooks of Henry James* (1987).

JOHN CARLOS ROWE, Professor of English and Comparative Literature at the University of California, Irvine, is the author of *Henry Adams and Henry James: The Emergence of a Modern Consciousness* (1976), *Through the Custom House: Nineteenth-Century American Literature and Modern Theory* (1982), and *The Theoretical Dimensions of Henry James* (1984), as well as of numerous essays on Henry James and on both literary and critical theory.

DANIEL R. SCHWARZ, Professor of English at Cornell University, is the author of numerous books, including *Conrad*: Almayer's Folly *to* Under Western Eyes (1980), *Conrad: The Later Fiction* (1982), *The Humanistic Heritage: Critical Theories of the English Novel from James to Hillis Miller* (1986), *Reading Joyce's* Ulysses (1987), *The Transformation of the English Novel 1890–1930* (1989), and *The Case for a Humanistic Poetics* (1991).

MARY DOYLE SPRINGER, Professor of English at St. Mary's College of California, is the author of *Forms of the Modern Novella* (1975) and of *A Rhetoric of Literary Character: Some Women of Henry James* (1978). On a fellowship at the Camargo Foundation, she is currently writing a book on Wallace Stevens.

ADELINE R. TINTNER, an independent scholar, is the author of *The Museum World of Henry James* (1986), *The Book World of Henry James: Appropriating the Classics* (1987), *The Pop World of Henry James: From Fairy Tales to Science Fiction* (1989), and *The Cosmopolitan World of Henry James* (1991), not to mention hundreds of articles on James and forthcoming books on James and the visual arts and on James's afterlife in modern and postmodern culture.

JAMES W. TUTTLETON, Professor of English at New York University, is the author of *The Novel of Manners in America* (1972) and the editor of the Norton Critical Edition of *The American* (1978), of *"The Sweetest Impression of Life":* *The James Family and Italy* (1990; coedited with Agostino Lombardo), and of *Edith Wharton: Contemporary Reviews* (1992; coedited with Kristin O. Lauer and Margaret P. Murray).

PHILIP M. WEINSTEIN, Professor of English at Swarthmore College, is the author of *Henry James and the Requirements of the Imagination* (1971), *The Semantics of Desire: Changing Models of Identity from Dickens to Joyce* (1984), and *Faulkner's Subject: A Cosmos No One Owns* (1992).